NEW YORK REVIEW BOOKS
CLASSICS

WE HAVE ONLY T

JEAN-PAUL SARTRE (1905–1980) was a hugely influential French philosopher, novelist, and playwright. The only child of Jean-Baptiste Sartre, a naval officer who died when his son was still an infant, and Anne-Marie Schweitzer, a first cousin of Albert Schweitzer, he was born in Paris and raised until the age of fourteen at his grandparents' in the suburb of Meudon. Tutored at home for several years, Sartre made a slow start in school but went on to study philosophy and psychology at the prestigious École Normale Supérieure, where he also began his lifelong companionship with Simone de Beauvoir. After passing his agrégation, Sartre taught in lycées in Le Havre and Paris from 1931 to 1945, interrupted by a year of study at the Institut français in Berlin and then by conscription into the French army in 1939, followed by ten months in a German prisoner-of-war camp. By the end of World War II, Sartre was well known in France both for his writings and for his activity in the Resistance. From then until 1970, when his eyesight began to fail, he enjoyed an international reputation as one of the dominant literary intellectual figures of the age. In 1964 he declined the Nobel Prize in Literature. Among his most well-known works available in English are *Nausea*, *Being and Nothingness*, *No Exit*, *Critique of Dialectical Reason*, and *The Words*.

RONALD ARONSON is the author of *The Dialectics of Disaster*, *After Marxism*, *Camus and Sartre*, and *Living Without God*. He is Distinguished Professor of the History of Ideas at Wayne State University.

ADRIAN VAN DEN HOVEN is professor emeritus at the University of Windsor and founding executive editor of *Sartre Studies International*. He has translated Sartre, Camus, and other French writers, and is the author of several books about Sartre. He was twice elected president of the North American Sartre Society.

WE HAVE ONLY THIS LIFE TO LIVE

The Selected Essays of Jean-Paul Sartre 1939–1975

Edited by

RONALD ARONSON *and*

ADRIAN VAN DEN HOVEN

NEW YORK REVIEW BOOKS

New York

THIS IS A NEW YORK REVIEW BOOK
PUBLISHED BY THE NEW YORK REVIEW OF BOOKS
435 Hudson Street, New York, NY 10014
www.nyrb.com

This work received support from the French Ministry of Foreign Affairs and
the Cultural Services of the French Embassy in the United States through their
publishing assistance program.

*Cet ouvrage publié dans le cadre du programme d'aide à la publication bénéficie du
soutien du Ministère des Affaires Etrangères et du Service Culturel de l'Ambassade
de France représenté aux Etats-Unis.*

Library of Congress Cataloging-in-Publication Data
Sartre, Jean-Paul, 1905–1980.
[Essays. English. Selections]
We have only this life to live : selected essays, 1939–1975 / by Jean-Paul Sartre ;
edited by Ronald Aronson and Adrian van den Hoven.
    pages cm. — (New York Review Books Classics)
Includes bibliographical references.
ISBN 978-1-59017-493-7 (alk. paper)
I. Aronson, Ronald, 1938- editor of compilation. II. Van den Hoven, Adrian,
1939– editor of compilation. III. Title.
PQ2637.A82A2 2013
848'.91409—dc23

                    2013001043

ISBN 978-1-59017-493-7

Printed in the United States of America on acid-free paper.
10 9 8 7 6 5 4

CONTENTS

INTRODUCTION

I.

WHEN, TOWARD the end of his life, Sartre was asked which of his hundreds of writings he hoped future generations would read, he picked five: a work of philosophy, *Critique of Dialectical Reason*; his biography of Jean Genet, *Saint Genet*; the novel *Nausea*; the play *The Devil and the Good Lord*; and *Situations*, ten sprawling and kaleidoscopic volumes of occasional writings on his contemporaries, philosophy, art, literature, politics, and life that had appeared at intervals over his career and covered its entire course—in effect, his collected essays. *Situations*, Sartre explained, was "the nonphilosophical work which comes closest to philosophy, critical and political."*

"Closest to philosophy," one might say, because at the heart of Sartre's philosophy are his ideas of freedom and situation, and nowhere does he so lucidly set forth both the constraints of human situations and the freedom and power of self-determination within these limits as in his essays. Through their immense variety, Sartre's essays reveal a distinct personality. Their sheer energy, whether encountered on first publication or today, marks their author as a self-conscious master of the form. "There is a crisis of the essay," he declared in 1943. "Elegance and clarity seem to demand that, in this kind of work, we employ a language deader than Latin: the language of Voltaire." But in trying to express "today's thoughts using yesterday's language, what a lot of metaphors, circumlocutions, and imprecise images ensue."

---

* Jean-Paul Sartre, "Self-Portrait at Seventy," in *Life/Situations*, trans. Paul Auster and Lydia Davis (New York: Pantheon Books, 1977), 24.

Indeed, in his critical study of Georges Bataille, Sartre confesses to being painfully aware that "as I write these lines . . . I am using an outdated instrument which academic tradition has preserved into our own day." Unlike that of the contemporary novel, he contends, "the style of the essay remains to be discovered."

This statement reveals one of Sartre's main goals as an essayist: to create a living language. Even in translation the reader can see the result, unfolding over forty years, as one of Sartre's greatest achievements. Above all, these essays are alive. No matter what the topic, Sartre's essays feel current, stirring, and demanding. And not only his prescient writings on political and social issues such as torture, third world immigrants in advanced societies, elections in Western democracies, and the continuing effects of colonialism and racism. Sartre's responses to days now long past, including the German occupation and the Resistance, his relations with Albert Camus, and the Vietnam War, still startle us with their energy.

Sartre writes with remarkable freedom, never settling into a single, predictable tone. He engages issues with extreme, attention-getting statements, vividly and forcefully taking a position on the question at hand. He can be direct, brutally honest, outrageous, even peremptory and abrupt, and yet at other times carefully nuanced, sympathetic, open to others' voices. Sartre writes quotable phrases, extended arguments, and over-the-top analyses. He describes, he argues, he theorizes, he asserts, he welcomes, he berates, he champions. His essays are revelations, unveilings of whatever he finds to be new and important; they take chances and place bets.

He almost always writes against conventional wisdom and received opinion, against the mainstream. He stresses that situations and people can change, that writers, artists, and movements never lose the capacity to create the genuinely unforeseen. No wonder that when reading Sartre's essays, even if long after their original composition, we often catch our breath as if watching a daring acrobat in a high-wire performance. Well into his thirties before he found his own path, Sartre made a habit of thinking against himself in dramatic ways right up to the end.

2.

Sartre's first essays are those of a restless young man figuring out what matters to him and where he wants to go. Sartre had been a brilliant philosophy student at the École Normale Supérieure, from which he graduated in 1929. He performed two years of military service, then taught in a lycée in Le Havre. For all his brilliance, he was at something of a loss. (*Nausea*, largely autobiographical in inspiration, would later capture his state of mind at the time.) His philosophical concerns had not yet come into focus. He had to prove himself as a writer of fiction. In Le Havre the young nonconformist taught psychology and philosophy and socialized freely with his students, with whom he shared his passion for cinema and the contemporary American novel. Then, on the advice of his friend (and later a political antagonist) Raymond Aron, Sartre spent the 1933–34 academic year in Berlin, studying Edmund Husserl's phenomenology. For Sartre this was a transformative event—here at last was a way of thinking that was adequate to lived experience! Sartre recorded it in the essay with which this collection begins. Written in Berlin but not published until 1939, it praises Husserl for having "given us back the world of artists and prophets: frightening, hostile, and dangerous, with havens of grace and love."

This is the tone of excited discovery, of intellectual recognition and existential encounter, that will become recognized as the hallmark of Sartre's essays. It is especially pronounced in these early years. Accordingly, Sartre embraces other writers and thinkers who express themselves in fresh ways. In John Dos Passos's journalistic style, he writes, "the aim is to show us *this* world, our world. To *show* it only, with no explanation or commentary." He is the "greatest writer of our time" because he has solved the novelist's problem of how to depict the individual's innermost self and social being at one and the same time by using the free indirect discourse of American journalism. In his celebrated and influential discussion of William Faulkner, Sartre reflects that "a novelistic technique always relates to the novelist's metaphysics. The critic's task is to identify the latter before evaluating the former.

It is blindingly obvious that Faulkner's metaphysics is a metaphysics of time." He vividly compares Faulkner's vision of the world to "that of a man sitting in a convertible and looking backward." And yet much as he admires Faulkner's originality, he criticizes him, as he also does Dos Passos, for presenting humans "deprived of possibilities," without a future. Here Sartre is pointing to what will become one of the distinguishing traits of his thought, a resistance to anything that deprives humans of the ability to freely shape themselves.

Sartre welcomes innovators and dismisses writers he finds conventional or backward-looking. His attack on the esteemed novelist François Mauriac (who later received the Nobel Prize) cleverly targets both Mauriac's novelistic technique and his Catholicism. Sartre is contemptuous of Mauriac's use of the omniscient narrator. He writes that Mauriac takes "the standpoint of God towards his characters. God sees the inside and the outside; he sees the depth of souls and bodies—the whole universe at a stroke."* This is both a philosophical and an aesthetic error, Sartre argues. It strips the novel of the uncertainty that is the essence of life. His conclusion is stinging: "God is not an artist and neither is M. Mauriac."†

Being unconventional is no guarantee of Sartre's praise, as his extended critique of sometime-surrealist Bataille shows. In his longest critical essay, Sartre sees Bataille's *The Inner Experience* (which came out in 1943, the same year as *Being and Nothingness*) not as breaking new ground but as escaping from reality. Dismantling the book from top to bottom, Sartre describes its irrationalist, even mystical, theory of knowledge as trying to express "silence with words." Bataille's fatalism, Sartre argues, is all too dangerously appealing: "It is not by chance that the word 'impossibility' flows frequently from his pen. He belongs, without a doubt, to that spiritual family whose members are susceptible, above all, to the acid, exhausting charm of impossible endeavors." Sartre, by contrast, defends his own activist approach to existence as an open-ended project filled with the sense of possibility.

* Jean-Paul Sartre, "Monsieur François Mauriac and Freedom," in *Critical Essays* (*Situations I*), trans. Chris Turner (London: Seagull, 2010), 62.
† Ibid., 80.

The beginning of Sartre's crucial relationship with Camus also dates from these years. While still in Algeria, Camus had written reviews of *Nausea* (he would go on to quote from the novel in *The Myth of Sisyphus*) and of the stories in *The Wall*, which he particularly admired. Sartre in turn looks at *The Stranger* in light of *The Myth of Sisyphus*, a book that he places within the classical French moralistic tradition. More than with anyone else he approaches in his early essays, Sartre expresses here a philosophical and stylistic kinship with Camus. He approvingly quotes Camus's description of absurdity (which paraphrases *Nausea*). And he is struck by the discontinuous nature of Camus's sentences:

> Each sentence is a present moment. But it is not a vague present that smudges and runs into the following one. The sentence is sharp, crisp, self-contained; an entire void separates it from the next one, just as Descartes's moment is separated from the moment that follows. Between each sentence and the next, the world is annihilated and reborn: as it emerges the world is a creation ex nihilo; a sentence in *The Stranger* is an island. And we tumble from sentence to sentence, from void to void.

3.

In September 1939, immediately after the outbreak of the Second World War, Sartre was mobilized by the army of the Third Republic. He spent the "Phony War" (before the German offensive in the late spring of 1940) in Alsace and Lorraine. Given the job of weather observer, he found time to write some twelve hours a day. After the fall of France, he was imprisoned in a German POW camp; there he lectured on Heidegger to the priests who were his fellow prisoners and worked on what was to become *Being and Nothingness*. He also wrote a play, *Bariona*, which was put on by the inmates at Christmas. Released in March 1941, Sartre returned to occupied Paris and, with Maurice Merleau-Ponty and other intellectuals, formed a Resistance group, Socialisme et liberté. Having been more or less politically disengaged in the 1930s (when in Berlin he appears to have taken little notice of the Nazis or of Husserl's dismissal from his university post because of his Jewish origins), Sartre now threw himself into activism. Within a few months, however, the group was disbanded, and Sartre went back to his writing desk. The essays on Camus and Bataille date from this period, as do *Being and Nothingness*, *The Flies*, and *No Exit*—the works for which he would soon become famous. He did, however, also contribute to three issues of the Resistance publication *Les Lettres françaises*. His first piece, appearing in April 1943, was a scathing attack on the novelist and collaborator Pierre Drieu La Rochelle, during the occupation the editor of France's foremost literary journal, *La Nouvelle Revue Française*.

In early 1944, Camus became the editor of the clandestine Resistance publication *Combat*. Sartre met and befriended Camus at the premiere of *The Flies* in May, and was the first writer honored with a byline when *Combat* began to appear openly and daily during the Paris insurrection in August. However limited his actual activities had been—some have accused him of complicity with the occupation—Sartre established himself in the months that followed as an important public commentator on the Resistance and the Liberation. His greatest contribution is the classic article "The Republic of Silence," published in September 1944 in the first open issue of *Les Lettres françaises*. The term "republic of silence" was widespread during the occupation, but Sartre gave it a precise and paradoxical new significance:

> Never were we freer than under the German occupation. We had lost all our rights, beginning with the right to speak. We were insulted to our faces every day and had to remain silent. We were deported en masse, as workers, Jews, or political prisoners. Everywhere—on the walls, on the movie screens, and in the newspapers—we came up against the vile, insipid picture of ourselves our oppressors wanted to present to us. Because of all this, we were free.

Because of this? Yes, the Nazis controlled and policed all public expression, so "every accurate thought was a triumph" and "every word became precious as a declaration of principle." The French truly knew freedom in this situation because every moment posed a danger and thus demanded a choice.

In "The Republic of Silence," Sartre addresses not just "the elite among us who were real Resistance fighters but . . . all the French people who, every hour of the night and day for four years, said 'No.'" Even those who only passively supported the Resistance but knew a few tidbits of important information—"and what Frenchman was not at one point or another in that position"—played an important role. They too, if arrested and interrogated, had faced the prospect of torture and the choice of talking or not talking. Thus does Sartre help to construct the postwar myth that all of occupied France engaged in some form of resistance against the Germans. And yet he indicated this narrative's mythic dimension in "The Liberation of Paris: An Apocalyptic Week," published on the first anniversary of the insurrection. There he reminds readers that by the time Paris rose up, the Allies were approaching the city and the Germans beginning their withdrawal. The insurrection, paradoxically, delayed their departure, but had nonetheless been necessary, Sartre argued. After four years of repression and humiliation, Parisians had risen up to demonstrate to themselves the power of their own freedom: "they wanted to affirm the sovereignty of the French people; and they understood that the only means they had of legitimizing the power of the people was to shed their own blood."

In 1945, *Combat* and *Le Figaro* sent Sartre to the United States as a reporter. He was there for some six months, touring the country, including New York, Washington, D.C., Chicago, Detroit, Tennessee, and California. The man who was later to be a scourge of the United States and its politics filed more than thirty, often enthusiastic articles on Hollywood, New York, jazz, and American society and culture. The space of New York, sweeping to the horizon, was a revelation—"a city for the long-sighted: you can 'focus' only at infinity"—and yet here and elsewhere in America, Sartre's feelings are ambivalent. Skyscrapers are monuments of an already bygone age; "talkies have not fulfilled the promise of the silent films"; jazz is "capable of limited development" and has already "had its day." (And yet two years later, in "Nick's Bar, New York City," he declared that jazz musicians "speak to the best part of you, the most unfeeling and most free, the part which doesn't want sad songs or sprightly ones but a moment of deafening explosion.") Sartre was genuinely impressed, however, by the social openness of the United States and its lack of class distinctions: "What is important is that here a worker never considers himself a 'proletarian' in the European sense of the word." Americans experience the world through a "professional individualism," and they display remarkable informality. *Combat* published one of Sartre's pieces under the title "'Hello, Jim,' Says Chicago's Bishop to the School's Janitor. 'Hello, Bishop!' Answers the Janitor"—and French readers could only have been shocked.

4.

In the fall of 1945, Sartre published *The Age of Reason* and *The Reprieve*, the first of two novels in a projected tetralogy, *Roads to a Freedom*, exploring France's recent slide into war and defeat, of which only three volumes were to be completed. At the same time, his companion, Simone de Beauvoir, published a novel of her own, *The Blood of Others*, while opening a successful play, *Useless Mouths*. De Beauvoir and Sartre gave public lectures; Sartre's, "Existentialism Is a Humanism," was an event. This was the "existentialist offensive" and its star couple had become a media sensation.

Sartre now enjoyed a previously unimaginable fame. With it—especially in the aftermath of the war—came a new sense of social and political responsibility that led him that same fall to launch a new intellectual monthly, *Les Temps modernes*, of which he would be the editor. In a ringing introduction (and perhaps glancing over his shoulder at his time spent on the sidelines and furthering his career during the occupation), he advocated a new program of political engagement.

We regret Balzac's indifference toward the revolutionary days of 1848; we regret Flaubert's panicky incomprehension when confronted with the Commune. We regret these unfortunate reactions for them: those events are something that they missed out on forever. We don't want to miss out on anything of our time. There may be better ones, but this one is ours: we have only this life to live, amid this war, and perhaps this revolution.

This new program was also reflected in the title, *Situations*, that Sartre gave to his first collection of essays, which he brought out in 1947. According to Michel Contat and Michel Rybalka, Sartre's indispensable bibliographers, he had first thought of calling the book "Significations," but then changed his mind. Sartre was famous, even notorious, for his emphasis on freedom. In *Being and Nothingness* hadn't he written that "the slave in chains is free to break them"?* *Situations*, by contrast, signaled his recognition of the constraints on human freedom—historical, social, political, and economic—that he was now determined to confront and transform.

Turning toward politics meant being torn between the most prominent forces in postwar France: communism and the United States. Sartre had kept his distance from the French Communist Party (PCF) during the 1930s, even though Paul Nizan and other friends had attached themselves to it; and though during the war he had written for communist-led organs, Sartre and existentialism had been viciously attacked by PCF intellectuals after the war was over, attacks that Sartre dismissed in "Existentialism: A Clarification" as "absurd" and based on "ignorance and bad faith." In the short-lived postwar movement Rassemblement Démocratique Révolutionnaire (RDR), Sartre sought radical change while maintaining neutrality between West and East, and in "Materialism and Revolution," published in 1946, he criticized the orthodox Stalinist "dialectical materialism" of the Party for reducing humans to things.

By 1948, with an eye toward Tito's break with Stalin in Yugoslavia, Sartre was proclaiming that "We must rethink Marxism, we must

---

* Jean-Paul Sartre, *Being and Nothingness*, trans. Hazel E. Barnes (New York: Philosophical Library, 1956), 550.

rethink man."* He was adrift for several months after the collapse of the RDR, during which time it became impossible to ignore the enormous presence of the PCF, with its powerful support from the working class and sheer political heft. More and more aware of the class struggle, Sartre slowly but surely was being pulled into the Party's gravitational field. In 1950, in the preface to Roger Stéphane's *Portrait de l'aventurier*, Sartre speculates on how to reconcile the adventurer's subjectivity and search for self with the obedience and courage of the militant (who has "neither depth nor secrets"), but he reaches no conclusion. In 1952 in "The Communists and Peace" he aligns himself with the PCF. But he stresses that he agrees "on precise and limited issues, reasoning from my principles and not theirs."† In elucidating those principles Sartre argues that support for the working class necessarily entails supporting the Communist Party, in spite of its faults. Industrial workers were atomized and passive and under attack from the French government, allied as it was with the United States in the cold war. Only the PCF could unify and mobilize them—not in spite of but because of the Party's bureaucratic and authoritarian character.

Sartre was now the most famous fellow traveler in the world. He wrote for a Party paper, *Libération* (he would co-found a publication of the same name in 1973), spoke at pro-Soviet events, denounced the West in a vitriolic essay on the execution of the Rosenbergs, and gave euphoric accounts of his travels in the Soviet Union and China. (Later Sartre would admit that he had allowed himself to be used by his Soviet hosts.)‡

Sartre's alignment with the communists also led to his break with Camus. In 1951, Francis Jeanson wrote a blistering review of *The Rebel* for *Les Temps modernes*, denouncing the book's moralism and romanticism, which drew an angry reply in the journal from Camus. In the

---

* Jean-Paul Sartre, "Faux savants ou faux lièvres," in *Situations VI* (Paris: Éditions Gallimard, 1964).

† Jean-Paul Sartre, *The Communists and Peace: With a Reply to Claude Lefort*, trans. Martha H. Fletcher and Philip R. Berk (New York: George Braziller, 1968), 168.

‡ See Jean-Paul Sartre, Philippe Gavi, and Pierre Victor, *On a raison de se révolter* (Paris: Éditions Gallimard, 1974).

same issue Sartre weighed in with "Reply to Albert Camus," which seconded Jeanson's critique and justified his new political turn: "To earn the right to influence human beings in struggle, you have first to take part in their fight; you have first to accept a lot of things if you want to try to change a small number." Sartre argued that violence and even brutality may be the only realistic path to a better world. Finally giving in to the slowly mounting compulsion to take sides, Sartre—no less than Camus—spent the next few years in a creative and intellectual void, virtually unable to say anything significant. Until the Soviet invasion of Hungary in 1956, Sartre, as he said in his eulogy of Camus, lost touch with "moral fact" and worshipped "the golden calf of realism."*

Already disappointed by the Party's inability to take a stand against the war in Algeria, he found it altogether impossible to overlook the suppression of the Hungarian revolution. He did not reject Marxism—indeed, in a project that produced *Search for a Method* and then *Critique of Dialectical Reason*, Sartre became one of the foremost thinkers of a reinvigorated Marxism. He broke with the PCF but not with the Soviet Union. It took another dozen years but finally, after tanks rolled into Prague in 1968, he denounced the Soviet leaders as agents of the "Thing." "The machine will not be repaired; the people must take it over and throw it out in the junkyard."

5.

As one of his first engaged essays in the aftermath of the Second World War (a group that included the long study *Anti-Semite and Jew*), Sartre contributed a preface, "Black Orpheus," to Léopold Sédar Senghor's anthology of black francophone poetry. Poets like Senghor and Aimé Césaire, Sartre argued, rejected the identities imposed on them by their colonial overlords and refashioned themselves as creative—and potentially revolutionary—subjects. With the outbreak of the

* Jean-Paul Sartre, "Albert Camus," in *Situations*, trans. Benita Eisler (New York: George Braziller, 1965), 110.

Algerian Revolution in 1954 and the brutal French effort to suppress it, which included a concerted campaign of torture, the third world struggle against colonialism became one of Sartre's central concerns.

In 1958, Sartre denounced French atrocities in Algeria in a review of Henry Alleg's *The Question*, published in *Les Temps modernes* under the title "A Victory." Alleg, a journalist, had been imprisoned and tortured by the French forces, treatment that his book vividly described. Sartre's essay takes up the common claim that torture "saves lives" and rejects it out of hand. "Was it to save lives that his nipples and his pubic hair were burned? No, they wanted to extract from him the address of the comrade who had sheltered him. If he had talked, they would have put another communist behind bars; that is all." The French authorities banned Sartre's essay for seeking "to demoralize the army," but a week later the popular satirical weekly *Le Canard enchaîné* published the whole thing anew as a scroll whose tiny characters could only be read using a magnifying glass. When a new edition of Alleg's book was published in Switzerland (from which it soon made its way into France), Sartre's essay appeared as the preface.

In 1960 Sartre and de Beauvoir visited Cuba in a show of solidarity with that country's revolution, and Sartre wrote a series of approving articles for the French press. His careful analysis of Patrice Lumumba's failure to unify the Congo confronts the difficulties that face postcolonial revolutionary governments. His most famous essay on the struggle against colonialism is his preface to Frantz Fanon's *The Wretched of the Earth*, in which he trumpets the liberatory power of violence. The essay contains a summons: "Europeans, open this book and enter into it. After a few steps in the night, you will see strangers gathered around a fire, draw closer, listen: they are discussing the fate they have in store for your trading posts, for the mercenaries who defend these." Colonialism, Sartre proceeds to argue, is a form of institutionalized daily violence. It is a regime of brutal dehumanization and it requires a violent response. The natives' "weapons are their humanity...they have to kill: to shoot down a European is to kill two birds with one stone, doing away with oppressor and oppressed at the same time: what remains is a dead man and a free man...."

6.

Sartre's political activities continued unabated throughout the 1960s, even as he worked on such major and massive works as the second volume of *Critique of Dialectical Reason* and *The Family Idiot*. He spurned the Nobel Prize, but he was to become something of an institution himself, an alternative ambassador roving the world from Brazil to the Soviet Union to Israel and Japan. His travels, arranged by left-wing governments, parties, and movements, became media events, featuring press conferences and interviews during which he was asked to comment on anything and everything. In 1967, Sartre presided over the Bertrand Russell International War Crimes Tribunal, during which the United States was accused and then judged guilty of committing genocide in Vietnam. In May 1968, he showed his support for the student movement by interviewing student leader Daniel Cohn-Bendit. He accepted the new movement's rejection of traditional authority, including his own, and used his celebrity to help the struggle. Interrupting work on his biography of Flaubert, he joined the activists in selling copies of the Maoist newspaper *La Cause du peuple* on the street. He remained an acute analyst of the changing world around him. "The Third World Begins in the Suburbs," from 1970, is a prophetic account of how colonial relationships have seeped into the cities of the advanced societies of the West; "Elections: A Trap for Fools," from 1973, argues that elections as we know them are intended to keep people passive and powerless.

The Israeli–Palestinian conflict, especially as it emerged around the time of the Six-Day War in 1967, was the one subject on which Sartre consistently and deliberately refused to take sides. While those close to him became pro-Arab and then pro-Palestinian on the one side or pro-Israeli on the other, Sartre insisted on the legitimacy of *both* sides, while encouraging them to listen to each other. In a 1969 interview he reached a balanced conclusion, which remains no less relevant today: "If I recognize that the child or a grandchild of a Jew who settled in Israel has the right to remain in his country because he lives there and shouldn't be expelled, I recognize that the

Palestinians, in virtue of the same principle, have the right to return to it."

The essays from Sartre's last two decades are not, however, exclusively devoted to politics. He writes about Kierkegaard and Tintoretto, among other philosophers, writers, and artists, and begins also to look back on his own life and work. In 1963 he had published his autobiography, *Les Mots*, and a number of essays from around the same time display the reflective awareness of that book. Sartre looks back to the 1930s and his relationship with his childhood friend Nizan, a gifted novelist and, for a time, a committed communist, who died in the war. He composes a long eulogy for Merleau-Ponty, regretting his break with the man who helped him to see the importance of politics. At the end of the decade, in a 1969 interview with the editors of *New Left Review*, Sartre looks back with astonishment at his early self: "The other day, I re-read a prefatory note of mine to a collection of these plays—*Les Mouches*, *Huis Clos*, and others—and was truly scandalized. I had written: 'Whatever the circumstances, and wherever the site, a man is always free to choose to be a traitor or not....' When I read this, I said to myself: 'It's incredible, I actually believed that!'" He continues: "This is the limit I would today accord to freedom: the small movement which makes of a totally conditioned social being someone who does not render back completely what his conditioning has given him."*

As his eyesight and energy deteriorated in the 1970s, Sartre depended more and more on interviews to develop his ideas. In "Self-Portrait at Seventy," a discussion with Michel Contat, he reflects on his achievements and failures, on the loss of his powers, and on the approaching end of his life. Contat inquires:

In short, so far life has been good to you?
    On the whole, yes. I don't see what I could reproach it with.
It has given me what I wanted and at the same time it has shown

---

* Jean-Paul Sartre, "Itinerary of a Thought," *New Left Review* 58 (November–December 1969): 44; reproduced in Jean-Paul Sartre, *Between Existentialism and Marxism*, trans. John Matthews (London: Verso, 1974), 33–64.

that this wasn't much. But what can you do? [The interview ends in wild laughter brought on by the last statement.] The laughter must be kept. You should put: "Accompanied by laughter."

7.

The essays in this book span the whole of Sartre's career and offer a representative sample of his various interests. They reflect the way his thinking changed over time and in relation to his times. Sartre's essays remain alive today, and his thoughts live in them. They are all responses to lived experience that value the experience supremely. They display the same sense of presence that Sartre brings to describing an Alexander Calder mobile, seeing it as "a little local party; an object defined by its movement and nonexistent without it."

These essays clearly illustrate the sharp political turn that Sartre's thinking took after the war. Of the twenty-one essays here that were written after 1944, fourteen are concerned with politics. Sartre was a brilliant advocate and a merciless polemicist. He belongs to a great French tradition of literary intervention that reaches from Pascal's "Provincial Letters" through Voltaire and Rousseau to Zola's "J'Accuse." Reading these essays at the beginning of the twenty-first century, how do we judge Sartre's engagements?

Sartre died in 1980. The Soviet Empire collapsed in 1989, followed by the Soviet Union itself. Sweeping post–cold war reappraisals of communism began to appear around the world, and especially in France,* where the reputation of anticommunists like Aron and Camus rose. Sartre's sank. Not that his philosophical or literary achievements were denied, but the activist Sartre, who supported the Communist Party, who eulogized revolutionary violence, fell into discredit. Bernard-Henri Lévy denounced the "totalitarian Sartre," whom he deemed guilty of "obtuse stupidity" and of writing "crazy,

---

* See Ronald Aronson, "Communism's Posthumous Trial," *History and Theory* 42, 2 (May 2003).

incomprehensible texts."* According to Tony Judt, "Sartre did not hesitate to advocate political murder as both efficacious and cleansing."†

Sartre's critics are in many respects right. He denounced the French campaign of terror and torture in Algeria, but at the same time gave a blank check to the Algerian National Liberation Front, which conducted a campaign of terror of its own that targeted not only French authorities but civilians and even other Algerian organizations. In the notorious Fanon essay, a consideration of the psychic damage inflicted by colonialism turns into a celebration of revolutionary bloodletting as therapy. Sartre spoke feelingly of terror as a "terrible weapon," and yet he never considered just how terrible its consequences might be.

Similarly Sartre was well acquainted with the horrors of communism but between 1952 and 1956 he was personally silent about show trials, forced-labor camps, the anti-Semitic Doctors' Plot, and the uprising in East Berlin. Indeed, after visiting the USSR in 1954, he spoke of it in glowing terms. His first response to Khrushchev's "Secret Speech" revealing Stalin's crimes was to dismiss it. Even after the invasion of Hungary, he addressed the Soviet leaders as comrades who had made a serious mistake and concluded that their admittedly ugly society was the only possible path to socialism. In May 1968, Sartre joined the students against the PCF as well as de Gaulle, yet only after the invasion of Czechoslovakia—not until 1969—did Sartre publicly denounce the communist system itself.

Sartre's inconsistencies and errors have led critics like Lévy to speak of "two Sartres." This enables Lévy to rescue the person he regards as the good Sartre from the one he regards as the bad Sartre, with the latter's regrettable attraction to "violence and revolutionary messianism." This is too easy. There is a single Sartre, perhaps nowhere more visible than in these essays; his strengths and weaknesses come from the same person, the same commitments, the same intellectual

---

* Bernard-Henri Lévy, *Sartre: The Philosopher of the Twentieth Century*, trans. Andrew Brown (Cambridge, UK: Polity, 2003), 321–38.
† Tony Judt, "The Rootless Cosmopolitan," *The Nation* (July 1, 2004), available at www.thenation.com/article/rootless-cosmopolitan.

and moral sources. Sartre's works fairly seethe with a hatred for colonialism, racism, anti-Semitism, and capitalism. He sees the world in Manichean terms, rooted in solidarity with the victims of oppression and fury against their exploiters.

Despite the PCF's faults, Sartre joined forces with them because of their ties to the French working class, and he sided with the Soviet Union because of its aspiration to build a society that would end exploitation. Similarly he insisted that the violence of the underdog must not be tabooed, repressed, or ignored: It was an essential part of the struggle to be human in the face of systemic violence. And yes, this stance also generated the romantic declaration that revolutionary violence, including terrorism, "is no less than man reconstructing himself." This is the voice of the single Sartre, a man of powerful commitments and terrible errors. The same man, for the same reasons, could be morally, politically, and historically right on many key issues of the twentieth century and morally, politically, and historically wrong on others—and both at the same time.

But as true as that may be, this judgment is too gentle on Sartre. And in any case, to explain is not to excuse. Sartre was uncritical toward those in struggle and, in more than one instance, was guilty of out-and-out dishonesty. Today, long after his passing, his writings continue to encourage a vicious climate on the radical left, one that accepts terrorism. He too easily justified violence and ignored the perilous structures, relationships, and attitudes that violence can generate. This is the heart of Camus's argument with Sartre, and on this point Camus was right.

But where do these criticisms leave us? These marks against Sartre do not change the fact that the essayist we find on the pages that follow was one of the great moralists of the twentieth century. Any full accounting must place, alongside his time of fellow-traveling with communism and his blindness to the costs of political violence, Sartre's radical hatred of oppression, his intense advocacy of freedom.

As an advocate of freedom, Sartre spoke concretely for human subjectivity and spontaneity, our self-determination and responsibility, and our capacity to create and resist—no matter what the circumstances. And in these essays and others he described many of the circumstances, and the hidden and overt violence, of oppressive practices and systems. This, after all, is what makes the Fanon essay impossible to ignore today.

Politically that meant taking responsibility, taking sides, and making mistakes. His hostility to oppression, whether that of systems or of deliberate practices, is also addressed to those of us who regard ourselves as bystanders. Sartre would not be a bystander—certainly not after the Liberation. He advocated for the oppressed and against their oppressors, so fiercely that he sometimes lost track of who was who, and exactly what were the roads to freedom. He insists that we cannot divorce ourselves from our society's practices and structures, inasmuch as these depend on our passive complicity if not our active consent. Its oppressions are carried out and rationalized in our name, Sartre argues, and insofar as we benefit from them, like it or not, we are responsible for them. The only way to avoid bad faith, he says, is to take responsibility, to break our complicity—to actively resist.

Sartre is not alone in posing this challenge. Questions of individual responsibility were central to the Nuremberg trials and continue to arise in democracies; part of the power of psychotherapy has been to encourage people to see that though they have been shaped by forces beyond their control, they can still take responsibility for their actions. But none of these sources is as sharp, radical, and urgent as Sartre: prodding people to assume responsibility for themselves and their world, demanding that they see their own links with societies and systems that injure others—demanding that they see themselves as active subjects and that they participate consciously in their societies and their histories. This, his great moral-political contribution, continues to resonate among us today.

—RONALD ARONSON

THE TEXTS

THE TEN volumes of *Situations* represent the most extensive collection of Sartre's essays, but they are far from exhaustive. The missing material includes pieces published in Resistance publications that have never before been reprinted; numerous newspaper articles that Sartre filed from the United States (still mostly uncollected) and Cuba (collected and translated into English as *Sartre on Cuba*); several shorter essays collected by Contat and Rybalka in *Les Écrits de Sartre* (subsequently translated as Sartre's *Selected Prose*); and a number of book-length essays.

The aim of our selection has been to provide the most substantial one-volume overview of Sartre's activity as an essayist available in English to date. We have with a single exception ("Merleau-Ponty") selected essays that can be read in one sitting—no longer, say, than "Black Orpheus" or "A New Mystic." Out of respect for the integrity of their forms, we have resisted the temptation to excerpt, except in the cases of *The Ghost of Stalin* and the interview "Self-Portrait at Seventy." We have also included a second interview, "Israel and the Arab World," inasmuch as it represents a rare public statement on a major issue that preoccupied Sartre over the years.

While being obliged to omit some crucial pieces for reasons of length—*Existentialism Is a Humanism* and *Anti-Semite and Jew*, for instance, were published and remain available as books—we have nonetheless succeeded in including outstanding work from each period in Sartre's life, work that also reflects his entire range of interests. In order to allow the reader to follow the logic of development of Sartre's thought, we have chosen to arrange the texts in what, to the best of our knowledge, is the order of their composition.

Three of the pieces here have never previously appeared in English translation: "Portrait of the Adventurer," "Israel and the Arab World," and "The Third World Begins in the Suburbs." In addition, Sartre's inaugural statement to the Russell Tribunal and the seven *Combat* articles on the American working class are gathered here in an English-language Sartre collection for the first time. We have also provided or added notes to many of the previously translated essays. Exceptions to this are the recent translations by Chris Turner for Seagull Books of *Situations, I, III,* and *IV* (*Critical Essays, The Aftermath of War,* and *Portraits*). We are grateful to Seagull Books and Chris Turner for making these translations available to us. For information on the publishing history of each selection, please see the respective Notes section.

Finally, the editors would like to acknowledge Monica van den Hoven and Phyllis Aronson for their patience, Edwin Dénommée for the many hours he spent checking the original French articles against the translations, David Drake and Jean-Pierre Boulé for their helpful comments on the introduction, and Carole Keller for her assistance at all stages of the project.

—Ronald Aronson
Adrian van den Hoven

WE HAVE ONLY
THIS LIFE TO LIVE

A FUNDAMENTAL IDEA OF
HUSSERL'S PHENOMENOLOGY:
INTENTIONALITY

"HE DEVOURED her with his eyes." This phrase and many other indications point up to some extent the illusion, common to both realism and idealism, that to know is to eat. After a hundred years of academicism, French philosophy is still at this point. We have all read Brunschvicg, Lalande, and Meyerson;[1] we all once believed that the Spider-Mind attracted things into its web, covered them with a white spittle, and slowly ingested them, reducing them to its own substance. What is a table, a rock, or a house? A certain assemblage of "contents of consciousness," an ordering of those contents. Oh alimentary philosophy! Yet nothing seemed more obvious: Isn't the table the current content of my perception? Isn't perception the present state of my consciousness? Nutrition, assimilation. The assimilation, as Lalande said, of things to ideas, of ideas among themselves, and of minds between themselves. The powerful bones of the world were picked apart by these painstaking diastases: assimilation, unification, and identification. In vain did the simplest and coarsest of us search for something solid, something that was not, ultimately, mere mind. But they encountered everywhere an insubstantial, though very distinguished, fog: themselves.

Against the digestive philosophy of empirio-criticism and neo-Kantianism and all forms of "psychologism," Husserl never tires of asserting that one cannot dissolve things in consciousness. Admittedly, you see this tree here. But you see it at the place where it is: beside the road, amid the dust, standing alone and distorted in the heat, twenty leagues from the Mediterranean coast. It cannot enter your consciousness, because it is not of the same nature as consciousness. You think you recognize Bergson's position in the first chapter of *Matter and Memory* here. But Husserl isn't in any way a realist: he doesn't make this tree, standing on its bit of cracked earth, an absolute that would subsequently enter into communication with us. Consciousness and the world are given at a single stroke: the world, external by its essence to consciousness is, by its essence, relative to consciousness. This is because Husserl sees consciousness as an irreducible fact, which no physical image can render. Except, perhaps, the rapid, obscure image of bursting. To know is to "burst out toward," to wrest oneself from moist, gastric intimacy and fly out over there, beyond oneself, to what is not oneself. To fly over there, to the tree, and yet outside the tree, because it eludes and repels me and I can no more lose myself in it than it can dissolve itself into me: outside it, outside myself. Don't you recognize your own exigencies and sense of things in this description? You knew very well that the tree wasn't you, that you couldn't take it inside your dark stomach, and that knowledge couldn't, without dishonesty, be compared to possession. And, in this same process, consciousness is purified and becomes as clear as a great gust of wind. There is nothing in it anymore, except an impulse to flee itself, a sliding outside of itself. If, impossibly, you were to "enter" a consciousness, you would be picked up by a whirlwind and thrown back outside to where the tree is and all the dust, for consciousness has no "inside." It is merely the exterior of itself and it is this absolute flight, this refusal to be substance, that constitute it as a consciousness. Imagine now a linked series of bursts that wrest us from ourselves, that do not even leave an "ourself" the time to form behind them but rather hurl us out beyond them into the dry dust of the world, onto the rough earth, among things. Imagine we are thrown out in this way, abandoned by our very natures in an indifferent, hostile, resistant world. If you do so, you will have grasped the profound meaning of the discovery Husserl expresses in this famous phrase: "All consciousness is consciousness *of* something." This is all it takes to put an end to the cozy philosophy of immanence, in which everything works by compromise, by protoplasmic exchanges, by a tepid cellular chemistry. The philosophy of transcendence throws us out onto the high road, amid threats and under a blinding light. Being, says Heidegger, is being-in-the-world. This "being-in" is to be understood in the sense of movement. To be is to burst forth into the world. It is to start out from a nothingness-of-world-and-consciousness and suddenly to burst-out-as-consciousness-in-the-world. If consciousness attempts to regain control of itself, to coincide, at long last, with itself, in a nice warm room with the shutters closed, it annihilates itself. Husserl calls this need on the part of consciousness to exist as consciousness of something other than itself "intentionality."

If I have spoken, first, of knowledge, I have done so to gain a better hearing: the French philosophy that shaped us is almost totally confined now to epistemology. But, for Husserl and the phenomenologists, the consciousness we have of things is not in any way limited to mere knowledge of them. Knowledge or "pure" representation is only one of the possible forms of my consciousness *of* this tree. I may also love it, fear it, hate it, and this surpassing of consciousness by itself that we call intentionality turns up again in fear, hatred, and love. To hate another person is one more way of bursting out toward him; it is to find oneself suddenly faced with a stranger whose objective "hateful" quality one experiences or, rather, first suffers. Suddenly, then, these famous "subjective" reactions of love and loathing, fear and liking, which were floating around in the foul-smelling brine of the Mind, tear themselves away from it; they are merely ways of discovering the world. It is things that suddenly disclose themselves to us as hateful, pleasant, horrible, or lovable. To be terrifying is a *property* of this Japanese mask, an inexhaustible, irreducible property that constitutes its very nature—not the sum of our subjective reactions to a piece of carved wood. Husserl has put horror and charm back into things. He has given us back the world of artists and prophets: frightening, hostile, and dangerous, with havens of grace and love. He has cleared the way for a new Treatise of Passions that would take its inspiration from this very simple truth that is so poorly understood by our finest minds: if we love a woman, it is because she is lovable. We can leave Proust behind now. And, with him, the "inner life": in vain would we seek, like Amiel,[2] or like a child kissing her own shoulder, the caresses and fondlings of a private intimacy, since, at long last, everything is outside. Everything, including ourselves. It is outside, in the world, among others. It is not in some lonely refuge that we shall discover ourselves, but on the road, in the town, in the crowd, as a thing among things and a human being among human beings.

ON JOHN DOS PASSOS AND *1919*

A NOVEL is a mirror. Everyone says so. But what is it to *read* a novel? I believe that it is to jump into the mirror. Suddenly, you find yourself through the looking glass, among people and objects that seem familiar. But this is simply an appearance; in fact we have never seen them before. And the things in our world are now external in their turn and have become mere reflections. You close the book, climb back over the rim of the mirror, and re-enter *this* honest-to-goodness world, and you are back with furniture, gardens, and people who have nothing to say to you. The mirror that has reconstituted itself behind you reflects them peacefully. After which you would swear that art is a reflection. And the cleverest will go so far as to speak of distorting mirrors. Dos Passos uses this absurd, obstinate illusion very consciously to prick us into revolt. He has done what was necessary for his novel to appear a mere reflection; he has even donned the dowdy garb of populism. But the fact is that his art is not gratuitous; he has something to prove. Yet consider what a curious enterprise this is: the aim is to show us *this* world, our world. To *show* it only, with no explanation or commentary. No revelations about the police's double-dealings, the oil barons' imperialism, or the Ku Klux Klan. And no cruel depictions of poverty. Everything he wants to show us is something we have already seen— and seen, as it initially seems, in just the way he wants to make us see it. We immediately recognize the sad abundance of these untragic lives. They are our lives, these thousand adventures sketched out, botched, immediately forgotten, but constantly begun again, which slide by without a trace, without ever connecting with anything, until the day when suddenly one of them, just like all the others, as though out of clumsiness and trickery, sickens a man forever and carelessly throws a machinery out of kilter. It is by depicting—as we ourselves could depict them—these all too well-known phenomena, which everyone normally accepts, that Dos Passos renders them unbearable. He infuriates those who have never been infuriated before, he frightens those who are frightened of nothing. Has there not perhaps been some sleight of hand here? I look around me and see people, cities, ships, warfare. But they aren't the real thing: they are discreetly suspect and sinister, as in nightmares. My indignation against that world also seems suspect. It merely *resembles* that other indignation, the indignation a little story in the newspaper can arouse—and it does so rather remotely. I am on the other side of the mirror.

Dos Passos's hatred, despair, and lofty contempt are genuine. But for just that reason, his world is not: it is a creation. I know of none, not even those of Faulkner or Kafka, in which the art is greater or better concealed. I know of none closer to us, more precious, more affecting. This is because he takes his material from our world. And yet there is no world further removed from our own or stranger. Dos Passos has invented only one thing: an art of storytelling. But that is enough to create a whole universe.

We live in time and it is in time that we count. The novel unfolds in the present, the way that life does. Only in appearance is the past preterit[1] the tense of the novel; we have to see it as a present *with aesthetic distance*, a staging device. In a novel, matters are not settled once and for all, for human beings in novels are free. They create themselves before our eyes; our impatience, our ignorance, and our expectation are the same as the hero's. By contrast, Fernandez[2] has shown that pure *narrative* is situated in the past. But narrative explains: there, chronological order, the order of life, barely conceals the causal order, the order of the understanding. Events in narrative do not move us; they are located midway between fact and law. Dos Passos's time is his own creation: it is neither novel nor narrative. It is rather, if you will, historical time. The past tenses are not employed to conform to the rules: the *reality* of Joe's or Eveline's adventures is that they are now past. The whole is narrated as if someone were remembering:

> *The years* Dick was little he never heard anything about his Dad ... All Eveline thought about *that winter* was going to the Art Institute ... They waited two weeks in Vigo while the official quarreled about their status and they got pretty fed up with it.[3]

The event in a novel is an unnamed presence: you cannot say anything about it because it is unfolding; we can be shown two men looking all around a city for their mistresses, but we are not told that they "don't find them" because that is not how it is: so long as there is still a street, a café or a house to explore, that is not how it is *yet*. With Dos Passos, we begin with the event being named. The die is cast, as in our memories:

> Glen and Joe only got ashore for a few hours and couldn't find Marcelline and Loulou.[4]

The facts have a clear outline to them; they are just ripe for *thinking about*. But Dos Passos never thinks about them. Not for a moment do we catch the order of causes beneath the order of dates. This is not narrative: it is the jerky unwinding of a raw memory full of holes, which sums up a period of several years in a few words, then lingers languidly over some tiny fact. In this it is just like our real memories, a jumble of frescoes and miniatures. There is no lack of relief, but it is artfully distributed at random. One step further and we would be back at the famous idiot's monologue in *The Sound and the Fury*. But that would still be to intellectualize, to suggest an explanation in terms of the irrational, to hint at a Freudian order behind this disorder. Dos Passos halts himself in time. As a result of which, past facts retain a savor of the present. They remain, in their exile, what they once were for a day, a single day: inexplicable tumults of color, noise, and passion. Each event is a—gleaming, solitary—*thing* that doesn't ensue from any other but emerges suddenly and adds itself to other things. It is irreducible. For Dos Passos, storytelling is an act of addition. Hence this loose air to his style: "and...and...and..." The great tumultuous phenomena—war, love, a political movement or a strike—fade and crumble into an infinity of little trifles that one can just place side by side. Here is the Armistice:

> In early November rumors of an armistice began to fly around and then suddenly one afternoon Major Wood ran into the office that Eleanor and Eveline shared and dragged them both away from their desks and kissed them both and shouted, "At last it's come." Before she knew it, Eveline found herself kissing Major Moorehouse right on the mouth. The Red Cross office turned into a college dormitory on the night of a football victory: It was the Armistice.
>
> Everybody seemed suddenly to have bottles of cognac and to be singing. *There's a long long trail awinding* or *La Madel-lon pour nous n'est pas sévère.*[5]

These Americans see war the way Fabrice del Dongo saw the battle of Waterloo.[6] And the intention, like the method, is clear when one thinks about it. But one must first close the book and reflect.

Passions and actions are also things. Proust analyzed them, connected them to previous states, and, as a consequence, rendered them necessary. Dos Passos wants to preserve their *factual* character. We can only say, "At that time Richard was like this, and at another time he was different." Love and decisions are great self-contained spheres. At best we can grasp a kind of *match-up* between psychological state and external situation: something like a color harmony. Perhaps, too, we will suspect that explanations are *possible*. But they seem frivolous and futile, like a spider's web lying on heavy red flowers. Nowhere, however, do we have the sense of novelistic freedom. Rather Dos Passos forces on us the unpleasant impression of an indeterminacy of detail. Acts, emotions, and ideas settle suddenly upon a character, make their nests, and then fly off, without the character himself having much to do with it. We should not say that he *undergoes* these things; he registers them, and no one can say what law governs their appearance.

Yet they did exist. This lawless past is irremediable. In his storytelling Dos Passos deliberately chose the perspective of history: he wants to make us feel that the die is cast. In *Man's Hope*, Malraux says, more or less, that the tragic thing about death is that it "transforms life into fate."[7] From the first lines of his book, Dos Passos has settled into death. All the existences he retraces have closed upon themselves. They are like those Bergsonian memories that float around, after the death of the body, full of shouts and smells and light, in some sort of limbo. We have a constant sense of these vague, humble lives as Destinies. Our own pasts are not like this: there is not one of our past acts whose value and meaning we could not still transform today. But, beneath their violent hues, these fine, gaily colored objects Dos Passos presents us with have something petrified about them. Their meaning is fixed. Close your eyes and try to remember your own life. Try to remember it like this. You will suffocate. It is this unrelieved suffocation Dos Passos has tried to express. In capitalist society, people do not have lives; they have only destinies. He doesn't say this anywhere, but he implies it everywhere. Discreetly and cautiously, he presses the point till he fills us with a desire to shatter our destinies. We are rebels now and his goal is achieved.

Rebels *behind the mirror*. For this isn't what the this-worldly rebel wants to change. He wants to change the *present* condition of human beings, the condition that evolves day by day. To relate the present in the past tense is to employ artifice, to create a strange and beautiful world, a world as rigid as one of those Mardi Gras masks that become terrifying when real, live human beings wear them on their faces.

But what are these memories that are unreeled in this way throughout the novel? At first sight, it seems as though they are the memories of the heroes—of Joe, Dick, Daughter,[8] and Eveline. And, on more than one occasion, this is true. It is true as a general rule, each time a character is sincere, each time he has a fullness in him of some sort or another:

> When he went off duty he'd walk home achingly tired through the strawberry-scented early Parisian morning, thinking of the faces and the eyes and the sweat-drenched hair and the clenched fingers clotted with blood and dirt ...[9]

But often the narrator doesn't coincide entirely with the hero. The hero couldn't precisely have said what he says, but one feels a discreet complicity between the two; the narrator recounts things from outside in the way the hero would like them to have been recounted. Under cover of this complicity, without alerting us to the fact, Dos Passos has us make the transition he was trying for: we suddenly find ourselves inside a horrible memory, and every recollection in it makes us ill at ease. It is a memory in which we lose our bearings, being neither that of the characters nor of the author. It is like a chorus remembering—a sentencious, yet complicit chorus:

All the same he got along very well at school and the teachers liked him, particularly Miss Teazle, the English teacher, because he had nice manners and said little things that weren't fresh, but that made them laugh. Miss Teazle said he showed a real feeling for English composition. One Christmas he sent her a little rhyme he made up about the Christ Child and the three Kings and she declared he had a gift.[10]

The narrative becomes a little stilted and everything we are told about the hero assumes the air of solemn, publicity-style information. "She declared he had a gift." There is no commentary on the sentence, but it acquires a kind of collective resonance. It is a *declaration*. And indeed, when we would like to know the thoughts of his characters, Dos Passos most often provides us, with respectful objectivity, with their declarations:

Fred ... said the last night before they left he was going to tear loose. When they got to the front he might get killed and then what? Dick said he liked talking to the girls but that the whole business was too commercial and turned his stomach. Ed Shuyler, who'd been nicknamed Frenchie and was getting very continental in his ways, said that the street girls were too naïve.[11]

I open *Paris-Soir* and read: "From our special correspondent: Charlie Chaplin says he has killed off the little tramp." Now I have it:

Dos Passos reports all his characters' words in the style of press releases. They are, as a result, immediately cut off from thought; they are pure words, simple reactions to be registered as such, after the fashion of the behaviorists, from whom Dos Passos takes occasional inspiration. But at the same time utterances assume a social importance: they are sacred, they become maxims. No matter what Dick had in his mind when he pronounced this sentence, thinks the satisfied chorus; all that matters is that it was pronounced. Besides, it came from way beyond him; it didn't form inside him. Even before he spoke, it was a high-sounding, ritualized noise; he merely lent it his power of assertion. It seems there is a celestial store of utterances and commonplaces from which each of us plucks the words appropriate to the situation. And a store of actions too. Dos Passos pretends to present us with actions as pure events, as mere *exteriors*, the free movements of an animal. But this is only a semblance: in relating them he actually adopts the standpoint of a chorus, of public opinion. Every one of Dick's or Eleanor's actions is a public manifestation, accompanied by a low murmur of flattery:

> At Chantilly they went through the château and fed the big carp in the moat. They ate their lunch in the woods, sitting on rubber cushions. J.W. kept everybody laughing explaining how he hated picnics, asking everybody what it was that got into even the most intelligent women that they were always trying to make people go on picnics. After lunch they drove out to Senlis to see the houses that the Uhlans had destroyed there in the battle of the Marne.[12]

Isn't this like the account of a veterans' dinner reported in a local newspaper? At the same time as the action dwindles merely to a thin film, we suddenly realize that it *counts*, in the sense both that it commits the characters and is sacred. Sacred for whom? For the vile consciousness of "everyone," for what Heidegger calls "das Man." But who brings this consciousness to life? Who represents it as I read? Why, I do. To understand the words, to give a meaning to the paragraphs, I first have to adopt the point of view of everyone's consciousness. I have to become the obliging chorus. That consciousness exists only through me; without me there would merely be black flecks on white sheets of paper. But at the very moment when I *am* this collective consciousness, I also want to wrench myself away from it, to assume the viewpoint of the judge—that is to say, to wrench myself away from myself. Hence this shame and unease Dos Passos is so good at imparting to his readers. I am complicit despite myself—though I am not so sure that it is despite myself—creating and rejecting taboos at one and the same time. I am, once again, to my very core—and against myself—revolutionary.

On the other hand, how I hate Dos Passos's people! Their minds are revealed to me for a second, just to show me that they are living beasts, and then there they are, interminably unfurling their tissue of ritual declarations and sacred acts. Not for them the divide between exterior and interior, between consciousness and the body, but one between the stammerings of an individual, timid, intermittent, inarticulate thinking and the viscous world of collective representations. What a simple procedure this is, and how effective! You have only to relate a life using the techniques of American journalism and life, like Stendhal's *"rameau de Salzbourg,"* crystallizes into something social.[13] By the same token, the problem of the transition to "the typical"— that stumbling block of the social novel—is solved. There is no need to present us with a typical worker, to put together, as Nizan does in *Antoine Bloyé*, an existence that is the precise average of thousands of existences. Dos Passos can devote all his attention to portraying the singularity of a life. Each of his characters is unique; what happens to them could happen only to them. And what matter, since social life has marked them more deeply than any particular circumstance could, since *they are* that social life? Beyond the chance workings of destiny and the contingency of details, we glimpse in this way an order more flexible than Zola's physiological necessity or Proust's psychological mechanism. It is a gentle, wheedling form of constraint that seems to let go of its victims, only to take hold of them again later without their suspecting it. It is, in short, a statistical determinism. They live as they are able, these people submerged in their own lives;

they pursue their various struggles and what happens to them wasn't determined beforehand. And yet neither their crimes, their efforts, nor their worst acts of violence can disrupt the regularity of births, marriages, and suicides. The pressure a gas exerts on the walls of its containing vessel doesn't depend on the individual history of the molecules that make it up.

We are still on the other side of the mirror. Yesterday you saw your best friend and told him of your passionate hatred of war. Now try to tell yourself that story in the style of Dos Passos. "And they ordered two beers and said that war was appalling. Paul stated he'd rather do anything than fight and John said he concurred and both were moved and said they were happy to agree. As he was going home, Paul decided to see more of John." You will immediately hate yourself. But it won't take you long to see that you *can't* speak of yourself in this tone. However insincere you might have been, at least you lived out your insincerity; you played it out on your own, you extended its existence at every moment in a process of continued creation. And even if you let yourself be dragged down into collective representations, you had first to live these out as an individual abdication. We are neither mechanisms nor possessed souls, but something worse: we are free. Entirely *outside* or entirely *inside*. Dos Passos's human is a hybrid, internal-external creature. We are with him and in him. We live with his vacillating individual consciousness and, suddenly, it falters, weakens, and flows off into the collective consciousness. We follow him and suddenly, here we are, outside, without having noticed it. This is the creature beyond the looking glass—strange, contemptible, and fascinating. Dos Passos knows how to achieve some marvelous effects with this perpetual slippage. I know of nothing more striking than the death of Joe:

> Joe laid out a couple of frogs and was backing off towards the door, when he saw in the mirror that a big guy in a blouse was bringing down a bottle on his head held with both hands. He tried to swing around but he didn't have time. The bottle crashed his skull and he was out.[14]

We are inside, with him, until the impact of the bottle on his head. Immediately afterward, we are outside, with the chorus: "and he was out." Nothing conveys the sense of annihilation more clearly. And every page you turn after that, speaking of other minds and a world that carries on without Joe, is like a spadeful of earth on his corpse. But this is a behind-the-looking-glass death. What we apprehend is, in fact, merely the fine *semblance* of nothingness. True nothingness can neither be felt nor thought. Of our real deaths neither we nor anyone after us will ever have anything to say.

Dos Passos's world, like Faulkner's, Kafka's, or Stendhal's, is impossible because it is contradictory. But therein lies its beauty. Beauty is a veiled contradiction. I regard Dos Passos as the greatest writer of our time.

ON *THE SOUND AND THE FURY*
Temporality in Faulkner

WHEN YOU read *The Sound and the Fury*, what strikes you first are oddities of technique. Why has Faulkner broken up the timeline of his story and scrambled the pieces? Why is the first window that opens onto this fictional world the mind of an idiot? The reader is tempted to search out markers and re-establish the chronology for himself: "Jason and Caroline Compson have had three sons and a daughter. The daughter, Caddy, has given herself to Dalton Ames and become pregnant by him. Forced to get hold of a husband quickly…" Here the reader stops, for he realizes that he is telling a different story. Faulkner didn't first conceive this orderly plot, then shuffle it like a pack of cards; he couldn't tell the story any other way. In the classical novel, there is a crux to the action: the murder of old Karamazov or the meeting of Édouard and Bernard in Gide's *The Counterfeiters*. One would look in vain for such a crux in *The Sound and the Fury*. Is it the castration of Benjy, Caddy's wretched amorous adventure, Quentin's suicide, or Jason's hatred for his niece? Each episode, as soon as you look at it, opens up and reveals other episodes behind it—all the other episodes. Nothing happens; the story doesn't unfold: you discover it beneath every word, like a cumbersome, obscene presence, more or less condensed in each case. It would be wrong to regard these anomalies as gratuitous shows of virtuosity: a novelistic technique always relates to the novelist's metaphysics. The critic's task is to identify the latter before evaluating the former. It is blindingly obvious that Faulkner's metaphysics is a metaphysics of time.

It is man's misfortune that he is a temporal being. "A man is the sum of his misfortunes. One day you'd think misfortune would get tired, but then time is your misfortune..."[1] This is the real subject of the novel. And if the technique Faulkner adopts seems at first a negation of temporality, this is because we are confusing temporality with chronology. It is man who invented dates and clocks: "Constant speculation regarding the position of mechanical hands on an arbitrary dial which is a symptom of mind-function. Excrement Father said like sweating."[2] To arrive at real time, we have to abandon this invented measure which in fact measures nothing: "time is dead as long as it is being clicked off by little wheels; only when the clock stops does time come to life."[3]

Quentin's act of smashing his watch thus has symbolic value: it takes us into clock-less time. And Benjy's time, too, is clock-less, he, the idiot, not knowing how to tell the time.

What is revealed at that point is the present. Not the ideal limit whose place is carefully marked between past and future. Faulkner's present is catastrophic in its essence. It is the event that comes upon us like a thief, enormous and unthinkable. That comes upon us and then disappears. Beyond that present, there is nothing, since the future doesn't exist. The present wells up from we know not where, chasing away another present. It is perpetually beginning anew: "And... and... and then..." Like Dos Passos, but much more discreetly, Faulkner turns his narrative into an addition. The actions themselves, even when they are seen by those who perform them, break up and scatter as they penetrate into the present:

> I went to the dresser and took up the watch with the face still down. I tapped the crystal on the dresser and caught the fragments of glass in my hand and put them into the ashtray and twisted the hands off and put them in the tray. The watch ticked on.[4]

The other characteristic of this present is a *sinking-down*. I use this word, for want of a better one, to point up a kind of motionless movement of this formless monster. There is never any progression in Faulkner, never anything that comes from the future. The present was not first a future possibility, as, for example, when my friend eventually appears, after having been *the man I am waiting for*. No, to be present means to appear without reason and to sink down. This sinking-down isn't part of some abstract vision: it is in things themselves that Faulkner perceives it and attempts to make his readers feel it:

> The train swung around the curve, the engine puffing with short, heavy blasts, and they passed smoothly from sight that way, with that quality of shabby and timeless patience, of static serenity...[5]

Or again,

> Beneath the sag of the buggy the hooves neatly rapid like motions of a lady doing embroidery, *diminishing without progress* like a figure on a treadmill being drawn rapidly off-stage.*

It seems as though, in the very heart of things, Faulkner grasps a frozen speed: congealed spurting presences brush up against him that grow pale, retreat, and reduce without moving.

Yet this elusive, unthinkable immobility can be halted and conceived of. Quentin can say, "I broke my watch." Only, when he says it, his act is already past. The past can be named and narrated; it can, to an extent, be grasped in concepts or recognized by the heart. We have noted, writing elsewhere of *Sartoris*, that Faulkner always showed events when they were finished. In *The Sound and the Fury*, everything happens behind the scenes: nothing happens, everything has happened. This is what enables us to understand the strange expression uttered by one of his heroes: "I was, I am not."[6] In this sense, too, Faulkner is able to make man a sum total without a future. He is "the sum of his climactic experiences," "the sum of his misfortunes," "the sum of what

---

*The italics are mine.

have you": at every moment a line is drawn under events, since the present is merely a lawless rumbling, a past future. It seems Faulkner's worldview can be compared to that of a man sitting in a convertible and looking backward. At each moment, formless shadows rear up to right and left; flickerings, subdued vibrations, wisps of light, which only become trees, people, and cars a little later, as they recede into the distance. The past acquires a sort of surreality in this: its outlines become crisp and hard—changeless. The present, nameless and fleeting, suffers greatly by comparison; it is full of holes and, through these holes, it is invaded by things past, which are fixed, still, and silent, like judges or stares. Faulkner's monologues are reminiscent of airplane journeys with lots of air pockets. With each new pocket, the hero's consciousness sinks back into the past, rises, and then sinks again. The present *is* not; it *becomes*; everything *was*. In *Sartoris*, the past was called "stories," because these were—constructed—family memories and because Faulkner hadn't found his technique yet.[7] In *The Sound and the Fury*, it is more individual and more undecided. But it is so obsessively there that at times it masks the present. And the present makes its way in the shadows like an underground river, reappearing only when it is, itself, past. When Quentin insults Bland,[8]* he doesn't even realize he has done so: he is reliving his dispute with Dalton Ames. And when Bland beats him up, the brawl is overlaid with the one between Quentin and Ames. Later, Shreve *will relate* how Bland struck Quentin: he will relate the scene because it has now become history, but when it was happening in the present, it was merely a veiled, furtive drift of events.

I was told once of a former deputy headmaster who had grown senile and whose memory had stopped like a broken watch: it now stood perpetually at the age of forty. He was sixty years old, but didn't know it and his last memory was of a school playground and the way he used to patrol its covered area each day. As a consequence, he interpreted his present in the light of this final stage of the past and walked around and around his table, convinced he was supervising school-

---

*The dialogue with Bland inserted into the dialogue with Ames, "Did you ever have a sister, did you?" etc., and the inextricable confusion of the two battles.

children at play. Faulkner's characters are like this. Worse: their past, though in order, isn't chronologically ordered. It is grouped into affective constellations. Around a number of central themes (Caddy's pregnancy, Benjy's castration, and Quentin's suicide), innumerable silent clumps of memories gravitate. Hence the absurdity of chronology, of "the assertive and contradictory assurance" of watch faces:[9] the order of the past is the order of the heart. We shouldn't believe that the present, as it passes, becomes our closest memory. Its metamorphosis may sink it to the bottom of our memories, just as it may also leave it on the surface: only its own density and the overall dramatic meaning of our lives determine its level.

Such is Faulkner's time. And is it not familiar? This ineffable present, everywhere, these sudden invasions by the past, this affective order that stands opposed to the order of the intellect and the will (which is chronological, but misses reality), these memories, monstrous, intermittent obsessions, these waverings of the heart—is this not the lost—and regained—time of Marcel Proust? I am not unaware of the differences. I know, for example, that salvation, for Proust, lies in time itself, in the reappearance of the past as something whole and entire. For Faulkner, by contrast, the past is never lost—unfortunately. It is always there, an obsession. Only by mystic ecstasies can one escape the temporal world. A mystic is always a man who wants to forget something: his self or, more generally, language or figural representations. For Faulkner, it is time that has to be forgotten:

Quentin, I give you the mausoleum of all hope and desire; it's rather excruciatingly apt that you will use it to gain the reductio ad absurdum of all human experience which can fit your individual needs no better than it fitted his or his father's. I give it to you not that you may remember time, *but that you might forget it now and then for a moment* and not spend all your breath trying to conquer it. Because no battle is ever won he said. They are not even fought. The field only reveals to man his own folly and despair, and victory is an illusion of philosophers and fools.[10]

It is because he has forgotten time that the hunted Negro of *Light in August* suddenly achieves his strange, dreadful happiness:

It's not when you realize that nothing can help you—religion, pride, anything—it's when you realize that you don't need any aid.[11]

But for Faulkner, as for Proust, time is above all *what separates*. We remember the astonishment of the Proustian heroes who can no longer return to their past loves, of those lovers depicted in *Les Plaisirs et les Jours*, clinging to their passions because they are afraid they may pass and know that they will. We find the same anxiety in Faulkner:

[P]eople cannot do anything that dreadful they cannot do anything very dreadful at all, they cannot even remember tomorrow what seemed dreadful today...[12]

and

[A] love or sorrow is a bond purchased without design and which matures willy-nilly and is recalled without warning to be replaced by whatever issue the gods happen to be floating at the time.[13]

In truth, Proust's novelistic technique *ought to have* been Faulkner's: it was the logical outcome of his metaphysics. But Faulkner is a lost man and it is because he feels lost that he takes risks, that he carries his thoughts through to their conclusions. Proust is a classicist and a Frenchman. The French lose themselves in a small-time sort of way and always end up finding themselves again. Eloquence, a taste for clear ideas, and intellectualism caused Proust to maintain at least the semblance of chronology.

The deep causes of the affinity between the two are to be sought in a very general literary phenomenon: most great contemporary authors—Proust, Joyce, Dos Passos, Faulkner, Gide, and Virginia Woolf —have, each in their own way, attempted to mutilate time. Some have shorn it of a past and future and reduced it to the pure intuition of the moment. Others, like Dos Passos, make it a dead, closed memory. Proust and Faulkner simply decapitated it. They took away its future: that is to say, the dimension of acts and freedom. Proust's heroes never undertake anything. Admittedly, they make plans, but their plans remain stuck to them alone; they cannot be thrown beyond the present, as bridges. They are dreams that reality puts to flight. The Albertine who appears isn't the one we were expecting, and the expectation is a mere inconsequential agitation, confined entirely to the present moment. As for Faulkner's heroes, they never see ahead; the car carries them off, facing backward. The future suicide that throws its dense shadow over Quentin's last day isn't a human possibility: not for a second does Quentin consider that he might *not* kill himself. That suicide is an immobile wall, a *thing* Quentin approaches backward, which he neither wants nor is able to conceive of: "You seem to regard it merely as an experience that will whiten your hair overnight so to speak without altering your appearance at all."[14] It isn't an *undertaking* but a fateful inevitability. By losing its character as possibility, it ceases to exist in the future. It is already present, and Faulkner's whole art is directed at suggesting to us that Quentin's monologues and his last walk *were already* Quentin's suicide. It is in this way, I think, that the following curious paradox is explained: Quentin thinks his last day in the past tense, like someone remembering. But who is doing the remembering, since the hero's last thoughts coincide more or less with the shattering of his memory and his annihilation? The answer has to be that the novelist's skill lies in the choice of the present from which he narrates the past. And the present Faulkner has chosen here is the infinitesimal moment of death, as Salacrou does in *L'Inconnue d'Arras*.[15] So, when Quentin's memory begins to unfurl his recollections ("Through the wall I heard Shreve's bed-springs and then his slippers on the floor hishing. I got up . . ."[16]), *he is already dead.* All this art and, to tell the truth, all this dishonesty are aimed simply at replacing the intuition of the future which the author lacks. Everything is then explained, beginning with the irrationality of time: since the present is the unexpected, the formless, it can acquire determinacy only by an overload of memories. We can understand, too, why duration is "man's characteristic misfortune": if the future has a reality, time distances us from the past and *brings us nearer* to the future; but if you abolish the future, time is now merely that which separates the present—which cuts it off—from itself. "You cannot bear to think that someday it will no longer hurt you like this." Man spends his time battling against time and it gnaws away at him like an acid, wrenches him away from himself, and prevents him from fulfilling his humanity. Everything is absurd: "Life is a tale told by an idiot, full of sound and fury, signifying nothing."[17]

But does human time have no future? I can see that, for a nail or a clod of earth, time is a perpetual present. But is man merely a thinking nail? If we begin by plunging him into universal time, the time of nebulae and planets, of tertiary flexures and animal species, as into a bath of sulfuric acid, then that is the case. But a consciousness buffeted about in that way from one moment to another would have to be a consciousness *first* and only *afterward* something temporal. Do we really believe that time can come to it from outside? Consciousness can "be in time" only on condition that it becomes time in the very movement that makes it consciousness; it must, as Heidegger says, temporalize itself.[18] Man can no longer be arrested at each present and defined as "the sum of what he has": the nature of consciousness implies, rather, that, of itself, it projects itself forward, toward the future; we can understand what it is only by what it will be and it is determined in its current being by its own possibilities. This is what Heidegger calls, "the silent force of the possible."[19] Faulkner's man, a creature deprived of possibilities, explained solely by what he was, is a being you will not recognize within yourself. Try to seize hold of your consciousness. Probe into it. You will see that it is hollow. You will find in it only futurity. I am not even speaking of your plans and expectations. But the very action you catch in passing has meaning for you only if you can project its completion outside of itself, outside of you, into the "not yet." This very cup with its bottom that you do not see—that you could see and that is at the end of a movement you have not yet made—this white sheet of paper, the underside of which is hidden (but you could turn it over), and all the stable, bulky objects surrounding us display their most immediate, most solid qualities in the future. Man is in no sense the sum total of what he has but the totality of what he doesn't yet have, of what he could have. And if we are immersed, in this way, in futurity, isn't the formless harshness of the present thereby attenuated? The event doesn't spring on us like a thief, since it is, by its very nature, a having-been-future. And, in seeking to explain the past, isn't it first the historian's task to research into its future? I rather suspect that the absurdity Faulkner finds in a human life is an absurdity he first put there himself. Not that human life isn't absurd: but there is another form of absurdity.

How does it come about that Faulkner and so many other authors chose that particular absurdity, which is so un-novelistic and so untrue? I believe we have to look for the cause in the social conditions of our present life. Faulkner's despair seems to me to precede his metaphysics. For him, as for all of us, the future is blocked off. Everything we see and experience suggests to us that "this cannot last," and yet change is not even conceivable, except in cataclysmic form. We are living in an age of impossible revolutions and Faulkner employs his extraordinary art to describe this world that is dying of old age and our suffocation in it. I love his art; I do not believe in his metaphysics. A blocked-off future is still a future. "Even when human reality still exists but has nothing more 'before it' and has 'settled [*abgeschlossen*] its account,' its Being is still determined by the 'ahead-of-itself.' Hopelessness, for example, doesn't tear human reality away from its possibilities, but is only one of its own modes of *Being-toward* these possibilities."[20]

THE STRANGER EXPLAINED

As soon as Albert Camus's *The Stranger* came off the press, it met with enormous acclaim. It was widely said to be "the best book since the armistice." Among the literary productions of its time, the novel was itself an outsider. It came to us from the other side of the line, from across the sea.[1] In that bitter coal-less spring, it spoke to us of the sun, not as an exotic marvel but with the weary familiarity of those who have had too much of it. It wasn't concerned with burying the old regime with its own hands once again nor with dinning into us the sense of our unworthiness. Reading it, we remembered that there had, in the past, been works that claimed to stand on their own merits and not prove anything. But, as the price to be paid for this arbitrariness, the novel remained rather ambiguous: what were we to make of this character who, the day after his mother had died, "was swimming in the sea, entering into an irregular liaison and laughing at a Fernandel film," who killed an Arab "because of the sun," and who, on the eve of his execution, stating that he had "been happy, and ... was still happy," wished "that there be a large crowd of spectators the day of [his] execution ... [to] greet [him] with cries of hate."[2] Some said: "He's a poor fool, an idiot"; others, more insightfully: "He's an innocent." And yet the sense of that innocence remained to be understood.

In *The Myth of Sisyphus*, which appeared a few months later, Camus provided us with an accurate commentary on his work: his hero was neither good nor evil, moral nor immoral. These are not categories that suit him: he is a member of a very peculiar species, for which the author reserves the name "*absurd*." But when Camus uses it, this term assumes two very different meanings: the absurd is both a state of fact and the lucid consciousness some people acquire of that state. The "absurd" man is the one who, from a fundamental absurdity, unfailingly draws the inevitable conclusions. There is the same shift in meaning here as when the young people who dance to "swing" music are called the "swing generation." What, then, is the absurd as a state of fact, as an original datum? It is nothing less than man's relation to the world. Primary absurdity is the expression, first and foremost, of a divorce—between man's aspirations toward unity and the insurmountable dualism of mind and nature, between man's longing for the eternal and the *finite* character of his existence, between the "concern" that is his very essence and the futility of his efforts. Death, the irreducible pluralism of truths and beings, chance and the unintelligibility of the real—between these poles lies the absurd. To tell the truth, these are not particularly new themes and Camus doesn't present them as such. They were enumerated as early as the seventeenth century by a certain sort of hard, terse, contemplative reason that is specifically French: they were commonplaces of classical pessimism. Wasn't it Pascal who stressed "the natural unhappiness of our feeble, mortal condition, so wretched that nothing can console us when we really think about it"? Wasn't it he who marked out reason's place? Wouldn't he wholly agree with Camus when he writes: "The world is neither (entirely) rational, nor so irrational either"? Didn't he show us that "custom" and "distractions" mask man's "nothingness, his abandonment, his insufficiency, his dependence, his impotence, his emptiness"? With the frosty style of *The Myth of Sisyphus* and with the subject matter of his essays, Camus places himself in the great tradition of those French moralists whom Charles Andler rightly calls the forerunners of Nietzsche. As for the doubts he raises about the scope of our reason, these are in the most recent tradition of French epistemology. Just think of scientific nominalism, of Poincaré, Duhem, and Meyerson,[3] and you will have a better understanding of the criticism our author makes of modern science: "[Y]ou tell me of an invisible planetary system in which electrons gravitate around a nucleus. You explain this world to me with an image. I realize then that you have been reduced to poetry..."[4] This is expressed separately, but almost at the same moment, by an author who draws on the same sources, when he writes: "(Physics) employs mechanical, dynamical or even psychological models interchangeably, as though, once freed from ontological pretensions, it were becoming indifferent to the classical antinomies of mechanism or dynamism, which presuppose an innate nature."[5] Camus makes a point of citing passages from Jaspers, Heidegger, and Kierkegaard, which, in my view, he doesn't always seem clearly to understand. But his real masters are to be found elsewhere. With the turn of his reasoning, the clarity of his ideas, his essayistic style, and a certain kind of sunlit, ordered, formal, desolate grimness, everything about him points to a man of classic temperament, a writer of the Mediterranean. Even his method ("Solely the balance between evidence and lyricism can allow us to achieve simultaneously emotion and lucidity"[6]) is redolent of the old "impassioned geometries" of Pascal and Rousseau, and brings him considerably closer, for example, to Maurras,[7] that other man of the Mediterranean from whom, however, he differs in so many ways, than to a German phenomenologist or a Danish existentialist.

But Camus would doubtless grant us all that. In his eyes, originality means taking his ideas to their limits; it is not his concern to make a collection of pessimistic maxims. Admittedly, the absurd is neither in man nor in the world, if we take the two separately. But, since it is of the essence of man to "be-in-the-world," the absurd is ultimately of a piece with the human condition. It is not in any sense, therefore, to be grasped as a simple notion; a gloomy insight reveals it to us. "Get up, streetcar, four hours in the office or factory, meal, streetcar, four hours of work, eat, sleep, Monday, Tuesday, Wednesday, Thursday, Friday and Saturday, according to the same rhythm,"[8] and then, suddenly, "the stage-sets collapse" and we arrive at a lucidity bereft of hope. Then, if we are able to reject the sham succor of religions or existential philosophies, we have acquired a number of essential self-evident truths: the world is chaos, "a divine equivalence born of anarchy"; and there is no tomorrow, since we die.

[I]n a universe suddenly divested of illusions and lights, man feels an alien, a stranger. His exile is without remedy since he is deprived of the memory of a lost home or the hope of a promised land.[9]

This is because man *is not*, in fact, the world:

If I were a tree among trees, . . . this life would have a meaning or rather this problem would not arise, for I should belong to this world. I should *be* this world to which I am now opposed by my whole consciousness . . . This ridiculous reason is what sets me in opposition to all creation.[10]

This already in part explains the title of the novel: the outsider is the man who stands in opposition to the world. To describe his work, Camus could just as easily have chosen the name of a novel by Gissing, *Born in Exile*.[11] The outsider is also the man among men. "[T]here are days when . . . we see the woman we had once loved as a stranger."[12] In the end, it is myself in relation to myself: in other words, the man of nature in relation to the mind: "the stranger who at certain seconds comes to meet us in a mirror."[13]

But this is not all there is to it: there is a passion of the absurd. The absurd man will not commit suicide: he wants to live, without abdicating any of his certainties, without tomorrows, without hope, without illusions, but without resignation either. The absurd man affirms himself in revolt. He confronts death with a passionate attention and that fascination liberates him: he knows the "divine irresponsibility" of the condemned man. Everything is permitted, since God doesn't exist and we die. All experiences are equivalent; it is just a matter of acquiring as many as possible. "The present and the succession of presents before a constantly conscious soul is the ideal of the absurd man."[14] All values crumble before this "ethics of quantity"; the absurd man, pitched into this world, in revolt and with no one to answer to, has "nothing to justify." He is *innocent*. Innocent like those primitives Somerset Maugham writes of, before the arrival of the parson who teaches them Good and Evil, tells them what is permitted and what forbidden.[15] For him, *everything* is permitted. He is innocent as Prince Myshkin,[16] who "lives in a perpetual present, varied only by smiles and indifference." An innocent in all senses of the term, and an "Idiot" too, if you will. And this time we fully understand the title of Camus's novel. The stranger he wishes to depict is precisely one of those terrible innocents who scandalize a society because they don't accept the rules of its game. He lives among strangers, but for them too he is a stranger. This is why some will love him, like Marie, his mistress, who likes him "because he is odd," and others will detest him for the same reason, like the crowd in the courtroom whose hatred he can immediately feel rising up toward him. And we ourselves who are not yet, when we open the book, entirely familiar with the feeling of the absurd, would seek in vain to judge him by our usual standards: for us, too, he is a stranger.

So when you opened the book and read, "It occurred to me that anyway one more Sunday was over, that Maman was buried now, that I was going back to work, and that, really, nothing had changed,"[17] the shock you felt was intended. It is the outcome of your first encounter with the absurd. But you were probably hoping that as you went on reading, you would find your sense of unease dissipating, that little by little everything would be cleared up, given a rational foundation, explained. Your hopes were dashed: *The Stranger* is not a book that provides explanations. The absurd man doesn't explain, he describes. Nor is this a book that furnishes proof. Camus merely proposes and doesn't trouble to justify that which is, in principle, unjustifiable. *The Myth of Sisyphus* will teach us how to receive our author's novel. We find in that work the theory of the absurdist novel. Although the absurdity of the human condition is its only subject, *The Stranger* isn't a novel that expounds a message; it doesn't emanate from a "self-sufficient" system of thought intent only on producing evidence for its position. On the contrary, it is the product of a form of thinking that is "limited, mortal and in revolt." It proves, in and of itself, the uselessness of abstract reason:

> The preference [great novelists] have shown for writing in images rather than in reasoned arguments is revelatory of a certain

thought that is common to them all, convinced of the uselessness of any principle of explanation and sure of the educative
message of perceptible appearance.[18]

Thus the mere fact of delivering his message in the form of a novel
reveals a proud humility on Camus's part. Not resignation, but the rebellious recognition of the limits of human thought. Admittedly, he
felt he had to provide a philosophical translation of his novelistic message and this is precisely what *The Myth of Sisyphus* does. We shall see
below what we are to make of this form of duplication. But the existence of this translation in no way detracts from the arbitrary nature of
the novel. The absurdist creator has lost even the illusion that his work
is necessary. On the contrary, he wants us to be constantly aware of its
contingency. He would like to give it the epigraph, "might never have
been," just as Gide wanted to add at the end of *The Counterfeiters* the
message, "could be continued." It might not have been, like this stone,
this stream, or this face. It is a present that simply is given, like all the
world's presents. It doesn't even have that subjective necessity that artists are inclined to claim for their works when they say, "I simply had to
write it; I had to get it out of my system." This is a theme familiar to us
from Surrealist terrorism, though it is exposed here to the harsh light
of classicism: the work of art is merely a leaf torn from a life. It does,
indeed, express that life: but it might have not done so. Moreover, everything is equivalent: writing Dostoevsky's *The Demons* or drinking a
coffee. Camus does not, then, require of his readers that attentive solicitude demanded by the writers who "have sacrificed their lives to
their art." *The Stranger* is one page of his life. And since the most absurd life must be the most sterile, his novel seeks to be magnificent in
its sterility. Art is a useless generosity. But let us not be too horrified
by this. Beneath Camus's paradoxes, I detect the presence of some very
wise remarks by Kant on the "purposeless purposiveness" of the Beautiful. At any rate, *The Stranger* is there, detached from a life, unjustified,
unjustifiable, sterile, instantaneous, already left behind by its author,
abandoned in favor of other presents. And this is how we should approach it, as a brief communion between two human beings, the author and the reader, in the absurd and beyond the realm of reason.

This gives us an indication of more or less how we are to view *The Stranger*'s central protagonist. If Camus had wanted to write a novel with a message, it would not have been difficult to show a civil servant lording it over his family, then suddenly gripped by a sense of the absurd, battling with it for a while, and finally resolving to live out the fundamental absurdity of his condition. The reader would have been convinced at the same time as his character—and by the same arguments. Or, alternatively, he would have recounted the life of one of those saints of absurdity whom he lists in *The Myth of Sisyphus* and of whom he is particularly fond: Don Juan, the Actor, the Conqueror, the Creator. This is not what he has done and, even for the reader familiar with the theories of absurdity, Meursault, the hero of *The Stranger*, remains ambiguous. We are, admittedly, assured that he is absurd, and pitiless lucidity is his chief characteristic. Moreover, he is, in more than one respect, constructed in such a way as to provide a concerted illustration of the theories advanced in *The Myth of Sisyphus*. For example, Camus writes in this latter work: "A man is more a man by the things he remains silent about than by the things he says." And Meursault is an example of this manly silence, of this refusal of idle chatter: "[He was asked] if he had noticed that I was ever withdrawn and all he would admit was that I didn't speak unless I had something to say." And, indeed, two lines before, the same witness for the defense declared that Meursault "was a man." When asked "what he meant by that...he stated that everyone knew what that meant."[19] Similarly, Camus holds forth at length about love in *The Myth of Sisyphus*: "We call love what binds us to certain creatures only by reference to a collective way of seeing for which books and legends are responsible."[20] And, in a passage that parallels this one, we read in *The Stranger*: "A minute later she asked me if I loved her. I told her it didn't mean anything but that I didn't think so." From this point of view, the debate that began in the court and in the mind of the reader around the question "Did Meursault love his mother?" is doubly absurd. First, as the lawyer says, "after all, is my client on trial for burying his mother or for killing a man?" But, above all, the word "love" is meaningless. Meursault probably put his mother in the old-age home because he was short of money and "they had no more to say to each other." Probably, too, he didn't go to see her often "because . . . it took up [his] Sunday—not to mention the trouble of getting to the bus, buying tickets and spending two hours traveling."[21] But what does this mean? Is he not entirely in the present, wrapped up wholly in his present moods? What we call a feeling is simply the abstract unity and the meaning of discontinuous impressions. I am not constantly thinking of those I love, but I claim to love them even when I am not thinking of them—and I would be capable of compromising my peace of mind in the name of an abstract feeling, in the absence of any real, immediate emotion. Meursault thinks and acts differently: he wants nothing to do with these great continuous and indistinguishable feelings. Love doesn't exist for him, nor even love *affairs*. Only the present and the concrete counts. He goes to see his mother when he wants to and that is all there is to it. If the desire is present, it will be powerful enough to make him take the bus, since another concrete desire will have sufficient force to make this lazybones run flat out and jump onto a moving truck. But he always refers to his mother affectionately and childishly as *maman* and he never misses a chance to understand her and identify with her. "Of love I know only that mixture of desire, affection, and intelligence that binds me to this or that creature."[22] We can see, then, that the *theoretical* side of Meursault's character shouldn't be overlooked. Similarly, many of his adventures are there mainly to bring out some particular aspect of fundamental absurdity. For example, as we have seen, *The Myth of Sisyphus* extols the "divine availability of the condemned man before whom the prison doors open in a certain early dawn"[23]—and it was to have us savor this dawn and this "availability" that Camus condemned his hero to capital punishment. "How had I not seen," he has him say, "that nothing was more important than an execution . . . and that, in a sense, it was even the only really interesting thing for a man!"[24] We could quote many more such passages. Yet this lucid, indifferent, taciturn man is not entirely constructed for the needs of the argument. No doubt, once the character was sketched out, it completed the picture itself; it assumed a substance all its own. And yet Meursault's absurdity appears not to be attained, but given. He is like that, and that is all there is to it. His epiphany will come on the last page, but he had always been living by

Camus's standards. If there were a grace of the absurd, we should have to say that he has grace. He doesn't seem to ask himself any of the questions that are aired in *The Myth of Sisyphus*; and we don't see him in revolt before he is condemned to death. He was happy, he followed his star, and his happiness doesn't even seem to have known that secret sting to which Camus refers several times in his essay and which comes from the blinding presence of death. Even his indifference often seems like indolence, as on that Sunday when he stays at home out of sheer laziness and when he admits that he "was a little bored." Thus, even to an absurdist gaze, the character retains an opacity all his own. He is by no means the Don Juan, nor the Don Quixote of absurdity; at many points, we might actually see him as its Sancho Panza. He is there, he exists, and we can neither entirely understand him nor judge him. In a word, he lives, and it is fictional density alone that can justify him in our eyes.

Yet we should not see *The Stranger* as an entirely arbitrary work. As we have said, Camus makes a distinction between the *feeling* and the *notion* of the absurd. On this, he writes: "Like great works, deep feelings always mean more than they are conscious of saying...Great feelings carry with them their own universe, splendid or abject."[25] And, a little further on, he adds: "The feeling of the absurd is not, for all that, the notion of the absurd. It lays the foundations for it, and that is all. It is not limited to that notion."[26] We might say that *The Myth of Sisyphus* aims to provide us with this *notion* and that *The Stranger* seeks to inspire in us the *feeling*. The order in which the two works appeared seems to confirm this hypothesis. *The Stranger*, published first, plunges us without further ado into the "climate" of the absurd; the essay follows, casting its light on the landscape. The absurd is a discrepancy, a gap. *The Stranger* will, as a result, be a novel of gaps and discrepancies, of disorientation. Hence its skillful construction: on the one hand, the amorphous, everyday flow of lived reality; on the other, the edifying reconstruction of that reality by human reason and discourse. The point is that the reader, having first been brought into the presence of pure reality, rediscovers it without recognizing it in its rational transposition. This will be the source of the feeling of the absurd or, in other words, of our incapability of *thinking* the events of the world with our concepts and words. Meursault buries his mother, takes a mistress, and commits a crime. These various facts are recounted at his trial by the assembled witnesses and explained by the public prosecutor: Meursault will have the impression they are talking about someone else. Everything is constructed so as to lead up suddenly to Marie's outburst. Having given an account framed in terms of human rules in the witness box, she bursts into tears: "it wasn't like that, there was something else and she was being made to say the opposite of what she thought."[27] These mirror games have been in common usage since Gide's *Counterfeiters*. This is not where Camus's originality lies. But the problem he has to solve will force him to adopt an original literary form. If we are to feel the gap between the prosecutor's conclusions and the actual circumstances of the murder, if, when we close the book, we are to retain the impression of an absurd justice that will never be able to comprehend, nor even ascertain the nature of, the acts it proposes to punish, we have first to have been brought into contact with reality or with one of these circumstances. But, in order to establish that contact, Camus, like the public prosecutor, has only words and concepts at his disposal. Using words and assembling ideas, he has to describe the world before words. The first part of *The Stranger* could, like a recent book, be called *Translated from Silence*.[28] We touch here on a problem shared by many contemporary writers, the earliest signs of which I see in the work of Jules Renard. I shall call it the obsession with silence. M. Paulhan[29] would certainly see it as an effect of literary terrorism. It has assumed a thousand forms, from the "automatic writing" of the Surrealists to the famous "theater of silence" of Jean-Jacques Bernard. This is because silence, as Heidegger says, is the authentic mode of speech. Only he who knows how to speak can be silent. Camus speaks a lot in *The Myth of Sisyphus*. He even chatters. And yet he tells us of his love of silence. He quotes Kierkegaard's phrase, "The surest of stubborn silences is not to hold one's tongue but to talk."[30] And he adds, himself, that, "A man is more a man by the things he remains silent about than by the things he says." So, in *The Stranger*, he set about being *silent*.

But how can one be silent with words? How, with concepts, can one render the unthinkable, disordered succession of present moments? It is a challenge that requires recourse to a new kind of technique.

What is that technique? "It's Kafka written by Hemingway," someone has suggested. I must admit that I don't see Kafka in it. Camus's views are wholly down-to-earth. Kafka is the novelist of impossible transcendence. For him, the universe is bristling with signs we do not understand. There is something behind the scenery. For Camus by contrast, the human tragedy is the absence of any transcendence.

> I don't know whether this world has a meaning that transcends it. But I know that I do not know that meaning and that it is impossible for me just now to know it. What can a meaning outside my condition mean to me? I can understand only in human terms. What I touch, what resists me—that is what I understand.[31]

There is no question then, for him, of finding arrangements of words that lead us to suspect an indecipherable, inhuman order. The inhuman is merely the disorderly, the mechanical. There is nothing dubious in his work, nothing disquieting, nothing suggested: *The Stranger* presents us with a succession of luminously clear views. If they disorient us, they do so only by their quantity and the absence of any unifying link. Mornings, clear evenings, relentless afternoons—these are his favorite times of day. The perpetual summer of Algiers is his season. There is scarcely any place for night in his universe. If he speaks of it, he does so in the following terms:

> I woke up with stars in my face. Sounds of the countryside were drifting in. Smells of night, earth, and salt air were cooling my temples with the smell of earth and salt. The wondrous peace of that sleeping summer flowed through me like a tide.[32]

The person who wrote these lines is as far as can be from the anguish of a Kafka. He is thoroughly calm amid the chaos. The stubborn blindness of nature irritates him certainly, but it also reassures him. Its irrationality is merely a negative factor: the absurd man is a humanist, he knows only the blessings of this world.

The comparison with Hemingway seems more fruitful. There is an obvious affinity of style. In both texts, we find the same short sentences: each refuses to profit from the impetus of the preceding one; each is a new beginning. Every sentence is like a snapshot of an action or an object. Each new action and each new object has its corresponding new sentence. And yet I am not satisfied: the existence of an "American" narrative technique has, without doubt, assisted Camus. But I doubt that it has, strictly speaking, influenced him. Even in *Death in the Afternoon*, which is not a novel, Hemingway retains this jolting mode of narration, which conjures each sentence out of nothingness in a kind of respiratory spasm: the style is the man. We already know that Camus has a different style, a ceremonial style. But even in *The Stranger*, he occasionally raises the tone: the sentence then has a broader, continuous flow:

> The cries of the newspaper vendors in the already languid evening air, the last few birds in the square, the shouts of the sandwich sellers, the screech of the streetcars turning sharply through the upper town and that hum in the sky before night engulfs the port, all this mapped out for me a route I knew so well before going into prison and which now I travel blind.[33]

Showing through Meursault's breathless narrative, I glimpse a broader underlying poetic prose, which must be Camus's personal mode of expression. If *The Stranger* bears such visible marks of the American technique, that is because there is a deliberate borrowing. Among the instruments available to him, Camus has chosen the one that seemed best to fit his purpose. I doubt if he will use it again in his future works.

Let us look more closely at the framework of his narrative. We shall get a clearer idea of his methods.

Camus writes: "Men too secrete the inhuman. At certain moments of lucidity, the mechanical aspect of their gestures, their meaningless pantomime makes silly everything that surrounds them."[34]

Here, then, is what must first be conveyed: *The Stranger* must put us, from the outset, into "a state of unease at man's inhumanity." But what are the particular occasions that can provoke in us this unease? *The Myth of Sisyphus* gives us an example:

A man is talking on the telephone behind a glass partition; you cannot hear him, but you see his incomprehensible dumb show: you wonder why he is alive.[35]

This tells us what we need to know. It almost tells us too much, for the example reveals a certain bias on the part of the author. The movements of the man on the phone, whom you cannot hear, are only *relatively* absurd: the fact is that he is part of an incomplete circuit. Open the door, put your ear to the receiver, and the circuit is re-established: human activity is senseless no longer. Sincerely, then, we would have to say that there are only relative absurdities—and then only by comparison with "absolute rationalities." Yet it is a question not of sincerity but of art. Camus has a ready-made method: he will insert a glass partition between the characters he is talking about and the reader. What could be more inept than men behind a window? The glass seems to let everything through, but it actually cuts out just one thing: the meaning of their actions. All that remains is to choose the window. In this case, it will be the Stranger's consciousness. It is, in fact, a transparent medium: we see everything that it sees. Only it has been so constructed as to be transparent to things and opaque to meanings:

From then on everything happened very quickly. The men moved towards the casket with a pall. The priest, his acolytes, the director and I all went outside. A woman I didn't know was standing by the door. "M. Meursault," the director said. I didn't catch the woman's name, I just understood that she was the nurse assigned by the home. Without smiling she lowered her long, gaunt face. Then we stepped aside to make way for the body.[36]

People are dancing behind a glass partition. Between them and the reader a consciousness has been inserted—almost nothing, a pure translucency, a purely passive thing recording all the facts. But this has done the trick: precisely because it is passive, the consciousness records only the facts. The reader has not noticed the interposing of the partition. But what, then, is the assumption implied by this kind of narrative? In short, a melodic organization has been turned into an assemblage of invariant elements; it is being claimed that the succession of *movements* is strictly identical with the *act* conceived as a totality. Are we not confronted here with the analytic presupposition that all reality is reducible to a sum total of elements? But if analysis is the instrument of science, it is also the instrument of humor. If I want to describe a rugby match and write: "I saw adults in short pants fighting and throwing themselves on the ground in an effort to get a leather ball between two wooden posts." I have summed up what I *saw*, but I have deliberately omitted its meaning: I have created something humorous. Camus's narrative is analytical and humorous. He lies—like every artist—because he is claiming to render raw experience and yet he is slyly filtering out all the meaningful connections, which are also part of the experience. This is what David Hume did when he announced that all he could find in experience was isolated impressions. This is what today's American neorealists do when they deny that there is anything between phenomena but external relations. Contrary to that view, contemporary philosophy has established that meanings are also immediate data. But that would carry us too far from our subject here. Let us simply note that the universe of the absurd man is the analytical world of the neorealists. In the literary world, this is an approach with a strong track record. It is Voltaire's approach in *L'Ingénu* and *Micromégas*, and Swift's in *Gulliver's Travels*. For the eighteenth century had its outsiders too—"noble savages" as a rule, who, when carried off to unfamiliar civilizations, perceived the facts before they could grasp their meaning. Wasn't the effect of this discrepancy precisely to prompt in the reader a sense of absurdity? Camus seems to remember this on several occasions, particularly when he shows us his hero pondering the reasons for his imprisonment.[37]

It is this analytic method that explains the use of the American technique in *The Stranger*. The presence of death at the end of our road has sent our futures up in smoke; there is "no tomorrow" to our lives; they are a succession of present moments. What does this express, other than that *the* absurd man applies his analytical spirit to time? Where Bergson saw a form of organization that cannot be broken down into smaller units, *his* eye sees only a series of instants. It is the plurality of the incommunicable instants that will, in the end, account for the plurality of beings. What our author borrows from Hemingway, then, is the discontinuity of his chopped-up sentences, which precisely apes the discontinuity of time. We are now better able to understand the cast of his narrative: each sentence is a present moment. But it is not a vague present that smudges and runs into the following one. The sentence is distinct, crisp, self-contained; an entire void separates it from the next one, just as Descartes's moment is separated from the moment that follows. Between each sentence and the next, the world is annihilated and reborn: as it emerges, the word is a creation ex nihilo; a sentence in *The Stranger* is an island. And we tumble from sentence to sentence, from void to void. It is to accentuate the solitude of each sentence unit that Camus chose to narrate his story in the present perfect tense (*le passé composé*).[38] The French past definite (*le passé simple*) is the tense of continuity: "*Il se promena longtemps.*" These words refer us to a *plu*perfect, and to a future. The reality of the sentence is the verb, the act, with its transitive character, its transcendence. "*Il s'est promené longtemps*" conceals the verbalness of the verb. The verb here is shattered, broken in two: on the one hand, we find a past participle that has lost all transcendence and is as inert as a thing; on the other, there is the verb "to be" which functions merely as a copula, joining participle to noun as it might join complement to subject. The transitive character of the verb has vanished and the sentence has become frozen; its reality now is the noun. Instead of projecting itself between past and future, like a bridge, it is merely a little, isolated, self-sufficient substance. If, moreover, one takes care to reduce it as much as possible to the main clause, then its internal structure becomes perfect in its simplicity; and it gains all the more in cohesiveness. It is truly indivisible, an atom of time. Of course, the sentences are not articulated together: they are merely juxtaposed. In particular, all causal relations are avoided, as they would introduce a glimmer of explanation into the narrative and bring an order to its moments that differed in some way from pure succession. Take the following passage:

> A minute later she asked me if I loved her. *I told her that it didn't mean anything but that I didn't think so. She looked sad.* But as we were getting lunch ready, and for no apparent reason, she laughed in such a way that I kissed her. It was at that point that we heard what sounded like a fight break out in Raymond's room.[39]

I have italicized two sentences which, as carefully as possible, conceal a causal link beneath the mere appearance of succession. When it is absolutely necessary to allude to the previous sentence, the words "and," "but," "then," and "it was at that moment that" are used, all of which suggest only disjunction, opposition, or pure addition. The relations between these temporal units are external ones, just like the relations new realism establishes between things. The real appears without being brought onto the scene and disappears without being destroyed. The world collapses and is reborn with each pulse of time. But do not go thinking it generates itself: it is inert. Every activity on its part would tend to substitute fearful powers for the reassuring disorder of chance. A nineteenth-century naturalist would have written, "A bridge spanned the river." Camus rejects such anthropomorphism. He will say, "Over the river there was a bridge." In this way the thing immediately imparts its passivity to us. It simply *is there*, undifferentiated:

> There were four men wearing black in the room . . . A woman I didn't know was standing by the door . . . Outside the gate stood the hearse . . . Next to it was the funeral director.[40]

It was said of Jules Renard that he would end up writing, "The hen lays." Camus and many contemporary authors would write, "There's the hen and she lays." The fact is that they like things for what they are in themselves; they do not wish to dilute them into the flow of time. "There is water": this is a little piece of eternity—passive, impenetrable, incommunicable, sparkling. What sensual delight if one can touch it! For the absurd man this is the one and only blessing of this world. This is why the novelist prefers this shimmering of short-lived moments of brilliance, each of which is a delight, to an organized narrative. This is why, in writing *The Stranger*, Camus is able to believe he is being silent: his sentences don't belong to the universe of discourse; they have neither ramifications, continuations, nor internal structure. A sentence from the novel might be defined, like Valéry's "Sylph" as

Unseen, never happened:
The instant of a naked breast
Between two shifts.

The span of time it takes for a silent intuition to emerge covers it very precisely.

Given this state of affairs, can we speak of a totality we might describe as Camus's novel? All the sentences in his book are equivalent, as are all the experiences of the absurd man. Each one takes its place in its own right and sweeps the others into the void. As a consequence, however, except in the rare moments when the author betrays his own principles and *makes* poetry, none stands out from the others. Even the dialogues are integrated into the narrative. Dialogue provides a moment of explanation, of meaning: to give it prominence would be to admit that meanings exist. Camus shaves it down, summarizes it, expressing it often in indirect style. He denies it any typographical distinction, so that the phrases uttered seem to be events just like any other; they shimmer for a moment and disappear, like a sudden pulse of heat or a sound or a smell. When you begin reading the book, you don't seem to be in the presence of a novel but rather of a monotonous chanting, of the nasal singing of an Arab. You have the impression that the book will be like one of those tunes Courteline[41] speaks of, which "drift away and never return" and which stop suddenly without you knowing quite why. Gradually, however, before the reader's very eyes, the work, by its own dynamic, assumes organized form; it reveals the solid substructure that underpins it. There isn't a single useless detail. Not one that isn't taken up again later and put to use. And when we have closed the book, we realize it could not have begun differently, that it could have had no other ending. In the world that is being presented to us as absurd, from which causality has been carefully extirpated, the tiniest incident has weight. Every single one contributes to leading the hero toward the crime and execution. *The Stranger* is a classical work, a work of order, written about the absurd and against the absurd. Is this entirely what the author intended? I do not know; it is the reader's opinion I am conveying.

And how are we to classify this crisp, clear work—a work that is so carefully put together beneath its apparent disorder, so "human" and so clear once one has the key to it? We cannot call it a *récit*; it substitutes causal order for chronological sequence. Camus calls it a "novel."[42] Yet the novel requires a continuous flow of time, a development, the manifest presence of the irreversibility of time. Not without some reluctance would I grant that name to this succession of inert present moments, beneath which we can just make out the mechanical economy of a deliberate contrivance. Or we could, in the manner of *Zadig* and *Candide*, see it as a moralist's short novel, one with a discreet strain of satire and a series of ironic portraits* which, despite what it takes from the German existentialists and the American novelists, remains ultimately very close to one of Voltaire's tales.

---

*Of the pimp, the investigating magistrate, the public prosecutor, etc.

DRIEU LA ROCHELLE,
OR SELF-HATRED

THERE are some literary men of easy virtue nowadays who write for the collaborationist press, go to Germany to drink to Goethe's honor with champagne stolen from the cellars of Epernay, and are trying to establish a "European" literature, the one in which, according to Alphonse de Chateaubriant in *La Gerbe*,[1] Hitler's speeches are the brightest jewels. We're not in the least surprised to find the drunkard Fernandez[2] and the pederast Fraigneau[3] among their number. But there are others who seem more decent. What could have led them to join forces with this gang? The lure of profit? But some of them are rich, and then the Germans pay badly. The truth is that they have more hidden, more disturbing motives than the healthy cupidity of classical traitors. Look at Drieu La Rochelle: a lyrical writer, he never stops talking about himself; he fills the pages of *La Nouvelle Revue Française*[4] with his little fits of anger and hysteria; and, since that's still not enough, he republishes his old writings with new prefaces in which he speaks about himself some more. All we have to do is put together what he has confided to us and we shall very swiftly understand the reasons for his choice. He's a long, tall, sad kind of guy with a great big battered head and the faded look of a young man who didn't know how to grow old. Like Montherlant, he fought for kicks in 1914. His patrons in high places sent him to the front when he asked them to and had him pulled back as soon as he became afraid of getting bored.

He ended up by going back to women again and being even more bored. The fireworks at the front had kept him from paying attention to himself for a while. When he came back home it was inevitable that he should make a scandalous discovery: he thought nothing, felt nothing, loved nothing. He was soft and cowardly, with neither physical nor moral resiliency, a "hollow man." His first move was to run from himself. He caroused and took drugs moderately, from lack of courage. And then, just as his hate-filled stupor at himself was threatening to take a tragic turn, he found the gimmick that enabled him to bear himself. It wasn't his fault if he was a bad little boy in a man's body. It was just that our epoch was one of great bankruptcies. He wrote, "I found myself confronted with a crushing fact: decadence." Now there's a good piece of work for you. It is always easier to be the innocent victim of a social upheaval than simply an individual who just couldn't make it himself. Thus from 1914 to 1918 millions of French peasants and workers got themselves killed defending their native soil, and from 1918 to 1939 millions of French peasants and workers tried courageously and patiently to live but M. Drieu La Rochelle, who was bored, declared that France had gone bankrupt.

The rest needs no further explanation. Gilles,[5] his wretched hero, tries at the end of the novel to heal his incurable boredom with the blood of others. Drieu wished for the fascist revolution the way certain people want war because they don't dare break up with their mistresses. He hoped that an order imposed from without and upon everyone would succeed in disciplining these weak and ungovernable passions that he had been unable to conquer, that a bloody catastrophe would succeed in filling the inner void he had been unable to fill, that the restlessness of power (like the sounds of battle in the past) would divert him better than morphine or cocaine from thinking about himself. And since that time he has in fact been speaking, getting excited, making a tiny little noise in the silence. He questions, exhorts, preaches to, and insults Frenchmen who are bound and gagged. The universal silence doesn't bother him. All he wants to do is talk. He writes that he is a naturally prophetic writer, that he prefers the German occupation to the prewar Jewish occupation. In part out of hatred for men, in part out of a taste for gossip, he denounces Free Zone writers to the Vichy government and threatens those in the Occupied Zone with prison. He enjoys himself as well as he can, wretchedly. But these little distractions are no more capable of tearing him away from himself than drugs; he's still hooked. When a journal in the ex–Free Zone digs into him, when the defunct *Esprit*[6] takes the liberty of calling *La Nouvelle Revue Française* the *N.R.B.*,[7] he howls and fills his journal with hysterical tantrums. This is not a man who has sold out: he lacks the untroubled cynicism. He has come over to Nazism through an elective affinity: at the bottom of his heart, as at the bottom of Nazism, there is self-hatred—and the hatred of man it engenders.

A NEW MYSTIC

On Bataille's Inner Experience

I

THERE is a crisis of the essay. Elegance and clarity seem to demand that, in this kind of work, we employ a language deader than Latin: the language of Voltaire. I have remarked on this before in relation to *The Myth of Sisyphus*.* But if we really try to express today's thoughts using yesterday's language, what a lot of metaphors, circumlocutions, and imprecise images ensue: you would think we were back in the age of Delille.[1] Some, like Alain[2] and Paulhan,[3] try to be economical with words and time, to rein in, by means of numerous ellipses, the florid prolixity that characterizes that language. But how obscure this becomes! Everything is covered with an irritating veneer, whose shimmering surface conceals the ideas. With the American writers, with Kafka, and with Camus in France, the contemporary novel has found its style. The style of the essay remains to be discovered. And the style of criticism, too, in my opinion, for I am not unaware, as I write these lines, that I am using an outdated instrument which academic tradition has preserved into our own day.

This is why we must point out a work like that of Georges Bataille as deserving of special attention. It is an essay that I would happily describe as agonized (and I have its author's authority to do so, since there are so many mentions of torture and torment in the book). Bataille

---

*See *Cahiers du Sud* (February 1943).

forsakes both the stony speech of the great wits of 1780[4] and with it, inevitably, the objectivity of the classics. He strips himself bare; he lays himself before us; he isn't pleasant company. If human wretchedness is his theme, then look, he says, at my sores and ulcers. And he opens his clothing to show them to us. Yet lyricism isn't his aim. If he shows himself, he does so in pursuit of proof. Barely has he let us glimpse his wretched nudity and he is covered up again and off we go with him in reasoned discussions of Hegel's system or Descartes's *cogito*. But then the reasoning comes to an abrupt halt and the man reappears. "I could say," he writes, for example, in the middle of an argument about God, that "this hatred is time, but that bothers me. Why should I say time? I feel this hatred when I cry; I analyze nothing."[5]

Actually, this form, which still seems so new, is already part of a tradition. The death of Pascal saved his *Pensées* from being written up into a strong and colorless Apologia. By delivering them to us all jumbled up, by striking down their author before he had the time to muzzle himself, that death made them the model for the genre that concerns us here.[6] And there is, in my view, more than a little of Pascal in Bataille, particularly the feverish contempt and the desire to get his words out quickly, to which I shall return. But it is to Nietzsche that he himself refers explicitly. And, indeed, certain pages of *Inner Experience*, with their breathless disorder, their passionate symbolism, and their tone of prophetic preaching, seem to come straight out of *Ecce Homo* or *The Will to Power*. Lastly, Bataille was once very close to the Surrealists and no one cultivated the agonized essay so much as the Surrealists. Breton's voluminous personality found itself at ease in that genre: coldly, in the style of Charles Maurras, he demonstrated the incomparable excellence of his theories, and then suddenly went off onto the most puerile details of his life, showing photographs of the restaurants in which he had had lunch and the shop where he bought his coal. There was, in that exhibitionism, a need to destroy all literature and, to that end, suddenly to reveal, behind the "monsters imitated by art," the true monster. There was probably also a taste for scandal, but mainly a preference for direct contact. The book had to establish a kind of fleshly closeness between author and reader. Lastly, in the case of these authors impatient for commitment, who felt contempt for the quiet occupation of writing, every work had to involve risk. As Michel Leiris did in his admirable *Manhood*,[7] they revealed of themselves everything that could shock, annoy, or prompt laughter, in order to lend their undertakings the perilous seriousness of a genuine act. Pascal's *Pensées*, Rousseau's *Confessions*, Nietzsche's *Ecce Homo*, *Les Pas Perdus* and *L'Amour Fou* by Breton, *Le Traité du Style* by Aragon, and *Manhood*—it is within this series of "passionate geometries" that Bataille's *Inner Experience* has its place.

Right from the preface, the author informs us that he wants to achieve a synthesis of *"rapture"* and *"rigorous intellectual method"*; that he is trying to make "rigorous, shared emotional knowledge (laughter)" and "rational knowledge" coincide.[8] No more is needed for us to see that we are going to find ourselves in the presence of a demonstrative apparatus with a powerful affective potential. But Bataille goes further. For him, feeling is both at the origin and at the end: "Conviction," he writes, "does not arise from reasoning, but only from the feelings which it defines."[9] We know these famous ice-cold yet fiercely blazing lines of reasoning, troubling in their harsh abstraction, that are deployed by the passionate and the paranoid: their rigor is, from the outset, a challenge and a threat; their suspicious immobility harbors forebodings of stormy lava flows. Bataille's syllogisms are like that. They are the proofs supplied by an orator, jealous lover, barrister, or madman. Not by a mathematician. We can sense that this plastic, molten substance, with its sudden solidifications that liquefy again as soon as we touch them, needs to be rendered in a special form and can never be at home with an all-purpose language. At times, the style is close to choking or drowning in its efforts to render the gasping suffocations of ecstasy or anguish (Pascal's "Joy, joy, tears of joy" will find a counterpart in such sentences as the following: "One must. Is this to moan? I no longer know. Where am I going to?" etc. . . . .[10]); at others, it is broken up with little bursts of laughter; at yet others, it sprawls out into the balanced periods of reasoning. The sentence of intuitive rapture, condensed into a single instant, is found side by side, in *Inner Experience*, with the leisurely discursive mode.

It is, in fact, only reluctantly that Bataille employs this discursive mode. He hates it and, through it, he hates all language. Bataille shares this hatred—which we also noted recently in Camus—with a great many contemporary writers. But the reasons he gives for it are all his own: it is the mystic's hatred to which he lays claim, not the terrorist's. First, he tells us, language is a project: the speaker has an appointment with himself at the end of the sentence. Speech is a construction, an undertaking; the octogenarian who speaks is as mad as the octogenarian who plants. To speak is to rend oneself apart; to put existence off until later, until the end of the discourse; to be torn between a subject, a verb, and a complement. Bataille wants to exist fully and immediately—this very instant. Moreover, words are "the instruments of useful acts": hence, to name the real is to cover it over or veil it with familiarity, to bring it into the ranks of what Hegel termed "das Bekannte": the *too well known*, which goes unnoticed. To tear away the veils and swap the opaque quietude of knowledge for the astonishment of non-knowledge, a "holocaust of words" is needed, that holocaust that has already been carried out by poetry:

> Should words such as *horse* or *butter* come into a poem, they do so detached from interested concerns . . . When the farm girl says *butter* or the stable boy says *horse*, they know butter and horses . . . But, *on the contrary, poetry leads from the known to the unknown.* It can do what neither the boy nor the girl can do: introduce a butter horse. In this way, it sets one before the unknowable.[11]

But poetry doesn't propose to communicate a precise experience. Bataille, for his part, has to identify, describe, persuade. Poetry confines itself to sacrificing words; Bataille aims to explain to us the reasons for this sacrifice. And it is with words that he must exhort us to sacrifice words. Our author is very conscious of this circle. It is partly for this reason that he situates his work "beyond poetry." As a result of this, he becomes subject to a constraint similar to those the [French neoclassical] dramatists imposed on themselves. Just as Racine could wonder "how to express jealousy and fear in rhyming alexandrines" and just as he drew his force of expression from that very constraint, so Bataille asks himself how he can express silence with words. Perhaps this is a problem that has no philosophical solution; perhaps, from this angle, it is merely a case of wordplay. But from our stand-point, it looks like an aesthetic rule as valid as any other, a supplementary difficulty the author freely imposes on himself, like a billiard player marking out limits for himself on the green baize. It is this difficulty freely consented to that lends the style of *Inner Experience* its particular savor. First, we find in Bataille a mimesis of the moment. Silence and the moment being one and the same thing, it is the configuration of the moment he has to impart to his thought. "The expression of inner experience," he writes, "must in some way respond to its movement."[12] He therefore eschews the carefully composed work and an ordered development of argument. He expresses himself in short aphorisms, spasms, which the reader can grasp at a single glance and which stand as instantaneous explosions, bounded by two blanks, two abysses of repose. He himself provides the following explanation:

> A continual challenging of everything deprives one of the power of proceeding by separate operations, obliges one to express oneself through rapid flashes, to free as much as is possible the expression of one's thought from a project, to include everything in a few sentences: anguish, decision and the right to the poetic perversion of words without which it would seem that one was subject to a domination.[13]

As a result, the work assumes the appearance of a string of remarks. It is odd to record that the anti-intellectualist Bataille meets up here with the rationalist Alain in his choice of mode of exposition. This is because this "continual questioning of everything" may just as well proceed from a mystic negation as from a Cartesian philosophy of free judgment. But the resemblance goes no further than this: Alain trusts in words. Bataille, by contrast, will attempt to consign them, in the very weft of his text, to the most minor role. They have to be shorn of their ballast, emptied out, and imbued with silence in order to lighten them to the extreme. He will try, then, to use "slippery sentences," like soapy planks that have us suddenly falling into the ineffable; slippery words too, like this very word "silence." He will write of "the abolition of the sound which the word is; among all words ... the most perverse and the most poetic."[14] Alongside those words which signify—words indispensable, after all, to understanding—he will slip into his argument words that are merely suggestive, such as "laughter," "torment," "agony," "rending," "poetry," etc., which he diverts from their original meaning to confer on them gradually a magical evocative power. These various techniques lead to a situation in which Bataille's deep thought—or feeling—seems entirely encapsulated in each of his *Pensées*. It doesn't build up, isn't progressively enriched, but rises, undivided and almost ineffable, to the surface of each aphorism, so that each presents the same formidable, complex meaning with a different lighting. By contrast with the analytical methods of the philosophers, we might say that Bataille's book presents itself as the product of a totalitarian thinking.

But this thinking itself, syncretic as it may be, could still aim for—and attain to—the universal. Albert Camus, for example, no less struck by the absurdity of our condition, has still attempted an objective portrait of "the absurd man," irrespective of historical circumstances, and the great exemplary Absurd individuals to whom he refers—such as Don Juan—have a universality that is every bit the equal of that of Kant's moral agent. Bataille's originality lies in his having, despite his angry, peevish reasoning, deliberately chosen history over metaphysics. Here again, we have to look back to Pascal, whom I would happily call the first *historical* thinker, because he was the first to grasp that, in man, existence precedes essence. There is, in his view, too much grandeur in the human creature for us to understand him on the basis of his wretchedness, too much wretchedness for us to deduce his nature from his grandeur. In a word, something *happened to* man, something undemonstrable and irreducible, and hence something *historical*: fall and redemption. As a historical religion, Christianity stands opposed to all metaphysics. Bataille, who was a devout Christian, has retained Christianity's deep sense of historicity. He speaks to us of the human condition, not of human nature: man is not a nature but a drama; his characteristics are *acts*: project, torment, agony, laughter—so many words referring to temporal processes of realization, not qualities given passively and passively received. This is because Bataille's work is, like most mystical writings, the product of a *re-descent*. Bataille is returning from an unknown region; he is coming back down among us. He wants to carry us with him: he describes our wretchedness which once was his; he tells us the story of his journey, his long-held delusions, his arrival. If, like the Platonic philosopher brought out from the cave, he had found himself suddenly in the presence of an eternal truth, the historical aspect of his account would probably have been eliminated, giving way to the universal rigor of Ideas. But his encounter was with non-knowledge, and non-knowledge is essentially historical, since it can be described only as a particular experience had by a particular person on a particular date. For this reason, we have to see *Inner Experience* both as a Gospel (though he doesn't impart any "good news" to us) and an Invitation to the Voyage.[15] Edifying Narrative—that is what he could have called his book. With this—through this mix of proof and drama—the work takes on an entirely original flavor. Alain first wrote his objective *Propos* (Remarks) and only later, as a conclusion to his life's work, his *Histoire de mes pensées* (History of My Thoughts).[16] But the two are in one here, entangled in the same book. Barely have the proofs been laid before us than they suddenly appear historical: a man thought them, at a certain point in his life, and became a martyr to them. We are reading not just Gide's *The Counterfeiters* but at the same time "Édouard's Journal"[17] and *The Journal of the Counterfeiters*.[18] In conclusion, the subjectivity closes over both the reasoning and the rapture. It is a man that stands before us, a man naked and alone, who disarms all his deductions by dating them, a man both repugnant and "captivating"—like Pascal.

Have I conveyed the originality of this language? One last feature will help me to do so: the tone is constantly scornful. It recalls the disdainful aggressiveness of the Surrealists; Bataille wants to rub his readers the wrong way. Yet he writes to "communicate." But it seems that he speaks to us reluctantly. And is he actually addressing us? Indeed he is not—and he is at pains to let us know. He "loathes his own voice." Though he regards communication as necessary—for ecstasy without communication is mere emptiness—he says: "I become irritated when I think of the time of 'activity' which I spent—during the last years of peacetime—in forcing myself to reach my fellow beings."[19]

And we must take this term "fellow beings" in its strictest sense. It is for the mystic's apprentice that Bataille writes, for the person who, in solitude, is making his way, through laughter and world-weariness, toward his final torment. But there is nothing comforting for our author in the hope that he will be read by this very particular sort of Nathanaël.[20] "Even in preaching to the converted, there is, in its predication, a distressful element."[21] Even if we were this potential disciple, we have the right to listen to Bataille, but not—he loftily warns us—to judge him: "There are no readers, nevertheless, who have in them anything to cause ... [my] disarray. Were the most perspicacious of them to accuse me, I would laugh: it is of myself that I am afraid."[22] This puts the critic at his ease. Bataille opens up here, strips himself bare before our very eyes, but at the same time he curtly rejects our judgment: it is for him alone to judge and the communication he wishes to establish is without reciprocity. He is on high, we are down below. He delivers us a message and it is for us to receive it if we can. But what adds to our difficulty is that the summit from which he speaks to us is at the same time the "abyssal" depth of abjection.

The proud and dramatic preaching of a man more than halfway committed to silence, who, to go as quickly as he can, reluctantly speaks a feverish, bitter, and often incorrect language and who exhorts us, without looking at us directly, to join him proudly in his shame and darkness—this is what *Inner Experience* seems at first to be. Apart from a little empty bombast and some clumsiness in the handling of abstractions, everything in this mode of expression is praiseworthy: it presents the essayist with an example and a tradition; it takes us back to the sources, to Pascal and Montaigne, and at the same time it offers us a language and a syntax better adapted to the problems of our age. But form isn't everything. Let us look at the content.

II

There are people you might call survivors. Early on, they lost a beloved person—father, friend, or mistress—and their lives are merely the gloomy aftermath of that death. Bataille is a survivor of the death of

God. And, when one thinks about it, it would seem that our entire age is surviving that death, which he experienced, suffered, and survived. God is dead. We should not understand by that that he does not exist, nor even that he now no longer exists. He is dead: he used to speak to us and he has fallen silent, we now touch only his corpse. Perhaps he has slipped out of the world to some other place, like a dead man's soul. Perhaps all this was merely a dream. Hegel tried to replace him with his system and the system has collapsed. Comte tried with the religion of humanity, and positivism has collapsed. In France and elsewhere, around the year 1880, a number of honorable Gentlemen, some of them sufficiently logical to demand they be cremated after their deaths, had the notion of developing a secular morality. We lived by that morality for a time, but then along came Bataille—and so many others like him—to attest to its bankruptcy. God is dead, but men have not, for all that, become atheists. Today, as yesterday, this silence of the transcendent, combined with modern man's enduring religious need, is the great question of the age. It is the problem that torments Nietzsche, Heidegger, and Jaspers. It is our author's central personal drama. Coming out of a "long Christian piety," his life "dissolved into laughter." Laughter was a revelation:

> Fifteen years ago . . . I was returning from I don't know where, late at night . . . Crossing the rue du Four, I suddenly became unknown to myself in this "nothingness" . . . I denied the gray walls that enclosed me, I plunged into a kind of rapture. I was laughing divinely: the umbrella that had come down over my head covered me (I deliberately covered myself with this black shroud). I was laughing as no one perhaps had laughed before; the bottom of every thing lay open, was laid bare, as though I were dead.[23]

For some time, he attempted to sidestep the consequences of these revelations. Eroticism, the all too human "sacred" of sociology, offered him some precarious havens. And then everything collapsed and here he is before us, lugubrious and comical, like an inconsolable widower[24] indulging, all dressed in black, in "the solitary vice" in memory of his dead wife. For M. Bataille refuses to reconcile these two immovable and contradictory demands: God is silent, I cannot budge an inch on that; everything in me calls out for God, I cannot forget Him. At more than one point in *Inner Experience*, you would think you had Stravogin or Ivan Karamazov before you—an Ivan who had known André Breton. From this there arises, in Bataille's case, a particular experience of the absurd. In fact, that experience is found in one form or another in most contemporary authors. One thinks of the "fissure" in Jaspers, death in Malraux, Heidegger's "abandonment," Kafka's temporarily reprieved creatures, the point-less, obsessive labor of Sisyphus in Camus, or Blanchot's *Aminadab*.

But it must be said that modern thought has encountered two kinds of absurd. For some, the fundamental absurdity is "facticity" or, in other words, the irreducible contingency of our "being-there," of our existence that has neither purpose nor reason. For others, faith-less disciples of Hegel, it resides in the fact that man is an insoluble contradiction. It is this absurdity M. Bataille feels most sharply. Like Hegel, whom he has read, he takes the view that reality is conflict. But, for him, as for Kierkegaard, Nietzsche, and Jaspers, there are con-flicts that have no resolution. He eliminates the moment of synthesis from the Hegelian trinity and, for the dialectical view of the world, he substitutes a tragic—or, as he would put it, dramatic—vision. The reader will perhaps be put in mind of Camus here, whose fine novel we commented on recently. But for Camus, who has barely dipped into the phenomenologists and whose thinking falls within the tradi-tion of the French moralists, the original contradiction is a matter of fact. There are forces in presence—which are what they are—and the absurdity arises out of the relation between them. The contradiction comes retrospectively. For Bataille, who is more intimately familiar with existentialism and has even borrowed his terminology from it, the absurd is not given but *produces itself.* Man creates himself as con-flict. We are not made of a certain stuff in which fissures might appear through wear and tear or the action of some external agent. The "fissure"* fissures only itself; it is its own substance and man is the

---

*This "*déchirure*" or "fissure" is found in Jaspers and in Bataille. Is this evidence of influence? Bataille doesn't quote Jaspers, but he seems to have read him.

unity of that substance: a strange unity that inspires nothing at all, but, rather, destroys itself to maintain the opposition. Kierkegaard called this ambiguity: in it contradictions coexist without merging; each one leads on indefinitely to another. It is this perpetual evanescent unity that Bataille experiences immediately within himself; it is this which provides him with his original vision of the absurd and the image he constantly employs to express that vision: the image of a self-opening wound whose swollen lips gape open toward the heavens. Should we then, you will ask, place Bataille among the existentialist thinkers? That would be too hasty. Bataille doesn't like philosophy. His aim is to relate a certain experience to us or, rather, we should say, a certain *lived experience*, in the sense of the German word *Erlebnis*.* It is a question of life and death, pain and delight, not tranquil contemplation. (Bataille's mistake is to believe that modern philosophy has remained contemplative. He has clearly not understood Heidegger, of whom he speaks often and ineptly.) As a result, if he does use philosophical techniques, he does so as a more convenient way of expressing an adventure that lies beyond philosophy, on the borders of knowledge and non-knowledge. But philosophy takes its revenge: this technical material, employed without discernment, bowled along by polemical or dramatic passion and dragooned into rendering the pantings and spasms of our author, turns against him. When inserted in Bataille's texts, words that had precise meanings in the works of Hegel or Heidegger lend it a semblance of rigorous thought. But as soon as you attempt to grasp that thought, it melts like snow. The emotion alone remains, that is to say, a powerful inner disturbance in respect of vague objects. "Of poetry, I will now say that it is ... the sacrifice in which words are victims," writes Bataille.[25] In this sense, his work is a burnt offering of philosophical words. As soon as he uses one, its meaning immediately curdles or goes off like warm milk. Moreover, in his haste to *bear witness*, M. Bataille regales us with thoughts from very different dates in no particular order, but he

---

*It is, in fact, only in the German language, as *Das innere Erlebnis*, that the book's title will have its full meaning. The French word "*expérience*" misrepresents our author's intentions.

doesn't tell us whether we are to regard them as the paths that have led him to his current state of feeling or as ways of seeing that he still holds to today. From time to time, he seems in the grip of a feverish desire to unify them; at other times, he relaxes, abandons them, and they go back to their isolation. If we attempt to organize this vague assemblage, we must first remind ourselves that each word is a trap and that he is trying to trick us by presenting as thoughts the violent stirrings of a soul in mourning. Furthermore, Bataille, who is neither a scholar nor a philosopher, has, unfortunately, a smattering of science and philosophy. We run up straightaway against two distinct attitudes of mind that coexist within him, without his realizing it, and that are mutually detrimental: the existentialist attitude and what I shall dub, for want of a better word, the scientistic. As we know, it was scientism that scrambled Nietzsche's message, deflecting him into childish views on evolution and masking his understanding of the human condition. It is scientism too that will distort the whole of Bataille's thought.

The starting point is that man is born from—"is begotten of"—the earth. We may take this to mean that he is the product of one of the countless possible combinations of natural elements. A highly improbable combination, we guess, as improbable as cubes with letters on them rolling on the ground arranging themselves in such a way as to spell out the word "anticonstitutional." "A single chance decided the possibility of this *self* which I am: in the end the mad improbability of the sole being without whom, *for me*, nothing would be, becomes evident."[26] There you have a scientistic, objective viewpoint if ever there was one. And, indeed, in order to adopt it, we have to assert the anteriority of the object (Nature) over the subject; we must, from the outset, place ourselves outside of inner experience—the only experience available to us. We have to accept the value of science as a basic assumption. And yet science doesn't tell us that we came from the earth: it simply tells us about earth. Bataille is scientistic in the sense that he makes science say much more than it really does. We are, then, it seems, poles apart from an *Erlebnis* on the part of the subject, from a concrete encounter of existence with itself: at the moment of the *cogito*, Descartes never saw himself as a product of Nature; he registered his own contingency and facticity, the irrationality of his "being-there," not his improbability. But here everything changes suddenly: this "improbability"—which can be deduced only from the calculation of the *chances* of the play of natural forces producing just *this*, this *Self*—is presented to us as the original content of the *cogito*. "The feeling of my fundamental improbability situates me in the world," writes Bataille.[27] And, a little further on, he rejects the reassuring constructs of reason in the name of the "experience of the *self*, of its improbability, of its insane demands."[28] How can he not see that improbability is not an immediate given but precisely a construct of the reason? It is the *Other* who is improbable, because I apprehend him from outside. But, in an initial conceptual slide, our author equates facticity, the concrete object of an authentic experience, with improbability, a pure scientific concept. Looking further, we find that, according to Bataille, this feeling brings us into contact with our deepest being. What a mistake! Improbability can only be a hypothesis that is closely dependent on earlier presuppositions. I am improbable if a certain universe is assumed to be true. If God created me, if I was subject to a particular decree of Providence, or if I am a mode of Spinozist substance, my improbability disappears. Our author's starting point is, then, *something deduced*; it is in no way encountered by feeling. But we shall see another piece of trickery: Bataille goes on to equate improbability with irreplaceability: "I," he writes, "that is to say, the infinite, painful improbability of an irreplaceable being, which I am." And this identification is even clearer a few lines later:

> The empirical knowledge of my similarity with others is irrelevant, for the essence of my self arises from this—that nothing will be able to replace it: the feeling of my fundamental improbability situates me in the world where I remain as though foreign to it, absolutely foreign.[29]

In this same way, Gide didn't need to advise Nathanaël to *become* the most irreplaceable of human beings: irreplaceability, which makes every person a Unique Entity, is given from the outset. It is a quality we are endowed with, since what is *unique* in me is, in the end, the "*single* chance" that "decided the possibility of this self."[30] Thus, in conclusion, this self is not me: it eludes me; it no more belongs to me than the movement belongs to the billiard ball. It was imparted to me from the outside. Bataille calls this external idiosyncrasy "ipseity," and the very name he gives to it reveals his perpetual confusion with regard to scientism and existentialism. The word "ipseity" is a neologism he takes from Corbin, Heidegger's translator. Corbin uses it to render the German term *Selbstheit*, which means existential return toward oneself on the basis of the project.[31] It is from this return to oneself that the *self* emerges. Hence, ipseity is a reflexive relationship that one creates by living it out. Once in possession of the word, Bataille applies it to knives, machines, and even attempts to apply it to the atom (then thinks better of it). This is because he understands it merely to mean *natural individuality*. The rest follows automatically: noticing its "ipseity," the product of the "most madly improbable chance," the self sets itself up defiantly above the void of Nature. We come back here to the inner attitude of existentialism: "Human bodies are erect on the ground like a challenge to the Earth . . ."[32] Improbability has been internalized; it has become a fundamental, lived, accepted, claimed experience. This brings us back to the "challenge" that lies, for Jaspers, at the beginning of all history. The self demands its ipseity; it wishes to "climb to the pinnacle." And Bataille tops Jaspers off with Heidegger: the authentic experience of my improbable ipseity is not given to me ordinarily, he tells us:

> As long as I live, I am content with a coming and going, with a compromise. No matter what I say, I know myself to be a member of a species and I remain in harmony, roughly speaking, with a common reality; I take part in what, by all necessity, exists—in what nothing can withdraw. The Self-that-dies abandons this harmony: it truly perceives what surrounds it to be a void and itself to be a challenge to this void.[33]

This is the meaning of human reality in the light of its "being-for-death." Just as Heidegger speaks of a freedom that launches itself against death (*Freiheit zum Tod*), so Bataille writes: "the *self* grows until it reaches the pure imperative: this imperative ... is formulated 'die like a dog.'"[34] Isn't this irreplaceability of "human reality," experienced in the blinding light of being-for-death, precisely the Heideggerian experience? Yes, but Bataille doesn't stop at that: the fact is that this experience, which ought to be pure, *suffered* apperception of the self by itself, bears within it a seed of destruction; in Heidegger we discover only the *inside* and we are nothing except insofar as we discover ourselves; being coincides with the movement of discovery. For his part, Bataille has poisoned his experience, since he actually makes it bear upon improbability, a hypothetical concept borrowed from external reality. In this way, the outside has slipped inside myself; death illumines only a fragment of Nature; at the point where the urgency of death reveals me to myself, Bataille has silently arranged that I should see myself through the eyes of another. The consequence of this piece of legerdemain is that "Death is in a sense an imposture." Since the Self is an external object, it has the "exteriority" of natural things.* This means, first of all, that it is *composite* and that the grounds of its compositeness lie outside itself: "A being is always a set of particles whose relative autonomies are maintained" and "This being *ipse*, itself constituted from parts and, as such—being result, unpredictable chance—enters the universe as the will for autonomy."[35] These remarks are made, once again, from the scientific standpoint: it is science which, by its desire for analysis, dissolves individualities and relegates them to the realm of appearances. And it is the scientist again who, looking at human life *from the outside*, can write:

> What you are stems from the activity which links the innumerable elements which constitute you to the intense communication of these elements among themselves. These are contagions of energy, of movement, of warmth, or transfers of elements, which constitute inevitably the life of your organized being. Life is never situated at a particular point; it passes rapidly from one point to another (or from multiple points to other points), like a current or like a sort of streaming of electricity. Thus,

---

*In the sense in which Hegel tells us, "Nature is exteriority."

where you would like to grasp your timeless substance, you encounter only a slipping, only the poorly coordinated play of
your perishable elements.[36]

Moreover, ipseity is subject to the solvent action of time. Bataille takes
over Proust's remarks on time as separator. He doesn't see the balancing element: namely, that duration also—and primarily—fulfills a
binding role. Time, he says, "signifies only the flight of the objects that
seemed true" and, he adds, "as is the case with time, the self-that-dies is
pure change, and neither one nor the other have real existence."[37]

What, then, but scientific time is this time that gnaws away and
separates—this time each instant of which corresponds to a position
of a moving object on a trajectory? Is Bataille sure that a genuine *inner*
experience of time would have yielded the same results? The fact remains that, for him, this "reprieved" self that is never finished, made
up of components external to one another is—though it reveals itself
to the dying subject—merely a sham. We see the emergence of the
tragic here: we are an appearance striving to be a reality, but whose
very efforts to leave its phantom existence behind are mere semblance.
We can, however, also see the *explanation* for this sense of the tragic:
the fact is that Bataille adopts two contradictory viewpoints simultaneously. On the one hand, he seeks—and finds—himself by a procedure analogous to the *cogito*, which reveals to him his irreplaceable
individuality; on the other hand, he suddenly steps outside himself to
examine that individuality with the eyes and instruments of the scientist, as though it were a thing in the world. And this latter point of
view assumes that he has taken on board a certain number of postulates on the value of science and analysis and on the nature of objectivity, postulates he would have to sweep away if he wanted immediate
access to himself. As a result, the object of his enquiry seems a strange,
contradictory entity, very similar to Kierkegaard's "ambiguous creatures": it is a reality that is, nonetheless, illusory, a unity that crumbles
into multiplicity, a cohesion that time tears apart. But these contradictions are not to be wondered at: if Bataille found them in himself,
that is because he put them there, forcibly introducing the transcendent into the immanent. If he had kept to the viewpoint of inner dis-

covery, he would have understood: 1) that the data of science have no part in the certainty of the *cogito* and that they have to be regarded as merely probable; if one confines oneself to one's inner experience, one cannot come out again to observe oneself from the outside; 2) that in the field of inner experience, there no longer are any appearances; or, rather, that, in that experience, appearance is absolute reality. If I dream of a perfume, it is not a real perfume. But if I dream that I take pleasure in smelling it, then that is *true* pleasure; you cannot dream your pleasure, you cannot dream the simplicity or unity of your *Self*. If you discover them, then they exist, because you give them existence by discovering them; 3) that there is nothing troubling about the famous temporal rending of the Self. For time also binds and the Self in its very being is temporal. This means that, far from being nullified by Time, it has need of Time to realize itself. And I shall have nothing of the objection that the Self fades away by fragments, by moments, for the Time of inner experience is not made up of moments.

But Bataille is at the second stage of the analysis now, the stage that will reveal to us the permanent contradiction that we *are*. The *ipse*, the unstable unity of particles, is itself a particle in larger entities. This is what Bataille calls *communication*. He notes quite rightly that the relations established between human beings cannot be limited to mere relations of juxtaposition. Human beings do not first exist and then communicate afterward; communication constitutes them in their being from the outset. Here again, we might at first believe we are in the presence of the latest philosophical advances of Phenomenology. Isn't this "communication" reminiscent of Heidegger's *Mitsein*? But, as before, this existential resonance appears illusory as soon as we look more closely. "A man," writes Bataille, "is a particle inserted in unstable and tangled groups," and elsewhere,

> Knowledge which the male neighbor has of his female neighbor is no less removed from an encounter of strangers than is life from death. *Knowledge* appears in this way like an unstable biological bond—no less real, however, than that of cells of a tissue. The exchange between two persons possesses in effect the power to survive momentary separation.[38]

He adds that "Only the instability of the relations ... permits the illusion of a being which is isolated ..." In this way, the *ipse* is doubly illusory: illusory because it is composite and illusory because it is a component. Bataille brings out the two complementary and opposing aspects of any organized ensemble: "constitution transcending the constituent parts, relative autonomy of the constituent parts."[39] This is a good description: it is akin to Meyerson's insights into what he termed "the fibrous structure of the universe."[40] But he was, precisely, describing the universe or, in other words, Nature outside the subject. To apply these principles to the community of subjects is to reinsert them into Nature. How, in fact, can Bataille apprehend this "constitution transcending the constituent parts"? It can only be by observing his own existence, since he is merely an element within an ensemble. The floating unity of the elements can be evident only to an observer who has deliberately placed himself outside this totality. But only God is outside. And even then, we would have to be speaking of a God that is different from Spinoza's. Moreover, the discovery of a reality that is not *our* reality can be made only through a hypothesis and its status is never anything more than probable. How are we to align the inner certainty of our existence with this probability that it may belong to these unstable ensembles? And, logically, shouldn't the subordination of the terms be reversed: isn't it our autonomy that becomes certainty and our dependency that is consigned to the realm of illusion? For if I am the consciousness *of* my dependency, then dependency is an object and consciousness is independent. Moreover, the law Bataille establishes isn't limited to the field of human interrelations. In the texts we have cited, he extends it expressly to the entire organized universe. If it applies, then, to living cells as much as to subjects, this can only be insofar as subjects are regarded as cells or, in other words, as things. And the law is no longer the simple description of an inner experience but an abstract principle, akin to those that govern mechanics and, at the same time, several regions of the universe. If it were sentient, the falling stone wouldn't discover the law of gravity in its own fall. It would experience its fall as a unique event. The law of gravity would, for that stone, be a law applying to *other stones*.

Similarly, when he legislates on "communication," Bataille is necessarily speaking of the communication of the Others amongst themselves. We recognize this attitude: the subject establishes a law by induction from the empirical observation of other human beings, then employs analogical reasoning to place himself under the sway of the law he has just established. This is the attitude of the sociologist. Not for nothing was Bataille a member of that strange and famous Collège de Sociologie that would have so surprised the honest Durkheim, whom it claimed, among others, as its inspiration and each member of which was using an emergent science to pursue extra-scientific designs. In the Collège Bataille learned to treat human beings as things. These volatile, incomplete totalities that suddenly form and become entangled, only to decompose immediately and re-form elsewhere, are more akin to the "unanimist lives" of Romains[41] and, above all, to the "collective consciousnesses" of the French sociologists than to Heideggerian *Mitsein*.

Was it by chance that these sociologists—Durkheim, Lévy-Bruhl, and, Bouglé[42]—were the ones, toward the end of the last century, who vainly attempted to lay the foundations of a secular morality? Is it any accident that Bataille, the bitterest witness to their failure, has taken over their vision of the social, transcended it, and stolen the notion of the "sacred" from them, in order to adapt it for his personal ends? But the point is that the sociologist cannot integrate himself into sociology: he remains the one creating it. He cannot be part of it, any more than Hegel can be part of Hegelianism or Spinoza of Spinozism. In vain does Bataille attempt to enter into the machinery he has set up: he remains outside, with Durkheim and Hegel and God the Father. We shall see, shortly, that he surreptitiously sought out that privileged position.

However this may be, we have now pinned down the contradiction: the self is autonomous and dependent. When it considers its autonomy, it wants to be *ipse*: "I want to carry my person to the pinnacle," writes our author.[43] When it experiences its dependence, it wants *to be everything*, that is to say, it wants to expand to the point where it embraces within itself the totality of the constituent parts:

> The uncertain opposition of autonomy to transcendence puts being into a position which slips: each being *ipse*—at the same

time that it encloses itself in autonomy, and for this very reason—wants to become the whole of transcendence: in the first place, the whole of the constitution of which it is a part, then one day, without limits, the whole of the universe.[44]

The contradiction becomes glaringly obvious: it lies both in the situation of the subject that is split in this way between two opposing exigencies and in the very end it wishes to attain:

The universal God ... is alone at the summit, even allows himself to be taken for the totality of things and can only arbitrarily maintain "ipseity" within himself. In their history, men are thus engaged in the strange battle of *ipse*, which must become everything and can only become it by dying.[45]

I shall not, with Bataille, go over the ins and outs of this vain struggle—this battle that is lost before it begins. At times man wishes to be everything (the desire for power, for absolute knowledge), at times "the individual, lost in the multitude, delegates to those who occupy its center the concern for taking on the totality of 'being.' He is content to 'take part' in total existence, which maintains, even in simple cases, a diffuse character."[46]

Our existence is, in any event, "an exasperated attempt to complete being."[47] The horror of our condition is such that most of the time we give up and attempt to escape from ourselves into the *project* or, in other words, into those thousand little activities that have a merely limited meaning and that mask the contradiction by the purposes they project forward. But in vain:

Man cannot, by any means, escape insufficiency, nor renounce ambition. His will to flee is the fear which he has of being man: its only effect is hypocrisy—the fact that man is what he is without daring to be so ... There is no concurrence imaginable, and man, inevitably, must wish to be everything, remain *ipse*.[48]

"Project" here is another existentialist's word. It is the received translation of a Heideggerian term. And, as a result, Bataille, who undoubtedly borrowed the word from Corbin, seems at times to conceive the project as a fundamental structure of human reality—as when he writes, for example, that "the world . . . of project is the world in which we find ourselves. War disturbs it, it is true: the world of project remains, but in doubt and anguish," and we "emerge through project from the realm of project."[49] But even though there still seems to be some vacillation in our author's thinking here, a rapid examination is enough to set us right: the project is only a particular form of flight: if it is essential, it is so only to the modern Western man. The equivalent is not so much to be sought in Heidegger's philosophy as in Kierkegaard's "ethical man." And the opposition between project and "torment" strangely resembles the opposition Kierkegaard establishes between the moral and the religious life. In fact the project pertains to the concern to compose one's life. The man who makes projects thinks of the morrow and the day after that. He sketches out the plan of his entire life and sacrifices each detail—that is to say, each moment—to the order of the whole. This is what Kierkegaard symbolized in the example of the married man, the head of the family. This perpetual sacrificing of immediate life to the laid-out, fissured life of discourse, Bataille likens to the *esprit de sérieux*: project is "the serious side of existence."[50] A wretched seriousness that *takes* time, that throws itself into time: "It is a paradoxical way of being in time: *it is the putting off of existence to a later point*."[51] But he is more scornful of the serious man than Kierkegaard was of the ethical: this is because seriousness is a flight into the future. M. Bataille is reminiscent of Pascal when he writes: "One has egotistical satisfaction only in projects . . . one falls in this way into flight, like an animal into an endless trap; on one day or another, one dies an idiot."[52] The fact is that the project is, in the end, identical with Pascal's distraction; our author would happily condemn the man of projects for "being unable to sit still in a room."[53] Behind our agitation, he uncovers—and wishes to get back to—an atrocious stillness. We shall speak of this in a moment. What we must note at this point is that, in his horror of the temporal fissure, Bataille has affinities with an entire family of thinkers who, whether mystical or sensual, rationalistic or otherwise, envisaged time as a separating, negating power and believed that man won himself from time by cleaving to himself in the moment. For these thinkers—Descartes must be ranked among them, as must Epicurus, Rousseau, and Gide—discourse, planning, utilitarian memory, abstract reasoning, and enterprise wrest us from ourselves. Against this they oppose the moment—the intuitive moment of Cartesian reason, the ecstatic moment of mysticism, the anguished, eternal instant of Kierkegaardian freedom, the moment of Gidean enjoyment, the instant of Proustian remembrance. What unites thinkers who are otherwise so different is the desire to exist right now and to the full. In the *cogito* Descartes believes he grasps himself in his totality as "res cogitans"; similarly, "Gidean purity" is the entire possession of oneself and the world in the enjoyment and plundering of the instant. This is the ambition of our author too: he too wishes to "exist without delay." His project is to exit from the world of projects.

It is laughter that will enable him to do this. Not that the man-in-project, so long as he continues to battle, is comical: "everything remains suspended within him." But a new vista can open up: with a failure or setback, suddenly laughter peals out, just as, for Heidegger, the world suddenly begins to glow with the prospect of machines getting out of kilter, tools being broken. We recognize this laughter of Bataille's: it isn't the plain, inoffensive laughter of Bergson. It is a forced laughter. It has its forerunners: it was through humor that Kierkegaard escaped the ethical life; it was irony that was to liberate Jaspers. But there is, above all, the laughter of Nietzsche: it is that laughter, first and foremost, that Bataille wants to make his own. And he quotes this note penned by the author of *Zarathustra*: "To see tragic natures sink and to be able to laugh at them, despite the profound understanding, the emotion and the sympathy which one feels—that is divine."[54] However, Nietzsche's laughter is lighter: he terms it "exuberance" and Zarathustra likens it explicitly to dance. Bataille's laughter is bitter and studied; it may be that Bataille laughs a lot when he is alone, but nothing of it passes into his work. He tells us that he laughs, but he doesn't make us laugh. He would like to be able to write of his work what Nietzsche writes of *The Gay Science*: "in practically every sentence of this book profundity and exuberance go hand in hand."[55] Yet the reader cries out here: profundity maybe, but exuberance!

Laughter is "a *communal* and *disciplined* emotional knowledge."[56] The laughing subject is "the unanimous crowd." By that, Bataille seems to accept that what is described is a collective phenomenon. Yet there he is, laughing alone. No matter: this belongs, no doubt, among those countless contradictions we shall not even attempt to point up. But *of what* is there knowledge here? This, our author tells us, is "the puzzle...which, solved, would itself solve everything."[57] That certainly pricks our curiosity. But what disappointment a little later on when we get the solution: man is characterized by his desire for sufficiency and laughter is caused by the sense of an insufficiency. More precisely, it *is* the sense of insufficiency.

> If I pull the rug out from under...the sufficiency of a solemn figure is followed suddenly by the revelation of an ultimate insufficiency.* I am made happy, no matter what, by failure experienced. And I myself lose my seriousness as I laugh. As if it were a relief to escape the concern for my sufficiency.[58]

Is this everything? So *all forms* of laughter are revelations of insufficiency? *All encounters with insufficiency* express themselves through laughter? I can hardly believe this: I could cite a thousand individual cases ... But I am not criticizing at this point, just laying out the argument. It is merely to be regretted that Bataille's "ideas" should be so formless and flabby when his feeling is so firm. To summarize, laughter now grows up: at first it has children and fools as its butt, whom it throws off toward the periphery, but in a reversal it turns back on the father, the leader, and all those charged with ensuring the permanence of social combinations and symbolizing the sufficiency of all that the *ipse* wishes to be:

---

*Here again, a German word would render M. Bataille's thought better, the word being *Unselbstständigkeit*.

If I now compare the constitution of society to a pyramid, it appears as domination by the summit...The summit incessantly consigns the foundation to insignificance and, in this sense, waves of laughter traverse the pyramid, contesting step by step the pretense of self-importance of the beings placed at a lower level. But the first pattern of these waves issued from the summit ebbs and the second pattern traverses the pyramid from bottom to top: in this instance the backwash contests the self-importance of the beings placed at a higher level...it cannot fail...to strike at [the summit]...And if it strikes at it, what ensues are the death throes of God in darkest night.[59]

A strong image, but sloppy thinking.* We are familiar with this wave that rises to the rafters and leaves only scattered stones in the shadows. But there is no other reason to call it laughter than Bataille's arbitrary decision to do so. It is also the critical spirit, analysis, dark revolt. It may even be noted that revolutionaries, who are the most convinced of the insufficiency of the commanding heights, are the most serious people in the world. Satire and pamphleteering come from on high. Conservatives excel at it; by contrast, it took years of labor to build up a semblance of revolutionary humor. And even then it looked less a direct insight into the ridiculous and more a painful translation of serious considerations.

However this may be, Bataille's laughter is not an inner experience. For himself, the *ipse* seeking "to become everything" is "tragic." But, by revealing the insufficiency of the total edifice in which we believed we occupied a reassuring, comfortable place, laughter, at its height, plunges us suddenly into horror: not the slightest veil subsists between ourselves and the dark night of our insufficiency. We are not everything; no one is everything; being is nowhere. Thus, just as Plato accompanies his dialectical movement with the *askesis* of love, we might speak in Bataille's thinking of a kind of *askesis* through laughter. But laughter here is *the negative* in the Hegelian sense. "At first I

---

*A conception akin to the Surrealists' notion of "black humor," which is also radical destruction.

had laughed, upon emerging from a long Christian piety, my life having dissolved, with a spring-like bad faith, in laughter."[60] This negative dissolution that wanders off into all the Surrealist forms of disrespect and sacrilege must, by dint of the fact that it is experienced, have its positive balancing element. Thus Dada, which was pure solvent laughter, transformed itself through reflection upon itself into the clumsy dogmatism of Surrealism. Twenty-five centuries of philosophy have left us familiar with those unforeseen turnabouts in which everything is saved when all seemed lost. Yet Bataille doesn't wish to save himself. Here, we might say, it is almost a question of taste: "What characterizes man . . . ," he writes, "is not only the will to sufficiency, but the cunning, timid attraction toward insufficiency."[61] This is perhaps true of mankind; it is certainly true of Bataille. How are we to explain this taste for abjection which makes him write, "I take pleasure today in being the object of disgust for the sole being to whom destiny links my life," a sentiment in which his sensitive pride is thoroughly steeped? Is it perhaps the remnant of a long period of Christian humility? At all events, this duly elaborated inclination has become a method: How could we believe that, after ten years of Surrealist sorcery, our author could quite simply plan to achieve salvation?

> Salvation is the summit of any possible project and the pinnacle where projects are concerned . . . At the extreme limit, the desire for salvation turns into the hatred of any project (of putting off existence until later), and of salvation itself, suspected of having a mundane motive . . . salvation *was* the sole means of dissociating eroticism . . . from the nostalgia for existing without delay.[62]

With Bataille, we remain entirely in the realm of black magic. If he quotes the famous maxim, "whosoever would save his life shall lose it, but whosoever would lose his life . . . shall save it," he does so only to reject it with all his might. The point is, indeed, to lose oneself. But "to lose oneself in this case would be to lose oneself and *in no way to save oneself.*"[63] This taste for perdition is utterly *outmoded*: we need only think back to the host of experiences the young people of 1925 engaged in: drugs, eroticism and all the lives lived on the toss of a coin out of a hatred for "making plans." But Nietzschean intoxication now comes and puts its stamp on this gloomy determination. Bataille sees this useless, painful sacrifice of self as the extreme of generosity: it is freely given. And precisely because of its gratuitousness, it cannot be done coolly; it makes its appearance at the end of Bacchic revels. Sociology can, once again, provide his imagery: what one glimpses beneath the icy exhortations of this solitary is nostalgia for one of those primitive festivals in which an entire tribe becomes inebriated, laughs, dances, and copulates randomly; for one of those festivals that are both consumption and consummation, in which everyone, in wild, joyous frenzy, engages in self-mutilation, gaily destroys a whole year's worth of patiently amassed wealth, and ends in self-destruction, going to their death singing, with neither God nor hope, carried by wine and shouting and rutting to the extremes of generosity, killing themselves *for nothing*. Hence a rejection of *askesis*. Asceticism would, in fact, put a mutilated man on the pyre. But for the sacrifice to be entire, it would have to consume man in his totality, with his laughter, passions, and sexual excesses: "If ascesis is a sacrifice, it is the sacrifice of only a part of oneself which one loses with the intention of saving the other part. But should one desire to lose oneself completely, one can do so from a movement of drunken revelry, but in no way without emotion."[64]

Here, then, is the invitation to lose ourselves without calculation, without quid pro quo, without salvation. Is it sincere? We spoke not so long ago of a turnabout. It seems to me that Bataille has masked his own turnabout, but he has not, for all that, eliminated it. For, in the end, this loss of self is, above all, *experience*. It is "the questioning (testing), in fever and anguish, of what man knows of the fact of being."[65] As a result, it realizes that existence without delay that we were seeking in vain. The *ipse* is drowned in it, no doubt, but another "oneself" arises in its stead: "'Oneself' is not the subject isolating itself from the world, but a place of communication, of fusion of the subject and the object."[66] And from this conversion Bataille promises us marvels:

I am and you are, in the vast flow of things, only a stopping-point favorable to resurgence. Do not delay in acquiring an exact awareness of this anguishing position. If it happened that you attached yourself to goals confined to limits in which no one was at stake but you, your life would be that of the great majority; it would be shorn of "the marvelous." A brief moment's halt and the complex, gentle, violent movement of worlds will make a splashing foam of your death. The glories, the marvels of your life are due to this resurgence of the wave that formed within you, to the immense cataract-like sound of the sky.[67]

And then anguish becomes frenzy, excruciating joy. Isn't this worth risking the journey for? Especially as one returns from it. For, in the end, Bataille writes; he has a job at the Bibliothèque Nationale; he reads, makes love, and eats. As he says, in a phrase that he surely couldn't blame me for laughing at, "I crucify myself when the fancy takes me."[68] Why not? And we are so *won over* to this little exercise that Bataille calls it, "the distance man has covered in search of himself, of his glory." He calls those who haven't been to the extremes of the possible, servants or enemies of man, not men. And suddenly this nameless destitution takes on shape: we thought we were irredeemably lost and we were, quite simply, thereby realizing our essence: we were becoming what we are. And, at the very end of our author's explanations, we glimpse a quite different way of losing ourselves irredeemably—namely, to remain willingly within the world of the project. In that world, man flees himself and loses himself on a daily basis. He hopes for nothing and he will receive nothing. But the auto-da-fé Bataille offers us has all the characteristics of an apotheosis.

However, let us look at this more closely. It is, we are told, a *death agony*. We have arrived at this agony through laughter, but we could have got to it by other methods. In particular, by systematic diligence in feeling our abjection. The key thing is that we should, from the outset, *experience* this fundamental truth: being is nowhere; we are not everything, there is no everything. As a result, we can no longer "desire to be everything."[69] And yet "man cannot, by any means, escape insufficiency, nor renounce ambition . . . There is no concurrence imaginable, and man, inevitably, must wish to be everything."[70] There is no contradiction. Or, rather, this new contradiction is in the subject:

we are dying from wishing for what we cannot give up wishing for. But this death agony is a passion: we have the duty to agonize, to raise up the whole of Nature with us to the point of agony. For it is through us that the world exists, through us, who are merely a delusion and whose ipseity is illusory. If we disappear, the world will fall back into darkness. And here we are, a flickering flame, always on the point of extinction; and the world flickers with us, it vacillates with our light. We take it in our hands and raise it to the heavens as an offering for the heavens to mark it with their seal. But the heavens are empty. Then man understands the sense of his mission. He is the One called on by all things to ask heaven for an answer that heaven refuses. "Completed 'being,' from rupture to rupture, after a growing nausea had delivered it to the emptiness of the heavens, has become no longer 'being,' but wound, and even 'agony' of all that is."[71] And this gaping wound, which opens in the earth, beneath the endless desert of the sky, is simultaneously supplication and challenge. It is a supplication and an imploring questioning, for it seeks in vain for the All that would give it its meaning, but which hides itself. It is challenge since it knows that the All conceals itself, that it alone is responsible for the inert world, that it alone can invent its own sense and the meaning of the universe. This aspect of Bataille's thinking is very deeply Nietzschean. He himself uses a "fragment" written by Nietzsche in 1880 to designate his "Experience" more precisely: "But where do those waves of everything which is great and sublime in man finally flow out? Isn't there an ocean for these torrents?—Be this ocean: there will be one," wrote Nietzsche. And Bataille adds: "the being lost of this ocean and this bare requirement: 'be that ocean,' designate experience and the extreme limit to which it leads."[72] Man, an absurd creature, protesting against creation, a martyr to absurdity but re-creating himself by giving himself a meaning of his own beyond the absurd, man defiant, laughing man, Dionysian man—here, it seems to me, are the foundations of a humanism common to Nietzsche and our author.

But, thinking about it, we are not so sure of ourselves anymore. Bataille's thought is changeable. Is he going to be content with this human, all too human heroism? First, let us note that he cannot properly hold to this Dionysian passion he proposes; as the reader may already have noticed, by the terms of the long argument that precedes it, that passion is a swindle, a more subtle way of identifying oneself with the all, the "everything." Didn't Bataille write, in a passage we quoted above, "Man (at the end of his quest) is…agony of *all that is*," and does he not prescribe for us, in the chapter devoted to Nietzsche, "a sacrifice in which everything is victim"?[73] At the bottom of all this, we find the old initial postulate of dolorism, formulated by Schopenhauer and taken over by Nietzsche, that the man who suffers takes up and founds within himself the pain and evil of the entire universe. This is what Dionysianism or the gratuitous affirmation of the metaphysical value of suffering amounts to. There are many excuses for such an affirmation: a little distraction is permitted when one is in pain, and the idea of taking on universal suffering may serve as a balm if one manages to convince oneself of this at the appropriate point. But Bataille wants to be sure. He has, then, to acknowledge his bad faith: If I suffer for *everything*, I am everything, at least where suffering is concerned. If my death throes are the death throes of the world, I am the world in its death throes. In this way, I shall, by losing myself, have gained *everything*.

Moreover, Bataille doesn't linger in this safe haven. Yet, if he leaves it, it is not for the reasons we have just stated. He does so because he wants more. The savor of Nietzschean thought derives from the fact that it is profoundly and solely earthly. Nietzsche is an atheist who harshly and logically draws all the consequences from his atheism. But Bataille is a shamefaced Christian. He has thrown himself into what he calls a dead end. His back is to the wall. He sums up the situation himself: "The sky is empty…The ground will give way beneath my feet. I will die in hideous conditions…I solicit everything negative that a laughing man can experience."[74] And yet this hard-pressed, cornered man will not make the admission we await from him: he will not acknowledge that *there is no* transcendence. He will prefer to play on the words, "there is no" and "transcendence." We have him here and his only thought is of escape. In spite of everything, he remains what

Nietzsche called one of the "Afterworldsmen"[75] (*Hinterweltler*).[76] With this, the work he sets before us assumes its true meaning: the Nietzschean humanism was merely a stopping point on his way. The true reversal comes a little later. We believed it was a question of finding man amid his wretchedness. But no, it was in fact God we had to find. Once we are aware of this, all the sophisms we have identified can be seen in a new light: they didn't arise inadvertently in some way or from precipitate judgments; they had their role to play; it was for them to persuade Bataille that a new kind of mysticism is possible. They were to lead us by the hand to mystical experience. It is this experience we are now going to contemplate.

III

Mysticism is *ek-stasis* or, in other words, a wresting from oneself toward, and intuitive enjoyment of, the transcendent. How can a thinker who has just asserted the absence of any transcendence achieve, in and by that very move, a mystical experience? This is the question our author has to face. Let us see how he answers it.

Jaspers showed him the way. Has Bataille read the three volumes of *Philosophy*?[77] I am assured that he has not. But he is probably aware of the commentary Jean Wahl has made of it in the *Études kierkegaardiennes*. The similarities of thought and vocabulary are disquieting. For Jaspers, as for Bataille, the key thing is the absolute, irremediable failure of any human enterprise, which shows existence to be a "thinking unintelligibility." On that basis, one must "make the leap where thought ceases." It is the "choice of non-knowledge" into which knowledge throws itself and in which it loses itself. For him, too, the abandonment of non-knowledge is passionate sacrifice to the world of darkness. "Non-knowledge," "rapture," " world of night," and "the extreme [limits] of possibility"—all these expressions are common to Wahl translating Jaspers and to Bataille.

Our author does, however, diverge from Jaspers on one essential point. I said just now that he was in search of God. But he wouldn't agree on this. "Mockery! that one should call me pantheist, atheist, theist! But I cry out to the sky, 'I know nothing.'" God is still a word, a notion that helps you to leave knowledge behind, but that remains knowledge: "God, final word meaning that all words will fail further on." Bataille starts out from a meditation on failure, as does Jaspers: "Lost and pleading, blind, half-dead. Like Job on the dung-heap, in the darkness of night, but imagining nothing—defenseless, knowing that all is lost."[78] Like Jaspers, he comes to know himself as thinking unintelligibility. But as soon as he has shrouded himself in non-knowledge, he refuses any concept enabling him to designate and classify what he then attains to: "If I said decisively: 'I have seen God,' that which I see would change. Instead of the inconceivable un-known—wildly free before me, leaving me wild and free before it—there would be a dead object and matter for the theologian."[79]

Yet not everything is so clear. He now writes: "I have of the divine an experience so mad that one will laugh at me if I speak of it" and, further on, "God speaks to me, the idiot, face to face..."[80] Lastly, at the beginning of a curious chapter that contains a whole theology,[81] he again explains his refusal to name God, but in a rather different way: "What, at bottom, deprives man of all possibility of speaking of God, is that, in human thought, God necessarily conforms to man insofar as man is weary, famished for sleep and for peace."[82] These are no longer the scruples of an agnostic who, faced with atheism and faith, intends to keep matters in suspense. This is genuinely a mystic speaking, a mystic who has seen God and rejects the all too human language of those who have not. The distance separating these two passages contains the whole of Bataille's bad faith. What has hap-pened?

We had left our author at a dead end, with his back to the wall. In a state of atrocious, unavoidable disgust. And yet, "man's 'possible' cannot be confined to this constant disgust at himself, this dying man's rejected denial."[83] It *cannot* be—and yet there is nothing else. The heavens are empty and man knows nothing. This is the situation Ba-taille rightly terms "torment" and that is, if not the torment of human beings in general, at least his individual torment, his initial situation.

There is no need, then, to go looking very far. This is the primary fact: Bataille disgusts himself. A fact considerably more terrifying in its simplicity than two hundred pages of loaded considerations on human wretchedness. Through it, I glimpse the man and his solitude. At present I know I can do nothing for him and he won't be able to do anything for me. He looks like a madman to me and I know, too, that he regards me as a madman. It is what he *is* that draws me onto the path of horror, not what he says.

But he has necessarily to fight back. Against himself. Has he not said as much? The torment he cannot escape is a torment he cannot bear either. Yet there is *nothing* but that torment. So it is this very torment that is going be doctored. The author admits this himself: "I teach the art of turning anguish to delight."[84] And here is where the slippage comes: I know nothing. All right. That means my knowledge goes so far and no further. Beyond that nothing exists, since nothing is for me only what I know. But what if I substantify my ignorance? What if I transform it into the "night of non-knowledge"? Then it becomes something positive: I can touch it, meld myself with it. "With non-knowledge attained, then absolute knowledge is simply one knowledge among others."[85] Better, I can settle into it. There was a light that lit up the darkness weakly. Now, I have withdrawn into the darkness and I look on the light *from the standpoint of darkness*:

> Non-knowledge lays bare. This proposition is the summit, but must be understood in this way: lays bare, therefore I see what knowledge was hiding up to that point, but if I see, I *know*. Indeed, I know, but non-knowledge again lays bare what I have known. If nonsense is sense, the sense which is nonsense is lost, becomes nonsense again (without possible end).[86]

Our author is not to be caught so easily. If he substantifies non-knowledge, he nonetheless does so with caution, as a movement, not as a thing. Nonetheless, he has pulled off the trick: non-knowledge, which previously was *nothing*, becomes the "beyond" of knowledge. By throwing himself into it, Bataille suddenly finds himself *in the realm of the transcendent*. He has broken clear: the disgust, shame, and nausea are left behind with knowledge. After that, little matter that he tells us "Nothing, neither in the fall nor in the void, is revealed,"[87] for the essential thing is revealed: that my abjection is a nonsense and there is a nonsense of this nonsense (which is not, in any way, a return to the original sense). A passage from Maurice Blanchot cited by Bataille* shows us the trick: "The night soon appeared to him to be darker, more terrible than any other night whatsoever, as it had really emerged from a wound of thought which could no longer think itself, *of thought captured ironically as object by something other than thought.*"[88]

But Bataille precisely will not see that non-knowledge is immanent to thought. A thinking that thinks it doesn't know is still thinking. It discovers its limits *from the inside.* Yet this doesn't mean it has an overview of itself. You might as well say that *nothing* has become something on the grounds that one has given it a name.

Indeed our author does go that far. It isn't hard to do so. You and I just write, quite straightforwardly, "I know nothing." But let us suppose I put inverted commas around this *nothing.* Suppose that I write, like Bataille, "And, above all, 'nothing,' I know 'nothing.'" This is a *nothing* that takes on a strange form; it detaches itself, isolates itself— it is not far from existing on its own. We have only now to call it the *unknown* and our goal is achieved. The nothing is what doesn't exist at all; the unknown is what in no way exists for me. By calling the nothing the unknown, I make it the entity whose essence it is to elude the grasp of my knowledge; and if I add that I know nothing, this means that I communicate with that entity by some means other than knowledge. Here again, Blanchot's text, to which our author refers, brings enlightenment:

> Through this void, therefore, it was his gaze and the object of his gaze which became mingled. Not only did this eye *that saw nothing* apprehend something, but it apprehended the cause of his vision. *It saw as an object that which caused him not to see.*[89]

---

*Albert Camus pointed out to me that *Inner Experience* is the exact translation of, and commentary on, Maurice Blanchot's *Thomas l'Obscur* (*Thomas the Obscure,* 1941).

Here, then, is this unknown, wild and free, to which Bataille at times gives—and at times refuses—the name of God. It is a pure hypostatized nothingness. One last effort and we shall ourselves dissolve into the night that previously only protected us: it is knowledge that creates the *object* over against the subject. Non-knowledge is "suppression of the object and of the subject: the only means of not resulting in the possession of the object by the subject."[90] There remains "communication" or, in other words, the absorption of everything by the night. Bataille forgets that he has, by his own hand, constructed a universal object: Night. And this is the moment to apply to our author what Hegel said of Schelling's absolute: "It is the night in which all cows are black."[91] It would seem that this abandonment to the night is a source of delight: that comes as no surprise. It is, in fact, one particular way of dissolving oneself into the *nothing.* But that nothing is skillfully contrived in such a way that it becomes *everything.* Bataille, as in the case of his Nietzschean humanism above, is here satisfying in a roundabout way his desire to "be everything." With the words "nothing," "night/darkness," "non-knowledge that lays bare," he has quite simply prepared a nice little pantheistic ecstasy for us. We remember what Poincaré said of Riemannian geometry: replace the definition of the Riemannian plane by the definition of the Euclidian sphere and you have Euclid's geometry. Similarly, just replace Bataille's absolute nothing by the absolute being of substance and you have Spinoza's pantheism. We must concede, of course, that Riemann's geometry isn't Euclid's. In the same way, Spinoza's system is a white and Bataille's a black pantheism.

We can, as a result, understand the function of scientism in our author's thinking. True inner experience is, in fact, poles apart from pantheism. When once one has found oneself through the *cogito,* there is no longer any question of losing oneself: farewell to the abyss and the night, man takes himself with him everywhere. Wherever he is, he casts light and sees only what he casts light on; it is he who decides the meaning of things. And if somewhere he apprehends an absurd being, even if that absurd being is himself, that absurdity is still a human signification and it is he who decides on it. Man is immanent to the human; man's universe is finite, but not limited. If God speaks, he is made in the image of man. But if he remains silent, he is still human. And if there is a "torment" for man, it is not being able to stand outside the human to judge himself, not being able to read the underside of the cards. Not because they are hidden from him but because even if he could see them, he would be able to judge them only by his own lights. From this point of view, mystical experience must be considered as one human experience among others; it enjoys no privilege. Those who find this torment of immanence unbearable devise ruses by which to see themselves with inhuman eyes. We have seen Blanchot resorting to the fantastic to present us with an inhuman image of humanity. With similar motivations, Bataille wants to get at the human without human beings, in much the same way as Loti described "India without the English."[92] If he manages to do this, then the game he is playing is already more than half won: he is already outside himself, has already situated himself in the realm of the transcendent. But—differing in this respect from the author of *Aminadab*—he doesn't resort to literary methods, but to the scientific attitude.

We remember Durkheim's famous precept that we should "treat social facts as things." This is what tempts Bataille in Sociology. If only he could treat social facts and human beings and himself as things, if his inexpiable individuality could only appear to him as a certain given quality, then he would be rid of himself. Unfortunately for our author, Durkheim's Sociology is dead: social facts are not things; they have meanings and, as such, they refer back to the being through whom meanings come into the world, to man, who cannot be both scientist and object of science at the same time. You might just as well try to lift the chair you are sitting on by grabbing it by its crossbars. Yet Bataille revels in this vain effort. It is not by chance that the word "impossibility" flows frequently from his pen. He belongs, without a doubt, to that spiritual family whose members are susceptible, above all, to the acid, exhausting charm of impossible endeavors. It would be more appropriate to symbolize his mysticism, rather than Camus's humanism, by the myth of Sisyphus.

What remains of such an undertaking? First, an undeniable

experience. I don't doubt that our author is familiar with certain ineffable states of anguish and torturous joy. I merely note that he fails in his attempt to impart to us the method that would enable us to obtain them in our turn. Moreover, although his avowed ambition was to write a mystical *Discourse on Method*, he confesses several times that these states come and go as and when it suits them. For my part, I see them, rather, as defensive reactions specific to Bataille, appropriate to his case alone. In the way that hunted animals sometimes react with what is known as "the fake death reflex," the supreme escapism, our author, pinned to the rear wall of his cul-de-sac, escapes his disgust by a sort of ecstatic fainting fit. But even if he were able to make available to us a rigorous method for obtaining these delights at will, we would be within our rights to ask: What of it? Inner experience, we are told, is the opposite of the "project." But we *are* projects, despite what our author says. And we are not so out of cowardice or to flee from anxiety: we are projects from the first. If such a state is to be pursued, then, it is to be sought as a basis for new projects. Christian mysticism is a project: it is eternal life that is at issue. But, if the joys to which Bataille invites us are to be purely self-referential, if they are not to be part of the fabric of new undertakings and contribute to shaping a new humanity that will surpass itself toward new goals, then they are of no greater value than the pleasure of drinking a glass of brandy or of sunning oneself on a beach.

Rather than with this unusable experience, then, we shall concern ourselves more with the man who reveals himself in these pages, with his "sumptuous, bitter" soul, his pathological pride, his self-disgust, his eroticism, his often magnificent eloquence, his rigorous logic that masks the incoherence of his thought, his passion-induced bad faith, and his fruitless quest for impossible escape. But literary criticism runs up against its limits here. The rest is a matter for psychoanalysis. Yet before anyone protests, I do not have in mind the crude, questionable methods of Freud, Adler, or Jung; there are other schools of psychoanalysis.

THE REPUBLIC OF SILENCE

NEVER were we freer than under the German occupation.[1] We had lost all our rights, beginning with the right to speak. We were insulted to our faces every day and had to remain silent. We were deported en masse, as workers, Jews, or political prisoners. Everywhere —on the walls, on the movie screens, and in the newspapers—we came up against the vile, insipid picture of ourselves our oppressors wanted to present to us. Because of all this, we were free. Because the Nazi venom seeped into our very thoughts, every accurate thought was a triumph. Because an all-powerful police force tried to gag us, every word became precious as a declaration of principle. Because we were wanted men and women, every one of our acts was a solemn commitment. The often atrocious circumstances of our struggle made it possible, in a word, for us to live out that unbearable, heartrending situation known as the human condition in a candid, unvarnished way. Exile, captivity, and, especially, death, which in happier times we artfully conceal, became for us the constant objects of our concern; we learned that they were not inevitable accidents or even constant, external dangers, but must be regarded as our *lot*, our destiny, the profound source of our human reality. Every second, we lived to the full the meaning of that banal little phrase: "Man is mortal!" And the choice each of us made of his life and being was an authentic choice, since it was made in the presence of death, since it could always have been expressed in the form: "Better dead than..." And I am not speaking here of the elite among us who were real Resistance fighters but of all the French people who, every hour of the night and day for four years, said "No." The very cruelty of the enemy drove us to the extremities of this condition by forcing us to ask ourselves questions we sidestep in peacetime. All those among us with any snippets of information about the Resistance—and what Frenchman was not at one point or another in that position—asked ourselves anxiously, "If they torture me, will I be able to hold out?" In this way, the very question of freedom was posed, and we were on the verge of the deepest knowledge human beings can have of themselves. For the secret of a human being is not his Oedipus complex or his inferiority complex. It is the very limit of his freedom, his ability to resist torture and death.

To those involved in underground activity, the conditions of their struggle afforded a new kind of experience. They did not fight openly like soldiers. They were hunted down in solitude, arrested in solitude, and it was in an abandoned, defenseless state that they resisted torture, alone and naked in the presence of clean-shaven, well-fed, smartly dressed torturers, who mocked their wretched flesh, and who, by their untroubled consciences and boundless sense of social strength, seemed fully to have right on their side. Yet, in the depths of this solitude, it was the others, all the others, they were protecting—all their Resistance comrades. A single word could have led to ten, or a hundred, arrests. Is not this total responsibility in total solitude the very revelation of our freedom? This abandonment, this solitude, this enormous risk—these were the same for everyone, for leaders and men alike. For those who carried messages without knowing what was in them and for those who directed the entire Resistance effort, the punishment was the same—imprisonment, deportation, and death. In no army in the world is such an equality of risk shared by private and commander in chief. And this is why the Resistance was a true democracy: for the soldier as for the commander, the same danger, the same responsibility, the same absolute freedom within discipline. Thus, in the shadows and in blood, the strongest of Republics was forged. Each of its citizens knew he had an obligation to all and that he had to rely on himself alone. Each, in the most total abandonment, fulfilled his role in history. Each, standing against the oppressors, made the effort to be himself irremediably. And by choosing himself in freedom, he chose freedom for all. This Republic without institutions, without army or police force, was something every French person had at every turn to conquer and assert against Nazism. We are now on the threshold of another Republic. Let us wish that this one will, in the full light of day, retain the austere virtues of that Republic of Silence and Night.

EXISTENTIALISM
A Clarification

NEWSPAPERS—including *Action*[1] itself—are only too willing these days to publish articles attacking existentialism. *Action* has been kind enough to ask me to reply. I doubt that many readers will be interested in the debate: they have many more urgent concerns. Yet if, among the persons who might have found principles of thinking and rules of conduct in this philosophy but have been dissuaded by these absurd criticisms, there were just one I could reach and straighten out, it would still be worth writing for him. In any case I want to make it clear that I am replying in my own name only: I would hesitate to involve other existentialists in this polemic.

What do you reproach us for? To begin with, for being inspired by Heidegger, a German and a Nazi philosopher. Next, for preaching, in the name of existentialism, a quietism of anguish. Are we not trying to corrupt the young and turn them away from action by urging them to cultivate a refined despair? Are we not upholding nihilistic doctrines (for an editorial writer in *L'Aube*, the proof is that I entitled a book *Being and Nothingness*. Nothingness, can you imagine!) during these years when everything has to be redone or simply done, when the war is still going on, and when each man needs all the strength he has to win it and to win the peace? Finally, your third complaint is that existentialism likes to poke about in muck and is much readier to show men's wickedness and baseness than their higher feelings.

I'll give it to you straight: your attacks seem to me to stem from ignorance and bad faith. It is not even certain that you have read any of the books you're talking about. You need a scapegoat because you bless so many things you can't help chewing out someone from time to time. You've picked existentialism because it's an abstract doctrine few people know, and you think that no one will verify what you say. But I am going to reply to your accusations point by point.

Heidegger was a philosopher well before he was a Nazi. His adherence to Hitlerism is to be explained by fear, perhaps ambition, and certainly conformism. Not pretty to look at, I agree; but enough to invalidate your neat reasoning. "Heidegger," you say, "is a member of the National Socialist Party; thus his philosophy must be Nazi." That's not it: Heidegger has no character; there's the truth of the matter. Are you going to have the nerve to conclude from this that his philosophy is an apology for cowardice? Don't you know that sometimes a man does not come up to the level of his works? And are you going to condemn *The Social Contract* because Rousseau abandoned his children? And what difference does Heidegger make anyhow? If we discover our own thinking in that of another philosopher, if we ask him for techniques and methods that can give us access to new problems, does this mean that we espouse every one of his theories? Marx borrowed his dialectic from Hegel. Are you going to say that *Capital* is a Prussian work? We've seem the deplorable consequences of economic autarky; let's not fall into intellectual autarky.

During the occupation, the slavish newspapers used to lump together the existentialists and the philosophers of the absurd in the same reproving breath. A venomous little mannered pedant named Albérès, who wrote for the Petainist *Echo des étudiants*,[2] used to yap at our heels every week. In those days, this kind of obfuscation was to be expected; the lower and stupider the blow, the happier we were.

But why have you taken up the methods of the Vichyssoise press again?

Why this helter-skelter kind of writing if it's not because the confusion you create makes it easier for you to attack both of these philosophies at once? The philosophy of the absurd is coherent and profound. Albert Camus has shown that he was big enough to defend it all by himself.[3] I too shall speak all by myself for existentialism. Have you even defined it for your readers? And yet it's rather simple.

In philosophical terminology, every object has an essence and an existence. An essence is an intelligible and unchanging unity of properties; an existence is a certain actual presence in the world. Many people think that the essence comes first and then the existence: that peas, for example, grow and become round in conformity with the idea of peas, and that gherkins are gherkins because they participate in the essence of gherkins. This idea originated in religious thought: it is a fact that the man who wants to build a house has to know exactly what kind of object he's going to create—essence precedes existence—and for all those who believe that God created men, he must have done so by referring to his idea of them. But even those who have no religious faith have maintained this traditional view that the object never exists except in conformity with its essence; and everyone in the eighteenth century thought that all men had a common essence called *human nature*. Existentialism, on the contrary, maintains that in man—and in man alone—existence precedes essence.

This simply means that man first *is*, and only subsequently is this or that. In a word, man must create his own essence: it is in throwing himself into the world, suffering there, struggling there, that he gradually defines say what this man *is* before he dies, or what mankind is before it has disappeared. It is absurd in this light to ask whether existentialism is fascist, conservative, communist, or democratic. At this level of generality existentialism is nothing but a certain way of envisaging human questions by refusing to grant man an eternally established nature. In Kierkegaard's thought it used to go together with religious faith. Today, French existentialism tends to identify itself with atheism, but this is not absolutely necessary. All I can say—without wanting to insist too much on the similarities—is that it isn't too far from the conception of man found in Marx. For is it not a fact that Marx would accept *this motto of ours for man: make, and in making, make yourself, and be nothing but what you have made of yourself*?

Since existentialism defines man by action, it is evident that this philosophy is not a quietism. In fact, man cannot help acting; his thoughts undertakings, he is nothing other than his life, and his life is the unity of his behavior. "But what about anguish?" you'll say. Well, this rather solemn word refers to a very simple reality. If man *is* not but *makes himself,* and if in making himself he makes himself responsible for the whole species, if there is no value or morality given a priori, so that we must in every instance decide alone and without any basis or guidelines, yet *for everyone,* could we possibly help feeling anguished when we have to act? Each of our acts puts the world's meaning and man's place in the universe in question. With each of them, whether we want to or not, we constitute a universal scale of values. And you want us not to be seized with fear in the face of such a total responsibility? Ponge, in a very beautiful piece of writing, said that man is the future of man. That future is not yet created, not yet decided upon. We are the ones who will make it; each of our gestures will help fashion it. It would take a lot of hypocrisy to avoid an anguished awareness of the formidable mission given to each of us. But you people, in order to refute us more convincingly, you people have deliberately confused anguish and neurasthenia, making who knows what pathological terror out of this virile uneasiness existentialism speaks of. Since I want to be thorough, I'll say then that *anguish, far from being an obstacle to action, is the very condition for it, and is identical with the sense of that crushing responsibility of all before all which is the source of both our torment and our grandeur.*

As for despair, we have to understand one another. It's true, that man would be wrong *to hope.* But what does this mean except that hope is the greatest impediment to action? Should we hope that the war will stop all by itself without us, that the Nazis extend the hand of friendship to us, that the privileged members of capitalist society give up their privileges in the celebration of a new "night of August 4"?[4] If we hope for all of this, all we have to do is cross our arms and wait. Man cannot want anything unless he has first understood that he can count only on himself: that he is alone, left alone on earth in the middle of his infinite responsibilities, with neither help nor succor, with no other goal but the one he will set for himself, with no other destiny but the one he will forge on this earth. It is this certainty, this intuitive understanding of his situation, that we call despair. You can see that it is no fine romantic frenzy but the sharp and lucid consciousness of the human condition. *Just as anguish is indistinguishable from a sense of responsibility, despair is inseparable from will.* With despair, true optimism begins: the optimism of the man who expects nothing, who knows he has no rights and nothing coming to him, who rejoices in counting on himself alone and in acting alone for the good of all.

Are you going to condemn existentialism for saying men are free? But you need that freedom, all of you. You hide it from yourselves hypocritically, and yet you incessantly come back to it in spite of yourselves. When you have explained a man's behavior by its causes, by his social situation and his interests, you suddenly become indignant at him and you bitterly reproach him for his conduct. And there are other men, on the contrary, whom you admire and whose acts serve as models for you. All right then, that means that you don't compare the bad ones to lice that infest vine roots and the good ones to useful animals. If you blame them, or praise them, you do so because they could have acted differently. The class struggle is a fact to which I subscribe completely, but how can you fail to see that it is situated on the level of freedom? You call us social traitors, saying that our conception of freedom keeps man from loosening his chains. What stupidity! When we say a man who's out of work is free, we don't mean that he can do whatever he wants and change himself into a rich and tranquil bourgeois on the spot. *He is free because he can always choose to accept his lot with resignation or to rebel against it.* And undoubtedly he will not be able to avoid great poverty; but in the very midst of his destitution, which is dragging him under, he is able to choose to struggle in his own name and that of all the others against all forms of destitution. He can choose to be the man who refuses to let destitution be man's lot. Is a man a social traitor just because from time to time he reminds others of these basic truths? Then the Marx who said, "We want to change the world," and who in this simple sentence said that man is master of his destiny, is a social traitor. Then all of you are social traitors, because that's what you think too just as soon as you let go of the apron strings of a materialism that was useful once but now has gotten old. And if you didn't think so, then man for you would be a thing, just a bit of carbon, sulfur, and phosphorus, and you wouldn't have to lift a finger for him.

You tell me that I work in filth. That's what Alain Laubreaux[5] used to say, too. I could refrain from answering here, because this reproach is directed at me as a person and not as an existentialist. But you are so quick to generalize that I must nevertheless defend myself for fear that the opprobrium you cast upon me will redound to the philosophy I have adopted. There is only one thing to say: I don't trust people who claim that literature uplifts them by displaying noble sentiments, people who want the theater to give them a *show* of heroism and purity. What they really want is to be persuaded that it's easy to do good. In fact, no! It isn't easy. Vichy literature and, alas, some of today's literature would like to make us think it is: it's so nice to be self-satisfied. But it's an outright lie. Heroism, greatness, generosity, abnegation; I agree that there is nothing better and that in the end they are what make sense out of human action. But if you pretend that all a person has to do to be a hero is to belong to the *ajistes,* the *jocistes,*[6] or a political party you favor, to sing innocent songs and go to the country on Sunday, you are cheapening the virtues that you claim to uphold and are simply making fun of everyone.

Have I said enough to make it clear that *existentialism is no mournful delectation but a humanist philosophy of action, effort, combat, and solidarity?* After my attempt to make things clear, will we still find journalists making allusions to "the despair of our eminent ones" and other claptrap? We'll see. I want to tell my critics openly; it all depends on you now. After all, you're free too. And those of you who are fighting for the Revolution, as we think we're fighting too: you are just as able as we are to decide whether it shall be made in good or bad faith. The case of existentialism, an abstract philosophy upheld by a few powerless men, is very slight and scarcely worthy. But in this case as in a thousand others, depending on whether you keep on lying about it or do it justice even as you attack it, you will decide what man shall be. May you grasp this fact and feel a little salutary anguish.

ON THE AMERICAN
WORKING CLASS

Combat, June 6, 1945

AMERICAN WORKERS ARE NOT YET PROLETARIANS

SAN FRANCISCO: In my presence they interviewed a liberal journalist from Baltimore about the situation of the American working class. He answered all questions willingly, but he seemed so obviously puzzled that I finally asked him what befuddled him so: "It's because you Frenchmen talk about the American working class as if it really existed," he replied.

Indeed, there is no doubt that the concept of class is foreign to American thinking. Once I even heard some old ladies declare that "the workers had profited the most from the war," and that "their wives now bought chicken and silk stockings." But these remarks, heard regularly in France after World War I, are definitely not the rule here. According to the average American, what separates the blue-collar worker from his white-collar employer is a difference in the nature of their work, not their class. In France, many bourgeois also prefer to ignore the reality of the working class.

What is important is that here a worker never considers himself a "proletarian" in the European sense of the word. An American, perfectly fluent in French, told me just yesterday that the term "worker" (which could be translated as "*travailleur*") has no equivalent in French because of the very specific connotations it possesses. Of course there is no doubt that in America, as in France, a "worker" is a wage earner, that is, a man who hires out his productive power and who owns neither the instruments nor the product of his labor. But if in that sense he remains the victim of the capitalist system, everything is organized in such a way that he is rarely conscious of it. This is the fact that has struck me the most during this trip.

How Kaiser Financed His Hospitals

In America, there is no generalized system of socialized medicine. Everything depends on the states and private initiative. It is one of the reasons for the disarray that typified the thirties: the government was taken aback because there was no federal organization to take care of the unemployed, specifically in California where there is no state health insurance. At the beginning of the war, when [Henry J.] Kaiser established his enormous shipyards, which employed more than 100,000 workers, he was confronted with a very practical problem: in order to obtain the highest productivity from this enormous crowd of workers, he had to take care of their health. Therefore he created, with Dr. Garfield's help, the famous Kaiser hospital, whose reputation has spread throughout the United States.

This hospital is financed as follows: Kaiser put up $700,000, part of which by the way was loaned to him by the federal government. But, at the same time, he deducted 50 cents per week from the wages of all those workers who wanted to benefit from these medical services; 63 percent of the workers accepted, which provided a weekly sum of $31,500. Kaiser was reimbursed in six months, and since the deductions continued to come in, he was able to build a second hospital, even bigger than the first. There are now 650 beds and 80 physicians and surgeons, all paid for by the weekly deductions of the subscribers.

In addition, even though the number of workers at Kaiser has dropped significantly, the money keeps coming in: they are now planning a training center for nurses as well as a medical research center for which they intend to hand out eight yearly scholarships of $5,000.

"Who Pays for All This?"—"Mr. Kaiser Does!"

Of course, the two hospitals and everything in them belong to the workers. It is they and no one else who pay the doctors and the nurses: it is with their money that research scholarships will be offered to young doctors. But—and this is what I wanted to get to—in these factories where the big left-wing union, the CIO [Congress of Industrial Organizations], has a significant number of members and where the communists exercise a considerable influence, nobody is conscious of the fact that the totality of these health facilities are the exclusive property of the workers.

Kaiser himself presides over these hospitals, and the vice presidents of these organizations are doctors, selected by him, together with perhaps one or two representatives from the city of San Francisco, but not one is a worker. There is no workers' control whatsoever and not even a consultative committee. It is as if the workers had paid for the total cost of these facilities and then, out of indifference, had donated them to their employer.

When I visited the hospital, I had already been informed of this state of affairs; however, I said nothing. On the contrary, I asked our guide, an engineer: "Who is paying for all this?" And he answered, honestly surprised, "But, Mr. Kaiser!" A little later, on the construction site, I had somebody ask a worker who the hospital belonged to and he answered quietly, "It's Kaiser's."

This mind-set can in part be explained by the fact that many Kaiser workers come from the Southwest; they are day workers from the countryside who come to work in the factories for six months or one year, attracted by the high wages. Upon their arrival, they discover an existing, perfectly organized health facility. Since the amount deducted from their wages is very small, and the advantages they enjoy considerable, it appears to them quite simply that all that is asked of them is a small fee in exchange for the services they receive.

Their attitude is ultimately understandable. But it is surprising that the union leaders or the communists don't try to make them understand that they have a claim to those hospitals and that, in a capitalist society, they own these facilities just as Kaiser owns his factory.

A Doctor Praises the System

I put the same question to a hospital doctor; he is a left-wing militant and an intelligent, capable, and energetic man who is totally devoted to the workers' cause, and he seemed surprised. "It's odd," he told me, "but all European visitors are equally amazed and indignant." "Because," I told him, "the European working class has a clearer understanding of its rights." "But that's absurd," he answered. "What can we do? Kaiser would never have accepted worker participation in the hospital's administration. Therefore, should we have sabotaged the undertaking? Look at the tremendous advantages it provides to our workers: last week a woman came in for a consultation; there was blood in her urine. A private doctor would have charged her $10 for this examination. Diagnosis: tuberculosis in her right kidney. It will require a $500 operation: here everything is free. Don't forget also that when a worker is hired, there never is a medical examination. Therefore it often happens that we look after workers whose diseases were contracted well before they were hired by Kaiser. And on top of that, it represents a terrible blow to private medicine. As you know, in America health is "big business" [in English in the text]; doctors are very expensive, and we have encountered terrible resistance from the American Medical Association. After the war, when the shipyards lost a lot of their importance, Kaiser's plan was to interest all the region's industrial enterprises in his hospital. That's how he will have contributed to the growth of socialized medicine."

What to answer him? That health care that is in the service of the big capitalists is not exactly socialized medicine? What would have been the use? What strikes me especially is that here workers do not have a sense of collective property. Since they do not own the hospitals as individuals, they immediately assume that they are the boss's personal property, that's how far removed they are from adopting a socialist point of view. And, finally, the manner in which they permit this hospital—that belongs to them—to be filched reminds me a little of what happens in the case of what is called in economics texts "profit." The worker is happy to be paid a wage. On the one hand, he can lay full claim to the product of his labor, but on the other, he is content with a lifetime interest in a medical facility that is properly his. In both cases, the plunder occurs with his consent.

I let my opinion be known to a worker in Detroit who replied, "I know, but what can we do? At international meetings, worker delegates from Europe often criticize American workers for not expressing solidarity with the international proletarians but that's because you are not aware of our situation; we are not yet proletarians." And he added bitterly, "Unfortunately!" This is the situation that I will try to explain in these articles.

———

Combat, June 7, 1945

THE UNITED STATES: A COUNTRY OF SETTLERS

SAN FRANCISCO: The American worker is not conscious of being riveted to his condition in the way his French or British comrades are. He is just "passing through."

When discussing Kaiser's factories, I referred to the considerable number of workers who are in reality day workers from Texas and Oklahoma and are here to make in two or three years the small amount of money necessary to buy a plot of land and start out on their own. During their stay in the city, they retain their peasant mentality: they seem like aliens to their worker buddies; their hopes and their deepest memories are attached to the earth and the fields; they hire themselves out, but they don't give themselves.

"Open Societies"

Besides, nowhere else is the small farmers' misery greater than in certain areas of Texas or New Mexico; as a consequence, for the day workers that come from there, becoming part of the working class represents an incredible improvement in their condition and approximates the attainment of bourgeois respectability. But of course they do not represent the majority. Except for those who were born of working-class parents and have worked in factories since their adolescence, the American class system appears, in Bergson's words, like an "open society."

Until the relatively recent period of massive immigration, immense regions remained undeveloped in this country, and natural resources greatly surpassed their potential for exploitation. In other regions, industrial progress and mechanization of agriculture allowed for the opening of new factories overnight, and as a result there was a continuous influx of foreign workers: the most recent arrivals were seen as the proletarians.

Upon arrival, the immigrants initially accepted their inferior jobs and low salaries. They largely retained the memory of the miserable existence they had fled and which made their present condition look like a paradise and, just as important, for them this condition was temporary. The point was to get a foothold in America and to be tolerated. Indeed, twenty years later, they had climbed one or two rungs up the social ladder, pushed up by new arrivals who replaced them in the low-paying jobs and who had to climb up the social ladder in turn. This is what allows [André] Siegfried to remark:

> The cotton industry in Massachusetts has in the last seventy-five years seen the character of its workers change several times. Towards 1870, the Irish and Scots still represented the majority; but since then, even though their numbers have not significantly declined, their relative place has undergone a strong decline, while they have tended to migrate towards the highly technical positions.
>
> Pressure from below obliged them to climb up the ladder. From 1870 to approximately 1880 a massive number of French-Canadians arrived. At the end of the decade, this group alone surpassed in number all other foreign nationalities. In accordance with their seniority, they succeeded in occupying all sorts of positions at all levels. Besides, they no longer occupied the bottom rung because in the last decade of the century, the heavy jobs were passed on to an improbable and colorful collection of Poles, Portuguese, Syrians, Greeks, and Russians.[1]

Hence class characteristics interfere with national ones: in 1920, a worker no longer knows whether he is a proletarian because he belongs by birth to the proletariat or because he is an Irishman who just got off the boat. On the other hand, national and religious solidarities persist for a long time among immigrants and explain the existence of those innumerable Irish, Jewish, Mexican, and Chinese neighborhoods that function as barriers and blind them to class solidarity.

Those Who Forged Their Own Destiny

Besides, these men have accepted their destiny and are proudly aware of having forged it themselves: they fled the miseries of Europe and in advance accepted a few difficult years in a new country which did not welcome them but in which they were sure to find their place. While a worker in France, born whether he wanted to be or not into an ancient proletariat, sees all horizons blocked from the start and learns as a child from bitter experience that his fate is tied to the entire working class, these men have freely accepted exiling themselves and have retained the impression of having "chosen" their fate. In America they did not experience that hopeless hereditary oppression that weighs on the European proletariat. Instead of having the stifling feeling of being swallowed up by an overwhelming destiny, they have acquired a kind of individualistic sense of their personal dignity because even if they are laborers or semiskilled, they know they have come to find their destiny on the other side of the ocean and they consider themselves responsible for it.

Of course, strictly speaking, this is true only for the immigrants of the first generation; but they raised their children with these sentiments, and Protestant individualism is responsible for the rest.

The Beginning of Americanization

America is a colonized country, and I would compare the American workers quite willingly to our French settlers in Morocco. In spite of the obvious and profound differences, they have the same consciousness of having established themselves freely in their place of work, and the result has been the same devotion to energy and action and the same profound conservatism.

The extraordinary opportunities many of them have encountered persuaded them that success depended on them. They did not understand that they were benefiting from an exceptional economic situation that was the result of the fact that America is a rich but underpopulated country. They attributed this state of affairs to the political constitution and to America's public spirit. And that was the beginning of the process of Americanization: without being intellectually and critically minded individualists, they acquired a professional individualism.

Combat, June 9, 1945

THE AMERICAN WORKER EATS JUST AS WELL AS HIS BOSS AND HEINZ PRODUCES 57 VARIETIES OF CANNED FOODS FOR ITS FELLOW CITIZENS

NEW YORK: Here people say frequently that the poorest American believes deep down that he can become a Rockefeller or move into the White House. Perhaps this is somewhat less true since the 1930s depression, but up until then this feeling was indeed quite widespread.

In this respect people pointed out a very important fact to me: at the beginning of that terrible depression, when millions of workers and employees found themselves out of work overnight, it was very difficult to persuade many of them to register at the unemployment office: they were ashamed. They were so used to counting on themselves that they were unable to see themselves as innocent victims of a collective catastrophe. It seemed to them that their misfortune was their own fault and that they had not been sufficiently clever or hardworking. Unable to grasp the meaning of collective property or of a collective event, how could they have been aware of the collective nature of their condition?

The Minimum Wage

I must admit that their standard of living, especially today, blinds them to their real problems. Of course, one must not exaggerate: there are still, if one includes the blacks, millions of workers whose wages are below the poverty line. About a month and a half ago, the federal government raised the minimum wage to 55 cents per hour; it had been 50 cents, which means that there were still a lot of people in America who made less than $100 per month. This is especially the case for workers in small shops and department stores as well as laundry workers, etc. But the "real" workers: the steelworkers, the miners, mechanics, and so on, enjoy a much higher standard of living and they are far more numerous than those underprivileged ones.

One Unmarried Worker in Fontana Village

Take as an example the Fontana Dam being constructed by the TVA [Tennessee Valley Authority]. Its workers make on average $6 per day. The legal work week is 40 hours and overtime is paid at one-and-a-half times the regular rate. The monthly wages range roughly from $330 to $360 a month and they are far from being the highest in America. At the official exchange rate of 50 francs to the dollar, they are making between 16,500 and 18,000 francs per month. But since life is nevertheless more expensive in America than in France (if one ignores for a moment the black market), it is better to evaluate the buying power this income confers on the worker.

Let us suppose he is unmarried because today everybody works in America, and if he is married, his wife's pay is added to his. He lives in Fontana Village, an artificial community made up of those "prefabricated houses" [in English in the text] which I talked about elsewhere. It is furnished and has three bedrooms, a kitchen, and bathroom, and he pays $31 per month rent. The furniture is ordinary, but completely new: it reminded me of the furniture from Dufayel, Bûcheron, or the Galeries Barbès. There are couches, leather armchairs, an electric oven, and a fridge.

This "housing" [in English in the text] policy is advantageous to the bosses: they are not out of pocket, because their enterprise is profitable and the workers rent from them and live on their property, which allows them to better control them. But it is also to the workers' advantage: they live in the most amazing comfort and it does not cost them too much.

Our "proletarian" buys his groceries in general food stores situated in the village itself and set up in agreement with the industry boss, and those stores sell him their goods at very low prices. If he prefers to eat out, he can eat for 40 cents in the company's cafeteria.

I have often eaten in these "cafeterias": there is lots of food and it is good. At the entrance, there is a reminder that the country is at war and the customers are asked not to order more food than they can eat: a clear indication that no one is starving to death. Life is so standardized here that I found no significant difference between the menus of the luxury restaurants and the canteens. In restaurants, you pay mostly for the cutlery, the service, and the atmosphere, but no matter where you go you find, whether it is in the "Automats" or the dining room of the great hotels, the same green peas whose color is so garish that you think they were hand-painted, the same unsalted white beans which are served in little dishes, the same brown and odd-looking gravy; it is semi-sweet, semi-salty, and they spread it on a refrigerated piece of beef, and especially the same canned foods Heinz provides to all of America—its 57 varieties of canned foods allow it to play a great role as equalizer. To finish up, the worker, just like his boss, eats a big piece of sponge cake with cream or an "ice cream" [in English in the text]. They drink the same chlorinated ice water and the same bad coffee.

The Worker's Budget

As a consequence, the worker seldom has the dim but haunting notion that the rich bourgeois American eats luxurious meals that he has to do without. For $30 or $40 a month he can eat the same food as "everybody" else, that food that is so American and that one finds from one end of the United States to the other and at all levels of society and which is presumably rich in vitamins but has so few that after their meals most people take vitamin pills apparently made especially to be swallowed rapidly and casually by people in a hurry.

Now we have spent $60 to $70; take out $20 to $30 for taxes, $60 to $70 for war bonds (the worker considers buying war bonds a patriotic duty and spends regularly 15 percent to 20 percent of his wages on them). This still leaves the worker $180 to $200 for clothes, miscellaneous expenses, and going out. If he wants to, he can become a shareholder and participate, to a certain degree, in the life of American capital.[2]

———

Combat, June 10 and 11, 1945

"HELLO, JIM," SAYS CHICAGO'S BISHOP TO THE SCHOOL'S JANITOR. "HELLO, BISHOP!" ANSWERS THE JANITOR.

NEW YORK: The figures I have provided on the American worker's living conditions should allow the reader to understand to what degree his mentality differs from his European comrade's.

Some time ago, a sociologist who was trying to describe the consumer habits of the French worker stressed the fact that the working class spent the smallest part of its budget on housing and clothes and the largest part on food. As a consequence, he indicated that most proletarian families were crammed into slums and that the worker abandoned family life in order to find in the street the social life that is indispensable to the most solitary individual.

There is nothing comparable to this in the case of America: undoubtedly one still encounters slums in the overpopulated Northeast, but decentralization and the "housing" [in English in the text] policy implemented by the government and management have reversed the situation. As we have seen, the worker spends as much, if not more, on housing as he does on food. That means that the American "proletariat" can enjoy a home life.

The "Community House"

Hence, it is not surprising that in each of the artificially created settlements near the big construction sites a "community house" [in English in the text] has been built, a huge shed composed of wooden boards where the workers get together after their work to smoke, read, and chat, and it is not surprising that the crowd gathering there at night resembles the people we encounter in working-class neighborhoods in our industrialized cities, but the resemblance is superficial: these halls created by the state's or the boss's paternalism preserve a puritanical air. Drinking doesn't take place there; playing rarely does. Tired and silent men dream there, alone or in small groups. One doesn't sense the presence of those powerful social forces that throng the streets and workers' cafés in Europe.

Also, the "community house" is mainly frequented by unmarried men who prefer that kind of "shared solitude" to complete loneliness.

In Public the American Worker Cannot Be Distinguished from the Bourgeois

The married workers live at home, just like the bourgeois; family life is just as important as his professional life. Similarly, in the cities' working-class neighborhoods, the streets do not look like our streets: you don't linger in them as we do for the joy of sensing oneself overwhelmed by a great unanimous wave: you cross them very quickly in order to go to work or to go home.

As you know, the Belgian writer [Hendrik] de Man spoke in the books he wrote before World War II of the presence of a certain "inferiority complex" in the European worker who sensed that he did not possess any specifically bourgeois values.[3] Here, nothing like that exists; the worker does not feel that he stands out because of the way he is dressed.

The numerous factories we visited struck me by their cleanliness: they resemble offices more closely than our dark and dirty factories: the workers are properly clothed, the women are attractively made up, they wear baseball caps and long cotton pants, and colorful blouses.

After work, the worker puts on a nice ready-made suit which is comparable to millions of the same suits manufactured in America because it is nearly impossible, especially today, for women and men to order clothes that are made-to-measure. There is a "Heinz" for clothes as there is for food.

In the street, you cannot tell the difference between a worker and a bourgeois; same outfit, same easy and nonchalant demeanor: the exterior class indications are nonexistent.

American Equality

This apparent equality also shows up in their public behavior: Why should the worker, the elevator attendant, the delivery boy be hostile to, or intimidated by, his boss or a rich customer? They think that what he is today, they will perhaps be tomorrow. The boss has been luckier than they are, that's all. And the bourgeois encourage this kind of familiarity, whose equivalent is found nowhere in Europe: first of all it is useful to them because it hides the profound differences of condition, but above all because they are very sincerely proud of American "equality."

Maybe they are more easily fooled than others. But this truly human kindness that pervades class relationships is surely one of the most charming and spontaneous characteristics of the United States.

In a restaurant, the waitress jokes with the customer, she teases him: if he comes back, she waves at him from afar as if he were an old acquaintance. Neither in stores nor in hotels is anyone obsequious; rather they are kindly and gruff in their approach. Taxi drivers become involved in the conversations of their passengers in the backseat of their cab.

Monsignor Shell, Chicago's bishop, was kind enough to show me around his school: in the gym we ran into the old caretaker, who was busily working. "Hello, Jim," said the bishop. And the caretaker, without turning around, tossed back at him, "Hello, Bishop!"

The Situation of the "Intellectuals"

The laborers and those who work in small shops do not have the impression that they are selling their labor but rather that they are performing a service; hence, most of them are, without ulterior motives, proud of their high wages. If you really want to talk about a complex, it would be better to talk about their superiority complex in respect to intellectuals, who after studying for ten years make less money than they do.

Recently, a French professor was on a boat with some twenty workers who were going back to America after having built a floating harbor somewhere on the European coast. They spoke to him in a friendly but disdainful manner.

"What," they said, "you studied so long and you make so little?" And they added proudly, "We, we never studied at all."

And, showing their hands, they remarked, "That's what we make our living with."

If they are upset by the huge salary of a Hollywood star or a radio singer, it is not because these amounts are high but because it seems to them that all these people are paid to do nothing.

Americans First

A French worker is definitely proud to be a manual laborer, but he affirms the superiority of his work all the more violently because the bourgeois hardly believe in it while they pretend to be the repositories of traditions, culture, and luxury to which he in principle has no access.

In the U.S.A., everybody is in agreement: this civilization is dominated by technology and it respects foremost the technician and the specialized worker. Cultural values follow far behind, and as far as traditions go, there are none. As a consequence, the American worker is not familiar with that internationalism based on poverty which before the war united the European proletariat. The famous cry "Workers of the world, unite!" leaves him cold. He is first of all an American.

Combat, June 12, 1945

A SADNESS COMPOSED OF FATIGUE AND BOREDOM
WEIGHS ON AMERICAN FACTORY WORKERS

NEW YORK: The American worker does not recognize his own suffering in that of his European brethren. He is inclined to attribute it to a lack of organization, and, if he thinks about it, he takes pride in his own country with its high salaries, its comfortable housing, its freedom and equality. And when he discerns the relationship between his high wages and the general prosperity of the U.S.A., he expresses solidarity with capitalism: it is within the framework of the capitalist system that he wants to improve conditions.

"Did You See Our Willow Run Plant?"

Before Roosevelt, many skilled workers voted for the Republican Party, which stood for large, organized production and had as its goal the increase of the nation's material wealth. In general, that American worker is proud of his country's riches, its overwhelming industrial power, and the scientific progress it accomplishes every day.

In Detroit, local CIO leaders asked me, glowing with pride, "Did you see our Willow Run plant?" (these are Henry Ford's main factories), just as the bourgeois of Amiens might ask before the war, "Did you see our cathedral?"

I have difficulty imagining the same pride in a French union leader working for Michelin or Goodrich. But an American feels as if the factory in which he works is "his own"; not that he participates in the profits or in its management for all that, but he considers himself a beneficiary of the cleanliness and hygiene that is strictly maintained in the workplace: every day, he is joyfully amazed over the most recent technological improvements. He even participates in them.

In most factories, initiatives and criticisms by the personnel are encouraged. If a worker invents a device that can improve the output or save time, they reserve a place of honor for it and his picture is displayed at the entry of the factory. All this allows one to understand that socialism has made no inroads into the American masses. The only attempts to create a socialist party were made in the agrarian Northwest and not in the East or in the industrialized Northeast; besides, these attempts have failed.

The Fear of Marxism

In the big cities, especially in San Francisco, there are a few communist cells. But the communists daren't speak their name: they hide under such fancy names as "progressives" or "reformers"; they lead a semi-clandestine existence. Marxism, about which the immense majority of Americans don't know the first thing, is America's bogeyman. Hundreds of times during this trip, in every kind of place, I have been asked in a genuinely apprehensive tone, "Is it true that France will fall to the communists?"

In the CIO, the most progressive labor union, there is a noisy and active minority who periodically demand the expulsion of the Marxists. What the workers especially fear is socialist policies that will reduce their standard of living and compromise America's prosperity. What estranges them from communism is their professional individualism.

In sum, the American worker "needs" capitalism; his attitude is firmly evolutionary and progressive, he rejects everything that smells of revolution. Rationalist optimism permeates him since it is one of the characteristics of Americanism that there is no problem that cannot be solved using common sense, goodwill, and mutual concessions.

The Mechanization of Labor

Can we say therefore, as some people maintain, that America is a worker's paradise and that goodwill and solidarity reign between management and the proletariat? If that were only the case!

First of all, the mechanization of labor has been pushed so far that the worker has lost all interest in what he does. He may well be proud of his factory, in the manner that we are proud of our works of art, but in his shop or construction site he suffers from the same sense of hopeless boredom that is now typical of the workers in our overly rationalized industries. The "joy of working" is just about completely foreign to him: and his time at work is a waste of a part his life; he sacrifices it to earn a living.

A young worker said before me, "A JOB [in English in the original] is work that one doesn't like."

There is a distinct sadness among the American working masses: it is composed of fatigue, boredom, and dreams. At night, the worker hurries off to the movies in order to get away and forget a long, inhuman day of work.

The movies play a social role here: many Americans call them the opium of the people.

It's because work, especially now during the war, has become a hell: it is not only completely mechanized, but management in agreement with the government has increased the output of the human machine to the maximum. In all factories, the number of operations that a worker must perform in one hour is rigorously determined. And it goes up from year to year.

A Fifteen-Minute Break Every Two Hours

The constantly increasing demands from management are at the origin of numerous conflicts. The worker is conscious of his exhaustion and that he is becoming an automaton. For two-thirds of the day, he is reduced to a series of identical gestures and his work is constantly speeded up and he is more and more hurried.

In a factory I visited it is customary to grant the worker a fifteen-minute break every two hours. That is how they hope to increase his productivity, because during the two hours that he is working, he does not have the right either to smoke or to raise his head.

I walked through the shops during the fifteen-minute break and I was struck by the gloomy stupor that showed on their faces. Everybody remained at his place, alone and in silence: most of them did not even smoke. They rolled a cigarette between their fingers but they did not even think of lighting it. They appeared to be plunged in a kind of nothingness in order "to recover their strength" from within the very depth of their being. Rather than speaking of fifteen minutes of rest, one should call it fifteen minutes of death. -

———

Combat, June 14, 1945

SINCE THE DEPRESSION OF THE THIRTIES, THE AMERICAN WORKER LIVES IN FEAR OF BEING UNEMPLOYED ONE DAY

NEW YORK: I have spoken of the pride with which the American workers showed off their high wages. But they have to protect these high wages constantly. The cost of living is rising: they have to fight in order to obtain raises that are in proportion. Often the conflicts are quite violent.

But the big fear of the American proletariat is to be unemployed. In that respect, the disastrous experience of the thirties has had a decisive impact. For the American people who had never known an economic crisis—at least not a crisis of such magnitude—it struck them like the revelation of evil. Few events have had such an impact on the history of the United States.

The working people feel profoundly terrorized; they may be enjoying an easy and luxurious existence, but they sense that it may well be ephemeral and they do not abandon themselves to it with confidence. Tomorrow, when the soldiers come back from the war and industry will be placed on a peacetime footing, workers may be out on the street without a penny. And the feeling that their situation is precarious may well be their greatest anxiety.

Last September, when all of America anticipated the swift collapse of the German army, a genuine panic occurred among the workers, and many quit their jobs in the war factories in order to find as quickly as possible a job in peacetime industries. One can sense that they are ready to do anything in order to avoid a return to the dark days of the 1930s.

I do not know if this is really management's intention, but it is true that in regard to their workers they practice a policy of enlightened despotism. The most progressive ones among the lot are completely in favor of improving the proletariat's condition where feasible. Henry Ford was the first to adopt the so-called "policy of high wages": since then, it has been imitated by the entire United States, and, as we know, Kaiser established a hospital with great effort. But they expect these improvements to be initiated by management: a lot is done for the worker, but it is not done by the worker.

Nowhere else but in America has it been so difficult to establish unions. The employers have fought them off violently. Not so long ago Henry Ford employed a team of goons to beat up the striking workers. Before 1936, management frequently fired workers suspected of belonging to "unions" [in English in the text].

Together with the CIO, radical moviemakers have produced an unusual film, *Native Land*, which I saw in a private showing; it describes the bitter and often bloody battles the unions had to undertake in order to be officially recognized. This film is already quite old, but it was officially withdrawn one week after it was shown in public. It shows strikes, bloody clashes, and lockouts and makes you grasp better this profound American contradiction: America is the most optimistic country in the world; its people have always considered war an avoidable accident and the use of force an unjustifiable tactic, but it is also a country that contains, in a latent state, the greatest possibilities for violence.

Management Against the Unions

Management has done what it could to imprison the worker in his so-called individual "freedom." Even today, many bosses are resolutely opposed to unions.

On April 9, B. E. Hutchison, vice president of the Chrysler Corporation and director of the National Association of Manufacturers (NAM), the most conservative management organization, stated that its committees were studying a plan whose preliminary outlines had been submitted to the Chamber of Commerce. It requests that it be declared illegal for workers' unions to prevent the adoption of modern techniques whose purpose it is to improve production and to call wildcat and illegal strikes. It also demands that the individual worker's rights against the unions be protected and he be permitted to work "without fear of any molestation or forms of violence exercised against his person or his property."

The Chamber of Commerce has not yet acknowledged this proposal, which would, if adopted, practically withdraw the right to strike from the unions and turn the workers away from union membership. But many fear that the return of the soldiers, the threat of unemployment, and the actions of conservative elements will, after the war, provoke in America a violent, antiunion movement. The tension between labor and management remains high.

———

Combat, June 30, 1945

IN THE STATES ONE-THIRD OF THE WORKERS BELONG TO TWO LARGE UNIONS: THE AFL WITH 5,800,000 MEMBERS, THE CIO WITH 5,200,000

NEW YORK: I've already written in *Combat* that tensions remain high between American workers and management. I should add that in the States what we call in Europe "the class struggle" is not viewed in the same light. Here workers view themselves as being involved in a struggle that has at its core the bad faith of some individuals rather than the very structure of society.

For them, the bosses are not the representatives of a social class whose interests are radically opposed to those of the proletariat. In order to adopt such a view, they would have had to perform a thorough analysis of capitalism and, as we have seen, nothing is farther from their mind. Rather, they see certain bosses as disloyal competitors or better yet as perfidious partners: in an economic system the workers accept that these bosses don't play the game; they prevent the workers from organizing, they don't raise wages when they should, they are not sufficiently worried about the return of unemployment, and, perhaps, they even secretly wish its return. That's what they criticize them for. They impute to them an egoistic hard-heartedness that undoubtedly stems from their situation but does not express the overall politics of a class.

The working masses feel deeply that they are in basic agreement with management: their common interest is to maintain the high living standard of the American people by raising production as much as possible. Thus, America's optimism and the preference for compromise solutions have resulted in the worker's ideal of permanent harmony between employers and employees, between capital and labor. A short overview of the American union movement will clarify this.

The Older of the Two Unions: The AFL

Only one-third of the workers are unionized. This disproportionately low number is explained first of all by their professional individualism of which we have already spoken, but another explanation lies in the fact that included among "workers" are all the day and farm laborers that the unions have not as yet tried to organize.

If one leaves aside the mine-workers' union, which accounts for at least a million men, the much less important "Brotherhood" [in English in the text] of railroad workers, and a handful of small independent unions, it can be said that in the United States there are two big occupational organizations.

The oldest union, and today also the most important, is the American Federation of Labor (AFL). As its name indicates, it is a federation of unions in which each union preserves its autonomy. It was created in 1881 but did not acquire its present name until 1886. Since that time, it has not stopped perfecting its tactics. It has demanded and obtained an improvement in labor legislation and sanitary conditions, wage increases, and a reduction in the work week. Its principal weapon is the strike, which is used judiciously and commonly called its "economic power."

The Workers' Attachment to Economic Liberalism

It views itself as a distributor of manpower; it distributes it as best as it can and in the workers' interests; if these cannot be guaranteed, it summarily rejects the jobs offered. But it has taken a clear position against socialism, and Samuel Gompers, its leader for forty years, prevented it from linking itself up permanently with a political party. Even today, after the 1930s depression, it remains hostile to state intervention and defends free enterprise. This does not mean that it never agrees to support a specific government action if it is shown to be necessary, but it wants to reduce its interference to the absolute minimum, because in principle it is suspicious of "planning" and it identifies democracy with economic liberalism.

On the question of race, it seeks to remain neutral, and in practice this pretty well means that blacks remain excluded from the federation. At present it has 5.8 million members and dominates the trades that have been unionized the longest, especially in the field of construction.

A Split in the AFL

Between 1930 and 1936 it was torn apart by a violent conflict: a certain number of its members accused it of having been incapable of unionizing the big mass-production industries: steel, autos, textile. Indeed, in these industries where the manufactured product is always the result of the cooperation of many skilled workers, the old-fashioned organization according to separate skills proved to be inefficient: fitters, bench hands, turners, finishers, even though they belong to different trades, have the same interests. Consequently, the minority that opposed the AFL proposed as a substitute for the federation system by skill a vertical structure that would unite in one single union all the workers of one particular industry. Therefore, the basic unit would no longer be the skill but the total industry of which the skills are a part. The conflict resulted in a split.

The CIO [Congress of Industrial Organizations], originally begun by a dissenting minority that left [the AFL], tried to organize the great industries according to these principles. It succeeded remarkably. Today it has 5.2 million members and its importance has become considerable, because the factories where it operated have been transformed for the most part into war plants.

The American Communists

Hence in principle, this new organization which grew out of the AFL only differs by structure and tactics from the federation from which it split. However, in fact it is made up of younger elements and it recruits its members in newer and more vibrant industries. Therefore, it must be considered as less conservative, which does not mean at all that it is influenced by socialist doctrine.

There are undoubtedly communists among its membership, but a minority is fiercely anticommunist and regularly demands their expulsion. Also, most American communists are workers sympathetic to the Soviet Union's cause who see America's future lying in close cooperation with the Soviets, but who absolutely do not want to see that type of government introduced into the United States.

Like the AFL, the CIO is particularly in favor of extracting the most from free enterprise, but it is more aware of the limits of economic liberalism and agrees that it should be corrected by using moderate interventionism where there are lacunae or weaknesses. It has supported Roosevelt's efforts at planning, specifically, the TVA, and accepts blacks as its members.

THE LIBERATION OF PARIS: AN APOCALYPTIC WEEK

THESE days, if a man isn't willing to say that Paris liberated itself, he is taken for an enemy of the people. And yet it seems quite clear that the city could not have even dreamed of rising up in revolt if the Allies had not been very close. And since they in turn could not have even dreamed of disembarking if the Russians had not stopped and beaten back the major part of the German divisions, it must be concluded that the liberation of Paris, an episode in a war of universal dimensions, was the common work of all the Allied forces. One does not, furthermore, drive out people who are leaving of their own free will, and by the time the insurrection first broke out the Germans had already begun to evacuate the city.

The goal of the members of the Resistance was just the opposite of that which is imputed to them today: they tried to slow down the enemy retreat and close Paris in on the occupying troops like a trap. And then, above all, they wanted to show future conquerors that the Resistance was not, as people outside the country still seemed all too ready to believe, a myth. In the eyes of governments who had dreamed for a time of having the liberated territories administered by their officers, they wanted to affirm the sovereignty of the French people; and they understood that the only means they had of legitimizing the power of the people was to shed their own blood.

Thus their undertaking owes its greatness to its limitations. The destiny of Paris was at stake fifty kilometers away; it was the German and the American tanks that would settle the issue. But the men of the Resistance did not want to be bothered with that. They did not even want to know the outcome of the struggle they had undertaken. In giving the signal for the uprising, they had unleashed vague and powerful forces capable from one moment to the next of crushing them. That's what gave this week in August the appearance of a classical tragedy. But fate was just what these men meant to deny. Whether or not the Germans blew up the Senate and a whole part of the city with it did not depend on them. Whether the retreating divisions attacked Paris and made another Warsaw of our city did not depend on them. But what did depend on them was to bear witness by their actions—and regardless of the outcome of the unequal struggle they had undertaken—to the will of the French people. So each of them refused to put his hope in anyone besides himself. The Parisians who were not fighting asked from hour to hour with anguish if the Allied troops would not be here soon. The fighters never thought about it, and it even seemed there was a tacit agreement which forbade them to talk about it: they were doing what they had to do.

One afternoon during that week, as I was going to see a friend who ran a Resistance newspaper in the building he had just taken over, someone came to tell him about German infiltrations around the building. "If they attacked tonight," he told me, "we'd be trapped like rats. There are only two ways out of here and both are guarded." "Do you at least have arms?" He shrugged his shoulders and replied, "No." Thus, surrounded by obscure dangers brushing them, these journalists did what they had to do, which was to print a paper. About everything else—that is, about everything concerning their personal security, their chances of coming out of the adventure alive—they didn't want to think. Since they were unable to influence the outcome of these things by their actions, they figured that none of it was any of their business.

This accounts for that other aspect of the Paris uprising, the festive air it never ceased to have. Whole sections of the city dressed up in their Sunday best. And if I ask myself just what they were celebrating,

I see that it was man and his strengths. It is reassuring that the anniversary of the Paris uprising fell so close to the first appearances of the atomic bomb. What the bomb represents is the negation of man. Not only because it risks destroying the whole of mankind but above all because it makes the most human qualities—courage, patience, intelligence, the spirit of initiative—vain and ineffectual. Most of the FFI,[1] on the contrary, had in August 1944 an obscure sense of fighting not only for France against the Germans but also for man against the blind powers of the machine. We had been told often enough that the revolutions of the twentieth century could not be like those of the nineteenth, and that it would take only one plane, only one big gun to put down a rebellious mob. We had been warned enough about the ring of guns the Germans had surrounded Paris with! We had been shown often enough that we could do nothing against their machine guns and tanks. Well, during that month of August the fighters you met in the streets were young people in shirtsleeves. All they had for weapons were revolvers, a few rifles, a few grenades and bottles of gasoline. Facing an enemy clad in steel, they became intoxicated with the feeling of the freedom and the lightness of their movements. The discipline which they invented with each passing moment won out over the discipline that had been learned. They tested, and made us test, the naked power of man. And we couldn't help thinking of what Malraux calls, in *Man's Hope*, the rehearsal of the apocalypse. Yes, it was the triumph of the apocalypse, of that apocalypse which is always defeated by the forces of order and which for once, within the narrow limits of this street fight, was victorious. The apocalypse: that is to say a spontaneous organization of revolutionary forces. All Paris felt during that week in August that man still had a chance, that he could still win out over the machine; and even if the battle had ended with the crushing of the Resistance forces, as it did in Poland, these few days would have been enough to prove the power of freedom. So it makes very little difference that the FFI did not, strictly speaking, liberate Paris from the Germans: at each instant, behind each barricade, and on each street they exercised freedom for themselves and for each Frenchman.

So what we're going to commemorate each year, officially and in an orderly manner, is the explosion of freedom, the disruption of the established order, and the invention of a spontaneous and effective order. It is to be feared that the festival will quickly lose its meaning. Yet there is a certain aspect of the insurrection which may endure in our ceremonies. When the mob of 1789 invaded the Bastille, they did not know the meaning, the consequences, of their gesture; it was only afterward and by degrees that they became conscious of it and raised it to the level of a symbol. What was striking in August 1944 was that the symbolic character of the uprising was already established while its outcome was still uncertain. Choltitz,[2] in hesitating to destroy Paris; the Allies, in agreeing to advance the date of their entry into the capital; the members of the Resistance, in choosing to fight their big battle there—all of them decided that the event would be "historic." All of them were remembering Paris's great day of wrath. All of them considered it one of the essential things at stake in the war. And each FFI, in fighting, felt that he was writing history. The whole history of Paris was there, in that sun, in those naked streets. That is why this tragedy, this risky affirmation of human freedom, was also something like a "ceremony." A pompous and bloody ceremony whose ordering was carefully controlled and which ended fatally in death, something like a human sacrifice. It is this triple aspect of tragedy denied, apocalypse, and ceremony that gives the insurrection of August 1944 its deeply human character and its continuing power to move us deeply. Is it not even, today, our best reason for hoping? It is vain and useless for us to imagine and proclaim that we liberated ourselves with our forces alone. Would you like to meet Maurras[3] on some side street and rattle on with him about the absurd "France, France, alone ..."? And similarly it is useless to stamp our feet, strike lofty poses, and insist daily on a place in the concert of nations we are daily denied. But is it not the insurrection of 1944 which, set against the inordinate powers the war brought into being, shows us our true strength? In that ceremonious and disproportionate battle, Paris affirmed, in opposition to the German tanks, the power of human beings. Is it not still our task today to defend the human, without great illusions and without too much hope, before the young and slightly inhuman forces which have just won victory?

NEW YORK, COLONIAL CITY

I KNEW I would love New York, but I thought I would be able to love it straightaway, as I had loved the red bricks of Venice at first sight or the solid, gloomy houses of London. I didn't know that for the European fresh off the plane, there is a "New York sickness," akin to sea sickness, air sickness or altitude sickness.

A bus had taken me from La Guardia airport to the Plaza Hotel at midnight. I had pressed my face against the window, but I could see only red and green lights and obscure buildings. The following day, without any transition, I found myself at the corner of Fifty-eighth Street and Fifth Avenue. I took a long walk beneath an icy sky. It was a forlorn January Sunday in 1945 and I was looking for New York and couldn't find it. It was as though it drew back from me, like a ghost town, as I advanced along an avenue that seemed coldly mediocre and unoriginal. What I was looking for was, no doubt, a European city.

We Europeans live by the myth of the city we forged in the nineteenth century. The Americans' myths are not ours and the American city isn't our city. It hasn't the same nature or the same functions. In Spain, Italy, Germany, or France, we find round cities originally encircled by ramparts, designed not only to protect the inhabitants from enemy invasion but also to conceal from them the inexorable presence of nature. These cities are, moreover, divided into similarly rounded, closed districts. The tangle of jumbled houses weighs heavily on the ground. They seem to have a natural tendency to grow closer to each other—so much so that, from time to time, we have to take an ax to them to clear new paths, as you might in virgin forests. Streets run into other streets. They are closed at each end and do not seem to lead out of the city. Inside them, you go around in circles. They are more than mere arteries: each one is a social milieu. These are streets where you stop, meet people, drink, eat, and linger. On Sundays, you dress up and take a stroll simply for the pleasure of greeting friends, of seeing and being seen. It is these streets that inspired Jules Romains' "unanimism." They are alive with a communal spirit that changes each hour of the day.

So, my shortsighted European eyes, venturing slowly and intently, strove in vain to find something to arrest them. Something, anything—a row of houses suddenly barring the way, a street corner or some old house bearing the patina of age. But to no avail. New York is a city for the long-sighted: you can "focus" only at infinity. My gaze met nothing but space. It slid over blocks of identical houses, there being nothing to arrest it on its journey to the indistinctness of the horizon.

Céline called New York "a vertical city." This is true, but it seemed to me first a lengthwise one. The traffic, at a standstill in the side streets, enjoys every possible privilege in the avenues, where it flows uninterrupted. How often the taxi drivers, who are happy to take passengers north or south, refuse point-blank to load up for east or west! The lateral streets have barely any other function than to mark the boundaries of the blocks between the avenues. The avenues cut through them and push them aside as they themselves rush on toward the north. It was for this reason, naïve tourist that I was, that I looked long and fruitlessly for distinct "neighborhoods." In France, our urban clusters surround and protect us. The rich neighborhood protects the rich from the poor; the poor neighborhood keeps us from the disdain of the rich; in the same way, the entire city protects us from nature.

In New York, where the main thoroughfares are parallel avenues, I was unable, except in lower Broadway, to find neighborhoods. I could find only atmospheres—gaseous masses stretching out longitudinally, with nothing to mark their beginning or their end. Gradually, I learned to recognize the atmosphere of Third Avenue, where, without even knowing each other, people meet, smile, and chat in the shade of the noisy elevated railway; and that Irish bar where a German, passing by my table, stopped for a moment to say, "You're French? I'm a Kraut"; the reassuring comfort of the stores on Lexington Avenue; the staid elegance of Park Avenue; the cold luxury and stuccoed impassiveness of Fifth Avenue; the merry frivolity of Sixth and Seventh; the "food fair" of Ninth and the no-man's-land of Tenth. Each avenue enwraps the neighboring streets in its atmosphere, but a block away you suddenly plunge into another world. Not far from the thrilling silence of Park Avenue, home to the limousines of the powerful, I find myself on First Avenue, where the ground permanently shakes beneath the weight of passing trucks. How can I feel safe on one of these interminable north–south trajectories when, a few feet away to east or west, other longitudinal worlds lie in wait for me? Behind the Waldorf Astoria and the white and blue canopies of the "elegant" buildings, I glimpse the "elevated," which carries with it something of the poverty of the Bowery.

The whole of New York is striped in this way with parallel, noncommunicating meanings. These long lines, running straight as a die, suddenly gave me a sense of space. Our European cities are built to protect us against this: the houses cluster together there like sheep. But space runs through New York, animating and dilating it. Space, the great empty space of the steppes and the pampas, runs in its veins like a draft of cold air, separating those who live on the right from those who live on the left. In Boston, an American friend showing me around the smart neighborhoods, pointed to the left of the street and said, "This is where the 'nice' people live." And, pointing to the right, he added ironically, "No one's ever found out who lives there." It is the same in New York: between the two sides of a street, there is the whole of space.

New York is halfway between a city for pedestrians and a city for cars. You don't go for a walk in New York, you move through it; it is a city in motion. If I walk quickly, I feel at ease there. If I stop, I get flustered and wonder, "Why am I on this street rather than on one of the hundreds of others like it?" Why in front of this drugstore, this branch of Schrafft's or Woolworth's, rather than any other one of the thousands like this?

And suddenly pure space appears. I imagine that a triangle, were it to acquire consciousness of its position in space, would be terror-stricken to learn of the rigor of its defining coordinates, and at the same time to discover that it is simply any old triangle, just anywhere. You never get lost in New York. You can see at a glance where you are: you are on the East Side, for example, at the corner of Fifty-second Street and Lexington. But this spatial precision is not accompanied by any emotional exactitude. Amid the numerical anonymity of streets and avenues, I am simply anyone, anywhere. Wherever I am, my position is established in terms of longitude and latitude. But there is no valid reason to justify my presence at one spot rather than at another, since one place is so like another. I am never astray, but always lost.

Am I lost in a city or in nature? New York affords no protection from the violence of nature. It is a city open to the skies. The storms flood its streets that are so wide and take so long to cross when it rains. The hurricanes, announced solemnly on the radio like declarations of war, shake the brick houses and rock the skyscrapers. In summer, the air shimmers between the buildings. In winter, the city drowns as though you were in some Parisian suburb with the Seine overflowing, but here it is merely the snow melting.

Nature weighs so heavily on New York that this most modern of cities is also the dirtiest. From my window I can see the wind whipping up heavy muddy litter, which flits around on the pavement. Going out, I walk in blackish snow, a kind of puffy crust of the same hue as the sidewalk, as though that itself were buckling. From the end of May, the heat descends on the city like an atomic bomb. It is evil. People go up to each other and say, "It's murder!" Millions of fleeing city dwellers take to the trains, leaving damp marks on the seats when they get off, like snails. It isn't the city they are fleeing but nature. Even in the depths of my apartment I suffer the depredations of a hostile, muffled, mysterious nature. I have the impression of camping in a jungle teeming with insects. There is the moaning of the wind, the electric shocks I get each time I touch a doorknob or shake a friend's hand, the cockroaches running around my kitchen, the elevators that make my stomach heave, the inextinguishable thirst that rages from morning to night. New York is a colonial city, a campsite. All the hostility and cruelty of nature are present in this city, the most prodigious monument humanity has ever raised to itself. It is a light city; its apparent weightlessness surprises most Europeans. In this immense, malevolent space, this desert of rock that tolerates no vegetation, they have built thousands of houses out of brick, wood, or reinforced concrete, all of which seem about to fly away.

I love New York. I have learned to love it. I have grown used to its massive clumps of buildings, its long vistas. My eyes no longer linger over the façades searching for one that might, by some remote chance, not be just like all the others. They rush immediately to the horizon, looking for blocks lost in fog, which are now mere volumes, merely the austere framing of the sky. When you know how to look at the two rows of buildings that line any major thoroughfare like cliffs, you get your reward: their mission is accomplished at the far end of the avenue in simple harmonious lines; a scrap of sky floats between them.

New York reveals itself only at a particular height, a particular distance, a particular speed. These are not the height, the distance, or the speed of the pedestrian. The city is strikingly like the great Andalusia plains—monotonous when you pass through on foot, superb and varying when crossed by car.

I have learned to love its sky. In the low-roofed cities of Europe, the sky crawls along the ground and seems tamed. The beauty of the New York sky comes from its being raised so far above our heads by the skyscrapers. Pure and lonely as a wild beast, it stands guard and watches over the city. And it isn't just a local protection: you feel that it stretches right out over the whole of America; it is the whole world's sky.

I have learned to love Manhattan's avenues. They are not somber little walkways enclosed by houses but national highways. As soon as you set foot in one of them you realize it has to go on as far as Boston or Chicago. Its vanishing point lies beyond the city and the eye can almost follow it out into the countryside. A wild sky above great parallel rails—that, first and foremost, is New York. In the heart of the city, you are in the heart of nature.

I had to get used to it, but now that I have, nowhere do I feel freer than amid the crowds of New York. This light, ephemeral city, which every morning and evening, beneath the curious rays of the sun, seems a mere juxtaposition of rectangular parallelepipeds, never oppresses or depresses. You can feel the anguish of solitude here, but not of being crushed.

In Europe we become attached to a neighborhood, a block of houses, or a street corner, and we are no longer free. But hardly have you plunged into New York than you live entirely on its scale. You can look over it in the evening from up on the Queensboro Bridge, in the morning from New Jersey, or at noon from the seventy-seventh floor of the Rockefeller Center, but you will never be captivated by any of its streets because none has a distinctive beauty all its own. Beauty is present in each of them, just as nature and the sky of the whole of America are present in them. Nowhere will you form a better sense of the simultaneity of human lives.

New York moves us Europeans despite its austerity. We have, admittedly, learned to love our old cities, but what touches us in them is a Roman wall forming part of the façade of an inn, a house where Cervantes lived, the Place des Vosges, or the town hall at Rouen. We love museum-cities—and all our cities are a little like museums where we wander amid our ancestors' dwellings. New York isn't a museum-city. Yet for Frenchmen of my generation it already possesses the melancholy of the past. When we were twenty—around 1925—we heard about the skyscrapers. For us they symbolized the fabulous prosperity of America. We discovered them with stupefaction in the movies. They were the architecture of the future, just as cinema was the art of the future and jazz the music of the future. Today we know all about jazz: it is more a music of the past than of the future. It is a popular black music, capable of limited development, but in gentle decline. It has had its day. And the talkies have not fulfilled the promise of the silent films: Hollywood is stuck in a rut.

The war clearly revealed to the Americans that America is the world's greatest power. But the age of easy living is over: many economists fear a new recession. Hence, no skyscrapers are being built now. It seems they are too difficult to rent out.

To the man who strolled through New York before 1930, the high-rise buildings towering over the city were the first signs of an architecture destined to radiate over the entire country. Skyscrapers then were living things. Today, for a Frenchman arriving from Europe, they are already mere historical monuments, witnesses to a bygone age. They still rise up into the sky but my spirit does not soar with them, and the New Yorkers pass by at their feet without so much as a glance. I cannot think of them without melancholy: they speak of an age when we thought that the last of the wars had just finished, an age when we believed in peace. They are already a little run-down: tomorrow, perhaps, they will be demolished. At any rate, to build them took a faith we no longer possess.

I walk between little brick houses the color of dried blood. They are younger than Europe's houses, but their fragility makes them seem much older. I see in the distance the Empire State and Chrysler buildings pointing vainly to the sky and it suddenly occurs to me that New York is on the point of acquiring a history and that it already has its ruins.

That is enough to soften somewhat the edges of the harshest city in the world.

NICK'S BAR,
NEW YORK CITY

Jazz, like bananas, has to be consumed on the spot. God knows there are plenty of records in France and gloomy imitators too. But they're just a pretext for shedding a few tears in good company. Certain countries have national entertainments and others don't. When the people impose strict silence on you during the first half of a demonstration and start to shout and stomp during the second, that's a national entertainment.

If you accept this definition, there is no national entertainment in France, except perhaps rummage sales and auctions. Nor in Italy, except perhaps robbery: they let the thief go to work in watchful silence (first part), and they stomp and shout "Stop thief!" while he runs away (second part). Belgium, on the contrary, has cockfights; Germany, vampires; and Spain, *corridas*. I found out in New York City that jazz is a national entertainment. In Paris they dance to it, but that's a mistake. Americans don't dance to the sound of jazz. For that they have a special music which is also used for first communions and marriages and is called *Music by Musak*. There are switches in apartments, you turn them on, and Musak is played: flirtation, tears, dancing. You turn off the switch, and the Musak stops playing: communicants and lovers are put to bed.

They celebrate nationally at Nick's Bar in New York. That is, they sit down in a smoke-filled room beside sailors, tough guys, unlicensed whores, and women of the world. There are tables and cubicles. No one talks. The sailors come in groups of four. With a justified hatred, they stare at the squares who sit down in the cubicles with their chicks. The sailors would like to have chicks; they don't. They drink; they're tough. The chicks are tough too: they drink and don't talk. No one budges; the jazz plays. They play jazz from ten at night to three o'clock in the morning. In France jazz musicians are handsome, lusterless men with flowing shirts and silk scarves. If listening bugs you, you can always look at them and take lessons in elegance. At Nick's Bar, it's advisable not to look at them; they're as ugly as the musicians in a symphony orchestra. Bony faces, mustaches, jackets, starched collars (at least at the beginning of the evening); and even their glance isn't soft. But their muscles bulge under their sleeves.

They play. Everybody listens. No one dreams. Chopin and André Claveau make you dream. But not the jazz at Nick's Bar. It fascinates you; it's all you think of. Not the least bit consoling. If you come in a cuckold, you leave a cuckold, without any tenderness. No chance to grab your girl's hand and let her know in a wink that the music translates your state of mind. It is harsh, violent, pitiless music. Not gay, not sad, inhuman. The cruel shrills of birds of prey. The musicians start to sweat, one after another. First the trumpet player, then the pianist, then the trombone player. The bass player looks beat. This music does not speak of love; it does not console. It's hurried. Like the people who take the subway or eat in Automats. It isn't the age-old chant of black slaves either. They don't give a damn about black slaves. Or the sad little dream of Yankees crushed by their machines. There's none of all that. There's a big man blowing his lungs out trying to follow the gyrations of his trombone, a merciless pianist, a bass player slapping his strings without looking at the others. They speak to the best part of you, the most unfeeling and most free, the part which doesn't want sad songs or sprightly ones but a moment of deafening explosion. They make demands on you; they don't baby you. Connecting rods, main shaft, milling machine. They throb, turn, grate. The rhythm is born. If you are tough and young and fresh, the rhythm grabs you and rocks you. You jump to the beat, faster and faster, and the girl next to you jumps with you. It's swinging around a circle down in hell. The trombone player sweats, you sweat, the trumpet player sweats, you sweat some more, and then you feel that something has happened up on the stand. They don't look the same. They speed it up, vibrate their haste to one another. They look tense and out of their minds; you'd say that they were looking for something else. Something like sexual pleasure. And you start to look for something yourself and you begin to yell. You have to yell: the combo has become an immense spinning top, and if you don't keep yelling it will tumble down. You yell. They dig, they blow, they are possessed. You are possessed. You yell out like a woman in childbirth. The trumpet player touches the pianist and transmits his own possession to him just the way it happened in the days when Mesmer mesmerized. You keep on yelling. A whole crowd of people is yelling in rhythm. You don't even hear the jazz anymore, you see people on the stand sweating in rhythm, you feel like whirling around and around, howling at death, hitting the girl next to you in the face.

And then suddenly the jazz stops. The bull has been run through; the oldest cock is dead. It's over. You've drunk your whiskey while you were yelling without even noticing that you were drinking it. An impassive waiter brings you another. You remain dazed for a moment, you shake yourself, you say to the girl next to you, "Not bad..." She doesn't answer, and it begins again.

You won't make love that night, you won't feel sorry for yourself, you didn't even succeed in getting drunk or shed blood, and you will have been swept away by a blind frenzy, by this convulsive crescendo which is like an angry, futile search for pleasure. You'll leave the place a little worn out, a little drunk, but in a sort of beat-down calm, as after great heaves of emotional storms.

Jazz is America's national entertainment.

INTRODUCING
LES TEMPS MODERNES

ALL WRITERS of bourgeois origin have known the temptation of irresponsibility. For a century now, it has been a traditional part of one's literary career. An author rarely establishes a link between his works and the income they bring. On the one hand, he writes, sings, or sighs; on the other, he is given money. The two facts have no apparent relation: the best he can do is tell himself that he's being paid in order to sigh. As a consequence, he views himself more as a student enjoying a scholarship than as a worker receiving wages for his efforts. The theoreticians of Art for Art's Sake and of Realism have confirmed him in that opinion. Have people noticed that they share the same purpose and the same origin? According to the former, the author's principal concern is to produce works that are useless; as long as they are quite pointless and thoroughly rootless, they have pretty well succeeded in appearing beautiful to him. That is how he places himself at the margins of society; or rather, he consents to appear there only in his role as pure consumer: just like the student on a scholarship. The Realist is also a willing consumer. As for producing, that is a different matter: he was told that science is not concerned with utility and he aspires to the sterile impartiality of the scientist. After all have we not been told often enough that he is "pouring over" the social groups he is intent on describing? Pouring over! Where was he, in that case? In the air? The truth is that unsure of his social position, too fearful to stand up to the bourgeoisie that pays him, and too lucid to accept it without reservations, he has chosen to judge his century and in that way he has convinced himself that he remains outside it, just as an experimenter remains outside the system of his experiment. Thus does the disinterestedness of pure science join with the gratuitousness of Art for Art's Sake. It is not by chance that Flaubert is simultaneously a pure stylist, a purist in his love of forms, and the father of Naturalism; it is not an accident that the Goncourt brothers were proud of the fact that they knew how to observe and had a highly aesthetic prose style.

That legacy of irresponsibility has bothered many minds. They suffer from a literary bad conscience and are no longer sure whether to write is admirable or grotesque. In former times, the poet took himself for a prophet, which was honorable. Subsequently, he became a pariah and felt "damned," which was still acceptable. But today he has been demoted to the rank of specialist, and it is not without a certain malaise that he lists his profession on hotel registers as "man of letters." Man of letters: that association of words is in itself sufficient to disgust one with writing. It makes you think of an Ariel, a vestal virgin, an enfant terrible, and also of a harmless maniac similar to a stamp collector or a weight lifter. The whole business is rather ridiculous. The man of letters writes while others fight. One day he's quite proud of it, he feels himself to be a cleric and guardian of ideal values; the following day he's ashamed of it, and finds that literature looks very much like a special form of affectation. In the company of the bourgeois who read him, he is aware of his dignity; but when dealing with workers, who don't, he suffers from an inferiority complex, as was seen in 1936 at the Maison de la Culture. It is certainly that complex which is the basis of what Paulhan calls "terrorism"; it is what led the Surrealists to despise literature, with which they made their living. After the other war, it was the occasion of a particular mode of lyricism: the best and purest writers confessed publicly to what might humiliate them the most and expressed their satisfaction whenever they succeeded in eliciting the disapproval of the bourgeoisie: they had produced a text which, because of its impact, looked a little like an act. Those isolated attempts could not prevent words from being devalued more and more every day. There was a crisis of rhetoric, then one of language. On the eve of this war, most practitioners of literature were resigned to being no more than nightingales. Finally came a few authors who pressed their disgust with writing to an extreme. Outdoing their elders they declared that publishing a book that was merely useless was not enough: they maintained that the secret aim of all literature was the destruction of language, and that it was sufficient, in order to attain this end, to speak so as not to say anything. Such voluble silence was in fashion for a while, and Hachette used to distribute capsules of silence, in the form of voluminous novels, to many a railroad station bookstore. Today things have gone sufficiently far that we have seen writers who once were blamed or punished for renting their pens to the Germans express a pained astonishment. "What do you mean?" they ask. "Does what you write actually commit you?"

We do not want to be ashamed of writing and we have no desire to write so as not to say anything. Moreover, even if we wanted to we would not succeed in doing so: no one can. Every text possesses a meaning, even if that meaning is far removed from the one the author dreamed of putting into it. Indeed, for us, an author is neither a vestal virgin nor Ariel: he is "in the game," whatever he does, he is marked and implicated, even in his farthest hiding place. If, at certain times, he uses his art to forge what Mallarmé called "trinkets of sonorous inanity," this in itself is a sign that there is a crisis in literature and, no doubt, in Society, or that the dominant classes have pushed him without his realizing it toward an activity that seems pure luxury, for fear that he might take off and join the ranks of the revolutionaries. What is Flaubert—who so raged against the bourgeoisie and believed he had withdrawn outside the social machine—for us if not a talented man living off his investments? And does not his meticulous art presuppose the comfort of Croisset, the solicitude of a mother or a niece, an orderly regimen, a prosperous commercial endeavor, dividends regularly received? It only takes a few years before a book becomes a social phenomenon, to be questioned like an institution or recorded as a statistical reality; not much time is needed for it to merge with the furnishings of an era, its habits, headgear, means of transport, and foodstuffs. A historian will say to us, "They ate this, read that, and dressed thus." The first railroads, cholera, the revolt of the Lyons silk workers, Balzac's novels, and the rise of industry all contributed equally to characterizing the July Monarchy. All this has been said and repeated since Hegel; what we want to do is draw the practical consequences. Since the writer has no way of escaping, we want him to embrace his era tightly. It is his only chance; it was made for him and he was made for it. We regret Balzac's indifference toward the revolutionary days of 1848; we regret Flaubert's panicky incomprehension when confronted with the Commune. We regret these unfortunate reactions for them: those events are something that they missed out on forever. We don't want to miss out on anything of our time. There may be better ones, but this one is ours: we have only this life to live, amid this war, and perhaps this revolution. Let it not be concluded from this that we are preaching a variety of populism: quite the contrary. Populism is an offspring of the very old, the sad scion of the last Realists; it is yet another attempt to get out of a difficult situation. We are convinced, on the contrary, that one cannot get out of this quandary. Even if we were as deaf and dumb as stones, our very passivity would be an action. The abstention of whoever wanted to devote his life to writing novels about the Hittites would in itself constitute taking a position. The writer is *situated* in his time; every word he utters has reverberations. As does his silence. I hold Flaubert and the Goncourt brothers responsible for the repression that followed the Commune because they didn't write a line to prevent it. Some will object that this wasn't their business. But was the Calas trial Voltaire's business? Was Dreyfus's sentence Zola's business? Was the administration of the Congo Gide's business? Each of those authors, at a particular time in his life, took stock of his responsibility as a writer. The occupation taught us ours. Since we act upon our time by virtue of our very existence, we decide that our action will be voluntary. Even then, it must be specified: it is not uncommon for a writer to be concerned, in his modest way, with preparing the future. But there is a vague, conceptual future which concerns humanity in its entirety and on which we have no particular light to shed: Will history have an end? Will the sun be extinguished? What will be the condition of man in the socialist society of the year 3000? We leave such reveries to futurist novelists. It is the future of *our time* that must be the object of our concern: a limited future barely distinguishable from it—for an era, like a man, is first of all a future. It is composed of its ongoing efforts, its enterprises, its more or less long-term projects, its revolts, its struggles, its hopes. When will the war end? How will the country be rebuilt? How will international relations be organized? What social reforms will take place? Will the forces of reaction triumph? Will there be a revolution, and if so what will it be? That future we make our own; we don't want any other. No doubt some authors have concerns which are less contemporary, and visions which are less shortsighted. They move through our midst as though they were not there. Where indeed are they? With their grandnephews, they turn around to judge that bygone age which was ours and whose sole survivors they are. But they have miscalculated: posthumous glory is always based on a misunderstanding. What do they know of those nephews who will come fish them out of our midst! Immortality is a terrible alibi: it is not easy to live with one foot in the grave and another beyond it. How might one expedite current business if one saw it from such a distance? How might one grow excited over a battle, or enjoy a victory? Everything is equivalent. They look at us without seeing us: in their eyes we are already dead, and they return to the novel they are writing for men they will never see. They have allowed their lives to be stolen from them by immortality. We write for our contemporaries; we want to behold our world not with future eyes—which would be the surest means of killing it—but with our eyes of flesh, our real, perishable eyes. We don't want to win our case on appeal, and we will have nothing to do with any posthumous rehabilitation. Right here in our own lifetime is when and where our cases will be won or lost.

We are not, however, thinking of instituting a literary relativism. We have little taste for the purely historical. Besides, does the purely historical exist anywhere but in the manuals of Monsieur Seignobos? Each age discovers an aspect of the human condition; in every era man chooses himself in confrontation with other individuals, love, death, the world; and when adversaries clash on the subject of disarming the Forces Françaises de l'Intérieur[1] or the help to be given the Spanish Republicans, it is that metaphysical choice, that singular and absolute project which is at stake. Thus, by taking part in the singularity of our era, we ultimately make contact with the eternal, and it is our task as writers to allow the eternal values implicit in such social or political debates to be perceived. But we don't care to seek them out in some intelligible heaven: they are of interest only in their contemporary guise. Far from being relativists, we proclaim that man is an absolute. But he is such in his time, in his surroundings, on his parcel of earth. What is absolute, what a thousand years of history cannot destroy is that irreplaceable, incomparable decision which he makes at this moment concerning these circumstances. What is absolute is Descartes, the man who escapes us because he is dead, who lived in his time, who thought it through day by day with the means available to him, who formed his doctrine on the basis of a certain state of the sciences, who knew Gassendi, Caterus, and Mersenne, who in his childhood loved a girl who was cross-eyed, who waged war and impregnated a servant girl, who attacked not the principle of authority in general but precisely the authority of Aristotle, and who emerges in his time unarmed but unvanquished, like a milestone. What is relative is Cartesianism, that errant philosophy, which is trotted out from century to century and in which everyone finds what he puts into it. It is not by running after immortality that we will make ourselves eternal; we will become absolutes not because we have allowed our writings to reflect a few emaciated principles (which are sufficiently empty and null to make the transition from one century to the next) but because we will have fought passionately within our own era, because we will have loved it passionately and accepted that we would perish entirely along with it.

In sum, our intention is to help effect certain changes in the Society that surrounds us. By which we do not mean changes within people's souls: we are happy to leave the direction of souls to those authors catering to a rather specialized clientele. As for us, who without being materialists have never distinguished soul from body and who know only one indivisible reality—human reality—we align ourselves on the side of those who want to change simultaneously the social condition or man and the concept he has of himself. Consequently, concerning the political and social events to come, our journal will take a position in each case. It will not do so politically—that is, in the service of a particular party—but it will attempt to sort out the conception of man that inspires each one of the conflicting theses, and will give its opinion in conformity with the conception it maintains. If we are able to live up to what we promise, if we succeed in persuading a few readers to share our views, we will not indulge in any exaggerated pride; we will simply congratulate ourselves for having rediscovered a good professional conscience, and for literature's having become again—at least for us—what it should never have stopped being: a social function.

Yet, some will ask, what is that conception of man that you pretend to reveal to us? We respond that it can be found on every street corner, and that we claim not to have discovered it but only to have brought it into better focus. I shall call this conception "totalitarian." But since the word may seem unfortunate, since it has been used to designate not the human individual but an oppressive and antidemocratic type of state, a few explanations are called for.

The bourgeoisie, it seems to me, may be defined intellectually by the use it makes of the analytic mode, whose initial postulate is that composite realities must necessarily be reducible to an arrangement of simple elements. In its hands, that postulate was once an offensive weapon allowing it to dismantle the bastions of the Old Regime. Everything was analyzed; in a single gesture, air and water were reduced to their elements, mind to the sum of impressions composing it, society to the sum total of individuals it comprised. Groups disappeared; they were no more than abstract agglomerations due to random combinations. Reality withdrew to the ultimate terms of the decomposition. The latter indeed—and such is the second postulate of analysis —retain unalterably their essential properties, whether they enter into a compound or exist in a free state. There was an immutable nature of oxygen, of hydrogen or nitrogen, and of the elementary impressions composing our mind; there was an immutable human nature. Man was man the way a circle is a circle: once and for all. The individual, be he transported to the throne or plunged into misery, remained fundamentally identical to himself because he was conceived on the model of the oxygen atom which can combine with hydrogen to produce water, or with nitrogen to produce air, without its internal structure being changed. Those principles presided over the Declaration of the Rights of Man. In society as conceived by the analytic cast of mind, the individual, a solid and indivisible participle, the vehicle of human nature, resides like a pea in a can of peas: he is round, closed in on himself, uncommunicative. All men are equal, by which it should be understood that they all participate equally in the essence of man. All men are brothers: fraternity is a passive bond among distinct molecules, which takes the place of an active or class-bound solidarity that the analytic cast of mind cannot even imagine. It is an entirely extrinsic and purely sentimental relation which masks the simple juxtaposition of individuals in analytic society. All men are free—free to be men, it goes without saying. Which means that political action ought to be strictly negative. A politically active individual has no need to forge human nature; it is enough for him to eliminate the obstacles that might prevent him from blossoming. Thus it was that, intent on destroying divine right, the rights of birth and blood, the right of primogeniture, all those rights based on the notion that there are differences in men's natures, the bourgeoisie confused its own cause with that of analysis and constructed for its use the myth of the universal. Unlike today's revolutionaries, they were able to achieve their goals only by abdicating their class consciousness: the members of the Third Estate at the Constituent Assembly were bourgeois precisely to the extent that they considered themselves to be simply men.

A hundred and fifty years later, the analytic frame of mind remains the official doctrine of bourgeois democracies, with the difference that it has now become a defensive weapon. It is entirely in the interest of the bourgeoisie to blind itself to the existence of classes even as it formerly failed to perceive the synthetic reality of the institutions of the Old Regime. It persists in seeing no more than men, in proclaiming the identity of human nature in every diverse situation; but it is against the proletariat that it makes that proclamation. A worker, for the bourgeoisie, is first of all a man like any other. If the Constitution grants that man the right to vote and freedom of expression, he displays his human nature as fully as does a bourgeois. A certain polemical tradition has too often presented the bourgeois as a calculating drone whose sole concern is to defend his privileges. In fact, though, one constitutes oneself as a bourgeois by choosing, once and for all, a certain analytic perspective on the world which one attempts to foist on all men and which excludes the perception of collective realities. To that extent, the bourgeois defense is in a sense permanent, and is indistinguishable from the bourgeoisie. It is not revealed in sordid calculations; within the world that the bourgeoisie has constructed, there is room for insouciance, altruism, and even generosity—except that the good deeds of the bourgeois are individual acts addressed to the universal: human nature insofar as it is incarnated in an individual. In this sense, they are about as effective as a skillful piece of propaganda, since the beneficiary of the good deeds is obliged to receive them on the terms on which they are offered—that is, by thinking of himself as an isolated human being confronting another human being. Bourgeois charity sustains the myth of fraternity.

But there is another form of propaganda which is of more specific interest to us, since we are writers, and writers have turned themselves into its unwitting agents. The legend of the irresponsibility of the poet, which we were criticizing awhile ago, derives its origin from the analytic frame of mind. Since bourgeois authors themselves think of themselves as peas in a can, the solidarity binding them to other men seems strictly mechanical to them, a matter, that is, of mere juxtaposition. Even if they have an exalted sense of their literary mission, they think they have done enough once they have described their own nature or that of their friends; since all men are made the same, they will have rendered a service to all by teaching each man about himself. And since the initial postulate from which they speak is the primacy of analysis, it seems quite simple to make use of the analytical method in order to attain self-knowledge. Such is the origin of intellectualist psychology, whose most polished example we find in the works of Proust. As a pederast, Proust thought he could make use of his homosexual experience in depicting Swann's love for Odette; as a bourgeois, he presents the sentiments of a rich and idle bourgeois for a kept woman as the prototype of love, the reason being that he believes in the existence of universal passions whose mechanism does not vary substantially when there is a change in the sexual characteristics, social condition, nation, or era of the individuals experiencing them. Having thus "isolated" those immutable emotions, he can attempt to reduce them, in turn, to elementary particles. Faithful to the postulates of the analytic frame of mind, he does not even imagine that there might be a dialectic of feelings, he imagines only a mechanics. Thus does social atomism, the entrenched outpost of the contemporary bourgeoisie, entail psychological atomism. Proust *chose himself* to be a bourgeois. He made himself into an accomplice of bourgeois propaganda, since his work contributes to the dissemination of the myth of human nature.

We are convinced that the analytic spirit has had its day and that its sole function at present is to confuse revolutionary consciousness and to isolate men for the benefit of the privileged classes. We no longer believe in Proust's intellectualist psychology, and we regard it as nefarious. Since we have chosen as an example his analysis of the passion of love, we shall no doubt contribute to the reader's enlightenment by mentioning the essential points on which we are totally at odds with him.

First of all, we do not accept a priori the idea that romantic love is a constitutive affect of the human mind. It may well be the case, as Denis de Rougemont has suggested, that it originated historically as a correlate of Christian ideology. More generally, we are of the opinion that a feeling always expresses a specific way of life and a specific conception of the world that are shared by an entire class or an entire era, and that its evolution is not the effect of some unspecified internal mechanism but of these historical and social factors.

Second, we cannot accept the idea that a human emotion is composed of molecular elements that may be juxtaposed without modifying each other. We regard it not as a well-constructed machine but as an organized form. The possibility of undertaking an analysis of love seems inconceivable to us, because the development of that feeling, like that of all others, is dialectical.

Third, we refuse to believe that the love felt by a homosexual offers the same characteristics as that felt by a heterosexual. The secretive and forbidden character of the former, its Black Mass aspect, the existence of a homosexual freemasonry, and that damnation toward which the homosexual is aware of dragging his partner are all elements that seem to us to exercise an influence on the feeling in its entirety and even in the very details of its evolution. We maintain that the various sentiments of an individual are not juxtaposed, but that there is a synthetic unity of one's affectivity and that every individual moves within an affective world specifically his own.

Fourth, we deny that the origin, class, environment, and nation of an individual are simple accessories of his emotional life. It seems to us, on the contrary, that every affect and for that matter every other form of his psychic existence manifests his social situation. A worker who receives a wage, who does not own the instruments of his craft, whose work isolates him from material reality, and who defends himself from oppression by becoming aware of his class can in no way feel the same way as does a bourgeois of analytic propensities, whose profession puts him into respectful relations with other members of his class.

Thus we will have recourse, against the spirit of analysis, to a synthetic conception of reality whose principle is that a whole, whatever it may be, is different in nature from the sum of its parts. For us, what men have in common is not a nature but a metaphysical condition by which we mean the totality of constraints that limit them a priori, the necessity of being born and dying, that of being *finite* and of existing in the world among other men. In addition, they constitute indivisible totalities whose ideas, moods, and acts are secondary, dependent structures and whose essential characteristic lies in being *situated*, and they differ from each other even as their situations differ in relation to each other. The unity of those signifying wholes is the meaning which they manifest. Whether he is writing or working on an assembly line, whether choosing a wife or a tie, a man constantly manifests himself. He manifests his professional surroundings, his family, his class, and ultimately, since he is situated in relation to the world in its entirety, the world itself. A man is the whole earth. He is everywhere present, everywhere active. He is responsible for all, and his destiny is played out everywhere, in Paris, Potsdam, Vladivostok. We adhere to these views because to us they seem true, because to us they seem socially useful at the present time, and because to us a majority of people seem to intuit them in their thinking and indeed to call them forth. We would like our journal to contribute in a modest way to the elaboration of a synthetic anthropology. But it is not, we repeat, simply a question of effecting an advance in the domain of pure knowledge: the more distant goal we are aiming at is a *liberation*. Since man is a totality, it is indeed not enough to grant him the right to vote without dealing with the other factors that constitute him. He must free himself totally, that is, make himself *other*, by acting on his biological constitution as well as on his economic condition, on his sexual complexes as well as on the political terms of his situation.

This synthetic perspective, however, presents some grave dangers. If the individual is the result of an arbitrary selection effected by the analytic frame of mind, doesn't one run the risk, in breaking with analytic conceptions, of substituting the domination of collective consciousness for the domination of the person? The spirit of synthesis cannot be apportioned its mere share: no sooner is he glimpsed than man as a totality would be submerged by his class. Only the class exists, and it alone must be delivered. But, it will be objected, in liberating a class is one necessarily freeing the men it comprises? Not necessarily. Would the triumph of Hitler's Germany have been the triumph of every German? Where, moreover, would the synthesis stop? Tomorrow we may be told that the class is a secondary structure dependent on a larger totality which will be, say, the nation. The great attraction which Nazism exercised on certain minds of the left undoubtedly came from the fact that it pushed the totalitarian conception to the absolute. Its theoreticians also denounced the ill effects of analysis, the abstract character of democratic freedoms; its propaganda also promised to forge a new man and retained the words "revolution" and "liberation." Except that for a class proletariat, a proletariat of nations was substituted. Individuals were reduced to mere dependent functions of their class, classes to mere functions of their nation, nations to mere functions of the European continent. If, in occupied countries, the entire working class rose up against the invader, it was undoubtedly because it felt wounded in its revolutionary aspirations, but also because it felt an invincible repugnance to allowing the individual to be dissolved in the collectivity.

Thus does the contemporary mind appear divided by an antinomy. Those who value above all the dignity of the human being, his freedom, his inalienable rights, are as a result inclined to think in accordance with the analytic frame of mind, which conceives of individuals outside their actual conditions of existence, which endows them with an unchanging, abstract nature, and which isolates them and blinds itself to their solidarity. Those who have profoundly understood that man is rooted in the collectivity and who want to affirm the importance of historical, technical, and economic factors are inclined toward the synthetic mode, which, blind to individuals, has eyes only for groups. This antinomy may be perceived, for example, in the widely held belief that socialism is diametrically opposed to individual freedom. Thus, those holding fast to the autonomy of the individual would be trapped in a capitalist liberalism whose nefarious consequences are clear; those calling for a socialist organization of the economy would be demanding a who knows what kind of unspecified totalitarian authoritarianism. The current malaise springs from the fact that no one can accept the extreme consequences of these principles: there is a "synthetic" component to be found in democrats of goodwill, and there is an "analytic" component in socialists. Recall, for instance, what the Radical Party was in France. One of its theoreticians wrote a book entitled *The Citizen Against The Powers That Be.*[2] The title sufficiently indicates how he envisaged politics: according to him, everything would be better if the isolated citizen, the molecular representative of human nature, controlled those he elected and, if need be, exercised his own judgment against them. But the Radicals, precisely, could not avoid acknowledging their own failure. In 1939 the great party had no will, no program, no ideology; it was sinking into the depths of opportunism, because it was intent on solving politically problems that were not amenable to a political solution. The best minds were astonished. If man was a political animal, how could it be that in granting him political freedom his fate had not been settled once and for all? How could it be that the unhampered interaction of parliamentary institutions had not succeeded in eliminating poverty, unemployment, and oppression by monopolies? How could it be that a class struggle had emerged on the far side of the fraternal competition between parties? One would not have to push things much further to perceive the limits of the analytic cast of mind. The fact that the Radicals consistently sought an alliance of leftist parties clearly indicates the direction in which their sympathies and confused aspirations were taking them, but they lacked the intellectual wherewithal that would have allowed them not only to solve but even to formulate the problems they intuited obscurely.

In the other camp, there is no less perplexity. The working class has made itself heir to the traditions of democracy. It is in the name of democracy that it demands its liberation. Now the democratic ideal, as we have seen, has manifested itself historically in the form of a social contract among free individuals. Thus do the analytic demands of Rousseau frequently interfere in many minds with the synthetic demands of Marxism. Moreover, the worker's technical training develops his analytic propensities. Similar in that regard to the scientist, he would resolve the problems of matter by way of analysis. Should he turn toward human realities, he will tend, in order to understand them, to appeal to the same reasoning that has served him in his work. He thus applies to human behavior an analytic psychology related to that of the French seventeenth century.

The simultaneous existence of those two modes of explanation reveals a certain uneasiness. The perpetual recourse, to the phrase "as though . . ." indicates sufficiently that Marxism does not yet have at its disposal a synthetic psychology adequate to its totalitarian conception of classes.

Insofar as we are concerned, we refuse to let ourselves be torn between thesis and antithesis. We can easily conceive that a man, although totally conditioned by his situation, can be the center of irreducible indeterminacy. The window of unpredictability that stands out within the social domain is what we call freedom, and a person is nothing other than his freedom. This freedom ought not to be envisaged as a metaphysical endowment of human "nature." Neither is it a license to do whatever one wants, or some unspecified internal refuge that would remain to us even in our chains! One does not do whatever one wants, and yet one is responsible for what one is: such are the facts. Man, who may be explained simultaneously by so many causes, is nevertheless alone in bearing the burden of himself. In this sense, freedom might appear to be a curse; it is a curse. But it is also the sole source of human greatness. On this score, the Marxists will agree with us in spirit, if not in letter, since as far as I know they are not reluctant to issue moral condemnations. What remains is to explain it, but this is the philosophers' business, not ours. We would merely observe that if society constitutes the individual, the individual, through a reversal analogous to the one Auguste Comte termed "the transition of subjectivity," constitutes society. Without its future, society is no more than an accumulation of raw data, but its future is nothing other than the project of the self, beyond the present state of things, of the millions of men composing it. Man is no more than a situation; a worker is not free to think and feel like a bourgeois. But for that situation *to become human*, an integral man, it must be lived and transcended toward a specific aim. In itself, it remains a matter of indifference to the extent that a human freedom does not charge it with a specific sense. It is neither tolerable nor unbearable, insofar as a human freedom neither resigns itself to it nor rebels against it, that is, insofar as a man does not choose himself within it, by choosing its meaning. And it is only then, within this free choice, that the freedom becomes a determinant, because it is overdetermined. No, a worker cannot live like a bourgeois. In today's social organization, he is forced to undergo to the limit his condition as an employee. No escape is possible; there is no recourse against it. But a man does not exist in the same way that a tree or a pebble does: he must *make himself* a worker. Though he is completely conditioned by his class, his wages, the nature of his work, conditioned even in his feelings and his thoughts, it is nevertheless up to him to decide on the meaning of his condition and that of his comrades. It is up to him, freely, to give the proletariat a future of constant humiliation or one of conquest and triumph, depending on whether he chooses to be resigned or a revolutionary. And this is the choice for which he is responsible. He is not at all free to choose: he is committed, forced to wager; abstention is also a choice. But he is free to choose at the same time his destiny, the destiny of all men, and the value to be attributed to humanity. Thus does he choose himself simultaneously as a worker and as a man, while at the same time conferring a meaning upon the proletariat. Such is man as we conceive him: integral man. Totally committed and totally free. And yet it is the free man who must be delivered by enlarging his possibilities of choice. In certain situations there is room for only two alternatives, one of which is death. It is necessary to proceed in such a way that man, in every circumstance, can choose life.

Our journal will be devoted to defending that autonomy and the rights of the individual. We consider it to be above all an instrument of inquiry. The ideas I have just presented will serve as our guiding theme in the study of concrete contemporary problems. All of us approach the study of those problems in a common spirit, but we have no political or social program; each article will commit its author alone. We hope only to set forth, in the long run, a general line. At the same time, we will draw from every literary genre in order to familiarize the reader with our conceptions; a poem or a novel, if inspired by them, may well create a more favorable climate for their development than a theoretical text. But that ideological content and those new intentions may also influence the very form and techniques of novelistic production; our critical essays will attempt to define in their broad lines the—new or old—literary techniques best suited to our designs. We will attempt to support our examination of contemporary issues by publishing as often as we can historical studies, when, as in the efforts of Marc Bloch or Pirenne on the Middle Ages, they spontaneously apply those principles and the method they entail to past centuries. That to say, when they forsake an arbitrary division of history into histories—whether political, economic, ideological, the history of institutions, the history of individuals—in order to attempt to restore a vanished age as a totality, one that they will consider as the age expresses itself in and through individuals and as individuals choose themselves in and through their age. Our chronicles will strive to consider our own era as a meaningful synthesis and will consequently envisage in a synthetic spirit the diverse manifestations of our contemporary situation—fashions as well as criminal trials and political events and works of the mind—always seeking to discover in them a common meaning far more than to appreciate them individually. Which is why, contrary to custom, we will no more hesitate to pass over in silence an excellent book which, from our point of view, teaches us nothing new about our era, than to linger, on the contrary, over a mediocre book which, in its very mediocrity, may strike us as revealing. Each month we will assemble, in addition to such studies, raw documents which will be selected in as various a manner as possible, simply requiring of them that they clearly demonstrate the interrelation of the collective and the individual. We will supplement those documents with polls and news reports. It strikes us, in fact, that journalism is one of the literary genres and that it can become one of the most important of them. The ability to grasp meanings instantly and intuitively, and a talent for regrouping them in order to offer the reader immediately comprehensible synthetic wholes, are the qualities most crucial to a reporter; they are the ones we ask of all our collaborators. We are aware, moreover, that among the rare works of our age destined to endure are several works of journalism, such as *Ten Days That Shook the World* and, above all, the admirable *Spanish Testament*.[3] Finally, in our chronicles we will devote a good deal of space to psychiatric studies, when they are written from the perspective that interests us. Our project is obviously ambitious: we cannot implement it by ourselves. At the start, we are a small team, who will have failed if, in a year, we have not increased our numbers considerably. We appeal to all men of goodwill; all manuscripts will be accepted, whatever their source, provided they be inspired by preoccupations related to our own and provided they possess, in addition, literary merit. I recall, in fact, that in "committed literature," commitment must in no way lead to a forgetting of literature, and that our concern must be to serve literature by infusing it with new blood, even as we serve the collectivity by attempting to give it the literature it deserves.

CALDER'S MOBILES

IF IT IS true that the sculptor is supposed to infuse static matter with movement, then it would be a mistake to link Calder's art with that of the sculptor's. Calder does not suggest movement, he captures it. It is not his aim to entomb it forever in bronze or gold, those glorious,[1] dumb materials doomed by their nature to immobility. With lowly, flimsy substances, with little bones or tin or zinc, he makes strange arrangements of stalks and palm leaves, of disks, feathers, and petals. They are resonators, traps; they dangle on the end of a string like a spider at the end of its thread, or are piled on a base, lifeless and self-contained in their false sleep. Some errant tremor passes and they get caught up in it, and breathe life into them. They channel it and give it fleeting form—a *Mobile* is born.

A Mobile: a little local party; an object defined by its movement and nonexistent without it; a flower that fades as soon as it comes to a standstill; a pure play of movement in the same way as there are pure plays of light. Sometimes Calder amuses himself by imitating a new form. He gave me an iron-winged bird of paradise. It takes only a little warm air that brushes against it as it escapes from the window and, with a little click, the bird smoothes its feathers, rises up, spreads its tail, nods its crested head, rolls and pitches, and then, as if responding to an unseen signal, slowly turns right around, its wings outspread. But most of the time he imitates nothing, and I know no art less untruthful than his.

Sculpture suggests movement, painting suggests depth or light.

Calder suggests nothing. He captures true, living movements and crafts them into something. His mobiles signify nothing, refer to nothing other than themselves. They simply *are*: they are absolutes.

In his mobiles, the "surprise element" is probably greater than in any other human creation.* The forces at work are too numerous and complicated for any human mind, even that of their creator, to be able to foresee all their combinations. For each of them Calder establishes a general grouping of movement, then abandons them to it: time, sun, heat, and wind will determine each particular dance. Thus the object is always midway between the servility of the statue and the independence of natural events. Each of its twists and turns is an inspiration of the moment. In it you can discern the theme composed by its maker, but the mobile weaves a thousand variations on it. It is a little Dixieland tune, unique and ephemeral, like the sky, like the morning. If you missed it, it is lost forever.

Valéry said the sea is always beginning over again. One of Calder's objects is like the sea and equally spellbinding: always beginning over again, always new. A passing glance is not enough; you must live with it, be fascinated by it. Then the imagination revels in these pure, interchanging forms, at once free and disciplined.

These movements whose sole purpose it is to please, to enchant our eyes, have nonetheless a profound and, as it were, metaphysical meaning. This is because the mobiles have to have some source of mobility. In the past, Calder drove them with an electric motor. Now he abandons to nature: in a garden, by an open window he lets them vibrate in the wind like Aeolian harps. They feed on the air, breathe it, and take their life from the indistinct life of the atmosphere. Their mobility is, then, of a very particular kind. Though they are human creations, they never have the precision and efficiency of de Vaucanson's automata.[2] But the charm of the automaton lies in the fact that it handles a fan or a guitar like a human being, yet its hands have the blind, implacable rigor of purely mechanical translated movements. By contrast, Calder's mobiles waver and hesitate. It is as though they make an error, then correct it.

---

*"The surprise element," or *la part du diable*, may be said to be everything that eludes understanding. It is the title of a 1942 work by Denis de Rougemont.

I once saw a hammer and gong hanging very high up in his studio. At the slightest draft of air, the hammer went after the rotating gong. It would draw back to strike, lash out at the gong and then, like a clumsy hand, miss. And just when you were least expecting it, it would come straight at it and strike it in the middle with an awful noise. And, besides, these movements are too artistically contrived to be compared to those, say, of a marble rolling on a rough plane, whose course depends solely on the uneven terrain: the movements of Calder's mobiles have a life of their own.

One day, when I was talking with Calder in his studio, a mobile, which had until then been still, became violently agitated right beside me. I stepped back and thought I had got out of its reach. But suddenly, when the agitation had left it and it seemed lifeless again, its long, majestic tail, which until then had not moved, came to life indolently and almost regretfully, spun in the air, and swept past my nose.

These hesitations and resumptions, gropings and fumblings, sudden decisions and, most especially, marvelous swanlike nobility make Calder's mobiles strange creatures, halfway between matter and life. At times their movements seem to have a purpose and at times they seem to have lost their train of thought along the way and lapsed into an inane swaying. My bird flies, floats, swims like a swan, like a frigate. It is one, one single bird. And then, suddenly, it breaks apart and all that remain are rods of metal traversed by futile little tremors.

These mobiles, which are neither entirely alive nor wholly mechanical, constantly disconcerting but always returning to their original position, resemble aquatic plants swaying in a stream; they are like the petals of the mimosa, the legs of a frog whose cerebrum has been removed, or gossamer threads caught in an updraft.

In short, although Calder did not want to imitate anything—because he wanted to do nothing except create scales and harmonies of unknown movements—his mobiles are at once lyrical inventions, almost mathematical technical combinations and the tangible symbol of Nature, of that great, indistinct Nature that squanders pollen and suddenly provokes a thousand butterflies to take wing, that Nature of which we shall never know whether it is the blind sequence of causes and effects or the timid, endlessly deferred, rumpled and ruffled unfolding of an Idea.

BLACK ORPHEUS

WHAT WERE you hoping, when you removed the gags that stopped up these black mouths? That they would sing your praises? Did you think, when the heads our fathers had ground into the dust had raised themselves up again, you would see adoration in their eyes? Here are black men standing, men looking at us, and I want you to feel, as I do, the shock of being seen. For the white man has, for three thousand years, enjoyed the privilege of seeing without being seen. He was pure gaze; the light of his eyes drew everything out of its native shade; the whiteness of his skin was another gaze, was condensed light. The white man, white because he was a man, white as day, white as truth, white as virtue, lit up Creation like a torch, revealed the secret, white essence of other creatures. These black men look at us today and our gaze is driven back into our eyes; black torches light the world in their turn, and our white faces are now just little lanterns swaying in the wind. A black poet, without even a thought for us, whispers to the woman he loves:

> Naked woman, black woman
> Dressed in your color which is life . . .

> Naked woman, dark woman!
> Ripe fruit with firm flesh, dark ecstasies of black wine.[1]

And our whiteness seems to us a strange pale varnish preventing our skin from breathing, a white undergarment, threadbare at the elbows and knees, beneath which, if could we take it off, you would find real human flesh, flesh the color of dark wine. We thought ourselves essential to the world, the suns of its harvests, the moons of its tides: we are merely beasts among its fauna. Not even beasts:

> These Gentlemen of the City
> These proper Gentlemen
> Who no longer know how to dance by the light of the moon
> Who no longer know how to walk on the flesh of their feet
> Who no longer know how to tell tales around the fire...[2]

We, who were once Europeans by divine right, were already feeling our dignity crumbling beneath the gaze of the Americans and Soviets; Europe was already nothing more than a geographical accident, the peninsula Asia juts out into the Atlantic. At least we were hoping to recover a little of our grandeur in the menial eyes of the Africans. But there are no menial eyes any longer: there are wild, free gazes that judge our earth.

Here is a black man wandering:

> to the end of
> the eternity of their
> cop-ridden boulevards...[3]

Here, another crying to his brothers:

> Alas! Alas! Spidery Europe moves its fingers and its phalanxes
>   of ships...[4]

And here,

> the insidious silence of this European night...[5]

where

… there is nothing time does not dishonor.

A Negro writes:

> Montparnasse and Paris, Europe and its endless torments
> Will haunt us sometimes like a memory or a malaise…[6]

and suddenly France seems exotic to our own eyes. It is no more now than a memory, an uneasy feeling, a white mist that lingers in sun-drenched souls, a tormented hinterland unpleasant to live in; it has drifted north, it is anchored off Kamchatka: it is the sun that is essential, the sun of the tropics and the sea "flea-ridden with islands" and the roses of Imanga and the lilies of Iarivo and the volcanoes of Martinique. Being is black, Being is fiery, we are accidental and distant, we have to justify *our* ways, our technologies, our half-baked pallor, and our verdigris vegetation. By these calm, corrosive eyes we are gnawed to the bone:

> Listen to the white world
> horribly weary from its immense effort
> its rebel joints cracking beneath the hard stars,
> its blue steel rigidities piercing the mystic flesh
> listen to its deceptive victories trumpeting its defeats
> listen to the grandiose alibis for its lame stumbling
> Pity for our all-knowing, naïve conquerors.[7]

We are *done for*. Our victories, upturned, expose their entrails, our secret defeat. If we want to break down this finitude that imprisons us, we can no longer count on the privileges of our race, our color, our technologies: only by tearing off our white undergarments to attempt simply to be human beings shall we be able to rejoin that totality from which these black eyes exile us.

Yet if these poems shame us, they do so inadvertently: they were not written for us. All the colonialists and their accomplices who open this book will have the impression that they are reading over someone else's shoulder, reading letters not addressed to them. It is to black people that these black people speak, and they do so to talk to them of black people: their poetry is neither satirical nor imprecatory: it is a *gaining of awareness.* "So," you will say, "of what interest is it to us other than documentary? We can't enter into it." I would like to indicate the route by which we can gain access to this jet-black world, and show that this poetry, that seems at first racial, is ultimately a song of all for all. In a word, I am speaking here to the whites and I would like to explain to them what black people know already: why it is necessarily through a poetic experience that the black person, in his present situation, must first become aware of himself and, conversely, why black French-language poetry is the only great revolutionary poetry of today.

It is not by chance that the white proletariat seldom employs poetic language to speak of its sufferings, its anger, or its pride in itself. I do not believe that the workers are less "gifted" than our well-heeled young men: "talent," that efficacious grace, loses all meaning when we claim to ascribe it more to one class than to another. Nor is it the case that the harshness of their labor deprives them of the strength to sing: slaves toiled even harder and we are familiar with slave songs. We have, then, to acknowledge the fact: it is the current circumstances of the class struggle that deter the worker from expressing himself poetically. Being oppressed by technology, it is a technician he wishes to become because he knows that technology will be the instrument of his liberation. If he is to be able one day to control the management of enterprises, he knows that only professional, economic, scientific knowledge will take him there.

Of what poets have dubbed nature he has a deep, practical knowledge, but it comes to him more through his hands than his eyes. Nature for him is Matter, that passive resistance, that inert, insidious adverse force to which he applies the instruments of his labor; Matter does not sing. At the same time, the present phase of his struggle calls for continuous, positive action: political calculation, exact prediction, discipline, mass organization; dreaming would be treason here. Rationalism, materialism, positivism—these great themes of his daily battle are the least conducive to the spontaneous creation of poetic myths. The last of these myths, the famous "new dawn,"[8] has retreated before the necessities of the struggle: the most urgent tasks have to be attended to; a particular position has to be won, then another; a wage has to be raised, a solidarity strike or a protest against the war in Indochina decided: effectiveness alone counts. And, without a doubt, the oppressed class has first to gain self-awareness. But this awareness is precisely the opposite of a descent into selfhood: it is a question of recognizing, in and through action, the objective situation of the proletariat that can be defined by the circumstances of the production or distribution of goods. United and simplified by an oppression exerted on each and all, and by a common struggle, workers know little of the internal contradictions that nourish the work of art and are detrimental to praxis. For them, to know themselves is to situate themselves in relation to the great forces around them; it is to determine the exact place they occupy within their class and the function they fulfill within the Party. The very language they use is free from the minor relaxing of order, the constant, mild impropriety and transmissive play that create the poetic Word. In their jobs they employ precisely determined technical terms. As for the language of the revolutionary parties, Parain has shown that it is pragmatic: it serves to deliver orders, slogans, information. If it loses rigor, the party falls apart. All this leads to the ever more complete elimination of the human subject. Poetry, by contrast, has to remain subjective in some way. The proletariat has not had a poetry that was social and yet drew its sources from subjectivity, a poetry that was social to the very extent that it was subjective, that was founded on a failure of language and yet was as stirring, as widely understood as the most precise of slogans or as the "Proletarians of all Countries, Unite!" that one finds over the entryways of Soviet Russia. Failing this, the poetry of the future revolution has remained in the hands of well-intentioned young bourgeois who drew their inspiration from their psychological contradictions, from the antinomy between their ideals and their class, from the uncertainty of the old, bourgeois language.

The Negro, like the white worker, is a victim of the capitalist structure of our society; this situation reveals to him his close solidarity, beyond nuances of skin color, with certain classes of Europeans who are oppressed as he is; it prompts him to plan for a society without privilege, where skin pigmentation will be regarded as a mere accident. But, though oppression is oppression, it comes in different forms, depending on history and geographical conditions: the black man is its victim *as black man*, as colonized native or transported African. And since he is oppressed in, and on account of, his race, it is of his race that he must first gain awareness. He has to force those who, for centuries, have, because he was a Negro, striven in vain to reduce him to the animal state, to recognize him as a human being. Now, no "way out" offers itself to him here, no deceit or "crossing of the floor": a Jew, who is a white man among white men, can deny that he is Jewish and declare himself a human being among human beings. The Negro cannot deny he is a Negro, nor lay claim to that colorless abstract humanity: he is black. He is, in this way, forced into authenticity: insulted and enslaved, he stands tall, picks up the word "Negro" that is thrown at him like a stone, and proudly, standing up against the white man, claims the name "black" as his own. The final unity that will bring all the oppressed together in a single struggle must be preceded in the colonies by what I shall term the moment of separation or negativity: this antiracist racism is the only path that can lead to the abolition of racial differences. How could it be otherwise? Can blacks count on the assistance of the distant white proletariat, its attention diverted by its own struggles, before they are united and organized on their own soil? And does it not, in fact, take a thorough analysis to perceive that deep down beneath the manifest difference of conditions their interests are the same? Despite himself, the white worker benefits a little from colonization: however low his standard of living, it would be even lower without it. In any event, he is less cynically exploited than the day laborer in Dakar or Saint-Louis. And then the technical installations and industrialization of the European countries make it possible to regard the effects of socialization as immediately there; seen from Senegal or the Congo, socialism appears, first and foremost, as a beautiful dream: for black peasants to discover that it is the necessary outcome of their immediate, local demands, they have first to learn to formulate those demands together and, therefore, to think of themselves as blacks.

But this consciousness differs in nature from the consciousness Marxism tries to awaken in the white worker. The European workers' class consciousness centers on the nature of profit and surplus value, on the current conditions of the ownership of the instruments of labor—in short, on the objective characteristics of their *situation*. By contrast, since the contempt whites display for blacks—which has no equivalent in the attitude of bourgeois toward the working class— aims to reach into the depths of their hearts, Negroes have to pit a more just view of black *subjectivity* against that contempt; race consciousness is, therefore, centered first on the black soul or, rather, since the term recurs often in this anthology, on a certain quality common to the thoughts and behavior of Negroes which is termed *negritude.*

Now, to form racial concepts, there are only two ways of operating: either one can convert certain subjective characteristics into something objective or one can attempt to internalize objectively identifiable behaviors. Thus the black man who lays claim to his negritude in a revolutionary movement places himself initially on the terrain of Reflection, either wanting to rediscover in himself certain traits that are objectively observed in African civilizations or hoping to discover the black Essence in the depths of his heart. It is in this way that subjectivity reappears, the subjectivity that is one's own relation to selfhood, the source of all poetry, which the worker has, in self-mutilation, cast off. The black man who calls on his colored brethren to acquire a consciousness of themselves will try to present them with the exemplary image of their negritude and delve into his soul to grasp it. He wants to be at once a beacon and a mirror; the first revolutionary will be the proclaimer of the black soul, the harbinger who will wrench negritude from himself to hold it out to the world; he will be half prophet, half partisan—in short, a poet in the precise sense of the word, *vates.* And black poetry has nothing in common with the outpourings of the heart: it is functional, it meets a need that defines it exactly. Leaf through an anthology of today's white poetry and you will find a hundred diverse subjects depending on the mood and concerns of the poet, his condition, and his country. In the anthology I am introducing here, there is only one subject, which all the poets attempt to deal with, more or less successfully. From Haiti to Cayenne, there is a single idea: to *show* the black soul. Negro poetry is evangelical, it announces the good news of negritude regained.

However, this negritude, which they wish to summon up from their uttermost depths, does not fall, of itself, under the soul's gaze: in the soul, nothing is *given*. Those heralding the black soul have attended the white schools, in accordance with that iron law that denies the oppressed any weapon they have not themselves stolen from their oppressors. It was when it ran up against white culture that their negritude passed from immediate existence to the reflective state. But, as a result, they more or less ceased to live it. By choosing to see what they are, they have become split; they no longer coincide with themselves. And, conversely, it is because they were already exiled from themselves that they have discovered this duty to *show*. They begin, then, with exile. A twofold exile: the exile of their bodies offers a magnificent image of the exile of their hearts. Most of the time they are in Europe, in the cold, amid the gray masses; they dream of Port-au-Prince, of Haiti. But that is not enough: in Port-au-Prince they were already exiled: the slave traders snatched their forefathers from Africa and scattered them. And all the poems in this book (except the ones written in Africa) will offer us the same mystical geography. A hemisphere; right at the bottom, in the first of three concentric circles, encompasses the land of exile, colorless Europe; then comes the dazzling circle of the islands and childhood, dancing around Africa; Africa, the last circle, the navel of the world, the hub of all black poetry, dazzling Africa, Africa afire, oily as snake's skin, Africa of fire and rain, torrid and dense, phantom Africa flickering like a flame between being and nothingness, truer than the eternal "cop-ridden boulevards," but absent, its black rays disintegrate Europe, yet invisible and beyond reach—Africa, the *imaginary* continent. It is the extraordinary good fortune of black poetry that the concerns of the colonized native find clear, grandiose symbols that have only to be meditated on and endlessly delved into: exile, slavery, the couple of Europe–Africa and the great Manichaean division of the world into black and white. This ancestral exile of bodies provides a metaphor for the other exile: the black soul is an Africa from which, amid the cold architectural structures of white culture and technology, the Negro is exiled. Negritude, present but hidden, haunts him, brushes against him, he brushes against its silky wing, it flutters, stretching out within him as his deepest memory and his highest demand, as his buried, betrayed childhood and the childhood of his race and the call of the earth, as the seething of the instincts and the indivisible simplicity of Nature, as the pure legacy of his ancestors and as the Ethics that should unify his truncated life. But if he turns around to look it in the face, it goes up in smoke; the walls of white culture stand between him and it— *their* science, *their* words, *their* ways:

> Give me back my black dolls, so that I may play
> the naïve games of my instinct with them
> remain in the shadow of its laws
> recover my courage
> my boldness
> feel myself
> a new self from what I was yesterday
>   yesterday
>   without complexity
>   yesterday
> when the hour of uprooting came...
> they have burgled the space that was mine.[9]

And yet one day the walls of the culture prison will have to be smashed, one day he will have to return to Africa: in this way, within the *vates* of negritude, the theme of the return to the native country and the re-descent into the vivid Hades of the black soul are indissolubly mingled. Involved here is a quest, a systematic stripping-down and an *askesis*, accompanied by a continuous effort to delve deeper. And I shall term this poetry "orphic" because this tireless descent of the Negro into himself puts me in mind of Orpheus going to reclaim Eurydice from Pluto. So, by an exceptional poetic felicity, it is by abandoning himself to trances, by rolling on the floor like a man possessed and under attack from himself, by singing his anger, his regret, or his hatreds, by baring his wounds, his life torn between "civilization" and the old black roots—in short, it is by displaying the greatest lyricism that the black poet most surely attains to great collective poetry. In speaking only of himself, he speaks of all Negroes: it is when he seems stifled by the serpents of our culture that he shows himself at his most revolutionary, for then he undertakes systematically to destroy what he has learned from Europe and that demolition in spirit symbolizes the great future uprising through which black people will break their chains. A single example will be enough to throw light on this last remark.

At the same time as they were struggling for their independence, most ethnic minorities in the nineteenth century tried passionately to revive their national languages. To be able to *call* oneself Irish or Hungarian, you have doubtless to belong to a community that enjoys broad economic and political autonomy, but to *be* Irish, you also have to *think* Irish, which means, first and foremost, to think in the Irish language.[10] The specific features of a society correspond exactly to the untranslatable expressions of its language. Now, what is likely dangerously to hold back the effort of black people to throw off our tutelage is the fact that the proclaimers of negritude are forced to frame their gospel *in French*. Scattered to the four corners of the earth by the slave trade, black people have no common language; to encourage the oppressed to unite, they have to resort to the words of the oppressor. It is French that will provide the black bard with the biggest audience among black people, at least within the boundaries of French colonization. It is into this language that gives you goose pimples, that is pale and cold as our skies and which Mallarmé described as "the neutral language par excellence, since the particular genius of this land demands that all over-vivid or riotous color be toned down"—into this language that is half dead for them—that Damas, Diop, Laleau, and Rabéarivelo will pour the fire from their skies and their hearts. Through it alone can they communicate. Like the scholars of the sixteenth century who could understand each other only in Latin, black people can meet only on the booby-trapped terrain the white man has prepared for them. Among the colonized, the colonialist has arranged to be the eternal mediator; he is there, always there, even when absent—even in the most secret meetings.

And since words are ideas, when the Negro declares in French that he is rejecting French culture, he takes with one hand what he rejects with the other; he installs the enemy's thinking apparatus in himself like a mechanical grinder. This would be of no importance, were it not for the fact that this syntax and this vocabulary, crafted in other times and distant climes, to meet other needs and refer to other objects, are unsuitable for providing him with the means for speaking of himself, his concerns and hopes. French language and thought are analytic. What would happen if the black spirit were, above all, a spirit of synthesis? The rather ugly term "negritude" is one of the only black contributions to our dictionary. But if this "negritude" is a definable, or at least describable, concept, it must be made up of other more elementary concepts, corresponding to the immediate data of Negro consciousness: Where are the words that would enable us to refer to these? How well one understands the lament of the Haitian poet:

> This nagging heart, that matches neither
> My language nor my customs,
> And into which bites, like a leach,
> Borrowed feelings and European
> Customs, do you feel this suffering,
> This unrivaled despair
> At taming, with the words of France,
> This heart that came to me from Senegal?[11]

However, it is not true that black people express themselves in a "foreign" language, since they are taught French from their earliest years and are perfectly at ease in it when they think as technicians, scientists, or politicians. We should speak rather of the slight, but constant, gap that separates what they say from what they mean as soon as they speak of themselves. It seems to them that a French spirit steals their ideas, gently inflects them, so that they mean more or less than they intended; that the white words soak up their thought the way sand soaks up blood. If they suddenly take control of themselves, gather their wits, and step back from what is happening, they see the words lying *over against them* in their strangeness, half signs and half things. There is no way they will speak their negritude with precise, effective words that always hit their target. There is no way they will speak their negritude *in prose*. But everyone knows that this sense of failure with regard to language considered as a means of direct expression is at the origin of all poetic experience.

The speaker's reaction to the failure of prose is, in fact, what Bataille calls the holocaust of words.[12] So long as we are able to believe that a preestablished harmony governs the relations between words and Being, we use words without seeing them, with a blind confidence. They are sense organs, mouths and hands, windows opened on the world. At the first failure, this easy chatter falls away from us; we see the whole system; it is nothing but a broken, upturned machine, its great arms still waving to *signal* in the void. We judge at a stroke the mad enterprise of naming. We understand that language is, in its essence, prose; and prose, in its essence, failure. Being stands before us as a tower of silence; if we still want to pin it down, it can only be by silence: "to evoke, in deliberate shade, the silenced object by allusive, ever-indirect words, reducing themselves to an equal silence."[13] No one has better expressed the idea that poetry is an incantatory attempt to evoke Being in and by the vibratory disappearance of the word. By going further in his verbal impotence, by driving words to distraction, the poet helps us to sense enormous silent densities beyond this self-canceling hubbub. Since we cannot stop speaking, we have to *make silence with language*. It strikes me that from Mallarmé to the Surrealists, the profound aim of French poetry has been this self-destruction of language. The poem is a camera obscura in which each word bangs insanely into the next. Colliding in the air, they set each other on fire and fall down in flames.

It is within this perspective that we have to situate the efforts of the black evangelists. To the colonialist's ruse, they reply with a similar, but opposite cunning: since the oppressor is present even in the language they speak, they will speak that language to destroy it. Today's European poet tends to dehumanize words in order to restore them to nature; the black herald, for his part, will *de-gallicize* them; he will pound them, break down their customary associations, join them together violently.

With little rain-of-caterpillar steps,
With little gulp-of-milk steps,
With little ball-bearing steps
With little seismic-shock steps
The yams in the soil are taking great star-gap strides.[14]

He adopts them only when they have disgorged their whiteness, making this language in ruins a solemn and sacred super-language, Poetry. By Poetry alone, the blacks of Antananarivo, Cayenne, Port-au-Prince, and Saint-Louis can communicate with each other unwitnessed. And since French lacks terms and concepts for defining negritude, since negritude is silence, to evoke it, they will use "allusive, ever-indirect words, reducing themselves to an equal silence." Short-circuits of language: behind the words falling down in flames, we glimpse a large, black, mute idol. It is not, then, simply the Negro's goal of depicting himself that seems to me poetic. It is also his own way of using the means of expression at his disposal. His situation prompts him to do so: even before he can think of singing, the light of the white words is refracted in him, polarized and altered. Nowhere is this more evident than in the use he makes of the coupled terms "black/white," which cover both the great cosmic divide between night and day and the human conflict between the native and the colonialist. But it is a hierarchical couple: in delivering it to the Negro, the schoolteacher also delivers a hundred habits of speech that confirm that the white man has precedence over the black. The Negro will learn to say "white like snow" to indicate innocence, to speak of "black looks" and the blackness of a soul or a crime. The moment he opens his mouth, he accuses himself, unless he makes an enormous effort to overturn the hierarchy. And if he overturns it *in French*, he is already being poetic: Can you imagine the strange flavor expressions like "the blackness of innocence" or "the shades of virtue" would have for us? It is this we savor on each of the pages of this book and, for example, when we read:

Your breasts of black satin, curvaceous and gleaming...
this white smile
of your eyes

in the shadow of your face
awaken in me, this evening,
the muffled rhythms ...
that inebriate
our black, naked sisters
over there in the land of Guinea
and stir in me
this evening
Negro twilights heavy with sensual feeling
for
the soul of the black country where the ancients sleep
lives and speaks
this evening
in the tremulous strength of your hollow loins ...[15]

Throughout this poem, black is a color or, rather, a light; its gentle, diffuse radiance dissolves our habitual perceptions: the black country where the ancients sleep is not a dark hell but a land of sun and fire. But on the other hand, the superiority of the white over the black isn't merely an expression of the superiority the colonialist claims over the native: at a deeper level, it expresses the adoration of *daylight* and our dread of the night, which is also universal. In this sense, the black writers re-establish this hierarchy they have just overturned. They do not want at all to be poets of the *night*, that is to say, of vain revolt and despair. They are announcing a dawn; they are hailing "the transparent dawning of a new day." As a result, the black recovers, in his writing, its sense of gloomy presage. "Negro, black as misery," exclaims one of them, and another: "Deliver me from the night of my blood."

So the word black turns out to contain both the whole of Evil and the whole of Good; it recovers an almost unsustainable tension between two contradictory classifications: the solar and the racial hierarchies. From this it acquires an extraordinary poetry, like those self-destructive objects produced by Duchamp and the Surrealists; there is a secret blackness of the white, a secret whiteness of the black, a frozen flickering of being and nonbeing that is nowhere so well expressed perhaps as in this poem by Césaire:

My great wounded statue a stone on its brow my great inatten-
tive pitilessly flecked daylight flesh my great night-time flesh
flecked with day[16]

The poet will go even further. He writes of "Our faces handsome as
the true operative power of negation."[17]

Behind this abstract eloquence redolent of Lautréamont, one
glimpses the boldest, most refined effort to give a meaning to black
skin and achieve the poetic synthesis of the two aspects of night.
When David Diop says of the Negro that he is "black as misery," he
presents the black as pure privation of light. But Césaire develops this
image and deepens it: the night is no longer absence, it is refusal.
Black is not a color; it is the destruction of that borrowed brightness
that comes down to us from the white sun. The Negro revolutionary
is negation because he seeks to be a pure stripping-bare: to construct
his Truth, he has first to wreck others' truths. Black faces, these
patches of night that haunt our days, embody the obscure work of
Negativity that patiently gnaws away at concepts. So, by a turnabout
that curiously recalls that of the humiliated, insulted Negro when he
claims for himself the name of "dirty nigger," it is the privative aspect
of the darkness that establishes its value. Freedom is night-colored.

Destruction, auto-da-fé of language, magical symbolism, conceptual ambivalence—the whole of modern poetry is here, from the negative standpoint. But this is not an arbitrary game. The situation of
black people, their original "having been torn away" and the alienation to which a foreign way of thinking subjects them in the name of
assimilation oblige them to reconquer their existential unity as Negroes, or, if you prefer, the original purity of their projects, by a progressive *askesis* beyond the universe of discourse. Negritude, like
freedom, is both starting point and final end: it is a question of shift-
ing it from the immediate to the mediate, of *thematizing* it. The black
person has, then, to let white culture die in him so that he can be reborn to the black soul, in the same way as the Platonic philosopher
dies to his body to be reborn to the truth. This dialectical, mystical
return to origins necessarily implies a method. But that method does
not present itself as a bundle of rules for the direction of the mind. It

is one with the person applying it; it is the dialectical law of the successive transformations that will bring the Negro to coincide with himself in negritude. It is not, for him, a question of *knowing*, nor of wrenching himself out of himself in ecstasy, but of discovering and, at the same time, becoming what he is.

To this original simplicity of existence there are two convergent means of access: the one objective, the other subjective. The poets in our anthology at times employ the one and at times the other. Sometimes they use both at once. There is, in fact, an objective negritude that is expressed in the mores, arts, songs, and dances of the African peoples. The poet will prescribe for himself, as spiritual exercise, a submissive fascination with primitive rhythms and let his thought flow into the traditional forms of black poetry. Many of the poems gathered here are called "tom-toms," because they borrow from the nocturnal drummers a percussive rhythm that is at times spare and regular, at others torrential and bounding. The poetic act is then a dance of the soul; the poet whirls like a dervish until he faints; he has attuned himself to the time of his ancestors, he feels its strange jolting rhythm; it is in this rhythmic flow that he hopes to find himself again. I would say that he is trying to give himself up to possession by the negritude of his people; he hopes the echoes of his tom-tom will awaken the immemorial instincts dormant in him. Leafing through this anthology, you will get the impression that the tom-tom is tending to become a genre of black poetry, as the sonnet and the ode were of ours. Others will take their inspiration, like Rabemananjara, from royal proclamations; yet others will draw on the popular source of the "hainteny."[18] The calm center of this maelstrom of rhythms, songs, and cries is, in its naïve majesty, the poetry of Birago Diop: it alone is at rest because it comes straight out of the tales of the *griots* and the oral tradition. Almost all the other attempts have something tense, forced, and desperate about them, because they aim to return to folk poetry rather than emanating from it. But, however distant he is from the "black country where the ancients sleep," the black poet is closer than us to the great age when, as Mallarmé puts it, "the word creates Gods." It is almost impossible for *our* poets to reconnect with popular tradition: ten centuries of refined poetry separate them from it and, besides, the folk inspiration has dried up; we could at best imitate its simplicity from the outside. By contrast, black Africans are still in the great period of mythic fecundity and black francophone poets do not merely amuse themselves with these myths as we do with our songs: they allow themselves to be entranced by them, so that at the end of the incantation, a magnificently evoked negritude emerges. This is why I call this method of "objective poetry" a weaving of spells or magic.

Césaire chose that his homeward journey would be made walking backward. Since this Eurydice will vanish in smoke if the black Orpheus turns around to look at her, he will descend the royal road of his soul with his back turned to the far end of the cave; he will descend beneath words and meanings—"to think of you, I left all my words at the pawnbrokers"[19]—beneath daily behavior and the plane of "repetition," beneath even the first reefs of revolt, his back turned, his eyes closed, so as to be able, at last, to touch the black water of dreams with his bare feet and let himself drown in them. Then desire and dream will rise up roaring like a tidal wave, will make words dance like flotsam, will throw them, pell-mell, shattered, onto the shore.

> Words transcend themselves, high and low permit of no distraction toward a heaven and an earth, the old geography is over and done with too . . . By contrast, a curiously breathable terracing occurs, real, but on one level. On the gaseous level of the organism, solid and liquid, white and black, day and night.[20]

We recognize the old Surrealist method here (for automatic writing, like mysticism, is a method: learning and practice must go into it; it must be set going). You have to plunge beneath the surface crust of reality, of common sense, of abstract reasoning, to reach the bottom of the soul and awaken the immemorial powers of desire. Of the desire that makes man a refusal of everything and a love of everything, a radical negation of natural laws and of the possible, an appeal to miracles; of the desire which, by its mad cosmic energy, plunges man back into the seething bosom of nature by affirming his right not to be satisfied. And Césaire is not, indeed, the only Negro writer to take this path. Before him, Étienne Lero had founded *Légitime Défense*.

"More than a magazine," says Senghor, "*Légitime Défense* was a cultural movement. Setting out from the Marxist analysis of the society of the 'isles,' it discovered the Caribbean as the descendant of black African slaves, kept for three centuries in the stultifying condition of proletarian. It asserted that only Surrealism could deliver him from his taboos and express him in his entirety."

But, precisely, if we compare Lero to Césaire, we cannot help being struck by their dissimilarities, and the comparison may allow us to measure the abyss that separates white Surrealism from its use by a black revolutionary. Lero was the forerunner. He invented the exploitation of Surrealism as a "miraculous weapon" and an instrument of research, a kind of radar that you beam out into the uttermost depths. But his poems are schoolboy exercises, they remain strict imitations: they do not "transcend themselves." Indeed, they close up on themselves:

> The old heads of hair
> Glues the bottom of the empty seas to the branches
> Where your body is but a memory
> Where the spring is doing its nails
> The helix of your smile cast into the distance
> On to the houses that we don't want...[21]

"The helix of your smile," "spring...doing its nails"—we recognize here the preciosity and gratuitousness of the Surrealist image, the eternal practice of throwing a bridge between the two most distant terms, hoping, without too much conviction, that this "throw of the dice" will deliver a hidden aspect of being. Neither in this poem nor in the others do I see Lero demanding the liberation of black people; at best, he calls for the formal liberation of the imagination. In this wholly abstract game, no alliance of words even distantly evokes Africa. Take these poems out of this anthology, conceal the author's name, and I defy anyone, black or white, not to attribute them to a European collaborator of *La Révolution Surréaliste* or *Le Minotaure*. This is because the aim of Surrealism is to recover, beyond race and condition, beyond class and behind the incendiary effects of language, a dazzling silent darkness that is no longer the opposite of anything, not even daylight, because day and night and all opposites melt and vanish in that darkness. One might speak, then, of an impassibility, an impersonality of the Surrealist poem, just as there is an impassibility and an impersonality of the Parnassian movement.

By contrast, a poem by Césaire flares and whirls like a rocket; suns burst from it spinning and exploding into new suns; it is a perpetual transcendence. It is not about joining in the calm unity of opposites, but of making one of the contraries of the black/white couple stand up like an erection in its opposition to the other. The density of these words, thrown into the air like rocks by a volcano, is negritude defining itself against Europe and colonization. What Césaire destroys is not all culture but white culture. What he brings out is not the desire for everything but the revolutionary aspirations of the oppressed Negro. What he reaches to in the depths of his being is not spirit but a certain form of concrete, determinate humanity. As a result, we can speak here of "committed," even directed automatic writing—not that reflection intervenes but because the words and images perpetually express the same torrid obsession. In the depths of himself, the white Surrealist finds release from tension; in the depths of himself, Césaire finds the relentless inflexibility of protest and resentment. Lero's words are organized flabbily, relaxedly, by a loosening of logical connections, around vague, broad themes. Césaire's words are pressed up against each other and cemented together by his furious passion. Between the most daring comparisons, the most distant terms, there runs a secret thread of hatred and hope. Compare, for example, "the helix of your smile cast into the distance," which is a product of the free play of the imagination and an invitation to daydreaming, with

and the radium mines buried in the abyss of my innocences
will leap as grains
into the birds' feeding trough
and the stere of stars
will be the shared name of the firewood
gathered from the alluvia of the singing seams of night

where the *disjecta membra* of the vocabulary arrange themselves to give us a glimpse of a black *Ars Poetica*.

Or read:

Our beautiful faces as the true operative power
of negation[22]

and then read:

and the sea flea-ridden with islands crunching between the
    fingers of the flamethrower roses
and my intact body of one thunderstruck.[23]

Here we have the apotheosis of the fleas of black destitution jumping around among the hair of the water, "isles" lying in the light, crunching beneath the fingers of the heavenly de-louser, the rosy-fingered dawn, that dawn of Greek and Mediterranean culture, snatched by a black thief from the sacrosanct Homeric poems, its slave-princess's fingernails suddenly made subservient by a Toussaint Louverture to squash the triumphant parasites of the Negro sea, the dawn that suddenly rebels and metamorphoses, pours out fire like the savage weapon of the whites and, as a flamethrower, weapon of scientists and torturers, strikes with its white fire the great black Titan, who rises intact and eternal to mount an assault on Europe and Heaven. In Césaire, the great Surrealist tradition completes itself, assumes its definitive meaning, and destroys itself: Surrealism, a European poetic movement, is stolen from the Europeans by a black man who turns it against them and assigns it a strictly defined function. I have stressed above how the entire proletariat closed their minds to this reason-wrecking poetry: in Europe, Surrealism, rejected by those who could have transfused their blood into it, languishes and withers. But at the very moment it is losing contact with the Revolution, here in the Antilles it is grafted onto another branch of the universal Revolution; it is blossoming into an enormous dark flower. Césaire's originality lies in his having poured his narrow, powerful concerns as Negro, oppressed individual, and militant into the world of the most destructive, freest, most metaphysical poetry, at a point when Éluard and Aragon were failing to give a political content to their verse. And finally, what is wrenched from Césaire like a cry of pain, love, and hatred is negritude-as-object. Here again, he is continuing the Surrealist tradition which wants the poem to *objectify*. Césaire's words do not describe negritude; they do not refer to it; they do not copy it from the outside as a painter does with a model: they create it, they compose it before our eyes. From this point on, it is a thing you can observe and come to know. The subjective method he has chosen reunites with the objective method we spoke of above: he thrusts the black soul out of itself at the point when others are trying to internalize it. The final result is the same in both cases. Negritude is that distant tom-tom in the nocturnal streets of Dakar; it is a voodoo cry issuing from a basement window in Haiti, slithering out at street level; it is a Congolese mask, but it is also a poem by Césaire, slobbery, bloody, mucus-filled, writhing in the dust like a severed worm. This double spasm of absorption and excretion beats out the rhythm of the black heart on every page of this collection.

So what, at the present time, is this negritude, the sole concern of these poets, the sole subject of this book? The first answer must be that a white man cannot properly speak of this, since he has no internal experience of it and since European languages lack words that would enable him to describe it. I should, then, let the reader encounter it as he reads these pages and form the idea of it that he sees fit. But this introduction would be incomplete if, having indicated that the quest for the black Holy Grail represented, in its original intention and its methods, the most authentic synthesis of revolutionary aspirations and poetic concern, I did not show that this complex notion is, at its heart, pure Poetry. I shall confine myself, therefore, to examining these poems objectively as a body of testimony and to cataloguing some of their main themes. "What makes the negritude of a poem," says Senghor, "is not so much the theme as the style, the emotional warmth that lends life to the words, that transmutes talk into the Word." What better indication is there that negritude is not a state, nor a definite set of vices and virtues, of intellectual and moral qualities, but a certain affective attitude to the world. Since the early part of this century, psychology has given up on its great scholastic distinctions. We no longer believe mental facts are divided into volitions or actions, cognitions or perceptions, and blind feelings or passivities. We know a feeling is a definite way of experiencing our relation to the world around us and includes in it a certain understanding of that universe. It is a tensing of the soul, a choice of oneself and others, a way of going beyond the raw data of experience—in short a *project*, just like an act of will. Negritude, to use Heideggerian language, is the Negro's being-in-the-world.

This is how Césaire puts it:

> my negritude is not a stone, its deafness hurled against
> the clamor of the day
> my negritude is not a spot of dead liquid on the earth's
> dead eye
> my negritude is neither tower nor cathedral
> it takes root in the red flesh of the soil
> it takes root in the ardent flesh of the sky
> it breaks through the opaque prostration with its upright
>   patience.[24]

Negritude is depicted in these beautiful verses far more as act than as disposition. But that act is an inner determination: it is not a question of *taking* the things of this world in one's hands and transforming them; it is a matter of *existing* in the world. The relation to the universe remains an *appropriation*. But it is not a technical appropriation. For the white man, to possess is to transform. Admittedly, the white worker works with instruments that he does not own. But at least his techniques are his own. If it is true that the major inventions of European industry are attributable to a personnel recruited mainly from the middle classes, at least the crafts of carpenter, joiner, and turner still seem to them a genuine heritage, though the direction taken by large-scale capitalist production tends to strip even them of the "enjoyment of their work." But it is not enough to say that the black worker works with borrowed instruments; the techniques too are borrowed.

Césaire calls his black brothers:

Those who have invented neither powder nor compass
those who could harness neither steam nor electricity
those who explored neither the seas nor the sky...[25]

This lofty claim to non-technicity reverses the situation: what could
pass for a failing becomes a positive source of riches. The technical relation to nature discloses it as pure quantity, inertia, exteriority: it dies.
By his lofty refusal to be *Homo faber*, the Negro gives it back its life.
As if, in the "man–nature" couple, the passivity of one of the terms
necessarily entailed the activity of the other. Actually, negritude is
not a passivity, since it "pierces the flesh of heaven and earth," it is a
"patience" and patience is seen as an active imitation of passivity. The
action of the Negro is, first, action on himself. The black man stands
up and remains still like a bird-charmer and things come and perch
on the branches of this false tree. This is indeed a harnessing of the
world, but a magical harnessing through silence and stillness: by acting first on nature, the white man loses *himself* as he loses *it*; by acting
first on himself, the Negro aspires to gain nature by gaining himself.

> [They] yield, captivated, to the essence of all things
> ignorant of surfaces but captivated by the motion of all things
> indifferent to conquering, but playing the game of the world
> truly the elder sons of the world
> porous to all the breathing of the world...
> flesh of the world's flesh pulsating with the very motion of the
> world![26]

On reading these lines, one inevitably thinks of the famous distinction
established by Bergson between intellect and intuition. And indeed
Césaire calls us "all-knowing, naïve conquerors." The white man
knows everything about tools. But the tool scratches the surface of
things; it knows nothing of duration, of life. Negritude, by contrast, is
an understanding through sympathy. The black man's secret is that
the sources of his Existence and the roots of Being are identical.

If we wanted to provide a social interpretation of this metaphysics,
we would say this was a poetry of farmers pitted against a poetry of

engineers. It is not true, in fact, that the black man has no technology: the relation of a human group of whatever kind with the outside world is always technical in one way or another. And conversely, it seems to me Césaire is unfair: Saint-Exupéry's plane, which folds the earth like a carpet beneath it, is an instrument of disclosure. But the black man is, first of all, a farmer; agricultural technique is "upright patience"; it has confidence in life; it waits. To plant is to impregnate the earth; one then must remain still and attentive: "each atom of silence is the chance of a ripe fruit" (Paul Valéry), every moment brings a hundred times more than the farmer gave, whereas, in the manufactured product, the industrial worker finds only what he put into it;* the man grows alongside his wheat; from one minute to the next he grows taller and more golden; attentive to this fragile swelling belly, he intervenes only to protect. The ripe wheat is a microcosm, because for it to grow, it took the contributions of sun, rain, and wind; an ear of wheat is at once the most natural of things and the most improbable piece of good fortune. Technologies have contaminated the white farmer, but the black one remains the great male of the earth, the sperm of the world. His existence is great vegetal patience; his work is the repetition year upon year of the sacred coitus. Creating and fed by what he creates. To plow, to plant, to eat is to make love with nature. The sexual pantheism of these poets is doubtless what will first strike the reader; it is in this respect that they connect with the phallic rites and dances of black Africans.

> Oho! Congo, lying on your bed of forests, queen of subdued
>   Africa.
> May the phalluses of the hills carry your banner high,
> For you are woman by my head, by my tongue, you are woman
>   by my belly[27]

---

*It is in this sense that Kant's critical idea expresses the viewpoint of the non-proletarian technician. The subject rediscovers in things that which he has put there. But he puts them there in spirit; these are operations of understanding. The scientist and the engineer are Kantians.

writes Senghor. And:

> Now I shall ascend the soft belly of the dunes and the gleaming
> thighs of the day...[28]

And Rabéarivelo:

> the blood of the earth, the sweat of the stone
> and the sperm of the wind.[29]

And Laleau:

> Beneath the sky, the conical drum laments
>   And it is the very soul of the black man
> Heavy spasms of rutting man, sticky lover's sobs
>   Offending the calm of evening.[30]

We are a long way here from Bergson's chaste, asexual intuition. It is
no longer a question of merely being in sympathy with life but of being in love with all its forms. For the white technician, God is first and
foremost an engineer. Jupiter ordains chaos and lays down laws for it;
the Christian God conceives the world by his understanding and creates it by his will: the relation of creature to Creator is never a fleshly
one, except for some mystics whom the Church regards with great
suspicion. And even then mystical eroticism has nothing in common
with fertility: it is the entirely passive wait for a sterile penetration. We
are *molded* from clay: statuettes produced by the *hand* of the divine
sculptor. If the manufactured objects around us could worship their
creators, they would doubtless adore us as we adore the Omnipotent
One. For our black poets, on the other hand, Being comes out of Nothingness like a male member becoming erect; Creation is an enormous,
perpetual giving-birth; the world is flesh and child of the flesh; in the
sea and in the sky, in the sand hills, the rocks and in the wind, the
Negro rediscovers the downy softness of human skin; he strokes himself against the belly of the sand, the thighs of the sky: he is "flesh of
the flesh of the world"; he is "porous to all breath," to all pollen; he is

by turns the female of Nature and its male; and when he makes love with a woman of his race, the sexual act seems to him the celebration of the Mystery of Being. This spermatic religion is like a tensing of the soul, balancing two complementary tendencies: the dynamic sense of being an erect phallus and the more muted, patient, feminine feeling of being a growing plant. So negritude, at its deepest source, is an androgyny.

> There you are
> standing naked
> clay you are and remember it
> but you are in reality the child of this parturiant shadow
> that sates itself with lunar lactogenic[31]
> then you slowly take the form of a cask
> on this low wall crossed by flower dreams
> and the scent of the resting summer
> feeling, believing that roots are growing at your feet
> and running and twisting like thirsting snakes
> toward some subterranean spring...[32]

And Césaire:

> Worn-out mother, leafless mother, you are a poinciana bearing
> only the seed pods. You are a calabash tree, and you are merely
> a host of gourds...[33]

This deep unity of plant and sexual symbols is certainly the most original feature of black poetry, particularly in a period when, as Michel Carrouges has shown, most white poets' images tend toward mineralizing the human. Césaire, by contrast, vegetalizes, animalizes sea, sky, and stones. More exactly, his poetry is a perpetual coupling of women and men, metamorphosed into animals, plants, and stones, with stones, plants, and animals metamorphosed into human beings. So the black poet bears witness to the natural Eros; he manifests it and embodies it. If we wanted to find something comparable in European poetry, we would have to go back to Lucretius, the peasant poet who celebrated Venus, the mother-goddess, in the days when Rome was little more than a great agricultural marketplace. In our own day, I can think of hardly anyone but Lawrence with a cosmic sense of sexuality. And, even then, that sense remains, in his case, highly literary.

But though negritude seems, fundamentally, this static outpouring, a union of phallic erection and vegetal growth, this single poetic theme does not exhaust it wholly. There is another motif that runs through this anthology like a major artery:

> Those who have invented neither powder nor compass...
> Know the furthest recesses of the land of suffering.[34]

Against the white man's absurd utilitarian agitation, the black man pits the authenticity he has derived from his suffering. Because it has had the horrible privilege of plumbing the depths of misfortune, the black race is a chosen one. And though these poems are anti-Christian through and through, one could, in this regard, speak of negritude as a Passion: the self-aware black sees himself in his own eyes as the man who has taken the whole of human pain upon himself and suffers for everyone, even the white man.

> Armstrong's trumpet will... on the Day of Judgment speak of man's pain.
>
> (Paul Niger)[35]

Let us note right away that this is in no way a resigned suffering. I spoke not so long ago of Bergson and Lucretius; I would be tempted now to quote that great adversary of Christianity, Nietzsche and his "Dionysianism." Like the Dionysian poet, the Negro seeks to penetrate beneath the brilliant fantasies of daylight and, a thousand feet beneath the Apollinian surface, he encounters the inexpiable suffering that is the universal human essence. If we were trying to be systematic, we would say that, insofar as he embodies sexual sympathy for Life, the black man merges with the whole of Nature and that he proclaims himself Man insofar as he is Passion of rebellious pain. We shall sense the basic unity of this twofold movement if we reflect on the ever-closer relationship psychiatrists are establishing between anxiety and sexual desire. There is but a single proud upsurge, which we can equally well describe as a desire, which plunges its roots into suffering, or a suffering that has driven itself like a sword through a vast cosmic desire. This "upright patience" evoked by Césaire is, in one single outpouring, vegetal growth, phallic erection, and patience against pain: it resides in the very muscles of the Negro; it sustains the black bearer walking a thousand miles up the Niger in overpowering sun with a fifty-pound load balanced on his head. But if we can, in a sense, equate the fertility of nature with a multitude of woes, in another sense—and this too is Dionysian—this fertility, by its exuberance, goes beyond pain, and drowns it in its creative abundance that is poetry, love, and dance. To understand this indissoluble unity of suffering, Eros, and joy, one has perhaps to have seen the blacks of Harlem dancing frenetically to the rhythm of those "blues" that are the most sorrowful tunes in the world.[36] It is rhythm, actually, that cements these many aspects of the black soul; it is rhythm that communicates its Nietzschean lightness to those heavy Dionysian intuitions; it is rhythm—tom-toms, jazz, the bounding movement of these poems—that defines the temporality of Negro existence. And when a black poet prophesies a better future for his brothers, he does so in the form of a rhythm that depicts to them their deliverance:

What?
a rhythm
a wave in the night through the forests, nothing—or a new soul
a timbre
an intonation
a vigor
a dilation
a vibration which, by degrees, flows out in the marrow, contorts
    in its march an old slumbering body, takes it by the waist
and whirls
and turns

and vibrates in the hands, the loins, the sex, the thighs and the
  vagina...[37]

But one must go even further: this fundamental experience of suffering is ambiguous; it is through it that black consciousness will become
historical. Whatever, in fact, the intolerable iniquity of his present
condition, the Negro does not first refer to *it* when he proclaims he
has plumbed the depths of human suffering. He has the horrible advantage of having known slavery. Among these poets, most of them
born between 1900 and 1918, slavery, abolished half a century earlier,
remains the most vivid of memories:

> My todays each have eyes glowering on my yesterdays
> Eyes rolling with rancor, with shame...
> I still feel my dazed condition of old
> from
> knotty blows with a rope from bodies
> charred from toe to charred back
> flesh killed by searing branding iron
> arms broken 'neath the raging whip...[38]

writes Damas, the Guyanan poet. And Brière, the Haitian adds:

> ...Often like me you feel old pains
> reawaken after the murderous centuries,
> And feel the old wounds bleed in your flesh...[39]

It was during the centuries of slavery that the Negro drank his fill of
the cup of bitterness; and slavery is a past fact that neither our authors
nor their fathers knew directly. But it is also an enormous nightmare
and even the youngest of them do not know whether they have completely awoken from it.* From one end of the earth to the other, black
people, separated because of their colonizers by languages, politics,

---

*And, indeed, what is the present condition of the Negro in Cameroon or the Ivory
Coast but slavery in the strictest sense of the term?

and history, share a collective memory. This comes as no surprise if we remember that, in 1789, French peasants were still subject to fearful panics that went back to the Hundred Years' War. So, when black people look back over their basic experience, it suddenly appears to them in two dimensions: it is both an intuitive grasp of the human condition and the still-fresh memory of a historical past. I am thinking here of Pascal who repeated tirelessly that man was an irrational combination of metaphysics and history—inexplicable in his grandeur if he emanates from the clay, inexplicable in his misery if he is still as God made him—and that, to understand him, one needed recourse to the irreducible fact of the Fall. It is in this same sense that Césaire calls his race "the fallen race." And, in a sense, I can quite understand how one can compare a black consciousness with a Christian consciousness: the iron law of slavery evokes the law of the Old Testament, which rehearses the consequences of Sin. The abolition of slavery recalls that other historical fact: the Redemption. The sickly sweet paternalism of the white man after 1848 and that of the white God after the Passion are similar. Except that the inexpiable Sin the black person discovers in the depths of his memory is not his own but that of the white man; the first fact of Negro history is, indeed, an original sin, but the black man is its innocent victim. This is why his conception of suffering is radically opposed to white dolorism. If these poems are, for the most part, so violently anti-Christian, this is because the religion of the whites appears even more as a hoax to the eyes of the Negro than it does to the eyes of the European proletariat: it wants him to share the responsibility for a crime of which he is the victim. It wants to persuade him that the abductions, massacres, rapes, and tortures that have soaked Africa in blood are a legitimate punishment, are deserved ordeals. Yes, you may say that, on the other hand, it proclaims the equality of all before God. *Before God.* I read recently in *Esprit* these lines from a correspondent from Madagascar:

> I am as convinced as you that the soul of a Madagascan is worth that of a white man . . . Precisely as the soul of a child is of the same worth before God as the soul of its father. And yet, dear

Editor, you do not allow your car, if you have one, to be driven by your children.

Christianity and colonialism could not be more elegantly reconciled. Against these sophisms, the black man, by the mere searching of his memory as onetime slave, asserts that pain is man's lot and, for all that, is still undeserved. He rejects with horror the depressing Christian attitude, its morose voluptuousness, masochistic humility, and all the tendentious promptings to resignation; he lives out the absurd fact of suffering in its purity, injustice, and gratuitousness and discovers in it that truth unknown or concealed by Christianity: suffering contains within itself its own rejection; it is, in its essence, refusal to suffer, it is the shadow side of negativity; it opens onto revolt and freedom. By so doing, he *historializes himself*,[40] insofar as the intuition of pain grants him a collective past and assigns him a future goal. Just a moment ago he was pure emergence into the present of immemorial instincts, pure manifestation of universal, eternal fecundity. Now he calls on his brothers of color in quite a different language:

> Black hawker of revolt,
> you have known the paths of the world
> since you were sold in Guinea ...

and

> Five centuries have seen you arms in hand
> and you have taught the exploiting races
> the Passion for freedom.[41]

There is already a black epic poem: first, the golden age of Africa; then the age of dispersion and captivity; then the awakening of consciousness, the somber, heroic days of the great revolts, of Toussaint Louverture, and the black heroes; then the historic moment of the abolition of slavery—"unforgettable metamorphosis," says Césaire—then the struggle for ultimate liberation.

You await the next call,
the inevitable mobilization,
for your war has known only truces,
for there is no land where your blood has not flowed,
no language in which your color has not been insulted.
You smile, Black Boy,[42]
you sing,
you dance,
you rock the generations in your arms
rising every hour,
on the fronts of labor and hardship,
who will rise up tomorrow against the Bastilles,
against the bastions of the future
to write in every tongue,
on the clear pages of every sky,
the declaration of your rights neglected
for more than five centuries...[43]

This is a strange, decisive turn: *race* has transmuted into *historicity*, the black Present explodes and temporalizes itself, negritude inserts itself with its past and its future into Universal History. It is no longer a state, nor even an existential attitude, it is a becoming. The black contribution to the development of humanity is no longer a savor, a taste, a rhythm, an authenticity, a cluster of primitive instincts, but an undertaking that can be dated, a patient construction, a future. Not so long ago, it was in the name of ethnic characteristics that the black man claimed his place in the sun; he now bases his right to life on his mission; and that mission, like the proletariat's, comes to him from his historical situation: because he has, more than all others, suffered from capitalist exploitation, he has, more than all others, the sense of revolt and the love of freedom. And because he is the most oppressed, when he works for his own deliverance he strives necessarily for the liberation of all:

Black messenger of hope
for you know all the world's songs

from the songs of the building sites by the Nile in times out of
mind...[44]

But can we still, after this, believe in the inner homogeneity of negritude? And how are we to say what it *is*? At times it is a lost innocence
that existed only in a distant past, at times a hope that will be realized
only in the radiant city of the future. At times it contracts in a moment
of pantheistic fusion with Nature and, at others, it expands to coincide with the whole history of Humanity; it is, at times, an existential
attitude and, at others, the objective totality of black-African traditions. Is it something one discovers? Is it something one creates? After
all, there are blacks who "collaborate"; after all, Senghor, in the notes
with which he has prefaced the work of each poet, seems to distinguish
degrees within negritude. Does the self-appointed proclaimer of negritude among his brothers of color invite them to become ever more
black or does he, rather, by a kind of poetic psychoanalysis, disclose
what they are to them? And is that negritude necessity or freedom?
For the authentic Negro, is it the case that his behavior flows from his
essence in the same way as consequences flow from a principle, or is
one a Negro in the same way as a religious believer has the faith—that
is to say, in fear and trembling, in a state of anguish, perpetually re-
morseful at never being sufficiently as one would like to be? Is it a fact
or a value? The object of an empirical intuition or a moral concept? Is
it something achieved by thought? Or does thinking poison it? Is it
only ever authentic when not reflected upon and immediate? Is it a
systematic explanation of the black soul or a Platonic archetype that
one approaches indefinitely without ever attaining it? Is it, for black
people, like our common sense, the most widely shared thing in the
world?[45] Or does it descend on some like grace and choose its elect?
The answer will no doubt come that it is all these things and many
more besides. And I agree: like all anthropological notions, negritude
is a glistening between "is" and "ought"; it makes you and you make it:
it is pledge and passion at one and the same time. But there is something more serious: the Negro, as we have said, creates an anti-racist
racism for himself. He in no way wishes to dominate the world: he
wants the abolition of ethnic privileges wherever their source; he

asserts his solidarity with the oppressed of all colors. The subjective, existential, ethnic notion of negritude "passes," as a result into the —objective, positive, exact—notion of proletariat. "For Césaire," says Senghor, "the 'white man' symbolizes capital in the same way as the 'Negro' symbolizes work. Through the black-skinned men of his race, he is hymning the struggle of the world proletariat." This is easy to say, but less easy to conceive. And it is doubtless not an accident that the most ardent spokesmen of negritude are, at the same time, Marxist activists. But, even so, the notion of race does not exactly match that of class: the former is concrete and particular, the latter universal and abstract; the one derives from what Jaspers calls understanding, the other from abstract thinking; the former is the product of a psycho-biological syncretism, the latter a methodical construction on the basis of experience. In fact, negritude is the weaker upbeat in a dialectical progression: the theoretical and practical affirmation of white suprem-acy is the thesis, the position of negritude as the antithetical value is the moment of negativity. But that negative moment is not sufficient in itself and the blacks who make use of it know this very well; they know its aim is to prepare the synthesis or realization of the human in a society without races. Thus negritude is bent upon self-destruction; it is transitional, not final; a means, not an end. At the moment the black Orpheuses embrace this Eurydice most tightly, they feel her pass out in their arms. A poem by Jacques Roumain, a black commu-nist, provides the most moving testimony of this new ambiguity:

> Africa I have retained a memory of you Africa
> you are in me
> Like the splinter in the wound
> like a tutelary fetish in the center of the village
> make me the stone in your slingshot
> make my mouth the lips of your wound
> make my knees the smashed columns of your degradation
> YET
> I want only to be of your race
> workers peasants of the world ...[46]

With what sadness he holds on, for a moment, to what he has decided to cast off! With what human pride he will shed, for other human beings, his pride as Negro! The person who says both that Africa is in him "like the splinter in the wound" and that he wants *only* to be one of the universal race of the oppressed, has not thrown off the hold of unhappy consciousness. One step more and negritude will disappear entirely: of what was the mysterious, ancestral seething of black blood, the Negro himself makes a geographical accident, the insubstantial product of universal determinism:

> ... Is it all these things climate range space
> that create the clan the tribe the nation
> the skin the race and the gods
> our inexorable dissimilarity?[47]

But the poet does not quite have the courage to accept this rationalization of the racial concept: we can see that he confines himself to questioning; beneath his desire for union, a bitter regret shows through. A curious path this: hurt and humiliated, black people search in the very depths of themselves to recover their most secret pride, and, when they have at last found it, that pride contests itself: by a supreme act of generosity they abandon it, as Philoctetus abandoned his bow and arrows to Neoptolemus. So Césaire's rebel discovers at the bottom of his heart the secret of his revolts: he is of royal lineage.

> It's true there's something in you that has never been able to bow the knee, an anger, a desire, a sadness, an impatience, in short a contempt, a violence ... and there's gold not mud in your veins, pride not servitude. A King, you were once a King.

But he immediately wards off this temptation:

> My law is that I run from an unbroken chain to the confluence of fire that sends me up in smoke, that purifies me and sets me

ablaze with my prism of amalgamated gold ... I will perish, but naked.[48] Intact.[49]

It is perhaps this ultimate nudity of man—tearing from him the cheap white rags that masked his black breastplate, before undoing, then rejecting, that breastplate itself—it is perhaps this colorless nudity that best symbolizes negritude: for negritude isn't a state; it is a pure surpassing of oneself, it is love. It is at the point where it renounces itself that it finds itself; it is at the moment it agrees to lose that it has won[50]: the colored man and the colored man alone can be asked to renounce the pride of his color. He is the one walking on a ridge between past particularism, which he has just come to grips with, and future universalism that will be the twilight of his negritude; the one who lives particularism to its limits, to find in it the dawning of the universal. And doubtless the white worker, too, achieves consciousness of his class in order to deny it, since he wishes for the coming of a classless society: but, let me say again, the definition of class is objective; it summarizes only the conditions of his alienation; whereas the Negro finds race at the bottom of his heart, and it is his heart he has to rip out. So, negritude is dialectical; it is not only, nor is it mainly, the flowering of atavistic instincts; it represents the transcendence of a situation defined by free consciousnesses. The painful and hope-filled myth of Negritude, born of Evil and pregnant with future Good, is as alive as a woman who is born to die and who senses her own death in the richest moments of her life; it is an unstable resting point, an explosive fixity, a pride that renounces itself, an absolute that knows itself to be transitory: for at the same time as it announces its birth and its death throes, it remains the existential attitude that is chosen by free men and lived *absolutely*, drained to the very dregs. Because it is this tension between a nostalgic past, of which the black man is no longer fully a part, and a future in which it will give way to new values, negritude decks itself in a tragic beauty that finds expression only in poetry. Because it is the living and dialectical unity of so many opposites, because it is a complex resistant to analysis, only the multiple unity of a song and this dazzling beauty of the poem, which Breton terms "fixed-explosive," can manifest it. Because any attempt to conceptualize its different aspects would necessarily lead to showing its relativity, whereas it is experienced in the absolute by regal consciousnesses and, because the poem is an absolute, it is poetry alone that will enable us to pin down the unconditional aspect of this attitude. Because it is a subjectivity that assumes objective form, negritude must be embodied in a poem, that is to say in an objective subjectivity; because it is an archetype and a value, it will find its most transparent symbol in aesthetic values; because it is a clarion call and a gift, it can be heard and given only through the work of art, which is a call to the freedom of the spectator and absolute generosity. Negritude is the content of the poem, it is the poem as—mysterious and open, indecipherable and allusive—thing in the world; it is the poet himself. We must go even further: negritude, the triumph of narcissism and the suicide of Narcissus, tensing of the soul beyond culture, words, and all psychical facts, luminous night of non-knowledge, deliberate choice of the impossible and of what Bataille terms "torture,"[51] intuitive acceptance of the world and its rejection in the name of the "law of the heart," a twofold contradictory postulate, protesting retraction and expansion of generosity, is, *in its essence, Poetry*. For once at least, the most authentic revolutionary project and the purest poetry emerge from the same source.

And if the sacrifice is one day consummated, what will happen? What will happen if black people, laying aside their negritude in favor of Revolution, will only see themselves anymore as proletarians? What will happen if they allow themselves to be defined by their objective condition alone; if they force themselves, in order to struggle against white capitalism, to assimilate the technical world of the white man? Will the source of poetry dry up? Or, in spite of everything, will the great black river color the sea into which it hurls itself? It does not matter: every age has its own poetry; in every age the circumstances of history elect a nation, a race, or a class to take up the torch, creating situations that can be expressed or overcome only through poetry; and sometimes the poetic élan coincides with the revolutionary, and sometimes they diverge. Let us hail, today, the historic opportunity that will enable black people to:

utter the great Negro cry with such firmness
    that the world will be
shaken to its foundations.[52]

THE QUEST FOR THE ABSOLUTE
On Giacometti's Sculpture

LOOKING at Giacometti's antediluvian face, it does not take long to divine his pride and his desire to place himself at the dawn of the world. He scorns Culture, and does not believe in Progress—at least not Progress in the Fine Arts. He sees himself as no more "advanced" than his chosen contemporaries, the people of Eyzies and Altamira. In those earliest days of nature and humanity, neither ugliness nor beauty existed. Nor taste nor people of taste nor criticism. Everything was still to be done: for the first time it occurred to someone to carve a man from a block of stone.

This was the model, then: the human being. Not being a dictator, a general, or an athlete, the human being did not yet have those airs and fanciful uniforms that would attract the sculptors of the future. He was just a long, indistinct silhouette walking along the horizon's edge. But you could already see that his movements were different from the movements of things; they emanated from him like first beginnings and hinted in the air at an ethereal future. They had to be understood in terms of their purposes—to pick a berry or push aside a briar—not their causes. They could never be isolated or localized. I can separate this swaying branch from a tree, but never one upraised arm or one clenched fist from a human being. A *human being* raises his arm or clenches his fist: the *human being* here is the indissoluble unit and the absolute source of his movements. And he is, besides, a charmer of signs; they catch in his hair, shine in his eyes, dance on his lips, perch on his fingertips. He speaks with the whole of his body: if he runs, he speaks; if he stops, he speaks; and if he falls asleep, his sleep is speech.

And now here is the material: a rock, a mere lump of space. From space, Giacometti has to fashion a human being: he has to inscribe movement in total stillness, unity in infinite multiplicity, the absolute in pure relativity, the future in the eternal present, the prattling of signs in the stubborn silence of things. The gap between material and model seems unbridgeable, yet that gap exists only because Giacometti has taken its measure. I am not sure whether to see him as a man intent on imposing a human seal on space or as a rock dreaming of the human. Or, rather, he is both these things, as well as the mediation between the two.

The sculptor's passion is to transform himself completely into extension, so that, from the depths of that extension, the whole statue of a man can spurt forth. He is haunted by thoughts of stone. On one occasion, he felt a terror of the void; for months he walked to and fro with an abyss at his side; that was space becoming aware within him of its desolate sterility. Another time, it seemed to him that objects, drab and dead, no longer touched the ground; he inhabited a floating universe, knowing in his flesh to the point of torture that there is, in extension, neither height nor depth, nor real contact between things. But at the same time he knew the sculptor's task was to carve from that infinite archipelago the complete form of the only being that can *touch* other beings.

I know no one else so sensitive as he to the magic of faces and gestures. He views them with a passionate desire, as though he were from some other realm. But at times, tiring of the struggle, he has sought to mineralize his fellow human beings: he saw crowds advancing blindly toward him, rolling down the avenues like rocks in an avalanche. So, each of his obsessions remained a piece of work, an experiment, a way of experiencing space.

"He's quite mad," you will say. "Sculptors have been working away for three thousand years—and doing it very well—without such fuss. Why doesn't he apply himself to producing faultless works by tried-and-tested techniques, instead of feigning ignorance of his predecessors?"

The fact is that for three thousand years sculptors have been carving only corpses. Sometimes they are called reclining figures and are placed on tombs; sometimes they are seated on curule chairs or perched on horses. But a dead man on a dead horse does not amount to even half a living creature. The rigid people found in museums, these white-eyed figures are deceiving us. The arms pretend to move but are held up by iron rods; the frozen forms struggle to contain an infinite dispersion within themselves. It is the imagination of the spectator, fooled by a crude resemblance, that lends movement, warmth, and life here to the eternal deadweight of matter.

So we must start again from scratch. After three thousand years the task of Giacometti and contemporary sculptors is not to add new works to the galleries but to prove that sculpture is possible. To prove it by sculpting, the way Diogenes, by walking, proved there was movement. To prove it, as Diogenes did against the arguments of Parmenides and Zeno. It is necessary to push to the limits and see what can be done. If the undertaking should end in failure, it would be impossible, in the best of cases, to decide whether this meant that the sculptor had failed or sculpture itself; others would come along, and they would have to begin anew. Giacometti himself is forever beginning anew. But this is not an infinite progression; there is a fixed boundary to be reached, a unique problem to be solved: how to make a man out of stone without petrifying him. It is an all-or-nothing quest: if the problem is solved, it matters little how many statues are made.

"If I only knew how to make one," says Giacometti, "I could make thousands..." While the problem remains unsolved, there are no statues at all, but just rough hewings that interest Giacometti only insofar as they bring him closer to his goal. He smashes everything and begins again. From time to time, his friends manage to rescue a head, a young woman, or an adolescent from the massacre. He leaves them to it and goes back to his work. In fifteen years he has not held a single exhibition. He allowed himself to be talked into this one because he has to make a living, but he remains troubled by it. Excusing himself, he wrote: "It is, above all, because I was goaded by the terror of poverty that these sculptures exist in this state (in bronze and photographed), but I am not quite sure of them. All the same they were more or less what I wanted. Barely."

What bothers him is that these moving approximations, still half-way between nothingness and being, still in the process of modification, improvement, destruction, and renewal, assumed an independent, definitive existence and embarked on a social career far beyond his control. He is going to forget them. The marvelous unity of this life of his is his intransigence in his quest for the absolute.

This persistent, active worker does not like the resistance of stone, which would slow down his movements. He has chosen for himself a weightless material, the most ductile, the most perishable, the most spiritual: plaster. He can barely feel it beneath his fingertips; it is the intangible counterpart of his movements.

What one notices first in his studio are strange scarecrows made of white blobs, coagulating around long russet strings. His adventures, ideas, desires, and dreams are projected for a moment onto his little plaster men; they give them form and pass on, and the form passes with them. Each of these perpetually changing agglomerations seems to be Giacometti's very life transcribed into another language.

Maillol's statues insolently fling their heavy eternity in our faces. But the eternity of stone is synonymous with inertia; it is a present that is fixed forever. Giacometti never speaks of eternity, never thinks of it. He said a fine thing to me one day about some statues he had just destroyed: "I was happy with them, but they were made to last only a few hours." A few hours: like a dawn, a momentary sadness, or a may-fly. And it is true that his figures, being designed to perish on the very night of their birth, are the only sculptures I know that retain the extraordinary but apparently perishable grace. Never was material less eternal, more fragile, more nearly human. Giacometti's material, this strange flour with which his studio is powdered, beneath which it is buried, slips under his nails and into the deep wrinkles of his face; it is the dust of space.

But space, even naked space, is still superabundance. Giacometti has a horror of the infinite. Not the Pascalian infinite, the infinitely large. There is another more insidious, secret infinite that runs through his fingers: the infinite of divisibility. "In space," says Giacometti, there is too much." This *"too much"* is the pure and simple coexistence of juxtaposed elements. Most sculptors have fallen into the trap; they have confused profligacy of extension with generosity; they have put too much into their works; they have delighted in the plump contour of a marble haunch; they have spread human gesture out, fleshed it out, bloated it.

Giacometti knows there is no excess in a living person, because everything is function. He knows space is a cancer of being that gnaws at everything. For him, to sculpt is to trim the fat from space, to compress it so as to wring all externality from it. The attempt may appear hopeless, and on two or three occasions Giacometti has, I believe, been on the verge of despair. If sculpting means cutting up and stitching together again within this incompressible milieu, then sculpture is impossible. "And yet," he said, "if I begin my statue the way they do, at the tip of the nose, it will take me more than an infinity of time to reach the nostril." That was when he made his discovery.

Take Ganymede on his pedestal. Ask how far he is from me and I will say I don't know what you're talking about. By "Ganymede," do you mean the youth carried off by Jupiter's eagle? If so, I'll say there's no *real* relationship of distance between us, for the very good reason that he does not exist. Or are you referring to the block of marble the sculptor has fashioned in the image of the handsome youth? If so, we are dealing with something real, with an existing block of mineral, and we can take measurements.

Painters have long understood all this, because, in paintings, the unreality of the third dimension necessarily entails the unreality of the other two. So the distance from the figures to my eyes is *imaginary*. If I step forward, I move nearer not to them but to the canvas. Even if I put my nose to it, I would still see them twenty paces away since for me they exist definitively at a distance of twenty paces. It follows also that painting escapes the toils of Zeno's paradox; even if I divided the space separating the Virgin's foot from Saint Joseph's into two, and split those two halves again and again to infinity, I would simply be dividing a certain length of the canvas, not the flagstones on which the Virgin and her husband stand.

Sculptors did not recognize these elementary truths because they were working in three-dimensional space on a real block of marble, and though the product of their art was an imaginary man, they thought they were producing it in real space. This confusion of two spaces has had some odd results. First, when they were sculpting from nature, instead of reproducing what they *saw*—that is to say, a model ten paces away—they shaped in clay that which *was* or, in other words, the model in itself. Since they wanted their statue to reproduce for the spectator ten paces away the impression the model had given them, it seemed logical to make a figure that would be for the spectator what the model had been for them. And that was possible only if the marble was *here* in the same way as the model had been *over there*.

But what does it mean to be *here* and *over there*? Ten paces from her, I form a certain image of this female nude; if I approach and look at her from close up, I no longer recognize her; the craters, crevices, cracks, the rough, black tufts, the greasy streaks, all this lunar orography simply cannot be the smooth fresh skin I was admiring from afar. Is this what the sculptor should imitate? But his task would be endless and, besides, no matter how close he came to her face, it would be possible to get closer.[1]

It follows that the statue will never truly resemble what the model *is* or what the sculptor *sees*. It will be constructed according to certain somewhat contradictory conventions, with some details that are not visible from so far away being shown, on the pretext that they exist, and certain others that exist just as much not being shown, on the pretext that one cannot see them. What does this mean other than that one relies on the eye of the spectator to recompose an acceptable figure? But in that case my relation to Ganymede varies with my position; if close, I will discover details I was unaware of from a distance. And this brings us to the paradox: that I have *real* relations with an illusion or, if you prefer, that my true distance from the block of marble has merged with my imaginary distance from Ganymede.

It follows from this that the properties of true space overlie and mask those of imaginary space. In particular, the real divisibility of the marble destroys the indivisibility of the character represented. Stone triumphs, as does Zeno. Thus, the classical sculptor slides into dogmatism because he believes he can eliminate his own gaze and, without men, sculpt the human nature in man; but, in fact, he does not know what he is making since he does not make what he sees. In seeking the truth, he has found convention. And since, in the end, he shifts the responsibility for breathing life into these inert simulacra onto the visitor, this seeker of the absolute ends up having his work depend on the relativity of the viewpoints from which it is seen. As for the spectator, he takes the imaginary for the real and the real for the imaginary; he searches for the indivisible and everywhere finds divisibility.

By taking a stance counter to classicism, Giacometti has restored an imaginary, undivided space to statues. By accepting relativity from the outset, he has found the absolute. This is because he was the first to take it into his head to sculpt human beings as one *sees* them—from a distance. He confers *absolute distance* on his plaster figures just as the painter does on the inhabitants of his canvas. He creates his figure "ten paces away" or "twenty paces away" and, whatever you do, that is where it stays. As a result, the figure leaps into unreality, since its relation to you no longer depends on your relation to the block of plaster—art is liberated.

With a classical statue, one must study it or approach it; each moment one grasps new details. The parts become singled out, then parts of the parts and one loses oneself in the quest. You do not approach a Giacometti sculpture. Do not expect this bosom to flesh out as you draw near; it will not change and, as you move toward it, you will have the strange impression of walking on the spot. As for the tips of these breasts, we sense them, divine them, are almost able to see them: one more step, two, and we are still sensing them; another step and everything vanishes. All that remains are creases in the plaster. These statues can be viewed only from a respectful distance. Yet everything is there: the whiteness and roundness, the flexible saggings of a well-developed breast. Everything except the substance. At twenty paces we feel we can see the wearisome wasteland of adipose tissue. But we cannot: it is suggested, outlined, signified, but not given.

We now know what press Giacometti used to condense space. There is only one: distance. He puts distance within reach. He pushes a distant woman before our eyes—and she keeps her distance even when we touch her with our fingertips. That breast we glimpsed and hoped to see will never spread itself before us; it is merely a hope. These bodies have only as much substance as is required to hold forth a promise. "Yet that's not possible," someone might say. "The same object can't at the same time be viewed close up and from afar." Hence it is not the same object. It is the block of plaster that is near; it is the imaginary person that is far away. "Distance should at least, then, effect its contraction in all three dimensions. But it is breadth and depth that are affected; height remains intact." This is true. But it is also true that human beings possess absolute dimensions for other human beings. If a man walks away from me, he does not seem to grow smaller, but his qualities seem rather to condense while his "bearing" remains intact. If he draws near to me, he does not grow larger, but his qualities open out.

Yet we must admit that Giacometti's men and women are closer to us in height than in width—as though they were taller than they should be. But Giacometti has elongated them deliberately. We must understand, in fact, that one can neither *learn* to know these figures, which are what they are wholly and immediately, nor observe them. As soon as I see them, I know them. They burst into my visual field like an idea in my mind. Ideas alone have this immediate translucency and are at a stroke what they are. Thus, Giacometti has in his way solved the problem of the unity of the multiple: he has quite simply suppressed multiplicity.

The plaster and the bronze are divisible, but this woman walking has the indivisibility of an idea or a feeling; she has no parts because she yields herself up all at once. It is to give tangible expression to this pure presence, to this gift of self, this instantaneous emergence, that Giacometti resorts to elongation.

The original movement of creation—that timeless, indivisible movement so beautifully figured in the long, gracile legs—runs through these El Greco–like bodies and lifts them heavenward. In them, even more than in one of Praxiteles's athletes, I recognize Man, the first beginning, the absolute source of the act. Giacometti has succeeded in imparting to his material the only truly human unity—unity of action.

I believe that such is the Copernican revolution that Giacometti has tried to introduce into sculpture. Before him, artists thought they were sculpting *being*, and that absolute dissolved into an infinity of appearances. He chose to sculpt *situated* appearance and it turned out that one reached the absolute that way. He gives us men and women *already seen*. But not already seen by himself alone. These figures are already seen in the way that a foreign language we are trying to learn is already spoken. Each of them shows us the human being as he *is seen*, as he is for other human beings, as he emerges in an interhuman milieu—not, as I said earlier for the sake of simplification, ten or twenty paces away, but at a human distance from us. Each imparts to us the truth that man is not there primarily in order subsequently to be seen, but is the being whose essence is to exist for others. When I look at this plaster woman, it is my cool gaze I encounter in her. Hence the pleasant uneasiness which the sight of her occasions. I feel constrained and know neither why nor by whom until I discover that I am forced to see and forced by myself.

Giacometti often takes pleasure, in fact, in adding to our perplexity—for example, by putting a distant head on a nearby body, so that we no longer know where to place ourselves or literally how to focus. But even without this these ambiguous images are disconcerting, so much do they clash with our most cherished visual habits. We were accustomed for so long to smooth, mute creatures, made to cure us of the sickness of having a body; these domestic genies watched over our childhood play and attest, in our gardens, to the fact that the world is risk-free, that nothing ever happens to anyone, and hence that nothing has ever happened to them except dying at birth.

Now, to *these* bodies something has happened. Do they come from a concave mirror, a fount of eternal youth, or a concentration camp? At first glance, we seem to be dealing with the emaciated martyrs of Buchenwald. But a moment later we have changed our minds: these slim, lissome creatures rise heavenward and we chance on a whole host of Ascensions and Assumptions; they dance, they *are* dances, made of the same rarefied substance as the glorious bodies promised to us by Scripture.[1] And while we are still contemplating this mystical élan, suddenly these emaciated bodies blossom and before us we have merely earthly flowers.

The martyred creature was merely a woman. But she was *all* of a woman—glimpsed, furtively desired, as she moved off and passed by with the comic dignity of those leggy, helpless, fragile girls whom high-heeled mules carry lazily from bed to bathroom with all the tragic horror of the hunted victims of fire or famine; all of a woman—given, rejected, near, remote; all of a woman, her delicious plumpness haunted by a secret slimness, and her atrocious slimness by a suave plumpness; all of a woman—in danger on the earth and no longer entirely on the earth, who lives and tells us the astounding adventure of flesh, *our* adventure. For, like us, she chanced to be born.

Yet Giacometti is not happy. He could win the game right away, simply by deciding he has won. But he cannot make his mind up to do so. He postpones his decision from hour to hour, from day to day. Sometimes, in the course of a night's work, he is on the point of admitting his victory; by morning, all is shattered. Does he fear the boredom that awaits him on the other side of triumph, that boredom that beset Hegel after he had imprudently rounded off his system? Or perhaps matter is taking its revenge? Perhaps that infinite divisibility he expelled from his work is being endlessly reborn between himself and his goal. The end is in sight: to reach it, he has to do better. And he does so, but now he has to do *a little* better still. And then *just a tiny bit* better. This new Achilles will never catch up with the tortoise. A sculptor has, one way or another, to be the chosen victim of space—if not in his work, then in his life. But above all, between him and us, there is a difference of position. He knows what he was trying to do and we do not; but we know what he has done and he does not. These statues are still more than half embedded in his flesh. He cannot see them. He has barely finished them and he is off dreaming of even thinner, even longer, even lighter women, and it is thanks to his work that he conceives the ideal against which he judges that work imperfect. He will never be done with it, merely because a man is always beyond what he does. "When I finish," he says, "I'll write, I'll paint, I'll enjoy myself." But he will die before he finishes.

Are *we* right or is *he*? To begin with, he is right because, as da Vinci said, it is not good for an artist to be satisfied. But we are right too—and right in the last instance. As he lay dying, Kafka asked to have his books burned, and Dostoevsky, in the very last stages of his life, dreamed of writing a sequel to *The Brothers Karamazov*. Both may have died in a bad mood, the former thinking he would slip from the world without even having scratched its surface, the latter feeling he had produced nothing of value. And yet both were winners, whatever they might have thought.

Giacometti is also a winner, and he is well aware of it. In vain does he hang on to his statues like a miser with his pot of gold; in vain does he procrastinate, temporize, and find a hundred ruses for stealing more time. People will come into his studio, brush him aside, and carry away all his works—even the plaster that covers his floor. He knows this. His hunted air betrays him. He knows that he has won in spite of himself, and that he belongs to us.

PORTRAIT OF
THE ADVENTURER

IT IS WITH pleasure that I add a few words to Roger Stéphane's remarkable essay on the adventurer. Not to praise or to recommend it: it recommends itself. The idea of bringing together these three names—T. E. Lawrence, André Malraux, and Ernst von Solomon—and their lives was ingenious; it will be up to the reader to decide whether it was fruitful. Nor would I want to comment on the work or attempt to complete it. I am afraid I would be reduced to paraphrasing it, so rich and clear are its ideas. Therefore I will attempt to highlight one parallel which is constantly implied but which the shrewd Roger Stéphane only alludes to briefly.

While reading this portrait of the adventurer (I would have preferred "of the man of action"), one immediately thinks of its opposite, the militant. It seems that it would even suffice to take the opposite of all that Stéphane proposes in order to arrive at an acceptable idea of the average communist. Yet the adventurer and the militant do not simply oppose each other as two abstract concepts. They are living men who are in conflict with each other, know and recognize each other sometimes as allies and sometimes as enemies. I would like to try, by way of a conclusion, to unravel some of the complex relationships that unite them, that is, to develop some of the ideas that Stéphane has suggested to me.

The more necessary the militant's entry into the Party appears, the greater confidence he inspires. And I don't mean to speak about that inner necessity that is always suspect and is the result of internal conflicts, complexes, moral aspirations, and what are more generally called "personal reasons." On the contrary, it is very much desirable that his membership be dictated by impersonal reasons such as hunger, for example, which is common to everyone, or the fear and anger that wreak havoc on the anonymous crowd: in short, he must still be part of nature and impelled by the great natural forces that impel primitive animals and incline them one way or another without their needing to possess a nervous system. Anger, fear, and hunger do not suffice to create a personality and that is why these are what is required. Because it is not true that they ask you to give up your ego: being able to dispose of an ego would still be too much. Becoming a member of the Party must correspond quite precisely to one's joining the human realm; rather than taking your ego from you, the Party gives it to you. I state this without irony: it is definitely pleasing to discover oneself in the fraternal look of the others. The new militant will in principle not suffer from their antipathy nor from mindless infatuation. Before all else, one will see in him a fellow, that is to say, a member of the Party: it is a consecration. In him, the Party changes itself into him and into all the others. As a creature of the Party, he will encounter the Party wherever he goes. The Party will be a necessary mediator between him and his closest friends. To a young communist they said, "Have your wife join the Party, that way no time will be lost." He is never alone because he discovers himself through the others. He possesses neither depth nor secrets. He is not permitted to have the slightest complex: they create him before his own eyes by means of rigorously objective criteria. He is explained by his class and his historical circumstances: he views his inner self as he is viewed from the outside: no secret compartments and no double bottom; it is for the sake of convenience that he does not use the third person to speak of himself. Besides, his existence is not a pure abstraction: he knows himself as a member of the class and Party that are making history. He knows that he is defined by precise tasks and by a great hope and he also knows that his heart is filled with hatred and friendship. For the rest, he distinguishes himself by his acts. Even so it is not the case that he "*creates by himself* . . . the most irreplaceable of beings."

The Party can do without irreplaceable beings. The militant remains halfway between the irreplaceable and the interchangeable: he serves, that is all. In 1935, Georges Politzer was doing what no one else could do: "concrete psychology."[1] But economists were needed. He abandoned psychology for social economics.[2] "And your research?" I asked him. "There is no urgency," he told me. "After the revolution, there will be other workers who will do it better than I can at the present."

Being a militant is not for everyone. If the ego comes first, one is forever isolated. In the bourgeoisie, it is created early. Already as a child André Gide threw himself in his mother's arms and cried out: "*I am not like the others.*" Being oneself means first of all that you are not like your neighbor; you are an original. As the saying goes: "The mold is broken." The mold must always be broken. Bourgeois civilization is "a civilization of solitude." And, undoubtedly, the bourgeois have to recognize each other first of all as men. But that abstract recognition focuses only on the universal in each of us and leaves us alone in our singularity. Ultimately one recognizes for us the right to be everything we want to be behind the wall of our private life. And the very term *private*, and the idea of privation that it evokes, shows clearly that the universality of the recognition is the universal refusal to recognize. Hidden behind the high circular walls, the bourgeois is a madman, an abandoned wild animal, a jumble of weeds. Don't people say that they belong to a different species? The militant's life is public even in the most secret recesses of his heart and, to the extent that he is transparent in all the others' eyes, he is the better acquainted with himself while the bourgeois is himself only for himself with all the shutters closed, and he remains in the shadows where he can't be recognized. If a certain young bourgeois suddenly becomes afraid of his solitude, it is too late: the Party can't help him. If they allow him to become a member, he is not likely to find in it the solutions to his problems: they are *personal*. He does not want them to provide him with another ego, all he wants is that they heal it. And besides, if he protests that he was attracted to the Party out of an inner need, they will tell him that such needs are a luxury and he will become suspect. The rejection of solitude is a bad start. Because in order to reject it, you must be aware of it and that is the way to make it exist most completely. To flee it, is to recognize it and to make it the motivation of all our acts. Will he attempt to get beyond himself by means of love? But that will be the love of a solitary person who is fleeing oneself: "To love is to flee from oneself," writes Malraux. That is the case if love is not wanted for itself but is seen as a means of getting beyond the self. And that is all it takes to make the evasion impossible: Kafka, another solitary figure, has spoken eloquently of that kind of love:

> It seemed to me that she was surrounded by armed men whose lances were pointing outward. Each time that I attempted to get closer I got caught on their tips; these wounded me and forced me to withdraw... I too was surrounded by armed men who pointed their lances inward and therefore against me. When I dashed toward the young girl, I was first caught by the lances of my own guards and I could not get beyond them. Perhaps I never even pushed up to the young girl and if I have never succeeded it was because I was bloodied by my own lances and without knowing it.[3]

The young worker entering the Party is fortunate in that he does not have an ego before he loves: he discovers himself in the gift he makes to the other and that the other *acknowledges*. For our young bourgeois to succeed in loving it is necessary for them to be willing to run the risk of letting themselves be acknowledged by others. However, it is already too late: they know too well what they are. At most they are left with the possibility of letting themselves be loved. Perhaps a woman, through her love, *will recognize* this singularity that bourgeois society refuses to acknowledge; perhaps she will know how to adopt "this monster, incomparable and preferable to everything, which every being is for himself and which he cherishes in his heart." But this word "cherish" is significant: they want to flee from themselves and yet they cherish themselves. It is not their ego they hate but their solitude, and they don't understand that to destroy one is to destroy the other.

Yet some people seem to have understood: it is precisely these people Stéphane talks about. And since action creates a bond between men, they are going to try and escape from their isolation by means of action. Through action one becomes other, one tears oneself away from oneself, one changes oneself by changing the world.

Still, one must aim at a goal and desire it profoundly. But in this case it is the goal that is essential and not the act which is simply the means of attaining it. For the militant the goal appeared first and with an absolute necessity: one has to live, fight off hunger, protect oneself against unemployment, rising prices, exploitation, the war. When he entered the Party, the goal metamorphosed itself under his eyes: he understood that his demands would only be realized by the creation of a socialist society. And he metamorphosed himself at the same time as the goal: in him and through him the Party pursued the realization of that absolute goal. The singular character that one acknowledged in him was the singular will to make that realization come true. An order was established: first the end exists and it is what defines the Party as the concerted totality of actions that will allow it to attain the goal. In turn each action seeks its instrument and in that way defines the person. The militant does not demand that his act justify him: he does not exist *first* in order to be justified afterward. But his personality envelops his own justification because it is constituted by the end to be attained. Consequently, he remains relative to the action which is relative to the goal. As far as the action itself is concerned, it must be called an enterprise because it is a slow and tenacious labor of edification that is spread out over an indefinite time period. There is no doubt that this work contains a negative element because one must struggle, undermine the old order, smash the resistance, and clear the terrain, but on the whole one must view it as a positive construction and the systematic and progressive production of new social forms. The militant, sustained and continuously re-created by this project that transcends him, finds himself sheltered from death: the enterprise that defines him exceeds the duration of a life by far; hence he works ceaselessly beyond his own death, and his disappearance will not modify the historical process any more than his appearance modified it. His will, which the Party lent him momentarily, will survive him and continue the work without him.

But for the young bourgeois who attempts to communicate with other men, action is the goal because this brings about the communication. The order has been reversed: he acts in order to save *himself* and chooses a goal in order to act. In principle any goal is good: it is enough that it justifies the action that will justify him. Even so his basic project is negative. Indeed, he cannot envisage receiving a new personality from other men: he wants the salvation of the one he has. This means that he wants his uniqueness to be recognized. For this to happen it is not enough that he serve their purposes: they would only recognize his services. If he wants them to recognize his unique nature, he has to hand it over to them. And since they don't need it, he will destroy it in a big ceremony and make them witness to his sacrifice. Perken, one of Malraux's heroes [in *The Royal Way*], wants "to exist in a great number of men and perhaps for a long time." And he adds this whimsical remark: "One kills oneself only in order to exist." Indeed, the dead person exists only for others; he comes to haunt their numerous solitudes, he is looked after again, willingly or reluctantly, but he is no longer alone. This public death comes close to what the Americans call "conspicuous consumption" and we call luxury. The moneyed class to which our men of action belong is characterized by saving only for a particular moment of its history. It consumes: this means it destroys itself by destroying its wealth through use while believing it is obtaining an exquisite possession of itself. At this stage the systematic squandering can become the sole means of communicating with others: it indulges in potlatches, the destruction of wealth to pay homage to others; it organizes feasts, the destruction of wealth in the presence of others; it gives generously, the destruction of wealth for the profit of others. The Roman aristocracy ruined itself with games; the French nobility also ruined itself: the sons of the well-to-do *wanted* ruination just as these young bourgeois want death. The adventurers will set fire to the enormous warehouse of merchandise that is bourgeois society and, in the end, will throw themselves in the flames. Potlatch, feasts, generosity: such will be their end. And I can't help but think of that other adventurer, Jean Genet, who wrote in *Funeral Rites*:

> We are acting with a view to a fine funeral, to formal obsequies.
> They will be the masterpiece, in the strict sense of the word, *the*

204 · JEAN-PAUL SARTRE

> major work, quite rightly the crowning glory of our life. I must
> die in an apotheosis, and it doesn't matter whether I know glory
> before or after my death as long as I *know* that I'll have it . . .[4]

The word "glory" is the key. It is not in fraternity—in which one
always abandons a little of one's self to the other—that they seek to
communicate but in glory where one exists for all without giving up
anything of one's self. The moment of death will be the apogee of their
life, they await it "with ecstasy." In that infinitesimal moment, still
alive and already dead, they will sense themselves becoming for others
what they were for themselves. While waiting for that supreme moment, they will satisfy themselves with "perfect moments"[5] in which
the universe will reflect to the living person the towering appearance
of the dead one that he will be. "We believe in the happiness of a
prompt decision." But if the decision commits an entire life, the life
that will follow will not stand out from a slow but sure death. Deciding in that manner is to hurry along the narrow crest that separates
extreme freedom from the cadaver's abdication, it means miming
one's own death. One recognizes their model: it is the *hero*, that man
fully occupied with his future funeral, a fatality for him and others,
and who does enjoy life only during a few privileged moments. It
should be noted that the militant is not a hero. Not that he does not
know how to die, but he does not seek out death if he can avoid it and,
if it strikes, he dies modestly. I know that some well-intentioned people have called the communists "the permanent heroes of our time."[6]
That insults them: those who did not speak when tortured simply
said, "I could not do otherwise." Their will was the incarnation of the
Party's Will, and the Will of the Party was that they must not speak.
And since they are not important in their own eyes, because their
project is to construct and that project will be completed without
them, and their wisdom is a meditation upon life, their death does
not appear to them to shatter the entire universe but is only an insignificant and regrettable accident.

Heroes, however, are the militants' parasites. A pretext is needed
for heroism otherwise it would only be suicide. And all the despair of
the destroyers would be ineffective if it was not carried along by the

immense hope of the masses. In order for their funerals to be solemn, in order for then to live a long time in people's memories, they have to have fought "for what in their era will have been charged with most powerful meaning and the greatest hope." For that reason they will strike alliances with a revolutionary movement or a party of national resistance. But these links are only provisional and the adventurer undertakes only negative tasks: he will be a terrorist or an officer. Besides, he will remain suspect to his allies and he does not like them: "I don't even like poor people, in fact those for whom I am going to fight. I prefer them purely because they are the vanquished." It is noteworthy that Lawrence and many of Malraux's heroes are *strangers* in the country in which they are fighting. In the nineteenth century the well-to-do author went outside his country to seek love and spend his money: as a foreign consumer in a society of workers, he enjoyed being the perfect image of the parasite. Today the writer-adventurer goes to risk his skin in the same countries: as a heroic parasite he asks his fellow fighters who did not choose their struggle to legitimate a death he has chosen; the difference in language and customs allows him to maintain his distance. The importance of the collective goals illuminates the adventurer's actions but it shines an indirect light on them.

Yet his position is untenable: the effectiveness of our adventurer is bestowed on him by passionate and tenacious men who only obey their orders in order to better exploit him. And the society that militants want to create rigorously excludes the desperadoes and their magnificent generosity. There is no place for them in a society of producers. Tchen knew full well that "the world that they were preparing together condemned him just as much as the world of his enemies."[7] In this world—in which men recognize each other in and through their work—there is no chance at all that the uniqueness of these human beings will be recognized. And what is worse, even their memory will be forgotten. Their very death appears compromised: one will no more be able to understand it as gratuitous generosity, it will be viewed in the same light as the obscure devotion of the militants. The moment of victory will be the beginning of their failure. Can they want the triumph of a Party that will bury them twice? But if they don't want it, their heroism collapses and only suicide remains. The adventurer's actions oscillate without ever halting between excessive generosity and the most self-serving suicide. These actions require faith and yet they destroy all faith: bamboozled if he believes in what he does and an impostor if he does not. He retracts himself, he clings to his destructive will. The Spanish Civil War in which he is fighting strikes him as a "hideous comedy," he contests the objective goal which contests him in his goals: "Who can tell me if the gains that economic liberation will bring will be greater than the losses introduced by the new society?" And as he noticed that he is going to die for nothing, he wants at the same time to affirm the vanity of any enterprise: "Men die for what does not exist." Committed to action in order to escape from solitude, he now finds himself ever more alone. We should not be surprised: this spendthrift who is wasteful for the fun of it will always be *other* than his allies; they will always consider him a suspect: he was not *obliged* to fight. And besides what does he want from them? Fraternity, comradeship, friendship? Yes, of course. But this means above all that he asks them to be witnesses to his death. The adventurer's comrades are his future mourners, the guardians of his destiny. As Malraux states: "There are no heroes without an audience."

Once again he returns to action; but this time to reduce it to what it is. He considers it lucidly, apart from the motivation that brought it into being and the ends that justified it, in its pure sterility: "No force, not even the *true* life, without being sure of, and being haunted by, the vanity of action." At that point he is going to want it for itself. For itself and for him, without worrying about witnesses anymore. Then for the short time that it lasts, it justifies him: "When my act withdraws itself from me ... my blood is also leaving me." But that is because it is no more than a *subjective state.* He undertook it to get beyond himself, he continues it to return to his inner self. He wants it in solitude and disgust without hiding its absurdity from himself, without hope or faith, for nothing. This action that was conceived to justify him is now justified by him. No transcendent goal can legitimize it. It depends on him alone, it is a pure and vain revolt against the way of the world and against human nature. It is no longer important to destroy by means of an act but to produce an act which destroys itself and whose very vanity underlines its antinatural character.

Since nothing calls out for him, since everything contests him, since everything is nature, chance, and misfortune, since a throw of the dice will never abolish chance,[8] precisely for that reason, as was the case for the poet Mallarmé, what remains to the adventurer is the realm of nonbeing. Man is a being who dies for what does not exist. Hence, action by engulfing it, points, like the "cipher" of failure for Jaspers,[9] to a supernatural reign of *being* which sparkles ever only through defeats, deaths, and betrayals. Besides the adventurer has a less lofty reason to situate his victory in failure: he wants his victory to be a failure. "Its realization, if it comes about, will be a great disillusionment." Let us hope therefore that it never arrives, that this future Eden never occurs; it is pitiless solely for the adventurer. "For the clear-sighted, failure was the only goal. We always had to believe in spite of everything that there was no victory aside from descending into death while struggling against and at the same time calling for defeat." The militant and the adventurer experience for the first time a true brotherhood in suffering and defeat: and in truth, it is the militant who changes, not the man of action. The latter had chosen to die; hence he will die, he has lost nearly nothing. But the former wanted to live, he wanted to achieve a goal which recedes in the distance and disappears; he was optimistic, he had faith in his leaders and properly carried out actions; everything becomes blurred, he discovers that they will perhaps never win. He was a peaceful functionary, with limited initiatives, used to recognizing his tamed face in the eyes of his comrades, sure of himself, sure to find in the bottom of his heart, solid like a rock, the Will of the Party. There he is abandoned in the inexpiable isolation of defeat, the Party has been vanquished, hope squashed, in the eyes of the triumphant enemy he discovers an unknown and savage face which is his. His ego, sustained by so many commands, speeches, and messages, collapses, another ego appears, a desperate uniqueness which oddly reminds him of bourgeois uniqueness; and his death which he had conjured away all through his life by pretending that he would die for the Cause, suddenly washes over him because the Cause has fallen to pieces and he is dying for nothing. Has he wasted his life? And the other, has he gained it?

I can see clearly that both require defeat to draw them to me. Even so I would wish a real defeat for the adventurer, that is to say the victory of the militant: the militant's triumph is morally right (and besides it is in line with the historical process). He is right in *every* respect: he gave himself selflessly to the party, he carried out his work without flinching, he loved all his comrades, and when one of them, through his own fault, was excluded from the Party, he ceased loving him immediately because he was no longer his comrade and the society he wanted to create was the only just one. The adventurer was wrong: he had all the vices of the bourgeoisie: egoism, pride, bad faith. Yet, after having applauded the victory of the militant, I will follow the adventurer in his solitude. Until the end he lived an *impossible* condition: fleeing from and at the same time looking for solitude, living to die and dying to live, convinced of the vanity of, *and* the necessity for, action, attempting to justify his enterprise by assigning it a goal in which he did not believe, searching for the complete objectivity of the result in order to dilute it in absolute subjectivity, wanting the failure that he rejected, rejecting the victory that he wished for, wanting to construct his life like a destiny and being pleased only by the infinitesimal moments that separate life from death. No solution to these antinomies and no synthesis of these contradictions is possible. Abandoned to itself, each couple would come undone, and each of the two terms would tumble back to its original position or they would destroy themselves and the two terms would cancel each other out. Yet, at the price of an intolerable tension, this man has at the same time held all of them together in their very incompatibility: he has been the permanent and conscious embodiment of this incompatibility. I see him move away, vanquished and victor, already forgotten in that society where there is no room for him, and I think that he is at once a testimony to the absolute existence of man and to his absolute impossibility. Better yet: he is proof that it is this impossibility of being which is the very condition of his existence and that man *exists* because he *is* impossible. And the militant? What can we wish for him at the dawn of his new day? That he learn how to salvage those who cannot be salvaged. I fully understand that Lawrence of Arabia merits a place only in the historical situation of 1914 and can be explained by starting with the role of British imperial colonialism and next by capitalism. I understand equally well that a man such as Lawrence will never recur, especially after the liquidation of the bourgeoisie. I also understand that the communists don't like him much and, in addition, he is closely linked to evil. Yet a socialist society in which future Lawrences would be radically impossible would strike me as sterile. And even if, in the eyes of the socialists, Lawrence was evil incarnate, I maintain that the goal must not be to suppress Evil but to preserve it in the greater Good.

"These are the last adventurers, after them there will only be militants anymore," Stéphane tells me. I would like this to be true but only if the militants inherit the virtues of the adventurers. I already know some who are at one and the same time: that ego that was *given* to them and which they received from others in order to struggle, they transcend it in the struggle and their true ego lies beyond this ego; they think by using their combative reasoning that the Party has provided them; but since their thinking rejects all obstacles, they push that constituted reasoning to the limit and metamorphose it into constituent reasoning.[10] And because they are completely devoted to obedience, they hold nothing of themselves in reserve, absolutely nothing, except for that freedom of which they give without reservation; completely committed to the daily struggle that is their exclusive concern, they remain at the same time completely on the outside because they know that the immediate objectives are secondary, even though they are determined to give their life to attain them and have decided that what is at stake is not man's happiness but that, in short, man has yet to be created. Adventurer or militant: I don't believe in that dilemma. I know all too well that an act has two aspects: adventure is the negative aspect and discipline is the constructive one. We must reintroduce negativity, anxiety, and self-criticism into discipline. We will only win if we draw all the consequences from this vicious circle: man has yet to be made and it is only man who can make man.

REPLY TO ALBERT CAMUS

My dear Camus,

Our friendship was not easy, but I shall miss it. If today you break it off, doubtless that means it had to end. Many things brought us together, few separated us. But those few were still too many: friendship, too, tends to become totalitarian; there has to be agreement on everything or it ends in a quarrel, and those who don't belong to any party themselves behave like members of imaginary parties. I shall not carp at this: it is as it must be. But, for just this reason, I would have preferred our current disagreement to be over matters of substance and that there should not be a whiff of wounded vanity mingled with it. Who would have said, who would have believed that everything would end between us in an authors' quarrel in which you played Trissotin to my Vadius?[1] I did not want to reply to you. Who would I be convincing? Your enemies, certainly, and perhaps my friends? And you—who do you think you are convincing? Your friends and my enemies. To our common enemies, who are legion, we shall both give much cause for laughter. That much is certain.

Unfortunately, you attacked me so deliberately and in such an unpleasant tone that I cannot remain silent without losing face. I shall, therefore, reply: without anger but, for the first time since I've known you, without mincing my words. A mix of melancholy conceit and vulnerability on your part has always deterred people from telling you unvarnished truths. The result is that you have fallen prey to a gloomy immoderation that conceals your inner difficulties and which you refer to, I believe, as Mediterranean moderation. Sooner or later, someone would have told you this, so it might as well be me. But do not fear, I shall not attempt your portrait; I do not want to incur the criticism you gratuitously level at Jeanson: I shall speak of your letter and of it alone, with a few references to your works if necessary.

It amply suffices to show—if I must speak of you the way the anticommunist speaks of the USSR; alas, the way *you* speak of it—that you have carried through your Thermidorian Reaction. Where is Meursault, Camus? Where is Sisyphus? Where today are those Trotskyites of the heart who preached permanent revolution? Murdered, no doubt, or in exile. A violent, ceremonious dictatorship has established itself within you, basing itself on a fleshless bureaucracy and claiming to enforce the moral law. You wrote that my collaborator "would like us to rebel against everything except the Communist Party and state," but I fear, in my turn, that you rebel more easily against the communist state than against yourself. It seems that the concern in your letter is to place yourself, *as quickly as possible*, beyond debate. You tell us this in the very first lines: it is not your intention to discuss the criticisms made of you nor to argue with your adversary as an equal. Your aim is to *teach*. With the praiseworthy, didactic concern to edify the readers of *Les Temps modernes*, you take Jeanson's article, which you assume to be symptomatic of the evil gnawing away at our societies and make it the subject of a lecture on pathology. It is as though we were in Rembrandt's painting, with you as the doctor and Jeanson the corpse, and you were pointing out his wounds to the astonished public.[2] For it is of no matter to you at all, is it, that the offending article discusses your book? Your book is not at issue; a God guarantees its value. It will merely serve as a touchstone for revealing the guilty man's bad faith. In doing us the honor of participating in this issue of *Les Temps modernes*, you bring a portable pedestal with you. Admittedly, you do change method partway through and abandon your professorial demonstration and your "tense serenity" to launch a vehement attack on me. But you were careful to say you were not defending your cause: What would be the point? Only Jeanson's criticisms—so tendentious that they could not possibly apply—run the risk of infringing inviolable principles and offending venerable personalities. It is these persons and principles you are defending: "It is not me...he has treated unfairly, but our reasons for living and struggling and the legitimate hope we have of overcoming our contradictions. In the event, silence was no longer an option."

But tell me, Camus, by what mystery can your works not be discussed without removing humanity's reasons for living? By what miracle do the objections made against you turn all at once into sacrilege? When *Passage du Malin*[3] received the reception it did, I don't remember François Mauriac writing to *Le Figaro* to say the critics had endangered the Catholic faith. The fact is that you have a mandate: you speak, you say, "in the name of that poverty that produces thousands of advocates and never a single brother." If this is the case, we have to throw in the towel: if it is true that poverty came to you and said, "Go and speak in my name," we cannot but be silent and listen to its voice. Only I admit I don't follow your thinking very clearly: You speak in its name, but are you its advocate, its brother, or its brother advocate? And if you are a brother to the poor, how did you become one? Since it cannot be by ties of blood, it must be a matter of the heart. But no, this cannot be either, since you *are selective about* your poor—I don't think you are a brother to the unemployed communist in Bologna or the wretched day laborer struggling against Bao Dai and the colonialists in Indochina. Did you become a brother to the poor by your condition? You may have been so once but you are no longer; you are middle-class, like Jeanson and me. Is it by devotion, then? But if that devotion is intermittent, how close we are here to Madame Boucicault and her charitable works.[4] And if, to dare to call oneself a brother to the wretched, one must devote every moment of one's life to them, then you are not their brother: whatever your concern, it is not your sole motive and you don't greatly resemble Saint Vincent de Paul or a "little sister of the poor." Their brother? No. You are an advocate who says "These are my brothers" because these are the words most likely to move the jury to tears. You'll appreciate that I've heard too many paternalistic speeches: permit me to distrust that kind of fraternalism. And poverty did not give you any message. I have not the slightest intention, I assure you, of denying you the right to speak of it. But if you do, let it be, like us, at your own risk, accepting in advance the possibility of disavowal.*

But what does all this matter to you? If we take the poor away from you, you will still have plenty of allies. The former Resistance fighters, for example. Jeanson, poor man, did not remotely intend to offend them. He merely wanted to say that French people of our kind were faced with a political choice in 1940 (for we were of the same kind then: the same educational background, principles, and interests). He was not claiming that resistance would have been easy; and, though he had not yet had the benefit of your lessons, he was not unaware of torture, shootings, and deportations, nor of the reprisals that followed resistance attacks and the excruciating dilemmas of conscience they posed for some. He had been told of these things, you may rest assured. But these difficulties emerged out of action itself; to know them, one had already to have committed oneself. If he remains convinced that the decision to resist was not difficult to *make*, he is in no doubt either that it took great physical and moral courage to *sustain* it. Yet he suddenly saw you appealing to the Resistance and—I blush here on your behalf—invoking the dead. "He does not necessarily understand that the Resistance ... never seemed to me either a happy or an easy form of history, anymore than it did to any of those who really suffered from it, who killed or died in it."

No, he does not necessarily understand that: he wasn't in France at the time but in a Spanish concentration camp, a result of trying to join the French Army in Africa.[5] But let us put these badges of honor aside. If Jeanson had lost an arm in the camp in which he almost died, his article would be neither better nor worse than it is. *The Rebel*[6] would be neither better nor worse if you hadn't joined the Resistance or if you had been deported.

But here is another protestor. Jeanson—rightly or wrongly, I shall not get involved—criticized you for a certain ineffectiveness of thought. Immediately summoned up, the old political activist comes

---

*You must have formed the habit of projecting the failings of your thought onto others to believe that Jeanson claimed to speak in the name of the proletariat.

onstage: he is the offended party. You, however, confine yourself to gesturing toward him and informing us that you are tired. Tired of receiving lessons in efficacity, admittedly, but, *above all*, tired of see-ing them given to mature family men by young upstarts. To this, one might, of course, reply that Jeanson was not speaking about political activists, young or old, but that he ventured, as is his right, an appre-ciation of that henceforth *historical* reality termed revolutionary syn-dicalism—for one may judge a movement ineffective while at the same time admiring the courage, spirit of enterprise, self-denial, even efficiency, of those who took part in it. Above all, one might reply that he was speaking about *you* who are not a political activist.

What if I were to quote an old communist activist to you, after making him rich in years and loading him down with the ills best calculated to evoke emotional effect? What if I brought him onstage and had him make the following comments:

> I'm tired of seeing bourgeois like you bent on destroying the Party that is my one hope when they are incapable of putting anything in its place. I don't say the Party is above criticism; I do say you have to earn the right to criticize it. I have had my fill with your moderation, Mediterranean or otherwise, and even less with your Scandinavian republics. Our hopes are not yours. And you may perhaps be my brother—fraternity costs so lit-tle—but certainly not my comrade.

What emotion, eh? I've trumped your activist with an activist-and-a-half. And we would lean, you and I, against the supports that hold up the stage set, receiving the applause of the public, each over-come by a healthy tiredness. But you know very well I do not play that particular game: I have never spoken except in my own name. And then, if I were tired, it seems to me I would be rather ashamed to say so: there are so many people who are more tired. If we are tired, Ca-mus, let's go and rest, since we have the means to. But let us not hope to shake the world by compelling it to take stock of our weariness.

What name am I to give to these methods? Intimidation? Black-mail? At the very least, their aim is to terrorize: the unfortunate critic, surrounded all of a sudden by this host of heroes and martyrs, ends up jumping to attention like a civilian lost among soldiers. But what a confidence trick! Are you really asking us to believe they have lined up behind you? Nonsense, it is you who have put yourself at their head. Have you changed, then, so much? You used to condemn the use of violence everywhere and now, in the name of morality, you subject us to virtuous violence; you used to be the first servant of your moralism and now you are making it serve you.

What is disconcerting in your letter is that it is too well "*written*." I have no quarrel with its ceremoniousness, which comes naturally to you, but I object to the ease with which you wield your indignation. I recognize that our age has its unpleasant aspects and that it must at times be a relief, for red-blooded natures, to bang on the table and shout. But I regret the fact that upon this disorder of the mind, for which there may well be excuses, you have based a rhetorical order. One is not as ready to show indulgence to controlled violence as to the involuntary kind. With what cunning you play the cool customer, so that your outbursts will astonish us the more; how artfully you let your anger show through, only to conceal it immediately beneath a smile that seeks to be falsely reassuring! Is it my fault if these techniques remind me of the law courts! Only the Public Prosecutor knows how to affect irritation at the opportune moment, to retain control of his anger even in the wildest outbursts and to switch, if need be, to a burst of "hearts and flowers." Did the Republic of Beautiful Souls appoint you its Public Accuser?[7]

I am here pulled aside and advised not to accord too much importance to stylistic devices. I would willingly give in, only it is difficult in this letter to distinguish devices in general from bad devices. You call me Monsieur le Directeur (M. Editor), when each of us knows we have been friends for ten years: this is, I agree, merely a device; you address yourself to me when your clear intention is to refute Jeanson: this is a bad device. Is it not your aim to transform your critic into an *object*, into a dead man? You speak *of him* as though of a soup tureen or a mandolin; you never speak *to him*. This indicates that he has placed himself beyond the bounds of the human: by your good offices, the Resistance fighters, the prisoners, the activists, and the poor turn him to stone. At times you succeed in annihilating him altogether, calmly writing "*your* article," as though I were its author. This isn't the first time you have used this trick: Hervé attacked you in a Communist journal[8] and someone mentioned his article in *L'Observateur*, describing it as "noteworthy" but offering no further comment. You asked the editor of that periodical how he could justify the adjective employed by his colleague and explained at length why Hervé's article was anything but "noteworthy." In short, you responded to Hervé but without addressing yourself to him: Does one speak to a communist? But I ask you, Camus, *who* are you to assume such a lofty stance? And what gives you the right to affect a superiority over Jeanson that *no one* grants you? Your literary merits are not in question; it matters little that you are the better writer and he the better thinker, or the other way about: the superiority you accord yourself, which gives you the right not to treat Jeanson as a human being, must be a *racial* superiority. Has Jeanson, by his criticisms, perhaps indicated that he differs from you in the way ants differ from human beings? Is there, perhaps, a racism of moral beauty? You have a handsome spirit and his is ugly: communication is not possible between you. And it is here that the device becomes intolerable because, to justify your attitude, you have to discover some blackness in his soul. And to discover it, isn't the easiest method first to put it there? For, what is this about? Jeanson didn't like your book. He said so and you didn't like it: so far, then, nothing exceptional. You wrote to criticize his criticism: you cannot be blamed for this; Monsieur de Montherlant does it every day.[9] You could go much further. You could say he had not understood a word and that I was a blockhead. You could cast aspersions on the intelligence of the whole editorial board of *Les Temps modernes*: that's part of the game. But when you write, "Your collaborator would like us to rebel against everything except the Communist Party and state," I confess I feel uneasy: I thought I was faced with a man of letters and I am, in fact, dealing with an investigating magistrate handling the case on the basis of tendentious police reports. And if only you would be happy just to call him a "communist mole," but you have to make him a liar and a traitor: "The author *has pretended* to mistake what he has read ... I found (in the article) neither generosity nor honesty, but the *futile desire to misrepresent* a position he could not express without putting himself in a situation where he would have to debate it properly." You propose to reveal the (evidently hidden) "intention" that leads him to "practice omission and make a travesty of the book's argument . . . to make you say the sky is black when you say it is blue, etc.," to avoid the real problems, to conceal from the whole of France the existence of Russian concentration camps which your book revealed. What intention? Well, let's take a look! The intention to show that any idea that is not Marxist is reactionary. And why, when all is said and done, does he do that? Here you are a little less clear-cut, but, if I understand you correctly, this shameful Marxist is afraid of the light. He was attempting with his clumsy hands to block all the openings of your thought, to halt the blinding rays of the obvious. For, if he had understood you fully, he *could no longer* call himself a Marxist. The unfortunate man believed it permissible to be both communist and bourgeois: he was hedging his bets. You show him that he must choose: join the Party or become bourgeois like you.* But that is precisely what he will not see. Here, then, are the findings of the investigation: criminal intent, deliberate misrepresentation of another's thought, bad faith, repeated lies. You can no doubt imagine the mixture of stupefaction and laughter with which those who know Jeanson and Jeanson's sincerity, uprightness, scruples, and concern for the truth will greet this indictment.

But what will be most appreciated, I suspect, is the passage in your letter when you invite us to come clean: "I would find it normal and almost courageous if, tackling this problem openly, you were to justify the existence of these camps. What is abnormal and betrays embarrassment is that you do not mention them at all." Here we are at the Quai des Orfèvres,[10] the cop is pacing up and down and his shoes are squeaking, as they do in the cinema: "We know the whole story, I tell you. Saying nothing isn't helping your case. Come on, admit you were involved. You knew these camps, didn't you? Just say you did and it will all be over. The court will take a favorable view of your confession." In heaven's name, Camus, how *serious* you are and, to employ one of your

---

*For you are bourgeois, Camus, like me; what else could you be?

own words, how frivolous! And what if you were wrong? What if your book merely revealed your philosophical incompetence? What if it were put together from secondhand information, hastily cobbled together? What if it merely afforded the privileged a good conscience, as might be attested by the critic who wrote the other day, "With Albert Camus, revolt is changing sides"? And what if your reasoning were not so very correct? If your ideas were vague and banal? And if Jeanson had quite simply been struck by the poverty of those ideas? If, far from obscuring your radiantly plain facts, he had been forced to turn on the lights to make out the contours of weak, obscure, garbled ideas? I do not say that this is the case, but could you not conceive *for one moment* that it might be? Are you so afraid of contradiction? Must you discredit all those who look you in the face as soon as you can? Can you accept only bowed heads? Was it not possible for you to defend your argument and maintain its correctness, while understanding that the other man thought it was wrong? Why do you, who defend *risk* in history, refuse it in literature? Why do you have to be defended by a whole universe of inviolable values instead of fighting against us—or with us—without divine intervention? You once wrote: "We are stifled among people who believe they are absolutely right, either in their political machines or their ideas." And it was true. But I'm very much afraid you may have gone over to the side of the stiflers and are abandoning forever your old friends, the stifled.

What really is too much is that you resort to the practice we heard criticized quite recently during a public meeting in which you took part—a practice termed, I believe, *conflation*. In certain political trials, if there are several defendants, the judge combines the charges so as to be able to combine the sentences: of course, this happens only in totalitarian states. Yet this is the procedure you have chosen. From one end of your indictment to the other, you pretend to confuse me with Jeanson. And how do you do this? It is simple, though it needed some thinking out: by an artifice of language, you disorient the reader to the point where he no longer knows which of us you are talking about. Step one: I am the editor of the journal, so it's me you are addressing—an irreproachable procedure. Step two: you invite me to acknowledge I am responsible for the articles published in it—I agree that this is the case. Step three: it *therefore* follows that I approve of Jeanson's attitude and, moving on quickly, that his attitude is also mine. Once this is established, it matters little which of us held the pen—in any event, the article is mine. Skillful use of the personal pronoun will complete the conflation: "*Your* article . . . *You* should have . . . *You* were entitled . . . *You* were not entitled . . . As soon as *you* spoke . . ." Jeanson, you imply, was merely embroidering on a canvas prepared by me. There is a double advantage here: you present him as my scribe and henchman, and there you have your revenge. And, then, here am I, a criminal in my turn: I am the one insulting the activists, the Resistance fighters, and the poor; I am the one who covers his ears when the Soviet camps are mentioned; I am the one seeking to hide your light under a bushel. One example will suffice to expose the method here: it will be clear that the "offense," which loses all substance if ascribed to its true author, turns into a crime when the charge is leveled against the person who did not commit it.

When you write, "No review of my book can leave aside the fact (of the Russian camps)," you are addressing Jeanson alone. It is the critic you are taking issue with for not speaking, *in his article*, about the concentration camps. Perhaps you are right. Perhaps Jeanson could reply that it is farcical to have the author decide what the critic is to say; moreover, you don't speak much of the camps in your book and it's not easy to see why you suddenly demand their being taken into consideration, unless some poorly primed informers have led you to believe you would thereby be embarrassing us. In any event, this is a legitimate debate that you and Jeanson could have. But when you then write, "*You* retain the relative right to ignore the fact of the camps in the USSR, so long as you do not tackle the questions raised by revolutionary ideology in general and by Marxism in particular, *you* lose it if you tackle those questions, and *you* tackle them *by speaking* about my book," or alternatively: "I would find it normal . . . if *you* justified the existence of the camps," then it is *me* you are addressing. Well, let me reply that these interrogations are deceitful: for you take advantage of the undeniable fact that Jeanson—*as was his right*—did not, in reviewing your book, speak of the Soviet camps, so that you may insinuate that I, the editor of a journal that claims to be politically committed, have never tackled the question—something which, if it were the case, might be said to be a serious offense against honesty. Only it just so happens that it is untrue: a few days after Rousset's declarations, we devoted several articles to the camps, together with an editorial to which I fully subscribed.[11] And, if you compare the dates, you'll see that the issue was put together *before* Rousset's declarations. But that matters little: I merely wanted to show you that we raised the question of the camps and took a stand at the very moment when French public opinion was discovering them. We returned to the subject a few months later *in another editorial* and clarified our point of view in articles and notes. The existence of these camps may enrage and horrify us; it may be that we are obsessed with them, but why should it *embarrass us*? Have I ever backed away when it came to saying what I thought about the communist attitude? And if I am a "crypto-communist," a shameful fellow traveler, why do they hate me and not you? But let us not boast about the hatreds we inspire: I will tell you honestly that I deeply regret this hostility; sometimes I might even go so far as to envy the profound indifference they show toward you. But what can I do about it, except precisely no longer say what I believe to be true? What are you claiming then, when you write, "You retain the relative right to ignore..." etc.? Either you are insinuating that Jeanson does not exist and is one of my pseudonyms, which is absurd, or you are claiming I've never said a word about the camps, which is slanderous. Yes, Camus, like you I find these camps unacceptable, but I also find unacceptable the use the "so-called bourgeois press" makes of them each day. I do not say that the Madagascan takes precedence over the Turkoman; I say we must not use the sufferings inflicted on the Turkoman to justify those *we* inflict on the Madagascan.

I have seen anticommunists delight in the existence of these jails, I have seen them use them to salve their consciences; and I did not have the impression they were helping the Turkomans, but, rather, exploiting their misery in the same way as the USSR exploited their labor. We might truly term this full employment for the Turkomans. But let's be serious, Camus: tell me, if you will, what sentiment Rousset's revelations could have stirred in an anticommunist's heart. Despair? Affliction? Shame at being human? Nonsense. It's difficult for a

Frenchman to put himself in the shoes of a Turkoman, to feel sympathy for that abstract being, the Turkoman, when seen from France. At best, I will concede that, among the best of Frenchmen, the memory of the German camps reawakened a kind of very spontaneous horror. And then, of course, fear too. But, don't you see, in the absence of any relationship with the Turkoman, what must provoke indignation, and perhaps despair, was the idea that a socialist government, supported by an army of bureaucrats, could have systematically reduced human beings to slavery? Now *that*, Camus, cannot affect the anticommunist, who *already believed the USSR capable of anything.* The only sentiment this information provoked in him was—and it pains me to say this—*joy*. Joy because he had, at last, his *proof* and that now "we should really see something." The point now was to act not on the workers—the anticommunist isn't so foolish—but on all the good people who remained "on the Left"; they had to be intimidated, stricken with terror. If they opened their mouths to complain about some outrage, it was closed immediately with a "What about the camps?" People were *commanded* to denounce the camps on pain of collusion with them. An excellent method, in which the unfortunates either offended the communists or were made to collude in "the greatest crime on earth." It was around this time that I began to find these blackmailers despicable. For, in my view, the scandal of the camps puts us all on our mettle. You as much as me. And everyone else: the Iron Curtain is merely a mirror and the two halves of the world reflect each other. To every turn of the screw *here* there is a corresponding turn *over there*; we both turn the screw and feel its bite. A tougher line in the United States, which expresses itself in a renewed outbreak of witch-hunting,[12] causes a harder line on the part of the Russians, which will perhaps be expressed in increased arms production and a higher number of forced laborers. The opposite may, of course, be true too. Those who condemn today must know that our situation will force them tomorrow to do worse things than they have condemned; and when I see this joke scrawled on the walls of Paris—"Take your vacations in the USSR, land of liberty" over gray shadowy figures depicted behind bars—it isn't the Russians I find disgusting. Don't misunderstand me, Camus: I know you have on a hundred occasions denounced and fought Franco's tyranny or the colonial policy of our government with all the powers available to you; you have won the *relative* right to speak of the Soviet concentration camps. But I shall make two criticisms of your position: you were fully entitled to mention the camps in a serious work, the aim of which is to provide us with an explanation of our times; indeed, it was your *duty*; what seems unacceptable to me is that you use this today as a piece of claptrap and that you, like the others, exploit the Turkoman and the Kurd the more surely to crush a critic who did not praise you.

And then I'm sorry you produce your sledgehammer argument to justify a quietism that refuses to distinguish between the different masters. For, as you say yourself, it is the same thing to treat all masters as the same as to treat all slaves as the same. And if you do not make any distinction between slaves, you condemn yourself to have only a theoretical sympathy for them. Particularly as it often happens that the "slave" is the ally of those you call the masters. This explains the embarrassment you get into over the war in Indochina. If we are to apply your principles, then the Vietnamese have been colonized and hence are slaves, but they are Communists and hence are tyrants. You criticize the European proletariat for not having publicly expressed disapproval of the Soviets, but you also criticize the governments of Europe because they are going to admit Spain into UNESCO; in this case I can see only one solution for you: the Galapagos Islands. It seems to me, by contrast, that the only way to help the slaves over there is to take the side of the slaves over here.

I was going to close on this, but, rereading your letter, I get the impression that your indictment claims also to take in our ideas.* It would seem, in fact, that in employing the words "unbridled freedom," you have our conception of human freedom in your sights.[13] Should I insult you by believing these to be your words? No, you are incapable of such an error; you have no doubt picked up the words

---

*It isn't my place to defend those of Marx, but allow me to tell you that the dilemma into which you have boxed those ideas (either Marx's "prophecies" are true or Marxism is merely a method) misses the whole of Marxist philosophy and everything in it that constitutes for me (who am not a Marxist) its profound truth.

"unbridled freedom" from the study by Troisfontaines.[14] Well, I shall at least share with Hegel the distinction of not having been read by you. But what a bad habit you have of not going back to sources! Yet *you know very well* that only the real forces of this world can be "bridled" and that the physical action of an object is restrained by acting on one of the factors affecting it. But freedom is not a force: this is not my decision; it is part of its very definition. Freedom either exists or does not, but, if it does, it lies outside the sequence of cause and effect; it is of another order. Would you not laugh if we spoke of Epicurus's unrestrained *clinamen*? Since that philosopher, the conception of determinism and, as a consequence, of freedom has become a little more complicated, but the idea of a break, a disconnection, or "solution of continuity" remains. I hardly dare advise you to refer here to *Being and Nothingness*;[15] to read it would seem to you pointlessly arduous: you detest difficulties of thought and are quick to decree that there is nothing to understand, so as to avoid in advance the criticism that you have not understood. The fact remains that in that book I explained precisely the conditions for this break. And if you had spent a few minutes reflecting on someone else's ideas, you would have seen that freedom cannot be restrained or bridled: it has neither wheels nor legs, nor jaws between which to put a bridle, and, since it is determined by the undertaking in which it is involved, it finds its limits in the positive, but necessarily *finite*, character of that undertaking.

We are on a journey, we have to choose: the *project* brings its own enlightenment and gives the situation its meaning, but, by the same token, it is merely one particular way of transcending that situation—of understanding it. Our project is ourselves: in the light of it, our relation to the world becomes clearer; the goals and the tools appear that reflect back to us both the world's hostility and our own aim. Having said this, you are quite at liberty to term "unbridled" the freedom that can alone ground *your own demands*, Camus (for if human beings are not free, how can they "demand to have a meaning"? Only, you don't like to think about that). But there will be no more sense to this than if you spoke of esophagus-less freedom or freedom without hydrochloric acid, and you merely have revealed that, like so many, you confuse politics and philosophy. Unbridled: of course. Without

224 · JEAN-PAUL SARTRE

police or the courts. If we grant the freedom to consume alcoholic
drink without setting limits, what will become of the virtuous wife of
the drunkard? But French Revolutionary thinking is clearer on this
than yours: the limit of one right (that is, of one freedom) is another
right (that is, another freedom) and not some "human nature" or
other; for nature, whether "human" or not, can crush human beings
but it cannot reduce them to the status of object; if man is an object,
he is so for another man. And it is these two ideas—which are, I agree,
difficult—that man is free and that man is the being by which man
becomes an object, that define our present status and enable us to understand *oppression*.

You had believed—on whose authority?—that I first ascribed a
paradisiacal freedom to my fellow creatures so as subsequently to clap
them in irons. I am so far from this conception that I see around me
only freedoms *already enslaved*, attempting to wrest themselves from
their *congenital* slavery. Our freedom today is merely *the free choice to
struggle to become free*. And the paradoxical aspect of this formula en-
capsulates the paradox of our *historical* condition. It is not a question,
as you see, of *caging* my contemporaries: they are already in the cage;
it is a matter, rather, of uniting with them to break down the bars.

For we too, Camus, are committed, and if you really want to prevent a popular movement from degenerating into tyranny, don't begin
by condemning it out of hand and threatening to withdraw into the
desert, particularly as your deserts are only ever a less frequented part
of our cage. To earn the right to influence human beings in struggle,
you have first to take part in their fight; you have first to accept a lot of
things if you want to try to change a small number. "History" presents
few more desperate situations than ours—this is what excuses the
pompous prophecies. But when a man sees the present struggles
merely as the imbecilic duel between two equally despicable monsters,
I contend that that man has already left us: he has gone off alone to his
corner and is sulking; far from seeming to me loftily to judge and
dominate an age on which he deliberately turns his back, I see him as
entirely conditioned by it and clinging obstinately to the refusal inspired in him by a very historical resentment. You pity me for having
a bad conscience and that is not the case, but, even if I were entirely

poisoned by shame, I would feel less alienated and more open than you: for, to keep your conscience in good order you need to condemn; you need a guilty party: if not yourself, then the universe. You pronounce your verdicts and the world responds with not a word; but your condemnations cancel themselves out on contact with it and you have perpetually to begin again. If you stopped, you might see yourself; you have condemned yourself to condemn, Sisyphus.

For us you were—and can again be tomorrow—the admirable conjunction of a person, an action, and a body of writings. That was in 1945: we discovered Camus, the Resistance fighter, as we had discovered Camus, the author of *The Stranger*.[16] And when we compared the editor of the underground *Combat* with that Meursault who carried honesty to the point of refusing to say that he loved either his mother or his mistress and whom our society condemned to death, when we knew, above all, that you had not stopped being either of these, the apparent contradiction increased our knowledge of ourselves and the world, and you were little short of exemplary. For you summed up the conflicts of the age in yourself and transcended them through your fiery determination to live them out. You were a *person*, the most complex and richest of persons: the latest and timeliest of the heirs of Chateaubriand and the resolute defender of a social cause. You had every good fortune and all the qualities, since you combined a sense of greatness with a passionate taste for beauty, a *joie de vivre* with an awareness of death. Even before the war, and against the bitter experience of what you call the *absurd*, you had chosen to defend yourself by scorn, but you were of the opinion that "every negation contains a flowering of *yeses*" and you tried to find the consent that underlay every rejection, "to hallow the accord between love and revolt." In your view, man is only entirely himself when he is happy. And "what is happiness but the simple accord between a being and the existence he leads. And what more legitimate accord can bind man to life than the twofold consciousness of his desire to endure and his mortal destiny?" Happiness was neither entirely a state nor entirely an act, but that tension between the forces of death and the forces of life, between acceptance and refusal, by which man defines the *present*—that is to say, both the moment and eternity—and turns into himself. Thus, when

you described one of those privileged moments that achieve a temporary accord between man and nature and which, from Rousseau to
Breton, have provided our literature with one of its major themes, you
were able to introduce into it an entirely new note of *morality*. To be
happy is to do one's job as a human being; you showed us "the duty of
being happy." And that duty merged with the affirmation that man is
the only being in the world who has a meaning, "because he is the only
creature to demand that he should." The experience of happiness,
similar to Bataille's "Torment,"[17] but richer and more complex, made
you stand up to an absent God as a reproach but also as a challenge:
"Man must affirm justice in order to combat eternal injustice, and create happiness to protest against the universe of misery." The universe
of misery is not *social* or, at least, not primarily so: it is indifferent,
empty Nature, in which man is alien and condemned to die; in a
word, it is "the eternal silence of the Divinity." So your experience
closely combined the ephemeral and the permanent. Aware of being
perishable, you wanted to deal only with truths "that must necessarily
rot." Your body was one of those. You rejected the fraudulence of the
Soul and the Idea. But since, in your own words, injustice is *eternal*—
that is to say, since the absence of God is a constant throughout the
changing course of history—the immediate relation, begun ever
anew, of the man who demands that he *have* a meaning (that is to say,
demands to be given one) to this God who eternally remains silent, is
itself transcendent with respect to history. The tension by which man
realizes himself—which is, at the same time, intuitive enjoyment of
being—is, therefore, a veritable conversion that wrests him from daily
"agitation" and "historicity" and reconciles him at last with his condition. We can go no further; no progress can have its place in this instantaneous tragedy. As an absurdist before his time, Mallarmé wrote
"(The drama) is resolved immediately in the time it takes to show the
defeat that occurs with lightning speed," and he seems to me to have
provided in advance the key to your theatrical works when he writes
"The Hero *releases*—the (maternal) hymn that creates him and is restored in the Theater which this was—from the Mystery in which
that hymn was shrouded."[18] In short, you remain within our great
classical tradition which, since Descartes and with the exception of

Pascal, is entirely hostile to history. But you, at last, achieved the synthesis between aesthetic pleasure, desire, happiness, and heroism, between satisfied contemplation and duty, between Gidean plenitude and Baudelairean dissatisfaction. You topped off Ménalque's immoralism[19] with an austere moralism; the content was not changed.

> There is only one love in this world. Embracing a woman's body also means holding in your arms this strange joy which descends from sky to sea. In a moment, when I throw myself down among the wormwood plants to bring their scent into my body, I shall know, whatever prejudice may say, that I am fulfilling a truth which is that of the sun and which will also be that of my death.[20]

But since this truth belongs to everyone, since its extreme singularity is precisely what makes it universal, since you were breaking open the shell of the pure present in which Nathanaël[21] seeks God and opening it to the "profundity of the world," that is to say, to death, then at the end of this somber, solitary pleasure, you rediscovered the universality of an ethics and human solidarity. Nathanaël is no longer alone; he is "conscious and proud of sharing" this love of life, stronger than death, "with a whole race." It all ends badly, of course: the world swallows up the irreconciled libertine. And you liked to cite this passage from *Obermann* : "Let us go down resisting, and if nothingness is to be our fate, let it not be a just one."[22]

You do not deny it then. You did not reject history because you have suffered from it and discovered its face to be horrendous. You rejected it before you had any experience of it, because our culture rejects it and because you located human values in man's struggle "against heaven." You chose and created yourself as you are by meditating on the misfortunes and anxieties that fell to you personally, and the solution you found for them is a bitter wisdom that strives to deny time.

However, with the coming of war you devoted yourself unreservedly to the Resistance; you fought an austere fight that offered no fame or elevation; the dangers incurred hardly brought one any glory: worse, one ran the risk of being demeaned and debased. That effort, always painful and often solitary, *necessarily* presented itself as a *duty*. And your first contact with history assumed for you the aspect of *sacrifice*. You wrote as much, in fact, and you have said that you were fighting "for that nuance that separates sacrifice from mysticism." Don't misunderstand me: if I say "your first contact with history," it is not to imply that I had another and that it was better. Around that time, we intellectuals had only that contact; and if I refer to it as *yours*, it is because you experienced it more deeply and totally than many of us, myself included. The fact remains that the circumstances of this battle entrenched you in the belief that one must sometimes pay one's tribute to history to have the right, later on, to return to the real duties. You accused the Germans of tearing you away from your battle with heaven to force you to take part in the temporal combats of men: "For so many years you have tried to *bring me into history*." And, further on, you write: "You did the necessary, *we entered history*; and for five years, it was no longer possible to enjoy the birds' singing."*[23] The history in question was the war; for you that was *other people's madness*. It does not create, it destroys: it prevents the grass from growing, the birds from singing, and human beings from making love. It so happened, in fact, that external circumstances seemed to confirm your point of view: *in peacetime* you were fighting a timeless battle against the injustice of our destiny and the Nazis had, in your view, sided with that injustice. In collusion with the blind forces of the universe, they were trying to destroy humanity. You fought, as you put it, "to save the *idea* of mankind."[24] In short, it was not your intention to "make history," as Marx says, but to prevent it from being made. Proof lies in the fact that, after the war, you merely had in mind a return of the status quo: "Our condition [continued to be] desperate." The meaning of the Allied victory seemed to you to be "the acquisition of two or three nuances that will perhaps have no other use than to help some of us to die better."

After serving your five years with history, you thought you (and the whole of humanity with you) could return to the despair in which man must find his happiness, and go back to "proving that we did not deserve so much injustice" (in whose eyes?) by resuming the desperate

*My emphasis.

battle human beings wage "against their repellent destinies." How we loved you in those days. We too were neophytes of history and endured it with repugnance, not understanding that the war of 1940 was merely one mode of historicity—neither more nor less so than the years preceding it. When we thought of you, we thought of Malraux's phrase, "May victory go to those who made war without liking it," and we felt a little sorry for ourselves as we repeated it; at that time we were under threat, like you and in you, without our realizing it.

It often happens that cultures produce their richest works when they are about to disappear, and those works are the fruits of the lethal marriage of the old values and the new ones that seem to render them fertile but actually kill them off. In the synthesis you were attempting, the happiness and the yea-saying came from our old humanism, but the revolt and the despair were intruders. They came from outside, from an outside where persons unknown looked on at our spiritual festivities with hatred in their eyes. You had borrowed that gaze from them to turn it on our cultural heritage; it was their simple, stark existence that *threw our tranquil pleasures into question*; of course, the defiance of destiny, the revolt against absurdity all came from you or passed through you: but, thirty or forty years earlier, you would have been made to drop these ill-bred ways and would have joined the ranks of the aesthetes or the Church. Your revolt assumed the importance it did only because it was prompted in you by this obscure crowd: you barely had time to deflect it against the heavens, where it vanished. And the moral demands you brought to light were simply the idealization of very real demands welling up around you that you had seized on. The equilibrium you achieved between these things could happen only once, for a single moment, in a single person: you had had the good fortune that the common struggle against the Germans symbolized for you, and for us, the unity of all human beings against inhuman fate. By choosing injustice, the German had, of his own volition, ranged himself among the blind forces of Nature and you were able, in *The Plague*,[25] to have his part played by microbes without anyone realizing the mystification. In short, you were, for a few years, the symbol and evidence of solidarity between the classes. This is also what the Resistance seemed to be and it is what you demonstrated in your earliest works: "Men rediscover their solidarity in order to enter the struggle against their repellent destinies."

In this way, a combination of circumstances, one of those rare concordances that, for a time, turn a life into the image of a truth, enabled you to conceal from yourself that man's struggle against Nature is both the cause and effect of another struggle, just as old and even more ruthless: the struggle of man against man. You were rebelling against death but, in the belts of iron that ring our cities, other people were rebelling against the social conditions that increase the mortality rate. When a child died, you condemned the absurdity of the world and that deaf, blind God you had created so as to be able to spit in His face. But the child's father, if he were a laborer or unemployed, condemned human beings: he knew very well that the absurdity of our condition isn't the same in Passy as it is in Boulogne-Billancourt.[26] And, in the end, the microbes were almost hidden from him by human beings: in the poor districts, the child mortality rate is twice what it is in the wealthy suburbs and, since a different distribution of income could save them,* half of the deaths, among the poor, seem like executions, with the microbe merely playing the hangman's final role.

You wanted to achieve—within yourself, through yourself—happiness for everyone by way of a *moral* tension. The somber masses we were beginning to discover called on us to give up our happiness so that they could become a little less unhappy. Suddenly, the Germans no longer mattered. It was almost as though they had never mattered. We had thought there had been only one way of resisting; we discovered that there were two ways of *seeing* the Resistance. And while you still personified the immediate past for us and were perhaps even the coming man of the near future, for ten million French people who did not recognize their only too real anger in your ideal rebellion, you had already become one of the privileged. The death, life, earth, rebellion, and God you spoke of, the "yes" and the "no" and the "love" were, they told you, mere aristocratic amusements. To others, they seemed like something out of a circus. You had written: "Only one thing is more tragic than suffering and that is the life of a happy man." And: "a cer-

---

*This is not entirely exact. Some are doomed come what may.

tain continuity in despair can give birth to joy." And: "I was not sure that this splendor of the world was not [the justification] of all men who know that an extreme point of poverty always connects us back to the luxury and riches of the world."[27] And admittedly, being like you, one of the privileged, I understood what you meant and I believe you have paid your dues to be able to say it. I imagine you have been closer to a certain kind of death and deprivation than many people, and I think you must have known genuine poverty, if not destitution. Coming from your pen, these lines *do not have* the meaning they would in a book by Mauriac or Montherlant. Moreover, when you wrote them, they seemed natural. But the key thing today is that *they no longer do*: we know that it takes, if not wealth, then at least culture, the inestimable and unjust riches of culture, to find luxury in the depths of deprivation. One feels that the circumstances of your life—even the most painful of them—have chosen you to attest that personal salvation was accessible to all; and the predominant thought in everyone's heart, a menacing, hate-filled thought, is that this is possible only for a few. A hate-filled thought, but what can we do about that? Hatred gnaws away at everything. Even in you, who tried not even to hate the Germans, there is a hatred of God that shows through in your books, and it has been said that you are even more of an "anti-theist" than an atheist. The whole value that oppressed persons may still have in their own eyes, they put into the hatred they bear to other human beings. And their friendship for their comrades also involves the hatred they bear for their enemies; neither your books nor your example can do anything for them; you teach an art of living, a "science of life," you teach us to rediscover our bodies, but their bodies when they get them back in the evening—after having them stolen from them all day—are merely great wretched things that encumber and humiliate them. These men are *made* by other men; their number-one enemy is man, and if the strange nature they find in the factory and, the building site still speaks to them of man, this is because it is men who have transformed these places into prisons for them.

What options remained open to you? To modify yourself in part, so as to retain some of your old loyalties, while satisfying the demands of these oppressed masses. You would perhaps have done this, had not their representatives insulted you, as is their habit. You stopped dead the slide that was taking place within you and insisted, with renewed defiance, on demonstrating to everyone the union of men in the face of death and the solidarity between classes, when the classes had already resumed their struggles before your very eyes. Thus, what for a time had been an *exemplary reality* became the utterly empty affirmation of an *ideal*—all the more so as this false solidarity had changed into struggle even in your own heart. You found history to be in the wrong and, rather than interpret its course, you preferred to see it as just one more absurdity. Basically, you resumed your initial attitude. You borrowed some sort of idea of the "divinization of man" from Malraux, Carrouges, and twenty other writers and, condemning the human race, you took your stand alongside it, but outside its ranks, like the last of the Mohicans.

Your personality, real and vital so long as it was fed by events, is becoming a mirage. In 1944 it was the future; in 1952 it is the past. And what seems to you the most intolerable injustice is that all this is happening to you from outside and without your having changed. It seems to you that the world offers the same riches as it did in the past and that it is human beings who no longer wish to see them. Well, try holding out your hand and you will see if it doesn't all vanish: even Nature has changed its meaning because the relationship of human beings to that Nature has changed. The memories and the language you are left with are increasingly abstract; you are only half living among us and you are tempted to leave us altogether to withdraw into some solitude where you can rediscover the drama that was supposed to be that of mankind and is no longer even your own—in other words, into a society that has remained at a lower level of technical civilization. What is happening to you is, in a sense, quite unjust. But, in another, it is pure justice: you had to change if you wanted to remain yourself and you were afraid of changing. If you find me cruel, have no fear: I shall speak of myself shortly, and in this same tone. There is no point trying to hit back at me; but, trust me, I shall see to it that I pay for all this. For you are absolutely unbearable, but you are, nonetheless, by force of circumstance, my neighbor.

Though engaged, like you, in history, I do not see it as you do. No doubt it has this absurd, fearful appearance for those who view it from Hades: this is because they no longer have anything in common with the human beings who are making it. And if it were a history of ants or bees, I am sure we would see it as a silly, macabre succession of crime, mockery, and murder. But if we were ants, perhaps we would take a different view. Until I reread your *Letters to a German Friend*, I did not understand your dilemma—"Either history has a meaning or it does not," etc.—but it all became clear to me when I found there this remark which you address to the Nazi soldier, "For years you have been trying to get me to enter history." "Good Lord," I said to myself, "since he believes he stands *outside* history, no wonder he lays down his conditions before coming *inside*." Like a girl testing the water with her toe and asking, "Is it warm?," you regard history warily. You stick in a finger, then very quickly pull it out again, asking, "Has it a meaning?" You didn't hesitate in 1941, but then you were being asked to make a sacrifice. It was quite simply a question of preventing the Hitlerian madness from smashing a world where solitary elation was still possible for some, and you were willing to pay the price for your future moments of elation.

Things are different today. It is no longer a question of *defending the status quo* but of changing it. This is something you will agree to only with the firmest of guarantees. And if I thought, as you do, that history is a pool full of dirt and blood, I would do as you do, I imagine, and look twice before diving in. But let us suppose that I am already in it; let us suppose that, from my point of view, your very aloofness is proof of your historicity. Suppose you receive the answer Marx would give you: "History does nothing... It is men, real living men who do everything; history is merely the activity of human beings pursuing their own ends." If this is true, the person who believes he is moving away from history will cease to share his contemporaries' ends and will be sensitive only to the absurdity of human restlessness. But if he rails against that restlessness, he will, against his will, re-enter the historical cycle, for he will involuntarily provide the side that is on the ideological defensive (that is to say, the one whose culture is dying) with arguments for discouraging the other. The person who, by contrast, subscribes to the aims of concrete human beings will be forced to choose his friends because, in a society torn apart by civil war, one can neither accept nor reject everyone's aims at the same time. But, as soon as he chooses, everything acquires a meaning: he knows why the enemies resist and why he fights. For only in historical action is the understanding of history vouchsafed. "Does history have a meaning?" you ask. "Does it have a purpose?" In my view, it is the question that is meaningless. For history, considered apart from those who make it, is merely an abstract, static concept, and we can neither say that it has a purpose nor that it does not. And the problem is not one of *knowing* its purpose but of *giving* it one.

Moreover, no one acts *solely* with an eye to history. Human beings are, in fact, engaged in short-term projects, illuminated by distant hopes. And there is nothing absurd about these projects: on the one hand, we have Tunisians rising up against the colonial power, on the other, miners striking for better conditions or on grounds of solidarity. Whether there are values transcendent to history is not the question: we shall merely note that *if there are* such values, they manifest themselves through human actions that are, by definition, historical. And this contradiction is essential to human beings: they become historical through pursuing the eternal, and discover universal values in the concrete action they take to achieve a particular outcome.

If you say this world is unjust, you have lost the game: you are already outside, comparing a justiceless world to a contentless justice. But you will discover justice in every effort you make to order your undertaking, to divide tasks between your comrades, to submit yourself to discipline or to apply it. And Marx never said history would have an end: How could he have? You might as well say that men would one day have no objectives. He merely spoke of an end to prehistory or, in other words, of an objective that would be achieved within history itself and then left behind, as all objectives are. It is not a matter of establishing whether history has a meaning and whether we accept to participate in it, but, given that we are in it up to our necks, of trying to give it what seems to us the best meaning, by not refusing our participation, no matter how small, in any of the concrete actions that require it.

Terror is an abstract violence. You became a terrorist and violent when history—which you rejected—rejected you in turn: this is because you were merely, then, the abstraction of a rebel. Your distrust of human beings led you to presume that any accused person was, *first and foremost*, a guilty one: hence your police methods with Jeanson. Your morality turned first into moralism; today it is merely literature; tomorrow it will perhaps be immorality. What will become of us I do not know: perhaps we shall end up on the same side, perhaps not. The times are hard and confused. In any event, it has been good to be able to tell you what I have been thinking. The journal is open to you if you want to reply, but I shall make no further reply to you. I have said what you were for me and what you are at present. But, whatever you may do or say in return, I refuse to fight with you. I hope our silence will lead to this polemic being forgotten.

From

THE GHOST OF STALIN

AFTER the crushing of the insurrection, on November 16, over Radio Budapest, a representative of the Factory Committees could be heard asking his comrades to go back to work conditionally. He spoke as a conqueror, with an admirable pride: they would stop the strike to come to the aid of the inhabitants of Budapest; they would start it again at once if the demands of the strikers were not satisfied. And he had this to say, in a building crammed full of cops, in the middle of a ravaged city where Russian tanks were patrolling: "The whole world knows our strength." We know it, it's true: 1.6 million workers are holding in check the most powerful of armies. Do people believe that those men would not have been capable by themselves of stamping out the counterrevolution? Of course it was necessary to take risks, to organize, to define a policy, to seek alliances: they were ready to do it. Was it then so mad a project? And which was better for the Country of the Workers: to gut a capital, decimate a population, ruin an economy already near bankruptcy, or to place confidence in a conscious, armed proletariat? A struggle had to be anticipated, yes, but it was a *true* struggle, that of the real forces of Hungary; the class conflict would have broken out in the open! Doubtless, but what is gained by hiding it? The USSR would have looked on, helpless, at the crushing of the forces of the left. Why? Couldn't it favor them? Grant substantial aid to a government in which the communists were strongly represented? Nothing is served by arresting the free develop-

ment of a country by force: it is up to it to overcome its own contradictions. But, one will say, the émigrés? the commandos? the West?
Come on! The USSR has just crushed the Hungarian resistance and
not one Western country budged. A distinguished speaker was saying
just the other day, at the Peace Movement: "Why bother with Hungary? No one will wage war for the Hungarians." This speaker was a
progressive and the communists applauded him. So? Do people believe that the USSR was unable to negotiate with the United States?
To compel the total neutrality of the West in exchange for its own? To
declare that it would hold the Western powers responsible for the
armed groups that would be organized on their territory and which
would try to cross the Hungarian border? To proclaim that it would
send two hundred thousand "volunteers"—as it did for Suez—in case
armed émigrés entered Hungary? The Western blabbermouths got
themselves detested by the Hungarians whom they pushed to revolt
only to abandon them afterward to their fate: however strong the
anti-Sovietism, couldn't the USSR count on the anti-Westernism? By
withdrawing its troops, wouldn't it have regained—at least in part—
the ground lost? Ah! that was taking risks. Yes. But does one imagine,
by chance, that one doesn't take greater ones still by having recourse
to force?

No one has the right to say that the events in Hungary made the
intervention inevitable. No one; not even those who decided it. Besides, the blunders and the repentances, the false starts, the returns,*
this strange paralysis of troops in the face of the strike, the announce-
ment of deportations broadcast by Radio Budapest itself and denied
the next day, the strange coming and going of trains crammed with
prisoners who were being taken toward the border "to be interrogated"
and subsequently brought back, the "shift to the right" of the Kadar

---

*Negotiations were still going on in Budapest between Russian and Hungarian
military elements when the order to attack was given. Our anticommunists didn't
miss this chance to stress Soviet perfidy. I don't believe in this perfidy: and first of
all the very power of the means brought into play made it unnecessary. It seems
rather that different groups in the Kremlin were seeking the solution to the Hungarian affair at the same time and by independent paths. Finally, the partisans of
repression won out.

government that seemed for a moment to embrace all Nagy's concessions (except neutralization), then its sudden hardening, the deportation of Nagy and his ministers, the pure and simple rejection of the
workers' demands, soon followed by a reopening of negotiations, then
by the dissolution of the committees:* all this goes to show the Soviet
hesitations. No: we are not dealing with the upsurge of a popular
power suddenly backed into a corner and faced with using violence or
accepting the irreparable: we are witnessing the incoherent action,
now feeble, now brutal and hasty, of a disunited government that is
bogged down in its internal divisions, in its own ideology, which becomes embarrassed when faced with the attitude of its soldiers and
discovers in amazement, but too late, the truth its lackeys hide from
it. What made the intervention inevitable is not the White Terror in
Budapest but the triumph of a certain policy in Moscow. They would
have us believe that it was necessary on the face of it and for univer-
sally valid reasons (that is to say, capable of being accepted by all men
of the left). It's not true: some men, by placing themselves *in a certain
political perspective*, based on an evaluation *which is their own* of the
international situation, judged it preferable to deny the socialist forces
of the new Hungary their chances and to plunge this country into
chaos. Never were the events in Budapest judged in and of themselves:
they were envisaged only by the repercussions they might have in
Central Europe and, in the end, in the two blocs.

Whoever will believe, indeed, that the Soviets sought, in Hungary,
to defend Hungarian socialism? If they thought they were doing so,
what naïveté and what a failure! What did they win? Nothing. What
did they lose? Everything. They kindled in peoples' hearts a hatred
that is far from dying out and that serves reaction. They disqualified
the Hungarian Party forever and forced it to repudiate itself by changing its name. They succeeded in ruining the economy and when, to
reconstruct it, the active collaboration of the whole people would be

---

*These are the committees that Kadar wishes to reconstitute today with the same
elected representatives and with respect to which he asserts the Gerő government
was thinking of organizing them before October 23, while Pravda condemns their
existence—in Yugoslavia.

needed, they raised the masses up against the government. They put in power a national communist whose popularity could have served them, but they discredited him in advance by obliging him to take upon himself the responsibility for the massacres. They provoked a general strike of protest that singles out for the whole world the Red Army, the Army of the Workers, as the enemy of the Hungarian workers. They don't dare have recourse to force openly to bring the workers back in the factories, and yet they multiply the arrests. They can't leave without having the peoples' anger sweep out the leaders that have been imposed upon them, nor stay without condemning Kadar's only resource, democratization, to remain a dead issue. Caught in their own trap, they are bogged down in an occupation which I hope their troops hold in horror and which is justified a bit more every day by the harm it is doing and the resentment it is engendering. Violence and oppression are progressively moving this martyred country away from the socialist camp; to keep it there, they have only one means left: oppression and violence. Before this month of October, they were winning across the board, they were turning out to be victors of the cold war, they were reconciling with Tito and restoring the unity of the socialist camp, they were extending their influence as far as India and the Middle East; in the bourgeois democracies, their cultural offensive was bearing fruit, the Twentieth Congress was disarming the propaganda of the adversary. Today, Nehru condemns them, the Afro-Asian countries are hesitant, worried, *Pravda* and *Borba*[1] are exchanging insults; the Budapest massacres have destroyed years of efforts for detente, for coexistence, for peace; never, in the West, have the Communists found themselves more isolated, never has their confusion been greater, never has the right triumphed so noisily. All that, one could foresee; in the dark days of November 2 and 3, when the radio was announcing the entrance of Soviet reinforcements into Hungary, the men of the left, the friends of the USSR and communists, in France and everywhere, were weighing the consequences of a *coup de force* and were saying to themselves: It's not possible, they won't do it.

They did it. But in the name of what, and what did they want to save? The answer is simple: Those who were responsible for the intervention acted in the conviction that a world conflict was inevitable, the politics from which they take their cue is the politics of the blocs and the cold war.

Where it comes from, what objectives it pursues, which men put it into practice, what its significance is for socialism, this is what I must now establish.

In our bourgeois countries, people know what had to be paid to carry through "primitive accumulation"; people haven't forgotten the tremendous waste of human lives, the forced labor, the poverty, the revolts, the repression. It seems that the industrialization of the USSR cost less; what a terrible effort it required, however; how much sweat, how much blood: it was a race against the clock, in an underdeveloped country almost entirely agricultural, encircled, which had to develop itself in spite of an economic blockade and under the constant threat of armed aggression. No one will ever be able to say to what point this "besieged fortress" could, without risking total destruction, reduce the suffering and hardships of its inhabitants; what is sure is that the communist leaders assumed the entire responsibility for the regime in its greatness and in its defects. The bourgeois liberal pleads not guilty: it's not he who made the world; he, like everyone, obeys the inexorable laws of the economy. But the Soviet revolutionaries, after some years of uncertainty, finally understood that socialism was not separable from economic planning. Moreover, the urgency of the dangers and the lack of culture of the masses made it necessary for the Russian government to declare itself for authoritarian planning; whereupon, the leaders became assimilated with the plan itself, the plan took on their faces, their voices, and their hands, it became the real government. This alienation of the head office from the enterprise could only accentuate the major contradiction of Soviet society: the long-term interests of socialist construction were opposed to the immediate interests of the working class. In a bourgeois democracy, indeed, the proletariat is per se, as Marx says, the "dissolution of society as a particular class."[2] In this negative situation, there is such an assimilation of its immediate reactions with its historical task that it is the masses who are the model of radicalism: their spontaneous demands result in accelerating the dissolution of capitalist society, at the same time that they express the fundamental character of the proletariat, "the secret of its own existence." Thus, the oppressed class has "a universal character because its sufferings are universal" and Marx can use the word "must" (*devoir*), which he borrows from ethics, to characterize demands whose origin is immediate self-interest. In other words, the needs of the worker, in a capitalist regime, his fatigue, his hunger, for example, have a socialist character in their very nakedness: the results of exploitation, these needs cannot be asserted without putting exploitation in question, they cannot be satisfied without diminishing profit and endangering capital. But, in Soviet Russia, the major concern of the leaders will be to achieve the material conditions that will permit the resolution of problems that the Revolution created. Now, the spontaneous reactions of the masses keep their negative character in relation to the general needs of the economy. In the period of postrevolutionary construction, at the moment when the socialist state wishes to endow the country with an industrial base, the movement of the masses in the direction of their demands threatens to compromise everything: the worker can refuse intensive work, demand a wage increase, clothing, shoes, a housing program. In a word, his immediate interest brings him to call for the development of consumer industries in a society that will perish if it does not first provide itself with heavy industry. Universal in a bourgeois society, his demand becomes particular in a postrevolutionary society: however his situation hasn't changed; it's true that he is no longer exploited, but "the contradiction between his human *nature* and his real life existence" has not disappeared: the Revolution, whatever it may be, does not work miracles, it inherits the poverty that the ancien régime produced. Of course, this conflict does not limit itself to setting the plan, the necessary condition for progress toward socialism, against the worker as labor power and a system of needs. It exists in both: for the worker wants the achievement of socialism at the same time as the satisfaction of his needs. In the name of the first, he is willing to restrict the second; one can ask great sacrifices of him. But a shift in his objectives takes place: in a capitalist regime, he was aiming at the overthrow of the bourgeoisie and the dictatorship of the proletariat through and beyond his concrete demands: the long-range goals made sense of the immediate

242 · JEAN-PAUL SARTRE

needs, the immediate needs gave a *real* content to these goals. The worker was in agreement with himself, and the leaders, while *organizing* the movement of the masses, couldn't escape their control: the leaders could lead the masses only where they wished to go. In a period of postrevolutionary construction, the worker's socialism rests on a solid base: the socialization of the means of production.* He knows that his efforts must sooner or later profit the working class itself and, through it, the whole population; work no longer appears to him as a hostile force but as a concrete link among the different social milieus. A rational understanding of the situation and of its necessities, the desire not to compromise what has been achieved, faithfulness to principles, to the goal: all this predisposes him to restrict his needs as much as he can, to consider his fatigue as an individual event that concerns only him, whereas he used to see in it, at the time of bourgeois exploitation, the expression of a universal fatigue of his class. All the same his socialist goals no longer are seen through the lived necessity that was the grounds for his demands; even if he wants to work more in order to free his sons from the constraint of needs, it's to his sons' needs that he ties the progress of industrialization and not to his own. It is not certain that this divorce would have been so clear if the Revolution of October 1917 had broken out in Germany or in England, rather than in Russia: in these already industrialized countries, the rhythm and the allocation of investments would have been of another nature. But since the USSR must *before everything* else provide itself with machinery, it will take a long time before the efforts and sacrifices of each person has a *visible* result of raising the standard of living. This real dichotomy of the worker in the first phase of socialist construction is curiously highlighted, in today's Poland, by the coexistence, for some enterprises, of management councils and union or-

---

*Even after the failure of the planned economies, in Hungary and in Poland the proletariat considers it has won something that it is ready to defend by arms: in neither country has it put socialism in question or allowed it to be put in question. It's a policy that it denounces (in Hungary it goes so far as to condemn the party responsible for this policy), but it remains faithful to the regime.

ganizations elected by the same workers. Bourdet[3] asked if these organisms didn't overlap; the workers told him no: "The management council, although emanating directly from us, is moved along by the general process of the economy; it represents us in our national universality as socialist workers and as such might well underestimate our concrete needs and immediate interests; it's for this reason that unions are necessary." Thus, the socialist contradiction carries with it the necessity for the same workers to have a double representation: the permanent opposition between the management council and the union only recapitulates objectively in broad daylight the conflict that each lives out in the shadows. Perhaps this objectification will go beyond the contradiction: in the USSR, in the heroic times of the first five-year plans, it was inconceivable. The proletariat was swollen daily by a mass of illiterate peasants whom the requirements of concentration were tearing away from the fields; the civil war had decimated the workers' elite; these confused masses, without political education, do not have a clear awareness of their tasks and their future; the conflict of the universal and the particular exists in them only in an embryonic state; overworked, underfed, they are distinguished above all by their needs. The contradiction is clearly seen, on the other hand, at the level of the leaders, but it appears above all as a problem to be resolved within the framework of the plan: the human needs appear as a factor of primary importance, but a negative factor, which tends to slow down production. It is humane, it is politic to make the widest concessions to them, having taken into account the vital needs of the Soviet economy. In this first phase, the masses lose the power of pointing the finger themselves at their own needs; it is the experts who decide what is suitable for them. In a prerevolutionary period, the cadres and the apparatus—however authoritarian—remained under the control of the working classes; after the Revolution, the socialist experiment partially escapes from this *human* control, it tends to substitute technical criteria for it. Forced to *figure out* the objective contradictions of the economic movement, the leaders become detached from the workers' condition; they become pure objective consciousness and authoritarian action resolving difficulties. Thus the mass becomes a passive and unconscious object of historical contradictions while the leaders decide investments, rates of work, and the standard of living by a veritable "rational calculation."

At about the same time, industrialization engenders a population upheaval that requires increasing agricultural productivity. These changes suddenly make apparent the contradictions that oppose the workers to the rural inhabitants: the former can compensate for the inadequacy of their wages only by authoritarian lowering and stabilizing agricultural prices; the latter demand that the lowering of prices be on manufactured products. The government sees itself obliged to achieve rural collectivization by force, large-scale operations have a better yield and are easier to control. The working class unreservedly supports this strong-arm policy of violence that serves the interests of urban concentrations; besides, the industrial workers consider the nationalization of industries as the greatest victory of the proletariat: agrarian collectivization appears to them as a necessary consequence of the socialization of industry. The rural inhabitants, on the contrary, even if they belong to a prosperous kolkhoz, do not stop resisting what they consider to be an expropriation. In fact both were put under the unconditional authority of the plan: it is nonetheless true that the demands of construction created the conditions for a genuine class struggle between workers and peasants and that this struggle became exacerbated to the point of becoming a civil war; deportations and executions cannot suppress this struggle: from 1930 on, the Soviet leaders are compelled to exercise in the name of the proletariat an iron dictatorship on a hostile peasantry.

Stalinism was born of this double contradiction. At first the plan engenders its own instruments: it develops a bureaucracy of experts, technicians, and administrators as rationalization; in capitalist countries it develops the "tertiary" sector.* It is absurd to pretend that this bureaucracy *exploits* the proletariat and that it is a *class*, for then words no longer have meaning. And it isn't true either that its only concern is to defend its own interests. Its members are much too well paid but

---

*To the extent that it cut the leaders off from the masses, it necessarily develops the only power that can assure its realization: the police.

they wear themselves out on the job; they put in more hours at work than the workers. Born of the plan, it is the plan that legitimizes their privileges: their personal ambition is not distinct from their devotion to socialism conceived as abstract economic planning, that is to say, ultimately, as the continuous increase of production. This total alienation allows them to consider themselves as organs of the universal to the extent that the plan must be established by their efforts; the demands of the masses, on the contrary, even if they take them into account, are for them particular accidents of a strictly negative character. And, in point of fact, their situation is contradictory in itself, for it is true that they represent the universal to the extent that they seek to involve the entire country in the building of socialism, and it is also true that they represent a simple *particularism* to the extent that their function has cut them off from the Russian people and their concrete lives. Between these "organizers" and the masses, the Party claims to play the role of mediator. In fact, it constantly keeps the bureaucracy in line. By incessant persecutions, by reorganizations and "purges," it keeps it in suspense and prevents it from getting entrenched. But the Party is, in itself, the political expression of economic planning; creator of myths, specialized in propaganda, it controls, stirs up, exhorts the masses, it can unite them for a moment in a unanimous movement, but no more than the unions does it reflect their immediate interests, their demands, nor the currents that keep them in ferment. The working classes close in on themselves and their real life falls into a kind of clandestinity: this estrangement engenders a reciprocal distrust. The leaders will ask themselves much later (they were putting the question to themselves in 1954, when I was in Moscow) how to interest the masses *as such* in production; but one formulates problems only when one has the means to resolve them. Today, the extraordinary progress of the Soviet economy permits envisaging real solutions: in a capitalist regime, the revolutionary movement is characterized by the profound unity of its long-term objectives and of its immediate goals, but this unity defines it as a negativity; at a certain stage of socialization the development of the Soviet economy can facilitate the unification of popular objectives in a positive process of construction. But in the period that follows the Revolution,

246 · JEAN-PAUL SARTRE

the prerevolutionary unity gives way to an insurmountable contradiction. It becomes necessary to create a workers' elite for whom the increase in productivity will express itself in material improvement and who will find its most immediate interest in the fulfillment and over-fulfillment of the plan. This connection between immediate well-being and the building of socialism is perfectly artificial: it is achieved by arbitrary authority, and for a few by drawing on the available surplus value. These "heroes of labor" are cited everywhere as an example, but the example is false; their small number is the very condition of their prosperity; at the same time, their existence alone is enough to carry along with it, sometimes without the knowledge of the masses, a general raising of norms. The necessities of socialization predispose the leaders to underestimate the revolutionary force of the proletariat; they work on it from the outside by propaganda, by a gentle force, by emulation, and in any case they prefer the Stakhanovites who were born of the plan like them and like them are sold on the increase in production. On their side, the working masses stick with the regime, but they don't have confidence in the bureaucracy. Certainly, between an alienated bureaucracy and a crushed peasantry, the industrial workers are the only ones to keep a certain independence and even—within well-defined limits—a certain right to criticize. It is nonetheless true that they feel governed from the outside. The proletariat is no longer the subject of history, it is not yet the concrete goal of socialization: it feels itself to be the *principal object* of administrative solicitude and the *essential means* of socialist construction. Precisely because of this, socialism remains its class "duty" and ceases to be its reality. Meanwhile, the bureaucracy hounds itself and relentlessly unifies itself. The contradictions of socialism and, quite particularly, the conflict between the proletariat and the peasants, compel the leaders to make abrupt turns, to change direction endlessly, and endlessly to correct the prior changes. The existence of a rightist faction and a leftist faction within the administration would cause economic planning to run the gravest risks: from what should be only a tactical retreat or a temporary toughening, the victory of *one* policy would be proclaimed, that is, the victory of one team and one program. In point of fact, the plan is only a hypothesis constantly submitted to the control of experience and that should be able to be corrected, without any other bias, in the light of the experience itself. The urgency of the corrections entails total agreement among the organizers; this agreement alone will prevent the momentary change of direction from becoming fixed, from changing into an *orientation*; it alone will allow the revocation of any harmful measure, even the one that has just been decided upon; it alone makes possible the leaders' constant submission to objectivity. Elsewhere, threats from abroad are becoming more explicit; and then the mute and hostile mass of rural inhabitants refuse to be mobilized; it is necessary to stress restraint; in fact a dictatorial group must first of all practice its dictatorship on itself. Thus, the external danger and the internal resistances require the indissoluble unity of the leaders. Without deep roots, without real support, the group of "organizers" will preserve its authority and assure national security only if it first achieves *from within*, by itself and over itself, its own security; events oblige it to push its own integration to the limit. But the limit is never achieved, for it is the biological and mental unity of the person that provides the best pattern for it. From this results this strange contradiction: each person becomes suspect in everyone else's eyes and even in his own eyes for the sole reason that his unity frustrates complete assimilation; but *only* a person is capable of becoming the example, the agent, and the ideal end product of a social process of unification. At the very moment when each individual considers himself inessential in relation to the group taken as a whole, this whole must remain a simple operational symbol, or the multiplicity of men must go beyond itself and unite in the sacred unity of one essential individual. Thus the cult of personality is above all else the cult of social unity in one person. And Stalin's function is not to represent the indissolubility of the group, but *to be* this very indissolubility and, at the same time, to forge it. No one can be surprised to see this idolatry surge up in a regime that denounces and rejects bourgeois individualism, because it is precisely the product of this rejection; each bourgeois resembles all the others in that he insists on his particular difference and on the worth of his own person; these primitive affirmations balance each other; the apparent reciprocity of the relationships universalizes them; the bourgeois respects in himself and claims to respect in others the absolute dignity of the human being. Consequently, this cult lapses into abstraction; each being sacred, none is. Under cover of this respect, the realistic appraisal of oneself and of others will depend on the particular content of this universal form: capabilities, actions, character. These material elements can constitute the object of a hierarchy but not of a cult: none of them is valued a priori. Therefore, individualism excludes all possibility of idolatry. The successful artist, the star, and the VIP, indispensable accessories of bourgeois ceremonies, certainly do not function to demonstrate the absolute superiority over everyone else; in everyone's eyes they incarnate his own possibilities; laden with honor, at the pinnacle of glory and power, their existence does more than the cleverest propaganda: contrary to all truth, it gives the impression that the highest positions are accessible to the humblest citizens. The function—as abstract power—is identified with the personality as pure form; this entity constitutes the object of the cult, it is sacred; but the *real* qualities of the individual aren't in it: every slightly pretty girl respects the star in Brigitte Bardot but remains persuaded that the qualities of this actress cannot entirely justify her eminence. There is such a lag between the concrete individual and what I will call the "personality function" that chance alone can lead the former to turn into the latter; now chance *is nothing*; thus every famous artist reflects for all the women of France their own possibilities of becoming sacred.*

By subordinating his person to the group, the Soviet man avoids the absurd vices of bourgeois personalism. But, by the same token, the ever more imperious necessity to maintain and reinforce unity causes his individual reality to go underground; despite the Constitution, this reality is deprived of status and remains only a factor of multiplicity, the possible source of a disunion, and the object of a latent dis-

---

*Bourgeois propaganda skillfully stresses the fact that public men, prestigious in their functions, have an ordinary private life like all lives. They are shown at home, celebrating with their wives (a very modest celebration), playing with their children. Their life story is told, showing them in their youth, ambitious, champing at the bit, like all young men when, suddenly, opportunity...! Thus, in his development as in his private life, the leader, the VIP, the successful artist is myself plus chance.

trust. The struggles, however atrocious, remain in the realm of objectivity: they are solutions and projects in opposition to each other, but ambition and the self-affirmation remain implicit, they never appear in the light of day; the plan covers and absorbs them. Without being manifested, individual wills can neither recognize themselves nor balance each other in a system that would be a universal guarantee against any hypertrophy into a cult of personality. Actually, Stalin does not appear at first as an individual superior to others but fundamentally like everyone. It is not the dignity of the person that he represents, it is social integration pushed to the limit. This indissolubility—which *happens* to be that of the individual—makes him the sole possible agent of unification, for it is unity alone that can unify multiplicity. He is identified with the coercive action that the group exercises on its own members; he will carry out the sentence the bureaucracy passes on itself; he gathers up and interiorizes the diffuse distrust of the revolutionary collectivity. In the name of all, he will be distrustful of each; but the group is not distrustful of him; within the bureaucracy, he would have represented only plurality and division; placed above it, he shows it the impossible collective unity. Stalin's right hand does not distrust his left hand nor his left ear his right ear. Stalin cannot become the spy of Stalin nor cease to be in accord with himself. The group cannot continue to exist without confidence, it is not enough to say that it trusts Stalin, but it places its own confidence in the confidence that Stalin has in himself. No one *enjoys* this confidence except Stalin in person; but each one knows that up there, in Stalin, the bureaucratic collectivity exists under a form of superior integration and that it is reconciled. Thus each member of the bureaucracy, far from seeing in Stalin an exaltation of the human person, discovers in this quintessence of collectivity the radical negation of his own self that contributes to unity. The ascending movement that goes from the group to Stalin is thus characterized by the total destruction of individuality. On the other hand, there is a descending movement: Stalin can resolve the problem of integration only by pushing social hierarchy to the limit. From the top to the bottom of the ladder, directly or indirectly, the officials get their power from him. Thus one sees the rebirth of the *person*. But the latter has nothing in common with the bourgeois individual. It derives its existence not from a universal status but from the unique person whom the necessities of integration place above the group. Its reality, always revokable, comes to it from its very functions; in its relations with its peers, it remains a factor of multiplicity, hence an object of distrust; for its subordinates, on the other hand, it is a hypostasis of Stalin, hence a factor of unification and an object of worship. At all levels of the hierarchy, we find the same contradiction; biological and mental autonomy appears as the element of plurality and as a symbol of integration; the same individual presents himself as a synthesizing force vis-à-vis his subordinates and denies his living reality in his relationships with his chiefs. In any case, what creates and what destroys the Soviet person is the impossible unity of the group. Stalin, alone, is pure unity: he is the act. It is not his own individual qualities that are worshiped in him; even less, some kind of "charismatic" power like that which the Nazis recognized in Hitler. His cult has nothing mystical; it is directed to a real unity insofar as it is a power of unification. It is inseparable moreover from terror: Stalin incarnating the collective distrust can overcome multiplicity only by trying to reduce it. The negative counterpart of hierarchization is this circulating terror that the bureaucracy practices on itself by Stalin's hands and that expresses itself by "purges" and deportations.

"Socialism in a single country," or Stalinism, does not constitute a deviation from socialism: it is the long way around it that is imposed on it by circumstances. The rhythm and evolution of this defensive construction are not determined by the consideration alone of Soviet resources and needs but also by the relations of the USSR with the capitalist world, in a word, by circumstances external to socialization that oblige it constantly to compromise its principles. The contradictions of this first phase provoke a class conflict between workers and peasants and cut off the leaders from the working masses: an authoritarian and bureaucratic system is established where everything is sacrificed to productivity. This system reflects its contradictions in its ideological superstructures: it appeals to Marxism-Leninism but this covering ill conceals a double value judgment on man and on socialism. On the one hand, the propaganda and the Pollyanna-like novels

of "socialist realism" appeal to a quite nauseating optimism: in a socialist country everything is good, there is no conflict except between
the forces of the past and those that are building the future; the latter
must necessarily triumph. The failures, suffering, death, all are caught
up and saved by the movement of history. It even seems opportune for
a while to produce novels without conflicts. In any case, the positive
hero knows nothing about internal difficulties and contradictions;
for his part, he contributes, without flinching and without mistakes,
to the construction of socialism, his model is the young Stakhanovite;
a soldier, he knows nothing of fear. These industrial and military fantasies appeal to Marxism: they depict for us the happiness of a classless
society. On the other hand, the exercise of dictatorship and the internal contradictions of bureaucracy necessarily engender an unavowed
pessimism: since one governs by force, men must be evil; these heroes
of labor, these so devoted high functionaries, these Party militants so
upright, so pure, a mere puff can blow out their most blazing virtues:
there they are counterrevolutionaries, spies, agents of capitalism; habits of integrity, of honesty, thirty years of faithfulness to the Party,
nothing can protect them against temptation. And if they deviate
from the line, one soon discovers that they were guilty *from birth.* The
great actions that merited for them so many honors and so much
praise, one discovers suddenly, were heinous crimes: one had to be
ready to revoke all judgments, to scorn the man whom one praised to
the skies without ever being surprised at having been mistaken so
long: in this dark and mixed-up world, one must affirm all the more
strongly today's truth for the fact that it will very likely be tomorrow's
error. The state, far from withering away, must reinforce itself: its
withering away will come when an authoritarian education has interiorized in everyone the constraints that the state practices; it is not the
emancipation of men that will succeed in making it unnecessary, it is
their self-domestication and their internal conditioning: it will not
disappear, it will move into peoples' hearts. It is this distrust of man
that is expressed in Stalin's famous "theoretical error": the class struggle is intensified in a period of socialist construction. It has been
claimed that he wished cynically to justify his "practice." Why? It is
practice, here, that engenders its own theory. Besides, this pessimism

turns up in foreign policy. The USSR doesn't want war but it sees it coming: for good reason, since Hitler's armies were to invade it in 1941. But these perfectly justifiable fears carry with them a gross over-simplification of problems: the capitalist world, out of reach, poorly known, becomes a purely destructive force that mercilessly pursues the extermination of the Soviet people and the liquidation of social-ism by force of arms; people still talk of the contradictions of the capitalist world, of the conflicts they can entail, of the peace forces that oppose the war forces in the West. People talk about them but they no longer believe in them, particularly after the failure of the Popular Front: for the only certain policy, in the state of isolation in which socialist Russia finds itself, is to arm, to arm ceaselessly *as if war were coming tomorrow*: thus foreign and domestic policy must be de-termined constantly in view of the risks of catastrophe, never in view of the chances of peace. So long as it has not caught up with the West-ern nations, the USSR must remain faithful to the pessimistic princi-ple: If you want peace, prepare for war (*Si vis pacem, para bellum*), which in French means: "You can always count on the worst" (*Le pire est toujours sûr*).

Must one give the name of socialism to this bloody monster that tears itself apart? I answer frankly: yes. This was even socialism *itself* during its primitive phase—there was no other, except perhaps in Plato's heaven, and we had to have that one or none at all.

A VICTORY

In 1943, in the rue Lauriston,[1] French people were crying out in anguish and in pain; the whole of France heard them. The outcome of the war was not certain and we did not want to think about the future; one thing seemed impossible to us, though: that one day, in our name, people could be made to cry out.

But nothing is impossible for the French: in 1958, in Algiers, people are being tortured regularly, systematically; everybody knows, from Monsieur Lacoste[2] to the farmers of the Aveyron, but nobody talks about it. Or hardly anybody: the sounds of thin voices fade into silence. France was scarcely more mute during the occupation; and then she did have the excuse that she was gagged. Abroad they have already concluded that we have not ceased to demean ourselves. Since 1939, according to some; according to others, since 1918. It is easily said: I do not believe so readily in the degradation of a people; I do believe in their stagnation and their stupor. During the war, when the British radio or the underground press had told us about Oradour,[3] we watched the German soldiers walking through the streets with an inoffensive air and we sometimes said to ourselves: "And yet they are

254 · JEAN-PAUL SARTRE

men who resemble us. How can they do what they do?" And we were proud of ourselves because we did not understand.

Now we know that there is nothing to understand: everything occurred unnoticed, by imperceptible abdications; and then, when we looked up we saw in the mirror an unfamiliar, hateful face: our own.

Deep in their stupor, the French people are discovering this terrible truth: if nothing protects a nation against itself, neither its past nor its loyalties, nor its own laws; if fifteen years are enough to change the victims into torturers, it is because circumstances alone dictate. Depending on the circumstances, anyone, at any time will become a victim or a perpetrator.

Fortunate are those who have died without ever having to ask themselves: "If they pull out my nails, will I talk?" But even more fortunate are those who have not been obliged, having scarcely left childhood, to ask themselves the other question: "If my friends, my brothers-in-arms, or my superior officers, before my eyes, pull out the nails of an enemy, what will I do?"

What do they know about themselves, these young men who, owing to circumstances, have their backs to the wall? They sense that the resolutions they make here will appear abstract and empty when the day comes, that their ideas will be fundamentally called into question by an unforeseeable situation, and that they will have to decide over there, alone, about France and about themselves. They go off, and others, who have measured their impotence, and most of whom maintain a resentful silence, return. Fear is born: fear of others, fear of oneself, spreading to all sectors. Victim and perpetrator are one and the same image: and it is our own image. In extreme cases, the only means of rejecting one of the two roles is effectively to assume the other.

This choice is not being imposed upon the people of France—or not yet; but this ambivalence weighs upon us: because of it we are both "the wound and the knife." The horror of being the latter and the fear of becoming the former govern and reinforce each other. Memories are awakened; fifteen years ago, the best members of the Resistance were less afraid of suffering than of giving in to their suffering. They would say: when he remains silent, the victim saves everything; when he talks, no one has the right to judge, not even those who did not talk: but the victim is coupled with the perpetrator, is his spouse, and this entwined couple is engulfed in the night of debasement. The night of debasement has returned: at El Biar.[4] it returns every night; in France it blackens our hearts. Whispered propaganda gives us to understand that, precisely, "everyone talks." Thus the torture is justified by human ignominy; since every one of us is a potential traitor, the tormentor in each of us would be wrong to hold back. Especially as the greatness of France demands it, as honeyed voices explain to us each day. And a true patriot must have a clear conscience. And if you have a guilty one you must be a defeatist.

Consequently, stupor turns to despair: if patriotism must thrust us into debasement, if there is no safeguard anywhere, at any time, to stop nations or the whole of humanity from falling into inhumanity, then why indeed should we take so much trouble to become or to remain human beings: it is the inhuman in us which is our truth. But if nothing else is true, if we must either terrorize or die of terror, why should we take the trouble to live and remain patriotic?

These thoughts have been put into our minds by force. Obscure and false, they all flow from the same principle: mankind is inhuman. Their aim is to convince us of our impotence. They achieve this as long as we do not look them in the face. Abroad people should know: our silence is not a sign of assent; it stems from nightmares which have been deliberately caused, sustained, and directed. I knew this already, but had been waiting for decisive proof of it for along time.

Here it is.

About two weeks ago, a book entitled *The Question* was published by Éditions de Minuit. Its author, Henri Alleg, who is still being held today in a prison in Algiers, recounts, without any superfluous commentary, and with admirable precision, the "interrogation" he has undergone. The torturers, as they themselves had promised him, have "seen to him": field telephone, water torture—as at the time of the Marchioness of Brinvilliers,[5] but with the technical improvements de rigueur in our times—torture by fire, by thirst, etc. A book not to be recommended to sensitive souls. And yet the first edition—twenty thousand copies—is already out of print, and despite a rushed second print run, demand cannot be met: certain booksellers are selling from fifty to a hundred copies a day.

So far those who have dared to provide evidence have been reservists, mostly priests. They had lived among the torturers, their brothers, our brothers; all they knew of their victims, more often than not, was their cries, their wounds, and their suffering. They showed us sadists bent over wrecks of human flesh. And what distinguished us from those sadists? Nothing, since we kept quiet: our indignation seemed sincere to us, but would we have maintained it had we been living over there? Would it not have given way to a universal disgust, a dull resignation? I myself read out of a sense of duty, I sometimes published, and I hated the accounts which mercilessly implicated us all and left no room for hope.

With *The Question*, everything changes. Alleg spares us despair and shame because he is a victim who has overcome torture. This reversal is not without a certain sinister humor; it is in our name that he was made to suffer, and we, because of him, at last rediscover a little of our pride: we are proud that he is French. Readers identify with him passionately, they accompany him to the limit of his suffering; with him, alone and naked, they hold out. Would they, would we, be capable of this *in reality*? That is another matter. What counts is that the victim frees us by letting us discover, as he himself discovers, that we have the power and the duty to endure anything.

We were fascinated by the abyss of the inhuman; but one hard and stubborn man, obstinately carrying out his role as a man, is sufficient to rescue us from our giddiness. The "question" is not inhuman; it is quite simply a vile, revolting crime, committed by men against men, and to which other men can and must put an end. The inhuman does not exist anywhere, except in the nightmares engendered by fear. And it is precisely the calm courage of a victim, his modesty and his lucidity, which awaken and demystify us: Alleg has just seized torture from the darkness that covers it; let us now have a closer look at it in broad daylight.

The perpetrators first of all, what are they? Sadists? Angry archangels? Warlords with terrifying whims? If we believe what they say, they are all of those things at once. But that is precisely it, Alleg does not believe them. What emerges from his account is that they would like to convince themselves and their victims of their total dominance: at times they are superhumans who have people at their mercy, and at times they are strict and strong men who have been given the task of taming the most obscene, the most ferocious, the most cowardly of animals: the human animal. You sense that they do not look too closely: the essential thing is to make the prisoner feel that he is not of the same race as they are. They undress him, they tie him up, they mock him; soldiers come and go, hurling insults and threats with a nonchalance meant to appear terrible.

But Alleg naked, shivering with cold, tied to a plank which is still black and sticky from old vomit, reduces all this posturing to its pitiful truth. It is an act played out by imbeciles. An act, the fascist violence of their comments, their promise to go and "fuck up the Republic." An act, the approach of the aide-de-camp of General Massu,[6] which finishes with these words: "All that's left for you to do now is commit suicide." All a vulgar, wooden act that they repeat, without conviction, every night, for every prisoner, and which they stop very quickly because they run out of time. For these dreadful workers are overburdened. Overworked: the prisoners queue up before the torture plank, they are tied, then untied, the victims are taken from one torture chamber to another. Seeing this disgusting hive of activity through Alleg's eyes, we realize that the torturers cannot cope with what they have to do.

At times, of course, they play it cool; they drink beer, very relaxed, over a battered body; and then, all at once, they jump to their feet, running everywhere, swearing, screaming with anger, very nervy men who would make excellent victims; at the first pasting they would start confessing.

Vicious, enraged, certainly; but sadists, no, not even that; they are in too much of a hurry. That is what saves them, moreover; they hold out by keeping up their momentum; they have to keep running or collapse.

Yet they like a job well done; if they judge it necessary, they will stretch their professional conscience to the point of killing. That is what is striking, in Alleg's account: behind these wild-eyed, colorless surgeons, one senses a lack of flexibility which goes beyond them and beyond their leaders themselves.

We would be fortunate indeed if these crimes were the acts of a handful of violent individuals: in truth, torture creates torturers. After all, these soldiers did not join an elite corps in order to torture the defeated enemy.

Alleg, in a few lines, describes for us those he has known and that is sufficient to mark the different stages of their transformation.

There are the youngest of them, powerless, overwhelmed, who murmur "It's horrible" when their flashlights shine on one of the tortured men; and then there are the torturers' assistants, who do not yet carry out the dirty work, who hold up and bring the prisoners; some of them are hardened, others not, all caught up in the system, all already inexcusable.

There is a blond fellow from northern France "with such a friendly face, able to talk about the torture sessions that Alleg underwent as if it were a match he was remembering and able to congratulate him, without embarrassment, as he would a cycle champion . . ." A few days later, Alleg saw him again "red in the face, disfigured by hatred, beating a Muslim on the stairs . . ." And then there are the specialists, the hard men who do all the real work, who like to see the convulsive movements of someone being electrocuted but who cannot stand hearing him scream; and then the madmen who go around in circles like dead leaves in the whirlwind of their own violence.

None of these men exists on his own account, none of them will stay as he is; they represent the stages of an inexorable transformation. Between the best and the worst of them, only one difference: the best are raw recruits and the worst are the old hands. They will all leave eventually and, if the war continues, others will replace them, blond lads from the north or little dark-haired southerners, who will have the same apprenticeship and will discover the same violence, with the same nervous tension.

In this business, the individual does not count; a kind of stray, anonymous hatred, a radical hatred of man, takes hold of both torturers and victims, degrading them together and each by the other. Torture is this hatred, set up as a system, and creating its own instruments.

When this is said quite timidly in the National Assembly, the pack is unleashed: "You are insulting the army!" These yapping dogs must be asked once and for all: What the hell has the army got to do with it? They torture *in the army*; that is a fact; the Safety Commission, despite the mildness of its report, did not feel it necessary to hide this fact. So what? Is it the *army* that tortures?

What rubbish! Do they think that the civilians are ignorant of their fine methods? If that is all it is about, let us put our trust in the Algiers police. And then, if a torturer in chief is needed, the whole of the National Assembly has designated him. It is not General S..., even less so General E..., not even General M..., though named by Alleg; it is Monsieur Lacoste, the man with full powers. Everything is done through him, by him, in Bône as in Oran. All the men who suffered a horrific death in the El Biar apartment block or in villa S..., died by his will. It is not I who say so: it is the members of assembly, it is the government. And what is more, the gangrene is spreading: it has crossed the sea: it has even been a rumor that people were being tortured in certain civilian prisons in France: I do not know whether there was any basis for it, but the persistence of it must have moved the authorities, since at the trial of Ben Saddok,[7] the public prosecutor solemnly asked the accused if he had been ill treated; the reply was, of course, known in advance.

No, torture is neither civilian nor military, nor specifically French: it is a pox which is ravaging the whole of this era. In the East as in the West there have been torturers. It is not so long ago that Farkas tortured the Hungarians; and the Polish do not hide the fact that their police, before Poznan, readily resorted to torture; as regards what happened in the USSR when Stalin was alive, the Khrushchev report is an indisputable account; not long ago, in Nasser's prisons, they "questioned" politicians who since then have been elevated, albeit with a few scars, to eminent positions. I could go on: today it is Cyprus and it is Algeria; all in all, Hitler was just a forerunner.

Disavowed—at times very feebly—but systematically applied behind the façade of democratic legality, torture may be defined as a semi-clandestine institution. Are its causes the same everywhere? Probably not, but everywhere it is a manifestation of the same malaise. Anyway, that is of little importance; and our task is not to judge the century. Let us put our own house in order first and attempt to understand what has happened to us, the French people.

You know what they say sometimes to justify torturers: that you have to bring yourself to torture one man if his confession enables hundreds of lives to be spared. What hypocrisy! Alleg was no more a terrorist than Audin[8] was; the proof is that he is charged with "threatening state security and reconstituting a disbanded organization."

Was it to save lives that his nipples and his pubic hair were burned? No, they wanted to extract from him the address of the comrade who had sheltered him. If he had talked, they would have put another communist behind bars; that is all.

What is more, people are arrested at random; any Muslim is "torturable" indefinitely: most of those tortured say nothing because they have nothing to say, unless they consent, so as not to suffer any more, to making a false statement or to gratuitously admitting to an unpunished crime, with which it seems opportune to charge them. As for those who could talk, we know full well that they remain silent. All or almost all of them. Neither Audin nor Alleg nor Guerroudj[9] opened their mouths. On this point the torturers of El Biar are better informed than we are. One noted after the first interrogation of Alleg: "He has at least gained a night to give his mates time to clear off." And an officer, a few days later: "For ten, fifteen years they have had the idea that, if they are caught, they must not say anything; and there is nothing that can be done to get that out of their heads."

Perhaps he only meant the communists. But do they think that the ALN[10] fighters are made of different stuff? This type of violence is not very productive: by 1944 the Germans themselves had ended up convincing themselves of that: it costs human lives and does not save any.

And yet the argument is not entirely false: in any case it enlightens us regarding the function of torture. As a clandestine or semi-clandestine institution, *torture* is indissolubly linked to the clandestine nature of resistance or opposition.

In Algeria, our army has been deployed throughout the whole territory: we have the numbers, the finance, and the weapons; the insurgents have nothing, except the trust and support of a large part of the population. We have defined, in spite of ourselves, the principal characteristics of this people's war: bomb attacks in the cities, ambushes in the country: the FLN has not chosen these actions; they do what they can, that is all; their forces in relation to ours oblige them to attack us by surprise: invisible, elusive, unexpected, they must strike and then disappear or else be exterminated. Hence our discomfort: we are struggling against a secret enemy; a hand throws a bomb in a street, a rifle shot injures one of our soldiers out on the road; we come running; there is no one there; later, in the vicinity, we will find Muslims who saw nothing. Everything links together: the people's war, a war of the poor against the rich, is characterized by the close ties between the rebel units and the population; as a result, for the regular army and the civilian authorities, this swarm of wretched people becomes the innumerable, daily enemy. The occupying troops are anxious about a silence which they have themselves engendered; one senses an elusive will to be silent, a circling, omnipresent secret; the rich feel hunted in the midst of the poor who say nothing; hampered by their own strength, the "forces of law and order" can do nothing to oppose the guerrilla fighters, apart from their searches and their reprisal expeditions, nothing to oppose terrorism other than terror. Something is being hidden: everywhere and by everybody; people must be *made to talk*.

Torture is a vain fury, born of fear: they want to extract from *one* throat, in the midst of the screams and vomiting of blood, *everyone's* secret. Useless violence: whether the victim talks or dies beneath the blows, the vast secret is elsewhere, always elsewhere, out of reach; the torturer turns into Sisyphus: if he applies torture, he will have to begin over and over again.

Yet even this silence, even this fear, even these ever present and ever invisible dangers cannot fully explain the tenacity of the torturers, their will to debase their victims, and ultimately the hatred of mankind which has taken hold of them without their consent and which has shaped them.

That people kill each other is the rule: we have always fought for collective or individual interests. But in torture, this strange combat, the stakes seem extreme; it is for the title of *man* that the torturer pits himself against the tortured, and the whole thing happens as if they could not both belong to the human species.

The aim of torture is not simply to force someone to talk, to betray: the victim must designate *himself*, by his cries and his submission, as a human animal. In everyone's eyes and in his own eyes. His betrayal must break and dispose of the victim forever. The intention is not just to force those who yield to torture to talk; they have had a status imposed upon them forever: that of a subhuman.

This extreme raising of the stakes is a feature of our times. The reason is that the condition of man needs to be realized. At no time has the will to be free been more conscious or stronger; at no time has oppression been more violent or better armed.

In Algeria, the contradictions are implacable: each of the conflicting groups demands the radical exclusion of the other. We took everything from the Muslims, then we forbade them everything, including even the use of their own language. Memmi[11] has clearly shown how colonization is achieved by the canceling out of the colonized. They no longer owned anything, they *were no longer anybody*; we liquidated their civilization while at the same time refusing them ours. They had requested integration, assimilation, and we said no: by what miracle would we maintain colonial overexploitation if the colonized enjoyed the same rights as the colonists? Undernourished, uneducated, impoverished, they were mercilessly pushed back by the system to the edge of the Sahara, to the limits of what is human; with population growth, their standard of living fell year on year. When despair drove them to revolt, these subhumans either had to perish or assert their humanity against us: they rejected all our values, our culture, our supposed superiority. Demanding the status of human beings and refusing French nationality amounted to one and the same thing for them.

This rebellion was not restricted to contesting the power of the colonists; they felt that their very existence was in question. For most of the Europeans of Algeria, there are two complementary and inseparable truths: the colonists are human beings by divine right, and the natives are subhumans. That is the mythical interpretation of a precise fact, since the wealth of the former depends on the extreme poverty of the latter.

Thus exploitation makes the exploiter dependent upon the exploited. And, on another level, this dependence is at the heart of racism; it is its profound contradiction and bitter misfortune: for the European in Algiers, being a man means *first of all* being superior to the Muslim.

But what if the Muslim, in turn, asserts himself as a man, as the colonist's equal? Well then, the colonist is wounded in his very being; he feels diminished, devalued: he not only sees the economic consequences of the accession of "niggers" [*bougnoules*] to the world of human beings, he also loathes it because it heralds his *personal* decline. In his rage, he sometimes dreams of genocide. But it is pure fantasy. He knows it, he is aware of his dependence; what would he do without an indigenous subproletariat, without a surplus workforce, without chronic unemployment that allows him to impose his salaries? And then if the Muslims are *already* human beings, all is lost, they do not even need to be exterminated anymore. No, the most urgent thing, if there is still time, is to humiliate them, to wipe out the pride in their hearts, to reduce them to the level of animals. The body will be allowed to live on but the spirit will be destroyed. Tame, train, punish: those are the words that obsess the colonist. There is not enough room in Algeria for two human species; the choice must be made between one and the other.

And I do not claim, of course, that the Europeans of Algiers invented torture, nor even that they encouraged the civil and military authorities to practice it; on the contrary: torture imposed itself, it had become routine practice even before we realized it. But the hatred of man apparent within it is the expression of racism. For it is indeed the man that they want to destroy, with all his human qualities: courage, will power, intelligence, loyalty—the very qualities to which the colonist lays claim. But if the European gets angry to the point of hating his own image, it is because that image is reflected by an Arab.

Thus, in these two inseparable couples—the colonist and the colonized, the torturer and the victim—the second is no more than a manifestation of the first. And, without any doubt, the torturers are not colonists, nor are the colonists torturers. The latter are frequently young men who come from France and who have lived twenty years of their life without ever worrying about the Algerian problem. But the hatred was a magnetic field: it passed through, corroded, and subjected them.

It is the calm lucidity of Alleg that allows us to understand all that. Even if he contributed nothing else, we would have to be profoundly grateful to him. But he did much more: by intimidating his torturers, he ensured that the humanism of the victims and the colonized triumphed over the excessive violence of certain soldiers and the racism of the colonists. And let not the word "victim" evoke any kind of tearful humanism: in the midst of these little chiefs, proud of their youth, their strength, their number, Alleg is the only hard man, the only one who is really strong. *We* may say that he paid the highest price for the simple right to remain a man among men. But he does not even think about it. That is why we are so moved by this sentence without affectation at the end of a paragraph:

> I felt suddenly proud and joyful at not having given in; I was convinced that I would hold out if they started again, that I would fight to the end, that I would not make their task easier by committing suicide.

A hard man, yes, and one who ended up frightening the archangels of anger.

In some of their words, at any rate, you feel that they sense and are trying to ward off a vague and scandalous revelation: when it is the victim who wins, farewell to supremacy and to the droit du seigneur; the archangelic wings stiffen and the lads ask themselves, embarrassed, "What about me? Would I hold out if I were tortured?" Here, at the moment of victory, one system of values has been replaced by another; the torturers, in their turn, come within an ace of feeling dizzy. But no, their heads are empty and their work exhausts them, and after all they scarcely believe in what they are doing.

Besides, what is the use of troubling the conscience of the torturers? If one of them faltered, his superiors would replace him: there are plenty more where they came from. Alleg's account in effect—and this is perhaps its greatest merit—finally dispels our illusions: no, it is not enough to punish or re-educate a few individuals; no, the Algerian war will not be humanized. Torture has established *itself* there: it was prompted by circumstances and required by racist hatred; in a certain manner, as we have seen, it is at the heart of the conflict and is, perhaps, what expresses its deepest truth. If we want to put an end to this revolting, dismal cruelty, save France from shame and the Algerians from hell, we have only one means, still the same, the only one we have ever had or will ever have: begin negotiations, make peace.

PAUL NIZAN

I

FEELING bored one day, Paul Valéry went over to the window and, gazing into the transparency of a pane, asked, "How to hide a man?" Gide was present. Disconcerted by this studied laconicism, he said nothing. Yet there was no lack of possible answers: any method would do, from poverty and hunger to formal dinners, from the county jail to the Académie française. But these two excessively renowned bourgeois had high opinions of themselves. Each day they buffed up their twin souls in public and believed they were revealing themselves in their naked truth. When they died, long afterward, the one morose, the other contented—both in ignorance—they had not even listened to the young voice crying out for all of us, their grandnephews: "Where has man hidden himself? We are stifling; we are mutilated from childhood: there are only monsters!"

The man denouncing our actual situation in these terms more than suffered in his own skin: while alive, there was not an hour that he did not run the risk of ruin. Dead, he faced an even greater danger: to make him pay for his clear-sightedness, a conspiracy of cripples tried to erase him from memory.

He had been in the Party for twelve years when, in September 1939, he announced he was leaving. This was the unpardonable crime, this sin of despair that the God of the Christians punishes with damnation. The communists do not believe in hell: they believe in oblivion.

It was decided that Comrade Nizan would be consigned to oblivion. One of many exploding bullets had hit him in the back of the neck, but that liquidation satisfied no one: it was not enough that he had ceased to live; he had to have never existed. They persuaded the witnesses to his life that they had not really known him: he was a traitor, a Judas; he worked secretly for the Ministry of the Interior and receipts had been found there bearing his signature. One comrade volunteered an exegesis of the works he had left behind, discovering in them an obsession with treason. "How can an author who puts informers in his novels know about their ways," asked this philosopher, "unless he were an informer himself?" A profound argument, one must admit, but a dangerous one. The exegete has, in fact, himself become a traitor and has just been expelled; should we criticize him now for having projected his own obsessions onto his victim? At any rate, the trick worked: the suspect books disappeared; the publishers were intimidated and left them rotting in cellars, as were the readers, who no longer dared ask for them. This grain of silence would germinate. Within ten years it would produce the most radical negation: the dead man would exit from history, his name would crumble into dust, his very birth would be excised from our shared past.

The odds were with them initially: a grave-robbery at night in a poorly guarded cemetery was no great task. If they lost the first phase of the battle, it was because they were too contemptuous of us. Blinded by mourning and glory, the Party intellectuals saw themselves as a chivalric order. They referred to each other as "the permanent heroes of the age" and it was around this time, I think, that one of my former students informed me, with sweet irony, "We communist intellectuals suffer, do you see, from a superiority complex!" In a word, subhumans unaware of their subhumanity. Hence their arrogance carried them so far as to try out their slanders on Nizan's best friends: to test them, as it were. The encounter proved decisive: challenged publicly to produce their evidence, they scattered in disarray, blaming us for never trusting them and for really not being very nice.

The second round in this battle spelled defeat for us: to confound them was a small matter; we needed to convince, to push home our advantage, to cut off our enemies' retreat. Our victory frightened us: at bottom we quite liked these unjust soldiers of Justice. Someone said, "Don't push it, they'll end up getting annoyed." We heard no more of the story, but it did the rounds of the Communist Party by word of mouth and new recruits in Bergerac and Mazamet learned in dispassionate but absolutely certain terms of the ancient crimes of an unknown by the name of Nizan.

When I think of it, our negligence seems suspect; in a pinch, I will admit we had honestly assumed that his innocence as a man had been re-established. But his works? Was it acceptable for us to do nothing to rescue them from oblivion? It was their aim to be disagreeable: that is their greatest strength; and I am certain at present that we found them so. I recall, indeed, that we had acquired beautiful, new souls, so beautiful that I still blush to think of it. Not wanting to waste anything, the nation decided to entrust to us those empty, insatiable pools in which it had no interest: pools of buried pain, the unsatisfied demands of the deceased—in short, all that is beyond recovery. These martyrs' merits were ascribed now to us; alive, we received posthumous decoration. We were, all in all, honorary dead men: a whispering campaign dubbed us Righteous; smiling, frivolous, and funereal, we took this noble vacuity for plenitude and concealed our unparalleled promotion beneath the simplicity of our manners. Alongside whiskey, Virtue was our chief diversion. We were everyone's friends! The enemy had invented classes in order to ruin us: in defeat, he took them with him. Workers, bourgeois, and peasants all communed in the sacred love of the fatherland. In the authorized circles, we thought we knew that self-sacrifice was rewarded in cash, that crime did not pay, that the worst does not necessarily happen, and that moral advance brings technical progress. We proved by our very existence and self-conceit that the bad are always punished and the good always rewarded. Wreathed in glory and pacified, the left had just entered upon the inexorable death throes that were to see it perish thirteen years later to the strains of military bands. Idiots that we were, we thought it was in fine fettle. Soldiers and politicians came home from Britain and Algeria; they crushed the Resistance before our eyes and spirited away the Revolution, and we wrote in the newspapers and our books that everything was in fine order: our souls had absorbed the exquisite essence of these annihilated movements into themselves.

Nizan was a killjoy. His was a call to arms and hatred. Class against class. With a patient, mortal enemy, no quarter can be given: it is kill or be killed, there is no middle way. And no time for sleep. All his life, with his graceful insolence and his eyes lowered to his fingernails, he had repeated, "Don't believe in Santa Claus." But he was dead. The war had just ended. In every French hearth, shoes and boots were laid out and Santa Claus was filling them with tins of American food. I am sure that those who thumbed through *Aden, Arabie* or *Antoine Bloyé*[1] at that time quickly broke off reading with lordly pity: "prewar literature, simplistic and decidedly passé." What need had we of a Cassandra? Had he lived, we thought he would have shared in our new subtlety or, in other words, our compromises. What had preserved his violent purity? A stray bullet, no more and no less. That was nothing to boast about. This wicked corpse was gently chuckling to himself: in his books he had written that, past the age of forty, a French bourgeois is merely a carcass. And then he disappeared. At thirty-five. At present we, his classmates and comrades, bloated with that flatulence we call our souls, are running about the town with garlands for both right and left. And we are forty. Protecting innocence is our job; we are the just and we dispensed Justice. But we left *Aden, Arabie* in the hands of the communists because we loathed all those who disputed our merits.

This attitude is an offense in French law: refusal to come to the assistance of a person in danger. If we had not morally liquidated this former colleague, it was because we did not have the means to do so. The rehabilitation was a farce. "Talk, talk, that's all you can do."[2] We talked: our beautiful souls spelled death for others; our virtue reflected our total impotence. It was, in fact, the job of the young to resurrect Nizan the writer. But the young people of the day—today quadragenarian carcass—gave no thought to that. Having just escaped an epidemic, what did the endemic disease of bourgeois death matter to them? Nizan asked them to look into themselves at a point when they believed they could at last look outward. Of course they would die. "Socrates is mortal." "Madame is dying, Madame is dead":

they had been given some famous passages to learn at school: "Le Lac," a sermon by Bossuet.[3] But there is a time for everything, and this was the time for living because for five years they had thought they were going to die. As adolescents they had been stunned by defeat: they had been heartbroken at no longer being able to respect anyone—either their fathers or the "best army in the world" that had run away without fighting. The biggest-hearted had given themselves to the Party, which had repaid them royally: with a family, a monastic rule, tranquil chauvinism, and respectability. In the aftermath of war, those young people went wild with pride and humility: they found pleasure in a sudden passion for obedience. I have said they were contemptuous of us all—by way of compensation. They twisted the arm of tomorrow to make it yield a radiant socialist future; one can imagine how the brassy song of these birds drowned out the thin, chill voice of Nizan, the short-lived voice of death and eternity. Other adolescents found their relaxation in cellars: they danced, made love, went to each other's houses, and threw their parents' furniture out of the windows in great, revolving potlatch ceremonies: in a word, they did all a young man can do. Some of them even read. In despair, of course. All of them were in despair: it was the fashion. And despairing of everything, except of course of the vigorous pleasure of despairing. Except of life. After five years, their futures were thawing: they had plans, the guileless hope of renewing literature through despair, of knowing the weariness of great global journeys, of the unbearable tedium of earning money or seducing women or, quite simply, of becoming a despairing pharmacist or dentist and remaining one for a long time, a very long time, without any other care than those of the human condition in its generality. How joyful they were! Nizan had nothing to say to them: he spoke little of the human condition and much of social matters and our alienations; he knew terror and anger better than he did the *douceurs* of despair; in the young bourgeois of his acquaintance he hated the reflection of himself, and, whether they were despairing or not, he despaired of them. His books were kept for the lean years, and rightly so.

Then, at length, came the Marshall Plan: the cold war hit this generation of dancers and vassals like a blow to the heart. We old-timers took a bit of a battering, as did our virtues. "Crime pays. Crime is re-warded." With the return of these fine maxims, our beautiful souls perished in a dreadful stench. And good riddance to them. But our juniors paid for everyone. The nightclubbers became dumbfounded, old young men. Some are going gray, some balding, others have a paunch. Their relaxed attitude has frozen into inertia. They do what has to be done, and do it simply; they earn their corn, own a Peugeot 403 and a country cottage, have a wife and children. These young men were getting ready for life, they were "starting out": their train came to a stop somewhere in the countryside. They will go nowhere now and do nothing. Sometimes a confused memory comes back to them from the glorious turbulent years; when this happens, they ask themselves, "What did we want?" and cannot remember. They are well-adapted, yet suffer from a chronic maladaptation that will kill them: they are tramps without poverty; they are well-fed, but they perform no service. I can see them at twenty—so lively, so joyous, so eager to relieve the old guard. I look at them today, their eyes ravaged by the cancer of astonishment, and I think to myself that they did not deserve this fate. As for the faithful vassals: some have not renewed their vows of fealty, others have fallen to a lower rank of vassalage. They are all wretched. The first group buzzes around at ground level, never able to land: dismayed mosquitoes who have lost everything, including weight. The second group, sacrificing their organs of locomotion, have taken root in the sand: the slightest breath of wind can whip up these plants into a swarm. Nomadic or sedentary, they are united in stupor: Where did their lives go? Nizan has an answer. For the desperate and for the vassals. Only I doubt whether they are willing or able to read it: for that lost, mystified generation, this vigorous dead writer tolls the knell.

But they have twenty-year-old sons, our grandsons, who register their defeats and ours. Until recently, the prodigal sons told their fathers where to get off, packed up, and joined the left. The rebel, following the classical pattern, became an activist. But what if the fathers are on the left? What is to be done? A young man came to see me: he loved his parents, but, he said severely, "They're reactionaries." I have aged and words have aged with me: in my head, they are as old as I am. I mistook him. I thought I was dealing with the scion of a prosperous family that was rather sanctimonious, with free-market beliefs perhaps, voting for Pinay.[4] He set me straight: "My father's been a communist since the Congress of Tours." Another, the son of a socialist, condemned both the SFIO[5] and the CP: "The one lot are traitors, the others are in a rut." And what if the fathers were conservatives? What if they supported Bidault?[6] Do we believe this great upturned, worm-ridden cadaver, the left, can attract the young? It is a stinking, decaying carcass; the power of the military, and dictatorship and fascism are being—or will be—born from its rotting corpse; it takes a strong stomach not to turn away from it. We, the grandfathers, were made by the left; we lived by it; in it and by it we shall die. But we no longer have anything to say to the young: fifty years of living in this backward province that France has become is degrading. We have shouted, protested, signed, and signed again. Depending on our habits of thought, we have declared, "It is not acceptable..." or "The proletariat won't stand for..." And yet, in the end, here we are; we have accepted everything. How to convey our wisdom and the fine fruits of our experience to these young unknowns? From abdication to abdication we have learned only one thing: our total powerlessness. Now, I admit that this is the beginning of Reason, of the struggle for life. But we have old bones, and, at an age when people are usually thinking about writing their wills, we are discovering that we have achieved nothing. Shall we tell them, "Be Cubans, be Russians or Chinese, as you like, be Africans"? They will tell us it is rather too late to change their place of birth. In short, accountants or tearaways, technicians or teddy boys, they are battling alone and without hope against asphyxiation. And do not think those who choose job and family are showing resignation: they have turned their violence inward and are destroying themselves. Reduced to impotence by their fathers, they cripple themselves out of spite. The others smash everything, hit anyone and everyone with everything and anything—a knife, a bicycle chain: to escape their malaise, they will send everything up in smoke. But nothing does go up in smoke and they end up at the police station, covered in blood. It was a great Sunday; next week they'll do better. Dishing out violence or taking it is all the same to them: there just has to be blood.

In the daze that follows the brawls, only their bruises hurt; they have the funereal pleasure of empty minds.

Who will speak to these "Angry Young Men"?[7] Who can explain their violence? Nizan is their man. Year by year, his hibernation has made him younger. Not so long ago he was our contemporary; today he is theirs. When he lived we shared his anger, but, in the end, none of us performed "the simplest Surrealist act" and now here we are, grown old. We have betrayed our youth so many times that mere decency demands we do not speak of it. Our old memories have lost their claws and their teeth. I must have been twenty once, but I'm fifty-five now and I would not dare write, "I was twenty. I won't let anyone tell me it's the best time of life." So much passion—and so lofty. Coming from my pen it would be demagogy. And then I would be lying: the unhappiness of the young is total, I know—I may perhaps have felt it once—but it is still human because it comes to them from human beings who are their fathers or their elders; ours comes from our arteries; we are strange objects half eaten away by Nature, by vegetation and covered with ants, we are like lukewarm drinks or the idiotic paintings that amused Rimbaud. Young and violent, the victim of a violent death, Nizan can step out of the ranks and speak to young people about youth: "I won't let anyone . . ." They will recognize their own voices. To some he can say, "Your modesty will be the death of you, dare to desire, be insatiable, let loose the terrible forces that are warring and whirling inside you, do not be ashamed to ask for the moon—we must have it." To the others, "Turn your rage on those who caused it, don't try to run away from your pain but seek out its causes and smash them." He can say anything to them because he's a young monster, a fine young monster like them, who shares their terror of dying and their hatred of living in the world we have made for them. He was alone, became a communist, ceased to be one and, died alone near a window on a stairway. His life is explained by his intransigence: he became a revolutionary out of a sense of rebellion; when revolution was necessarily eclipsed by the war, he rediscovered his violent youth and ended as a rebel.

We both wanted to write. He finished his first book long before I penned a word of mine. At the point when *La Nausée*[8] appeared, if we had valued such solemn presentations, *he* would have prefaced *my* book. Death has reversed the roles. Death and systematic defamation. He will find readers without my assistance: I have said who his natural readership will be. But I thought this foreword was necessary for two reasons: to show everyone the cunningly abject nature of his detractors and to warn the young to lend his words their full weight. They were once young and hard, those words; it is we who have caused them to age. If I want to restore to them the brilliance they had before the war, I must recall the "marvelous age" of our refusals and make it live again, with Nizan, the man who said "no" to the very end. His death was the end of a world: after him, the Revolution became constructive and the left came to define itself by assent—to the point where, one day in the autumn of 1958, it expired, with a last, dying "yes" on its lips.[9] Let us attempt to recover the days of hatred, of unquenched desire, of destruction, those days when André Breton, barely older than we were, spoke of wishing to see the Cossacks watering their horses in the fountains of the Place de la Concorde.

II

The error I want to avoid readers committing is one I made myself during his lifetime. Yet we were close—so close that we were sometimes mistaken for each other. In June 1939, Léon Brunschvicg[10] met the two of us at the publisher Gallimard's offices and congratulated me on having written *Les Chiens de garde*:[11] "although," as he told me without bitterness, "you were rather hard on me." I smiled at him in silence. Alongside, Nizan smiled too: the great idealist left without our having disabused him. This confusion had been going on for eighteen years; it had come to define us socially and, in the end, we accepted it. From 1920 to 1930, in particular, as schoolboys and then students, we were indistinguishable. Nevertheless, I did not see him as he was.

I could have drawn his portrait: medium height, dark hair. He squinted, as I did, but in the opposite direction, that is to say attractively. My divergent strabismus turned my face into an unplowed field;

his was convergent and lent him a mischievous faraway look, even when he was paying attention. He followed fashion closely, insolently. At seventeen, his trousers were so tight around the ankles that he had difficulty pulling them on. A little later they flared into bell-bottoms, to the point where they hid his shoes. Then, all of a sudden, they turned into flares, up around his knees and billowing out like skirts. He carried a rattan cane and wore a monocle, wing collars or little round ones. He exchanged his iron-rimmed spectacles for enormous tortoiseshell ones which, with a touch of the Anglo-Saxon snobbery that raged among the youth of the time, he called his "goggles."

I tried to emulate him, but my family mounted effective resistance, even going so far as to bribe the tailor. And then someone must have put a spell on me: when I wore them, fine clothes changed into rags and tatters. I resigned myself to gazing at Nizan in amazement and admiration. At the École normale, no one gave much thought to how they dressed, with the exception of a few provincials who proudly wore spats and sported silk handkerchiefs in their jacket. However, I don't remember anyone disapproving of Nizan's outfits: we were proud to have a dandy among us.

Women liked him, but he kept them at arm's length. To one who came right up to our very room and offered herself to him, he replied, "Madam, we would be defiling each other." In fact, he liked only girls, and he chose the virgins and the fools among them, drawn by the dizzying secret of stupidity—our only true profundity—and by the glossy brilliance of a flesh with no memories. Indeed, during the only liaison I ever knew him to have, he was constantly tormented by the most needless jealousy: he could not bear the thought that his mistress had a past. I found his behavior quite incomprehensible, and yet it was very clear. I stubbornly insisted on seeing it as a personality trait. I also saw his charming cynicism and his "black humor" as personality traits, together with his quiet, implacable aggressiveness; he never raised the tone of his voice; I never saw him frown nor heard him strain his voice: he would bend back his fingers and, as I have said, fall to contemplating his nails, loosing his violent remarks with a sly, deceptive serenity.

276 · JEAN-PAUL SARTRE

Together we fell into every trap there is: at sixteen, he offered me the role of superman and I eagerly accepted. There would, he said, be the two of us. Since he was a Breton, he gave us Gaelic names. We covered all the blackboards with the strange words R'hâ and Bor'hou. He was R'hâ. One of our classmates wanted to share our newfound status. We devised ordeals to test him. He had, for example, to declare out loud that the French army and the flag could go to hell; these remarks were not so daring as we imagined: they were commonplace at the time and reflected the internationalism and antimilitarism of the old prewar days. However, the aspirant declined the task and the two supermen remained alone, eventually forgetting their superhumanity.

We would spend hours, days, strolling around Paris: we discovered its flora, its fauna, and its stones, and were moved to tears when the first electric signs appeared; we thought the world was new because we were new in the world. Paris was the bond between us; we loved each other through the crowds of this gray city, beneath its light spring skies. We walked and talked; we invented our own language, an intellectual slang of the kind all students make up.

One night, the supermen climbed the hill of Sacré-Coeur and turning, saw a disorderly collection of jewels spread out beneath their feet. Nizan stuck his cigarette into the left-hand corner of his mouth, which he twisted into a horrible grimace, and announced, "Hey, hey, Rastignac." I repeated, "Hey, Hey!" as I was meant to, and we walked down again, satisfied at having so discreetly marked the extent of our literary knowledge and the measure of our ambition. No one has written about those walks or that Paris better than my friend. Reread *La Conspiration*[12] and you will recapture the fresh, yet quaint charm of that world capital, quite unaware as yet that it would later become a provincial backwater. The ambition, the sudden mood swings, the gentle, livid rages—I took it all in my stride. That was the way Nizan was, calm and perfidious, charming. That was how I loved him.

He described himself in *Antoine Bloyé* as "a taciturn adolescent, already plunged into the adventures of youth, deserting childhood with a kind of avid exhilaration."[13] And that is how I saw him. I experienced his taciturnity to my own cost. In *hypokhâgne*,[14] we fell out for six months, which I found painful. At the École normale, where we roomed together, he went for days without speaking to me. In the second year, his mood grew even darker: he was going through a crisis and could see no way out. He disappeared, and was found three days later, drunk, with strangers. And when my fellow students asked me about his "escapades," I could answer only that he was "in a foul mood." Yet he had told me of his fear of death, but, being mad enough to believe myself immortal, I criticized him for this and thought that he was wrong: death wasn't worth a thought. Nizan's horror of death was like his retrospective jealousy—eccentricities that a healthy morale should combat.

When he couldn't stand things any longer, he left: he became a tutor with an English family in Aden. This departure scandalized the rest of us, rooted in the École as we were, but, since Nizan intimidated us, we found a benign explanation: love of travel. When he came back the following year, he did so at night when no one was expecting him. I was alone in my room. I had been plunged into a state of pained indignation since the previous day by the loose morals of a young lady from the provinces. He entered without knocking. He was pale, a bit breathless, and rather grim. He said, "You don't look too cheerful." "Neither do you," I replied. Whereupon we went off to have a drink and set the world to rights, happy that the good feeling was restored between us.

But this was simply a misunderstanding: my anger was a mere soap bubble, his was real. He gagged on the horror of returning to his cage with his tail between his legs. He was looking for the sort of help no one could give him. His words of hate were pure gold, mine were false coin. He ran off the very next day. He lived with his fiancée, joined the Communist Party, married, had a daughter, nearly died of appendicitis; then, after passing the *agrégation*, taught philosophy at Bourg and stood for election to parliament. I saw him less. I was teaching at Le Havre and there was also the fact that he had a family. His wife had given him a second child—a son—but it was mostly the Party that came between us: I was a sympathizer but not an initiate. I remained his friend from adolescence, a petty bourgeois that he liked.

Why did I not understand him? There was no lack of signs: Why would I not see them? It was out of jealousy, I think: I denied the feelings that I couldn't share. I sensed from the very first that he had incommunicable passions, a destiny that would separate us. I was afraid and I blinded myself to these things. At fifteen, this son of a pious woman had wanted to take holy orders: I found out only many years afterward. But I can still remember my scandalized bewilderment when, walking round the schoolyard with me, he said, "I had lunch with the pastor." He saw my stupor and explained in a detached tone, "I may convert to Protestantism." "You," I said, indignantly, "but you don't believe in God." "Well, no," he replied, "but I like their morality."

Madame Nizan threatened to cut off his allowance and the plan was dropped, but the moment had been enough for me to glimpse, beyond this "childish whim," the impatience of a sick man writhing around to escape his pain. I did not want him to have this inaccessible pain: we shared superficial melancholies and that was enough; otherwise, I tried to force my optimism on him. I kept telling him we were free: he did not reply, but his thin, sidelong smile was eloquent.

On other occasions, he proclaimed himself a materialist—we were barely seventeen—and I was the one smiling scornfully. Materialist, determinist: he felt the physical weight of his chains; I did not want to feel the weight of mine. I hated him engaging in politics because I felt no need to do so myself. He was a communist, then a follower of Georges Valois,[15] then a communist again. It was easy to mock him and I wasn't slow to do so; in fact, these enormous swings were evidence of his stubbornness: there was nothing more excusable than that he should hesitate between two extremes at the age of eighteen.

What did not vary was his extremism: whatever happened, the existing order had to be destroyed. For my part, I was quite happy at the existence of that order and the opportunity to hurl my bombs—my words—in its direction. This real need to unite with other men to move away the stones that were weighing them down seemed to me a mere dandy's extravagance: he was a communist in the same way that he was a monocle-wearer, out of a trivial desire to shock.

He was unhappy at the École normale and I criticized him for it: we were going to write, we would write fine books that would justify our existences. Since I wasn't complaining, why was he? In the middle of the second year, he suddenly declared that literature bored him and he was going to be a cameraman; a friend gave him a few lessons. I was annoyed with him. In explaining to me that too much reading and writing had turned him against words and he now wanted to act on things and transform them into silence with his hands, he was, as I saw it, merely compounding his offense: this defector from the word could not condemn writing without passing sentence on me. It never occurred to me that Nizan was seeking, as we said at the time, his salvation, and these "written cries" do not save.

He did not become a cameraman and I was delighted. But only briefly: his departure for Aden annoyed me. For him it was a matter of life and death, as I guessed. To reassure myself, I chose to see it as a further eccentricity. I had to admit to myself that I did not mean much to him, but, I ask myself today, whose fault was that? Where would you find a more stubborn refusal to understand and, hence, to help? When he came back from one of his binges, his panic-stricken flights, drunk and with death at his heels, I would welcome him tight-lipped without a word, with the dignity of an old wife who has resigned herself to such outrages, so long as it is understood that she is keeping score. It is true he was hardly encouraging. He would go and sit down at his table, gloomy, his hair tousled, his eyes bloodshot; if I happened to speak to him, he would give me a distant, hate-filled look. No matter, I still reproach myself for the fact that I had only these four words in my head: "What an awkward so-and-so!" and that I never tried, even out of curiosity, to find an explanation for these escapades. His marriage I got all wrong. I was friendly with his wife, but bachelorhood was a moral principle with me, a rule of life. It could not, I assumed, be otherwise for Nizan. I decided he had married Rirette because that was the only way he could have her. In all honesty, I didn't realize that a young man in the grip of a dreadful family can break free only by starting one of his own. I was born to be a bachelor all my days. I did not understand that the single life weighed down the bachelor living at my side, that he detested casual affairs—because they have a taste of death about them—just as he detested travel, and that, when he said "man is a sedentary animal" or "give me my field . . . my needs, my men," he was simply demanding his share of happiness: a home, a wife, and children.

When he published *Aden, Arabie*, I thought it a good book and I was delighted. But I saw it only as a lightweight pamphlet, a whirl of frivolous words. Many of his classmates made the same mistake: we were set in our thinking. For most of us, for me, the École normale was, from the very first day, the beginning of independence. Many can say, as I do, that they had four years of happiness there. But here was a wild man flying at our throats: "The École normale...a ridiculous and more often odious thing, presided over by a patriotic, hypocritical, powerful little old man who respected the military." In his eyes, we were "adolescents worn out by years of lycée, corrupted by a classical education, and by bourgeois morality and cooking."[16] We chose to laugh about it: "He didn't moan about the place when he was here, did he? He seemed to have quite a good time with the worn-out adolescents." And we would recall our harmless pranks, in which he had gladly taken part. Forgetting his escapades, his scorn, and the great breakdown that took him off to distant Arabia, we saw his passion merely as excessive rhetoric. Personally, I felt foolishly offended because he tarnished my memories. Since Nizan had shared my life at the École, he had to have been happy there, or else our friendship was dead even then. I preferred to rescue the past. I said to myself, "It's all a bit over the top!" Today, I think our friendship was already dead, through no fault of our own, and that Nizan, consumed with loneliness, needed to be fighting among men rather than bandying words with an unfaithful and all-too-familiar reflection of himself. I was the one who maintained our friendship and embalmed it, by premeditated ignorance, by lying. In truth, our paths had always been moving apart. It has taken many years, and I have had to come at last to understand my own path through life, before being able to speak sure-footedly about his.

The more dismal life is, the more absurd is death. I do not claim that a man busy with his work and full of hope cannot be struck, as if by lightning, by an awareness of death. I do say that a young man is afraid of death when he is unhappy with his fate. Before he is led by the hand to the seat that is kept for him, a student is the infinite, the undefined: he passes easily from one doctrine to another, detained by none of them; he finds all systems of thought equivalent. In fact, what we call "classics" in school curricula is merely the teaching of the great errors of the past. Shaped by our republics in the image of Valéry's Monsieur Teste—that ideal citizen who never says or does anything but who knows what the score is all the same[17]—these young men will take twenty years to understand that ideas are stones, that there is an inflexible order to them and they have to be used for building. So long as worn-out old men, discreet to the point of transparency, carry bourgeois objectivity so far as to ask their students to adopt the standpoint of Nero, Loyola, and Monsieur Thiers, each of these apprentices will take himself for pure Mind, that colorless, tasteless gas that at times expands to the galaxies and at others condenses into formulae. The young elite are everything and nothing: in other words, they are supported by the state and by their families; beneath this vaporous indistinctness their life burns away; suddenly pure Mind is brought up short against the stumbling block of Death. In vain does it try to encompass it in order to dissolve it: death cannot be thought. A body is struck down by an accident; a brute fact must put an end to the brilliant indeterminacy of ideas. This shocking realization awakens more than one terrified adolescent at night: against capital punishment and its incomprehensible particularity, universal Culture provides no defense. Later, when the individuality of his body is reflected in the individuality of the work he has undertaken, a young man will integrate his death into his life and view it as just one more risk among others— among all those that threaten his work and family. For those men who have the rare good fortune to be able to enjoy what they do, the final disaster, the less terrifying as one approaches it, is converted into the small change of everyday concerns.

I have described our common fate. That is nothing; but when the anxiety outlasts adolescence, when it becomes the profound secret of the adult and the mainspring of his decisions, the invalid knows his afflictions: his terror at the idea that he will soon be no more simply reflects his horror at still having to live. Death is the irremediable sentence; it condemns the wretched, for eternity, to have been only that: disgusting calamities. Nizan dreaded that fate: this monster crawled randomly among monsters; he feared one day he would burst and nothing would remain. He had known for a long time when he put these words into the mouth of one of his characters, that death was the definitive illumination of life: "If I think about my death, it's for a good reason. It's because my life is hollow and death is all it deserves." In the same book, Bloyé takes fright at "the uniform countenance of his life . . . and [this fear] comes from a deeper region than the bleeding places in the body where the warnings of disease are formed."[18]

What, when all is said and done, did he suffer from? Why did I sound ridiculous to him, more than to anyone else, when I talked about our freedom? If he believed, from the age of sixteen, in the inflexible chain of causes, it was because he felt constrained and manipulated: "We have within us divisions, alienations, wars, debates . . ." "Every man is split between the men he can be . . ."[19] Having been a solitary child, he was too conscious of his singularity to throw himself, as I did, into universal ideas: having been a slave, he came to philosophy to free himself, and Spinoza provided him with a model: in the first two types of knowledge, man remains a slave because he is incomplete; knowledge of the third type breaks down the partitions, the negative determinants: so far as the mode is concerned, it is one and the same thing to return to infinite substance or to achieve the affirmative totality of one's particular essence. Nizan wanted to beat down all walls: he would unify his life by proclaiming his desires and assuaging them.

The easiest desire to name comes from sex and its frustrated appetites: in a society that reserves its women for old men and the rich, this is the first source of unhappiness for a poor young man and a premonition of his future troubles. Nizan spoke bitterly of the old men who slept with our women and sought to castrate us. But, all in all, we were living in the age of the Great Desire: the Surrealists wanted to awaken that infinite concupiscence whose object is simply Everything. Nizan was looking for remedies and took what he could find; through their works he came to know Freud, who became part of his pantheon. As revised by Breton and by a young writer in peril, Freud looked like Spinoza: he tore away the veils and cobwebs, he imposed harmony on the enemies massacring each other in our tunnels, dissolved our raging monsters in light, and reduced us to the unity of powerful appetites. My friend tried him for a while, not without some happiness.

Even in *Antoine Bloyé* we find traces of this influence. It gave us the following fine sentence, for example: "As long as men are not entire and free, they will dream at night." Antoine dreams: about the women he has not had and has not even dared to long for. On waking, he refuses to hear "this voice of wisdom." The fact is that "the wakeful man and the sleeper seldom see eye to eye."[20] Antoine is an old man, but here Nizan speaks from experience, I know; he used to dream, he dreamed until the day of his death: his wartime letters are filled with his dreams.

But it was only a working hypothesis, a temporary way of unifying himself. He adored the passing women in the street, those pale forms eclipsed by the light, by the smoke of Paris, those fleeting tokens of love; but he loved, above all, their being inaccessible to him: this well-behaved, literary young man intoxicated himself with privations; that is useful to a writer. But let us not suppose that he found chastity difficult to bear: one or two affairs—short and painful—and, the rest of the time, nice young girls whom he touched lightly as they slipped by. He would have been only too happy to find in himself merely a conflict between the flesh and the law; he would have decided the matter by finding the law guilty: "Morality is an asshole," he used to say at twenty. In fact, taboos are more insidious, and our very bodies collude with them. Morality never showed itself but, with all women other than virgins, his unease was accompanied by a strong sense of revulsion. Later, when he had his "field" and his "men," he praised the beauty of the *whole* female body to me with a shocked, but precise, sense of wonder. I had wondered what had kept him from such a general discovery at the time of his devastating affairs. Now I know: it was disgust, an infantile repugnance for bodies he regarded as stale from past caresses. As adolescents, when we looked at women, I wanted them all; he wanted only one, and one who would be his. He could not conceive that it was possible to love unless one loved from dawn till nighttime, or that there could be possession when you did not possess the woman and she did not possess you. He thought that man was a sedentary being and that casual affairs were like travel—abstractions. A thousand and three women are a thousand and three times the same, and he wanted one woman who would be a thousand

and three times another; as a promise against death, he would love in her even the secret signs of fecundity.

In other words, the non-satisfaction of the senses was an effect, not a cause. Once married, it disappeared: the Great Desire fell back into line, became one need among others again, a need one satisfies poorly, too quickly, or not at all. In fact, Nizan suffered from his present contradictions only because he deciphered them by the light of the future. If he formed the intention, one day, of killing himself, it was to put an immediate end to what he believed merely to be a recommencement. He was marked from childhood by Breton piety; too much or too little for his happiness; contradiction had settled beneath his roof. He was the child of old parents: the two adversaries had begotten him during a cease-fire; by the time he was born, they had resumed their quarrel. His father, first a manual worker, then an engineer on the railways, provided him with an example of adult, atheistic, technical thinking and, when he talked, betrayed a sorrowful loyalty to the class he had left behind. This mute conflict between a childish old bourgeoise and a renegade worker was something Nizan internalized from his earliest childhood; he made it the future foundation of his personality. However humble his position may be, the child of a housekeeper has a part in the future of his family: his father makes plans. The Nizans had no future: the yardmaster was almost at the height of his career—what had he to look forward to? A promotion that was due to him, a few honors, retirement, and death. Madame Nizan lived both in the crucial moment—when the onions have to be "browned" or the juices "sealed" in the chops—and in that fixed moment termed Eternity. The child was not far from his starting point and the family not far from its point of fall: carried along in this fall, he wanted to learn and build, whereas everything was visibly coming apart, even the marital quarrel. Externally, it had transformed itself into indifference; it existed nowhere, except within him. In the silence, the child heard their dialogue: the ceremonious, futile babble of Faith was occasionally interrupted by a harsh voice, naming plants, stones, and tools. These two voices consumed each other. At first the pious language seemed to be winning out: there was talk of Charity, Paradise, of Divine Purpose, and all this eschatology did battle with the precise activity of the technicians. What was the point of building locomotives? There are no trains to heaven. The engineer would leave the house as soon as he could. Between the ages of five and ten, his son would follow him into the fields, take his hand, and run along at his side. At twenty-five, he had fond memories of those men-only walks that were so obviously directed against the wife, against his mother. I note, however, that he gave his preference not to the Sciences but to the weary urbanity of the Word. A worker becomes an engineer, feels the deficiencies in his education, and his son tries to get into the École Polytechnique; the pattern is a classic one. But Nizan showed a suspect repugnance for mathematics: he did Greek and Latin. As the stepson of a Polytechnique graduate, I had the same dislike, but for different reasons: we liked vague, ritualistic words, myths. Yet his father took his revenge: under the influence of his positivism, my friend sought to wrest himself from the baubles of religion. I have mentioned the stages of this release: the mystical transport—the last gasp of Catholicism—that almost took him into holy orders, his flirtations with Calvin, and the metamorphosis of his pious Catharism into political Manichaeism, royalism, and, in the end, Marxism. For a long time the two of us continued to use a Christian vocabulary: though atheists, we had no doubt we had been brought into the world to find our salvation, and, with a little luck, the salvation of others. There was only one difference: I felt certain I was one of the elect, Nizan often wondered if he were not damned. From his mother and Catholicism he got his radical scorn for the things of this world, the fear of succumbing to worldly temptations, and the taste—which he never lost—for pursuing an absolute Purpose. He was persuaded that, hidden within him, beneath the tangle of daily concerns, was a beautiful totality, flawless and unsullied; he had to hoe and weed, to burn the brushwood, and the indivisible Eternity would manifest itself in all its purity. And so, at this period, he regarded his father's job as manic, pointless agitation: the order of supreme purposes was being sacrificed to that of mere technical resources; man was being lost to the machine. He soon stopped believing in the white pills of life called souls, but he retained the obscure feeling that his father had lost his.

These ancient superstitions do not prevent you from living, *provided that you have the Faith*. But technology, ruled out of court, took its revenge by wringing the neck of religion. Nizan's dissatisfactions stayed with him, but they were rootless now and disconnected. Worldly activities are farcical, but, if nothing exists but the earth and the human animals scraping a living from it, then the children of men must take over and begin scraping: for there is no other occupation, short of doctoring the old Christian words. When Nizan offered me the strange prospect of becoming a superman, it was not so much pride that drove him as an obscure need to escape our condition. Alas, it was merely a matter of changing names. From that time on, until he left for Aden, he carried a constant millstone around his neck and kept on forging symbols of escape.

But one would understand nothing of Nizan's *angst* if one did not recall what I said earlier: he deciphered this arduous, disenchanted present, broken as it was only by brief periods of exhilaration, in the sinister light of a future that was nothing other than his father's past. "I was afraid. My departure was a product of fear." Fear of what? He says it right here in this book: "mutilations ... awaited us. After all, we knew how our parents lived."[21] He expanded upon this sentence in a very fine, long novel, *Antoine Bloyé*, where he recounts the life and death of his father. As for Nizan, though he barely appears in the book, he continually speaks of himself: first, he is the witness to this process of decay; and second, Monsieur Nizan confided in no one— all the thoughts and feelings attributed to him are torn from the author's own person and projected into that old, disordered heart. This constant dual presence is a sign of what psychoanalysts term "identification with the father."

I have said that, in his early years, Nizan admired his father, that he envied that sterile but visible strength, those silences and those hands that had toiled. Monsieur Nizan used to talk about his former comrades: fascinated by these men who knew the truth about life and who seemed to love each other, the little boy saw his father as a worker and wanted to be like him in every way—he would have his father's earthly patience. It would take nothing less than the obscure inner density of things, of matter, to save the future monk from his mother, from Monsieur le Curé, and from his own idle chatter. "Antoine," he said admiringly, "was a corporeal being. He did not have a mind so pure that it separated itself from the body that nourished it and for so many years had provided it with the admirable proof of existence."[22]

But the admirable man stumbled; suddenly, the child saw him begin to come apart. Nizan had committed himself unreservedly to his father: "I shall be like him." He now had to watch the interminable decomposition of his own future: "That will be me." He saw matter come to grief; the maternal prattle triumphed—and with it the Spirit, that foam that remained after the shipwreck. What happened? Nizan tells the story in *Antoine Bloyé*: for reasons I do not understand—because, while staying quite close to the truth in his book, he undoubtedly changed the circumstances—the man who served as the model for Antoine sought, as early as forty years of age, to take stock of his life. Everything had begun with that false victory, a "crossing of the line," at a time when the bourgeoisie was promising everyone a "great future of equal opportunity," a time when every working-man's son carried in his schoolbag "a blank certificate of membership in the middle classes." Since the age of fifteen, his life had been like the express trains he would later drive, trains "carried along by a force that was all certainty and breathlessness." And then, in 1883, he graduated from the École des Arts et Métiers, eighteenth out of a class of seventy-seven. A little later, at twenty-seven, he married Anne Guyader, his yardmaster's daughter. From that point on, "everything was settled, established. There was no going back." He sensed this at the very moment the *curé* united them and then he forgot his worries: years passed, the couple went from town to town, constantly moving in and out without ever settling. Time wore on, and life remained provisional; yet every day was like all the others in its abstraction. Antoine dreamed, without too much conviction, that "something would happen." Nothing happened. He consoled himself: he would show what he was made of in the real battles. But while he waited for the great events, the little ones ate into him and imperceptibly wore him down. "True courage consists in overcoming small enemies." Yet he rose irresistibly. First, he experienced "the most insidious peace," he heard the bourgeois siren song: he was able to derive from the false duties assigned to him—toward the Company, towards Society, *even* toward his former comrades—what might be called a vital minimum of good conscience. But "the years piled up"; desires, hopes, and memories of youth drove down "into that shadowy realm of condemned thoughts into which human forces sink." The Company devoured its employees: for fifteen years there was no man less self-aware than Antoine Bloyé: he was driven by "the demands, the ideas and the judgments of work"; he barely even scanned the newspapers: "the events they speak of take place on another planet and are of no concern to him." He passionately devoured "descriptions of machines" in technical journals. He lived, or rather his body imitated the attitudes of life. But the mainsprings of his life, the motives for his action were not in him. In fact, "complex powers prevent him from having his feet firmly set on the earth." Changing just a few words, changing nothing, one could apply to him what Nizan writes about a rich Englishman in Aden: "Each of us is divided among the men he might be, and Mr. C. has allowed to triumph within him that man for whom life consists of making the price of... Abyssinian leather go up or down... Fighting abstract entities such as firms, unions, merchants' guilds—are you going to call that action?"[23] Of course, Bloyé does not have so much power, but what of that? Isn't everything about his job abstract: the plans, the specifications, the paperwork—isn't it all *preordained* somewhere else, a long way away, by other people? The man himself is merely a subsidiary of the Company: this "full employment" of himself leaves him both unoccupied and available. He sleeps little, works unstintingly, carries sacks and beams on his back, is always the last to leave his office, but, as Nizan says, "all his work conceals his essential lack of an occupation." I know. I spent ten years of my life under the thumb of a *polytechnicien*. He worked himself to death—or rather, somewhere, no doubt in Paris, his work had decided it would kill him.

He was the most trifling of men: on Sundays he would withdraw into himself, find a desert within and lose himself in it; he held on, though, saved by his somnolence or by rages of wounded vanity. When they retired him, it was, fortunately, during wartime: he read the newspapers, cut out articles, and glued them into a notebook. At least he was straight about it: his flesh was abstract. For young Bloyé, however, the scandal lay in an unbearable contradiction: Antoine had a real body that was tough, capable, and had once been eager; and that body imitated life: driven by distant abstractions, scuttling his rich passions, he transformed himself into a creature of the mind:

> Antoine was a man who had a profession and a temperament, that was all. That is all a man is, in the world in which Antoine Bloyé lived. There are nervous shopkeepers, full-blooded engineers, morose workers and irascible notaries: people say these things and think they have worked on defining a man; they also say a black dog, a tabby cat. A doctor... had told him, "You're the highly-strung, full-blooded type, you are." There, that said everything. Everyone could handle him like a coin of known value. He circulated with the other coins.[24]

The boy worshipped his father: I do not know if he would have noticed this inner wretchedness on his own. Nizan's misfortune lay in the fact that his father was better than the next man: after ignoring many danger signs, Monsieur Nizan came—too late—to see what he was and was horrified at his life; in other words, he saw his death and hated it. For almost half a century he had lied to himself, he had tried to persuade himself he could still "become someone new, someone different, who would be truly himself." He realized suddenly that it was impossible to change. This impossibility was death in the midst of life: death draws the line and tots up the score; but, for Nizan's father, the line was already drawn, the score already counted. This schematic, half-generalized creature shared a bed with a woman who was no more a particular person than he was, but more a relay station for the pious thoughts manufactured in Rome, and one who had no doubt, like himself, repressed simple, voracious needs. He proclaimed their double failure to his frightened son. He would get up in the night:

> He carried his clothes over his arm and dressed at the foot of the staircase... He would go out... "I'm unnecessary," he would tell himself, "I'm not wanted, I'm useless, already I don't exist; if I threw myself into the water no one would notice, there would just be the announcement of my death. I'm a failure, I'm

finished..." He would come back in...shivering; he would
draw his hand over his face and feel how his beard had grown
during the night. Near the house, his wife and son, awakened,
would be looking for him, calling to him: he could hear their
high-pitched cries from a way off, but did not reply; he left them
to worry till the very last moment, as if to punish them. They
were afraid he had killed himself...When he got near them,
stifling his anger, he would say, "Haven't I the right to do as I
like?" and he would go back up to his room without any concern for them.[25]

These nocturnal escapades are no novelist's invention: Nizan
talked to me about his father and I know all this is true. Meditating
on death inclines you to suicide, out of a feverishness, an impatience.
I ask you to imagine the feelings of an adolescent whose mother wakes
him at night with the words, "Your father isn't in his bedroom; this
time I'm sure he's going to kill himself." Death enters him, hunkers
down at the crossroads of all his possible routes in life; it is the end
and the beginning: dead in advance, his father wants to join the lists
ahead of time—this is the meaning and conclusion of a stolen life.

But this paternal life occupied Nizan like a foreign power; his father infected him with the death that was to be his end. When this
disenchanted old man—the doctors called him "neurasthenic"—fled
the house goaded by fear, his son feared two deaths in one: the first, in
its imminence, presaged the other and lent it its aspect of horror. The
father bayed at death[26] and the child died of fright each night. In this
return to nothingness of a life that was nothing, the child believed he
saw his destiny; "everything was settled, established. There was no going back." He would be this superfluous young man, then this empty
shell, then nothing. He had identified with the strong maturity of another man; and when that man displayed his wounds, my friend was
alienated from that mortal wretchedness. The engineer's unseemly
nocturnal wanderings increased when Nizan turned fourteen; now,
between fifteen and sixteen, the adolescent took out an insurance
policy on eternal life: in one last effort, he asked the Church to grant
him immortality. Too late: when the faith is lost, disgust with one's

times is not enough to restore it. He lived out his alienation: he believed himself to be another, interpreted every moment in the light of another existence. Everywhere he came upon the traps that had been laid for his father. Kindly and deceitful people got around him with flattery or by granting him false victories: academic honors, little gifts, invitations. The engineer's son would enter the teaching profession. And afterward? Teachers, like railway yardmasters, move around a lot, pass hurriedly from town to town, take wives from the provincial lower middle class, and align themselves, out of self-interest or weakness, with their masters. Are they less divided than the technicians? And which is better: building locomotives to serve a few overlords and the bourgeois state, or imparting a foretaste of death to children by teaching them dead languages, a loaded history, and a mendacious morality? Do academics show more indulgence "for their great pain, for the adventures coiled in the crevices of their bodies"? All these petty bourgeois are alike: they have an imbecilic dignity imposed on them, they unman themselves, they have no sense of the real purpose of their work, and they wake up at fifty to watch themselves die.

From the age of sixteen, I thought we were united by the same desire to write; I was wrong. As a clumsy hunter, I was dazzled by words because I always missed them; the more precocious Nizan had a game bag full of them. He found them everywhere—in dictionaries, in books, even at large on people's lips. I admired his vocabulary and the way he dropped into the conversation, with ease and at the first attempt, the terms he had just acquired—among others, "bimetallism" and "percolator." But he was far from fully committed to literature: I was inside it; the discovery of an adjective delighted me. For his part, he wrote better and watched himself write, doing so with his father's cheerless eyes. The words died or turned into withered leaves: Can you justify yourself with words? The smoldering fires of death made literature seem a mere party game, a variant on canasta. It is quite natural for a teacher to write; he is encouraged to do so. And the same traps will work with both the engineer and the writer: flattery and temptation. At forty, all these flunkeys are mere shells of themselves. Valéry was buried beneath honors; he met with princes, queens, and powerful industrialists and dined at their tables. And he did so because he was working for them: the glorification of the word serves the interests of people in high places; you teach people to take the word for the thing, which is not so costly. Nizan understood this: he was afraid of wasting his life gathering together mere wisps of voices.

He set about *repeating* his father's dark follies: he recommenced that man's nocturnal excursions and escapades. He would be walking in the street and suddenly "he felt he was going to die (and) was suddenly a man apart from all the passers-by... It was a thing he knew in a single act of cognition, a thing of which he had a particular, perfect knowledge."[27] It wasn't an idea, but "an absolutely naked anxiety... far beyond all individual forms." At such moments he believed he possessed a fundamental, material insight; he believed he understood the undivided unity of his body through the unity of its radical negation. But I don't think it was anything of the sort: we do not even have that, do not even have such unmediated communication with our nothingness. In reality, a shock had revived his old, learned pain-response: in him his father's life was draining away, the eye of *other death* reopened, tainting his modest pleasures: the street became a hell.

In those moments he loathed us: "the friends he met, the women he glimpsed were life's accomplices, drawing drafts on time." He would not even have dreamed of asking our help: we lacked awareness, we would not even have understood him: "Which of these madmen loved him so shrewdly as to protect him from death?"[28] He fled our rapacious faces, our eager mouths, our greedy nostrils, our eyes ever set on the future. Gone missing. A three-day suicide, ending in a hangover. He was *reproducing* his father's nighttime crises; these grew more acute and ended in drink—and yet more words: I think he exaggerated the tragic element, being unable to achieve the perfect, gloomy sincerity of the fifty-year-old. No matter: his anxiety did not lie; and if you want to know the deepest, most specific truth, I would say that it was *this* and this alone: the death throes of an old man gnawing at the life of a very young one. He had fire and passion about him, and then that implacable stare froze everything; to judge himself on a daily basis, Nizan had placed himself beyond the tomb. In fact, he was going around in circles: there was, of course, the rush to get to the end, and the panic fear that he would do so; there was the time that was wearing away, "the years piling up," and those traps he just managed to avoid, that manhunt, the sense of which he didn't quite understand; but there was also, in spite of everything, his muscles, his blood: How could you stop a well-fed young bourgeois from trusting in the future? He did have times of somber enthusiasm, but his own excitement frightened him, aroused mistrust: What if it were a trap, one of the lies you tell yourself to choke back your anxiety and pain? The only thing he liked in himself was his revolt: it proved he was still holding out, that he was not yet on the track that leads, irresistibly, to life's railroad sidings. But when he thought about it, he was afraid that his resistance might weaken: they have thrown so many blankets on me that they've almost got me; they will start again. What if I were to get used, little by little, to the condition they are preparing for me?

Around 1925–26, this was what he feared madly: habituation. "So many ties to break, secret timidities to conquer, little battles to fight... One is afraid of being... unbearably singular, of no longer being just like anyone... false courage waits for great opportunities; true courage consists in defeating the little enemies each day." Would he manage to defeat these gnawing enemies? And in five or six years' time, would he still be capable of breaking all these ties, which daily increased in number? He was living in enemy country, surrounded by the familiar signs of universal alienation: "Just try, while still in your arrondissements and sub-prefectures, to forget your civic and filial obligations."[29] Everywhere there were invitations to slumber, to abandonment, to resignation: he had got to the point of cataloguing his abdications: "the terrible old habits." He was also afraid of that alibi so dear to the cultured: the empty noise in his head of torn and precious words. Meditation on death has, in fact, other consequences, more serious than these intermittent conversations: it disenchants. I was running after sparks that for him were merely ashes. He wrote, "I tell you, all men are bored." Now, the worst damage done by boredom, "that continuous forewarning of death," is to generate a by-product for sensitive souls: the inner life. Nizan feared his very real loathings might end up by giving him an overrefined subjectivity, and he was afraid that he might lull his grievances to sleep with the purring of "empty thoughts, and ideas that are not ideas at all." These aborted offspring of our impotence deflect us from facing up to our wounds, our bleeding. But Nizan, with his eyes wide open, felt sleep rising in him.

So far as the sons of the bourgeoisie are concerned, I think this revolt can be termed exemplary, because it has neither hunger nor exploitation as its direct cause. Nizan sees all lives through the cold windowpane of death: in his eyes, they become balance sheets; his fundamental alienation is the source of his insight: he can sniff out any kind of alienation. And how serious he is when he asks each of us, in the presence of our death, like a believer, "What did you do with your youth?" What a deep, sincere desire to knit together the scattered strands in each of us, to contain our disorders in the synthetic unity of a form: "Will man never be anything but a fragment of man—alienated, mutilated, a stranger to himself; how many parts of him left fallow... how many things aborted!"[30]

These cries of protest on the part of a "subhuman" form the outline in negative of the man he wanted to be. He put his mystical flights to one side, his taste for adventure and his word castles. The inaccessible image remains simple and familiar: man can be said to be a harmonious, free body. There is a bodily wisdom—constantly stifled, but constantly present since Adam; "in the most obscure part of our being are hidden our most authentic needs." It is not a question here of being madly in love or of undertakings that exceed our powers: man is sedentary; he loves the earth because he can touch it; he enjoys producing his life. The Great Desire was just empty words: *desires* remain, modest but concrete, balancing each other out; Nizan felt an affection for Epicurus, on whom he later wrote very well:[31] *there* was a man who spoke to everyone, to prostitutes and to slaves, and he never lied to them.

We may be reminded here of Rousseau and not without reason: out of loyalty to his childhood, Nizan the town dweller retained a kind of rustic naturalism. We may also wonder how this noble savage could have adapted to the needs of socialist production and interplanetary nomadism. It is true: we shall not recover our lost liberty unless we invent it; there can be no looking back, even to gauge the extent of our "authentic" needs.

But let us leave Epicureanism and Rousseau to one side: to do otherwise would be to take fleeting hints to extremes. Nizan began with individualism, like all the petty bourgeois of his day: he wanted to be *himself* and the entire world was separating him from himself; against the abstractions and symbolic entities they tried to slip into his heart, into his muscles, he defended his own, individual life. He never wasted effort describing the fullness of moments or passions: for him it did not exist. It is what is stolen from us. But he said that love was true and we were prevented from loving; that life could be true, that it could bring forth a true death, but that we were made to die even before we were born. In this upside-down world, where ultimate defeat is the truth of a life, he showed that we often have "encounters with death" and each time confused signs awaken "our most authentic needs." A little girl is born to Antoine and Anne Bloyé; she is doomed and they know it; grief draws closer together these abstract characters, who have been living in solitude despite being crowded together. For only a short while, the singularity of an accident will never be able to save individuals.

From the age of fifteen, Nizan had understood the key things about himself: this had to do with the nature of his suffering. Some alienations are, in fact, the more formidable for the fact that they are covered up by an abstract sense of our freedom. But he never felt free: there had been *possession*; his father's "bungling unhappiness" occupied him like a foreign power; it imposed itself upon him, destroying his pleasures and impulses, governing by diktat. And one could not even say this wretched fate had been produced by the ex-worker; it came from all quarters, from the whole of France, from Paris. Nizan had tried for a time—in the days of mysticism, of R'hâ and Bor'hou— to struggle alone, by way of words and moral uplift, against his revulsions and the discords within him. But to no avail: the fabric of our social being crushes us. Spinoza came to his aid: you have to act on the causes. But what if the causes are not in our hands? He deciphered his experience: "What man can overcome his dividedness? He will not overcome it on his own for its causes are not within him." This is the juncture at which to bid a scornful farewell to spiritual exercises: "I was under the impression that human life disclosed itself through revelation: what mysticism!"[32] It is clearly the case that one has to fight and that one can do nothing on one's own. Since everything comes from elsewhere—even the innermost contradictions that have produced the most singular features of one's character—the battle will be waged elsewhere and everywhere. Others will fight for him *there*; *here*, Nizan will fight for others: for the moment, it is simply a question of seeing clearly, of recognizing one's brothers-in-darkness.

As early as his second year at the École normale, he had been drawn to the communists: in short, his decision was made. But decisions are taken in the night and we battle for a long time against our own will, without recognizing what that will is. He had to knock on all the doors, to try everything, to test out solutions he had long since rejected. He wanted, I think, to experience the good things of this world before making his vow of poverty. He left in order to bury his bachelor life. And then the fear mounted and he had to break it off. Aden was his last temptation, his last attempt to find an individual way out. His last escapade too: Arabia attracted him in the same way as, on certain evenings, the Seine had attracted his father. Did he not later write of Antoine Bloyé that he "would have liked to abandon this existence . . . to become someone new, someone foreign, who would really be himself"? He imagined himself ". . . lost, like a man who has left no address and who is doing things and breathing." He had to get away from us and from himself.

We lost him, but he did not shake himself off. He was gnawed at now by a new abstraction: to run from one place to another, to chase after women was to hold on to nothing. Aden is a compressed version of Europe, heated to a white-hot temperature. Nizan one day did what his father—when still living—never dared: he took a convertible and set out on the road without a cap at noon. They found him in a ditch, unconscious but unharmed. This suicide attempt swept away some old terrors. On coming to, he looked about him and saw "the most naked state, the economic state." The colonies lay bare a regime that is seen only through a mist in the home countries. He came back: he had understood the causes of our servitude; the terror within him became a force of aggression: it turned to hatred. He was no longer fighting insidious, anonymous infiltrations; he had seen exploitation and oppression in the raw and understood that his adversaries had names and faces: they were human beings. Unhappy, alienated human beings, no doubt, like his father and himself. But "defending and preserving their unhappiness and its causes with cunning, violence, obstinacy and cleverness." On the night of his return, when he came knocking at my door, he knew he had tried everything, that he was up against it, that all the exits were blind alleys except one: war. He came back to his enemies' heartland to fight: "One must no longer be afraid to hate. One must no longer be ashamed to be a fanatic. I owe them some pain. They almost lost me."[33]

It was over: he found his community and was received into it; it protected him from them. But, since I am presenting him here to the young readers of today, I must reply to the question they will unfailingly ask: Did he at last find what he was looking for? What could the party offer to this sensitive soul, wracked to the core of his being by the horror of death? We have to ask this conscientiously: I am telling the story of an exemplary existence, which is the absolute opposite of an edifying life. Nizan turned over a new leaf and yet the old man— the old, young man—remained. Between 1929 and 1939, I saw less of him, but I can give an impression of these meetings which, though shorter, are the more vivid for it. I am told people choose family ahead of politics today. Nizan had chosen both—together. Aeneas had tired of carrying gloomy old Anchises for so long: with a heave of his shoulders he dropped him flat on his back; he became a husband and father in great haste, in order to kill his own father. But fatherhood alone is an insufficient remedy for childhood. Far from it. The authority of the new head of the family condemns him to repeat the age-old childishnesses that Adam bequeathed to us through our parents. My friend knew the score: he wanted to strike a definitive blow against the father who, in the passage from father to son, is repeatedly murdered and repeatedly revived. To do so, he would become *a different person* and, through a public discipline, would take care to avoid family quirks. Let us see whether he succeeded.

The doctrine fully satisfied him. He detested reconciliation, and among conciliators he most detested Leibniz, their Grand Master. Forced by the syllabus to study the *Discourse on Metaphysics*, he took his revenge by making a talented drawing of Leibniz in full flight, wearing a Tyrolean hat, with the imprint of Spinoza's boot on his right buttock. From the *Ethics* to *Capital*, by contrast, the transition was easy. Marxism became second nature for Nizan, or, rather, became equivalent to Reason itself. His eyes were Marxist, and his ears too. And his head. He was at last able to explain to himself his incomprehensible wretchedness, the holes in his life, his anxiety: he saw the world and saw himself in it. But, above all, the doctrine—while lending legitimacy to his hatreds—reconciled in him the opposing voices of his parents. Technical rigor, scientific exactitude, and the patience of reason—everything was preserved. But, at the same time, the pettiness of positivism was overcome and its absurd refusal to "know through causes"; the sad world of means—and of means to means—was left to the engineers. For the troubled young man trying to save his soul, there were absolute goals on offer: playing midwife to history, making revolution, readying Man to come into his kingdom. There was no talk of salvation or personal immortality, but survival, in fame or anonymity, was granted as part of a shared undertaking that ended only when the human race came to an end. He put everything into Marxism: physics and metaphysics, the passion for action and for rehabilitating his actions, his cynicism and his eschatological dreams. Man was his future: but this was a time for cleaving things apart; others would have the job of stitching them back together; to him fell the pleasure of merrily smashing everything to pieces for the good of humanity.

Everything suddenly took on substance, even words: he had distrusted them because they served bad masters. Once he could turn them against the enemy, everything changed. He used their ambiguity to confound, their dubious charms to beguile. With the Party's guarantee, literature could even become idle chatter; the writer, like the ancient sage, would, if he wanted, turn a triple somersault. All the words belonged to man's enemies; the Revolution gave permission to steal them; that was all. But it was enough: Nizan had been pilfering for ten years and suddenly he came forth with the sum total of his thefts: his vocabulary. He understood his role as a communist writer and understood that discrediting the enemies of man or discrediting their language were, for him, one and the same thing. It was "no-holds-barred," the law of the jungle. The masters' Word is a lie: we shall take apart their sophisms and shall also invent sophisms against them; we shall lie to them. We shall even go so far as to clown around, so as to prove, as we speak, that the masters' speech is clownish.

These games have become suspect today: the East is building; it has given our provinces a new respect for the "trinkets of high-sounding inanity."[34] I have said we were serious, caught between two kinds of false coin, one coming from the East, the other from the West. In 1930, there was only one sort and, with us in France, the Revolution was simply at the destructive stage: it was the intellectual's mission to spread confusion and muddle the threads of bourgeois ideology; marauding troops were setting fire to the brush and whole linguistic sectors were being reduced to ashes. Nizan seldom played the fool and had little time for sleight of hand. He lied, like everyone in that golden age, when he was quite certain he would not be believed: slander had just been born, a nimble, joyous thing verging on poetry. But he found these practices reassuring: we know that he wanted to write against death, and death beneath his pen had turned words into dead leaves; he had been afraid of being duped, afraid of wasting his life toying with trifles. Now he was being told he had not been wrong, that literature was a weapon in the hands of our masters, but he was being given a new mission: in a negative period, a book can be an act if the revolutionary writer applies himself to deconditioning language. Everything was permitted—even to create a style for himself: for the wicked, this would be a gilding of a bitter pill; for the good, it would be a call to vigilance: when the sea sings, do not jump in. Nizan studied the negative form: his hatred produced pearls; he took the pearls and cast them before us, delighted that it fell to him to serve common ends by producing so personal a body of work. Without changing its immediate target, his battle against the particular dangers menacing a young bourgeois became a sacred charge: he spoke of impotent rage and hatred; he wrote of the Revolution.

The writer, then, was made by the Party. But the man? Had he at last found "his field"? His fulfillment? Was he happy? I do not believe so. The same reasons deprive us of good fortune as make us forever incapable of enjoying it. And then, the doctrine was clear and fit his personal experience: his alienations, being linked to the present structures of society, would disappear when the bourgeois class disappeared. Now, he did not believe that he would see socialism in his lifetime nor, even if he saw it in the last days of his life, that such a metamorphosis of the world would leave time to transform the old habits of a dying man. Yet he had changed: his old bouts of desolation never returned; he was never again afraid he was wasting his life. He had an invigorating violence about him, and felt joy: he accepted in good heart being only the *negative man*, the writer of de-moralization and de-mystification.

Was there enough in this to satisfy the serious child he had continued to be? In a sense, yes. Before he joined the Party, he clung to his rejections. He clung to the idea that, since he could not achieve true being, he would be empty: he would derive his sole value from his dissatisfaction, from his frustrated desires. But, sensing a torpor coming over him, he was terrified of letting go and of one day subsiding into consent. As a communist, he consolidated his resistances: up until then he had continually feared that dunce, the "social man." The Party socialized him without tears: his collective being was none other than his individual person; it was enough merely that his restless agitations were now *sanctioned*. He saw himself as a monstrous, misbegotten thing; he was heaved onto the stage, where he showed off his wounds, saying, "See what the bourgeois have done to their own children." Once he had turned his violence against himself: now he made it into bombs which he hurled at the palaces of industry. The buildings sustained no damage, but Nizan found deliverance. He presided over a sacred fury, but he no more felt it than a fine singer hears his own voice; this *mauvais sujet* turned himself into a terrible object.

It was not so easy to free himself from death, or rather from the shadow it cast over his life. But the adolescent ravaged by an alien anxiety acquired, as an adult, the right to die his own death. Marxism revealed his father's secret to him: Antoine Bloyé's loneliness was the product of betrayal. This worker-turned-bourgeois thought constantly of:

the companions he had had in the yards of the Loire and among the watchmen at the goods depots, who were on the side of the servants, on the side of life without hope. He said … something he would strive to forget, which would disappear only to reappear at the time of his decline, on the eve of his own death: "So I am a traitor." And he was.[35]

He had crossed the line, betrayed his class, and ended up as a simple molecule in the molecular world of the petty bourgeois. On a hundred occasions, he felt his friendlessness—one day in particular, during a strike, seeing the demonstrators marching by:

> These men of no importance bore far away from him the strength, friendship and hope from which he was excluded. That evening, Antoine felt he was a man of solitude. A man without communion. The truth of life lay with those who had not "succeeded." They are not alone, he thought. They know where they are going.[36]

This renegade had fallen apart; now he was whirling around in the bourgeois pulverulence. He knew alienation, the misfortune of the rich, as a result of having thrown in his lot with those who exploited the poor. This communion of the "men of no importance" could have armed him against death. With those men, he would have known the fullness of misfortune and friendship. Without them, he remained unprotected: dead before his time, a single blow of the scythe had severed his human bonds and cut short his life.

Was Monsieur Nizan really this tearful deserter? I do not know. At any rate, his son saw him that way: Nizan discovered or thought he discovered the reason for the thousand tiny resistances he put up against his father: he loved the man in him but loathed the betrayal. I beg those well-intentioned Marxists who have studied my friend's case, and have explained it by the obsession with betrayal, to reread his writings with open eyes, if they can, and not reject the glaring truth. This son of a traitor does, admittedly, often speak of betrayal; in *Aden* he writes, "I could have been a traitor, I might have suffocated."

302 · JEAN-PAUL SARTRE

And in *Les Chiens de garde*, he writes: "If we betray the bourgeoisie for humanity, let us not be ashamed to admit that we are traitors." A traitor to men, Antoine Bloyé; a traitor still, in *La Conspiration*, the sad Pluvinage, the son of a cop and a cop himself. And what does it mean, then, this word repeated so often? That Nizan was in the pay of Daladier? When they speak of others, the right-thinking characters of the French left are shamefully hungry for scandal; I know of nothing dirtier or more puerile, except perhaps "decent" women gossiping about a free woman. Nizan wanted to write, he wanted to live: What need had he of thirty pieces of silver from secret political funds? But as the son of a worker who had become a bourgeois, he wondered what he might become: Bourgeois or worker? His chief concern was undoubtedly this civil war within him; as a traitor to the proletariat, Monsieur Nizan had made his son a betraying bourgeois; this bourgeois-despite-himself would cross the line in the opposite direction: but that is not so easy. When the communist intellectuals want a bit of fun, they call themselves proletarians: "We do manual work in our garrets." Lacemakers, so to speak. Nizan, more clear-sighted and more demanding, saw them—saw himself, indeed—as petty bourgeois who had chosen the cause of the people. That does not actually close the gap between a Marxist novelist and an unskilled worker: they can exchange smiles from either side of the intervening gulf, but if the author takes a single step, he falls in. All this is true when we are speaking about a bourgeois who is the son and grandson of a bourgeois: against the fact of birth, fine feelings are powerless. But Nizan? He was close to his new allies by ties of blood: he remembered his grandfather who "remained on the side of the servants, on the side of life without hope"; he had grown up, like the sons of the railwaymen, in landscapes of iron and smoke; yet a diploma in the "liberal arts" had been enough to make his a lonely childhood, to force an irreversible metamorphosis on the whole family. He never crossed the line again: he betrayed the bourgeoisie without rejoining the enemy army and had to remain something of a "Pilgrim" with one foot on either side of the frontier; right to the end he was the friend—but he never managed to become the brother—of "those who have not succeeded." It was nobody's fault but those bourgeois who had taken his father into their class. This discreet absence, this emptiness always troubled him a little: he had heard the bourgeois siren song. Retaining his scruples, he remained anxious: for want of participating in the "communion of servants, of those who live without hope," he never saw himself as sufficiently protected from temptations, from death; he knew the comradeship of fellow militants without escaping his loneliness, which was the legacy of a betrayal.

His life would not be stolen from him; released now from an alien death, he contemplated his own: it would not be the death of a railway yardmaster. But this negative man, robbed of the humblest plenitude, knew he would ultimately suffer an irreparable defeat. With his passing, nothing might be said to have happened but the disappearance of a refusal. All in all, a highly Hegelian demise: it would be the negation of a negation. I doubt if Nizan drew the slightest consolation from this philosophical view. He made a long journey to the USSR. On his departure, he had told me of his hopes: over there, perhaps, these men were immortal. The abolition of classes closed up all the divides. United by a long-term undertaking, the workers would change themselves by death into other workers, and those into others in their turn; the generations would succeed each other, always different and always the same.

He came back. His friendship for me did not entirely exclude the propagandist's zeal: he told me the reality had exceeded all his expectations. Except on one point: the Revolution freed men of the fear of living, but it did not remove the fear of dying. He had questioned the best among them: they had all replied that they thought about death and that their zeal for the shared task gave no protection from that obscure personal disaster. Disabused, Nizan forever renounced the old Spinozist dream: he would never know that affirmative plenitude of the finite mode which, at the same time, shatters its own limits and returns to infinite substance. In the midst of the collective commitment, he would retain the particularity of his disquiet. He tried not to think of himself anymore, and he succeeded, concentrating only on objective necessities: yet he remained, as a result of this hollow, indissoluble nothingness—this bubble of emptiness within him—the most fragile and the most "irreplaceable" of human beings. Individualized in spite of himself, a few scattered phrases show that he ended up choosing the most individual solution: "It takes a great deal of strength and creation to escape nothingness... Antoine understood, at last, that he could only have been saved by creations he had produced, by exercising his power."[37] Nizan was not an engineer. Nor a politician. He wrote; he could exercise power only through the practice of style. He put his trust in his books: he would live on through them. Into the heart of this disciplined existence, which grew more militant each day, death injected its cancer of anarchy. This lasted somehow for ten years. He devoted himself to his party, lived a dissatisfied life, and wrote with passion. From Moscow there came a squall—the Trials—which shook but did not uproot him. He held out. But to no avail: this was a revolutionary without blinders. His virtue and his weakness were that he wanted everything *right now*, the way young people do. This man of negation did not know renunciation of assent. About the trials he remained silent and that was all there was to it.

I regarded him as the perfect communist, which was convenient: in my eyes, he became the spokesman for the Political Bureau. I saw his moods, illusions, frivolities, and passions as attitudes agreed on by the Party leadership. In July 1939, where I met him by chance for the last time, he was cheerful: he was about to take a ferry to Corsica. I read in his eyes the cheeriness of the Party; he spoke about war, expressing the view that we were going to escape it. I immediately translated in my head: "the Political Bureau is very optimistic, its spokesman declares that the negotiations with the USSR will bear fruit. By the autumn," he says, "the Nazis will be on their knees."

September taught me it was prudent to dissociate my friend's opinions from Stalin's decisions. I was surprised by this. And annoyed: though apolitical and reluctant to commit myself in any way, my heart was on the left, as was everyone's. Nizan's rapid career had flattered me; it had given me some sort of revolutionary importance in my own eyes. Our friendship had been so precious and we were still so often confused for each other that it was I too who wrote the foreign politics leaders in *Ce Soir*—and I knew quite a bit about all that! Now, if Nizan knew nothing, what a comedown: we were back to being a pair of real idiots. Sent back to the ranks. Unless he had deliberately deceived me. This conjecture amused me for a few days: what a fool I was to have believed him; but this way he retained his high-flying role, his perfect insight into what in those days we called "the diplomatic chessboard." Deep down, I preferred this solution.

A few days later in Alsace, I learned from the newspapers that the spokesman for the Political Bureau had just left the Party, making a great splash about the break. So I had been wrong about everything, from the very outset. I don't know why I wasn't completely stunned by this news: perhaps my frivolousness protected me; and then, at this same time, I discovered the monumental error of a whole generation—our generation—which had actually been sleepwalking. Through a fierce period of preparation for war, when we thought we were strolling on the calm lawns of Peace, we were actually being impelled toward massacres. At Brumath I experienced our immense anonymous awakening; I lost my distinctiveness once and for all and was drawn in.[38]

Today I recall this learning experience without displeasure and I tell myself that at the same time, Nizan was engaged in *unlearning*. How he must have suffered! It is not easy to leave a party: there is its law, which you have to wrench from yourself if you are to break it, its people, whose beloved, familiar faces will become filthy enemy "mugs," that somber crowd continuing on its stubborn march which you will watch disappear into the distance. My friend became an interpreter: he found himself alone in the north of France among British soldiers: alone among the British, as he had been at the worst time of his life in Arabia, fleeing beneath the sting of the gadfly, separated from everyone and saying "no."

He gave political explanations, of course. His former friends accused him of moralism; he criticized them for not being Machiavellian. He approved, he said, of the lofty cynicism of the Soviet leaders: all means were permitted when it came to saving the socialist fatherland. But the French communists had neither imitated this cavalier attitude nor understood that they had to distance themselves in appearance from the USSR; they were going to lose their influence for failing to put on a timely act of indignation.

He was not the only one to give these reasons—how frivolous they seem today! In fact, this recourse to Machiavelli was merely a riposte to his critics: Nizan was attempting to prove his realism; he was a tactician condemning a tactic: nothing more—and, above all, he didn't want anyone to think that he was resigning for emotional reasons or because his nerves were shot! His letters prove, on the contrary, that he was distraught with anger. We know the circumstances and documents better today, we understand the reasons driving Russian policy: I tend to think his decision was a headstrong one and that he should not have broken with his friends, with his real life. Had he lived, I believe the Resistance would have brought him back into the fold, like so many others. But that is none of my business: I want to show that he was cut to the quick, wounded to the heart, that his unexpected turnabout revealed his nakedness to him again, sent him back to his desert, to himself.

He was writing for *Ce Soir* at the time; he had been put in charge of foreign affairs, where a single theme prevailed—union with the USSR against Germany. He had argued this so many times that he had become convinced of it. When Molotov and Ribbentrop were putting the last touches to their pact, Nizan, in his harshest tones, was demanding a Franco-Soviet rapprochement with threats. In the summer of 1939, he saw some of the leaders in Corsica: they talked with him in a friendly way, congratulated him on his articles, and, when he had gone to bed, held long secret meetings. Did they know what was in store for us? There is some chance they did not: the September revelation struck a vacationing Party like a thunderbolt. In Paris we saw journalists assuming the most serious responsibilities blindly and with a sense of dismay. At any rate, Nizan never doubted for a moment that he had been lied to. It pained him, not in his vanity, nor even in his pride, but in his humility. He had never crossed the class boundary—he knew; suspect in his own eyes, he saw the silence of his party bosses as a sign of the people's distrust. Ten years of obedience had not allayed it: they would never forgive this dubious ally for his father's betrayal.

That father had worked for others, for gentlemen who robbed him of his strength and life; against this, Nizan had become a communist.

Now he learned that he was being used as a tool, with the real objectives hidden from him; he learned that lies had been put into his mouth and he had repeated them in good faith: from him too, unseen, remote individuals had stolen his strength, his life. He had put all his obstinacy into rejecting the gentle, corrosive words of the bourgeoisie and, all of a sudden, in the Party of the revolution, he was back with what he feared most: alienation from language. Communist words, so simple, virtually raw—what were they? Leaking gas. He had written that his father "[had performed] solitary acts that had been imposed on him by an external, inhuman power, ... acts that had not been part of an authentic human existence, that had produced nothing enduring. They were merely recorded in bundles of dusty files ..."[39] At present, his actions as a militant came back to him and they were virtually identical to those of the bourgeois engineer: "nothing enduring"; articles scattered in dusty newspapers, hollow phrases imposed by an external power, the alienation of a man to the necessities of international politics, a frivolous life emptied of its substance, "the vain image of that headless human being walking in the ashes of time, with hurried tread, directionless and disorientated."[40]

He came back to his eternal concern: he became politically active to save his life and the Party stole his life from him; he was fighting death and death was coming to him from the Party itself. He was, I think, wrong: it was the Earth that gave birth to the slaughter and it broke out in all parts at once. But I am relating what he felt: Hitler had a free hand now, he was going to hurl himself against us; Nizan, dumbfounded, imagined that our army of workers and peasants would be exterminated with the consent of the USSR. To his wife he spoke of another fear: he would return too late and exhausted from an interminable war; he would survive only to ruminate on his regrets and his rancor, haunted by the false coin of memory. Against these rediscovered threats, only revolt remained—the old desperate, anarchic revolt. Since human beings were betrayed on all sides, he would preserve the little bit of humanity that remained by saying "no" to everything.

I know the angry soldier of 1940, with his prejudices, principles, experience, and intellectual resources was not much like the young adventurer who set out for Aden. He wanted to be rational, to see things clearly, weigh everything up and maintain his links with "those who have not succeeded in life." The bourgeoisie awaited him, affable and corrupting: they had to be thwarted. Having been betrayed, as he saw it, by the Party, he felt anew a pressing duty not to betray in his turn; he persisted in calling himself a communist. He pondered patiently how he was to correct the deviations without falling into idealism. He kept notebooks and logs; he wrote a great deal. But did he really believe he could redirect the inflexible thrust of these millions of human beings on his own? A lone communist is lost. The truth of his last months was hatred. He had written that he wanted "to fight real men." At that juncture, he had in mind the bourgeois, but the bourgeois has no face: the person you think you detest slips away, leaving behind Standard Oil or the Stock Exchange. Right up to his death, Nizan harbored particularized grudges: out of cowardice, such and such a friend hadn't supported him; another had encouraged him to break with the Party, then condemned him for it. His anger was fueled by some undying memories; in his mind's eye he saw eyes, mouths, smiles, skin tones, a harsh or sanctimonious look, and he hated these all-too-human faces. If ever he had an experience of fullness, it was in these violent moments when, selecting these hunting trophies, his rage turned to delight. When he was totally alone, "directionless and disorientated," and reduced to the inflexibility of his refusals, death came and claimed him. *His* death, stupid and savage, in keeping with his constant fears and forebodings.

An English soldier took the trouble to bury his private notebooks and his last novel, *La Soirée à Somosierra*, which was almost finished. The earth devoured this testament: when his wife, following precise instructions, tried to recover his papers in 1945—the last lines he had written about the Party, the war, or himself—there was nothing left of them. Around this time, the slander against him began to be taken seriously: the dead man was found guilty of high treason. What a funny old life: a life alienated, then robbed, then hidden, and saved even in death because it said "no." Exemplary too, because it was a scandal, like all the lives that have been lived, like all the lives that are manufactured today for young people; but a conscious scandal and one that publicly declared itself such.

Here is his first book. We thought he had been obliterated; he is reviving today because a new audience demands it. I hope we shall soon have restored to us his two masterpieces: *Antoine Bloyé*, the finest, most lyrical of funeral orations, and *The Conspiracy*. But it is no bad thing to begin with this raw revolt: at the origin of everything, there is refusal. So now, let the older generation withdraw and let this adolescent speak to his brothers: "I was twenty. I won't let anyone tell me it's the best time of life."

MERLEAU-PONTY

HOW MANY friends I have lost who are still alive. It was nobody's fault: sometimes it was them, sometimes me. Events made us and brought us together; they also separated us. And Merleau-Ponty, I know, said just this when he happened to think of the people who had been part of his life and left it. Yet he never lost me, and he has had to die for me to lose him. We were equals, friends, but we were not alike; we had understood this immediately and our differences amused us at first. And then, around 1950, the barometer plummeted: a stiff breeze blew through Europe and the world; the swell it whipped up knocked us against each other, then a moment later tossed us to opposite poles. Though so often strained, the ties between us were never severed: if you ask me why, I must say we had a lot of luck and, sometimes, a degree of merit. We each tried to remain true to ourselves and loyal to the other, and we more or less succeeded. Merleau is still too alive for it to be possible to paint his portrait; it will be easier to achieve a likeness—perhaps unconsciously—if I tell the story of that quarrel that never took place: our friendship.

At the École normale, we knew each other without being part of the same set. He lived outside the college and I was a boarder: each of these two groups regarded themselves as an elite and the others as mere commoners. Then came military service: I was a private, he became a second lieutenant: two different orders again.* We fell out of touch with each other. He had a chair at Beauvais, I think; I taught at Le Havre. Yet, without knowing it, we were preparing to meet: each of us was trying to understand the world as best he could with the resources at hand. And we had the same resources—which were then called Husserl and Heidegger—because we were part of the same world.

One day in 1947 Merleau told me he had never got over an incomparable childhood: it was a time of the coziest happiness, and only age drove him out of it. Being from adolescence a Pascalian, even before reading Pascal, he experienced his singular selfhood as the singularity of an adventure: a person is something that happens and fades, though not without tracing out the lines of a future ever new and ever renewed. What was his life but a lost paradise? An amazing piece of undeserved good luck—a free gift—turned, after the Fall, into adversity; it depopulated the world and disenchanted it in advance. The story is an extraordinary one and yet it is common: our capacity for happiness depends on a particular balance between what our childhood has granted and denied us. If we are entirely deprived or entirely satisfied, we are doomed. The lots that fall to us are infinite in number: it was his lot to have won in life too early. Yet he had to live: it remained for him to make himself, until the end, as events had made him. As they had made him and different: seeking the golden age. His archaic simplicity, crafting from that golden age his myths and what he has since termed his "style of life," set up preferences—both for traditions, which recall the ceremonies of childhood, and for the "spontaneity" that evokes its superintended freedom—discovered the meaning of what is happening from what *has happened*, and, lastly, turned inventory and acknowledged fact into prophecy. This is what he felt as a young man, without being able to express it yet; these are

---

*I do not know whether, in 1939, on contact with those whom their leaders refer to curiously as "men," he regretted leaving the condition of simple soldier. But when I saw my officers, those incompetents, I regretted my prewar anarchism: since we had to fight, we had been wrong to leave command in the hands of those vain imbeciles. We know that, after the brief interim Resistance period, it remained in their hands; this in some measure explains our misfortunes.

the byways by which he came to philosophy. He felt a sense of wonderment and that is all there is to it: everything is played out in advance and yet you carry on; why? Why lead a life discredited by
absences? And what is it to live?

Our teachers, serious and ineffectual, knew nothing of history:
they took the view that such questions should not be asked, that they
were badly framed or—as a stock response of the time had it—that
"the answers were in the questions." To think is to measure, said one
of them, who did neither. And all of them argued that man and nature can be treated in terms of universal concepts. This was precisely
what Merleau-Ponty couldn't accept: tormented by the archaic secrets
of his prehistory, he felt irritation at these well-meaning souls who
saw themselves as bees and whose philosophy soared above the earth,
forgetting that we are bogged down in it from birth. They pride themselves, he was later to say, on looking the world in the face: Are they
not aware that it envelops and produces us? The most penetrating mind
bears the mark of this and one cannot form a single thought that is
not deeply conditioned, from the outset, by that Being about which it
claims to speak. Since we are each of us ambiguous histories—good
and bad fortune, reason and unreason—the origin of which never lies
in knowing but in events, it isn't even imaginable that we could express our lives, these unraveling stitches, in terms of knowledge. And
what can be the value of human thinking about human beings, since
the human being himself is both making the judgment and vouching
for it? This was how Merleau "ruminated on his life." But the comparison with Kierkegaard is not apposite here: it is too early for that.
The Dane was thoroughly averse to Hegelian knowledge; he invented
opacities for himself out of a horror of transparency: if the light passed
through him, Søren would be done for. With Merleau-Ponty, it was
precisely the opposite: he wanted to understand, to understand *himself*; it wasn't his fault if he discovered in practice that universalist idealism was incompatible with what he would call his "primordial
historicity." He never claimed to grant unreason precedence over rationalism: he merely wanted to bring history into play against the immobility of the Kantian subject. It was, as Rouletabille said, coming at
reason from the right end and nothing more.[1] In short, he was looking

for his "point of anchorage." We can see what he lacked for beginning at the beginning: "intentionality," "situation," and twenty other tools that were to be had in Germany. Around this time I, for quite other reasons, had need of the same instruments. I came to phenomenology through Levinas and went off to Berlin where I stayed for almost a year. When I came back, we were both, without realizing it, at the same point; until September 1939, we went on with our reading and research; at the same pace, but separately.

Philosophy, as is well-known, has no direct efficacy: it took the war to bring us together. In 1941, groups of intellectuals formed all over France, aspiring to resist the victorious enemy. I belonged to one of them: Socialism and Liberty. Merleau joined us. Our meeting again was no chance matter: being each of us a product of the Republican petty bourgeoisie, our tastes, tradition, and professional conscious-ness prompted us to defend the freedom of the writer. It was through this freedom that we discovered all the others. Apart from this, we were innocents. Born in enthusiasm, our little unit caught a fever and died a year later, for want of knowing what to do. The other groups in the occupied zone met the same fate, doubtless for the same reason: by 1942, none was left. A little later, Gaullism and the Front National swept up these early Resistance fighters. As for the two of us, despite our failure, Socialism and Liberty had brought us together. The times helped us too: there was an unforgettable openness of heart between Frenchmen, which was the reverse side of hatred. By way of this na-tional friendship, which liked everything about everybody from the outset so long as they hated the Nazis, we recognized each other; the essential words were spoken: phenomenology, existence; we discov-ered our real concerns. Being too individualistic to pool our research, we developed a reciprocity, while remaining separate. Left to our-selves, each of us would have persuaded himself too easily that he had understood the phenomenological idea; together, we embodied its ambiguousness for each other: this was because each of us regarded the alien—and sometimes hostile—labors the other was engaged in as an unexpected deviation from his own work. Husserl became at once the distance between us and the foundation of our friendship. On that terrain, we were, as Merleau, writing about language, has rightly put it: "differences without terms or, rather, terms engendered by the differences which appear among them."[2] He retained a nuanced recollection of our talks. Ultimately, he merely wanted to deepen his own understanding, and discussions distracted him. And then I made too many concessions to him, and too hastily: he criticized me for this later, in the dark times, and for having exposed *our* viewpoint to third parties without taking account of *his* reservations; he told me he attributed this to pride, to some kind of contempt for others. Nothing can be more unjust: I have always taken the view, and take the view now, that Truth is one and indivisible; on the points of detail it seemed to me then that I had to abandon my views if I had not been able to convince my interlocutor to abandon his or hers. Merleau-Ponty, by contrast, found security in the multiplicity of perspectives: he saw in it the facets of Being. As for remaining silent about his reservations, if I did so it was in good faith. Or almost: Does one ever know? My fault was, rather, to drop the decimals so as to achieve unanimity more quickly. In any event, he was not too displeased with me, as he retained the thoroughly amicable idea that I was a reconciler. I do not know if he derived any benefit from these discussions: sometimes I doubt it. But I cannot forget what I owe to them: a thinking that had been aired. In my opinion, this was the purest moment of our friendship.

Yet he did not tell me everything. We no longer spoke about politics except to comment on the news on the BBC. I had lapsed into a distaste for politics which I did not overcome until I was able to join up with a well-established organization. Merleau, formerly more reserved about our joint venture, was slower to forget it: it offered him in miniature the image of an event: it transported the human being back to what he was—to the accident that he was and continued to be, the accident he produced. What had they been through, what had they wanted, and, in the end, what had they done, those teachers (including ourselves), students, and engineers, suddenly thrown together and just as suddenly separated by a whirlwind?

Merleau-Ponty was, at the time, inquiring into perception; it was, he thought, one of the beginnings of the beginning: this ambiguous testing-out yields up our body by way of the world and the world by way of our body; it is the pivot and the *point of anchorage*. But the world is also history; perhaps we are historical first. In the margins of the book he was slowly writing, he reflected on what, ten years later, seemed to him the fundamental anchoring point. *Phenomenology of Perception*[3] bears the marks of these ambiguous meditations, but I was not able to recognize them; it took him ten years to get to what he had been seeking since adolescence, this *being-event* of human beings, which we may also term existence. Should I say that phenomenology remained a "static" in his thesis and that he was going to transform it gradually into a "dynamic" by a deepening, of which *Humanism and Terror*[4] represented the first stage? This would not be wrong; exaggerated, no doubt, but clear. Let us say that this magnification at least enables us to glimpse the movement of his thought: gently, cautiously, inflexibly, it turned around on itself to reach back, through itself, to the original. In these years preceding the Liberation he had not got far: he knew already, however, that History cannot, any more than Nature, be looked straight in the face. The fact is that it envelops us. How? How did it envelop us, the totality of future time and time past? How were we to discover the others in ourselves as our deep truth? How were we to perceive ourselves in them as the rule of their truth? The question already arises at the level of perceptual spontaneity and "intersubjectivity"; it becomes more concrete and urgent when we resituate the historical agent within the universal flow. Our labors and travails, our tools, government, customs, and traditions—how were persons to be "inserted" into this? Conversely, how could they be extracted from a web they were constantly spinning and that was, in its turn, constantly producing them?

Merleau had expected to make a peacetime living; a war had made him into a warrior and he, for his part, had made war. What if this strange whirligig marked the scope and limits of historical action? He had to look closely into this. As investigator, witness, defendant, and judge, he went back and, in the light of our defeat and of the future German defeat—of which, after Stalingrad we felt assured—examined the false war he had fought, the false peace he had thought he was living through, and himself, as ever, at the pivot of these things, the shoe now on the other foot, the mystifier mystified, both victim and accomplice, despite a good faith that was not in doubt and yet had, nonetheless, to be questioned.* All this went on in silence: he had no need of a partner to cast this new light on the singularity of his times, on his own singularity. But we have the evidence that he was constantly reflecting on his times; as early as 1945 he wrote: "When all is said and done, we have learned history and it is our contention that we must not forget it."[5]

This was a courtesy "we": it would take me a good few years yet to learn what he knew. Having known deep satisfaction from birth, then frustration, he was destined, by his experience, to discover the force of circumstance, the inhuman powers that steal our acts and thoughts from us. As a man invested with a role and yet encircled, a man pre-destined but free, his original intuition disposed him to understand *the event*, that adventure that comes out of everywhere and nowhere, with no consistency or signification until it has filled us with its hazardous shades, until it has forced us to grant its iron necessity freely and in spite of ourselves. And then he suffered from his relations with others: everything had been too good too quickly; the Nature that at first enveloped him was the Mother Goddess, his mother, whose eyes bestowed upon him what he saw; she was the *alter ego*; by her and in her he lived that "intersubjectivity of immanence" he has often described and which causes us to discover our "spontaneity" through another. With childhood dead, love remained, just as strong, but disconsolate. Being sure that he could never recover the lost intimacy, he didn't know what to ask of his friends: everything and nothing; at times too much, at others not enough. He moved quickly from demands to lack of interest, not without suffering from these failures which confirmed his exile. Misunderstandings, estrangements, separations with wrong on both sides: private life had already taught him that our acts register themselves in our little world in a manner different from what we had wished, making us other than we were by retrospectively lending us intentions we did not have but will have had from now on. After 1939 he saw these errors of reckoning, these un-

---

*Not, as I did in 1942, by an eidetics of bad faith but by the empirical study of our historical allegiances and the inhuman forces perverting them.

necessary expenses that must be accepted because one has failed to foresee them, as the very characteristics of historical action. In 1945 he wrote, "We have been led to accept and regard as our own not only our intentions, the meanings our acts have for us, but also the consequences of those acts externally, the meaning they assume in a certain historical context." He saw "his shadow cast on history as on a wall, that form which his actions assumed for the outside world, that objective Spirit that was himself."[6] Merleau felt sufficiently engaged to have constantly a sense of restoring the world to the world, sufficiently free to objectivize himself in history by that restitution. He was happy to compare himself to a wave: one crest among others, with the whole of a head sea holding in a hem of foam. As a mix of strange chance occurrences and generalities, historical man appears when his act, performed and planned remotely, to the point of the most alien objectivity, introduces the beginnings of reason into the original irrationality. To his adversaries, Merleau replied, in all certainty, that his feeling for existence did not set him in opposition to Marxism and, in actual fact, the well-known saying, "Men make history, but not in circumstances of their own choosing" could pass, in his eyes, for a Marxist version of his own thinking.

The communist intellectuals made no mistake on this point. As soon as the lull of 1945 was over, they attacked me: my political thinking was confused, my ideas could do harm. Merleau, by contrast, seemed close to them. A flirtation began: Merleau-Ponty often saw Courtade, Hervé, and Desanti;[7] his traditionalism found solace in their company: after all, the Communist Party is a tradition. He preferred its rites, its thought baked and hardened by twenty-five years of history, to the speculations of those who belonged to no party.

He was not, however, a Marxist: he did not reject the Marxist idea but he rejected Marxism as dogma. He did not accept that historical materialism was the sole light of history, nor that that light emanates from an eternal source which stands, in principle, outside the vicissitudes of historical events. He criticized this objectivistic intellectualism, like classical rationalism, for looking the world in the face and forgetting that in fact it enwraps us. He would have accepted the doctrine if he could have seen it merely as a net cast upon the sea, unfurled

318 · JEAN-PAUL SARTRE

and refurled by the swell, its truth dependent, precisely, on its perpetual participation in the sea's endless commotion. He could see it as a system of reference, but, on condition that, in referring to it, we change it; he could see it as an explanation, on condition that it change shape as it explain. Should we speak of "Marxist relativism"? Yes and no. Whatever the doctrine, he mistrusted it, fearing he might find it to be a construction of that philosophy that "soars above the earth." A relativism, then, but a precautionary relativism; he believed in just the one absolute: our point of anchorage, life. What, then, ultimately was his criticism of the Marxist theory of history? Crucially this and nothing else: it allowed no room for contingency:

> Every historical undertaking has something of an adventure about it, being never guaranteed by any *absolutely* rational structure of things. It always involves a utilization of chance, one has always to be crafty with things (and with people) since one has to extract from them an order that was not given with them. The possibility of an enormous compromise remains, of a corruption of history in which the class struggle, which is powerful enough to destroy, would not be powerful enough to build, and in which the broad outlines of history as mapped out in the *Communist Manifesto* would fade away.[8]

The contingency of each and all, the contingency of the human adventure; within this, the contingency of the Marxist adventure— we come back here to Merleau-Ponty's fundamental experience. He had first reflected on the singularity of his life, then, moving on to contemplate his historical existence, he had discovered they were both cut from the same cloth.

With these reservations, he accepted historical materialism as a grid, as a regulative idea, or, if one prefers, as a heuristic schema:

> There have been enough writers in the last fifteen years who have falsely gone beyond Marxism for us to take care to distinguish ourselves from them. To go beyond a doctrine, you have first to have come up to its level and you have to explain what it

explains better than it does itself. If we raise some questions with regard to Marxism, this is not to prefer a conservative philosophy of history that would be even more abstract.

In short, he was a Marxist for want of anything better.

Let us be clear about this: Marxism is basically a practice that has its origins in class struggle. Deny that struggle and nothing remains. In 1945—and so long as the Communist Party shared power with the bourgeois parties—that struggle was not clearly decipherable. The Party's young intellectuals believed in it devoutly. They were not wrong; I say they *believed* in it because they could not *see* it behind the deceptive mask of national unity. Merleau-Ponty often irritated them because he only half believed in it. He had reflected on the consequences of victory: no more allies, two giants face-to-face. These latter, concerned to avoid friction, had recast the globe at Yalta: I'll have the sunset lands, you have the sunrise; for peace they had little concern; it was beyond doubt that there would be a Third World War; each of the two, anxious to win it as soon as possible, came to an arrangement with the other, to postpone it until such time as they had acquired the better positions. The balance of forces remained, however, temporarily in favor of the West: hence, in that moment of history, revolution became impossible in Europe; neither Churchill, Roosevelt, nor, in the end, Stalin would have tolerated it. We know what happened to the Greek resistance and how it was liquidated. Everything is clear today: the whole earth became united in a single history; there ensued this contradiction, indecipherable at the time, that the class struggle transformed itself in places into conflicts between nations—hence into deferred wars. Today the Third World shows us the truth of this; in 1945, we could neither understand the change that had taken place nor accept it. In short, we were blind; Merleau-Ponty, who had one good eye, came to conclusions that were astonishing because they seemed inevitable: if the revolution can be halted from outside by the concern to preserve the international balance, if external forces can nip it in the bud, if the workers must look not to themselves but to a planetary conflict for their emancipation, then the revolutionary class has gone on leave. The bourgeoisie continued to exist, surrounded by

the immense mass of workers it exploited and atomized. But the proletariat, that invincible force that passed sentence on capitalism and
whose mission was to overturn it, was out to lunch. It was quite possible that it would return; perhaps tomorrow, perhaps in half a century; it may, also, never return. Merleau-Ponty registered this absence,
deplored it as seemed fitting, and proposed that we organize immediately just in case it should continue. He went so far as to outline a
program in a text which I quote from memory, though I'm certain I
do so quite accurately: "In the meantime, let us undertake to do nothing that might prevent the rebirth of the proletariat; better, we should
do all we can to help it to reconstitute itself; in short, we should follow
Communist Party policy." I can, at any rate, vouch for these last
words, as I was so struck by them: born out of the class struggle, the
Communist Party developed its policy as a function of that struggle;
in the capitalist countries, it would not survive the disappearance of
the proletariat. Now, Merleau-Ponty no longer believed in civil war,
contesting by that very token the legitimacy of communist organization: the paradox is that he proposed, at the same moment, that we
should align ourselves with the Party.

There was another paradox. Go and find a bishop and, just as an
experiment, tell him: "God is dead, I doubt he'll revive but, in the
meantime, I'm with you." You will be thanked for your kind offer, but
it will not be possible to accept it. Now, Merleau's communist friends
had taken the opposite stance: they said some harsh things to him in
polite terms, but they didn't reject him. Thinking about it, this is no
surprise. The Party had come out on top from the Resistance: it was
less strict about the choice of its fellow travelers. But, above all, its intellectuals were uneasy about their lives: being radical by their position, they would have liked the proletariat to set about gaining new
ground, to resume its forward march; the bourgeoisie, terrorized by
the publicity given to its betrayals, would have put up no opposition.
Instead of this, action was postponed. They said, "Let's seize power"
and the reply came back: the British and Americans would land
within the hour. A new contradiction appeared within the movement
for political advance since, to save peace and the socialist countries, a
revolution demanded from the inside by the masses could be counter-

manded from the outside. These young people, who had come to the Party through the Resistance, did not lose their trust in it; but there were doubts and frictions. After all, France was a bourgeois democracy; what was the Communist Party doing in the tripartite government? Was it not a hostage to capital? They faithfully transmitted the slogans that troubled them: "you have to know how to end a strike" and "the reconstruction of the country is the revolutionary objective." But they couldn't keep Merleau's conclusions from worrying them a little. At the edges. After all, he approved of the Party's reformist policy, that policy of which they themselves, out of sheer obedience, were the agents. Could they blame him for repeating out loud what they sometimes said under their breath: Where is the proletariat? In actual fact, it was there. But bridled and muzzled. And by whom? They became irritated a little more each day by Merleau-Ponty, that Cassandra; Merleau-Ponty became irritated with them—each as wrongly as the other.

Merleau misunderstood the rootedness of his friends. He returned to the question fifteen years later, in the preface to *Signs*. There, by contrast, he stresses the status of the party activist who is embedded and entrusted with a mission and who must, nonetheless, contribute by his allegiances and actions to making the party that makes him. It is an ambiguous expression of regret, which leads him, above all, to justify resignations from the Party: it is all very well to have fun judging a policy calmly and serenely from the outside. When those who produce that policy on a day-to-day basis, if only through their acquiescence, discover its meaning, and when they see their shadows cast on the wall, they have no alternative but to break with it. But the argument can be turned around and I believe he knew it: for all these young people of 1945, floundering about between their sincerely held beliefs and their sworn allegiance, by way of actions they assumed daily and whose meaning they saw change in their hands, on more than one occasion the thinker "soaring" above the fray was Merleau-Ponty.

His friends were mistaken about him in their turn: they did not know the path he had followed. From some conversations we had later, I was left with the feeling that he had been closer to Marxism before 1939 than he ever was afterward. What distanced him from it? I imagine it was the trials; the fact that he spoke about them at such length in *Humanism and Terror* shows that he continued to be very affected by them. After that, the Nazi-Soviet pact made little impression on him: he amused himself by writing rather "Machiavellian" letters to "distribute blame." Friends and the writings of Rosa Luxemburg had converted him to the idea of that "spontaneity of the masses" that saw the general movement as being closely related to its particular form; when he saw Reason of State gleaming out from behind it, he turned away.

He had been a Christian at twenty but ceased to be so because, as he said, "You believe you believe, but you don't believe." More exactly, he wanted Catholicism to reintegrate him into the unity of immanence and that was precisely what it couldn't do: Christians love each other in God. I shall not say that he went straight from there to socialism: that would be too schematic. But there came a time when he encountered Marxism and asked what it had to offer: he concluded that it offered the future unity of a classless society and, in the meantime, a warm friendship in struggle. After 1936, there can be no doubt: it was the Party that troubled him. One of his most constant characteristics was to seek the lost immanence everywhere, to be thrown back by that immanence itself toward some transcendent entity and thereupon to take his leave. Yet he did not remain at this level of the original contradiction: between 1950 and 1960, he gradually conceived a new connection between being and intersubjectivity; but in 1945, though he dreamed perhaps of going beyond it, he had found no way to do so.

In short, he had been through a great deal when, despite the feelings of revulsion he had at times experienced, he proposed his severe, disillusioned, *attentiste* Marxism. And it was true that he had "learned history" without having any taste for it, from his vocation and out of obstinacy. It was true, too, that he was never again to forget it. This is something his communist friends did not see at the time, tending, as they did, more toward unconditional commitments than precise, limited agreements. For his part, being concerned only with deepening his relation to history, he would have been unaffected by their criticisms, I imagine, and would have remained stubbornly silent, if we had not, by chance, founded *Les Temps modernes*. He now possessed the instrument of expression and was virtually compelled to express the detail of his thinking.

We had dreamed of having the review since 1943. If the Truth is indivisible, I thought, then we must, as Gide said of God, seek it "only everywhere." Every social product, every attitude—the most private and the most public—are allusive incarnations of it. An anecdote reflects a whole age as effectively as a political constitution. We would be seekers after meaning; we would speak the truth about the world and our lives. Merleau thought me overoptimistic: Was I sure there was meaning everywhere? To which I might have replied that the meaning of non-meaning exists and it was up to us to find it. And I know what he would have replied in turn: cast as much light on barbarism as you will, you will not dispel its obscurity. The discussion never took place: I was more dogmatic, he was more nuanced, but that is a matter of temperament or, as they say, of character. We had a single desire: to get out of the tunnel, to see things clearly. He wrote: "Our only recourse lies in a reading of the present that is as complete and faithful as possible; a reading that does not prejudge its meaning and even recognizes its chaos and non-meaning where they are to be found, but is not averse to discerning a direction and an idea in that present, where they exist."[9]

This was our program. Today, after Merleau's death, it is still the program of the review. We would have to say that the real difference was our inequality. After he had learned history, I was no longer his equal. I was still stuck in the questioning of facts while he was already attempting to make events speak.

Facts *repeat* themselves. They are, of course, always new—but what of it? The annual play by the boulevard playwright is new. He had to come up with the idea and then he thought about it and worked on it; every speech was a stroke of inspiration, and the actors in their turn had to "get inside" the piece. For days they said "I don't feel the part" and then, suddenly, "I feel it." And in the end, on the day of the dress rehearsal, the unexpected happens: the play became what it was—namely, just the same as all the others. Facts confirm and begin anew: they reveal customs, old contradictions, and sometimes, more deeply, structures. The same adultery has been committed for fifty years, every evening, before the same bourgeois audience in the heart of Paris. By looking only for permanencies of this kind, I was hoping unconsciously that we would become the ethnographers of French society.

Merleau-Ponty didn't hate these permanencies. Indeed, he loved the childlike return of seasons and ceremonies. But for this very reason, pining hopelessly for his childhood, he knew it would not return. It would be something too wonderful if, in the world of adults, the adult could be visited by the grace of his earliest years: life would be too perfect. Merleau, the exile, had *felt* at an early stage what I could only *know*: you cannot go back; you cannot take a second turn; by its irreversibility, the sweet contingency of birth transforms itself into a destiny. I was not unaware that you descend life's course and never reverse its direction; but, duped by the bourgeois myth of progress, I cherished for a long time the illusion that I was a little better each day. Progress: the accumulation of capital and virtue; you keep everything. In short, I was approaching excellence; it was the masking of death, which today stands naked. He was moving away from it: being born to die, nothing could restore the immortality of his earliest years; this was his original experience of *the event*.

In the middle of the last century, he would have lived time backward, though in vain, as Baudelaire did after the "*fêlure*": the golden age is past; there is room now only for decline. It is to Merleau's credit that he avoided this reactionary myth: let there be as much decline as you will, but it is our decline, we cannot suffer it without creating it or, in other words, without producing man and his works through that decline. The event swoops on us like a thief and throws us into a ditch or hoists us up onto a wall; dazed, we see nothing. Yet hardly has it gotten away than we find ourselves so deeply changed that we no longer even understand how we could love, live, and act before. Who in 1945 would have remembered the 1930s? They were preparing quietly for retirement; the occupation had killed them off; only bones remained. Some still dreamed of a return to prewar days. Merleau knew it would not happen and it was criminal and futile to wish for it: when he wondered in 1945 whether the human adventure would sink into barbarism or rescue itself through socialism, he was putting the question to universal history as though it were his own life: Time lost? Time regained? Divergence, deviation, drift—these words from his pen, a hundred times rewritten, attest to the fact that we gain nothing without a loss, that the future, even the nearest, most docile future, betrays our hopes and calculations. But most of the time it betrays them by bringing them to fruition: our past acts come back to us, from the depths of future time, unrecognizable, but nonetheless our own; one either had to despair or find in those acts the changing reason for change and, not being able to restore the old facts, at least establish them in the heart of the event that repudiates them. We would try to govern the strange slippage we call history from within, by seeking, in the movement that carries us along, the implicit objectives of human beings, so as to propose those objectives to these human beings explicitly. This meant questioning the event in its unpredictability—without prejudging anything—to find a logic of temporality in it. One might be tempted to call that logic "dialectical" if Merleau had not already objected to that term and had not, ten years later, more or less repudiated it.*

All in all, the prewar period denied time: when a cyclone had blown down our walls, we searched for the survivors among the rubble and told them, "It's nothing." The most extraordinary thing is, they believed us. Merleau-Ponty "learned history" quicker than we did because he took a full and painful pleasure in passing time. This is what made him our political commentator, without his even having wished to be and without anyone even noticing.

Les Temps modernes had at that point an editorial board that was anything but homogeneous: Jean Paulhan, Raymond Aron, and Albert Ollivier were all friends of ours, of course. But, though no one knew this, least of all ourselves,[10] we did not share any of their ideas. In fact, our inert coexistence had been, not so long before, a lively comradeship: some had just come from London, others from underground. But the Resistance fragmented: everyone returned to their natural home, some to *Le Figaro*, others to the RPF [Rassemblement

*He had not pronounced on this question in 1945: he thought the word too ambitious to apply it to the modest activity of *Les Temps modernes*.

du peuple français], yet others to the *Nouvelle Nouvelle Revue Française*. The communists themselves, having participated in the first issue in the person of Jean Kanapa, took their leave. This was a heavy blow for those of us who remained: we lacked experience. Merleau saved the review by agreeing to take charge of it: he was editor in chief and political editor. This happened naturally. He didn't offer me his services and I didn't take the liberty of "selecting" him: we both realized, after a certain time, that he was filling these two posts and that he couldn't leave them without the review going under. We discussed only one matter: since the editorial board had disappeared from the cover, I suggested printing Merleau's name there alongside my own: we would have been the two "directors." He turned me down flat. I put the same offer to him a hundred times in the ensuing years, always on the simple grounds that it would have been a truer reflection of the actual position. A hundred times, relaxed and smiling, he turned me down again, citing circumstantial reasons, but never the same ones. Since his reasons changed constantly, but his position did not, I concluded that he was concealing his true motives from me. I confronted him with this and he rejected the idea, though with no great vigor: he was not trying to deceive me, but merely wanted to put a stop to the discussion. And then, whatever the subject, he never liked the debate to get to the crux of the matter. On this point, he won: I know no more of his reasons today than I did in 1945. Was it modesty? I doubt it: this wasn't about sharing honors but responsibilities. On the other hand, I have been told, "At the time you were better known: he was too proud to accept the fruits of that fame." It is true that I was better known and it was nothing to boast of: it was the time of the *rats de cave*,[11] of existential suicides; the respectable newspapers heaped dirt on me and so did the gutter press: I had fame, but it was born of misconceptions. But those who read *Samedi Soir*'s interesting account of a virgin whom I apparently lured to my room to show her a camembert did not read *Les Temps modernes* and were not even aware of its existence. On the other hand, the real readers of the review knew both of us equally; they had read our essays and preferred the one or the other of us, or felt no great preference but no animosity either. Merleau knew this as well as I did: we had received letters and shown them to each other. All in all, his audience and mine—the audience of *Les Temps modernes*—were the same people. And the best people one could wish for, not shooting the pianist, and judging him on his work and not concerning themselves with other matters. From my dubious reputation Merleau could neither suffer nor profit. Was he perhaps afraid of being compromised? Nothing was less like him: he proved this in the review itself, publishing articles that provoked scandal and signing them with his own name. So, what can we say? Why did he stubbornly persist in signing editorials with the letters T. M., when, though I accepted them unreservedly, he had conceived and written every word? All the writings to which he didn't own up were randomly attributed to me: there was some logic to this, since I claimed to be in sole charge. And last year, leafing through some foreign bibliographies, I discovered that I was the author of his article on the Soviet camps—the very one he recognized and legitimized in his last book.[12] Why had he not signed it in 1950, given that he was later to republish it? Why did he republish it ten years later, when he hadn't wanted to sign it? Why create all these "bastards" for the review when it was wholly within his power to "regularize" their status? This is the question; I cannot claim to have an answer. Yet one had to get on with life; I contented myself with the most convenient explanation: he valued his independence and would have felt as a burden any bond but the tacit understanding, renewed with each issue, that committed no one and that either of us could break at a moment's notice. This is a possible explanation, and yet I think today that he mistrusted me: he knew my incompetence, and he feared my zeal; if I should begin talking politics, then where would we be? I have no evidence of this distrust except for the following. In 1947, I published "What Is Literature?" in the review. He read the first proofs and thought he had found in them a sentence which, as was the fashion at the time, equated fascism with "Stalinism" beneath the common appellation of "totalitarian regimes." I was in Italy and he wrote to me immediately; I received the letter in Naples and I remember my stupefaction. It said, more or less: "If you really apply the same yardsticks to communism and Nazism, then I beg you to accept my resignation." Fortunately, as I was able to prove to him, it was simply a typographical error. We left matters there. But when I reflect on it, it reveals the extent of his distrust: first, the text, at the proof stage, was incomprehensible and clearly mangled; second, as Merleau knew, I had never indulged in that kind of silliness; last, his resignation was offered rather too eagerly. All in all, it is very clear that he was expecting the worst. But what strikes me most is that his fear was that I would defect to the *right*. Why? Did he see me as temperamentally right-wing? Or was he simply afraid that the hyena with the fountain pen, frozen out by the jackals, would seek admission to the Pen Club? In any event, he was taking precautions against possible blunders on my part: if one should prove inexcusable, he could be away within twenty-four hours. This emergency exit was still in place five years later when a political disagreement drove us apart: yet Merleau did not use it; so long as he could hope that our contradictions would be overcome, he remained. His letter of 1947 proves he would have left the review there and then if I had let it fall into a rightist rut. When I moved to the left, he accepted being compromised: he believed he could already see the ditch and that we would imminently be pitched into it, yet he remained at my side, determined to jump only as a last resort. For a long time I thought he was wrong not to have joined me in the stocks: public collaboration would have forced us, I told myself, to make concessions on both sides; we would have been tactful with each other to save the collegiate editorship. Yet for some time now I have tended to believe he was right: in 1952, our differences could neither be masked nor overcome. They arose not out of our temperaments but from the situation: since the name of Merleau wasn't mentioned, we were able to delay matters a little longer. The secret nature of the bond between us, which had been conceived to make withdrawal easy for him, enabled us to stay together till the last moment. The separation was a quiet one, we had no need to proclaim it or, in other words, to turn it into a publicized quarrel. This is perhaps what saved our friendship.

In our closest circles, all these precautions afforded him the reputation of an éminence grise. This was quite wrong, particularly as he was nobody's adviser: master of his sphere, as I was of mine, his role—like mine—was to make decisions and to write.

He was, however, extremely keen that I should read his articles, both those which he signed T. M., which spoke in the name of the review, and the others bearing his own name, which committed only himself. Let me be clear here: this attitude *seems like* that of an employee, a functionary having his actions "covered" by the competent authority. It was, in fact, quite the opposite: Merleau was entirely his own boss. He knew his way around the ambiguous world of politics better than I did and I knew that. It would be an understatement to say I trusted him: it seemed to me that, when I read him, he revealed my own thinking to me. But our gentlemen's agreement demanded that he consult me: writing anonymously, he did not want me to be saddled with his writings. He was as tactful as possible about it: I was still a stammerer in this new language he already spoke and he was not unaware of this. Reluctant either to coerce or inveigle me, he brought me his manuscripts without comment. In the early days, he had to make a lot of effort to be read: the political labyrinth confused me, I approved everything in advance and in haste, and then ran off. He'd find out my hiding place and track me down to it. I'd find him suddenly standing there, smiling, and holding out his manuscript: "I agree," I'd stammer. "That's good," he'd reply, not moving, "But all the same," he'd add patiently, indicating with his left hand the sheets of paper in his right, "you should read these."

I read and learned, and in the end I was passionate about my reading. He was my guide; it was *Humanism and Terror* that caused me to take the plunge. That little book, so densely written, showed me the method and the object: it gave me the nudge I needed to wrest me from my immobility. As is well known, it provoked scandal everywhere. Communists who see no harm in it today loathed it at the time. But, particularly to our right, it raised a fine hullabaloo. One sentence in particular, which equated opponents with traitors and traitors with opponents, triggered the reaction. In Merleau's mind, this sentence applied to those anxious, threatened societies that huddle together around a revolution. But attempts were made to present it as a sectarian condemnation of any opposition to Stalin. In just a few days, Merleau became the bloodthirsty revolutionary. When Simone de Beauvoir visited them in New York, the editors of *Partisan Review* made no effort to conceal their disgust: we were being manipulated; it

330 · JEAN-PAUL SARTRE

was the hand of Moscow that held the pen of our *père Joseph*.[13] What idiots! One evening, at Boris Vian's, Camus took Merleau to task, accusing him of justifying the Moscow trials. It was painful: I can still see them, Camus outraged, Merleau-Ponty courteous and firm, a little pale, the one permitting himself, the other forbidding himself, the splendors of violence. Suddenly Camus turned away and left. I ran after him, accompanied by Jacques Bost, and caught up with him in the empty street. I tried as best I could to explain Merleau's thinking, which Merleau himself had not deigned to do. The only result was that we parted on bad terms; it took more than six months and a chance meeting to bring us together again. This is not a pleasant memory for me: what a stupid idea to try to play the peacemaker! I was, admittedly, to the right of Merleau and to the left of Camus; what black humor can have prompted me to play go-between to two friends who were both not long afterward to criticize my friendship for the communists, and who are both dead, unreconciled?

In fact, with this little sentence, which caused such a violent reaction, but which everyone accepts today as a basic truth with a universal validity beyond the limits set for it by its author, Merleau had done nothing but apply to other circumstances what the war had taught him: we will not be assessed on our intentions alone. As much as, and more than, the intended effects of our acts, the basis on which we are judged will be the unintended consequences that we have divined and exploited, and for which, in any event, we have assumed responsibility. "The man of action," he wrote later, quoting Hegel, "has the certainty that, through his action, necessity will become contingency and contingency necessity." In so doing, he was asking the true philosophical question of history: What is a detour and what does it mean to veer off course? We started out in rough weather and a headwind, we battled on stoically and have grown old in hard times; this, here, is what we have achieved. What remains of the old goals? What has disappeared? A new society has been born along the way, shaped by the undertaking and deflected by its deflection. What can it accept? And what must it reject or risk doing itself a serious mischief? And, whatever the heritage, who can say whether we have traveled the shortest path or whether we must attribute the meanderings to everyone's failings?

Through this rough justice of injustice, in which the bad are saved by their works and men of good faith condemned to hell for acts committed with a pure heart, I finally discovered the reality of the event. In a word, it was Merleau who converted me: at heart I was an anarchist laggard, I saw a chasm between the vague fantasies of collectivities and the precise ethics of my private life. He set me straight: he taught me that this ambiguous undertaking that is both rational and mad, ever unpredictable and always foreseen, attaining its objectives when it forgets them, missing them when it tries to remain loyal to them, destroying itself in the false purity of failure and dissipating itself in victory, abandoning its prime mover on the way or denouncing him when he no longer believes himself responsible for it, was something I found everywhere, both in the most intimate recesses of my life and in the broad daylight of history, and that there is only one undertaking and it is the same for everyone—the event that makes us by becoming action, the action that unmakes us by becoming, through us, event—and, since Hegel and Marx, it bears the name *praxis*. In a word, he revealed to me that I made history in the same way as Monsieur Jourdain made prose. The course of events broke down the last ramparts of my individualism and swept away my private life, and I discovered myself in just those very places where I began to slip beyond my own grasp. I came to know myself: and I was more obscure, in the full light of day, than I believed myself to be, and two billion times richer. The time had come: our age demanded a dissertation on French politics from all men of letters. I prepared myself for that ordeal; Merleau instructed me without teaching, by his experience, by the consequences of his writings. If philosophy is to be, as he said, an "educative spontaneity," I may say he was for me the philosopher of his politics. As for his politics, it is my claim we could have had no other and that it was appropriate. If one is to last, one must begin well: the beginning came from him and it was excellent. Proof of this is that our readers have taken all the subsequent twists and turns with us; it will soon be seventeen years since we published the first issue of *Les Temps modernes*; we have regularly gained subscribers and at the very most a few dozen have left us.

It was possible in 1945 to choose between two positions. Two and no more. The first and best was to address ourselves to the Marxists, to them alone, and to denounce the way the Revolution had been nipped in the bud, condemn the murder of the Resistance and bemoan the fragmentation of the left. A number of periodicals adopted this line courageously and disappeared, unheeded; it was the happy time when people had ears so as not to hear and eyes so as not to see. Far from believing that these failures condemned the attempts, I take the view that we could have imitated them without going under: the strength and weakness of these publications was that they confined themselves to the political sphere; ours published novels, literary essays, reportage, and nonfiction material: these kept it afloat. However, in order to denounce the betrayal of the Revolution, one had first to be revolutionary: Merleau was not, and I was not yet. We didn't even have the right to declare ourselves Marxist, despite our sympathies for Marx. Now, revolution is not a vague sentiment: it is a daily practice illuminated by a theory. And, though it is not enough to have read Marx to be a revolutionary, you connect with him sooner or later when you campaign for revolution. The conclusion is clear: only men shaped by that discipline could criticize the left effectively; at the time, then, they had to belong, in one way or another, to Trotskyist circles; but, without it being at all their fault, that affinity disqualified them: within that mystified left that dreamed of unity, they were regarded as "splitters." Merleau-Ponty saw the threats clearly too; he noted that the working class's forward march was halted and he knew the reasons for it. But if he had shown the workers gagged, chained, mystified, and defrauded of their victory, this petty-bourgeois intellectual—even if he had wept hot tears for them, even if he had made his readers weep them—would have been laying the demagogy on thick. When, on the other hand, he concluded that the proletariat had gone on vacation, he was being sincere and true to himself, and I was being true to myself when I backed his conclusions. Revolutionaries, us? Come off it! At the time, revolution seemed the most likable of myths, a Kantian idea, so to speak; I repeated the *word* with respect, but I knew nothing of the *thing*. We were moderate intellectuals whom the Resistance had pulled to the left; but not enough; and then again, the Resistance was dead; left to ourselves, what could we be but reformists?

There remained the other attitude. We had no choice to make; it forced itself upon us. As products of the middle classes, we attempted to form a link between the intellectual petty bourgeoisie and the communist intellectuals. That bourgeoisie had engendered us; its culture and values were our heritage; but the occupation and Marxism had taught us that neither the culture nor the values were to be taken for granted. We called on our friends in the Communist Party to supply us with the requisite tools to wrest humanism from the bourgeoisie. And we asked all our friends on the left to do the work with us. Merleau wrote: "We were not wrong in 1939 to want freedom, truth, happiness, and openness between human beings, and we are not renouncing humanism. [But] the war...taught us that these values remain nominal...without an economic and political infrastructure to bring them into existence."[14] I can see that this position, which might be termed eclectic, was not viable in the long run, but I can also see that the French and international situations made it the only one possible. Why would we have taken things to extremes? We had, admittedly, forgotten the class struggle but we were not alone in that. Events had chosen us to bear witness to what the petty-bourgeois intelligentsia wanted in 1945, at the moment when the communists had lost both the means and the intent to overthrow the regime. Paradoxically, that intelligentsia, as it seems to me, wanted the Communist Party to make reformist concessions and the French proletariat to regain its revolutionary aggression. The paradox is merely an apparent one: this chauvinistic class, exasperated by five years of occupation, was afraid of the USSR, but would have come to an accommodation with a "homegrown" revolution. There are, however, degrees in being and thought: whatever the appeal of this revolutionary, chauvinistic reformism, Merleau did not care for being the herald of a proletariat in French colors. For his part, he had undertaken—as did others in other countries at around this same time—an enormous labor of confrontation: he threw our abstract concepts out to the Marxists, and their Marxism changed, as they assimilated those concepts, into what we know it to be today.

Today, the task is easier: this is because the Marxists—communists or otherwise—have taken it up themselves. In 1948, it was very thorny, particularly as the Communist Party intellectuals felt no compunction about telling these two suspect, empty-handed bourgeois, who had volunteered themselves as fellow travelers, where to get off. We had to defend Marxist ideology without concealing our reservations and hesitations; to travel with men to whom we expressed our goodwill and who, in return, called us *intellectuels-flics*; to make our ripostes without being insulting or breaking off relations; to criticize, moderately but freely, these hypersensitive souls who could not tolerate any reservations; to assert, despite our solitude, that we were marching at their side, alongside the working class—the bourgeois fell about laughing when they read us—and yet allow ourselves, when necessary, to run ahead of the Communist Party, as we did at the beginning of the war in Indochina; to struggle for peace and détente in our little magazine, as though we were running a mass-market daily; to deny ourselves any righteous passions, particularly self-importance and anger; to speak in the wilderness as though we were addressing the assembled nation and yet not lose sight of our extreme smallness; to remember at every moment that you don't need success to persevere but that the point of persevering is to achieve success. Despite the jibes and the cheap shots, Merleau-Ponty did the work decently, tastefully, and unflinchingly: it was his job. He cannot claim to have uncovered the reality of the second half of the 1940s (who can?), but he took advantage of illusory French unity to stay as close as possible to the communists, to begin necessary—and yet impossible—negotiations with them, and to lay the foundations, beyond Marx, of what he sometimes called "a left-wing thought." In a sense, he failed: left-wing thought is Marxism, no more and no less. But history salvages everything except death: if Marxism is becoming *the whole of left-wing thought* today, we owe this, in the first place, to the efforts of a handful of people of whom he was one; the petty bourgeoisie, as I have said, were veering to the left; efforts to stop their slide came from all directions, but it came to a halt on some advanced positions: to the shared desire for democratic union and reforms Merleau gave the most radical expression.

Two years of calm and then the outbreak of the cold war. Behind Marshall's homilies, Merleau was immediately able to see, and denounce, the generosity of an ogre. It was the time when groups were forming. The Communist Party hardened its line, our right fled off toward the center; at the same point, we were beginning to hear the sound of the RPF rousing its support. The bourgeoisie raised its head again, dubbed itself "the third force," and developed the policy of the cordon sanitaire. We were being pressed to take sides and Merleau refused. He had at times to cling tightly to the tiller: the Prague coup, revolving strikes, the end of the tripartite government, the Gaullist landslide at the municipal elections. He had written, "The class struggle is masked"; it unmasked itself. We persisted stubbornly with our offers of mediation, which no one took seriously, all the more confident that we were, in our two persons, achieving the unity of the left because it had at the time no other representative. The RDR[15] was born, a mediating neutralism between the blocs, between the advanced fraction of the reformist petty bourgeoisie and the revolutionary workers. I was asked to join and, allowing myself to be persuaded it shared our objectives, I accepted. Merleau, receiving requests from elsewhere, joined nevertheless so as not to disown me. It did not take me long to see I had been wrong. To live in the closest proximity to the Communist Party, to have it accept certain criticisms, we had, first, to be politically ineffectual and they had to sense that we were effectual in other ways. Merleau-Ponty was just that, standing alone with neither supporters nor champions, his thought, ever new and ever recommenced, relying entirely on its own merits. By contrast, the Rassemblement, small as it was and small as it consented to be, put its faith in force of numbers. As a result, despite its immediate desire to suspend hostilities, it immediately triggered them: Where would it recruit its revolutionary supporters from, if not from communist or related circles? The Party, up in arms, treated it from the first as an enemy, to the astonishment of the Rassemblement's members. It was the ambiguity of this situation that gave rise to our internal divisions: some, in disgust, allowed themselves to drift to the right—in general, these were the "organizers." The others—the majority—sought to remain unshakable and to align themselves with the social action of the PCF.[16] This latter group, which included us, criticized the others for abandoning the initial program: "Where's your neutralism?" we asked and they immediately retorted, "Where's yours?"

Did Merleau discover our mistake before I did? Did he learn that political thinking cannot easily be embodied unless it is pushed to its own logical extreme and taken up somewhere by those who have need of it? Was it not rather that, in 1948 as in 1941, he couldn't help feeling a little scorn for groups that were too young, that had no roots and traditions? The fact is that he never came to the Steering Committee, even though he was a founder member: this, at least, is what I've been told as I did not often go either. He may justifiably have feared that we were distorting his project and that *Les Temps modernes* might come to be seen as the monthly organ of the RDR: he said nothing of this to me, either because he shared my incautiousness or because he did not want to reproach me with it, counting on events to remove the scales from my eyes. In short, he carried on editing the review as usual and let me carry on battling, alone and intermittently, under the banner of neutrality. In the spring of 1949, however, we were agreed that the RDR was not viable. The Mouvement de la Paix, led at the time by Yves Farge, was to hold a congress in Paris.[17] As soon as we became aware of this, the suggestion came up within the Rassemblement that we should invite a number of American personalities and, a few days after the congress, devote some "Study Days" to peace. Clearly, we could count on the right-wing press to spread the news; in short, these pacifist "days" were merely a political machination, backed, if not indeed inspired, by the Americans. Having been invited a little too insistently by the U.S. embassy to take part, a worried Richard Wright came to see me: Where were we heading? Merleau joined us: we decided that the three of us would not appear at these events and we wrote a letter in all our names to explain why we were staying away; the war between the two peaces was waged without us; at the *Vél d'Hiver*, an American was to be heard vaunting the merits of the atom bomb but we were not present. The activists were outraged; in June 1949, they went to the leadership to tell them what they thought of them and I took their side. We killed off the RDR and I left for Mexico, disappointed but at peace with myself. Merleau had not appeared at the congress but there could be no doubting his opinion: I realized I needed this unpleasant experience to appropriate his thought in its entirety. In fact, the so reasonable unreason of politics had been within an inch of tipping us into an anticommunism which we vomited and to which we would, nonetheless, have had to adapt.

I saw him again in autumn: I told him I had understood his position. There would be no more active politics: the review and the review alone. I put some plans to him: Why not devote an issue to the USSR? We were, it seemed, in entire agreement on this: we were becoming interchangeable. I was, then, all the more astonished that so little came of my proposals. It would have been all right if he had shown me they were absurd: but he simply let them drop, silently and glumly. The fact was that we were getting wind of the Soviet camps. Documents were sent to us at the same time as Rousset received them, but from another source. Merleau's editorial appeared in the January 1950 issue; it was to be republished in *Signs*; this time I went so far as to ask him to show it to me even before he had offered. I didn't miss a word and approved the whole piece, not least the author's consistency with his previous positions. He laid out the facts and ended the first paragraph in the following terms:

> If there are ten million concentration camp inmates—while at the other end of the Soviet hierarchy salaries and standard of living are fifteen to twenty times higher than those of free workers—then quantity changes into quality. The whole system swerves and changes meaning; and in spite of nationalization of the means of production, and even though private exploitation of man by man and unemployment are impossible in the USSR, we wonder what reasons we still have to speak of socialism in relation to it.[18]

How could the Soviet workers tolerate this disgraceful return of slavery on their soil? It was, he answered, because it had come about gradually "without deliberate intention, from crisis to crisis and expedient to expedient."[19] Soviet citizens know the [Corrective Labor] Code, they know there are camps: what they are not perhaps aware of is the extent of the repression; if they discover it, it will be too late: they have become habituated to it in small doses.

> A good number of young Soviet heroes ... [and] many civil ser-
> vants who were favorably endowed ... who never knew discus-
> sion and the critical spirit in the sense of 1917, continue to think
> the prisoners are hotheads, asocial persons, men of bad will ...
> And communists throughout the world expect that, by a sort of
> magical emanation, so many canals, factories and riches shall
> one day produce whole men, even if in order to produce them it
> is necessary to reduce ten million Russians to slavery.

The existence of the camps, he said, made it possible to gauge how
deluded the communists were today. But he immediately added:

> It is ... this illusion which forbids confusing communism and
> fascism. If our Communists accept the camps and oppression,
> it is because they expect the classless society to emerge from
> them ... No Nazi was ever burdened with ideas such as the rec-
> ognition of man by man, internationalism, classless society. It is
> true that these ideas find only an unfaithful bearer in today's
> communism ... The fact remains that they are still part of it.[20]

He added even more explicitly:

> We have ... the same values as a Communist ... We may think
> he compromises them by embodying them in today's commu-
> nism. The fact remains that they are ours, and that on the con-
> trary we have nothing in common with a good number of
> communism's adversaries ... [T]he USSR is on the whole situ-
> ated ... on the side of those who are struggling against the
> forms of exploitation known to us ... [W]e do not draw the
> conclusion that indulgence must be shown towards commu-
> nism, but one can in no case make a pact with its adversaries.
> The only sound criticism is thus the one which bears on exploi-
> tation and oppression, inside and outside the USSR.[21]

Nothing could be clearer: whatever its crimes, the USSR had this
formidable advantage over the bourgeois democracies: the revolution-

ary aim. An Englishman said of the camps, "They are their colonies." To which Merleau replies, "Our colonies are, then, *mutatis mutandis*, our labor camps." But those camps have no other aim than to enrich the privileged classes; the Russians' camps are perhaps even more criminal since they betray the revolution; the fact remains that they were built in the belief of serving it. It may be that Marxism has been bastardized, that domestic difficulties and external pressure have distorted the regime, warped its institutions, and deflected socialism from its course: still Russia cannot be compared with other nations; it is permissible to judge it only if one accepts its project and in the name of that project.

In short, five years after his first article, in a moment of extreme seriousness, he was going back to the principles of his politics: alongside the Party, cheek by jowl with it, never inside it. We oriented ourselves by the Party alone and outside opposition was our only attitude to it. To attack the USSR alone was to absolve the West. This uncompromising position echoes Trotskyist thinking: if the USSR is attacked, said Trotsky, we have to defend the foundations of socialism. As for the Stalinist bureaucracy, it is not for capitalism to deal with that; the Russian proletariat will see to it.

But Merleau's voice grew somber: he spoke coldly and even his anger lacked passion and was virtually lifeless. It was as though he were feeling the first symptoms of that weariness of soul that is our general malaise. Look again at the 1945 articles and compare them and you will be able to gauge his disappointments, the attrition of his hopes. In 1945, he wrote, "We pursue the policy of the Communist Party with no illusions." In 1950: "we have the same values as a communist." And, as if the better to demonstrate the weakness of this purely moral bond: "A Communist, it will be said, has no values ... He has values *in spite of himself*."[22] To be in agreement with the communists was to attribute our maxims to them while knowing they rejected them; as for a political understanding, there was no longer the slightest prospect of it. In 1945, Merleau forbade himself any thought or action that could possibly hinder the rebirth of the proletariat. In 1950, he simply refused to attack oppression in Russia alone: it should either be denounced everywhere or nowhere. The fact was that the USSR of 1945 seemed "ambiguous" to him. There were "both signs of progress and symptoms of regression." It was a nation emerging from a terrible ordeal and hope was permissible. In 1950, after the revelation of the concentration-camp system: "[W]e wonder what reasons we still have to speak of socialism in relation to it."[23] One single concession: the USSR was, all in all, on the right side of the fence, with the forces fighting exploitation. No more than that: the revolutionary objective of "produc[ing] whole men" was reduced in the 1950 context to being merely an illusion of the communist parties. We might say that Merleau was, around this time, at the parting of the ways, but he was still reluctant to choose. Was he going to continue favoring the USSR in order to remain true to himself and the disadvantaged classes? Was he going to lose interest in this society based on concentration camps? If it were proved that it was made of the same clay, why would one expect any more from it than from the predatory powers? One last scruple held him back: "The decadence of Russian communism does not make the class struggle a myth . . . or Marxist criticism in general null and void."[24]

Were we so sure we could reject the Stalinist regime without condemning Marxism? I received an indignant letter from Bloch-Michel. In substance, he wrote: "How is it that you cannot understand that the Soviet economy needs a servile labor force and that each year it systematically recruits millions of underfed, overexploited workers?" If he were right, Marx had pitched us from one barbarism into another. I showed the letter to Merleau who was not convinced by it. We thought there was a legitimate passion in it, reasons of the heart but no actual Reason. No matter: perhaps if it had been better thought out, backed by proven facts and by argument, who knows whether it would not have won us over? The difficulties of industrialization in a period of socialist accumulation, encirclement, the resistance of the peasantry, the need to secure food supplies, demographic problems, distrust, terror, and police dictatorship—this whole set of facts and consequences were quite enough to overwhelm us. But what would we have said or done if it had been demonstrated that the concentrationary regime were required by the infrastructure? We would have needed to have a better knowledge of the USSR and its production regime: I went there some years later and was relieved of these fears at the point when the camps were being opened. During the winter of 1950, we were still grimly uncertain: the communists' strong point was that we couldn't worry about them without worrying about ourselves; however inadmissible their politics might be, we could not distance ourselves from them—at least in our old capitalist countries —without resolving on some sort of betrayal. To ask "How far can they go?" was the same as asking "How far can I follow them?" There is a morality of politics—a difficult subject that has never been clearly examined—and when politics has to betray its morality, choosing morality means betraying politics. Just try to sort all that out—especially when politics has set the coming of humanity's rule as its objective. At the point when Europe was discovering the Soviet camps, Merleau was at last catching the class struggle without its mask; strikes and repression, the massacres in Madagascar, the war in Vietnam, McCarthyism and the Red Scare in America, the Nazi revival, and the Church in power everywhere, mealy mouthed, protecting renascent fascism beneath its cloak: How could we not smell the stench of the decaying carcass of bourgeois rule? And how could we publicly condemn slavery in Eastern Europe without abandoning the exploited here at home to their exploiters? But could we agree to work with the Party if it meant putting France in chains and covering it with barbed wire? What were we to do? To kick out aimlessly to right and left at two giants who would not even register our blows? This was the least-bad solution: Merleau suggested it, for want of anything better. I could see no other way, though I was worried: we had not moved an inch, but our "yes" had simply changed to a "no." In 1945, we said, "Gentlemen, we are everyone's friends and, first and foremost, friends of our dear Communist Party." Five years later, we were saying, "We are everyone's enemies and the Party's only privilege is that it is still entitled to the full measure of our severity." Without even talking about it, we both sensed that this "soaring" objectivity would not take us far. When everyone was being forced to choose, we had not chosen; and we had perhaps been right. At present, our universal peevishness could perhaps put off the choice for a few months more. But we knew that, had we been editors of a daily or a weekly, we should long ago have had to take the plunge or go to the wall. The relatively small-circulation character of the review gave us some respite, but our—initially politi-cal—position was in danger of turning gradually into moralism. We never descended to the level of the "beautiful soul," but fine senti-ments flourished in our vicinity while manuscripts became scarcer: we were losing momentum, people no longer wanted to write for us.

In China, they showed me the statues of two traitors in a ditch; people have been spitting on them for a thousand years and they are all shiny, eroded by human saliva. We were not yet shiny, Merleau and I, but the process of erosion had begun. We were not being for-given for rejecting Manichaeism. On the right, butchers' boys had been recruited to insult us: they were given carte blanche; they showed their behinds to the critics and the critics took off their hats to them, proclaiming them the "new generation." Ultimately, all the fairies had watched over their cradles but one, the "talent fairy," and they disap-peared for lack of it: they needed just a hint of it, no more, but it had been denied them at birth. They would be starving to death today if the Algerian War were not feeding them: crime pays. They made a lot of noise, but did little harm. On the other flank, things were more serious: our friends in the Communist Party had not come to terms with the article on the camps. We had left ourselves open to attack and we really got it from them. It didn't bother me. I was called a rat, a hyena, a viper, and a skunk, but I liked this bestiary; it took me out of myself. Merleau was more upset by it: he still remembered the com-radely relations of 1945. There were two phases: at first, he was insulted in the morning papers, then late in the evening his communist friends made their highly secretive excuses. This went on until a day came when, in order to simplify matters, these same friends combined the two jobs, writing the articles at dawn and apologizing for them at dusk. Merleau suffered less from being insulted by intimates than from no longer being able to respect them. I would say today that they were possessed by a literally insane violence that was the product of a war of attrition being fought elsewhere, the effects of which were felt in our provincial backwater: they were trying to see themselves as other than they were and couldn't quite manage it. Merleau saw their faults, I think, and not their problem, this provincialism. This is understand-able, since he knew them in everyday life. In short, he moved away from them because they wanted him to: the Communist Party had tolerated these fringes of critical sympathy on its periphery, but it had not liked them. From 1949 onward, it decided to eliminate them: the friends outside the Party were requested to shut their mouths. If any of them publicly expressed reservations, they sickened him until he turned into an enemy. In this way the Party proved to its activists—and each activist thought he proved to himself—that free examination of the dogma was the beginning of betrayal. It was *themselves* that Merleau's friends loathed in him. How much anguish there was in all this and how it all came out after the seismic shock of the Twentieth Congress! Merleau knew the score: the communists' bad tempers did not reduce him to anticommunism. He took the blows but gave none back: his attitude was simply to do right and let others say what they wanted. In short, he carried on with the project. No matter: they denied him oxygen; they exiled him once again into the thin atmosphere of solitary life.

The Communist Party, born of a historical upheaval, a party that had its traditions and its constraints, had appeared to him in the past, even from afar, as offering a possible community: now he lost it. He had many friends who were not communists, of course, and who remained true to him: But what did he find in them or for them, but the affectionate indifference of the prewar period? They met together around a table and ate together, so as to pretend for a moment they had a common task: but these very varied human beings, still shattered by history's intrusion into their private lives, shared nothing but a scotch or a leg of lamb. This amounted, of course, to recognizing that something had died: he realized at last that the Resistance had crumbled; but these perceptions have no deep truth to them unless we feel them to be our own death gaining ground on us. I saw Merleau often in the winter and spring; he showed little sign of nerves, but was extremely sensitive: without entirely understanding him, I felt he was dying a little. Five years later, he would write: "The writer well knows that there is no possible comparison between the rumination on his life and the clearer, more precise things it may have produced (in his work)." This is true: everyone ruminates; one broods on the insults one has suffered, the disgust one has felt, the accusations, recriminations, and pleadings—and then one tries to piece together fragmented experiences that have neither rhyme nor reason to them. Like each of us, Merleau knew those wearisome repetitions from which a sudden enlightenment sometimes springs. That year, there was neither light nor a bolt from the blue. He tried to take the measure of things, to put himself back at that crossroads where his own story intersected with the history of France and the world, where the course of his thinking emerged from the course of events: this is what he had tried to do, and succeeded in doing, as I have said, between 1939 and 1945. But in 1950 it was both too late and too early. "I'd like to write a novel about myself," he told me one day. "Why not an autobiography?" I asked. "There are too many questions without answers. In a novel I could give them imaginary solutions." We must not let this recourse to the imagination mislead us: I would remind the reader of the role phenomenology allots to it in the complex movement that ends in the intuiting of an essence. And yet, even so, his life defied explanation; in meditating upon it, patches of shade emerged, breaks in continuity. Didn't the fact that he had pitched himself, against his will, into this open conflict with his former friends mean that he had made a mistake at the outset? Or was he not bound to take upon himself—at the risk of becoming torn by it—the shifts and turns of an immense movement that had produced him, the mainsprings of which lay beyond his control. Or, alternatively—as he had suggested in 1945 as a mere conjecture— had we not fallen, for a period at least, into non-meaning? Perhaps there was nothing left for us to do but *endure* by holding on to a few rare values? He kept his post at *Les Temps modernes* and chose not to change any of his activities. But "ruminating on his life," taking him back toward his origins, slowly took him away from day-to-day politics. This was his good fortune; when people leave the marginal zone of the Communist Party, they have to go somewhere: they usually walk for a time and end up on the right; Merleau never committed this betrayal: rejected, he took refuge in the depths of his inner life.

Summer came. The Koreans began fighting each other. We were separated when the news reached us: each of us commented off on his own, as we saw fit. We met up at Saint-Raphaël, in August, for a day: too late. We were happy to see each other's gestures again, hear each other's voices, to meet up again with all those familiar oddities for which friends the world over love their friends. There was only one flaw: our ideas, already formed, were incommunicable. From morning to night we talked only of the war, first sitting still by the water, then over dinner, then on the terrace of a café surrounded by scantily clad vacationers. We debated as we walked and then again at the station as I waited for my train. But to no avail; we were deaf to each other. I spoke more than he did, I fear, and not without vehemence. He replied gently and curtly: the sinuous thinness and childlike mischievousness of his smile made me hope he was still hesitating. But no: he never trumpeted his decisions; I had to accept he had made up his mind. He repeated gently, "All that remains is for us to keep silent."

"Who is us?" I said, pretending not to understand.

"Well, we at *Les Temps modernes*."

"You want us to shut up shop?"

"No, but I want us to say no more about politics."

"Why?"

"They're fighting."

"Yes, they are, in Korea."

"Tomorrow they'll be fighting everywhere."

"But even if they were fighting here, why would we keep quiet?"

"Because... It's brute force that will decide. Why speak, since brute force has no ears?"

I got on the train. Leaning out of the window, I waved, as one does, and I saw he was waving back, but I sat dumbfounded till I reached my destination.

I charged him, very unjustly, with wanting to gag criticism at the point when the guns were beginning to rumble. This was far from his mind; he had merely come up against an overwhelming fact: the USSR, he thought, had attempted to compensate for its inferiority in weaponry by acquiring a strategic position. The first thing this meant was that Stalin thought war inevitable: it was no longer a question of averting war but of winning it. But war had only to appear inescapable to one of the blocs for it to become so. It would have been all right if the capitalist world had attacked first: the world would have been blown up, but humanity's venture would have retained a meaning, even when shattered. Something would be dead, but it would at least have made an effort to be born. But since the preventive aggression was coming from the socialist countries, history would merely have been the shroud of our species. The game was up. For Merleau-Ponty, as for many others, 1950 was the crucial year: he thought he saw the Stalinist doctrine without its mask and he judged it to be a Bonapartism. Either the USSR was not the homeland of socialism—in which case, socialism existed nowhere and was probably impossible—or else socialism was indeed this: this abominable monster, this police state, this predatory power. In short, Bloch-Michel had been unable to convince Merleau that socialist society rested on serfdom; but Merleau convinced himself that it had engendered—whether by chance, necessity, or both together—an imperialism. This did not, of course, mean that he had opted for the other monster, capitalist imperialism. "But what can you say?" he said. "They are as bad as each other." This was the great change: he had no desire to rail against the Soviet Union— "Why should I? People are exploited, massacred, and plundered the world over. Let's not take it all out on the one party." It merely lost all privilege in his eyes; it was a predatory power like all the others. He believed at this point that the internal workings of history had perverted its course once and for all; it would carry on in a state of paralysis, deflected by its own dejecta, till it finally came to grief. All meaningful discourse could only, therefore, be lies: all that remained was to withhold one's complicity, to remain silent. He had wanted at first to retain what he felt to be valid in the two systems; he wanted to make a gift to the better one of what the other had achieved. In his disappointment, he had subsequently resolved to denounce exploitation wherever it occurred. After further disappointment, he calmly decided not to denounce anything anywhere ever again, till such point as a bomb, from either East or West, put an end to our brief histories. Being first affirmative, then negative, then silent, he had not shifted an inch. This moderation would be difficult to understand, however, if one did not see it as the calm exterior of a man committing suicide: I have already said that his worst acts of violence were depth charges that harmed only himself. Even in the most wildly raging anger, some hope remains: in this calm, funereal refusal, there was none.

I didn't think these things through as he did; that is what preserved me from melancholy. Merleau made light of the Koreans, but I could see nothing else. He moved too quickly to global strategy and I was mesmerized by the blood: the fault, as I saw it, was with the horse traders at Yalta who had cut the country in two. We were both wrong, out of ignorance, but not without some excuse: where at the time would we have acquired our knowledge? Who would have revealed to us that a military canker was gnawing at the United States and that civilians, in Truman's day, already had their backs to the wall? How in August 1950 would we have guessed MacArthur's plan and his intention to take advantage of a conflict to give China back to the Chinese lobby? Did we know of Syngman Rhee, the feudal prince of a state reduced to poverty, and of the designs of the agricultural South on northern industry? The communist press barely spoke of any of this: they knew little more about it than we did and merely denounced the crime of the imperialist forces, i.e., the Americans, without taking the analysis any further. And, then, they compromised their credibility with a preliminary lie: the only fact that had been established was that the northern troops had been the first to cross the 38th Parallel; now, the communist press stubbornly maintained the opposite. We know the truth today, which is that the U.S. Army, in league with Seoul's feudal overlords, drew the communists into a trap: there were frontier incidents daily and they took advantage of them; the South made such obvious troop movements that the North, deceived, committed the enormous error of striking first to forestall an attack that was never intended. It is a failing of mass parties that they think they can connect with popular thinking—the only deep, true thought—by offering it truths adjusted to its taste. I no longer have any doubt, for example, that in this wretched business the warmongers were the feudal South and the U.S. imperialists. But I have no doubt either that the North attacked first. The Communist Party's task was not easy: when it acknowledged the facts, if only to bring out their meaning, its enemies everywhere presented it as "confessing" to them. If it denied the facts, its friends discovered the lie and backed away. It chose to deny them in order to remain on the offensive. But it was less than a year ago that we had discovered the existence of the Soviet camps: we were still distrustful and ready to believe the worst. In reality, the

USSR deplored this conflict, which might drag it into a war that it could not easily win: yet it had to support the North Koreans for fear of losing its influence in Asia. By contrast, the young China entered the fray, knowing itself to be the object of American designs, but everything required it to do so: revolutionary fraternity, its permanent interests, and its international policy. We, however, had not enough information in the summer of 1950 to see who was playing which role. Merleau believed in Stalin's guilt because he had to believe in it. I didn't believe in anything; I was floundering about, uncertain. This was my good fortune; I didn't have the same temptation to believe that the lights were going out or that it was the year 1000 and the curtain was going up on the Apocalypse: I viewed this blaze from afar and could make out nothing distinct.

In Paris, I met up again with Merleau. Colder and darker. Some of our friends, his wife told me, were devoutly hoping I would blow my brains out the day the Cossacks crossed our borders. Naturally, they were calling for Merleau's brains too. Suicide did not tempt me and I laughed; Merleau-Ponty observed me and did not. Thoughts of war and exile came to his mind. Lightly, with that puckish air I always saw him adopt when things might be turning serious: he would, he said, be a elevator attendant in New York. An embarrassing joke: this was another version of suicide. If war broke out, it would not be enough just to stop writing, you would have to refuse to teach. Trapped in an elevator, he would simply push buttons and mortify himself with silence. Such seriousness is not common and may surprise the reader. Yet he had it, we had it, and I do still. On one point we were in agreement with the good people who wanted our skins: in politics, you have to pay. We were not men of action, but wrong ideas are crimes at par with wrong acts. How did he judge himself? He did not say, but he seemed worried and worrying: "If ever," I said to myself, "he passes judgment on himself, his concealed rage will push him immediately to the point of carrying it out." I often wondered later how his cold anger against the USSR could have turned into a surliness directed against himself. If we had fallen into barbarism, then we could not say a word or even keep silent without behaving as barbarians: Why did he blame himself for sincere, carefully thought-out articles? The world's absurdity had simply stolen his thoughts; there was nothing more to it. He answered this point in *Signs* with an explanation of Nizan that also covers his own case:

> One can understand, then, the objections Sartre makes today to the Nizan of 1939 and why they are without weight against him. Nizan, he says, was angry. But is that anger a matter of mood? It is a mode of understanding which is not too inappropriate when fundamental meaning-structures are at stake. For anyone who has become a Communist and has acted within the party day after day, things said and done have a weight because he has said and done them too. In order to take the change in line of 1939 as he should, Nizan would have had to have been a puppet. He would have to have been broken ... I recall having written from Lorraine, in October, 1939, some prophetic letters which divided the roles between us and the USSR in a Machiavellian fashion. But I had not spent years preaching the Soviet alliance. Like Sartre, I had no party: a good position for severely doing justice to the toughest of parties.[25]

Merleau-Ponty was never, by any stretch of the imagination, a communist; he was not even tempted to be. There was no question of him "acting within the Party," but he lived its daily life through friends he had chosen. He did not blame himself for things said and done, but for the comments he had penned about them, for his decision never to offer a critique before having attempted to understand and to justify. He had been right, however, and one knows something only if one gives of oneself. But the consequence was that he suffered for having given of himself for nothing. He had said, "Historical man has only one way of suffering barbarism, and that is to make it." He was the victim of those he had defended so patiently because he had made himself their accomplice. In a word, he abandoned politics the moment he felt he had lost his way in it. With dignity, but guiltily: he had dared to live; now, he walled himself up. He was of course to change his mind about all this later and come to other conclusions; but that was in 1955: this sorrow weighed on his heart for five years.

There was no shortage of people to explain his turnabout in class terms: he was, they said, a liberal petty bourgeois; he went as far as he could and then stopped. How simple that is! And those who say this are petty bourgeois raised as liberals who, nonetheless, opted for the Manichaeism he rejected. It was, in fact, history's fault that the thread was broken: she wears out the men she uses and rides them to death like horses. She chooses actors, transforms them to their very core by the role she forces on them, then, at the slightest change, dismisses them and takes on entirely new ones, whom she throws untutored into the scrimmage. Merleau began work in the milieu that had been produced by the Resistance: with the Resistance's passing, he believed the unity it had produced lived on to a degree in some sort of future humanism which the classes, by their very struggle, could construct together. He "followed the Communist Party line," yet refused to condemn the cultural heritage of the bourgeoisie out of hand. Thanks to this effort to hold on to both ends of the chain, the circulation of ideas in France was never entirely halted: as everywhere, there was a loathing for intelligence, but until 1958 we never knew any intellectual McCarthyism. Moreover, the official thinkers of the Communist Party condemned his ideas, yet the best of them always knew those ideas had to be taken up and that it was necessary that Marxist anthropology assimilate them. But for Merleau, is it conceivable that Tran Duc Thao would have written his thesis and attempted to annex Husserl to Marx?

In many archaic religions, there are sacred personages who perform the function of *binders*: everything has to be linked and attached through them. Politically, Merleau played such a role. He had come to politics in a time of union and refused to break up that union; his role was to bind. I believe the ambiguity of his heuristic Marxism—he said that it could not be sufficient, but also that we had nothing else—created a favorable climate for encounters and discussions that will continue. In this way, he made the history of this postwar period, as much as an intellectual can. Conversely, while being made by him, history also made him. Refusing to set his seal on breaches between people, hanging on with each hand to continents that were drifting apart, he returned in the end, without illusions, to his old idea of catholicity: on either side of the barricade there are only human beings; hence human inventiveness is being born everywhere: it is to be judged not on its origins but on its content. It is enough that the "binder" strain every sinew to keep the two terms of the contradiction together, that he hold back the explosion for as long as he is able: creative works, the product of chance and reason, will attest that the reign of the human is possible. I cannot decide whether this idea was behind its time or ahead of it in October 1950. One single thing is sure: it was not timely. The globe was cracking apart. There wasn't a single thought that didn't express some prejudice and aim to function as a weapon, not a single bond that didn't form without others breaking; to serve one's friends, everyone had to spill the blood of enemies. Let us be clear here: others, besides the "binder," condemned Manichaeism and violence. But they did so precisely because they were Manichaean and violent: in a word, to serve the bourgeoisie. Merleau-Ponty was the only one who did not celebrate the triumph of discord, the only one not to tolerate—in the name of our "catholic" vocation—love everywhere becoming the obverse of hatred. History had given him to us; well before his death, it took him away.

At *Les Temps modernes*, we had put politics on the back burner. It must be admitted that our readers did not notice this straightaway: we were, at times, so far behind that we got around to talking about things when everyone had forgotten them. However, in the long run, people grew angry: being uncertain, they called for enlightenment and it was our bounden duty either to provide them with it or to confess that we were as lost as they were. We received irritated letters; the critics weighed in too; in an old issue of *L'Observateur* I recently found a "Review of reviews" that took us sternly to task. We were each aware of these criticisms, sometimes learning of them from each other, but we never discussed them: that would have meant reopening the debate. It rather got on my nerves: Did Merleau realize he was *imposing* his silence upon us? But then I reasoned to myself: the review belonged to him, he had defined its political orientation and I had followed him; if our silence were the ultimate consequence of this, I had to go on following him. His smiling sullenness was harder to bear: he seemed to be reproaching us for having accompanied him into this hell on earth, and sometimes for having dragged him into it. The truth is that he could sense our discord growing and it pained him.

We emerged from this impasse without having made any decisions, without speaking. Dzelepy and Stone sent us good, well-informed articles that showed up the war, as it was happening, in a new light. I found that these articles confirmed my opinions. As for Merleau, they didn't contradict his own: we didn't go back over the origins of the conflict. However, he didn't like the articles much, but he was too honest to reject them: I didn't dare insist that we take them. I can't claim that we published them: they published themselves and we found them in the review. Others followed, finding the way to the printers by themselves. This was the beginning of a surprising transformation: having lost its political director, *Les Temps modernes* stubbornly went on obeying him, despite his change of heart. That is to say, it took a radical turn of its own volition. We had longstanding collaborators, most of whom did not meet us often: they changed position to remain as close as they could to the Communist Party, believing they were following us in this, when in fact they were dragging us along with them. Young people came into the review on the basis of the reputation Merleau had made for it: it was, they thought, the only publication which, in this age of iron, retained both its preferences and its clear-sightedness. None of these newcomers was a communist, yet none wanted to veer from the Party line. In this way they put *Les Temps modernes* back, in other—more brutal—circumstances, in the position Merleau had given it in 1945. But this meant overturning everything: to keep our distance from the communists, it was necessary in 1951 to break with all the rest of what still called itself the left. Merleau remained silent: more exactly, he gagged himself with a hint of sadism. He forced himself, out of professionalism and the demands of friendship, to let through this stream of tendentious articles, which addressed themselves to our readership over his head and which, in a roundabout way—by way of anything, even a film criticism—gave vent to a confused, muddled, impersonal opinion that was no longer his without yet being entirely mine. In this way we both discovered that, over these six years, the review had acquired a kind of independence and that it directed us as much as we directed it. In a word, during the interregnum years 1950–52, a skipperless vessel itself recruited officers who kept it afloat. In those days, when Merleau looked at this little sardine rushing along in the wake of a whale, if he still told himself "That is the fruit of my labors! . . ." then he must have swallowed many draughts of gall. He had fixed himself fast to the review, to which he had given life and which he kept alive day after day. I think he found himself in the position of a father who, having only yesterday treated his son as a child, suddenly finds himself face-to-face with a mulish, almost hostile adolescent, who has "got into bad company." Sometimes I tell myself that our common mistake was to remain silent *even then*, when we were still uncertain and uncommitted . . . But no, the die was cast.

The world developed a war psychosis and I developed a bad conscience. All over the West, people wondered in nonchalant tones, but wild-eyed, what the Russians would do with Europe when they had occupied the whole of it. "For they certainly will," said the drawing-room generals. The same people spoke smugly of the Breton redoubt, that bridgehead the Americans would maintain in Finistère to facilitate future landings. Fine: if there was fighting on our soil, no problem: none of us would be spared. But other oracles thought the United States would look to other continents for the real battlefields and would abandon us, out of convenience, to the USSR. What would we do in that case? One answer was given by some young middle-class maidens: in a girls' grammar school in Paris, an entire class vowed to resort to collective suicide. The black heroism of these poor children said a great deal about the fright their parents felt. I heard some very dear friends, former Resistance fighters, coldly declare that they would take to the hills. "This time," I said, "there's a danger you'll be shooting at Frenchmen." I saw from their eyes that that would not trouble them, or rather that they had stubbornly arrived, out of hysteria, at this unreal decision. Others chose realism: they would take a plane to the New World. I was, in those years, a little less mad: for no other reason, perhaps, than a lack of imagination, I didn't believe in the Apocalypse. Yet my mood grew somber; in the Metro a man shouted out, "I'll be glad when the Russians get here!" I looked at him: his life story was etched on his face; in his place, I would perhaps have said the same. I asked myself, "What if, nonetheless, this war did take place?" People kept telling me, "You'd have to leave. If you stay, then either you'll broadcast on Soviet radio or you'll go to a camp and we won't hear from you again." These predictions didn't frighten me much, because I didn't believe in an invasion. Yet they made an impact on me: they were, in my eyes, mind games which, pushing things to extremes, revealed to everyone the need to choose and the consequences of their choices. Staying, they told me, meant collaboration or death. And leaving? To live in Buenos Aires with the wealthy of France, while abandoning my poor compatriots to their fate, would also be a way of collaborating: with the enemy class. But it was your class, you will say. Yet what does that mean? Is that any proof it is not still the enemy of humanity? If there must be betrayal, as Nizan said in *The Watchdogs*, let it be the smallest number doing it for the good of the largest. These gloomy fantasies made me feel really up against it. Everyone had chosen; in my turn, I tried for a moment to linger in neutralism: several of us supported Rivet's candidacy;[26] but the Communist Party had diverted away the potential supporters to his right: he suffered a crushing defeat.

Some communists came to see me about the Henri Martin affair.[27] They were trying to bring together intellectuals of every stamp, from the well-regarded to the smarmy and the wanton, to bring the matter before the public. As soon as I'd taken a look at the business, it seemed so stupid that I joined in unreservedly with the protestors. We decided to write a book about the affair and I left for Italy; it was spring. From the Italian newspapers I learned of Duclos's arrest, the theft of his notebooks, and the carrier pigeons farce.[28] These sordid childish tricks turned my stomach: fouler things were done, but none that was so revealing. My last ties were broken, my view transformed: an anticommunist is a dog; this is my firm opinion and I shall not change it. People will think me very naïve and, indeed, I had seen many other things of this kind that had not stirred me. But after ten years of ruminations, I had reached breaking point; only the merest trifle was needed. In the language of the Church, this was a conversion. Merleau too had been converted, in 1950. We were both conditioned, but in opposite ways. Our disgusts, slowly accumulated, caused us in an instant to discover, in the one case, the horror of Stalinism, in the other,

the horror of his own class. On the basis of the principles it had incul-
cated in me, on the basis of its humanism and its "humanities," on the
basis of liberty, equality, and fraternity, I swore a hatred of the bourgeoisie that will end only when I do. When I hastily returned to Paris,
I had to write or suffocate. I wrote, day and night, the first part of
"The Communists and Peace."[29]

Merleau could not be suspected of any indulgence for the police
methods of a dying regime: he seemed surprised by my eagerness, but
he strongly encouraged me to publish this essay, which was supposed
to be merely article-length. When he read it, he needed only a glance:
"The USSR wants peace," I said, "it needs it, the only threat of war
comes from the West." I said not a word about the Korean War, but,
despite that precaution, it seemed I had premeditatedly taken a systematically opposite line to our political director, that I had contradicted his views point by point. I had in fact written at breakneck
speed, with rage in my heart, joyously and tactlessly. When the best-
prepared conversions explode, one finds the joy of the storm: all
around is blackest night, except where the lightning is striking. Not
for a moment did I think to spare his feelings. For his part, he chose
rather to be amused by my hotheadedness and was not angry. Awhile
later, however, he pointed out that some of our readers were not with
me on this: of course they shared my opinion on the way our government had acted, but in their view I was being too soft on the communists. "What do you tell them?" I asked. It so happened that printed
below this first study were the words: "To be continued." "I tell them,"
he said, "next installment in the next issue." Around 1948, the non-
communist left had, in fact, drawn up an essay plan that acquired
classic status: 1. Thesis: rehearsal of the vileness of the government and
its crimes against the working classes; the Communist Party was pronounced right; 2. Antithesis: the unworthiness of the Political Bureau
was highlighted, together with the mistakes it had made; 3. Conclusion: both were as bad as each other and a middle course was pointed
out, with unfailing mention here of the Scandinavian countries. As
Merleau saw it, I had developed only the thesis; he was still hoping—
though without too many illusions—that the antithesis would follow.

It did not. Nor was the continuation printed in the next issue. I was, in reality, out of breath. And I realized I knew nothing. Just railing against a Prefect of Police doesn't bring insight into one's times. I had read everything, but everything had to be read again. I had only one guiding thread, but it was enough: the inexhaustible, difficult experience of the class struggle. I did the rereading. I had some intellectual muscle and I set about using it, not without tiring myself. I met Farge. I joined the Peace Movement. I went to Vienna. One day I took my second article to the printers, though it was, in fact, merely an outline. I had entirely set aside the "Third Force"–style essay plan: far from attacking the communists, I declared myself a fellow traveler. At the end, once again, I wrote, "To be continued," but there could no longer be any doubt. Merleau didn't see the article until the second proofs. Adding to my guilt, I didn't show them to him myself: he read them at the point when we had to make up the issue. Why hadn't I shown him my manuscript when he always showed me his without fail? Had I decided, once and for all, to take myself seriously? I don't believe so. And I don't believe either that I wanted to escape his admonishments or objections. I would blame, rather, that heedlessness of rage that aims straight for the goal and brooks no precautions. I believed; I knew; I had cast off my illusions: as a result, I would not climb down over anything. In our virtually private publication, you had to shout to be heard: I would shout; I would place myself alongside the communists and would proclaim this to all and sundry. I shall not give the objective reasons for my attitude: they are of no importance here; I shall simply say that they alone counted, that I regarded them as urgent, and that I still do. As for the emotional reasons, I can see two: I was propelled along by the new team; they wanted us to take the leap; I could count on their approval. And then I now see that I bore a bit of a grudge against Merleau for having imposed his silence on me in 1950. The review had been drifting for two years and I couldn't bear it. Let each one judge: I have no excuse, I don't want any. What may be of interest in this adventure—which we both found painful—is that it shows in what ways discord may arise in the heart of the most loyal friendship and the closest agreement. New circumstances and an outdated institution—there were no other reasons for our conflict. The institution was our silent contract. Valid when Merleau spoke and I said nothing, this agreement had never clearly defined our respective domains. Each of us, without speaking of it even to himself, had appropriated the review. There was on the one hand, as in *The Caucasian Chalk Circle*, an official, nominal paternity, mine—and in everything connected with politics it was only that*—and, on the other, an adoptive paternity, five years of jealous care. Everything came to a head suddenly and exasperatedly. We realized that each of us, by his silences as much as by his words, was compromising the other. We needed to have only one set of ideas; and this was the case so long as I did not think for myself. But once there were two heads under the same hat, how were we to choose the right one? Looking at the matter from outside, it will seem that events themselves decided: this is true, but it is rather a facile explanation. It is true, in general, that empires crumble and parties collapse when they are not swimming with the tide of history. Even so, we must admit that this idea, which is perhaps the most difficult of all, is handled incautiously by most writers. But how can we use what may be applied—though not without care—to the great social forces, to explain the growth, life, and death of microorganisms like *Les Temps modernes*? The overall movement was not without its small-scale catastrophes. And, then, however it might be, we had to live the venture ourselves, to accept the sentence passed on us, to carry it out and, as he said later, institute it. With wrong on each side and, in each of us a futile goodwill.

Merleau could have broken things off; he could have provoked a quarrel or written something against me. He abstained, eloquently, from all these things. For a time we remained this strange couple: two friends who still liked each other, each of whom was stubbornly opposed to the other and who had between them only one voice. I admire his moderation all the more for the fact that there were, at the time, several loudly trumpeted defections from the review: one of our longest-standing collaborators left us in a great hurry for the *Nouvelle Nouvelle Revue Française*, where he began by rounding on the "Hitlero-Stalinists" and by speaking in glowing terms of Lucien Rebatet.[30]

---

*In the other fields I would say not that the situation was reversed but that we worked together.

I wonder what there is left of him now: perhaps a rather too self-conscious smattering of ennui, somewhere in the provinces, and nothing more.

The years that followed brought several entertaining crack-ups of the same kind. To fill these gaps and drum up articles, I assembled our collaborators at my flat every other Sunday. Merleau-Ponty attended assiduously, being always the last to arrive and the first to leave, conversing in hushed tones with anyone and everyone on all subjects except *Les Temps modernes*. Yet he had allies in the camp: Claude Lefort, who disapproved of my position; Lefèvre-Pontalis,[31] who wasn't interested in politics; Colette Audry, who feared my excesses; and Erval.[32] It would not have been hard for Merleau to assume the leadership of a strong opposition: he refused to do so on principle—a review isn't a parliamentary assembly—and from friendship. He forbade himself to influence the group, while noting, without liking the fact, that the group was influencing me. The majority was, as it happened, lining up before his eyes behind the critical fellow-traveler position he had just abandoned; given the virulence of anticommunism, the majority was even contemplating toning down the critical aspect and stressing the "fellow-traveling." Above all, I think Merleau found these meetings laughable and their product worthless. In the long run they became so and his silence had its part in bringing this about. But what would he have said? I never failed to ask his opinions; he never ventured them. It was as though he was letting me know it was no good asking me about details when I hadn't deigned to consult him on the main issue. He probably took the view that I was salving my conscience cheaply and didn't want to help me in that. In fact, my conscience was clear and I felt Merleau was wrong to refuse to participate. This grievance will seem misplaced; when all is said and done, I was asking him to work on a venture he had openly disavowed. I recognize this: but, after all, he remained one of our number and then, from time to time, he couldn't stop himself taking some initiative—usually a felicitous one. Though he had abandoned his role of political director after 1950, he still remained editor. In these ambiguous situations, which one maintains in being to avoid a break, everything both parties do turns bad.

But there were more serious reasons for our misunderstanding and they were of a different order. I saw myself as remaining faithful to his thinking of 1945, while he was abandoning it. He saw himself as remaining faithful to himself and felt that I was betraying him. I claimed that I was carrying on his work and he accused me of wrecking it. This conflict came not from either of us but from the world. And we were both right. His political thinking came out of the Resistance; in other words, it emerged from the united left. Within that unity, it could slide toward the most extreme radicalism, but he needed this triple-entente environment: the Communist Party guaranteed the practical efficacy of common action; the allied parties assured him that that action would retain its humanism and certain traditional values, while lending them real content. When, around 1950, everything broke apart, he saw only wreckage; in his eyes, it was my folly to cling to one bit of flotsam, expecting that the pieces of wreckage would rebuild the lost vessel on their own. For my part, I made my decision when the left was smashed to pieces; my opinion was that it had to be reconstituted, though not at the top but from the bottom up. We had, of course, no contact with the masses and hence no power. But our task remained clear: in the face of the unholy alliance between the bourgeoisie and the socialist leaders, there was no other course than to snuggle up to the Party and call on the others to join us. We had to attack the bourgeoisie unrelentingly, expose its policies and defuse its feeble arguments. We would not, of course, recoil from criticizing the Communist Party and the USSR. But we recognized that changing them was out of the question—an impossible task. We wanted to foreshadow future agreements for our readers by setting before them this tiny example of an accord with the communists that had in no way detracted from our freedom of judgment. I was able, in this way, honestly to take the view that I was espousing Merleau-Ponty's attitude.

In fact, the contradiction was not in *us* but, from 1945 onward, in our position. To be for the whole was to refuse to choose between its parts. The privilege Merleau accorded the communists wasn't a choice in their favor: merely a preferential regime. When the moment to choose came, he remained faithful to himself and jumped ship so as

360 · JEAN-PAUL SARTRE

not to survive the shipwrecked unity. I, however, as a newcomer, chose the Party precisely in the name of unity: that unity could not be rebuilt, I thought, unless it were done around the Party. In this way, at a few years' remove, the same idea of union had led the one of us to reject a choice it had forced upon the other. Structures and events together determined everything; France is so constituted that the Party will not take power there on its own: we have therefore to think, first, in terms of alliances. Merleau could still see the tripartite government as a legacy of the Popular Front. But in 1952, without the demographic structure of the country having changed, I could no longer see the Third Force—a mere mask for the right—as coterminous with the unity of the masses. Yet, power could not be taken from the right without gathering together all the forces of the left: the Popular Front remained the necessary means to triumph at the point when the cold war rendered it impossible. While waiting for an alliance to come about that seemed only a distant possibility, we had to maintain that possibility day after day by forming local alliances with the Party. Not choosing on the one hand, choosing on the other—but for the five years' difference, the two attitudes were pursuing the same objective. Two attitudes? There was, rather, just the one, which set us against each other as adversaries, by compelling each of us to stress one of its two contradictory components. In order to remain true to what he wouldn't accept, Merleau forgot his desire for union. And, to give future unity its chance, I forgot my universalism and chose to begin by increasing the disunion. These words will seem abstract; in fact we had to live through these historical determinations: that is to say, we put our whole life into them, our passions, our skins. I mocked his "spontaneity": in 1945, union seemed to be achieved, he could just let himself be carried along. He mocked my naïveté and voluntarism; in 1952, there was no union any longer. Was wishing for it in the abstract enough to bring it about? The truth is that we each found the job to suit our talents: Merleau when it was time for subtleties, myself when the time of the hired killers had arrived.

Lefort and I had some lively discussions and I suggested that he criticize me in the review itself. He accepted and submitted a rather nasty article. I got angry and wrote a reply in the same tone. As a friend to both of us, Merleau found himself, against his wishes, with a new task: he had to play the role of mediator. Lefort had had the courtesy to submit his article to Merleau and I did the same with mine. My article exasperated him: with his customary sweetness, he informed me that he would leave once and for all if I didn't remove a certain paragraph, which was, as it seems to me, needlessly violent. I seem to remember that Lefort made some sacrifices too. All the same, our two texts had a spiteful tone to them. Merleau was fond of both of us and felt every one of the blows we dealt each other. Without being entirely in agreement with Lefort, he felt closer to him than to me: this freed his tongue. And mine. We launched into a long and futile argument that cascaded from one subject to another, one conversation to another. Is there such a thing as the spontaneity of the masses? Can groups derive their cohesion from themselves? Ambiguous questions which sent us off at times to politics, to the role of the Communist Party, to Rosa Luxemburg and Lenin, and at times to sociology, to existence itself, or, in other words, to philosophy, to our "styles of life," to our "anchorage points," to ourselves. With every word we bounced from a consideration of world affairs to the development of our own moods and back again. Beneath our intellectual divergences of 1941, which we had accepted so serenely when we were just arguing over Husserl, we discovered to our stupefaction conflicts that had their source in our childhoods—and even in the elementary rhythms of our organisms. We went on to uncover the surreptitious presence in one of us of a slyness, a smugness, and a mania for activism that covered over his disorientation and, in the other, retractile sentiments and a determined quietism. Naturally, nothing in this was entirely true or entirely false: our ideas became confused because we were putting the same ardor into convincing, understanding, and accusing each other. This passionate dialogue, carried on at a halfway point between good and bad faith, began in my office, continued in Saint-Tropez and was recommenced in Paris at the Café Procope and later at my flat. I traveled. He wrote me a very long letter. I replied, on a day when it was one hundred degrees in the shade, which didn't improve matters. What were we hoping for? Ultimately, for nothing. We were doing our "breakup work" in the sense in which Freud has so well demonstrated that mourning is "work." I believe this sullen two-handed rumination, this endless repetition that led us nowhere, was going to end in gradually exhausting our patience, in breaking the bonds between us one by one by little angry bursts, in casting shadows on the transparent nature of our friendship to the point of making us strangers to each other. If this undertaking had reached its end, we would have quarreled. Fortunately, an incident intervened that interrupted it.

A Marxist I had bumped into by chance offered to write for us on "the contradictions of capitalism." This was, he said, a familiar subject, but little understood, and he would shed new light on it. He was not a member of the Party but a party unto himself and one of the most rigid; he had such a sense that he was doing me a favor that he convinced me. I forewarned Merleau, who knew the man but said nothing. I had to be out of Paris and the article was submitted in my absence. It was worthless. As editor in chief, Merleau-Ponty could not be persuaded to allow it to appear without adding an introductory paragraph, which was, all in all, an apology to our readers. He took the opportunity to criticize the author in two lines for not having even mentioned the contradictions of socialism: this would be for another day, no doubt? On my return, he told me nothing of all this; one of our collaborators warned me and I got myself a set of proofs and read the article beneath its introductory paragraph. The less defensible the article seemed to me, the more irritated I was by that paragraph. Having put the issue "to bed," as they say, Merleau was in his turn away from the office and I wasn't able to get hold of him. Alone and in a state of merry rage, I took out the introductory paragraph and the article appeared without it. You can guess the rest. A few days later, Merleau received the final proofs of the review, noticed his text had been cut, and took it extremely badly. He grabbed the telephone and informed me of his resignation—for good this time. We spoke for more than two hours. Sitting in an armchair by the window, a very gloomy Jean Cau heard half the conversation and thought he was witnessing the last moments of the magazine.[33] We accused each other of abusing our power; I offered him an immediate meeting and tried in every way possible to make him reverse his decision: he was immovable. I didn't see him again for a few months; he didn't come to *Les Temps modernes* and never had anything else to do with it.

If I have told this idiotic story, I have done so, first and foremost, for its pointlessness. When I think back to it, I feel both that it was heartbreaking and that it "had to end like that." Like that: badly, stupidly, inevitably. The stage was set, the end decided in advance. As in commedia dell'arte, it only remained for us to improvise the breakup; we handled it badly, but, for good or ill, we acted out the scene and moved on to the next ones. I don't know which of us was the more guilty and it's not a question that excites me much: in fact, the ultimate guilt was a preordained part of our two roles; we had established, long before, that we would part with wrong on both sides and on some puerile pretext. Since we could no longer continue to work together, we had to part or have the review disappear.

Without *Les Temps modernes*, the events of 1950 would have had little impact on our friendship: we would have discussed politics more often or taken more care not to speak of it. Ordinarily politics affects people obliquely and they are unaware of anything except a muffled tremor or an indecipherable anxiety. Unless, that is, it seizes them by the throat and sends them flying: even in that case, they will not realize what has happened to them. But chance has only to put the tiniest means of influencing or expressing the movement of history into their hands and the forces that shape our lives are immediately laid bare and show us the shadow we cast on the dazzling wall of objectivity. The review was nothing: it was just a sign of the times like a hundred others. But no matter: it belonged to history and through it the two of us experienced our standing as historical objects. It was our objectivization; through it the course of events provided us with our charter and our twofold role: we were at first more united than we would have been without it, then more divided. This is only natural: once caught in the mechanism, we are completely dragged into it; the little freedom that remains to us lies entirely in the moment when we decide whether to get involved or not. To put it succinctly, beginnings are our affair; thereafter we have to will our destinies.

The beginning was not a bad one. It was so for a single reason that is still a mystery to me: against the desire of all our collaborators, and

364 · JEAN-PAUL SARTRE

against my desire, Merleau had claimed the weakest position from day one. The position of doing everything and not being named, of refusing to have a status to defend him against my moods or attacks: it was as though he had wanted to derive his power only from a living agreement, as though his fragility would be his most effective weapon, as though his moral authority would alone have to underwrite his functions. He had no sort of protection: for that reason, he was not bound by anything or anyone. He was present among us and as much in charge as I was. And he could be light and free as air. If he had agreed to his name going on the cover, he would have had to fight me and perhaps even overthrow me: but he had envisaged this possibility from the first day and declined on principle a battle that would have needlessly demeaned us both. When the fateful day came, a telephone call sufficed. He had made his decision, he informed me of it and disappeared. Yet there were sacrifices: for him, for me, and for *Les Temps modernes*. We were all victims of this cleansing murder: Merleau cut off a part of himself, leaving me to grapple with fearful allies who, he thought, would grind me down or reject me as they had rejected him; he abandoned *his* review to my incompetence. This aggressive expiation must have absorbed the greater part of his resentment: in any event it allowed us to interrupt our breakup "work" and rescue our friendship.

To begin with, he avoided me. Did he think the sight of me would revive his grievances? Perhaps. It seems to me, however, that he wanted to keep open the prospect of some kind of shared future. I would meet him at times; we stopped a moment to talk together; when we were about to part, I would suggest we meet up again the next day or the next week. He replied politely and firmly, "I'll call you," but he did not. Yet, another "work" had begun: the stilling of grievances and a rapprochement. This was halted by grief: in 1953 Merleau lost his mother.

She meant as much to him as his own life; more exactly, she *was* his life. He owed his infant happiness to the attentions she had lavished on him; she was the clear-sighted witness of his childhood: thanks to that, when exile came, she remained its guardian. Without her, the past would have been swallowed by the sands; through her, it was preserved, out of reach but intensely felt; until the time came to mourn his mother, Merleau-Ponty experienced that golden age as a paradise that retreated a little more each day and as the fleshly, daily presence of the woman who had bestowed it on him. All the connivances of mother and son carried them back to ancient memories; thus, as long as she lived, Merleau's banishment retained a degree of sweetness and could be reduced at times to the bare difference that separates two inseparable lives. As long as there were two of them reconstructing and, at times, reviving the long prehistory of his actions, his passions, and his tastes, he still had hope of regaining that immediate concord with everything that is the good fortune of children who have been loved. But when his mother died, the wind slammed all the doors shut and he knew they would never open again. Memories *à deux* are rites: the survivor is left only with dried leaves, with words. Meeting Simone de Beauvoir a little after this, Merleau-Ponty told her, quite casually and with that sad cheerfulness with which he masked his sincere remarks, "I am more than half dead." Dead to his childhood—for the second time. He had dreamed of achieving salvation: in his youth through the Christian community, as an adult through his political companionships. Twice disappointed, he suddenly discovered the reason for these defeats: to "save" oneself on all levels, "in all orders," would be to recommence one's earliest years. We repeat ourselves endlessly, but we never begin again. Seeing his childhood go under, he understood himself: he had never wished for anything but to return to it and that impossible desire was his particular vocation, his destiny. What was left of it? Nothing. He had already been silent for some time: silence not being enough any longer, he turned into a recluse, leaving his office only to go to the Collège de France. I did not see him again until 1956 and his best friends now saw him less.

I have, however, to indicate what was happening in him during the three years that separated us. But, as I have forewarned my readers, my object is merely to recount the adventure of a friendship. I am, for this reason, interested in the history of his ideas rather than in the ideas themselves, which others will be able to describe in detail, and better than I would. It is the man I want to restore, not as he was for himself but as he lived in my life, as I experienced him in his. I do not know how truthful I shall be. I shall seem questionable and it will seem I am depicting myself negatively by the way I paint him: this I admit. I am, at any rate, sincere: I am describing what I took to be the case.

Pain is emptiness: others might have remained simulacra of hermits, hollow men. But, at the same time as it cut him off from us, his pain led Merleau back to his initial meditation, to the good fortune that had made him so unfortunate. I am struck by the unity of Merleau's life. Since the prewar years, this young Oedipus who had revisited his origins had wished to understand the rational unreason that produced him. Just as he was getting close to it and writing the *Phenomenology of Perception*, history jumped at our throats. He wrestled with it without interrupting his quest. Let us call this the first period of his thinking. The second began in the last years of the occupation and continued until 1950. His thesis completed, he seemed to abandon that investigation and turn to the questioning of history and the politics of our time. But his concern had changed only in appearance: everything connects up, since history is a form of envelopment and we are "anchored" in it, since we have to situate ourselves historically not in an a priori fashion, by some "soaring" thought, but through the concrete experience of the movement that carries us along: if we read him closely, Merleau's commentaries on politics are merely a political experience becoming, by itself and in all senses of the term, a *subject* of meditation; if writings are acts, let us say that he acts in order to appropriate his action and to find himself, at a deep level, in that action. From the general perspective of history, Merleau is an intellectual from the middle classes, radicalized by the Resistance and blown off course by the fragmentation of the left.* Seen for himself, his was a life that turned around on itself to grasp the emergence of the human in its singularity. Cruel as it was, it is clear that his disappointment of 1950 was to be of use to him: it removed him from our sad arenas, but, in so doing, it offered him an arena that was neither quite the same nor entirely different—that enigma that is the self. Not that he sought, like Stendhal, to understand the individual that he was but,

---

*Clearly, we could all be defined in this same way, except that the degrees of drift are variable and sometimes run in the opposite direction.

rather, in the manner of Montaigne, he wanted to comprehend the person, that matchless mix of the particular and the universal. Yet that was not enough: there remained knots to untie; he was tackling these when the death of his mother supervened and cut through them. It is admirable that, in his sadness, he made this ill fortune his own, elevating it to the status of strictest necessity. Though it had been foreshadowed for some years, the third period of his meditation began in 1953.

In the beginning, it was both a renewed investigation and a wake. Thrown back on himself for a third time by death, he tried to use it to cast light on his birth. To the newborn, this visible-seer who appears in the world of vision, something must *happen*: something, anything, even if it is only dying. This initial tension between appearance and disappearance he terms "primordial historicity": it is in and through this that everything occurs; it hurls us, from the very first moment, into an inflexible irreversibility. To survive birth, if only for a moment, is an adventure; and it is an adventure also not to survive it: one cannot escape this unreason he terms our contingency. It is not enough to say that we are born to die: we are born to death.

But at the same time, being alive, he prevented his mother from disappearing entirely. He no longer believed in an afterlife; if, however, in his last years, he happened to reject being numbered among the atheists, this was not out of consideration for his onetime burst of Christianity but to leave a chance for the dead. Yet this precaution was not enough: In reviving a dead woman through the worship of her, what was he doing? Was he reviving her in fantasy or *instituting* her?

Life and death; existence and being: to carry out his two-pronged investigation, he tried to pitch his tent at this crossroads. In a sense, none of the ideas he advanced in his thesis changed; in another, nothing was recognizable any longer: he plunged into the dark night of non-knowledge, in search of what he now called the "fundamental." In *Signs*, for example, we read: "What interests the philosopher in anthropology is just that it takes man as he is, in his actual situation of life and understanding. The philosopher it interests is not the one who wants to explain or construct the world, but the one who seeks to deepen our insertion in being."[34]

At the level of presence and absence, the philosopher appears, blind and all-seeing: though *knowledge* claims to explain or construct, he does not even want to *know*. He lives in this mix of oxygen and thin gases called the True, but he doesn't deign to itemize the truths—not even to distribute them to our schools or textbooks. He does nothing but deepen himself: he allows himself to slide, while still alive, without interrupting his undertakings, into the sole, derisory abyss accessible to him; to seek within himself the door that opens onto the night of what is not yet self. This is to define philosophy as a meditation in the Cartesian sense of the word—that is to say, as an indefinitely sustained tension between existence and Being. This slim, ambiguous dividing line is the origin: to think, one must *be*; the tiniest thought exceeds being, instituting it for others; this happens in an instant: it is birth, absurd and definitive, that indestructible *e*vent that changes into *ad*vent and defines the singularity of a life by its calling to death: it is the work [*oeuvre*], opaque and wild, retaining being in its folds; it is the undertaking, an unreason that will endure in the community as its future raison d'être; it is, above all, language, this "fundamental," for the Word is merely the Being cast into the heart of man to extenuate itself in a *meaning*; in short, it is man, emerging at a stroke, moving beyond his presence to Being and toward his presence to others, moving beyond his past and toward his future, moving beyond everything and himself toward the sign: for this reason, Merleau tended, toward the end of his life, to grant ever greater scope to the unconscious. He doubtless agreed with Lacan's formula, "The unconscious is structured like a language." But, as a philosopher, he had placed himself at the opposite pole to psychoanalysis: the unconscious fascinated him both as a fettered speech and as the hinge of Being and existence.

One day, Merleau-Ponty was irritated by dialectics and abused it. Not that he didn't accept the division on which it is based; he explains in *Signs* that the positive always has its negative and vice versa; they will, as a consequence, pass eternally one into the other. These things go around, so to speak, and the philosopher will go around with them. It is for him to follow the circuits of his object scrupulously and in a spirit of discovery; he must spiral down into the darkness. Merleau-

MERLEAU-PONTY · 369

Ponty acquired the habit of pursuing every "No" until he saw it turn into a "Yes" and every "Yes" until it changed into a "No." He became so proficient, in his latter years, at this game of dissembling that he positively made a method of it. I shall term this inversion. He jumped from one standpoint to another, denied and affirmed, changed more into less and less into more: all things are contraries and all are also true. I shall give just one example of this: "At least as much as he explains adult behavior by a fate inherited from childhood, Freud shows a *premature* adult life in childhood, and ... for example, a first choice of his relationships of generosity or avarice to others."[35] *At least as much*: in his writings contradictory truths never fight against each other; there is no risk of shackling the movement, of causing a breakup. And are they indeed, strictly speaking, contradictory? If this were even admitted, it would have to be acknowledged that contradiction, weakened by this girating impulse, loses its role as "engine of history" and represents in his eyes the sign of paradox, the living mark of fundamental ambiguity. In short, Merleau is quite happy with thesis and antithesis; it is the synthesis he rejects: he reproaches it with turning the dialectic into a construction set. By contrast, his revolving structures leave no room for a conclusion; each in its way illustrates the merry-go-round of Being and existence. As children of clay, we should reduce ourselves to imprints on the earth if we did not begin by denying it. Let us invert, then: We, whose most immediate existence is the negation of what is, what do we do from our first moment to our last but announce Being, institute it, restore it by and for others, in the milieu of intersubjectivity? Institute it, announce it—all well and good. As for seeing it face-to-face, that we must not expect: we know only its signs. Thus the philosopher will never stop running around in circles, nor will the roundabout stop turning:

> This being—which is glimpsed through time's stirrings and always intended by our ... perception and our carnal being, but to which there can be no question of our being transported because to abolish its distance would be to take away its consistency of being—this being "of distances," as Heidegger will put it, which is always offered to our transcendence, is the dialectical

idea of being as defined in the *Parmenides*—beyond the empirical multiplicity of existent things and as a matter of principle
intended through them, because separated from them, it would
be only lightning flash or darkness.*

Merleau still has his flirtatious moments: he still speaks in this text
of dialectics. Yet it isn't to Hegel he refers but to Parmenides and
Plato. The appropriate method with meditation is to draw an outer
line around one's subject and revisit the same places time and again.
What is it, then, that meditation can make out? An absence? A presence? Both? Refracted by a prism, the outer being scatters, becomes
multiple and inaccessible; but, as part of the same movement, it is also
internalized, becomes the inner being—entirely and constantly present, yet not losing its intangibility. And, naturally, the opposite is also
true: the inner being within us, our innermost recess, fiercely guarded
and grave, constantly manifests its oneness with Nature, that indefinite deployment of outer being. Thus, circling and meditating, Merleau remains faithful to his spontaneous thinking, a slow rumination
shot through with bolts of lightning: it is this which he sets up discreetly as a method, in the form of a decapitated dialectic.

In the end, it was this descent into Hell that enabled him to find
the profoundest merry-go-round of all. It was a discovery of the heart,
as is proved by its striking, somber density. I shall tell how he informed me of it almost two years ago: the man paints himself, subtle
and laconic as he was, in these remarks, tackling problems head-on
when he seems merely to be brushing at them from the side. I asked
him if he was working. He hesitated: "I'm perhaps going to write on
Nature." To whet my appetite, he added: "I read a sentence in White-
head that made an impression on me: 'Nature is in tatters.'" As the

*Merleau-Ponty, *Signs*, 156. It was a question at that point of characterizing the
present moment of philosophical research. Merleau lent it these two features: "existence and dialectics." However, a few months before, he had given a lecture at
the Rencontres Internationales de Genève on the thought of our time. Remarkably,
he did not say one word about Dialectics: rather, in referring to our problems, he
avoided the word contradiction and wrote: "Embodiment and the question of the
other are the labyrinth of thinking and sensibility among our contemporaries."

reader will already have guessed, not another word was added. I left him without having understood: at that time I was studying "dialectical materialism" and for me the word "Nature" evoked the full extent of our physical and chemical knowledge. Another misunderstanding: I had forgotten that Nature for him was the tangible world, that "decidedly universal" world in which we encounter things and animals, our own bodies and others. I did not understand him until his last article, "Eye and Mind," was published.[36] That long essay was, I imagine, supposed to form part of the book he was writing: at any rate, he constantly refers and alludes there to an idea that was going to be expressed but remains unformulated.

More hostile than ever to intellectualism, Merleau inquires into painters and their manual, untutored thinking: he tries to grasp the meaning of painting from the works themselves. On this occasion, Nature reveals its "threads and tatters" to him. How, he says more or less, does that mountain in the distance announce itself to us? By discontinuous and, at times, intermittent signals, sparse, insubstantial phantasms, shimmerings, shadowplay; this dusty thing strikes us by its sheer insubstantiality. But our eye is, precisely a "computer of Being";[37] these airy signs will settle into the heaviest of terrestrial masses. The gaze no longer contents itself with "glimps[ing] ... being ... through time's stirrings": it would seem now that its mission is to form its—ever-absent—unity out of multiplicity. "And so that unity does not exist?" we shall ask. It does and it does not, just like the defunct coat whose presence haunts the threads and tatters like Mallarmé's rose that is "absent from all bouquets." Being *is* through us, who *are* through it. All this, of course, requires the Other; this is how Merleau understands Husserl's "difficult" assertion that "transcendental consciousness is intersubjectivity." No one, he thinks, can see, unless he is at the same time visible: How would we grasp what *is* if we *were not*? We are not speaking here of a mere "*noesis*," producing its noematic correlative through appearances. Once again, in order to think, one must first *be*. The thing, constituted by each of us out of all things—always a unity, but an indefinitely beveled unity—consigns each of us, through the others, to our ontological status. We are the sea; as soon as it emerges each piece of driftwood is as uncountable as the waves, through them and like them absolute. The painter is the privileged artisan, the best witness of this mediated reciprocity. "The body is caught in the fabric of the world, but the world is made of the stuff of my body." A new spiraling, but deeper than the others since it relates to the "labyrinth of embodiment." Through my flesh, Nature is made flesh; but, conversely, if painting is possible, then the lineaments of being that the painter perceives in the thing and fixes on the canvas must designate, in the very depths of himself, the "flexions" of his being. "Only on condition of being self-figuring does the painting relate ... to anything whatever among empirical things; it is a spectacle of things only by being the spectacle of nothing ... showing how things make themselves things and the world a world." It is just this that gives "the painter's occupation an urgency that exceeds all others." By representing outer being, he presents others with inner being, *his* flesh, their flesh. But "present" is too weak a word here: culture, says Merleau, is a "coming-into-being." So the artist has this sacred function of instituting being amid men; this means going beyond the "layers of raw being of which the activist is unaware" toward that eminent being that is *meaning*. The artist has this function, but each of us has it also. "Expression," he says, "is the *fundamental* quality of the body." And what is there to express except Being: we do not make a single movement without restoring being, instituting it, and rendering it present. Primordial historicity, our being born unto death, is the surging from the deep through which the event becomes man and, by naming things, recites his being. This is also the history of groups in its most radical aspect: "What but history are we to call this [milieu] in which a form burdened with contingency suddenly opens up a cycle of futurity and commands it with the authority of that which is established?"

These are, in their beginnings, his last thoughts: of his last philosophy, "burdened with contingency," gnawing patiently at chance, and interrupted by that chance, I have said that I saw it begin with a discovery of the heart. Against mourning and absence, it was he in his turn who was discovering himself: he was the true "computer of Being." He had a handful of memories and relics left, but our gaze reveals the being of the mountain with fewer resources than that: from the tatters of memory, the heart will wrest the being of the dead; out of the *e*vent that killed them it will make their *ad*vent; it is not simply a question of restoring their eternity to the lost smile and the words: to live will be to deepen them, to transform them into themselves a little more each day, by our words and our smiles, without end. There is a progress of the dead and it is our history. In this way, Merleau made himself his mother's guardian, as she had been the guardian of his childhood; born through her unto death, he wanted death to be a rebirth for her. For this reason, he found more real powers in absence than in presence. "Eye and Mind" contains a curious quotation: Marivaux, reflecting in *Marianne* on the strength and dignity of the passions, praises men who take their own lives rather than deny their being.[38] What Merleau liked about these few lines is that they uncovered an indestructible slab of stone beneath the transparency of the shallow stream that is life. But let us not be tempted to think he is returning here to Cartesian substance: hardly has he closed the quotation marks and taken up his pen on his own account than the slab shatters into discontinuous flickerings, becomes that ragged being that it is our lot to be, which is perhaps merely a disordered imperative, and which a suicide will sometimes put back together better than a living victory. By a movement of the same kind, since this is our rule, we shall institute the being of the dead in the human community by our own being, and our being by that of the dead.

How far did he go, then, in these dark years that changed him into himself? At times, reading him, one would say that Being invents man in order to be *manifested* by him. Did it not happen from time to time that Merleau, inverting the terms and standing things on their head, thought he glimpsed in us, "ungraspable in immanence," some sort of transcendent mandate? In one of his articles, he congratulates a mystic on having written that God is below us. He adds, more or less, "Why not?" He dreams of an Almighty who would need human beings, who would be in question in everyone's heart and would remain the total Being, the one that intersubjectivity is reinstituting infinitely, the only one we would push to the limit of its being and which would share with all of us the insecurity of the human adventure. This is clearly just a metaphorical indication. But the fact that he chose it cannot be seen as insignificant. It has everything in it: both stroke of inspiration and risk; if *L'Être*[39] is below us, a gigantic ragged pauper, it will take only an imperceptible change for it to become *our task*. God, the task of man? Merleau never wrote that, and he forbade himself to think it: there is nothing to say that he did not sometimes dream of it, but his researches were too rigorous for him to put forward anything he had not established. He worked unhurriedly; he was waiting.

It has been claimed that he had moved closer to Heidegger. There is little doubt of this, but we must be clear what we mean. So long as his childhood was safeguarded for him, Merleau had no need to radicalize his quest. With his mother dead, and his childhood swept away with her, absence and presence, Being and Non-Being flowed into each other. Merleau, through phenomenology and without ever leaving it, wanted to connect with the imperatives of ontology; that which is no longer, is not yet, never will be: it was for man to give Being to beings. These tasks emerged out of his life, out of his mourning; he found in them the opportunity to reread Heidegger, to understand him better, but not to give in to his influence: their paths crossed and that was all. Being is the sole concern of the German philosopher; despite what is at times a shared vocabulary, man remains the main concern of Merleau. When the former speaks of "openness to being," I smell alienation. Admittedly, we should not deny that the latter has sometimes penned some troubling words. These, for example: "The irrelative henceforth is not nature in itself or the system of the apprehensions of the absolute consciousness, nor indeed is it man, but that 'teleology' that must be written and thought between quotation marks—the framework and articulation of the being that is accomplished through man." The quotation marks don't make any difference. All the same, it was said only in passing. It is regrettable that a man can write today that the absolute is not man; but what he denies to the human realm, he does not grant to any other. His "irrelative" is, in fact, a relation of reciprocity that is closed upon itself: man is designated by his basic calling, which is to institute Being, but Being is similarly designated by its destiny, which is to accomplish itself through man. I have told how, twice at least—in the Christian community and in the fraternity of political combat—Merleau had sought to envelop himself in immanence and had run up against the transcendent. While more than ever avoiding recourse to the Hegelian synthesis, his last thinking attempts to resolve the contradiction he experienced in his life: the transcendent will be poured into immanence; it will be dissolved in it, while being protected, by its very intangibility, from annihilation; it is now merely absence and supplication, merely infinite weakness dragging its omnipotence along. Is this not, in a sense, the fundamental contradiction of all humanism? And can dialectical materialism—in the name of which many will want to criticize this meditation—do without an ontology? Looking closer, indeed, and if we set aside the absurd theory of reflection, would we not find in it, discreetly announced, the idea of a layer of raw being producing and underpinning action and thought?

No, the man who a few months before his death wrote, "When the lightning flash that is man blazes out, everything is given in that very instant," never ceased to be a humanist. And then what? To accomplish Being is indeed to consecrate it: but that means to humanize it. Merleau does not claim that we should lose ourselves so that Being may be but, quite the contrary, that we shall institute Being by the very act that causes us to be born to the human [*naître à l'humain*]. More Pascalian than ever, he reminds us once again: Man is absolutely distinct from the animal species, but precisely in the respect that he has no original equipment and is the place of contingency, which sometimes takes the form of a kind of miracle ... and sometimes the form of an unintentional adversity.[40]

This is sufficient to say that man is never either the animal of a species or the object of a universal concept but, from the moment he emerges, the splendor of an event. But he draws the same lesson from the humanist Montaigne: Montaigne "rejects in advance the explanations of man a physics or metaphysics can give us, because it is still man who 'proves' philosophies and sciences, and because they are explained by him rather than he by them ..."[41] Man will never think man: he *makes* him at every moment. Is not this the true humanism: man will never be a total object of knowledge; he is the subject of history.

In the last works of the somber philosopher, it is not difficult to find a certain optimism: nothing comes to anything, but nothing is lost. An endeavor is born, institutes *its* man at a stroke—the whole of the man in a lightning flash—and perishes with him or survives him extravagantly to end, in any event, in disaster; yet, at the very moment of calamity, it opens a door to the future. Spartacus struggling and dying is the whole of man: Who can say better than this? A word is the whole of language gathered into a few sounds; a picture is the whole of painting. "In this sense," he says, "there both is progress and there is not." History is constantly establishing itself in our prehistoric milieu; with each lightning flash, the whole is illuminated, instituted, frays at the edges, and, deathless, disappears. Apelles of Cos, Rembrandt, and Klee each in their turn *presented Being to the gaze* in a particular civilization and with the means available to them. And long before the first of them was born, the whole of painting was already made manifest in the caves of Lascaux.

Precisely because he is constantly summing himself up in this ever-recommenced lightning flash, there will be a future for man. Contingency of Good, contingency of Evil: Merleau no longer either favored or condemned anyone. Adversity had brought us within an inch of barbarism; miracles, always and everywhere possible, would bring us out of it. Since, "spontaneously, every gesture of our body and language, every act of political life ... takes others into consideration and surpasses itself, in its singularity, in the direction of the universal," then even though it is in no sense necessary or promised, and even though we call on it not so much to improve us in our being as to clean up the detritus of our lives, a *relative* progress has to be the most probable conjecture: "Experience will, very probably, end up eliminating the false solutions." It is in this hope, I believe, that he agreed to write a number of political commentaries for *L'Express*. The Soviet and Western blocs were two growth economies, two industrial societies, each riven by contradictions. Above and beyond the different regimes, he would have liked to have identified common demands at the infrastructural level or lines of convergence at least: it was a way of remaining faithful to his own thinking. Once again, the point was to reject the Manichaean option. There had been unity; after the loss of that minor paradise, he had wanted to denounce exploitation everywhere, then he had walled himself up in silence: he came back out to seek after reasons for hope everywhere. Without any illusions—"*la virtù*" and nothing more. We are twisted creatures: the ties binding us to others are distorted; there is no regime that could, in itself, rectify that distortion, but perhaps the men who will come after us—all men together—will have the strength and the patience to undertake this task.

The course of our thinking separated us a little more each day. His mourning and voluntary reclusiveness made a rapprochement more difficult. In 1955, we almost lost each other completely, by abstraction. He wrote a book on the Dialectic in which he attacked me fiercely.[42] Simone de Beauvoir replied no less fiercely in *Les Temps modernes*: it was the first and last time we argued in print. By publishing our differences, it seemed we would inevitably render them irremediable. Quite the contrary: at the point when friendship seemed dead, it began to blossom again imperceptibly. We had no doubt been too careful to avoid violence: it needed a little to eliminate the last remaining grievances and for him to get everything off his chest once and for all. In short, the quarrel was short-lived and we met up again not long afterward.

It was in Venice in the early months of 1956, where the European Society of Culture had organized discussions between East and West European writers. I was there. As I sat down, I noticed that the seat alongside mine was empty. I leaned over and saw Merleau-Ponty's name on the card: we had been put together because they thought it would be to our liking. The discussion began, but I was only half listening; I was waiting for Merleau—not without trepidation. He came. Late as usual. Someone was speaking. He slipped behind me on tiptoe and touched me lightly on the shoulder; when I turned around, he smiled. The conversations went on for several days: we were not entirely in agreement, except that we both became irritated listening to an over-eloquent Italian and an excessively naïve Englishman whose mission was to scuttle the project. But among so many people of such diversity, some older than us, others younger, we felt united by the very same culture and experience, meaningful only to us. We spent several evenings together, a little uneasily and never alone. It

378 · JEAN-PAUL SARTRE

was all right. Our friends who were present protected us from ourselves, from the temptation of prematurely reestablishing our intimacy. As a consequence, we merely talked to each other. Though neither of us had any illusions about the significance of the Venice discussions, we both wanted them to take place again the next year— he because he was a "connector," I to "privilege" the left: when it came to drafting the final communiqué, we found ourselves of the same mind. It was nothing, and yet it was proof that a shared task could bring us together.

We met again—in Paris, in Rome, and again in Paris. Alone: this was the second stage. The unease was still there, but was tending to disappear; another feeling emerged, one of tender affection: such disconsolate, mildly funereal affection brings together exhausted friends, to whom strife has left nothing in common but their quarrel and whose quarrel has one day ended for want of anything to argue over. That thing had been the review: it had united, then separated us; it no longer even separated us. Our cautiousness in our relations with each other had almost led us to fall out: aware of this now, we were careful never to spare each other's feelings. But too late. Whatever we did, each of us now failed to engage the other. When we explained our positions, it seemed to me rather as though we were exchanging news of our respective families—auntie Mary is having an operation, nephew Charles has got his diploma—and we were sitting side by side on a bench with blankets over our knees, tracing out signs in the dust with the ends of our walking sticks. What was missing? Neither affection, nor esteem, but a shared undertaking. Our past activity had been buried without it having being able to separate us, but it took its revenge by making "retired" old friends of us.

We had to wait for the third stage without forcing things. I waited, certain that our friendship would be recovered. We were united in condemning the war in Algeria unreservedly; he had sent his *légion d'honneur* back to the Guy Mollet government and we were both opposed to the fledgling dictatorship that was Gaullism. We were not perhaps agreed on how to fight it, but that would come: when fascism is on the rise, it reunites lost friends. I saw him in March of that same year. I was giving a lecture at the École normale and he came along. I was touched by this. For years it had been I who was always angling for meetings, proposing rendezvous. For the first time, he spontaneously went out of his way. Not to hear me rehearse ideas that he knew by heart but to see me. At the end of the lecture, we met up together with Hyppolite and Canguilhem. For me, it was a happy moment. Later, however, I learned that he had apparently felt a persistence of the unease between us. This was not remotely the case, but unfortunately I had the flu and was rather groggy. When we parted, he had uttered no word of his disappointment but for a moment I sensed a stiffening. I took no notice of it: "Everything is as it was," I told myself, "it will all begin again." A few days later, I learned of his death and our friendship ended on this last misunderstanding. Had he lived, it would have been dissipated as soon as I returned. Perhaps. With his death, we shall remain for each other what we always were: unknowns.

Without a doubt, Merleau's readers can know him; he has "made an appointment with them in his work"; every time I become his reader, I shall know him and know myself better. A hundred and fifty pages of his future book have been saved from the wreckage,[43] and then there is "Eye and Mind," which says everything, provided one knows how to decipher it: we shall, all of us together, "institute" this thinking we find in tatters; it will be one of the prisms of our "intersubjectivity." At a moment when M. Papon, the Prefect of Police, sums up the general view when he states that nothing surprises him any longer, Merleau provides the antidote by being surprised by everything. He is a child scandalized by our futile grown-up certainties, a child who asks the scandalous questions the adults never answer: Why do we live? Why do we die? Nothing seems natural to him—either the fact that there is a history or that there is a nature. He doesn't understand how it can be that every necessity turns into contingency and every contingency ends up in necessity. He says this and we, reading him, are dragged into this whirligig, from which we shall never extract ourselves. Yet it is not us he is questioning: he is too afraid we shall bump up against reassuring dogmatisms. This questioning will be something between himself and himself, because "the writer has chosen insecurity." Insecurity: our basic situation and, at one and the same time, the difficult attitude that reveals this situation to us. It is

380 · JEAN-PAUL SARTRE

not appropriate for us to ask for answers from him; what he teaches us is how to deepen an initial inquiry; he reminds us, as Plato did, that the philosopher is the person who experiences wonderment, but, more rigorous in this than his Greek master, he adds that the philosophical attitude disappears the minute that wonderment ceases. Conversely, to those who predict that philosophy will one day take over the world, he replies that if man were one day happy, free, and transparent to other men, we ought to be as amazed by that suspect happiness as we are at our present misfortunes. I would happily say, if the word did not seem suspect to him through overuse, that he had managed to rediscover the internal dialectic of questioner and questioned, and that he had pushed it as far as the fundamental question we avoid with all our alleged responses. To follow him, we have to give up two contradictory securities between which we constantly waver, for we reassure ourselves ordinarily by the use of two concepts that are opposite in nature but equally universal. Both of these take us as objects, the first telling each of us that he is a man among men and the second that he is an Other among others. But the former is worthless because man is constantly making himself and can never think of himself in his entirety. And the latter deceives us, because we are in fact similar, insofar as each of us differs from all. Jumping from the one idea to the other, the way monkeys jump from one branch to another, we avoid singularity, which is not so much a fact as a perpetual postulation. Severing our links with our contemporaries, the bourgeoisie confines us within the cocoon of private life and cuts us up with its scissors into *individuals*—that is to say, molecules without history that drag themselves from one moment to the next. Through Merleau we find ourselves singular again, through the contingency of our anchorage in nature and in history or, in other words, through the temporal adventure that we represent within the human adventure. Thus history makes *us* universal to precisely the same degree that we make *it* particular. This is the considerable gift Merleau bestows on us by his relentless determination to keep on digging in the same spot: starting out from the well-known universality of the singular, he arrives at the singularity of the universal. It was he who exposed the crucial contradiction: every history is the whole of history; when the lightning flash that is man blazes out, all is said: all lives, all moments, all ages—contingent miracles or misfires—are *incarnations*: the Word becomes flesh, the universal establishes itself only by way of the living singularity that distorts it as it singularizes it. We should not see here a rehashing of the "unhappy consciousness": it is precisely the opposite. Hegel is describing the tragic opposition between two abstract notions, the very ones that are, as I said, the two poles of our security. But, for Merleau, universality is never universal, except for "soaring" thought: its birth is dependent on the flesh and, as flesh of our flesh, it retains, in its most subtle degree, our singularity. This is the admonition anthropology—be it analysis or Marxism—should not forget. Nor, should it forget, as Freudians do too often, that every man is the whole of man and that we must have regard in all human beings for the *lightning flash*, that singular universalization of universality. Nor, as novice dialecticians do, should it be forgotten that the USSR is not the mere beginning of the universal revolution but also its incarnation, and that 1917 will bestow ineradicable features on future socialism. This is a difficult problem: neither banal anthropology nor historical materialism will free themselves from it. Merleau didn't think he was providing solutions. On the contrary, had he lived, he would have dug down even further into the problem, spiraling as ever, until he had radicalized the elements of the question, as we can see in "Eye and Mind" from what he says of primordial historicity.[44] He did not reach the end of his thinking or, at least, he did not have time to express it in its entirety. Is this a failure? No, it is something like a reprise of the initial contingency by the final contingency: singularized by this twofold absurdity and meditating upon singularity from the beginning to his death, Merleau's life takes on an inimitable "style" and justifies by itself the warnings contained in the work. As for that work, which is inseparable from the life, a lightning flash between two chance events, lighting up our darkest night, we could apply to it, word for word, what he wrote at the beginning of this year:

> [I]f we cannot establish a hierarchy of civilizations or speak of progress—neither in painting nor in anything else that matters —it is not because some fate holds us back; it is, rather, because

the very first painting in some sense went to the farthest reach of the future. If no painting comes to be *the* painting, if no work is ever absolutely completed and done with, still each creation changes, alters, enlightens, deepens, confirms, exalts, re-creates or creates in advance all the others. If creations are not established advances, this is not only because, like all things, they pass away; it is also that they have almost all their lives still before them.[45]

As a question without an answer, a *virtù* without illusion, Merleau entered universal culture as something singular; he took his place as something universal in the singularity of history. Changing, as Hegel said, the contingent into the necessary and the necessary into the contingent, it was his mission to embody the problem of embodiment. On this question, we can all find a meeting place in his work.

I, who had other meetings with him, do not want to lie about our relations nor end on such fine optimism. I can still see his face that last night I saw him—we parted in the rue Claude-Bernard—a face disappointed, suddenly impenetrable. It remains with me, a painful wound, infected by regret, remorse, and a little rancor. Transformed into what it will now be, our friendship is summed up in it forever. Not that I accord the slightest privilege to the last moment, nor allot it the task of telling the final truth about a life. But everything was, in fact, gathered in that face: frozen in that silent expression are all the silences he met me with after 1950, and at times, I, for my part, still feel the eternity of his absence as a deliberate mutism. I can clearly see that our final misunderstanding—which would have amounted to nothing if I could have seen him alive again—is cut from the same cloth as the others: it jeopardized nothing, and in it you can just see our mutual affection, our shared desire not to spoil anything between us. But you can see also the way our lives were out of phase, so that the initiatives we took were always out of kilter; and then, adversity intervening, it suspended our dealings, without violence, *sine die*. Like birth, death is an embodiment: his death, a nonsense full of obscure meaning, brought into being, where we were concerned, the contingency and necessity of an ill-starred friendship. Yet there was something there worth striving for: with our qualities and our shortcomings, the published violence of the one, the secret excesses of the other, we were not so badly suited. And what did we make of all that? Nothing, except that we avoided falling out. Everyone may apportion blame as they see fit: at any rate, we were not very guilty, so that sometimes I see in our adventure nothing but its necessity: this is how men live in our times; this is how they love each other: badly. That is true; but it is true also that it was we, we two, who loved each other badly. There are no conclusions to draw from this except that this long friendship—neither established nor undone, but simply wiped out at the point when it was either about to be reborn or break up—remains in me like an ever-open wound.

THE WRETCHED OF THE EARTH

NOT SO very long ago, the earth numbered two billion inhabitants, that is five hundred million human beings and 1.5 billion natives. The former possessed the Word, the rest borrowed it. Between the former and the latter, corrupt kinglets, feudal landowners, and an artificially created false bourgeoisie served as intermediaries. In the colonies, the naked truth revealed itself; the mother countries preferred it dressed; they needed the natives to love them, like mothers, in a way. The European elite set about fabricating a native elite; they selected adolescents, marked on their foreheads, with a branding iron, the principles of Western culture, stuffed into their mouths verbal gags, grand turgid words which stuck to their teeth; after a brief stay in the mother country, they were sent back, interfered with. These living lies no longer had anything to say to their brothers; they echoed; from Paris, from London, from Amsterdam we proclaimed the words "Parthenon! Fraternity!" and, somewhere in Africa, in Asia, lips parted: "...thenon!...nity." It was a golden age.

It came to an end: the mouths opened of their own accord; the yellow and black voices still talked about our humanism, but it was to reproach us for our inhumanity. We listened without displeasure to these courteous expressions of bitterness. At first there was a proud astonishment: "What? Can they talk on their own? Look what we have made of them, though!" We did not doubt that they accepted our ideals since they accused us of being unfaithful to them; then,

Europe believed in its mission: it had hellenized the Asians, created that new species, Greco-Roman Negroes. And we pragmatically added, just among ourselves: anyhow, let them mouth off, it makes them feel better; their bark is worse than their bite.

Another generation came that shifted the argument. With incredible patience, its writers and poets tried to explain to us that our values were poorly suited to the reality of their lives, that they could neither entirely reject them nor assimilate them. By and large, that meant: you are making monsters of us; your humanism claims that we are universal but your racist practices set us apart. We listened to them, very relaxed: colonial administrators are not paid to read Hegel, and in any case they read him very little, but they have no need of this philosopher to know that an unhappy consciousness gets entangled in its contradictions—result, zero effectiveness. Let us therefore perpetuate their unhappiness: only hot air will come of it. If there were the hint of a demand in their moaning, the experts told us, it would be for integration. There was no question of granting it, of course: that would have ruined the system which rests, as you know, on overexploitation. But it would suffice to hold this carrot before their eyes: they would gallop. As for their revolting, we were quite untroubled: What sensible native would go and massacre the fine sons of Europe with the sole aim of becoming European like them? In short, we encouraged this melancholy and were once not averse to awarding the Prix Goncourt to a Negro: that was before 1939.

Now listen in 1961. "Let us not waste time on sterile litanies or on nauseating mimicry. Let us quit this Europe which talks incessantly about Man while massacring him wherever it meets him, on every corner of its own streets, in every corner of the world. For centuries... in the name of a supposed 'spiritual adventure,' it has been suffocating almost the whole of humanity." This tone is new. Who dares to adopt it? An African, a man of the Third World, a former colonial subject. He adds: "Europe has reached such a mad and uncontrollable speed that it is heading toward an abyss from which it would be better to move away." In other words: it has had it. This is a difficult truth to admit, but one of which we are all—are we not, my dear fellow continentals?—convinced deep down.

We must express a reservation, however. When a French person, for example, says to other French people: "We've had it!"—which, as far as I know, has been happening more or less every day since 1930—it is a passionate discourse, burning with rage and love; the orator puts himself in the same boat as all his compatriots. And then he generally adds: "Unless...." We can see clearly what this means: no further mistake can be made; if his recommendations are not followed to the letter, then and only then will the country disintegrate. In short, it is a threat followed by advice and these comments are all the less shocking because they spring from a shared national consciousness. When Fanon, in contrast, says of Europe that it is heading toward ruin, far from giving a cry of alarm, he offers a diagnosis. This doctor wishes neither to condemn it without hope—miracles can happen—nor to give it the means to recover: he notes that it is in its death throes, based on external observation and going by the symptoms he has been able to gather. As for treating it, no; he has other worries on his mind; he does not care whether it lives or dies. His book is scandalous for that reason. And if you murmur, in a joking and embarrassed way, "He's hassling us!" the real nature of the scandal escapes you: for Fanon is not hassling you at all; his work—so burning hot for others—remains ice-cold for you; in it, the author often talks about you, but never to you. No more black Goncourt winners, no more yellow Nobel Prize winners: the time of colonized laureates will never return. A French-speaking ex-native bends this language to new requirements, makes use of it, and addresses only the colonized: "Natives of all underdeveloped nations, unite!" What a decline: for the fathers, we were the sole interlocutors; the sons no longer even consider us as qualified interlocutors: we are the object of their discourse. Of course, Fanon mentions in passing our famous crimes—Sétif, Hanoi, Madagascar[1]—but he doesn't waste his effort condemning them: he uses them. If he dismantles the tactics of colonialism, the complex play of relations that unite and divide the colonialists from the "metropolitan" French, it is *for his brothers*; his goal is to teach them to outsmart us.

In short, the Third World is discovering *itself* and talking to *itself* through this voice. We know that it is not homogenous and that we still find subjugated peoples there, others who have acquired a false independence, others who are fighting to win sovereignty, and others, finally, who have won total freedom but who live under the constant threat of imperialist aggression. These differences were born of colonial history, in other words, of oppression. Here, the mother country contented itself with paying a few feudal landowners: there, by dividing and ruling, it has artificially created a bourgeoisie of the colonized; elsewhere it has killed two birds with one stone by establishing a colony of exploitation *and* settlement. Thus Europe has multiplied divisions and oppositions, forged classes and sometimes racisms, attempted by every means to cause and to increase the stratification of the colonized societies. Fanon hides nothing: to fight against us, the former colony must fight against itself. Or rather, the two are one and the same thing. In the heat of the combat, all internal barriers must melt, the powerless bourgeoisie of racketeers and traders, the urban proletariat which is always privileged, the *lumpenproletariat* of the shantytowns, all must fall into line with the stand taken by the rural masses, the real reservoir of the national revolutionary army. In those lands whose development colonialism deliberately halted, the peasantry, when it revolts, appears very quickly as the *revolutionary* class: it knows naked oppression, it suffers from it much more than the workers of the towns and to prevent itself from dying of hunger will take nothing less than a complete shattering of all existing structures. If it triumphs, the national revolution will be socialist; if its momentum is halted and the colonized bourgeoisie takes power, the new state, despite formal sovereignty, remains in the hands of the imperialists. This is illustrated rather well by the example of Katanga.[2] Thus the unity of the Third World is not established: it is an enterprise in progress which goes via the unity, in each country, both before and after independence, of all the colonized under the command of the peasant class. That is what Fanon explains to his African, Asian, and Latin American brothers: we shall achieve revolutionary socialism everywhere together, or we shall be defeated one by one by our former tyrants. He hides nothing; neither the weaknesses, nor the discords, nor the mystifications. Here the movement gets off to a bad start; there, after resounding successes, it loses momentum; elsewhere it has stopped: if people want it to resume, the peasants must drive their bourgeoisie into the sea. The reader is strictly warned against the most dangerous types of alienation: the leader, the personality cult, Western culture, and just as much, the return of the distant past of African culture: the real culture is the Revolution; that means it must be forged while hot. Fanon speaks aloud; we Europeans can hear him: the proof is that you hold this book in your hands; does he not fear that the colonial powers might use his sincerity to their advantage?

No. He fears nothing. Our practices are no longer valid: they may sometimes delay emancipation, but they will not stop it. And let us not imagine that we can adapt our methods: neocolonialism, that lazy dream of the mother countries, is hot air; "Third Forces" do not exist or they are bogus bourgeoisies that colonialism has already placed in power. Our Machiavellianism has little hold over this wide-awake world that has detected our lies one after the other. The colonist has only one recourse: force, when he still has some; the native has only one choice: servitude or sovereignty. What difference can it make to Fanon whether you read his work or not? It is to his brothers that he denounces our old acts of malice, sure that we have no replacements for them. It is to them that he says: Europe has got its paws on our continents, we must slash them until it removes them; the moment favors us: nothing happens in Bizerte, Elisabethville, or in the Algerian countryside without the entire world knowing; the blocs occupy opposite positions, they hold each other in check, let us benefit from this paralysis, let us enter into History and may our sudden appearance make it universal for the first time; let us fight: in the absence of other arms, the patience of the knife will suffice.

Europeans, open this book and enter into it. After a few steps in the night, you will see strangers gathered around a fire, draw closer, listen: they are discussing the fate they have in store for your trading posts, for the mercenaries who defend these. They will see you perhaps, but they will continue to talk among themselves without even lowering their voices. Their indifference strikes at our hearts: their fathers, creatures of the shadows, *your* creatures, were dead souls, you dispensed light to them, they talked only to you, and you did not bother to reply to these zombies. The sons ignore you: a fire which is not yours lights and warms them. Standing at a respectful distance, you will feel furtive, nocturnal, chilled to the bone; everyone has their turn; in this darkness out of which will come a new dawn, you are the zombies.

In that case, you will say, let us throw this book out of the window. Why read it since it has not been written for us? For two reasons, the first of which is that Fanon is explaining you to his brothers and is dismantling for them the mechanism of our alienations: take advantage from this to discover yourselves in your true light as objects. Our victims know us by their wounds and their chains: that is what makes their testimony irrefutable. It is enough for them to show us what we have done with them for us to understand what we have done with ourselves. Is this useful? Yes, because Europe is in great danger of dying. But, you will continue, we live in mainland France and disapprove of the excesses. It is true: you are not *colons*, but you are no better. They are your pioneers, you sent them overseas, they made you rich; you had warned them: if they caused too much blood to be spilled, you would disown them reluctantly; in the same manner, a state—whichever it may be—maintains abroad a horde of agitators, agents provocateurs, and spies whom it disowns when they are caught. You who are so liberal, so humane, and take the love of culture as far as affectation, pretend to forget that you have colonies and that people are being massacred there in your name. Fanon reveals to his comrades—to some of them, above all, who remain a little too Westernized—the solidarity of the "metropolitan" French and their colonial agents. Have the courage to read it, because it will make you ashamed, and shame, as Marx said, is a revolutionary sentiment. So you see: I cannot free myself from subjective illusion either. I, too, say to you: "Everything is lost, unless...." I, a European, steal the book of an enemy and use it as a means to cure Europe. Make the most of it.

The second reason is this: discarding Sorel's fascist chatter,[3] you will find that Fanon is the first since Engels to bring back to light the midwife of History. And do not imagine that hot-bloodedness or an unhappy childhood have given him some sort of strange taste for violence: he offers himself as the interpreter of the situation, nothing more. But that is enough for him to establish, step by step, the dialectic which liberal hypocrisy hides from you, and which has produced us just as much as him.

In the last century, the bourgeoisie regarded the workers as envious and warped by vulgar appetites, but they were careful to include these rough brutes in our species: If they were not men, and free, how could they freely sell their labor? In France, and in England, humanism claimed to be universal.

With forced labor, it is quite the opposite: there is no contract; what is more, you have to intimidate and so oppression manifests itself. Our soldiers overseas reject metropolitan universalism, and apply a numerus clausus to humankind: since no one can rob, enslave, or kill their fellow human beings without committing a crime, they establish the principle that the colonized are not fellow human beings. Our strike force has been charged with the mission of turning that abstract certainty into reality: they have been given orders to reduce the inhabitants of the annexed territory to the level of a superior monkey to justify the *colon*'s treating them as beasts of burden. Colonial violence does not only aim to keep these enslaved people at a respectful distance; it also seeks to dehumanize them. No effort will be spared to liquidate their traditions, substitute our languages for theirs, destroy their culture without giving them ours; they will be rendered stupid by exploitation. Malnourished and sick, if they continue to resist, fear will finish the job: the peasants have guns pointed at them; along come civilians who settle the land and force them with the riding crop to farm it for them. If they resist, the soldiers shoot and they are dead men; if they give in, they degrade themselves and they are no longer human beings; shame and fear fissure their character and shatter their personality. The business is carried out briskly by experts: "psychological services" are by no means a new invention. Nor is brainwashing. And yet, despite so much effort, the goal has not been attained anywhere: no more in the Congo, where Negroes' hands were cut off, than in Angola, where quite recently the lips of malcontents were pierced and padlocked together. And I am not claiming that it is impossible to change human beings into animals: I am saying that you cannot succeed without weakening them considerably; blows are never enough, one has to push malnutrition hard. That is the trouble with servitude: when we domesticate members of our own species, we diminish their output and, however little you give them, farmyard human beings end up costing more than they bring in. For this reason, the *colons* are obliged to stop the training halfway: the result, neither man nor beast, is the native. Beaten, undernourished, sick, frightened—but only up to a certain point—yellow, black, or white, they always have the same characteristics: they are lazy, sly, and thieving, live off nothing and understand only force.

Poor *colons*: that is their contradiction stripped naked. They should kill those whom they pillage, as the devil is said to do. Yet that is impossible, because they do have to exploit them, of course. Because they do not take massacre as far as genocide, and servitude as far as reducing them to beasts, they lose their grip, the operation goes into reverse, an implacable logic will lead it to decolonization.

But not immediately. First of all, the Europeans reign: they have already lost but do not realize it; they do not yet know that the natives are false natives: they hurt the natives, so they claim, to destroy or to repress the evil in them; three generations of this, and their pernicious instincts will never return. What instincts? Those which drive slaves to massacre their masters? Why can they not recognize their own cruelty turned against them? Why can they not recognize in the savagery of those oppressed peasants their savagery as *colons* which the natives have absorbed through every pore and from which they cannot recover? The reason is simple: these imperious characters, panic-stricken by their omnipotence and the fear of losing it, only dimly remember that they were human beings: they take themselves to be riding crops or guns; they have come to believe that the domestication of the "inferior races" can be attained by conditioning their reflexes. They neglect human memory, the indelible recollections which mark it; and then, above all, there is something they have perhaps never known: that we become what we are only by a profound and radical negation of what others have made of us. Three generations? By the second generation, scarcely had the sons opened their eyes when they saw their fathers being beaten; in psychiatric terms, there they were, "traumatized" for life. But these constantly repeated acts of aggression, far from causing them to submit, plunge them into an unbearable contradiction for which the European, sooner or later will pay. Following that, whether we train them in their turn, whether we teach them shame, pain, and hunger, we will only provoke in their bodies a volcanic rage whose force is equal to the pressure applied to them. You were saying they only understand force? Of course; to begin with, it will only be that of the *colon* but soon it will be theirs alone, that is to say, the same violence rebounding on us just as our reflection comes from the depths of the mirror to meet us. Do not be mistaken; it is through this mad rage, this gall, and this bile, their permanent desire to kill us, the permanent contraction of powerful muscles which are afraid to loosen that they are men—also through and against the *colons*, who want them as their lackeys. Hatred—blind, still, and abstract—is their only treasure: the Master provokes it because he seeks to reduce them to beasts; he fails to break it because his interests stop him halfway; thus the false natives are still human, owing to the oppressors' power and powerlessness which, in them, are transformed into a stubborn rejection of the animal condition. As for the rest, we have got the message; of course they are lazy, but that is sabotage, of course they are sly and thieving, but their petty thefts mark the beginning of an as yet unorganized resistance. That is not enough: some of them assert themselves by throwing themselves empty-handed at the guns; these are their heroes; others again become men by assassinating Europeans. They are slaughtered: the suffering of these bandits and martyrs exalts the terrified masses.

Terrified, yes: at this new juncture, colonial aggression is internalized as Terror by the colonized. By that, I mean not only the fear they experience when confronted with our inexhaustible methods of repression but also the fear which their own fury inspires in them. They are trapped between the arms we point at them, and the frightening impulses and murderous desires which rise from the depths of their hearts and which they do not always recognize: for it is not in the first place *their* violence that grows and tears them apart but ours returned; and the first reflex of these oppressed people is to bury deeply this unspeakable anger censured by both, their morality and ours, and yet which is simply the last refuge of their humanity. Read Fanon: you will know that, in their time of powerlessness, murderous madness is the collective unconscious of the colonized.

This contained fury, instead of exploding, goes nowhere and ravages the oppressed themselves. To free themselves of it, they end up massacring each other: the tribes fight against each other because they cannot challenge the real enemy—and you can count on colonial policies to nurture their rivalries; the brother raising the knife against his brother imagines he is destroying, once and for all, the detested image of their shared debasement. But these expiatory victims do not quench their thirst for blood; they stop themselves marching into the machine guns only by becoming our accomplices: they, by their own initiative, will accelerate the progress of the dehumanization which they reject. Under the amused eye of the *colon*, they protect themselves from themselves by supernatural barriers, sometimes resurrecting old and terrible myths, sometimes binding themselves with meticulous rites: thus the obsessed flee their profound need by inflicting upon themselves fetishes that do not release them for an instant. They dance: that occupies them, that loosens their painfully contracted muscles; and then dance secretly mimes, often without their knowing, the No they cannot say, the murders they dare not commit. In some regions, they make use of that last resort, possession by spirits. What in the past was simply a straightforward religious act, a sort of communication between the faithful and the sacred, they turn into a weapon against despair and humiliation: the *zars*, the *loas*, all the sacred idols descend into them, govern their violence and dissipate it in trances ending in exhaustion. At the same time, these elevated figures protect them: in other words, the colonized defend themselves against colonial alienation by taking religious alienation to greater lengths. The only result ultimately is that they combine the two alienations and each reinforces the other. Thus, in certain psychoses, hallucinating patients, weary of being insulted every day, decide one fine day to hear an angel's voice complimenting them; the jibes do not, for all that, cease, but from now on they alternate with approbation. It is a defense but also the end of their adventure: the personality has become dissociated, the patient is on the way to insanity. Add to this, for some rigorously selected unfortunates, that other possession I mentioned above: Western culture. In their position, you will say, I would prefer my *zars* to the Acropolis. All right: you have understood. You have not understood completely, though, for you are not in their position—not yet. Otherwise you would know that they cannot choose:

they add one thing to the other. Two worlds make two possessions: they dance the whole night, and then at dawn they pack into the churches to hear mass; day by day the crack widens. Our enemy betrays his brothers and makes himself our accomplice; his brothers do the same. The *indigenous condition* is a neurosis introduced and maintained by the *colon* among the colonized *with their consent*.

The contradiction of both claiming and renouncing the human condition is an explosive one. And explode it does, as you and I well know. And we are living in the age of the conflagration: if the rise in births increases the famine, and if the new arrivals come to fear living a little more than dying, the torrent of violence will sweep away all barriers. In Algeria and Angola, Europeans are massacred on sight. It is the moment of the boomerang, the third stage of violence: it comes back and hits us, and no more than on the other occasions can we understand that it is our own violence. The "liberals" are dumbfounded: they recognize that we were not polite enough with the natives, that it would have been fairer and more prudent to grant them certain rights as far as possible; they asked for nothing better than to be admitted in batches and without sponsors into that very exclusive club—our species: and now this barbaric and mad outbreak spares them no more than the bad *colons*. The left in metropolitan France is embarrassed: they know the true fate of the natives, the merciless oppression to which they are subjected. They do not condemn their revolt, since they know that we did all we could to provoke it. But all the same, they think, there are limits: the guerrillas must have their hearts set on showing that they are chivalrous; that would be the best way to prove that they are men. Sometimes, they reprimand them: "You're going too far: we will no longer support you." They don't care [*Ils s'en foutent*]: for all the good the left's support does them, they might just as well stick it up their rear ends. As soon as their war started, they saw the painful truth: we are all as bad as each other, we have all profited from them, they have nothing to prove, they will give favorable treatment to no one. They have a single duty, a single objective: to drive out colonialism by *any* means. And the shrewdest among us would consent to it, in extreme circumstances, but they cannot prevent themselves from seeing in this test of strength the utterly inhuman method taken by subhumans to win a charter of humanity for themselves: let it be granted as quickly as possible and let them then attempt, by peaceful undertakings, to deserve it. Our well-meaning souls are racist.

They will benefit from reading Fanon; this irrepressible violence, as he demonstrates perfectly, is not an absurd storm, nor the resurrection of savage instincts, nor even an effect of resentment: it is no less than man reconstructing himself. We knew this truth, I think, but we have forgotten it. No gentleness can efface the marks of violence; it is violence alone that can destroy them. And the colonized cure themselves of the colonial neurosis by driving out the *colon* with weapons. When their rage explodes, they recover their lost transparency, they know themselves in the same measure as they create themselves; from afar, we regard their war as the triumph of barbarism; but it leads by itself to progressive emancipation of the fighters, it progressively liquidates the colonial darkness within and outside them. Once it starts, it is merciless. One must remain terrified or become terrible; that is to say: abandon oneself to the dissociations of a falsified life or conquer native unity. When the peasants pick up guns, the old myths pale, prohibitions are one by one overturned: the fighters' weapons are their humanity. For, at this first stage of the revolt, they have to kill: to shoot down a European is to kill two birds with one stone, doing away with oppressor and oppressed at the same time: what remains is a dead man and a free man; the survivor, for the first time, feels *national* soil under his feet. At this instant, the nation does not desert him: it is found wherever he goes, wherever he is—never any farther away, it merges with his freedom. But, after the first surprise, the colonial army reacts: it must unite or be massacred. Tribal discords diminish and tend to disappear: first because they endanger the Revolution, and more importantly, because their only purpose was to divert the violence toward false enemies. When they remain—as in the Congo —it is because they are kept alive by the agents of colonialism. The nation moves into action: for every brother, it is everywhere where other brothers are fighting. Their fraternal love is the opposite of the hate they have for you: they are brothers in that each of them has killed, can kill, from one instant to the next. Fanon demonstrates to his readers the limits of "spontaneity," the necessity and the dangers of "organization." But, however immense the task may be, at every stage of its undertaking, revolutionary awareness deepens. The last complexes vanish: let them come and talk a little to us about the "dependency complex" of the ALN soldiers. Freed from his blinders, the peasant becomes aware of his needs: they used to kill him and he tried to ignore them; but now he sees in them an infinite necessity. In this violence of the people—to hold out for five years, eight years as the Algerians have done—military, social, and political necessities cannot be distinguished from one another. Even if only in asking the question of command and responsibilities, war institutes new structures which will be the first institutions of peace. Here, then, human beings are established even in new traditions, the future daughters of a horrible present, here they are legitimated by a right which is about to be born, which is being born each day in the fire: when the last *colon* is killed, shipped back home, or assimilated, the minority species disappears, giving way to socialist fraternity. And that is not yet enough: these fighters rush ahead; you can be sure they are not risking their skin to find themselves in the same position as the old colonial man. Look at their patience: perhaps they dream sometimes of a new Dien Bien Phu; but do not believe that they really expect it: they are beggars struggling, in their wretchedness, against rich people, powerfully armed. While waiting for the decisive victories and, often, without expecting anything, they make their adversaries feel nauseated. This is not possible without terrible losses; the colonial army becomes ferocious: controlling, combing the terrain, rounding up, carrying out punitive expeditions; women and children are massacred. They know: these new men begin their life as human beings at the end of it; they consider themselves potential dead men. They will be killed: it is not just that they accept the risk of it but rather that they are certain of it; these potential dead men have lost their wives, their sons; they have seen so many agonies that they prefer victory to survival; others will benefit from the victory, not them: they are too weary. But this weariness of heart gives rise to an incredible courage. We find our humanity on this side of death and despair; they find it beyond torture and death. We have sown the wind; they are the whirlwind. Sons of violence, at every instant they draw their humanity from it: we were human beings at their expense; they are making themselves human beings at ours. Different human beings, of better quality.

Here Fanon stops. He has shown the way: the spokesman of the fighters, he has called for the union, the unity of the African continent against all the discords and all the particularisms. His goal has been attained. If he wanted to describe the historic fact of decolonization completely, he would have to talk about us, which is certainly not his intention. But, when we have closed the book, it continues to work in us, in spite of its author: for we experience the force of peoples in revolution and we respond with force. There is thus a new moment of violence and this time we must return to ourselves, for it is changing us to the same degree as the false native is changed by it. It is up to everyone to reflect as they see fit, provided, however, that they do reflect: in today's Europe, thoroughly dazed by the blows being delivered to it, in France, in Belgium, and in Britain, the slightest distraction of thought is criminal complicity with colonialism. This book had no need of a preface. Even less so because it is not addressed to us. I have written one, however, to bring the dialectic to its conclusion: we, the people of Europe, are also being decolonized, that is to say the *colon* within each of us is being removed in a bloody operation. Let us look at ourselves, if we have the courage, and see what is happening to us.

We must first face up to that unexpected spectacle: the striptease of our humanism. Here it is, completely naked and not beautiful: it was nothing but an illusory ideology, the exquisite justification for pillage; its tenderness and its affectation sanctioned our acts of aggression. The nonviolent are looking pleased with themselves: neither victims nor executioners![4] Come on! If you are not victims, since the government for which you voted, since the army in which your young brothers have served, carried out a "genocide" without hesitation or remorse, then you are unquestionably executioners. And if you choose to be victims, to risk one or two days in prison, you are just extricating yourself while you can. But you cannot extricate yourself; you must stay in to the bitter end. Understand this for once: if the violence had started this evening, if exploitation or oppression had never existed on earth, perhaps this display of nonviolence could settle the dispute. But if the entire regime and even your nonviolent thoughts are a condition born of an age-old oppression, your passivity only serves to place you on the side of the oppressors.

You know very well that we are exploiters. You know very well that we took the gold and the metals and then the oil of the "new continents" and brought them back to the old mother countries. Not without excellent results: palaces, cathedrals, industrial capitals; and then whenever crisis threatened, the colonial markets were there to cushion or deflect it. Europe, stuffed with riches, granted de jure humanity to all its inhabitants: for us, a human being means "accomplice," since we have all benefited from colonial exploitation. This fat and pallid continent has ended up lapsing into what Fanon rightly calls "narcissism." Cocteau was irritated by Paris, "the city which is always talking about itself." What else is Europe doing? Or that super-European monster, North America? What empty chatter: liberty, equality, fraternity, love, honor, country, and who knows what else? That did not prevent us from holding forth at the same time in racist language: filthy nigger, filthy Jew, filthy North Africans. Enlightened, liberal, and sensitive souls—in short, neocolonialists—claimed to be shocked by this inconsistency; that is an error or bad faith. Nothing is more consistent, among us, than racist humanism, since Europeans have only been able to make themselves human beings by creating slaves and monsters. As long as there was an *indigenous people*, this imposture remained unmasked; we saw in the human race an abstract principle of universality that served to conceal more realistic practices: there was, on the other side of the seas, a race of subhumans who, thanks to us, in a thousand years would perhaps reach our status. In short, we confused the human race with the elite. Today, the natives are revealing their truth; as a result, our exclusive club is revealing its weakness: it was a minority, no more and no less. And worse than that: since the others are making themselves human beings through their opposition to us, it appears that we are the enemies of the human race; the elite is revealing its true nature: a gang. Our cherished values are losing their sparkle: looking at it closely, there is not a single one that is not stained with blood. If you need an example, remember those grand words: "How generous France is!" Generous, us? What about Sétif? And those eight years of ferocious war that have cost the lives of more than a million Algerians? And the torture? But you must understand that we are not being reproached for having betrayed some mission or other, for the good reason that we did not have one. It is generosity itself which is at issue; this beautiful melodious word has only one meaning: the granting of statutory rights. For the men on the other side, new and liberated, no one has the power or the privilege to give anything to anyone. Everyone has all rights to anything. And our species, when one day it is completely formed, will not define itself as the sum of the world's inhabitants but as the infinite unity of their reciprocal relations. I shall stop here; you will finish the job without difficulty; it is enough to take a good look, for the first and the last time, at our aristocratic virtues: they are in their death throes. How could they outlive the aristocracy of subhumans that engendered them? A few years ago, a bourgeois—and colonialist—commentator could find nothing better to defend the West than this: "We are not angels. But at least we feel remorse." What an admission! In the past, our continent had other devices to keep it afloat: the Parthenon, Chartres, the Rights of Man, the swastika. We now know what they are worth: and now the only thing they claim can save us from shipwreck is the very Christian sentiment of our guilt. This is the end, as you can see: Europe is taking on water everywhere. What then has happened? Quite simply this: in the past we were the subjects of History, whereas we are now its objects. The balance of power has been reversed, the process of decolonization is in progress; all that our mercenaries can attempt is to delay its completion.

But for that, the old "mother countries" would have to spare no expense and commit all their might to a battle lost in advance. At the end of the adventure, we again encounter the old colonial brutality, which provided the Bugeauds[5] with their dubious glory, now increased tenfold and insufficient. We sent the troops to Algeria where they have remained for seven years without effect. The violence has changed direction: when we were victorious, we employed it without appearing to be corrupted by it: it decomposed the others, while for us human beings, our humanism remained intact; united by profit, the people of the mother country baptized the community of their crimes "fraternity" and "love"; today, that same violence, everywhere obstructed, returns to us via our soldiers, is internalized and takes possession of us. Involution is starting: the colonized are reconstructing themselves, whereas we, the extremists as well as the liberals, the *colons* as well as the people of metropolitan France, are decomposing. Already rage and fear are naked: they are shown quite openly in the attacks on Arabs in Algiers. Where are the savages now? Where is the barbarity? Nothing is missing, not even the tom-tom: the car horns blare out "Algeria is part of France" while the Europeans have the Muslims burned alive. Not very long ago, Fanon reminds us, psychiatrists at a conference deplored the crimes of the natives: these people are killing each other, they said, that is abnormal. The Algerian's cortex must be underdeveloped. In central Africa, others have established that "the African uses his frontal lobes very little." Today, these scientists could usefully pursue their research in Europe, and particularly among the French. For we too, for some years now, must have been affected by cerebral laziness: the patriots have been murdering a few of their compatriots; if they are not at home, they blow up their concierge and their house. That is just the start: civil war is expected in the autumn or next spring. Our lobes, however, appear to be in perfect condition: Could it not rather be the case that, because it has been unable to crush the native, the violence is rebounding on itself: mounting within us and seeking an outlet? The union of the Algerian people is producing the disunion of the French people: throughout the territory of mainland France, tribes are dancing and preparing for combat. Terror has left Africa and established itself here, for there are quite simply fanatics here who want to make us pay with our blood for the shame of having been beaten by the natives. And then there are the others, all the others, who are also guilty (did anyone take to the streets to say "Enough" after Bizerte and the September lynchings?[6]), but who are more composed: the liberals, the hard nuts of the soft left. In them, too, the fever is mounting. And so too is aggression. But they are scared stiff! They mask their rage from themselves with myths and complicated rites; to delay the final reckoning and the hour of truth, they have placed at our head a Grand Sorcerer whose function is to keep us in the dark at all costs. To no effect—proclaimed by some, repressed by others, the violence is going around in circles: one day it explodes in Metz, the next in Bordeaux; it has passed through here, it will pass through there, it is like the parlor game of passing the bottle. We in turn, step by step, are going down the path that leads to the *indigenous people*. But for us to become total natives, our soil would have to be occupied by the former colonized and we would have to be dying of starvation. That will not happen: no, what possesses us is fallen colonialism, it is that which will soon be riding us, senile and haughty. That is our *zar* and our *loa*. And after reading Fanon's last chapter, you will be convinced that it is better to be a native at the worst hour of misery that a former *colon*. It is not a good thing for a police officer to be obliged to torture ten hours a day: at that rate, his nerves will crack up unless torturers are forbidden, in their own interest, to work overtime. When one wants to protect, with the full rigor of the law, the morale of the Nation and the army, it is not a good thing for the latter to systematically demoralize the former. Nor is it a good thing that a country with a republican tradition should entrust its young people in their hundreds of thousands to putschist officers. It is not a good thing, my fellow Frenchmen, you who are aware of all the crimes committed in our name, it is really not a good thing that you do not breathe a word of it to anyone, not even your own soul, for fear of having to be judged. At the start you did not know, I can believe that; then you suspected; now you know, but you continue to remain silent. Eight years of silence have a degrading effect. And all to no avail: today, the blinding sun of torture is at its zenith and illuminates the whole country; in this light, there is no laughter that does not sound false, no face that is not made up to conceal anger or fear, no act that does not betray our disgust and complicity. Whenever two French people meet now, there is a dead body between them. In fact, did I say one? . . . In the past, France was the name of a country; let us take care that it is not, in 1961, the name of a neurosis.

Will we recover? Yes. Violence, like Achilles's spear, can heal the wounds that it has made. Today we are in chains, humiliated, sick with fear, at our lowest ebb. Luckily, that is not yet enough for the colonial aristocracy: they cannot accomplish their delaying mission in Algeria unless they first complete the colonization of the French. Every day we shy away from the fight, but you can be sure that we will not avoid it: the killers need it; they will wade in and let us have it. Thus will end the time of sorcerers and fetishes: you will have to fight or rot in the camps. It is the last stage of the dialectic: you condemn this war, but do not yet dare to declare your solidarity with the Algerian fighters; have no fear, count on the *colons* and the mercenaries: they will make you take the plunge. Perhaps then, with your back to the wall, you will finally unleash this new violence aroused in you by old rehashed crimes. But that, as they say, is another story. That of man. The time is coming, I am sure, when we will join those who are writing it.

KIERKEGAARD
The Singular Universal

THE TITLE of our colloquium is "The Living Kierkegaard." It has the merit of plunging us to the very heart of *paradox*, and Søren himself would have appreciated this. For if we had gathered here today to discuss Heidegger, for example, no one would have dreamed of entitling our debate "The Living Heidegger." The living Kierkegaard, in other words, turns out to mean "the dead Kierkegaard." But not just this. It means that for us he exists, that he forms the object of our discussions, that he was an instrument of our thought. But, from this point of view, one could use the same expression to designate anyone who became part of our culture after he died. One could say, for example, "The Living Arcimboldo,"[1] since surrealism has allowed us to reappropriate this painter and cast him in a new light; but this would amount to making an *object* of him within what Kierkegaard called the *world-historical*. But, precisely, if Søren is in our eyes a sort of radioactive object, of whatever potency and virulence, then he can no longer be this living being whose subjectivity necessarily appears—insofar as it is lived—as other than what we know of it. In short, he sinks into death. The abolition of the subjective in a subject of History—the reduction of one who was an agent to an object—is an explosive historical scandal in the case of all who disappear from among us. History is full of holes. But nowhere is this more obvious than in the case of the "knight of subjectivity." Kierkegaard was a man who set out to pose the problem of the historical absolute, who emphasized the scandalous paradox of the appearance and disappearance of this absolute in the course of History. If we cannot revive this martyr of interiority other than in the form of an object of knowledge, a determination of his praxis will forever escape us: his living effort to elude knowledge through reflective life, his claim to be, in his very singularity and at the heart of his finitude, the absolute subject, defined in interiority by his absolute relationship with being. In other words, if death is historically no more than the passage of an interior to exteriority, then the title "The Living Kierkegaard" cannot be justified.

If we retain something of this life which, in its time and place, removed all traces of itself, then Kierkegaard himself is the scandal and the paradox. Unable to be understood as anything other than this immanence which for forty years never stopped designating *itself* as such, either he eludes us forever and the world rid itself, in 1856, of *nothing*; or else the paradox exposed by this dead man is that a historical being, beyond his own abolition, can still communicate as a non-object, as an absolute subject, with succeeding generations. What will attract our attention then will not be the religious problem of Christ incarnate nor the metaphysical problem of death, but the strictly historical paradox of survival: we shall plumb our knowledge of Kierkegaard in order to locate what in a dead man eludes knowledge and survives *for us* beyond his destruction. We shall ask ourselves whether the presence, that is the subjectivity of someone else, always inaccessible to cognition in its strict sense, can nevertheless be given to us by some other means. Either History closes back over our knowledge of this death, or the historical survival of the subjective ought to change our conception of History. In other words either Kierkegaard today, April 24, 1964, is dissolved by the enzymes of knowledge or he persists in demonstrating to us the still virulent scandal of what one might call the transhistoricity of a historical man.

He posed the fundamental question in these terms: "Can History act as the point of departure for an eternal certitude? Can one find in such a point of departure anything other than a historical interest? Can one base eternal happiness on a merely historical knowledge?"

And of course what he has in mind here is the scandalous paradox of the birth and death of God, of the historicity of Jesus. But we must go further; for if the answer is yes, then this transhistoricity belongs to Søren, Jesus's witness, just as much as to Jesus himself; and to us as well, Søren's grandnephews. As he says himself, we are all contemporaries.[2] In a sense, this is to explode History. Yet History exists and it is man who makes it. Thus posteriority and contemporaneity mutually imply and contradict each other. For the moment we cannot proceed further. We must go back to Kierkegaard and question him as a privileged witness. Why privileged? I am thinking of the Cartesian proof of the existence of God through the fact that *I exist with the idea of God*. Kierkegaard is a singular witness—or, as he says, the Exception—by virtue of a *redoubling* in himself of the subjective attitude: in our eyes he is an object of knowledge insofar as he is a subjective witness of his own subjectivity, that is to say, insofar as he is an existent announcer of existence by virtue of his own existential attitude. Thus he becomes both object and subject of our study. We should take this subject-object insofar as it demonstrates a historical paradox that transcends it; we shall question its testimony insofar as its historicity—he said such-and-such on such-and-such a date—transcends itself and makes the paradox of the object-subject burst within History. By integrating *his* words into our language, in translating him with *our* words, will the limits of knowledge be revealed? And by virtue of a paradoxical reversal of meaning, will this knowledge point to the signifier as its silent foundation?

In principle everything about him can be *known* [*connu*]. Doubtless he kept his secrets well. But one can press him hard and extract statements from him and interpret them. The problem can now be formulated: When everything is *known* [*su*] about the life of a man who refuses to be an object of knowledge and whose originality rests precisely in this refusal, is there an irreducible beyond this? How are we to seize it and think it?[3] The question has two sides to it—prospective and retrospective. One can ask what it means to have lived when all the determinations of a life are *known*. But one can also ask what it means to live when the essential core of these determinations has been foreseen. For the singularity of the Kierkegaardian adventure is that, as it unfolded, it revealed itself to itself as known in advance. Thus it lived within and in spite of knowledge. It must be borne in mind that this opposition between foreseen and lived experience was made manifest around 1850 in the opposition between Hegel and Kierkegaard. Hegel had gone, but his system lived on. Søren, whatever he did, acted within the limits of what Hegel had called the unhappy consciousness—that is to say he could only realize the complex dialectic of the finite and the infinite. He would never be able to surpass it. Kierkegaard knew that he already had his place within the system. He was familiar with Hegel's thought, and he was aware of the interpretation it conferred *in advance* on the movements of his life. He was trapped and held in the beam of the Hegelian projector; he either had to vanish into objective knowledge or demonstrate his irreducibility. But, precisely, Hegel was dead and this death pronounced his knowledge as dead knowledge, or as knowledge of death. While Kierkegaard showed by the simple fact of his life that all knowledge concerning the subjective is in a certain sense false knowledge. Foreseen by the system, he disqualified its legitimacy by not appearing in it as a moment to be surpassed and at the site assigned to him by the master but, on the contrary, by emerging quite simply as a survivor of the system and its prophet, as one who, despite the dead determinations of an anterior prophecy, had to live this foreseen life as if it were indeterminate at the outset and as if its determinations had arisen of their own accord within free "non-knowledge" [*non-savoir*].

The new aspect of the problematic that Kierkegaard reveals to us is the fact that in his personal life he did not contradict the content of knowledge but illegitimized knowledge of any content. By negating the concept through the very fashion in which he realized its prescriptions in another dimension, he was traversed through and through by the light of knowledge—for others and also for himself, as he was acquainted with Hegelianism—but at the same time remained utterly opaque. In other words, this preexistent knowledge revealed a being at the heart of future existence. Thirty years ago, the contradictions of colonialism constituted, in the eyes of the generation of colonized born into it, a being of misery, anger, blood, revolt, and struggle; a few among the best-informed of the oppressed and of the colonialists themselves were aware of this. Or to take a quite different example, a vacancy created high up or low down on the social scale creates a destiny, that is to say a future but foreseeable being for the person who will fill it, even though this destiny remains for each candidate, if there is more than one, no more than a *possible being*. Or, in the narrow particularity of private life, the structures of a specific family (seen as a local example of an institution produced by the movement of History) permit the psychoanalyst, in theory at least, to foresee the future destiny (to be lived and undergone) that will be a particular neurosis for a child born into this milieu. Kierkegaard *foreseen* by Hegel is but a privileged example of such ontological determinations which predate birth and allow themselves to be *conceptualized*.

Søren identified with the problem because he was conscious of it. He knew that Hegel, in pointing to him as a moment of universal History vainly posed for itself, attained him in the being which he suffered as a schema to be accomplished in the course of his life, and which he called his Untruth, or the error that he was at the start of his life, as a truncated determination. But this was the point: Hegel's designation attained him like the light from a dead star. The untruth *had to be lived*; it too belonged to his subjective subjectivity. And so he could write, in the *Fragments*: "My own Untruth is something I can discover only by myself, since it is only when I have discovered it that it is discovered, even if the whole world knew of it before."[4] But when it is discovered, my Untruth becomes, at least in the immediate, my Truth. So subjective truth exists. It is not knowledge [*savoir*] but self-determination; it can be defined neither as an extrinsic relation of knowledge [*connaissance*] to being, nor as the internal imprint of a correspondence, nor as the indissoluble unity of a system. "Truth," he said, "is the act of freedom." I would not know how to be my own Truth even if its premises were given in me in advance: to reveal it means to produce it or to produce myself as I am; to be for myself what I have to be.

What Kierkegaard highlighted was the fact that the opposition between non-knowledge and knowledge is an opposition between two ontological structures. The subjective has to be what it is—a singular realization of each singularity. One would have to go to

Freud for the most illuminating commentary on this remark. In fact psychoanalysis is not knowledge nor does it claim to be, save when it hazards hypotheses on the dead and thus allows death to make it a science of death. It is a movement, an internal labor, that at one and the same time uncovers a neurosis and gradually makes the subject capable of supporting it. With the result that at the term (actually an ideal) of this process, there is a correspondence between the being that has developed and the truth it once was. The truth in this case is the unity of the conquest and the object conquered. It transforms without teaching anything and does not appear until the end of a transformation. It is a non-knowledge, an effectivity, a placing in perspective that is present to itself insofar as it is realized. Kierkegaard would add that it is a decision of authenticity: the rejection of flight and the will to return to oneself. In this sense *knowledge* cannot register this obscure and inflexible *movement* by which scattered determinations are elevated to the status of being and are gathered together into a tension which confers on them not a signification but a synthetic meaning: what happens is that the ontological structure of subjectivity escapes to the extent that the subjective being is, as Heidegger has put it so well, in question in its being, to the extent that it never *is* except in the mode of having to be its being.

From this point of view, the moment of subjective truth is a temporalized but transhistorical absolute. And subjectivity is temporalization itself: it is *what happens to me*, what cannot be but in happening. It is myself insofar as I can only be a random birth—and, as Merleau-Ponty said, insofar as I must, no matter how short my life, *at least* experience the occurrence of death; but it is also myself insofar as I try to regain control of my own adventure by assuming—we shall come back to this point—its original contingency in order to establish it in necessity. In short, insofar as *I* happen to myself. Dealt with in advance by Hegel, subjectivity becomes a moment of the objective spirit, a determination of culture. But if nothing of lived experience [*le vecu*] can elude knowledge, its *reality* remains irreducible. In this sense, lived experience as concrete reality is posed as *non-knowledge*. But this negation of knowledge implies the affirmation of itself. Lived experience recognizes itself as a projection into the milieu of meaning, but at the same time it fails to recognize itself there since, in this milieu, an ensemble is constituted which aims randomly at objects and since, precisely, it is itself not an object. Doubtless, one of the principal concerns of the nineteenth century was to distinguish the being of an object from one's knowledge of it, in other words to reject idealism. Marx attacked Hegel not so much for his point of departure, as for his reduction of being to knowledge. But for Kierkegaard, as for ourselves today when we consider the Kierkegaardian scandal, the question is one of a certain ontological region in which being claims at once to elude knowledge and to attain itself. Waelhens has rightly written: "With the advent of Kierkegaard, Nietzsche, and Bergson, philosophy ceased to be *explanation at a distance*, and claimed to be henceforth *at one* with experience itself; it was no longer content to throw light on man and his life, but aspired to become this life in its full consciousness of itself. It seemed that for the philosopher this ambition involved an obligation to renounce the ideal of philosophy as a rigorous science, since the basis of this ideal was inseparable from the idea of a detached ... spectator."

In short, the determinations of lived experience are not simply heterogeneous to knowledge, as the existence of thalers was heterogeneous for Kant to the concept of thaler and to the judgment that combined the two. It is the very way in which these determinations attain themselves in the redoubling of their presence to themselves that reduces knowledge to the pure abstraction of the concept and, in the first moment at least (the only one Kierkegaard described) turns an object that is a subject into an objective *nothing* in relation to a subjective subjectivity. Knowledge [*savoir*] itself has a being; bodies of knowledge [*connaissances*] are realities. For Kierkegaard, even in his lifetime, the being of knowledge was obviously radically heterogeneous to that of the living subject. Thus we can designate the determinations of existence with words. But *either* this designation is nothing but a place-marker, a set of references without conceptualization, *or else* the ontological structure of the concept and of its links—i.e., objective being, being in exteriority—is such that these references, grasped as notions, cannot but yield a false knowledge when they present themselves as insights into being in interiority.

In his life, Kierkegaard lived this paradox in passion: he desperately wanted to designate himself as a transhistorical absolute. In humor and in irony, he revealed himself and concealed himself at the same time. He did not refuse to communicate, but simply held on to his *secrecy* in the act of communication. His mania for pseudonyms was a systematic disqualification of *proper names*: even to *assign* him as an individual before the tribunal of others, a welter of mutually contradictory appellations was necessary. The more he becomes Climacus or Virgelin Hufnensis, the less he is *Kierkegaard*, this Danish citizen, this entry in civil registry.

This was all very well so long as he was alive: by his life he gave the lie to a dead man's predictions that are a knowledge of death. That is to say he ceaselessly fabricated himself by writing. But on November 11, 1855, he died, and the paradox turned against him without ceasing to be scandalous in *our eyes*. The prophecy of a dead man condemning a living being to exist as an unhappy consciousness, and our knowledge of this living being once he has died, reveal their homogeneity. In fact in our own time Käte Nadler—to cite but one example—has applied to the late Kierkegaard the prediction of the late Hegel. A dialectical pair is formed, in which each term denounces the other: Hegel foresaw Kierkegaard in the past, as a superseded moment; Kierkegaard gave the lie to the internal organization of Hegel's system by showing that superseded moments are conserved, not only in the *Aufhebung* that maintains them as it transforms them but in themselves, without any transformation whatever; and by proving that even if they arise anew, they create, merely through their appearance, an anti-dialectic. But once Kierkegaard died, Hegel regained possession of him. Not *within the System*, which visibly crumbled insofar as it was a finished totality of Knowledge which, as a system, was subsequently totalized by the onward movement of History itself—but simply by virtue of the fact that the late Kierkegaard has become *in our eyes* homogeneous with the descriptions that Hegelian knowledge gives of him. The fact remains, of course, that he contested the whole system by appearing in a place that was not assigned to him: but since the system itself is an object of knowledge and as such is contested, this anachronism provides us with nothing really new. By contrast, the Knowledge that *we* have of him is knowledge of a dead man and thus knowledge of death; as such it rejoins the Hegelian intuition which produced and conceptualized a future death. In ontological terms, Kierkegaard's prenatal being was homogeneous with his postmortem being and his existence seemed merely to be a way of enriching the first so that it could equal the second: it was no more than a provisional *malaise*, an essential means of getting from one to the other, but, in itself, an inessential fever of being. The notion of the unhappy consciousness became Søren's insurpassable destiny as well as the generality enveloping our most particularized items of knowledge concerning his dead life. Or if you like, to die meant to be restored to being and to become an object of knowledge. That at least is the recurrent lazy conception whose aim is to close a breach. Is it true? Should we say that death terminates the paradox by revealing that it is nothing more than a provisional appearance, or on the contrary, that it pushes it to the extreme and consequently, since we die, the whole of History becomes paradoxical—an insurmountable conflict between being and existence, between non-knowledge and knowledge? It was Kierkegaard's merit that he formulated this problem *in the very terms of his life*. Let us come back to him.

Let us note at the outset that between him and us, History has *taken place*. No doubt it is still going on. But its richness puts a distance, *an obscure density* between him and us. The unhappy consciousness will find other incarnations, and each of them will contest this consciousness by his life and confirm it by his death, but none of them will reproduce Kierkegaard by virtue of a kind of resurrection. Knowledge has its foundations in this instance in non-coincidence. The poet of faith left texts behind. These writings are dead unless we breathe our life into them; but if revived they bear the stamp of thoughts committed to paper long ago, somewhere else, with the means to hand—they only partially answer to our present requirements. Nonbelievers will pronounce *the Kierkegaardian proof to be unconvincing*. Theologians, in the name of dogma itself, may declare themselves unsatisfied and find the attitude and declarations of the "poet of Christianity" insufficient and dangerous. (They may reproach him in the name of his own admission, through the very title of poet that he gave himself, with not having got beyond what he himself called the "aesthetic stage." Atheists will *either*—a formula dear to him—reject any relationship with this absolute and opt firmly for a relativism, or else define the absolute in History *in other terms*—and regard Kierkegaard as the witness of a false absolute or a false witness of the absolute. Believers, on the other hand, will declare that the absolute Kierkegaard aimed at is certainly that which exists, but that the relation of historical man to transhistoricity, which he tried to establish, was involuntarily deflected and lost by him in the night of atheism. In each case, his attempt is pronounced a *failure*.

There is more: the failure is *explained*. In different ways, it is true, but by convergent approximations. Mesnard, Bohlen, Chestov, and Jean Wahl are all agreed in stressing the psychosomatic significance of the "thorn in the flesh."[5] This means that, in the case of this dead man, lived experience itself is contested. Later conceptual judgment renders the life itself inauthentic. Kierkegaard lived out badly—in the sense of obscurely, disguisedly—determinations that we can perceive better than he. In short, in the eyes of historical knowledge, one lives to die. Existence is a mild surface ripple that is soon stilled in order to allow the dialectical development of concepts to appear; chronology dissolves into homogeneity and in the end, into timelessness. Every lived venture ends in failure for the simple reason that History continues.

But if life is a scandal, failure is even more scandalous. First we describe and denounce it by collections of words that aim at a certain object named Kierkegaard. In this sense the "poet of faith" is a signified—like this table, like a socioeconomic process. And it is true that death first presents itself as the fall of the subject into the realm of absolute objectivity. But Kierkegaard in his writings—today inert or living with our life—proposes a usage of words that is the converse of this: what he seeks is a dialectical regression from signified and significations to signifier. He presents himself as a signifier, and at a stroke refers us back to our transhistoricity as signifiers. Should we reject this regression a priori? To do so is to constitute ourselves as relative—relative to History if we are unbelievers, relative to Dogmas and mediated by the Church if we believe. Now if such is the case, then everything should be relative, in us and in Kierkegaard himself, *except his failure*. For failure can be *explained* but not *resolved*: as nonbeing it possesses the absolute character of negation. In fact historical negation, even at the heart of a relativism, is an absolute. It would be a negative absolute to declare that at Waterloo *there were no* fighter planes. But this negative declaration remains a formality: as the two adversaries were equally without air power and were both incapable of missing it, this ineffectual absence is no more than a formal proposition devoid of interest, that merely registers the *temporal distance* from Waterloo to the present. There are, however, other negative absolutes and these are concrete: it is correct to state that Grouchy's army *did not* link up with the emperor;[6] and this negation is historical in the sense that it reflects the frustrated expectation of the head of an army, and the fear turned to satisfaction of the enemy. It is effective in the sense that Grouchy's delay in all probability *settled* the outcome of the battle. It is thus an absolute, an irreducible but a concrete absolute. Similarly in the case of the failure: the fact that an ambition is not realized in objectivity means that it returns to subjectivity. Or, more precisely, the interpretations of such a failure aim via moderate negations (he didn't consider..., he couldn't be aware at the time, etc.) to reduce it *to the positive*, to erase it before the affirmative reality of the Other's victory, whatever it may be.

But at once this relative positivity slips back and reveals what no knowledge could ever transmit directly (because no historical advance could recuperate it): failure lived in despair. Those who died of anguish, of hunger, of exhaustion, those defeated in the past by force of arms, are so many gaps in our knowledge insofar as they existed: subjectivity constitutes *nothing* for objective knowledge since it is a non-knowledge, and yet failure demonstrates that it has an absolute existence. In this way Søren Kierkegaard, conquered by death and recuperated by historical knowledge, triumphs at the very moment he fails, by demonstrating that History cannot recover him. As a dead man, he remains the unsurpassable scandal of subjectivity; though he may be known through and through, he eludes History by the very fact that it is History that constitutes his defeat and that he lived it in anticipation. In short, he eludes History because he is historical.

Can we go further? Or must we simply conclude that death irrevocably filches the agents of past History from the historian? Here it is necessary to question *what remains* of Kierkegaard, his verbal remnants. For he constituted himself in his historicity as an absolute contesting the historical knowledge that would penetrate him after his death. But the kind of interrogation with which we are concerned is of a particular type: it is a paradox itself. Kant situated himself in the realm of cognition in order to test the validity of our knowledges. We, the living, can approach him through the realm of cognition, question his words with words, and cross-examine him on concepts. But Kierkegaard stole language from knowledge in order to use it against knowledge. If we approach him, as we are compelled to do, through the realm of cognition, our words encounter his and are disqualified by disqualifying them. The fact is that his use of the Word and our own are heterogeneous. Thus the message of this dead man is scandalous through the very fact of its existence, since we are incapable of considering this residue of a life as a determination of knowledge. On the contrary, the paradox reappears since his thought expressed in words constitutes itself within knowledge as irreducible non-knowledge. Our interrogation must then either disappear without a trace, or be transformed and itself become non-knowledge questioning non-knowledge. That is to say, the questioner is called into question in his very being by the questioned. Such is the fundamental virtue of the pseudo-object called the works of Kierkegaard. But let us push our examination to the very moment of this metamorphosis.

This philosopher was an anti-philosopher. Why did he reject the Hegelian system and, in a general way, the whole of philosophy? Because, he says, the philosopher seeks a first beginning. But why, one may ask, did he who rejected beginnings take as his point of departure the Christian dogmas? For to accept them a priori without even testing their validity is tantamount to making them the uncontested principles of thought. Is there not a contradiction here? Did not Kierkegaard, having failed to establish a solid beginning himself, take the beginning of others as the origin and foundation of his thought? And as he failed to test it through criticism, and as he neglected to doubt it to the point where it could no longer be doubted, did it not retain for him, even in his most intimate thought, its character of otherness?

This is, indeed, the unfair question that knowledge puts to existence. But, in Kierkegaard's pen, existence replies by rejecting knowledge's case. To deny dogma, it says, is to be mad and to proclaim the fact. But to prove dogma is to be an imbecile: while time is wasted proving that the soul is immortal, living belief in immortality withers away. At the absurd limit of this logic, the day would come when immortality was finally proved irrefutably—except that no one would believe in it anymore. There is no way we could better understand that immortality, even if proven, could never be an object of knowledge: it is a particular absolute relationship between immanence and transcendence that can only be constituted in and through lived experience. And of course this is sufficient for believers. But for the non-believer that I am, what this means is that the real relation of man to his being can only be lived, in History, as a transhistorical relationship.

Kierkegaard replies to our question by rejecting philosophy or rather by radically changing its end and aims. To seek the beginning of knowledge is to affirm that the foundation of temporality is, precisely, timeless, and that the historical individual can wrench himself free of History, de-situate himself and relocate his fundamental timelessness by a direct vision of being. Temporality becomes the means of intemporality. Naturally Hegel was aware of the problem since he placed philosophy at the end of History, as truth-that-has-come-into-being and retrospective knowledge. But this is the point: History is never finished, so this atemporal reconstitution of temporality, understood as the unity of the logical and the tragic, becomes in turn an object of knowledge. From this point of view, there is no being at all at the beginning of Hegel's system, but only the person of Hegel, such as it had been fashioned, such as it had fashioned itself. This is the sort of ambiguous discovery that can lead, from the point of view of knowledge, only to skepticism.

To avoid this, Kierkegaard took as his point of departure the *person* envisaged as non-knowledge, that is to say inasmuch as he both produces and discovers, at a given moment in the temporal unfolding of his life, his relation to an absolute which is itself inserted in History.

In short, far from denying the beginning, Kierkegaard testified to a beginning that is lived.

How is it possible that, in the context of History, this historical situation does not contest the claim of the thinker to have disclosed the absolute? How can a thought *that has appeared* testify on its own behalf after its *disappearance*? This is the problem Kierkegaard set himself in the *Philosophical Fragments*. Of course, this paradox was first and foremost a religious one. What was at stake was the appearance and disappearance of Jesus. Or equally, the transformation of one sin—Adam's—into original and hereditary sin. But it was just as much the personal problem of Kierkegaard the thinker: How could he establish the transhistorical validity of a thought that had been produced within History and would disappear into it? The answer lay in "reduplication": the insurpassable cannot be knowledge, but must be the establishment in History of an absolute and non-contemplative relation with the absolute that has been realized in History. Rather than knowledge dissolving the thinker, it is the thinker who testifies on behalf of his own thought. But these ideas are obscure and can appear to be merely a verbal solution so long as one has not understood that they proceed from a novel conception of thought.

The beginning of the thinker's existence is analogous to a birth. This is not a rejection but a displacement of the beginning. Before birth there was nonbeing; then comes the leap, and the moment they are born to themselves, the child and the thinker find themselves immediately situated within a certain historical world that has produced them. They discover themselves as a particular adventure, whose point of departure is a set of socioeconomic, cultural, moral, religious, and other relations, which proceeds with whatever means are to hand, that is to say within the limits of these relations, and which gradually becomes inscribed in the same set. The beginning is reflective—I saw and touched the world, and so see and touch myself, this self who touches and sees the surrounding things; in this way I discover myself as a finite being, one that these same objects I touched and saw condition invisibly in my very sense of touch and sight. As against the constant and nonhuman beginning that Hegel postulated, Kierkegaard proposed a start that is in flux, that is conditioned and is conditioning, whose foundation approximates to what Merleau-Ponty called *envelopment*. We are enveloped: being is behind us and in front of us. He-who-sees is visible, and sees only by virtue of his visibility. "My body," said Merleau-Ponty, "is caught in the fabric of the world, but the world is made from the stuff of my body." Kierkegaard knew he was enveloped: he saw Christianity and in particular the Christian community in Denmark with the eyes that this community had given him. This is a new paradox: I see the being that fashioned me. I see it as it *is* or as it made me. "Overview thought" [*"pensée de survol"*] has an easy solution to this: having no qualities, the understanding grasps the objective essence without its own nature imposing particular deviations on it. Idealist relativism has an equally simple solution: the object fades away; what I see, being the effect of causes modifying my vision, contains no more than what these latter determine me to be. In each case, being is reduced to knowledge.

Kierkegaard rejects both solutions. The paradox, for him, is the fact that we discover the absolute in the relative. Kierkegaard was a Dane, born at the beginning of the last century into a Danish family, and conditioned by Danish history and culture. He came across other Danes as his contemporaries, people who were formed by the same History and cultural traditions. And at the same time, moreover, he could *think* the historical traditions and circumstances that had produced them all and produced himself. Was there either deviation or appropriation? Both. If objectivity has to be unconditioned knowledge, then there can be no true objectivity: to see one's surroundings, in this instance, would be to see without seeing, to touch without touching, to possess in oneself an a priori intuition of the other and, at the same time, to grasp him on the basis of common presuppositions that can never wholly be uncovered. Even in broad daylight my neighbor is dark and impenetrable, separated from me by his apparent resemblances; and yet I sense him in his underlying reality when I penetrate deeper into my own inner reality and attain its transcendental conditions. Later, much later, the presuppositions inscribed in things will be correctly deciphered by the historian. But at this level, the mutual comprehension that takes the existence of a communal envelopment for granted will have disappeared. In short, contemporaries understand each other without knowing each other, whereas the future historian will know them but his greatest difficulty—a difficulty bordering on the impossible—will be to understand them as they understood each other.

In fact—and Kierkegaard was aware of this—the experience which turns back upon itself, after the leap, comprehends itself more than it knows itself. In other words, it sustains itself in the milieu of the presuppositions that are its foundation, without succeeding in elucidating them. Hence a beginning that is a dogma. A particular religion produced Kierkegaard: he could not pretend to emancipate himself from it so that he could rise above it and see it as historically constituted. Note however that other Danes, from the same society, from the same class, became nonbelievers: but even they could do nothing to prevent their irreligion questioning or challenging *these* dogmas, this particular Christianity which had produced them—and hence their past, their religious childhood, and finally themselves. Thus whatever they did, they remained wedded to their faith and their dogmas while vainly attempting to negate them by using other words to express their demand for an absolute. Their atheism was in fact a Christian *pseudo-atheism*. As it happens, one's envelopment determines the limits within which real modifications are possible. There are times when disbelief can only be verbal. Kierkegaard doubted as a youth, and hence was more consequential than these "freethinkers": he recognized that his thought was not free and that whatever he might do or wherever he might go his religious determinations would follow him. If in spite of himself he saw Christian dogmas as irreducible, then it was perfectly legitimate for him to locate the beginning of his thought at the moment when it retraced its steps to them to get at its roots. Such a thought was doubly embedded in history: it grasped its envelopment as a conjuncture, and it defined itself as an identity between the beginning of thought and thought of the beginning.

If such was the case, what then was to become of the universality of historical determinations? Must we deny in absolute terms that there is any social sphere, with structures, pressures, and developments of its own? Not at all. We shall see that Kierkegaard testified to a double universality. The revolution consisted in the fact that historical man, by his anchorage, turned this universality into a particular situation and this common necessity into an irreducible contingency. In other words, far from this particular attitude being, as in Hegel, a dialectical incarnation or the universal moment, the anchorage of the individual made this universal into an irreducible singularity. Did not Søren say to Levin one day: "How lucky you are to be a Jew: you escape Christianity. If I had been protected by your faith, I would have enjoyed a quite different life"?[7] This was an ambiguous remark, for he often reproached Jews with being inaccessible to religious experience. There could be no doubt that dogma was truth, and the Christian who was not religious remained inauthentic, outside himself, lost. But there was a sort of humble birthright which meant, in the case of a Jew, a Muslim or a Buddhist, that the chance occurrence of their birth in one place rather than another was transformed into a statute. Conversely, Kierkegaard's deepest reality, the fabric of his being, his torment and his law appeared to him in the very heart of their necessity as the accidental outcome of his facticity. Again this contingency was common to all members of his society. He came across others which belonged only to him. In 1846 he wrote: "To believe is to lighten oneself by assuming a considerable weight; to be objective is to lighten oneself by casting off burdens . . . Lightness is an infinite weight, and its altitude the effect of an infinite weight." He was clearly alluding to what he called elsewhere the "thorn in the flesh." Here we are confronted with pure contingency, the singularity of his conditionings. Søren's unhappy consciousness was the product of random determinations which Hegelian rationalism did not take into account: a gloomy father who was convinced that he would be struck by a divine curse on his children; the mournings that seemed to bear out these expectations and ended by persuading Søren that he would die by the age of thirty-four; the mother, mistress, and servant, whom he loved insofar as she was *his* mother and whom he reproved insofar as she was an intruder in the household of a widower and testified to the carnal lapses of his father, and so on. The origin of singularity is the random at its most radical: if I had had a different father . . . if my father had not blasphemed, etc. And this prenatal accident reappears in the individual himself and in his determinations: the thorn in the flesh was a complex disposition whose inner secret has not yet been unearthed. But all authors are agreed in seeing a sexual anomaly as its kernel. A singularizing accident, this anomaly *was* Kierkegaard, it *made* him; it could not be cured, and hence could not be surpassed; it produced his most intimate self as a pure historical contingency, which might not have been and in itself meant nothing. Hegelian necessity was not negated, but it could not be embodied without becoming a singular and opaque contingency; in an individual the rationality of History is experienced irreducibly as madness, as an inner accident, expressive of random encounters. To our questioning, Kierkegaard replies by revealing another aspect of the paradox: there can be no historical absolute that is not rooted in chance; because of the necessity of anchorage, there can be no incarnation of the universal other than in the irreducible opacity of the singular. Is it Søren who says this? Yes and no: to tell the truth he says *nothing* if "to say" means the same as "to signify," but his work refers us back, without speaking, to his life.

But here the paradox has a twist to it, for to experience original contingency means to surpass it. Man, irremediable singularity, is the being through whom the universal comes into the world; once fundamental chance starts to be lived, it assumes the form of necessity. Lived experience, we discover in Kierkegaard, is made up of nonsignificant accidents of being insofar as they are surpassed toward a significance they did not possess at the beginning, and which I will call the singular universal.

To gain more insight into this message, let us come back to the notion of sin which lies at the center of Kierkegaard's thought. As Jean Wahl has noted correctly, Adam exists in a pre-Adamite state of innocence, i.e. of ignorance. Nevertheless, although the Self does not yet exist, this being already envelops a contradiction. At this level, the spirit is a synthesis which unites and divides: it brings body and soul together and, in doing so, engenders the conflicts which oppose them. Dread makes its appearance as the interiorization of being, that is to say, its contradiction. In other words, being has no interiority prior to the appearance of dread. But since the spirit can neither flee nor fulfill itself, since it is a dissonant unity of the finite and the infinite, the possibility of choosing *one* of the terms—the finite, the flesh, in other words the Self which does not yet exist—makes its appearance in the form of dread, at the moment when God's Thou Shalt Not resounds. But what is this prohibition? In actual fact, communication is not possible—no more than it was possible between Kafka's Emperor and the subject he wanted to touch but whom his message does not reach.[8] But Kierkegaard gave this Shalt Not its full value when he deprived the Serpent of the power to tempt Adam. If the Devil is eliminated and Adam is not yet Adam, who can pronounce the prohibition and at the same time suggest to the pre-Adamite that he turn himself into Adam? God alone. A curious passage from the *Journal* explains why:

> Omnipotence...should make things dependent. But if we rightly consider omnipotence, then clearly it must have the quality of so taking itself back in the very manifestation of its all-powerfulness that the results of this act of the omnipotent can be independent... For goodness means to give absolutely, yet in such a way that by taking oneself back one makes the recipient independent...Omnipotence alone...can create something out of nothing which endures of itself, because omnipotence is always taking itself back...If...man had even the least independent existence (in regard to *materia*) then God could not make him free.[9]

The pre-Adamite state of innocence is the final moment of dependence. At any moment God will withdraw from his creature as the ebbing tide uncovers a piece of flotsam; and by this movement alone he creates dread—as the possibility of independence. In other words, God becomes at once the Prohibiter and the Tempter. Thus dread is the abandonment of being to the forbidden possibility of choosing finitude by a sudden retreat of the infinite. Dread is the internalization of this forsaken condition and it is completed by the free realization of the sole possible future of Adam abandoned—the choice of the finite. The moment of sin is defined by the restitution of original being as *meaning*. Being was the contradictory unity between the finite and the impalpable infinite, but this unity remained in the indistinction of ignorance. Sin as *re-exteriorization* makes the constituent contradiction reappear. It is the determination of it: the Self and God appear. God is infinite withdrawal but yet immediate presence, insofar as sin bars the way to any hope of return to Eden. The Self is chosen finitude, nothingness affirmed and delimited by an act; it is determination conquered by defiance; it is the singularity of extreme estrangement. Thus the terms of the contradiction are the same and yet the *state* of ignorance and sin are not homogeneous: the finite is now constituted as loss of the infinite, freedom as the *necessary* and irremediable foundation of the formation of the *Ego*. Good and Evil make their appearance as the meaning of this exteriorization of the interiority that is sinful freedom. Everything happens as though God *needed sin* in order that man might produce himself in front of him, as if he had solicited it in order to bring Adam out of his state of ignorance and *give* meaning to man.

But we are all Adam. Thus the pre-Adamite state is one with the contingency of our being. For Kierkegaard, what produces it is a disunited unity of accidents. In this sense, sin becomes the *establishment* of Kierkegaard as a surpassal of these scattered data *toward a meaning*. The contingency of our being is the beginning; our necessity only appears through the act which assumes this contingency in order to give it a *human meaning*, in other words to make of it a singular relationship to the Whole, a singular embodiment of the ongoing totalization which envelops and produces it. Kierkegaard was well aware of this: what he called sin is, as a whole, the supersession of the (pre-Adamite) *state* by the advent of freedom and the impossibility of retreat. Thus the web of subjective life—what he called passion, and Hegel called *pathos*—is nothing other than the freedom that institutes the finite and is lived in finitude as inflexible necessity.

If I wished to summarize what Kierkegaard's non-signifying testimony has to offer to me, a twentieth-century atheist who does not believe in sin, I would say that the state of ignorance represents, for the individual, being-in-exteriority. These exterior determinations are interiorized in order to be re-exteriorized by a praxis which *institutes* them by objectifying them in the world.

This is what Merleau-Ponty was saying when he wrote that History is the milieu in which "a form burdened with contingency suddenly opens up a cycle of the future and commands it with the authority of the instituted." The cycle of the future is a *meaning*: in the case of Kierkegaard, it is the Self. Meaning can be defined as the future relation of the instituted to the totality of the world or, if you like, as the synthetic totalization of scattered chance occurrences by an objectifying negation, which inscribes them as necessity freely created in the very universe in which they were scattered, and as the presence of the totality—a totality of time and of the universe—in the determination which negates them by posing itself for itself. In other words, man is that being who transforms his being into *meaning*, and through whom *meaning* comes into the world.

The singular universal is this meaning: through his *Self*—the practical assumption and supersession of being as it is—man restores to the universe its enveloping unity, by engraving it as a finite determination and a mortgage on future History in the being which envelops him. Adam temporalizes himself by sin, the necessary free choice and radical transformation of what he is—he brings human temporality into the universe. This clearly means that the foundation of History is freedom in *each man*. For we are all Adam insofar as each of us commits on his own behalf and on behalf of all a singular sin: in other words finitude, for each person, is necessary and incomparable. By his finite action, the agent alters the course of things—but in conformity with what this course itself ought to be. Man, in fact, is a mediation between a transcendence behind and a transcendence in front, and this twofold transcendence is but one. Thus we can say that through man, the course of things is deviated in the direction of its own deviation. Kierkegaard here reveals to us the basis of his own paradox and of ours—and the two are the same. Each of us, in our very historicity, escapes History to the extent that we make it. I myself am historical to the extent that others also make history and make me, but I am a transhistorical absolute by virtue of what I make of what they make of me, have made of me, and will make of me in the future—that is, by virtue of my historiality [*historialité*].

We still need to understand properly what the myth of sin holds for us: the *institution* of a man is his singularity become law for others and for himself. What is Kierkegaard's body of work but himself insofar as he is a universal? But on the other hand the content of this universality remains his contingency—even if elected and surpassed by his choice of it. In short, this universality has two sides to it: by virtue of its meaning it raises contingency to the level of concrete universality. This is its luminous and yet unknowable recto side—to the extent that knowledge refers to the "world-historical" by the mediation of an *anchorage*. Its verso side is in darkness, and refers back to the contingent set of analytical and social data which define Kierkegaard's being before his *institution*. Two errors in method are thereby denounced. The first of them, the world-historical, would define Kierkegaard's message in its abstract universality and as the pure expression of general structures; thus Hegelians would categorize it as the unhappy consciousness, incarnation of a necessary moment in universal History, or interpreters like Tisseau[10] would view it as a radical definition of faith, an appeal by a true Christian addressed to all Christians.

The other error would be to deem his work a simple effect or translation of original chance occurrences: this is what I would call psychoanalytic skepticism. Such a skepticism is founded on the fact that the whole of Kierkegaard's *childhood* is present in his work and forms the basis of its singularity, and that in a sense, there is nothing more in the books he wrote than the life he instituted. Søren's works are rich in Freudian symbols, it is true, and a psychoanalytic *reading* of his texts is quite possible. The same holds good for what I would call skeptical Marxism, that is to say bad Marxism. Although its truth here is mediate, there is no doubt that Kierkegaard was radically conditioned by his historical environment: his disdain for the masses, and aristocratic demeanor, his attitude to money, leave no trace of doubt as to his social origins or his political position (for example his liking for absolute monarchy), which, though well concealed, surface time after time and obviously form the basis of his ethical and religious opinions.

But this is the point: Kierkegaard teaches us that the Self, action and creation, with their dark side and light side, are absolutely irreducible to the one or to the other. The shadow is wholly in the light because it is *instituted*: it is true that every act and every text expresses the whole of the Self, but this is because the Self-as-institution is homogeneous with action-as-legislator. It is impossible to make the general conditions the *basis of it*: this would be to forget that they are general in a "world-historical" sense—for example the relations of production in Denmark in 1830—but that they are lived as nonsignificant chance by each individual, who is inserted in them fortuitously. By virtue of the fact that the individual expresses the universal in singular terms, he singularizes the whole of History which becomes at once *necessity*, through the very way in which objective situations take charge of themselves, and *adventure*, because History is forever the general experienced and instituted as a particularity which at first is non-signifying.

In this way the individual becomes a singular universal by virtue of the presence within himself of agents defined as universalizing singularities. But conversely, the side in shadow is already in light because the same individual is the moment of interiorization of exterior contingency. Without this pre-instituting unity, the person could lapse into scattered disorder; too frequently psychoanalysis reduces meaning to non-meaning because it refuses to acknowledge that dialectical stages are irreducible. But Kierkegaard was perhaps the first to show that the universal enters History as a singular, insofar as the singular institutes itself in it as a universal. In this novel form of historiality we encounter paradox once again: here it acquires the insurpassable appearance of ambiguity.

But as we have seen, the *theoretical* aspect of his work, in the case of Kierkegaard, is pure illusion. When we *encounter* his words, they immediately invite us to another use of language, that is to say of our own words, since they are the same as his. Kierkegaard's terms refer to what are now called, in accordance with his precepts, the "categories" of existence. But these categories are neither principles nor concepts nor the elements of concepts: they appear as lived relationships to a totality, attainable by starting with the words and following their trajectory back from speech to speaker. This means that not a single one of these verbal alliances is *intelligible*, but that they constitute, by their very negation of any effort to know them, a reference back to the foundations of such an effort. Kierkegaard made use of irony, humor, myth, and non-signifying sentences in order to communicate indirectly with us. This means that if one adopts the traditional attitude of a reader to his books, their words engender a series of pseudo-concepts which are organized under our eyes into false knowledge. But this false knowledge denounces itself as false at the very moment of its formation. Or rather it is constituted as knowledge of something which pretends to be an object but in fact cannot be other than a subject. Kierkegaard made *regressive* use of objective and objectifying ensembles in such a way that the self-destruction of the language necessarily unmasked he who employed it. In this way the surrealists were later to think that they could unmask being by lighting fires in language. But being was still, they believed, *in front of their eyes*; if the words—whatever they were—were burned, being would be unveiled to infinite desire as a surreality, something which was also ultimately a non-conceptual sur-objectivity. Kierkegaard by contrast constructed his language in such a way as to reveal within his false knowledge certain lines of force which allowed the possibility of a return from the pseudo-object to the subject. He invented regressive enigmas. His verbal edifices were rigorously logical. But the very abuse of this logic always gave rise to contradictions or indeterminacies which implied a complete reversal of our own perspective. For example, as Jean Wahl has pointed out, even the title *The Concept of Dread* is a provocation. For in Kierkegaard's terms dread could never be the object of a concept. To a certain extent, insofar as dread is the source of a free and temporalizing choice of finitude, it is the non-conceptual foundation of all concepts. And each of us ought to be able to understand that the word "dread" is a universalization of the singular, and hence a false concept, since it awakens universality in us to the very extent that it refers to the Unique, its foundation.

It is by turning his words upside down that one can understand Kierkegaard in his lived and now vanished singularity, that is to say in his instituted contingency. His finitude, excluded, corrupted, and ineffective, victim of the curse that he believed his father had brought on the whole family, could be described as impotence and as alterity. He is *other* than *all* others, other than himself, other than what he writes. He institutes his particularity by his free choice to be singular, that is to say he establishes himself at that ambiguous moment when interiorization, pregnant with future exteriorization, suppresses itself so that the latter may be born. Kierkegaard, who was afraid of being alienated by inscribing himself in the transcendence of the world, opted for identification with this dialectical stage, the perfect *locus of the secret*. Of course, he could not refrain from exteriorizing himself, as interiorization can only be objectification. Yet he did his best to prevent his objectification from defining him as an object of knowledge, in other words to ensure that the inscription of his person in the realm of reality, far from condensing him into the unity of ongoing History, should remain *as such* indecipherable, and refer back to the inaccessible secret of interiority. He performs brilliantly at a social function, laughing and making others laugh, and then notes in his journal that he wishes he could die. He could make people laugh because he wanted to die, and he wanted to die because he made people laugh. In this way his exteriority—a sparkling wit—was deprived of meaning, *unless* it is to be seen as the intentional contestation of every action reduced to its objective result, *unless* the *meaning* of any manifestation is not precisely incompletion, nonbeing, non-signification forcing he who wishes to decipher it to return to its inaccessible source, interiority. Kierkegaard instituted his accidents by choosing to become the knight of subjectivity.

Now that he is dead, Søren takes his place in knowledge as a bourgeois who came to Denmark in the first half of the last century, and was conditioned by a specific family situation, itself an expression of the movement of history in its generality. But he takes his place in knowledge as unintelligible, as a disqualification of knowledge as a virulent lacuna, that eludes conceptualization and consequently death. We have now gone full circle and can reconsider our initial question. We asked what it was that prevented the late Kierkegaard from becoming the object of knowledge. The answer is that he was not such while he was alive. Kierkegaard reveals to us that death, which we took to be the metamorphosis of existence into knowledge, radically *abolishes* the subjective but does not change it. If Kierkegaard, in the first instance, can appear to be an assemblage of items of knowledge, the reason is that the *known* is not contested in any immediate fashion by *lived experience*. But at the next moment it is knowledge which radically contests itself in the pseudo-object that this dead man is to us. It discovers its own limits as the object of study, impotent to become an autonomous determination of the exterior, escapes it.

The paradox, at this level, can be seen in a new light: Can the contestation of knowledge by itself be surpassed? Can it be surpassed in the face of the living being who bears witness to his secret? Can it be surpassed when this living being has utterly disappeared? To these questions, Kierkegaard has but one reply, and it is always the same: the regression from signified to signifier cannot be the object of any act of intellection. Nevertheless, we can grasp the signifier in its real presence through what Kierkegaard calls *comprehension*. But the knight of subjectivity does not define comprehension, and does not conceive it as a new action. However, through his work, he offers his life to us *to be comprehended*. We encounter it in 1964, in History, fashioned as an *appeal to our comprehension*.

But is there anything left to be understood if death is utter abolition? Kierkegaard replied to this with his theory of "contemporaneity." In relation to the dead man Søren, there remains one thing to be understood, and that is ourselves. Søren, alive in his death, is a paradox for us: but Søren had already himself encountered the same paradox in relating to Jesus, in starting from Adam. And his first solution was to say that one comprehends what one becomes. To comprehend Adam is to become Adam. And certainly if an individual cannot become Christ, at least he can comprehend his unintelligible message without any temporal mediation by becoming the man to whom this message was destined—by becoming a Christian. Thus Kierkegaard lives on if it is possible for us to become Kierkegaard or if, conversely, this dead man is ceaselessly instituted by the living—borrowing their life, flowing into their life, and nourishing his singularity with our own. Or if, in other words, he appears at the heart of knowledge as the perpetual denouncer, in each of us, of non-knowledge, of the dialectical stage in which interiorization turns into exteriorization; in short, of existence.

Yes, says Kierkegaard; you may become myself because I may become Adam. Subjective thought is the reflective grasp of my being-an-event, of the adventure that I am and which necessarily ends in my becoming Adam—that is, in recommencing original sin in the very movement of my temporalization. Sin in this case is choice. Every man is at once himself and Adam renewed, precisely to the extent that Kierkegaard was at once himself and his father, the blasphemer whose blasphemy he took upon himself through his own sin. Every sin is singular insofar as it institutes, in particular conditions, a unique individual and, at the same time, it is sin in general insofar as it is the choice of finitude and blasphemous defiance of God. In this way the universality of sin is contained in the singularity of choice. By virtue of it, every man always becomes all man. Each individual moves History forward by recommencing it, as well as by prefiguring within himself new beginnings yet to come. From this point of view, if Kierkegaard could become Adam, it was because Adam was already at the heart of his sinful existence the premonition of a future Kierkegaard. If I can become Kierkegaard it is because Kierkegaard was in his being already a premonition of us all.

If we take up the question again in the initial terms in which we posed it, it comes to this: Kierkegaard's words are our words. To the extent that, within the framework of knowledge, they are changed into non-knowledge and are referred back via the paradox from the signified to the signifier, we are the signifier they regressively disclose. Reading Kierkegaard I reascend back to myself; I seek to grasp Kierkegaard and it is myself I hold; his non-conceptual work is an invitation to understand myself as the source of all concepts. Thus the knowledge of death, by discovering its own limits, does not issue into sheer absence, but comes back to Kierkegaard. I discover myself as an irreducible existent, that is to say as freedom that has become my necessity. I understand that the object of knowledge *is* his being in the peaceful mode of perennity and by the same token that I am a non-object because I have to be my being. In fact my being is a temporalizing and hence suffered choice—but the nature of this sufferance is to be *freely* suffered, and thus to be sustained as a choice.

Kierkegaard is restored as my adventure not in his unique meaning but at the level of my being-as-adventurer, insofar as I have to be the event that happens to me from outside. Insofar as History, universalized by things—the bearers of the seal of our action—becomes, through each new birth of man, a singular adventure within which it enfolds its universality, Søren could continue to live after his death as my forerunner before birth, when I begin anew in different historical conditions. Curiously, this relationship of reciprocal interiority and immanence between Kierkegaard and each of us is established, not in the relativity of circumstances but rather at the very level where each of us is an incomparable absolute. And what can demonstrate to us the reality that is common to all and yet in each case is singular, but words? Words are signs turned back on themselves, tools of indirect communication referring me to myself because they refer uniquely to him.

Kierkegaard lives on because, by rejecting knowledge, he reveals the transhistorical contemporaneity of the dead and the living. In other words, he unmasks the fact that every man is all man as a singular universal or, if you like, because he shows temporalization, in opposition to Hegel, to be a transhistorical dimension of History. Humanity loses its dead and begins them absolutely anew once more in its living. Kierkegaard is not myself, however—I am an atheist. Nor is he the Christian who will reproach him tomorrow for his negative theology. Let us say that he was, in his own time, a unique *subject*. Once dead he can be revived only by becoming a *multiple subject*, that is to say an inner bond linking our singularities. Each of us *is* Søren in our capacity as adventure. And each of our interpretations, contesting the others, nevertheless subsumes them as its negative depth. Just as each of them, conversely, is contested but subsumed by the others to the extent that, refusing to see in it a complete reality or knowledge concerning reality, they conceive of its possibility by referring to the susceptibility of Kierkegaard to several different interpretations: in fact, divergence, contradiction, and ambiguity are precisely the determinate qualifications of existence. Thus it is today's Other, my real contemporary, who is the foundation of Kierkegaard's profundity, his way of remaining *other* within myself, without ceasing to be mine. Conversely he is, in each of us, the denunciation of ambiguity in himself and in others. Kierkegaard, comprehensible in the name of each ambiguity, is our link, a multiple and ambiguous existential relation between existent contemporaries, themselves lived ambivalences. He remains within History as a transhistorical relation between contemporaries grasped in their singular historiality. Within each of us he offers and refuses himself, as he did in his own lifetime; he is my adventure and remains, for others, Kierkegaard, the other—a figure on the horizon testifying to the Christian that faith is a future development forever imperiled, testifying to myself that the process of *becoming-an-atheist* is a long and difficult enterprise, an absolute relationship to these two infinites, man and the universe.

Every enterprise, even one brought to a triumphant conclusion, remains a *failure*, that is to say an incompletion to be completed. It lives on because it is open. The particular failure, in Kierkegaard's case, is clear. Kierkegaard demonstrated his historicity but failed to find History. Pitting himself against Hegel, he occupied himself over-exclusively with transmitting his instituted contingency to the human adventure and, because of this, he neglected praxis, which is rationality. At a stroke, he denatured *knowledge*, forgetting that the world we know is the world we make. Anchorage is a fortuitous event, but the possibility and rational meaning of this chance is given by general structures of envelopment which found it and which are themselves the universalization of singular adventures by the materiality in which they are inscribed.

Kierkegaard is alive in his death inasmuch as he affirms the irreducible singularity of every man to the History which nevertheless conditions him rigorously. He is dead, within the very life that he continues to lead within ourselves, inasmuch as he remains an inert interrogation, an open circle that demands to be closed by us. Others, in his own time or shortly thereafter, went further than him and completed the circle by writing: "Men make history on the basis of prior circumstances." In these words there is and is not progress beyond Kierkegaard: for this circularity remains abstract and risks excluding the human singularity of the concrete universal, so long as it does not integrate Kierkegaardian immanence within the historical dialectic. Kierkegaard and Marx: these living-dead men condition our anchorage and institute themselves, now vanished, as our future, as the tasks that await us. How can we conceive of History and the transhistorical in such a way as to restore to the transcendent necessity of the historical process and to the free immanence of a historicization ceaselessly renewed, their full reality and reciprocal interiority, in theory and practice? In short, how can we discover the singularity of the universal and the universalization of the singular, in each conjuncture, as indissolubly linked to each other?

RUSSELL VIETNAM WAR CRIMES TRIBUNAL INAUGURAL STATEMENT

OUR TRIBUNAL was formed, at the initiative of Lord Bertrand Russell, to decide whether the accusations of "war crimes" leveled against the government of the United States as well as against those of South Korea, New Zealand, and Australia, during the conflict in Vietnam, are justified.

During this inaugural session, the origin, function, aims, and limits of the Tribunal are going to be clarified: the Tribunal plans to explain itself clearly about the question of what has been called its "legitimacy."

In 1945, something absolutely new in history appeared at Nuremberg with the first international Tribunal formed to pass judgment on crimes committed by a belligerent power. Until then there had indeed been a few international agreements, such as the Briand-Kellogg pact, which were aimed at limiting the *jus ad bellum*;[1] but as no other body had been created to implement them, relations between the powers continued to be ruled by the law of the jungle. It could not be otherwise: the nations which had built their wealth upon the conquest of great colonial empires would not have tolerated being judged for their own behavior in Africa or Asia. From 1939, the Hitlerian furies spread such danger in the world that the horrified Allies decided, since they were victorious, to judge and condemn the wars of aggression and conquest, the maltreatment of prisoners and the tortures, as well as the racist practices known as "genocide," unaware that they were condemning themselves, in this way, for their own practices in the colonies.

For this reason, that is to say because they were simultaneously condemning the Nazi crimes, and, in the more universal sense, they were opening the way to a genuine jurisdiction for the denunciation and condemnation of war crimes wherever committed, and whoever the culprits, the Nuremberg Tribunal still demonstrates a change of crucial importance: the substitution of *jus ad bellum* by *jus contra bellum*.[2]

Unfortunately, as happens whenever a new body is created by the demands of history, this Tribunal possessed certain serious weaknesses. It was criticized for having been the simple diktat of the victors upon the vanquished and, which amounts to the same thing, that it was not really international: one group of nations was judging another. Would it have been better to have selected the judges from neutral countries? I cannot say. What is certain, however, is that, although the decisions were perfectly just by ethical standards, they did not convince all Germans. And that means that the legitimacy of the judges and their sentences is contested to this day. Also, people have declared that, if the fortunes of war had been otherwise, a tribunal of the Axis could have condemned the Allies for the bombing of Dresden or for that of Hiroshima.

A body that was legitimate would not have been difficult to set up. It would have been enough to continue the body created for judging the Nazis after it completed its original task, or that the United Nations, drawing all the consequences of what had just been achieved, would have, by a vote of the General Assembly, consolidated it into a permanent tribunal and empowered it to investigate and judge all accusations of war crimes, even if the accused were among the countries whose judges had been responsible for the sentencing at Nuremberg. Thus the implicit universality of the original intention would have been clearly defined. However, we know what happened: hardly had the last guilty German been sentenced than the Tribunal vanished in thin air and was never heard of again.

Are we then so pure? Have there been no war crimes since 1945? Have we never again resorted to violence or to aggression? Have there been no more "genocides"? Has no large country ever tried to destroy by force the sovereignty of a smaller one? Has there never been reason in the entire world for denouncing more Oradours or Auschwitzes? You know the truth: in the last twenty years, the great historical fact has been the struggle of the Third World for its freedom. The colonial empires have crumbled, and in their place sovereign nations have arisen or have reclaimed their previous and traditional independence which had been destroyed by colonialism. All this has happened amidst suffering, sweat, and blood. A tribunal such as that of Nuremberg has become a permanent necessity. I have already said that, before the Nazi trials, war was lawless. The Nuremberg Tribunal, an ambiguous reality, no doubt was created according to the highest legal principles but, at the same time, it opened a future possibility, by creating a precedent and the embryo of a tradition. Nobody can go back, deny what once existed, nor, when a small and poor country is the object of aggression, be kept from recalling those trials and saying to oneself: this is the very same thing that was condemned then. In this way, the hasty and incomplete measures taken and then abandoned by the Allies in 1945 have created a real gap in international affairs. Painfully, we lack an organism—which had been created and affirmed in its permanency and universality and which had irreversibly defined its rights and duties, but which has left a gap which *must* be filled and yet which no one is filling.

There are, in fact, two sources of power for such a body. The first is the state and its institutions. However, in this period of violence most governments, if they took such an initiative, would fear that it might one day be used against them and that they would find themselves in the dock with the accused. And also, for many, the United States is a powerful ally: Who would dare ask for the resurrection of a tribunal whose first undertaking would be to order an inquiry into the Vietnam conflict? The other source is the people, who in a time of revolution change their institutions. But, although the struggle is implacable, how could the masses, divided by borders, succeed in uniting and imposing on the various governments an institution which would be a true Court of the People?

The Russell Tribunal was born of this doubly contradictory

realization: the Nuremberg judgment made necessary the existence of an institution to inquire into war crimes and, if necessary, to judge them; today neither governments nor the masses are capable of creating one. We are perfectly aware that we have not been given a mandate by anyone; however, we initiated such a tribunal knowing that nobody could give us a mandate. It is true that our Tribunal is not an institution. But *this is because it is not a substitute for any existing institution*: it is the result of a void and fills a real need. We were not recruited or invested with real powers by governments: but, as we have just seen, investiture at Nuremberg was not enough to give the jurists unquestioned legitimacy... The Russell Tribunal believes, on the contrary, that its legitimacy comes from both its absolute powerlessness and its universality.

We are powerless: this is the guarantee of our independence. There is nothing to help us except for the participation of the supporting committees which are, like ourselves, meetings of private individuals. As we do not represent any government or party, we cannot receive orders. We will examine the facts "to the best of our knowledge and belief," as the expression goes, or, if one prefers, with full independence of mind or judgment. None of us can say, today, how the discussions will turn out and whether we answer yes or no to the accusations, or whether we will come to a conclusion at all, perhaps deciding that the evidence, though real, is insufficiently proven. What is certain, in any case, is that our impotence, even if we are convinced by the evidence brought before us, prevents us from imposing punishment. What can even the lightest sentence mean if we do not have the means to put it into effect? We will therefore limit ourselves, should this arise, to declaring that this or that act does in fact fall under the jurisdiction of Nuremberg, and that it is therefore a war crime, and that, if the law were applied, it would be appropriate for this or that sentence to be carried out. In this case, if possible, we will name the guilty. Thus, the Russell Tribunal will have no other function, in this inquiry and its conclusions, than to make everybody understand the necessity for an international institution—which it has neither the means nor the ambition to become. Its essence would be to revive the *jus contra bellum*, stillborn at Nuremberg, and to substitute legal, ethical rules for the law of the jungle.

From the very fact that we are only citizens, we have been able, in drawing our members from all over the world, to give our Tribunal a more universal structure than was the case at Nuremberg. Not only are a larger number of countries represented; from this point of view there remain still many gaps. But, most of all, while in 1945 the Germans were represented only in the dock, or sometimes as witnesses, here several members of the jury are from the United States. This means that they come from the country whose very policies are being scrutinized and that they have, therefore, a way of understanding it that is unique to them. Whatever may be their conclusions, the intimate relation with their own country and its institutions and traditions will necessarily be reflected in this Tribunal's conclusions.

Whatever may be our desire for impartiality and universality, we are very conscious of the fact that this does not legitimize our undertaking. We really want this legitimacy to be retrospective, or a posteriori. In fact we are not working for ourselves nor for our own edification, and we do not presume to impose our conclusions like a bolt of lightning. In truth, we want, with the help of the press, to maintain constant contact between ourselves and the masses who, in all parts of the world, are painfully watching the tragedy in Vietnam. We hope that they will be learning as we are learning, that together with us they will discover the reports, the documents and statements by the eyewitnesses, that they will evaluate them and gradually arrive at their own conclusions. Whatever these conclusions may be, we hope that they arrive at them at the same time as we do and perhaps even before then. This session is a communal undertaking for which the final term should be, as a philosopher said, "a truth that has become."[3] If the masses ratify our judgment, it will become truth, and we, at the very moment when we step back so that the people will become the guardians and powerful supporters of that truth, will then know that we have been legitimized. When the people show their agreement they will also unveil a greater demand: namely, that a real "War Crimes Tribunal" be created on a permanent basis in order that these crimes may be denounced and not sanctioned anywhere or at any time.

These last remarks allow me to reply to a critical comment made, without hostility by the way, by a Paris newspaper: "What a strange Tribunal: it has a jury but no judge." It is true, we only form a jury, we have no power to condemn, nor to acquit anyone. Therefore, no Ministry of Justice. There will not even be a real bill of indictment. Instead Judge Matarasso, president of the Legal Commission, will read a list of the charges that are being leveled. The jurors, at the end of the session, will have to pronounce on these: Are they justified or not? Besides, judges exist everywhere. They are the peoples of this world and, in particular, the American people. We are working for them.

ISRAEL AND THE ARAB WORLD

What is your opinion of the unfolding developments of the Middle East drama and in particular of General de Gaulle's policies[1] in this respect?

I am in favor of a negotiated peace treaty. Both for political reasons and because I am friendly toward both camps. In general, the Arabs have not much liked my statements and neither have the Israelis. Even so, my belief that a negotiated peace treaty is needed is inspired by what I consider to be everybody's interests. Obviously, in my mind that means 1) that, in one way or the other, Israel will have to give back the occupied territories and even that it should make the decision to do so on its own initiative and without being pressured; 2) that Israel's sovereignty must be recognized; and 3) that from the start the Palestinian problem must be the object of the first negotiations because that problem is crucial. (Obviously, it is regrettable that the Palestinian problem is never dealt with in the declarations of the Israeli government.)

Do you see the negotiations taking place under the aegis of the United Nations or of some other international organization? Or do you think that the Jews and the Arabs can arrive at these negotiations all by themselves? But that does not seem to be happening.

I find it deplorable that a decision can be dictated by the great powers; I would find it deplorable if finally everything should result in a negotiated settlement between the Soviets and the Americans and then was imposed on the two parties. The true solution, the only solution, must be the result of direct negotiations. But since the situation, hardly lends itself to it, there is indeed only one place where that can and must be undertaken and that is the United Nations. Unfortunately, the UN's decision will probably reflect that of the great powers. No: not the four great powers because that is a sham. The two other powers [France and Great Britain] should not be allowed to participate. Neither [France] nor Great Britain should be seriously consulted. There is no more reason to consult us than those others who have a greater stake in the problem or who are in fact more important.

Having said that, I don't see that an abrupt and angry gesture can be helpful at all. [De Gaulle's] arms embargo is really an unacceptable capricious gesture that is meaningless. It is a way for France to draw attention to itself and to want to be associated with those who are really going to settle the conflict.

Couldn't the other "great powers"—Great Britain, the Soviet Union, and the United States—be urged to suspend their arms shipments to the Arabs as well as of course to the Jews? You know that de Gaulle has pretended, I don't know if it is true, that the Arabs had not received any arms at all for a year and a half. Hence if the four "great powers" really implemented such a decision on a bilateral basis—

De Gaulle has given arms to Iraq, and you know that there are Iraqi troops ready to intervene in the conflict. Besides, I don't think that France's decision to impose an embargo will be imitated by the great powers. General de Gaulle's decision will have no impact, none whatsoever. It must really be recognized that everything General de Gaulle has been doing for the last several years is never of any consequence. There are never any results, except negative ones. In general, one shouldn't play at being a great power when you aren't one. In addition, this brutal intervention is at the same time dishonest: a contract has been signed, money has been received. Hence, in exchange one must deliver the product specified in the contract. No honest person has ever violated such a contract. And that can't lead to anything except to inflame passions. Because the Israelis will be even harder to deal with when they become aware that they had friends in France and that suddenly it is no longer the case. The Palestinians, on the other hand, will see in it a sign that their cause has met with complete approval. Therefore the conflict will intensify on both sides.

Ultimately the solution of not giving arms to anybody will result in this: the Israelis will in fact manufacture their own and Egypt will receive them from the Soviets. But let's suppose that ideally no one has arms anymore; at that point you will have eighty million people against two million. If you eliminate the firepower on both sides, you will solve the problem by abandoning these two million people to those eighty million people. I am not saying that some people don't wish such a solution. I simply note that, if you pretend to arrive at a peace treaty by taking away everybody's weapons, you will in fact deliver the State of Israel into the hands of the Arabs.

But where then do you see hope for peace? Especially if you believe that the United Nations does not possess sufficient moral authority to impose an eventual peace treaty?

I believe that a lot of things are in Israel's hands. And I find that Israel's policies are very dangerous in particular since they are letting doubt hover over the occupied territories. Nobody knows if they are occupied militarily simply for security reasons or if these are territories that are going to be annexed. Nobody knows because no statements have been made on this subject in the Knesset. No minister has broached the subject. Besides, it would have to be proved that hanging on to them is militarily necessary: on the contrary, to have such long borders could present a danger for two million mobilized men. For example, I know that at the same time that they are occupying these areas, they are leaving areas along the Lebanese border exposed—and it is very volatile right now. To protect the Lebanese border, they would have to evacuate other parts of the territories. And then again, what has been the experience of these last years? As was the case for the English, the French, or the Dutch, an occupied country never remains so for a long time. We have had to abandon all our colonies; and in this case we are not talking about colonies, these territories are under military occupation. But, in the long run, such a costly operation is ruinous. And, in addition, the adversaries' forces become more and more active and one ends up abandoning [the territories] while it would have been more advantageous to have done so as quickly as possible.

Do you see signs indicating that at least a handful of important and intelligent people in Israel wish to change this military policy?

I think so. There are signs of that. Or at least there were, because Israeli opinion is changing given the nature of current developments. The left wing of the Mapam[2]—and I personally know some of its members very well—was in favor of such a change; it would have consisted of an immediate declaration that the occupied territories are so only militarily and [Israel] is even willing to envisage a withdrawal of the troops (perhaps with guarantees). On the other hand, those left-wing Mapam members proposed first of all to resolve the problem of the Palestinian refugees. For example, one of its most intelligent members told me: "For the Israelis the valid interlocutor is El Fatah." You see, there are people who were pursuing this direction. Unfortunately, they are a minority.

But could Israel, without running immense dangers, absorb that mass of obviously very poor refugees who are perhaps less diligent workers than the Israelis? Wouldn't they represent a terrible dead weight?

You know there are already many Israeli Arabs and they are far from representing a dead weight. But they also suffer quite often from a certain kind of discrimination. In some ways, this is not the fault of the Israelis because they far outnumber the Arabs: as a result, the Arabs carry barely any weight in the opposition. Economically, the Arabs are very often second-class citizens. Once again, this is first of all a natural fact because the birth rate among the Arab population is greater than among the Israelis. As they say, put a young Arab couple and a young Israeli couple in two completely identical homes and, ten years later, the Israeli couple with one child will have a standard of living twice as high as the Arab couple which will have several children. But, at the same time, in other areas there is definite economic segregation: Arab workers don't have access to certain trades; they're not allowed the opportunity for technical training; they are found especially in construction and agriculture.

But the Palestinian problem must be resolved aside from these considerations. First of all it must be raised as the subject of negotiations, because the Palestinians have the strict right to return to their homeland.

Hence, in your estimation the Palestinians have the legal and historical right to the land of Israel equally with the Jews? Because, on the one hand, people, depending on their feelings or their prejudices, will tell you: "But what about Jerusalem . . . the Wailing Wall . . . etc.: since all of Antiquity these are Israel's holy places." And then again others will reply: "Yes, but the Arabs have lived there for seven or eight hundred years. It is their homeland too."

I don't see the problem at all like that but rather as follows. For me, Israel's sovereignty consists in this: among those who are over forty years old, most Israeli Jews who settled in Israel since the beginning of the century or later have not exploited these territories *in a colonial manner* because one cannot speak of a colonial exploitation of the Arabs. To the extent that it exists, it is a capitalist exploitation, if you like, just as there are exploited Israeli Jews—and we are not speaking of an excessive kind of exploitation. These people who settled there have had children and there are even those who are grandchildren of pioneers. Those who are born in the country and don't have a place elsewhere have acquired a trade: they work. They have the right to sovereignty over that country.

As far as the Palestinians are concerned, I don't know how long they were there. But I have seen them, I went to see them in Gaza: for a fairly large part they are still relatively young and hence they have really been expelled from *their* country and now they are living in a huge slum. Simply because they have been expelled, they have the right to return. You'll tell me: "They weren't expelled, it was at the behest of the mufti's appeals that they left, etc." All that is quite complicated; it is certain that there were at that moment mixed responsibilities. Nevertheless, they became afraid and left their country and because they were terrified they left in great numbers and in a perfectly unjust manner. If I recognize that the child or a grandchild of a Jew who settled in Israel has the right to remain in his country because he lives there and shouldn't be expelled, I recognize that the Palestinians, in virtue of the same principle, have the right to return to it.

You know very well that the Jews refuse to the Palestinians the right to that term that you just used: homeland. They say, "Arab countries are their homeland. Since they are Arabs, the neighboring countries should have accepted them."

But no; their homeland is after all the place where they work, where they were born. It would be as if we Frenchmen were chased out of France and told that our country can be any European country whatsoever, since we are Europeans. In that case we should have no choice but to find our home in Germany? . . . That does not make a lot of sense.

The Arabs who have been expelled live in unacceptable conditions. They have children who were born in very bad conditions and grandchildren who are quite rightly haunted by the idea of returning to Palestine. Let me repeat myself: one can't take away sovereignty from the Israelis because they are living in Palestine for several generations and don't exploit the country in a colonial manner. But I also say in a similar vein: the people who have been expelled must have the right to return.

Then what would you foresee . . . a federation?

Just a second . . . I am not a politician, I am an intellectual. I am telling you what I see simply in the name of international law, that's all . . .

But what I would like to add is that if you say, "The Arabs are exploiting the issue," I would answer that when I was in Egypt I saw such misery among the peasants (in spite of the very real efforts of the government to improve their condition) that I told myself: "To accuse the Egyptians of not wishing to absorb this mass of peasants while they are having such difficulty in providing for their own peasants, and while the Aswan Dam—that marvelous undertaking—is going to prove insufficient and be overtaken by the demographic increase, is after all an example of bad faith."

However, the Jews reply: "We find ourselves in the same situation, we are not rich, all we have is our hands and our courage. We don't want those poverty-stricken people who will be a burden and be much more like dead weights than productive citizens."

That's not where the problem lies, it is matter of rights. As long as the problem is not faced directly, there will be El Fatah, there will be the Palestinian Liberation Front, that's absolutely certain. As a result, there will be increased tension and ultimately a new war. There are certainly people who despair in Israel, who occasionally think that, perhaps, there will no longer be an Israel. But others think, on the contrary, that precisely in order to ensure Israel's survival, the Palestinian problem must be solved. As long as that is not the case, the Arab countries will protect their own, that is to say the Palestinians. Therefore El Fatah, and consequently war.

In any case, I don't think terrorism is the answer.

Listen, unfortunately, I don't see any other solution at this moment. I can't reproach the Palestinians for doing what I approved of when it was the Algerian FLN that did it, nor for fighting with the means available to them. If they were sufficiently numerous, they would use other means to fight—terrorism is a weapon of the poor and has always existed—but ultimately it is also in certain cases the road toward a people's war... Neither do I reproach the Israelis for counterattacking, because one can't ask them to let themselves be killed systematically without reacting. Especially since this process is likely to grow given that the members of El Fatah possess a courage that is admirable—and at the same time are a little desperate. There is no reason that it shouldn't continue . . .

All this has begun badly, because with El Fatah we are dealing with individual groups that act while Israel responds at the government level. As a result one gets the kind of comments that I consider to be in bad faith: "Israel has attacked a country that never declared war on it even during the Six-Day War, and it went to Beirut to destroy weaponry." But that was Israel's only possible reaction. Because the other reaction would have been to go and massacre the inhabitants of a village of whom it would have been said that they were members of El Fatah, but who in fact—after all this is true in certain cases—may well be innocent villagers. That's not a solution either. Hence, on that level, the Israelis are in a corner, because it is not on the same level.

That is to say that the acts are the same: but it appears to be more serious coming from Israel because it is more "official."

Precisely. Therefore, given these conditions, there is only one possible solution: a negotiated settlement. And in that case one can ask more of Israel than the others. But even so, the peace treaty has to be negotiated on bases that make discussion possible: the withdrawal of Israeli troops could even precede the opening of discussions. Or at least, right now, preceding the troop withdrawal, Israel could announce that the occupation of the territories is temporary. Immediately thereafter would follow the discussion of the Palestinian problem even if this is done through intermediaries. These are the things that will allow one to ask the Arabs to recognize Israel's borders and its sovereignty. I don't see any other solution.

The 1948 borders?

Yes. There is however also the question of Eilat. It appears that the

Israelis didn't have it in 1948, but, truthfully, I don't think it is a problem and Israel must be left an outlet to the Red Sea . . . Let me repeat, the problem is exclusively a return to the borders as they existed with respect to Jordan and Sinai, and then to discuss all the questions.

All that is, let's admit it, infinitely complex, because there are a lot of possibilities. There could be two federated countries . . . But there are a thousand possibilities, and it's not up to me to discuss them.

In any case it is a pity that no Israeli official has ever stated publicly: "We want to negotiate the refugee problem." All the Israelis I know and who are on the left think the opposite; for them it is the first problem that should be resolved.

Do the Arab officials appear in favor, at least on paper, of negotiations?

Perhaps I wouldn't go that far. But the tone has certainly changed recently; I believe that the idea could soon become acceptable in Egypt. First, I believe that Nasser didn't want war at all; it broke out because of a series of misunderstandings. All at once, everybody was caught in the web. There was an article in *Al Ahram* that *New Outlook* quoted a few months ago and that had been written four days before the war broke out, at the time when the UN troops had already withdrawn. This article stated: "War will break out because Israel can't accept what we have done." A curious article because in a certain way it said: "Dayan is going to attack us because we did all that is necessary for him to attack us." From my viewpoint, this was already a warning against the hotheads that exist down there.

I had seen Nasser three months earlier in March–April 1967. He knew I was going to Israel, therefore I will say what he told me. And I have maintained, and I still do so, that the man I saw didn't want war. I asked him a question solely on this one point.

"The Palestinians must return to their homeland," he said.

"But," I said, "will Israel accept—"

And Nasser answered: "Israel can't accept."

We were left with that contradiction.

"Well, then what—" I said.

And he replied: "Do you want to say there will be war? Hmm! How difficult, how painful!"

Hence his point of view was: "There is a contradiction we aren't able to resolve. But solving it through war doesn't appear to be the right solution."

That's where we left off in March 1967. Since that time...

THE SOCIALISM THAT CAME
IN FROM THE COLD

The voices heard in this book were raised between 1966 and the first months of 1968; a timid dawn shed its light on the Slovakian Carpathians, the Moravian plain, the mountains of Bohemia. Had there been just a bit more light, we might have seen these men—men who had been hidden from our eyes by clouds ever since we turned them over to the Nazis in return for twelve months of peace—in broad daylight.[1]

It was not dawn, no lark was singing; since then socialism has been plunged back into the long night of its Middle Ages. I remember what my Soviet friend used to tell me around 1960: "Be patient; it will take time perhaps, but you'll see. The process is irreversible." But sometimes I have the feeling that nothing has been irreversible except the continuous, implacable degradation of Soviet socialism. These Slovak and Czech voices remain, bouquets of snipped-off puffs of breath, still warm and alive, disavowed and unrefuted. One cannot hear them without feeling ill at ease; they speak of a sinister and grotesque past, they tell us that it is buried forever, and yet this resuscitated past has once again become the interminable present of Czechoslovakia; they prudently gave voice to a better future that a great gust of wind soon snuffed out like a candle. One is tempted to compare these voices to the light that comes to us from dead stars, all the more so since they bore a message, before the country was once again plunged into silence, that was not addressed to us. However, we today *must* understand them; I shall try to explain here why these voices concern us.

Fourteen interviews, fifteen accounts, or if you prefer, fifteen confessions. For a confession, in the sense in which Rousseau took the word, is the exact opposite of self-criticism. Those who speak here—Nobel Prize winners, dramatists, poets, essayists, and even a philosopher—seem relaxed, even-tempered, rarely harsh, and often ironic; if they burn with revolutionary rage, they scarcely show it. They affirm less than they question, less than they question themselves. Aside from this, they differ in every respect. Some of them are sons of workers, of peasants, of teachers. Jiří Mucha's father was a painter, Milan Kundera's a musician, and Václav Havel comes from the prewar upper middle class. Some are Czechs, others Moravians, and others Slovaks. Laco Novomeský, the eldest, was sixty-two when these interviews took place; the youngest, Havel, who was thirty-two, could well have been his son. Novomeský saw the birth, in 1918, and the collapse, in 1938, of the first Czechoslovakian Republic; he was one of the known leaders of the Slovak National Uprising; and as a cabinet minister after the war he helped make his country what it has become, though this did not prevent him a little later from acquiring, like so many others, firsthand experience of what a prison was like.

Havel was two years old at the time of the surrender at Munich, fifteen when the trials began.[2] The mature men's ages range between the ages of these two. They represent three generations, the first of which was the destiny of the third, and the third of which willingly made itself the judge of the two others; the second, both victim and accomplice, was attracted to both the others by undeniable affinities while, at the same time, it kept itself apart from them because of definite antagonisms. This is what this book is about—intellectuals take a look around them and inside them and ask themselves: "What happened?"

I fear that these last words will put more than one reader off: "Intellectuals? This mandarin caste has no right to speak in the name of the people." These witnesses have therefore been very careful not to do this; they speak as Czech citizens to their fellow citizens. Not to you. And the people to whom they are really addressing themselves seem to have been less supercilious than you are, since for several decisive years, culture, as Liehm puts it, took over the role of politics. The reason for this is that despite their divergences, their opposition, it is possible by reading between the lines to reconstruct a common discourse on twenty-five years of Czechoslovakian history from their various shades of meaning, their hesitations, and the diversity of their characters. It is this discourse—such as I understood it when I read it—that I would like to analyze with you before you read the accounts themselves.

"What happened?"

Novomeský, the first of these intellectuals to question himself, goes straight to the heart of the matter: Czechoslovakia's present misfortunes stem from its having adopted a ready-made socialism. He is in the best position to speak of the years that immediately followed the war: In 1945, nobody wanted to restore the First Republic. It had collapsed *before* the occupation, in Munich. For these angry young men capitulation was not only the fault of their allies, but first and foremost the fault of their national middle class.

The humanism of Edvard Beneš[3] was nothing but a plaster mask, a mask that had crumbled to dust. Behind it there was no human face, not even a pitiless one—only cogs in a machine. As a proof of this: Why had the united Czech people not risen up against the German *diktat* in 1938? Would this have been useless? Would insurrection have resulted in a bloodbath? Perhaps. But perhaps, too, an uprising would have forced the Allies to revise their policy. In any event, resistance was better than passivity. But what was the cause of this passivity? Beyond the shadow of a doubt it stemmed from the relationship of people to production, that is to say, from bourgeois institutions. The country's high degree of industrialization developed "massifying" forces that destroyed the unity of the workers and tended to make each of them a solitary molecule; the reign of profit, which is a thing, imposed the dispersion and the inertia of things on men. When the insurgents came to power after the liberation, they swore that no more would be seen of this powerless society.

Socialism for them was first and foremost the overthrow of the golden calf, the integration of everyone in a *human* collectivity, full citizenship for everyone, full rights to participate in the economic, political, and social administration of the country; they would strike while the iron was hot and obtain this national unity that they had been unable to obtain when circumstances demanded it, putting the fate of all in the hands of all, which could be done only on one basis: the socialization of the means of production.

The reasons that a nation has for coming to socialism matter little; the essential thing is for the nation to build it with its own hands. The truth, Hegel writes, is something that has *become*.[4] And this is also the underlying principle of psychoanalysis: It would be useless, or harmful, if one knew the secrets of the patient (which is not possible), to reveal them to him, to *give* him his truth like a hard blow on the head with a cudgel; the only proper way to do this is for him to look for it himself and change himself by the very act of searching, in such a way that he will discover it when he is prepared to bear it. What applies to the individual in this case also applies to great collective movements: The proletariat must emancipate itself on its own, forge its arms and its class consciousness in daily battle, so as to take power when it is capable of exercising it. This was not the case in the USSR, but the fact remains that one makes oneself a socialist by making socialism, as much by the efforts one forces oneself to make to set up the required structures and destroy the old ones, both outside oneself and within, as by the functioning of the institutions that have been set up. This is what Lenin said, pointing to Soviet men who were uncertain, still imbued with ideologies of the old regime, and for the most part illiterate: It was *with them* and *by them* that the new society was to be built. And this is exactly what the revolutionaries wanted in Bohemia, in Slovakia: To change themselves by changing the world, to make themselves, by the patient and stubborn building of *their* socialism, socialists who have *become*. Today, as you will see in this book, several of them call Yalta "another Munich." At the time, they were full of gratitude toward the USSR, which had just freed them, and dazzled by its victory, which they held to be the triumph of a free society over a great capitalist power, or, more simply, the triumph of Good over Evil. All they asked was to remain within the zone of Soviet influence, not dreaming of denying the leadership of their "big brother." What they wanted was to benefit from its experience and its advice but do the work themselves, taking their own problems, their own particular situation, their own resources, their own history, and their own culture as the point of departure. This little binational country, Czechoslovakia, highly industrialized, a hundred times invaded and enslaved, had no model to copy. It was necessary for it to invent its own path, by way of errors surmounted, deviations corrected, distortions set to rights—as was to be the case with Cuba fifteen years later—so as to be able one day to recognize itself in its work.

The country was spared this trouble. The two great powers each made a contribution: after Yalta, the Marshall Plan. We know what followed. In 1948 the communists took power and the big brother gave its little brother a prefabricated socialism as a gift. In the USSR, this socialism had evolved as best it could, turning out more on the very bad side than on the fairly good side.[5] At least it was an answer— during the first years—to the difficulties of a vast country that was almost entirely agricultural and still in the process of being industrialized, without a middle class and almost without a proletariat after the civil war and its massacres, a country which the bloc of capitalist powers forced to be autonomous—that is to say, to sacrifice the peasant class to the production of heavy equipment. Since there was no working class and since it therefore could not exercise its dictatorship, the party saw itself forced to exercise it in its place, or rather, in the place of a future working class.

Most people are familiar with the extraordinary demographic upheaval that was both the means and the result of socialist accumulation. In order to rebuild the secondary sector, money was skimmed off the primary sector, as happens everywhere, but the metamorphosis was so hasty that the party had to forge the new working class by forcing the peasants required by industry into a mold. These mutants had none of the traditions of the old revolutionary proletariat. Where could they have come by them? It was necessary to proceed with an accelerated acculturation through various manipulations: In the face of the stubborn vestiges of the old ideologies, that "first nature" that passed itself off as spontaneity, an effort was made to create a "second nature" which would wipe out the first by conditioning reflexes and weighing down people's memories with a ballast of mini-Marxist maxims that would assure that the thought of the masses would have the required stability, weight, and inertia. Driven by the necessities of the moment, the party, far from *expressing* the consciousness of the workers, was forced to *produce* it. The only real force in this immense invertebrate country, it saw itself obliged to enhance its powers: Instead of contributing to the state's withering away through its critical independence, the party reinforced the state by identifying itself with it, but it was thereby afflicted with administrative sclerosis; constituting a majority in all elected assemblies, this gigantic apparatus was half paralyzed by its omnipotence: In its omnipresence and its solitude, it could not *see itself*. At first all this was only a means to cope with problems as speedily as possible, only a dangerous deviation (Lenin was aware of this), a provisional means that doubtless could be corrected, until the bureaucracy, the inevitable product of the accumulation of responsibilities, transformed it into a definite system. Soviet society little by little built a structure around this spinal cord and in half a century became what it is today.

Everybody is familiar with this history; it is useless to ponder whether things could have turned out differently. What is certain is that the relationship of people to production was *set up* in the USSR because of the pressure of a vital need: production at any price. This end, at least, was *forced upon* an almost entirely agricultural country which had just socialized the means of production; electrification gobbled up the Soviets, but it was at least partially successful in that it was a necessity in that place, at that time.

Czechoslovakia, for its part, had gone beyond the phase of primitive accumulation and was very embarrassed by the sort of socialism so politely bestowed upon it. Czechoslovakia had no need of developing its heavy industry since its resources came, before the war, from prosperous processing industries. As for autonomy—that horse medicine which, in the beginning, the USSR forced down its own throat*—this little nation that lived on exchanges with the outside, exporting consumer goods and importing most of its heavy equipment, had no reason and, despite the richness of its subsoil, no means to bring this about. With firm ties to the socialist zone, all Czechoslovakia needed to do was to change customers.† The extension of its production and above all the absurd reversal of its top-priority objectives was to rapidly lead it to *produce for the sake of producing*, when it should on the contrary have reorganized its already existing industries to conform to the needs of the people and to the *just* demands of its new clientele, and when, above all, it should have sought to improve its productivity. Though the identification of the party and the state had been necessary—or had appeared to be necessary "in fateful circumstances"[6]—in order to control demographic trends in an agricultural country in the process of industrialization, what sense did it make for a nation of fourteen million inhabitants, a considerable portion of which was made up of an intact proletariat that during the First Republic had acquired, through its struggles, its defeats, its very powerlessness, an undeniable class conscience and strong workers' traditions? Czechoslovakia could have been the first power to pass successfully from an advanced capitalist economy to a socialist economy, thereby offering the proletariat of the West, if not a model, at least an incarnation of their revolutionary future. It lacked nothing, neither the instruments nor the men; if administration of a country by workers was possible anywhere, it was in Prague and Bratislava. To its misfortune, the string-pullers in Moscow, manipulated by their own manipulations, couldn't even grasp that brand of socialism. They imposed *the system* instead. This imported, unsuitable model, without real foundations but supported from the outside by the solicitude of "big brother," thus presented itself as an idol—that is to say, as a fixed whole made up of unconditional demands which neither could be nor were discussed, which could not be explained and which remained unexplained. The Czech workers had freed themselves of the reign of

---

* Also because the USSR had the means to live on its own resources.

† Which, moreover, it did, substituting the USSR for Germany, though under conditions that are common knowledge.

456 · JEAN-PAUL SARTRE

profit only to fall into that of fetishized production. One nail drives out another; the "thing in power" in the old republic was driven out and replaced by another "thing," one alienation substituted by another alienation. As soon as the heavy machine was put in working order it dislocated the country's structures and ravaged it, slowly at first, then more and more rapidly.

One can, of course, say that this socialism bestowed on Czechoslovakia was made by the Czechs and Slovaks, or rather through them. The trouble is that it did not socialize them. Let us be clear on this point: The men of 1945 were convinced revolutionaries and most of them remained so, but the system forbade them to experience the building of socialism themselves. In order to change them, they would have had to be taken as they were; the system took them as they were not. Instead of presenting itself as an open set of problems requiring at one and the same time a rational transformation of the structures and a continual, thoroughgoing re-examination of ideas—in short a reciprocal and dialectical conditioning of praxis and theory—it lay claim, with incredible conceit, to being a gracious gift of providence, a socialism without tears—in other words, without a revolution and without the slightest chance of being called into question. The tasks were already defined, and needed only to be performed; knowledge was a closed area and needed only to be learned by heart.

Let us not be surprised if, under such conditions, the men of the first generation, those who militated within the Czech Communist Party before the war and resisted under the occupation, returned, as Novomeský says, to their 1920 options after 1956. Having been unable to build anything, they changed nothing; boxed in, hidden by the slogans raining down like stones, the memories of former times, the hopes of their youth were intact; all the more so in that, for many, they provided a silent refuge from the official line. It is their misfortune that this memory, however vivid it may seem to them, smells of mold. What a mad idea—to relive one's twenties when one is sixty! In the same way, and for the same reason, the old collective base was not touched.

Our fifteen witnesses insist on this point: Families, churches, local or national traditions, currents of thought, ideologies, the entire heritage that would have been superseded or modified by a socialism in the process of becoming, was either maintained or strengthened under the established order. We hear of the growing influence of Catholicism in Brno, while some of our witnesses report that the relations between Bohemia and Slovakia, which were always somewhat tense, have steadily deteriorated rather than improved, as perhaps they would have done if both peoples had been engaged in a great common undertaking. Even though the old ways have remained virulent beneath the mantle of semisecrecy, we must not conclude that human relations have not been changed by the new regime. From 1948 to 1956 they worsened day by day; a false relationship of people to a production economy was established because the economy had been doctored and power had been reified.

Let it be said, first of all, that the system deprived citizens of any real participation in this national undertaking at the very moment when it was calling upon them to work together. I shall not even try to speak here of self-management by workers, nor of control exercised by regularly elected assemblies; the system, as has been seen, is allergic to these passing fancies on the part of leftists. I am thinking of this inevitable corollary of imported socialism: the radical, dizzying depoliticalization of a country which the occupation and the resistance had profoundly politicalized. All our witnesses agree on this point. The "thing," obviously, could not function without men. It recruited men who were things, blockheads that it changed into brickheads; these then became men literally possessed by power, hierarchized bureaucrats, each of whom ruled in the name of another, his superior, this other in the name of yet another, and the man highest on the ladder in the name of the "thing" itself. The "thing" is, by its very essence, incapable of adapting itself or of progressing. (The least little shift threatens to shatter it.) It therefore has no need to renew its cadres, or rather, it need *not* renew them. If a bureaucrat disappears, he is replaced by another who resembles him like a twin and is hardly any younger than he is. The "system" keeps things in existence and keeps itself in existence; it has no other end than to persevere in its being; for this reason it has a tendency to produce a gerontocracy, for old

people are generally conservative. As a consequence, the "first generation," the one that brought the system in, carefully kept the second
generation out of all the key posts. "We were eternal dauphins," says a
forty-year-old witness. And Kundera says:

> My generation was far from uniform.... Some emigrated, oth-
> ers became silent, still others adapted themselves, while others
> —including myself—adopted a kind of legal, constructive op-
> position. None of these postures was very dignified .... The
> emigrants soon ceased to be involved, internal emigration suf-
> fered from isolation and impotence, the "loyal opposition"
> could not help but be inconsistent and too prone to compro-
> mise, and those who completely adjusted are now dead, both
> morally and artistically. Nobody can really be satisfied with
> himself, and this bitter knowledge is the common basis of our
> whole paradoxical generation. When we are attacked by the
> youngsters, we no longer even have the desire to defend our-
> selves.

Powerless and compromised, kept out of public affairs by their elders, attacked by young people for having had too large a share in
them despite this—such is the "middle" generation; the members of
this generation rarely judge their elders very harshly, however; once
they've said that they were total failures and frauds, they occasionally
add, with a pity that is not without tenderness: "They had so little
chance to have any effect on anything." As for the aggressive young
people who sometimes revile them—much less than their elders—
they are afraid both of and for these youngsters; this generation is
skeptical and cynical, they explain, because they feel that they can do
nothing about anything. Raised in ignorance, at a time when knowledge was being degraded, they feared these youngsters would suffer a
fate worse than their own; they would yearn for the First Republic
because they would never discover how rotten it was, then they would
be progressively taken over by the regime, and, because it would be
necessary to live somehow, would perpetuate the regime without believing in it. That at least was what adults were predicting for their

younger brothers and sisters before the winter of 1967–1968. They were right about one thing: This third generation rejected, with horror and disgust, that prefabricated socialism which was supposed to be its fate. It was a fruitless rejection because, up until 1967, this generation had no purchase on anything. But what their elders did not understand was that one day all it would take would be an opening, some sort of possibility of undertaking a common action, for this impotent cynicism to change into revolutionary demands and for these "absurdist" young people to become, in the eyes of everyone, the generation of Jan Palach.* For this generation, in fact, the process of turning man into a mineral had barely begun.

Kosík and Kundera give us precious information about the nature of this process, which is all the more instructive in that they consider it from different points of view. The essential point is that the "thing" thought of Man only through the intermediary of its servants and, it goes without saying, conceived of him as a thing. Not as the subject of history but, necessarily, as its object. Blind and deaf to Man's specifically human dimensions, it reduced him to a mechanical system, not only in theory but in day-to-day practice—"a concept of Man," Kosík says, "implicit in the regime's political, economic, and moral functioning, one which was, at the same time, mass-produced by the regime because it required precisely this sort of human being."

What distinguishes *Homo bureaucraticus* is a whole concatenation of negative traits. He does not laugh. "The ruling political group in Czechoslovakia considered laughter totally irreconcilable with their...position." This is tantamount to saying that they had unlearned how to laugh. And if someone, contrary to the nature that had been forced upon him, permitted himself a joyful outburst, he ran grave risks and compromised everybody around him as was proved by the misadventure—recounted by Liehm—of the young scatterbrains who thought that they could poke fun at [the poet Vítězslav] Nezval with impunity. This grotesque episode, I imagine, was the origin of Kundera's book *The Joke*.[7] It is forbidden to *want* to laugh. A

---

* On January 15, 1969, the twenty-one-year-old Jan Palach immolated himself in St. Wenceslaus Square in Prague to protest the Soviet occupation of his country.

luminous imperative, which follows rigorously from the premise: Laughter calls things into question, so when the revolution is conservative, it is counterrevolutionary. The "official man," as Kosík says, doesn't die either "because ideology refused to acknowledge death." And for good reason: A robot isn't alive, and therefore it can't die; when it gets out of order, it is either repaired or scrapped. "In fact," Kosík adds, "he didn't even have a body." This means that the system has cogs and drive belts, but no organs, and that those who "think" in their place and for their benefit don't have eyes to see the organisms, those antibureaucratic integers that might risk taking themselves for ends if too much attention were paid to them. The Czech philosopher adds that *Homo bureaucraticus* knows neither the grotesque, nor the tragic, nor the absurd, because these existential categories have no discernible connection with production, and consequently no reality; they are merely mirages of the daydreaming bourgeoisies in the West. To conclude: "Official man had no conscience, since this category likewise did not officially exist." What in the devil would he do with one, as a matter of fact?

The paths are all laid out, the tasks ready and waiting; his reflexes will be conditioned by proven methods, including that cerebral reflex improperly referred to as thought. This marvelous object outside himself, moved by outside forces, works solely by virtue of Pavlovian mechanics; he is eminently manipulatable and infinitely liable to forced labor. "People," Kosík says, "are not born as ambitious career-seekers, blind to the needs of others, unthinking, unfeeling, prone to demoralization; rather, a certain system requires such people for its smooth functioning, and so it creates them."

The men of the system, those products of fetishized production, are suspect *by essence*; in fact, doubly suspect because they are turned into things and because they are never completely mere things. Robots can be manipulated and are, therefore, potential traitors; since those in power know how to work their controls, why couldn't foreign agents find out how to work them, too? And how does one know who is pulling the puppet's strings in that case? But to the very degree that men's mineralization is not complete—and it never is, for these mineral bipeds are men who live their mineralization in a human way—

their very existence constitutes a danger to the regime. To laugh, weep, die, or even sneeze is to give proof of a lurking spontaneity that is perhaps of bourgeois origin.

To live, in short, is to question things; if not in fact, at least potentially. A live man is a man to watch. The regime benefits twice over from this double suspicion. First of all—having no other end than itself and, owing to its lack of either outside control or mediations, a victim of its own unlimited power unable to recognize itself, unable to even conceive of the possibility that it might be criticized—it lays down the principle that one must suspect men rather than institutions. It therefore suits it that the animal in these animal-machines should sometimes reappear beneath the machinery. Animality is Evil, the irreducible residue of a succession of corrupted millennia. Criticism never reveals an imperfection in the system, but rather the profound vice of the man who made it, that serf-will which impels Man as a whole to sin sooner or later, at least in spirit, against the building of socialism. But, above all, the principle of the permanent corruptibility of *Homo bureaucraticus* has two undeniable advantages: It legitimizes the recourse to Machiavellian practices—buying or terrorizing, it allows the "thing" to liquidate its own ministers if need be. When the machine stalls or creaks, it eliminates a few men in charge rather than give itself over to be repaired—which, moreover, would be useless. These leaders are traitors who have sold out to the enemy; the motor itself was working quite nicely, its inexplicable "misfirings" were simply due to the fact that someone was trying to sabotage it. In short, the "thing" is forced to use men but it mistrusts them, scorns them, detests them, just as the master does his slaves or the boss his workers. Mistrust, hatred, and scorn will not cease so long as these noble sentiments essentially determine the relations of men among themselves and the relation of each man to himself.

But does it succeed in doing so? Our witnesses reply that there is no doubt that it does. At least in certain cases and up to a certain point. Who, then, allows it to? Those who have sold out, those who are cowards, those who are ambitious? On the contrary: the best men, the most sincere, the most devoted, the most scrupulous communists. Kundera tells us why. The mechanistic vision of Man is not, as Kosík

462 · JEAN-PAUL SARTRE

seems to think, the cause of bureaucratic socialism; it is the product of it and, if you like, of the ideology.

The Revolution of 1917 brought with it immense hopes; Marxist optimism existed side by side with old dreams of 1848, with Romantic ideals, with Babeuf's egalitarianism, with Utopias of Christian origin. When "scientific socialism" took over, it did not hesitate to discard this humanist bric-a-brac; it claimed to be the heir and the realizer of these idealistic but deep-seated ambitions; it was a question of freeing the workers from their chains, of putting an end to exploitation, of replacing the dictatorship of profit, where men are the products of their products, with a free classless society where they are their own product. When the party, once bureaucratized, came to identify itself with the state, these principles, these ideals, these great objectives did not disappear for all that; on the contrary, the spokesmen for power made frequent references to them in their speeches, at a time when numerous Muscovites had acquired the habit of not going to bed until the first light of dawn, after having assured themselves that the milkman had already come by.

The bureaucratic system had, of course, given rise to its own ideology long before. But this ideology was never explicit; present everywhere in people's acts, it could be glimpsed only in the turn of a phrase, a fleeting form, in the official speeches; it was masked by the other ideology, the one proclaimed *ad usum populi*, a vaguely Marxian humanism. This is what led the young Slovaks and the young Czechs astray. In 1945, galvanized by words, they fell into the trap. Is it not striking that Vaculík, one of the most implacable critics of the system, joined the party enthusiastically—he was twenty years old—because he had read Stalin's tract "Dialectical and Historical Materialism"? It is for this reason that Kundera, without pretending to compare German society to Soviet society, declares that Hitlerism was in one respect much less dangerous than what he calls Stalinism. Where the former was concerned, one at least knew what to expect. It spoke out loud and clear; rarely has the Manichaean vision of the world been more clearly stated. But Stalinism was something altogether different; one got lost in it. There were two points of reference in it, two visions of the world, two ideologies, two kinds of reason, the one dialectical, the other mechanistic. People repeated to you Gorky's irritating slogan: "The word 'Man' has a proud ring to it,"[8] while functionaries were deciding to send *individual men*, who were weak and sinful by nature, to state detention camps.

How could one find one's bearings? The socialist idea seemed to have gone mad. It hadn't, actually, but the servants of the "thing" demanded, without the slightest cynicism (so there is every reason to believe) that the system be accepted by their fellow citizens and by themselves in the name of socialist humanism. They presented—perhaps in good faith—the man of the future as the ultimate end of a daring and sublime undertaking in the name of which his ancestor, the man of the present, was called upon to allow himself to be treated, and to treat himself, like a thing *and* like a guilty man. This was not entirely their fault; their brains were afflicted with an ailment ordinarily located in the bladder: It was suffering from stones. But for all those who tried to look at themselves with the eyes of Medusa, out of loyalty to the principles of socialism, there resulted a generalized distortion of thought. This explains the apparent paradoxes that Kundera bitterly enumerates: "In art, the official doctrine was realism. But it was forbidden to speak of the real. The cult of youth was publicly celebrated, but our enjoyment of our own youth was frustrated. In those pitiless times, all we were shown on the screen was a series of tender and bashful lovers. Official slogans were full of joy, yet we didn't dare to play even the slightest prank." He would have better accounted for this situation, perhaps, if he had written: *In the name of realism*, we were forbidden to depict reality; *in the name of the cult of youth*, we were prevented from being young; *in the name of socialist joy*, joyousness was repressed.

And the worst part of it all was that this crude ruse found willing accomplices. So long as they still believed in bureaucratic socialism—at least as the thankless and painful way that leads to true socialism—these men used their living dialectical reason to justify the reign of petrified reason, which necessarily led them to give assent to the condemnation of the former by the latter. Convinced by propaganda that, as Mirabeau put it, "The road that leads from Evil to Good is worse than Evil," first they resigned themselves to Evil because they saw in it the one way to attain Good, then, goaded by what one of them has named "the demon of consent," they saw in it Good itself, and took their own resistance to the process of petrification to be Evil. Cement poured into them through their eyes and ears, and they considered the protests of their simple good sense to be the residue of a bourgeois ideology that cut them off from the people.

All the witnesses who are in their forties recognize this to be true; they felt a need to reject every temptation to criticize in advance, for fear that it might be a sign of the resurrection of individualism in them. They tell of how they carefully buried the slightest astonishment, or any unexpected discomfort, in the darkest corner of their memory, of how they forced themselves not to see anything that might have shocked them. There was a great risk, to be sure; a single doubt would have sufficed to put the whole system in question, and then, they were certain, questioning the system would have reduced them to ignominious solitude. Born during the First Republic, they bore the ineradicable marks of a culture which they must rid themselves of, at any cost, if they wanted to find themselves in agreement with the masses. As a matter of fact, the party line of the "thing" passed itself off as the very *thought* of the working class, and the proof of this was plain as day since the "thing" exercised its dictatorship in the name of the proletariat and was the consciousness of that class. No one really *thought* of the declarations of the "thing," for they represented precisely the *unthinkable*. But, at the time, each individual took them to be the certified expressions of Objective Spirit and, while waiting to understand them, learned them by heart and set them up, like mysterious icons, each in his own inner shrine. Everyone—whether worker, peasant, or intellectual—was unaware that he was the victim of an alienation and a new atomization. Each individual, accusing himself of subjectivism, wanted to break through his molecular isolation and rediscover the passionate unity of partisan and revolutionary action, in which each person comes to each other person not as *another* but as the *same*, and no one dared realize that what he was asked to do to erase his suspect individual differences was to deny himself, to make himself *other than himself* in order to join the others insofar as each of them was trying to make himself other than himself. These serialized men communicated among themselves only by the intermediary of *that-which-is-other-than-Man*. They thus plunged even deeper into solitude by the very efforts they made to escape it; and each, to the very degree that he mistrusted himself, mistrusted the other. In his introduction to this book, Liehm has vividly described the ultimate hysterical temptation, the logical consequence of the whole process: getting down on one's knees so as to believe, and replacing the process of reasoning by faith—*credo quia absurdum*. Which amounts to saying that in the reign of fetishized production every real man appears to himself, in his simple daily existence, as an obstacle to the building of socialism and can escape the crime of living only by doing away with himself altogether.

This obviously is an extreme consequence. For many workers it primarily meant a growing disinterest in public affairs, darkness, numbness. To make up for this, a title was bestowed on them; they were all "public servants." A fairly large number of intellectuals, on the contrary, were frenetic partisans of self-destruction. It must be noted that they were accustomed to such a role; in the bourgeois democracies as in the popular ones, these specialists of the universal are often encumbered by their singularity. But, as Kundera remarks, in the West their masochism is completely harmless; nobody notices it there, while, in the socialist countries, they are looked down upon and the powers that be are always ready to give them a helping hand if they want to destroy themselves. In Czechoslovakia they hastened to plead guilty at the slightest reproach, using their reason only to work the absurd accusation over until they had made it acceptable, and working themselves over until they could accept it. In the party, furthermore, the best leaders—who were not all intellectuals; far from it—also worked themselves over out of loyalty.

It is only when they are seen in this light that the confessions during the trials of the 1950s can be understood. They did not come about without the process of self-destruction being pushed to extreme limits; no longer was it a question of tacitly working the accusations over in order to give them some semblance of truth; the "referents" had permission to stimulate the critical faculties of the accused by threats, beatings, deprivation of sleep, and other techniques in order to make

them accept *those very parts of the accusation that were unacceptable.*
But if the percentage of failures was practically nil, this was due to the
fact that the Czech had long been trained to confess. Essentially suspect to his leaders, to his neighbors, to himself, a separatist in spite of
himself merely because of his molecular existence, a potentially guilty
man in the best of cases, a criminal in the worst, without being in on
the secret of his crime, devoted despite everything to the party which
was crushing him—to him confession, provided that it was forced
upon him, seemed to promise an end to his unbearable discomfort.
Even if he had the inner certainty that he had not committed the errors he was being taxed with, he would confess to them out of self-
punishment. Thus certain anxiety-ridden people, tortured by some
inexplicable feeling of guilt, steal in order to get caught and are at
peace again once they are in prison; in condemning them for a minor
crime, society has in fact punished their original sin; they have paid.

There is something else. Goldstücker here recounts how after being let out of prison he read the work of an analyst who saw in confession an "identification with the aggressor," and he adds that to judge
from his own experience this interpretation is not very far from the
truth. The aggressor is the party, his reason for living, which excludes
him and looms up before him like a wall that cannot be scaled and
that makes him answer each denial with the voice of a policeman:
"There is only one truth—yours." When the truth wants to be taken
for the Great Wall of China, how can a mere man oppose it with fragile subjective convictions ("I wasn't in Prague that day; I've never seen
Slánský")? It is better for the poor victim to secretly join the party
once again, by identifying with it and with the cops that represent it,
by embracing the scorn and the hatred that they show toward him in
the name of the party; if he finally manages to look at himself with
the paralyzing eyes of the Gorgon in power, he will cause the dreary
little incongruity that separates him from it—his life—to disappear.
Guilty! How dizzy this makes him! He will know peace, torpor,
death. As regards this subject, I feel it my duty to add to Goldstücker's
story an account whose authenticity I guarantee. In another popular
democracy, on the occasion of another series of trials, a former woman
partisan, who had risen very far in the hierarchy, was accused of espio-

nage and thrown in prison. She worked for the intelligence service; during the armed resistance, her husband had denounced her and she had arranged to have him fall into an ambush, in which he was killed. After several months' "treatment," she confessed everything, and the indignant tribunal condemned her to life imprisonment. Her friends later found out that she was no longer being tortured, that she didn't talk much to her fellow prisoners but appeared to have recovered her equanimity. The affair had been so crudely handled that she hadn't convinced anybody; after another group of leaders had taken over, the young woman was freed and rehabilitated. She disappeared, and it was learned that she was hiding with her family. The first person who forced his way into her room, at the entreaty of her parents, found her curled up on a sofa, her legs tucked under her, absolutely silent. He spoke to her for a long time without getting any reply, and when she finally managed to utter a few pained words, it was to tell him in an anguished voice: "What's the matter with all of you? *After all, I'm guilty.*" What the condemned woman could not bear was neither the mistreatment she had undergone, nor her downfall, nor her imprisonment, but her rehabilitation.

As can be seen, mineralized thought can bring repose; one sets it up like a gravestone in a tormented head and it stays there, heavy, inert, bringing "security," erasing doubts, reducing the spontaneous movements of life to an unimportant swarming of insects. Without going this far, confession is within the logic of the system; one might even say that it is the final outcome of it. First of all, because the "thing" is possessed of neither understanding nor reason, and therefore does not require that one actually believe what one says, but only that one say it publicly. And secondly, because in this imported socialism—which was meant to convince the Czech workers of 1950 that, when all was said and done, they were nothing but Russian peasants of 1920—the truth could be defined as institutionalized lying. Those who set up the system in good faith or who persuaded themselves that it suited Czechoslovakia were sooner or later to come to the point of lying desperately, without believing in their lie, so as to approximate what they took to be the truth.

The young woman I spoke of was brought out of the state she was in by electric shock treatments. This is a somewhat Stalinist way of going about things, but it is not inappropriate when it is a question of de-Stalinizing brains. Because they were not so seriously ill, a single electric shock sufficed for our sixteen witnesses: "the report [attacking Stalin] attributed to Khrushchev," as *L'Humanité* put it at the time. As a matter of fact, the report had this in common with the horse medicine that "cured" the innocent-in-spite-of-herself: It was a bolt of lightning and nothing more. Not an idea, not an analysis, not even an attempt at interpretation. A "tale told by an idiot, full of sound and fury, signifying nothing." Let us be clear on this point: Khrushchev's intelligence doesn't enter into the argument; he simply spoke in the name of the system; the machine was a good one, though its principal servant had not been; fortunately, this saboteur rid the world of his presence and the machine was going to work nicely again.

In short, the new personnel eliminated a cumbersome corpse as the old personnel had eliminated living victims. It was *true*, however, that Stalin had ordered massacres and transformed the country of socialist revolution into a police state; he was *truly* convinced that the Soviet Union would never reach communism without first passing through concentration camp socialism. But as one of the witnesses very astutely points out, when power judges it useful to tell the truth, it is because it has no better lie at hand. Immediately this truth passes through official mouthpieces and becomes a lie corroborated by the facts.

Stalin was a wicked man. So be it. But how had Soviet society perched him on the throne and kept him there for a quarter of a century? The new personnel flung these four words in the face of those who were worried: "the cult of personality." Let them be content with this bureaucratic formula, a typical example of the *unthinkable*. The Czechs and the Slovaks had the feeling that an enormous block of stone had fallen on their heads and was shattering all the idols as it broke up. It was, I imagine, a painful awakening. An awakening? The word doubtless is not the right one, for as one of them writes, this did not come as a great surprise; it seemed to them that they had always known what they were now suddenly being told. Moreover, far from rediscovering the world where one is awake and it is daylight, everything seemed unreal to them; those who attended the rehabilitation trials came back openmouthed: The dead were being acquitted with the same words, the same speeches that had served to condemn them. It was, certainly, no longer criminal to be alive. But this was *just a feeling*, and couldn't be proved; the institutionalized lie still existed. Inert and intact.

The witnesses of a gigantic, distant avalanche, they smelled something rotten in the Soviet state; they learned from an authoritative source, however, that in their own country the model imported from the USSR had never functioned better. The machine was running smoothly. Everything had changed, but nothing had changed. Khrushchev gave ample witness of this when the Hungarian people made an ill-timed attempt to draw conclusions from the Twentieth Congress. Obviously, they no longer believed in the institutionalized lie, but they were very much afraid that they would have nothing left to believe in. Up to that point they had lived in what one of them called "the socialist fog"; now that this fog was dissipating somewhat, they could survey the ruins: The ravaged economy threatened to collapse; the factories, now many years old, were spewing out products of mediocre quality, and no attention was being paid to the real needs of the moment; the level of technical and professional skills was falling day by day; "year by year there is an irresistible decline in humanist education" (Kundera); the country had literally no idea of what it was doing, for official lies and the faking of statistics had not only destroyed what knowledge there had once been but also completely halted surveys and socioeconomic research on the realities of the situation. Let us, above all, not believe that the leaders knew the truth and kept it under wraps: the truth simply did not exist, and no one had the means of establishing it.

Young people were, beyond the shadow of a doubt, the worst off: "Young people's knowledge is fragmentary, atomized ... our schools have not yet found a method of enabling a student to form a unified picture of anything—not even of our national history, for example. As for world history, let us not even speak about it; there the situation is disastrous." (Goldstücker)

Our witnesses found themselves in an unknown country, on an

unknown planet, between the secret East and the forbidden West. They suspected that the tragicomic speech on "Stalin's crimes" would prove to be true if it were incorporated into a *Marxist* analysis of Soviet society. But how could they continue to trust Marxism when the "thing" in power continued to claim that its bases were Marxist? If it was the official lie, how could it at the same time be the truth? And if there were two Marxisms, one false and one true, how would they themselves—who were products of the false one—be able to recognize the true one? They realized then that they themselves were the strangest natives in this strange land. (It is said that when Joseph Le Bon, a member of the Convention, was questioned in 1795 by his judges as to the reasons for his repressive policy in the Pas-de-Calais, he replied with a sort of dazed astonishment: "I don't understand...it all happened so fast...")

Nothing went very fast in Czechoslovakia from 1948 to 1956, but—what with fatigue, force of habit, resignation, lack of imagination, and willed self-delusion—there was doubtless a dreary truthfulness in untruth, a normality in the abnormal, a daily life in the unlivable, and a fog covering the whole thing. Once the curtain of fog was torn, there were only wisps drifting over the plain and these disillusioned men also said, "I don't understand." Who were they to have lived the unlivable, tolerated the intolerable, taken the destruction of their economy for the construction of a socialist economy, abandoned reason for faith in the name of scientific socialism, and finally, admitted faults or confessed to crimes they had not committed? They were unable to remember their past lives, to measure "the weight of things done and said," to call up their most intimate memories without falling into the slightly dazed state that Freud calls "alienation." Their reactions were quite different at first. Disgust, shame, anger, scorn.

Kundera chose black humor. "I was born on the first of April. That has its metaphysical significance." And also: "In my generation...our egos don't live in much harmony with themselves. I, for example, don't particularly care for myself." What Kundera calls "the Stalinist distortion" drove him to absolute skepticism: "Stalinism...was based upon a majestic human movement...and was more dangerous for all its virtues and ideals, because it...gradually converted them into their opposite: love of humanity into cruelty, love of truth into denunciation.... In the midst of the Stalinist era I wrote my first book, in which I tried to combat the prevailing inhumanity by appealing to universal human principles. But when this era was over, I asked myself: Why? Why should one have to love people, anyway? Today when I hear anyone mention the innocence of childhood or one's sacred duty to increase and multiply or the justice of history, I know what all this really means. I've been through the mill." This lyrical writer abandons poetry so as to recapture lost categories: laughter, the grotesque. He writes *The Joke* and by this title means to point not only to the innocent jest of the hero but to the whole system within which a trivial, childish prank inevitably causes the prankster to be imprisoned.

Václav Havel, for his part, discovers at one and the same time the absurdity of the world and his own absurdity. Coming from a bourgeois family, embarrassed since childhood at finding himself a rich kid among poor kids and therefore rootless and confused, Havel became, after the war, the victim of the discrimination whose target was Jews and people from a bourgeois background; numerous jobs were not open to him and he could not enter the university—with the result that, with admirable stubbornness, he kept vainly requesting permission to take courses in drama at the University of Prague and was admitted only after having proved himself as a dramatist. He was alienated, however, from the sovereign "thing." A little less than the others, perhaps. Many of them sought integration, but he knew that this was impossible for him because he wasn't wanted. The result was that he soon tended to feel absurd in an absurd world. The "revelations" of 1956 only increased his feeling of estrangement, and it is for this reason that his theater has been compared to that of the "practitioners of the absurd" in the West.*

In short, whether they felt themselves unreal in an unreal and drearily ceremonious society, the victims, witnesses, and accomplices of a monumental, nightmarish farce, or whether they floated like ab-

---

* With this difference however: His plays have a political content that cannot escape his compatriots. In *The Memorandum*, he clearly indicated that nothing could change as long as the system remained in existence and secreted its bureaucracy.

surd imps in a bottle in a milieu built on a fundamental absurdity of such a sort that any attempt to adapt to it or change it was absurd from the outset, all the men who speak here suffered what psychiatrists call an "identity crisis" in the first years following the Twentieth Congress. They were not the only ones—a deaf, dumb malaise was spreading all through the masses—but doubtless they were the ones most seriously affected. What could they do? Kill themselves or try to live?

From certain allusions that the reader will find in the interviews, one can guess that certain of them opted for the first of these alternatives; the others wanted to use the right to exist that had recently been officially granted them. These latter had no choice: To live was first of all to tear oneself away from a depersonalization that risked becoming an excuse, to know oneself, to recognize what one was in order to reconstruct oneself. And how could they tell themselves their own story without going to seek it out where it lay concealed, in the last fifty years of their national history?

Their individual adventures and the great adventure of the Czech people mirrored each other: In the extremely urgent situation in which they found themselves, with neither categories nor concepts for thinking about what is real, for thinking about themselves, they realized that each of these two adventures could be reconstructed only through the other. Subjectivism? No, modesty. They were forced either to find the truth or die. Not the truth of the system; they were not yet armed with the weapons to attack it; that would come later. The truth, rather, of their lives, of the lives of all Czechs and Slovaks, amid brute reality, with nothing in their hands, nothing in their pockets, holding themselves aloof from any ideological interpretation: going back to the facts, first of all, to the hidden, misrepresented facts which [former president Antonín] Novotný frankly said should not be bowed to in too servile a way.*

---

* An idea which in the last analysis is quite correct, and which to all appearances is opposed to *Realpolitik*, but which, coming from Novotný, meant in fact that no notice should be paid these facts when they contradicted the decisions of those in charge.

Slowly, stubbornly, to their great credit these men, amid all their confusion, publicly undertook this Oedipal search despite censorship and the threats of those in power. The reader will see in this book how Jaroslav Putík left journalism for literature. At one time, doubtless to avoid questioning the great synthesis of Stalinism, Putík immersed himself in facts about the outside world, as reported by radio and the press throughout the world, fruits disguised in the East by the pedantic boredom of the media, and in the West by a cagey "objectivism." "The need to write my own things, to express myself in my own way, arose only after 1956. I cannot say that the revelations of Stalinist deformations shook my whole world....There were many things I had already guessed long before. Nevertheless, this was the final...blow. It was then that I became acutely aware that I wasn't really doing what I really wanted to do." What he wanted to do was write, to know himself, and as most of the novelists who speak in this book put it, to "know men," to rediscover them in "their existential dimensions." "During the last few years," Kosík says, "Czechoslovak culture focused its attention on existential human problems, and the 'common denominator' was the question: What is Man?" It was, never fear, not a question of piecing a humanism together. They had known two sorts of humanism—that of Edvard Beneš and that of Josef Stalin. Both of whom, as one of our witnesses nicely put it, "hid men from them." Both had fallen to pieces, and no one had any intention of putting the pieces back together again. The exciting and difficult task they were undertaking was the only one possible, the only one necessary—that of approaching their fellow man without any sort of philanthropic prejudice. And from this point of view, the question posed by Kundera is the mark of a healthy radicalism: "Why should one have to love people, anyway?" Yes, why? They would know the answer some day, or perhaps they never would. For the moment it mattered little. Kundera's skepticism is certainly not a soft pillow, but let us not believe that it leads to despair. This author expressly says that he sees in it the renaissance of thought: "Skepticism doesn't annihilate the world; it only turns it into questions." Profiting from their alienation, they want nothing to be taken for granted, no truth to be established once and for all. For them as for Plato, astonishment is the beginning of philosophy, and for the moment they do not want to go beyond that point. Rather than affirmations of power—those replies that precede the questions so as to prevent questions from being raised—they prefer questions that have no answers; thought will not rid itself of calcareous concretions, which damage or divert it, by setting other concretions in opposition to them, but rather by dissolving them in a problematical framework. This does not prevent research; quite the contrary, it stimulates it, sets tasks and temporary limits for it. In April 1968, Václav Havel foresaw a social art with a profoundly realistic cast, which will show "Man as an individual" and "the social structure in which he is placed, his private life, marriage, children, material conditions. Soon we may be able to write about things as they really are.... I believe that a new type of social realism will emerge, as well as a new psychological realism, sounding and exploring the unexplored."*

Goldstücker does not say otherwise—and Marx (and Freud, too) said it before him—when, to show that the quest of these new Oedipuses is meant to be exhaustive, he declares: "Realism...has shown its inability to capture the essence of reality by describing its superficial manifestations."

This zeal will make more than one Western reader smile. We in the "free" world have gone beyond that! We have long been inured to reflective knowledge, metapsychology, analysis. It is true that we have another way of not knowing ourselves, that we talk more willingly of our complexes than of our material situation or of the socioprofessional context we have placed ourselves in, that we would much rather ask ourselves about the homosexual component of our behavior than about the history that has made us and that we have made. We, too, are victims and accomplices of alienation, reification, mystification. We, too, collapse beneath "the weight of things done and said," of the lies we have accepted and passed on without really believing them. But we don't want to know this. We are sleepwalkers walk-

---

*As will have been noted, the art which Havel foresaw and which he hopes to call forth has nothing in common with his previous "absurdism." This is because today he hopes that the society presently gestating will at last be able to take in the exiles gravitating around the dying system.

ing on a rain gutter dreaming of our balls rather than looking at our feet. The Czechs too, of course, have to rethink these problems which the puritanism of the fifties hid from their view.*· But as one of them said to Liehm: "How lucky we would be if that was all we had to think about!" The fact is that they must say *everything* or disappear. The questions that we ask ourselves lightly, abstractly, and a thousand others that we would never think of asking ourselves, they ask *passionately* and concretely; if they do not yet know themselves completely, it is because their experience is too rich; it takes time to put it in order.

This is not the only reason. I remember my conversation with a Latin American writer in 1960; he was worn out, more lucid than disillusioned, and still a militant. I knew that his life was full of battles, of victories and failures, that he had experienced exile and prison, that he had been thrown out by his comrades and then taken in again, and that in the course of this ceaseless struggle he had kept his loyalties though he had lost his illusions. "You ought to write this story—your story," I said. He shook his head—it was the only time that he let his bitterness show—and said, "We communists don't have a story." And I realized that the autobiography I had just spoken to him about, his or that of one of his comrades, had little chance of seeing the light, either there or elsewhere. No stories, no memory; none. The party has both, but they are both fake!

Anyone who writes the history of the Communist Party from the outside, from legal evidence, documents, and firsthand accounts, risks being hampered by his prejudices; in any event he lacks one irreplaceable experience. If he has left the party he chokes on his own rancor and dips his pen in bile. If he writes from the inside, in collaboration with the leaders, he becomes an official historiographer, and either lies or dodges questions according to the positions of the day. What can a militant who would like to understand his life cling to, since the organization that he has found his niche in and that has produced him and that, furthermore, discourages this sort of subjective undertaking in principle, will tend to make him bear false wit-

---

* In the interviews several of them refer explicitly to psychoanalysis as a means of access to "underlying reality."

ness against himself even in his most secret heart of hearts? What does he have at his disposal? Reconstructed memories, dried up or canceled out by a succession of self-criticisms, or other memories that may still be vivid but are insignificant or incomprehensible. After having successfully "negotiated" so many turns in the party line, how can he remember the direction he thought he was taking in the beginning? How can he know where he is heading this very moment? And who in the party can boast that the key he uses to interpret his actions today will still be the same a year from now? Men false to the core see to it that they keep one dimension of themselves secret, like Mr. X, the Russian whose friends told me has twelve levels of sincerity, and I've only gotten as far as the fourth. This latter sort keeps his mouth shut. The others have given their lives to their party twice over; they have often risked their lives on party orders, and from day to day, out of discipline, they have let them pile up like sand behind them, in dunes where the slightest gust of wind suffices to erase their footprints.

The Czechs and the Slovaks who speak in this book are for the most part members of the Communist Party. They, too, have given their lives with enthusiasm and then lost sight of them for several years. It is they, however, who today have undertaken in these interviews, in novels, in a hundred different articles,* the task of retrieving them, which seemed impossible in 1960 and which encounters the same difficulties today. For this reason, it was necessary to proceed step by step, to shatter their inner resistances, to scrutinize almost invisible tracks, to raise tombstones to see what was buried underneath. And above all—this was the crux of the matter—to find the right *lighting*. Fortunately, their memories are still vivid: In 1956 the "socialist fog" was only eight years old.

Khrushchev's report, however absurd it may have been, gave them the "final shock" that allowed them to speak of themselves and the party as they should. They did not attempt to fly high above this great body of which they are an integral part; it is their anchorage. If they

---

* From this point of view, I know nothing as thoughtful, as tough, and as lucid as Artur London's admirable firsthand account: *Confession*.

fell under the sway of the system, they also know that they made it—even though it was prefabricated, it at least had to be installed—and that the very struggle which they all carried on to limit certain of its excesses was merely a certain way of accepting it. They therefore spoke of it *from the inside*, since that is where they still are, and with an undeniable solidarity, without ever condemning it in hatred and rage the better to proclaim their innocence, but rather taking their distance *inside*, thanks to the displacement brought on by their *alienation*, which suddenly shed light on practices that had been so much a matter of routine that they had engaged in them without even seeing them. As if they could retrieve their lives, in the very name of constants to be located, of loyalties to be recaptured, only by internal criticism of the party, and as if they could question the role of the party only by a radical questioning of themselves, while at the same time not questioning their actions and their consequences, their omissions, their failures, and their compromises. What may seem to be a vicious circle will be seen, when these interviews are read, to be in fact a dialectical movement which was to permit all their readers, as well as themselves, to find their lost truth, the concrete, continually detotalized, contradictory, problematical totalization that never doubles back on itself, that never is ended, and that nonetheless is one, a totalization that must be the starting point of any theoretical research, the point from which Marxism took off with Marx and then again after him with Lenin, with Rosa Luxemburg, with Gramsci, though it never thereafter returned to this point.

What would they use as a basis to maintain the *distancing* necessary for the pursuit of their inquiry? The answer is clear: their national culture. Is this any reason to tax them with nationalism as the old guard of mummified Stalinists did? No. Read them and you will see. Is it their fault if the tide of pseudo-Marxism revealed, as it ebbed, that their historical traditions remained intact because people had not worked on them and gone beyond them on the way to a true socialism? Is it their fault if they have perceived that the recourse to their history, however insufficient it may be, is temporarily a more useful tool for understanding their present than the hollow concepts they were obliged to use? They do not deny that there must later be a return to a Marxist interpretation of these very facts; quite the contrary. But in order to meet the most immediate needs, it is necessary to take simple, known facts as a point of departure: The configuration of the soil, the geopolitical situation of the country, its small size, all of which have made both Bohemia and Slovakia battlefields for their powerful neighbors; the annexation to the Austro-Hungarian Empire which in the past "re-Catholicized" them by force as today there has been an attempt to "re-Stalinize" them—all these factors, so many mortgages on their future and so many explanations of their present. The two peoples have always struggled against the occupiers of their country, whoever they might be, and against their ponderous, invincible armies by permanently reaffirming their cultural unity. "The Czechs," Liehm says, "are the only people in Europe to have passed through most of the seventeenth century and all of the eighteenth without possessing a national aristocracy and thus were deprived of this traditional center of education, culture, and political power. As a result of the violent Germanization and counterreformation, which characterized these two centuries in our land, modern Czech political consciousness emerged as an attempt to revive the national language and culture.... Thus, the connection between culture and politics had an organic basis from the very start."

During the period of Stalinization the problems were different, but the weapons of the Czechs remained the same: Affirming their cultural personality in the face of the socialism that came in from the cold. Protecting national culture, not to preserve it just as it is, but to use it as a basis for constructing the socialism that will change it and at the same time preserve its imprint. This is what the Czech intellectuals discovered in the 1960s; this allowed them to place themselves better on this planet; they were not strangers among strangers, as they had thought. If they made this mistake it was because the reign of the "thing" had reduced them to mere atoms; in order to dethrone it without falling into "subjectivism," it was necessary that each of them recognize each of his neighbors as his *brother*; that is to say, as the product of one and the same cultural history. The struggle will be a hard one, and its outcome is uncertain. They know that they are "living in the century of the taking-over of small groups by large ones." One of them even declares that "the process of one country taking over another threatens (sooner or later) to swallow up all the little nations." What can be done in this case? They do not know; ever since they closed their catechism books they wanted to be sure of nothing. All they know is that at this precise moment the struggle of Czechoslovakia for its cultural autonomy is part of a larger battle which many nations, large and small, are waging against the policy of the big powers in the name of peace.

Uncertain, already sapped by inner conflicts, those in power thought it prudent to get rid of some ballast; for fear that the new commitment of cultivated men might lead them to leave "socialist realism" for "critical realism"—two concepts that are *unthinkable*, but the servants of the "thing" do not react to the dangers that threaten it unless they can find them already defined in the catalogue handed out to them—they opened the door to disengagement: If you lack the means to express your confidence in the system, you are allowed to talk without saying anything. It was too late. Those who express themselves in this book—and many others whom they represent—rejected this tolerance. Goldstücker puts it perfectly: "Concepts such as realism and nonrealism simply obscure the real issue—namely, the issue of presenting reality as the writer sees it, a task which calls for a personal analysis of reality which may differ from the official picture." It was not a question for them of calling for the return of bourgeois liberalism but, since truth is revolutionary, of claiming the revolutionary right to tell the truth.

Those in power could not even understand this demand. For them the truth had already been spoken, everyone knew it by heart, and the duty of the artist was to repeat it. A dialogue of the deaf. But it so happened that the masses suddenly caught fire; what may have seemed, at the outset, to be the concern of a caste of privileged professionals became the passionate demand of an entire people. It is necessary to explain here how that which was so sorely lacking in France a month later—the unity of the intellectuals and the working class—came to be realized in Czechoslovakia.

The economic situation in the 1960s became more and more alarming; there was no lack of Cassandras among economists. Their cries of alarm had not yet reached the general public. Everything happened inside the party; that is to say, the struggle to repair the machine became synonymous with the struggle for power. At the top levels, the conflict between the bureaucrats of the past and those of today became even more acute. The former, whom Liehm calls "amateurs," justified their universal incompetence by the Stalinist principle of the autonomy of politics; the latter, who were younger, almost all belonged to the generation of "eternal dauphins"; without questioning the system, they spoke in favor of the primacy of economics, if only temporarily.* In short, they were reformists. The nature of power was not questioned; those in power, old men, legitimized their authority by resorting to the old slogan calling for the intensification of the class struggle; those seeking power, young men, based their demand on their abilities and on the urgent necessity of setting the economy in order. These authoritarian reformists did not see the contradiction they had fallen into when they based the unchanged principle of the autonomy of politics on the immediate demands of the economic infrastructure. They planned to abolish the fetishism of production from the top, readjusting it to the resources and the needs of the country; they planned to allow consumer demand to regulate it, to a certain extent. The conflict of these two despotisms, one of them obscurantist and the other enlightened, led both of them to turn toward the working class. It was this class that was to be the arbiter.

At the beginning, this class seemed to have sided with the old leaders. Depoliticalized by the dreary routine they had been forced into, many workers had misgivings about a change that risked threatening their job security. In order to win them over, the other clan had to allow a certain control over production by this class too and to promise the workers a "law on the socialist enterprise." In short, the reform that was envisaged involved, ipso facto, a certain *liberalization* of the

---

*It is striking that the leaders in East Germany have simultaneously prevented conflicts at the top and applied the whip to the East German economy by giving technocrats a share in the exercise of power. As a consequence, their control over the masses is stricter than in the other socialist countries.

regime: there was talk of decentralization, of self-management. There was *talk* about it, but as long as the system existed, these words had no meaning whatsoever. The Yugoslavian experience has proved that self-management remains a dead issue when political power remains in the hands of a privileged group based on a centralized organization. It was to the credit of the intellectuals and the Slovaks that they profited from the paralysis of power, which had been brought to a standstill by its internal contradictions, in order to incite the workers to respond to the offers of reformist liberalism by pressing their revolutionary demands for socialist democratization. In all truth, no one in either group was fully aware at first of what was happening. The intellectuals, fascinated by reformism, wanted above all to help bring the masses over to the side of the reformers by writing articles. But their writings (those that the reader will read in this book and many others as well), which were the result of the long period of reflection that had begun in 1956, had a wider and deeper effect than they themselves suspected. By seeking the truth and proclaiming it, they stripped the system bare, and by shedding light on their own experience they showed readers that in the case of the Czech people it was not a question of putting an end to the "abuses" of the regime but rather of liquidating the whole system.

The trials, the confessions, the paucity of thought, the institutionalized lie, atomization, universal mistrust—these were not abuses; they were the inescapable consequences of prefabricated socialism; no repair work, no patching could make them disappear, and regardless of what team was in power it, too, would be petrified or crushed, despite its good will, unless both Czechs and Slovaks fell upon the machine with hammers and pounded like deaf men until it fell to pieces and was ruined beyond repair. They learned firsthand the real content of their thought at the end of 1967, when their writings had the honor of attracting the lightning bolts of a power that had grown weary. Gagged—though only for a short time—they saw their ideas go down into the streets; the young students—that generation they were so afraid of—had taken possession of them and were brandishing them like battle flags. The victory of reformism in January 1968 was no longer their victory, despite the temporary alliance of the masses and technocracy. Their real triumph came later when the working class, roused from its torpor, remembered its old maximalist demand, the only one that really came from this class: power to the workers. There were discussions wherever people worked; they learned direct democracy; in some factories the workers did not even wait for the passage of a law to force the director out and put his *elected* replacement under the control of a workers' council. The new leaders were outdone and had to revise their draft law in order to take account of the pressure brought to bear by the people. But it was too late; it was becoming clear that the process of democratization could not be halted. In this great popular movement, the intellectuals realized that their thought had been radicalized, and thus, radicalized themselves, they intensified their struggle against the system without being hostile toward the new team in power.

The press and radio have never been freer than in Czechoslovakia during the spring of 1968. But what strikes the Westerner is that the struggle of the intellectuals for total freedom of expression and information was helped along by the workers, who quickly had come to believe that the right to total information was part of their fundamental demands. It was on this basis that the union of workers and cultivated men was sealed.* This underlines quite clearly how much the problems of a popular democracy differ from ours. French workers will not go out on strike if the government attacks the freedom of the press, and in the present situation this is understandable on their part. Power rarely needs to muzzle the newspapers; profit can take care of that. Workers read *Le Parisien Libéré* without believing a

---

* This union still existed when I went back to Prague in November 1969. The students had occupied certain departmental offices at the university to protest the effective re-establishment of censorship. One could still speak with a certain degree of freedom about the occupier, however, and at the request of a student I was able to tell an audience that filled the hall that I considered the intervention of the Five to be a war crime; they demanded freedom of information within the perspective of the maximalist demand that I spoke of above. Without too much conviction, the government had been considering dealing harshly with them when the personnel of important Czech factories set a limit to its caprices by letting it be known that they would go on strike immediately if measures were taken against the students.

word of it, with the thought that the problems of the press will find their solution with the pure and simple abolition of profit. They know, perhaps, that censorship exists in the USSR or in Poland, but this doesn't keep them from sleeping. In those countries, they have been told, the proletariat exercises its dictatorship; it would be a crime to allow counterrevolutionary gazettes, in the name of principles that are both abstract and bourgeois, to persistently poison the air with their lies.

In 1968, after twenty years of Stalinism, it was quite different for the Czechs and Slovaks; in the beginning they, too, had had their fill of lies, though they had never known just how fed up they were and were only beginning to learn. The dictatorship of the proletariat was the dictatorship of a party that had lost all contact with the masses. As for class struggle, how could they have believed that it had intensified with the progress of socialism since they realized that socialism had done nothing but go backwards ever since it had been established? Censorship in their eyes was not just a lesser evil since it represented the censorship of truth by lies. Quite the contrary; as they became aware of their maximalist demand, the full truth, in its function both as theoretical knowledge and as practical knowledge, became indispensable to them, for the simple reason that the power of the workers cannot be exercised even on the job if they are not constantly kept informed at all levels. This demand, one suspects, concerned not only the dissemination of national and international news by the mass media from day to day.

It took on its real meaning by searching deeper: In order to orient, correct, control production, in order to situate their activities both within their own country and the world at large, and in order to remain, despite the distances involved, in permanent contact with each other, the Czech and Slovak workers demanded full participation in the scientific and cultural life of the nation. This demand, which in the "Prague springtime" had barely begun to be conscious of itself, would sooner or later have brought on a revolution in culture and teaching.

Thus, within a vast revolutionary movement, workers and intellectuals were a reciprocal and permanent factor in radicalization; the latter became convinced that they could fulfill their function—the search for truth—only in a socialist society in which power is exercised by all; the former, inflamed by the polemics that went on in the newspapers, became convinced that they would not bring about true socialism without breaking the monopoly of knowledge (it exists both in the East and the West), and without insuring the widest possible dissemination of truth, which, being indissolubly both theoretical and practical, would reach full development in the dialectical unity of these two postulates.

There is no doubt that all the agents of this process were far indeed from knowing where they were going and what they were doing. But neither can one doubt that they were trying to *bring about true socialism* by liquidating the system and establishing new relationships between people and production. The team in power, which was outstripped but clearheaded, made no mistake about this, as is evidenced by the timid plan for "revisions of the statutes of the party" published in *Rudé Právo* [the official newspaper of the Communist Party of Czechoslovakia] on August 10, 1968, which forbade "holding a plurality of public offices in the Party and in the State." It was the bureaucracy itself that was forced to administer the first hammer blows that were to break the machine.

We know what happened next. No sooner had this socialism been born than it was smothered to death by counterrevolution. This is what *Pravda* says, and I am in complete agreement with Soviet newspapers except on the minor question of cardinal points: The counterrevolutionary forces did not come from the West.

For once it was not Western imperialism that crushed the shift toward democratization and re-established the reign of the "thing" by force and violence. The leaders of the USSR, horrified to see socialism on the march once again, sent their tanks to Prague to stop it. They just barely managed to save the system, and another set of leaders, rapidly installed in power, prolonged the existence of the institutionalized lie by publicly congratulating itself on the Soviet intervention. Nothing is changed except that the socialism that was thrust upon them, by becoming an oppressive socialism, has been unmasked. The party line goes on amid the silence of fourteen million men who don't believe a word of it. Those who repeat it at the top are as lonely as the French collaborators during the German occupation; they know that they are lying, that the "thing" is the enemy of Man. But the lie has gotten hold of them and will no longer let them go; the invitation to inform on others is within the logic of the system: In order to endure, it demands that everyone mistrust both others and himself. But mistrusting oneself is now a thing of the past; after the Twentieth Congress and the act of aggression of 1968, the system will no longer get Czechs and Slovaks to do this; it has yet to make everyone a potential informer and therefore a suspect in the eyes of his neighbors. Despite a few precautions which were, moreover, quite useless, the five invaders have taken few pains to conceal the eminently *conservative* nature of their intervention. Our Western bourgeoisie was not taken in: The entry of tanks into Prague *reassured* it. Why not end the cold war and conclude a "holy alliance" with the USSR that would maintain order all over the world? This is the point we have arrived at. The cards are on the table and it is no longer possible to cheat.

We are still cheating however. The left *protests*, waxes indignant, blames, or "regrets"; *Le Monde* often publishes texts inspired by a virtuous wrath, followed by a long list of signatures that always include the same names—mine, for example. But let us sign! Let us go ahead and sign! Anything is better than a silence that might be construed as acceptance. Provided that this moral stance is not made to serve as an excuse. And indeed what the Five have done is not very edifying. They should be ashamed! But if you knew how little they care! Even if they did care about the European left, the thing they would most want would be for it to stamp its foot and yell "Boo!" So long as we restrict ourselves to the field of ontology, the system can rest easy: They are guilty, but didn't they act as socialists? They thus could do what they did. They are the only ones before the bar; the regime cannot be called into question. But if we read these interviews and use them to decipher the Czech experience we will soon discover that these leaders, who have been recruited and trained by the system and who exercise power in the name of the "thing," could act no differently than they did. It is the regime that ought to be attacked, the relationships established between people and production which gave it its structure and which have been reinforced and frozen by its action.

After the month of August 1968, it is necessary to abandon the handy shelter of moralism and reformist illusions where the regime is concerned. The machine will not be repaired; the people must take it over and throw it out in the junkyard.

The revolutionary forces of the West have only one way of helping Czechoslovakia effectively in the long run: Listening to the voices that talk to us about her, gathering together the documents, reconstructing the events, and trying to analyze them in depth, beyond the present situation, insofar as they show the structures of Soviet society, those of the popular democracies, and the relations of the latter with the former, and profiting from this analysis to think, without presuppositions and without bias, second thoughts about the European left, its objectives, its tasks, its possibilities, its various types of organization, with the aim of answering today's fundamental question: How to unite, how to liquidate the old ossified structures, how to produce new ones so as to prevent the coming revolution from giving birth to *this sort of socialism*.

THE THIRD WORLD BEGINS
IN THE SUBURBS

READING this book makes one understand that the situation African workers find themselves in—and of course this is equally true for many other immigrant workers—is not the result of negligence and is not only due to racism; the capitalist French economy requires the overexploitation of the African worker. One often says about Americans that they have their colonies "at home" in their own country; well, France is trying to reconstitute within its borders the colonies it lost. Specifically, this book shows how the system functions that integrates the African worker into our economy.

First of all, this book is quite clear about one thing: the notion of the illegal worker is a farce: it is an integral part of immigration policy. As one of the Africans, who was questioned, put it so well: "You can't come from Senegal on foot. One comes on a boat and when this boat arrives in a port, Marseilles, for example, thirty to fifty African workers could not disembark if the police did not close their eyes." This tolerance is, on the one hand, dictated very clearly by the employers' policies; on the other hand, this tolerance is dearly paid for by the African workers themselves. In so many words, they pay to enter the country and now that they are here people say: "But these people came without being invited; we don't know them, we have no responsibility toward them. What, they live in slums? But that's because there are too many of them!" They are too numerous but not so numerous that some of them aren't useful to the French economy. It also allows for arbitrary threats of expulsion, precisely because they have not been invited.

You see, to start with one must consider the obvious farce known as illegal immigration which is, in fact, the very kind of immigration that the employers want. Indeed, in the past, France imported raw materials from the colonies and of course it still does so in a neocolonialist way. That is what explains, as has already been so well stated, the destruction of the infrastructures of African countries to the benefit of the old colonial powers. And it also explains this vicious circle: immigrant workers are more numerous than in the past precisely because in their countries the situation is becoming more and more difficult. And when it comes to these men, what are we importing now? They are imported as so-called "raw human material," because one wants them to be unskilled workers: unskilled exactly because the skilled positions are reserved for the French workers; consequently, they are simply denied all opportunities for upgrading. One of them—we find this in the book—who asked to train for a job with better qualifications was told: "Here we don't need trained workers or skilled tradesmen; we need manual laborers."

The result is quite clear; one wants to reduce the workers to their lowest potential. And when trained workers show up among the Senegalese or the Africans in general, one either puts them to work in positions that are very much below their qualifications (there are cooks in Le Havre who have worked for thirty years as dishwashers, even though they know their trade perfectly well), or if they accept them in their trade, they are paid at a rate very much below their skills. As an example, there is a truck driver who is in fact employed as such—I forget in which municipality—but who is paid as a road repairman.

Thus we are really dealing with a general policy. This policy has huge advantages for the employers. First, those who are brought in are "mature" men; that is to say the employers—and, in a general way, the French economy—don't need to pay for their early education in which, quite rightly, they would otherwise have had to invest. In order to work legally one must be at least fourteen or fifteen years old.

Consequently, from birth to the moment you start working, in a factory or anywhere else, the system is faced with fifteen unproductive years. Those fifteen years are totally eliminated when mature men are brought in—men who, for example, after three days of apprenticeship immediately start to work. Thus these men, and there a million of them—I am not only speaking of the Senegalese—account for considerable savings to the French employers. Second, they do work that French workers are less and less likely to perform and, because of this, as has already been very well stated, they do not integrate into the French working class. On the contrary, they are rejected and they are seen as inferior. This is how one creates a racism that is quite useful to the capitalists. After this, one does everything to make sure they don't become members of French society or progress in it as does any other Frenchman. One does everything to make sure they keep their native tongue and don't acquire a second language that would allow them to communicate with their French comrades. In fact, literacy is not promoted among them. Each time there is a need for it, volunteers, and in general French radicals, undertake the task. Officially, there is nothing to promote literacy. Why? Because "where there is no elite, there are no problems"—this was said in the Belgian Congo (and afterward this caused many problems...).

They have just barely been allowed to set up an association: UGTSF (the Union of Senegalese Workers in France); it is what is called a "foreign" association. However, it takes only an arbitrary decree by the Ministry of the Interior to dissolve it and, as a result, any possibility of making it permanent is always up in the air. Finally, when it comes to social assistance, France will realize significant financial benefits, for they receive family allowances only if their families are with them. Now, it is quite obvious that most Africans don't take their families along because they come here precisely in order to send money home to feed their families. As a result, these allowances are either not paid at all or, if they are paid, it is at a much lower rate. Yet the African workers are told: "But we are not cheating you because all the moneys will go into the social action fund with which, for example, homes will be built." Do you realize the incredible swindle that this represents? Because in the end they ask these African workers to use their money to build the homes that will belong to the state and which they will never be able to enjoy for long. In general this is because of the well-known turnover which permits their replacement by others when these mature men are worn out because they are sick or tired. As a consequence, they will never live more than two or three years in a home they have paid for. We are dealing here with a swindle that represents at the same time an additional benefit for French industry. The result is that the African worker is overexploited, and he is additionally overexploited precisely because the French economy cannot maintain its competitive position in Europe unless it uses men who are underpaid and given salaries below those of French workers.

We are familiar with all the horrible consequences that follow, the kind of housing in which they actually live because the lodgings that are to be built for them in fact remain unbuilt. Then there is the discrimination, the constant possibility of being expelled, and, in addition, the actual expulsions (the book contains a list of all those expelled since 1968). And, in a more general way, men are destroyed by the tens of thousands; they are being sent back to their homelands without having acquired real skills, after having contracted diseases due to the change of climate and the unhealthy conditions in which they live. They have constantly been exploited and overexploited solely and deliberately because of France's need for a truly colonial workforce.

For these reasons everyone must read this book. People must become aware by means of the facts—and not in a theoretical fashion but solely by means of the facts—of the mechanism of overexploitation. In France we really possess our colonies just like the Americans, with the difference that the situation of black Americans is in spite of everything not quite as bad as that of the Africans who work in France.

ELECTIONS: A TRAP FOR FOOLS

In 1789 the vote was given to landowners: that meant the vote had been given not to men but to their *real estate*, to bourgeois property, which could only vote for itself. The system was profoundly unfair, since it excluded the greater part of the French population, but it was not absurd. The voters, of course, voted separately and in secret. This was in order to segregate them from one another and allow only incidental connections between their votes. But all the voters were property owners and thus already isolated by their land, which closed around them and with its physical impenetrability kept out everything, including people. The ballots were discrete quantities that reflected only the separation of the voters. It was hoped that when the votes were counted, they would reveal the common interest of the greatest number, that is, their class interest. At the same time, the Constituent Assembly adopted the Le Chapelier law,[1] whose ostensible purpose was to put an end to the guilds but which was also meant to prohibit any association of workers against their employers. Thus these property-less, passive citizens who had no access to indirect democracy, in other words, no access to the vote which the rich were using to elect *their* government, were also denied permission to form groups and exercise popular or direct democracy. The only form of democracy appropriate to them, since they could not be separated from one another by their property.

Four years later, when the convention replaced the landowners' vote by universal suffrage, it still did not choose to repeal the Le Chapelier law. Consequently the workers, deprived once and for all of direct democracy, had to vote as landowners even though they owned nothing. Popular rallies, which took place often even though they were prohibited, became illegal even as they remained legitimate. What rose up in opposition to the assemblies elected by universal suffrage, first in 1794, then during the Second Republic in 1848, and lastly at the very beginning of the third in 1870, were spontaneous though sometimes very large rallies of what could only be called the popular classes, or the people. In 1848 especially, it seemed that a worker's power, formed in the streets and in the National Workshops, was opposing the chamber elected by the recently regained universal suffrage. We know the outcome: in May and June of 1848, legality massacred legitimacy. Confronted with the legitimate Paris Commune, the very legal Bordeaux Assembly, transferred to Versailles, had only to imitate this example.

At the end of the last century and the beginning of this one, things seemed to change. The workers' right to strike was recognized, and the organization of trade unions was tolerated. But the presidents of the council, the heads of legality, were not in favor of the intermittent thrusts of popular power. Clemenceau in particular became known as a strikebreaker. All of them were obsessed by fear of the two powers. They rejected the coexistence of legitimate power, which had come into being here and there out of the real unity of the popular forces, with the falsely indivisible power which they exercised and which really depended on the infinitely wide dispersal of the voters. In fact, they had fallen into a contradiction which could only be resolved by civil war, since the function of the first was to disarm the second.

When we go to vote tomorrow, we will once again be substituting legal power for legitimate power. The first, which seems precise and perfectly clear-cut, separates the voters in the name of universal suffrage. The second is still embryonic, diffuse, unclear even to itself. At this point it is indistinguishable from the vast libertarian and antihierarchical movement which one encounters everywhere but which is not at all organized yet. All the voters belong to the most diverse groups. But to the ballot box they are not members of a group but *citizens*. The polling booth standing in the lobby of a school or town hall is the symbol of all the acts of betrayal that the individual may commit against the group he belongs to. To each person it says: "No one sees you, you have only yourself to look to; you are going to make your decision in complete isolation, and afterward you can hide that decision or lie about it." Nothing more is needed to transform all the voters who enter that hall into potential traitors to one another. Distrust increases the distance that separates them. If we want to fight against atomization, we must try to understand it first.

Men are not born in isolation: they are born into a family which *forms* them during their first years. Afterward they will belong to different socio-professional communities and will start a family themselves. They are atomized when large social forces—work conditions under the capitalist regime, private property, institutions, and so forth—bring pressure to bear upon the groups they belong to, breaking them up and reducing them to the units which supposedly compose them. The army, to mention only one example of an institution, does not look upon the recruit as an actual person; the recruit can only recognize himself by the fact that he belongs to existing groups. The army sees in him only the *man*, that is, the soldier—an abstract entity which is defined by the duties and the few rights which represent his relations with the military power. This "soldier," which is just what the recruit is not but which military service is supposed to reduce him to, is in himself *other* than himself, and all the recruits in the class are *identically* other. It is this very identity which separates them, since for each of them it represents only his predetermined general relationship with the army. During the training period, therefore, each is other than himself and at the same time identical with all the Others who are other than themselves. He can have real relations with his comrades only if they all cast off their identity as soldiers—say, at mealtimes or during the evening when they are in the barracks. Yet the word "atomization," so often used, does not convey the true situation of people who have been scattered and alienated by institutions. They cannot be reduced to the absolute solitude of the atom even though institutions try to replace their concrete relations with people by incidental connections. They cannot be excluded from all social life: a soldier takes the bus, buys the newspaper, votes. All this presumes that he will make use of "collectives" along with the Others. But the collectives address him as a member of a series (those of newspaper buyers, television watchers, etc.). He becomes in essence identical with all the other members, differing from them only by his serial number. We say that he has been serialized. One finds serialization of the action in the practico-inert field, where matter mediates between men to the extent that men mediate between material objects. For example, as soon as a man takes the steering wheel of his car he becomes no more than one driver among others and, because of this, helps reduce his own speed and everyone else's too, which is just the opposite of what he wanted, since he wanted to possess a car *himself*.

At that point, serial thinking is born in me, thinking which is not my own thinking but that of the Other which I am and also that of all the Others. It must be called the thinking of powerlessness, because I produce it to the degree that I am Other, an enemy of myself and of the Others, and to the degree that I carry the Other everywhere with me. Let us take the case of a business where there has not been a strike for twenty or thirty years, but where the buying power of the worker is constantly falling because of the "high cost of living." Each worker begins to think about a protest movement. But twenty years of "social peace" have gradually established serial relations among the workers. Any strike—even if it were only for twenty-four hours—would require a regrouping of those people. At that point serial thinking—which separates them—vigorously resists the first signs of group thinking. Serial thinking will take several forms: it will be racist ("The immigrant workers would not go along with us"), sexist ("The women would not understand us"), hostile to other categories of society ("The small shopkeepers would not help us any more than the country people would"), distrustful ("The man next to me is an *Other*, so I don't know how he would react"), and so forth. All the separatist arguments represent not the thinking of the workers themselves but the thinking of the *others* whom they have become and who want to keep their identity and their distance. If the regrouping should come about successfully, there will be no trace left of this pessimistic ideology. Its only function was to justify the maintaining of serial order and of an impotence that was in part tolerated and in part accepted.

Universal suffrage is an institution, and therefore a collective which atomizes or serializes individual men. It addresses the abstract entities within them—the citizens, who are defined by a set of political rights and duties, or in other words by their relation to the state and its institutions. The state makes citizens out of them by giving them, for example. the right to vote once every four years, on condition that they meet certain very general requirements—to be French, to be over twenty-one—which do not really characterize any of them.

From this point of view all citizens, whether they were born in Perpignan or in Lille, are perfectly identical, as we saw in the case of the soldiers. No interest is taken in the concrete problems that arise in their families or socio-professional groups. Confronting them in their abstract solitude and their separation are the groups or parties soliciting their votes. They are told that they will be delegating their power to one or several of these political groups. But in order to "delegate its power," the series formed by the institution of the vote would itself have to possess at least a modicum of power. Now, these citizens, identical as they are and fabricated by the law, disarmed and separated by mistrust of one another, deceived but aware of their impotence, can never, as long as they remain serialized, form that sovereign group: the People, from which, we are told, all power emanates. As we have seen, they have been granted universal suffrage for the purpose of atomizing them and keeping them from forming groups.

Only the parties, which were originally a group—though more or less bureaucratic and serialized—can be considered to have a modicum of power. In this case it would be necessary to reverse the classic formula, and when a party says "Choose me!" understand it to mean not that the voters would delegate their sovereignty to it but that, refusing to unite in a group to obtain sovereignty, they would appoint one or several of the political communities already formed, in order to extend the power they have to the national limits. No party will be able to represent the series of citizens, because every party draws its power from itself, that is, from its communal structure. In any case, the series in its powerlessness cannot delegate any authority. Whereas

496 · JEAN-PAUL SARTRE

the party, whichever one it might be, makes use of its authority to influence the series by demanding votes from it. The authority of the party over the serialized citizens is limited only by the authority of all the other parties put together.

When I vote, I abdicate my power—that is, the possibility everyone has of joining others to form a sovereign group, which would have no need of representatives. By voting I confirm the fact that we, the voters, are always other than ourselves and that none of us can ever desert the seriality in favor of the group, except through intermediaries. For the serialized citizen, to vote is undoubtedly to give his support to a party. But it is even more to vote for voting, as Kravetz[2] says; that is, to vote for the political institution that keeps us in a state of powerless serialization.

We saw this in 1968 when de Gaulle asked the people of France, who had risen and formed groups, to vote—in other words, to lie down again and retreat into seriality. The noninstitutional groups fell apart and the voters, identical and separate, voted for the UDR.[3] That party promised to defend them against the action of groups which they themselves had belonged to a few days earlier. We see it again today when Séguy[4] asks for three months of social peace in order not to disturb the voters, but actually so that elections will be *possible*. For they no longer would be if fifteen million dedicated strikers, taught by the experience of 1968, refused to vote and went on to direct action. The voter must remain lying down, steeped in his own powerlessness. He will thus choose parties so that they can exert *their* authority and not his. Each man, locked in his right to vote just as the landowner is locked inside his land, will choose his masters for the next four years without seeing that this so-called right to vote is simply the refusal to allow him to unite with others in resolving the true problems by praxis.

The ballot method, always chosen by the groups in the assembly and never by the voters, only aggravates things. Proportional representation did not save the voters from seriality, but at least it used *all* the votes. The assembly accurately reflected political France, in other words repeated its serialized image, since the parties were represented proportionally, by the number of votes each received. Our voting for a single ticket, on the other hand, works on the opposite principle—that, as one journalist rightly said, 49 percent equals zero. If the UDR candidates in a voting district obtain 50 percent of the votes in the second round, they are all elected. The opposition's 49 percent is reduced to nothing: it corresponds to roughly half the population, which does not have the right to be represented.

Take as an example a man who voted communist in 1968 and whose candidates were not elected. Suppose he votes for the Communist Party again in 1973. If the results are different from the 1968 results, it will not be because of him, since in both cases he voted for the same candidates. For his vote to be meaningful, a certain number of voters who voted for the present majority in 1968 would have to grow tired of it, break away from it, and vote further to the left. But it is not up to our man to persuade them; besides, they are probably from a different milieu and he does not even know them. Everything will take place elsewhere and in a different way: through the propaganda of the parties, through certain organs of the press. As for the Communist Party voter, he has only to vote; this is all that is required of him. He will vote, but he will not take part in actions that seek to change the meaning of his vote. Besides, many of those whose opinion can perhaps be changed may be against the UDR but are also deeply anticommunist. They would rather elect "reformers," who will thus become the arbiters of the situation. It is not likely that the reformers will at this point join the Socialist Party–Communist Party. They will throw their weight in with the UDR which, like them, wants to maintain the capitalist regime. The UDR and the reformers become allies—and this is the objective meaning of the communist person's vote. His vote is in fact necessary so that the Communist Party can keep its votes and even gain more votes. It is this gain which will reduce the number of majority candidates elected and will persuade them to throw themselves into the arms of the reformers. There is nothing more to be said if we accept the rules of this fool's game.

But insofar as our voter is himself, in other words insofar as he is one specific man, he will not be at all satisfied with the result he has obtained as an identical Other. His class interests and his individual purposes have coincided to make him choose a leftist majority. He will have helped send to the assembly a majority of the right and center in which the most important party will still be the UDR. When this man, therefore, puts his ballot in the box, the box will receive from the other ballots a different meaning from the one this voter wished to give it. Here again is serial action as it was seen in the practico-inert field.

We can go even further. Since by voting I affirm my institutionalized powerlessness, the established majority does not hesitate to cut, trim, and manipulate the electoral body in favor of the countryside and the cities that "vote the right way"—at the expense of the suburbs and outlying districts that "vote the wrong way." Even the seriality of the electorate is thereby changed. If it were perfect, one vote would be equal to any other. But in reality, 120,000 votes are needed to elect a communist deputy, while only 30,000 can send a UDR candidate to the assembly. One majority voter is worth four Communist Party voters. The point is that the majority voter is casting his ballot against what we would have to call a supermajority, meaning a majority which intends to remain in place by other means than the simple seriality of votes.

Why am I going to vote? Because I have been persuaded that the only political act in my life consists of depositing my ballot in the box once every four years? But that is the very opposite of an act. I am only revealing my powerlessness and obeying the power of a party. Furthermore, the value of my vote varies according to whether I obey one party or another. For this reason the majority of the future assembly will be based solely on a coalition, and the decisions it makes will be compromises which will in no way reflect the desires expressed by my vote. In 1956 a majority voted for Guy Mollet[5] because he claimed he could make peace in Algeria sooner than anyone else. The socialist government which came to power decided to intensify the war, and this induced many voters to leave the series—which never knows for whom or for what it is voting—and join clandestine action groups. This was what they should have done much earlier, but in fact the unlikely result of their votes was what exposed the powerlessness of universal suffrage.

Actually, everything is quite clear if one thinks it over and reaches the conclusion that indirect democracy is a hoax. Ostensibly, the elected assembly is the one which reflects public opinion most faithfully. But there is only one sort of public opinion, and it is serial. The imbecility of the mass media, the government pronouncements, the biased or incomplete reporting in the newspapers—all this comes to seek us out in our serial solitude and load us down with wooden ideas, formed out of what we think others will think. Deep within us there are undoubtedly demands and protests, but because they are not echoed by others, they wither away and leave us with a "bruised spirit" and a feeling of frustration. So when we are called to vote, I, the Other, have my head stuffed with petrified ideas which the press or television has piled up there. They are serial ideas which are expressed through my vote, but they are not *my* ideas. The institutions of bourgeois democracy have split me apart: there is me and there are all the Others they tell me I am (a Frenchman, a soldier, a worker, a taxpayer, a citizen, and so on). This splitting-up forces us to live with what psychiatrists call a perpetual identity crisis. Who am I, in the end? An Other identical to all the others, inhabited by these impotent thoughts which come into being everywhere and are not actually thought anywhere? Or am I myself? And who is voting? I do not recognize myself anymore. There are some people who will vote, they say, "just to change the old scoundrels for new ones," which means that as they see it the overthrow of the UDR majority has absolute priority. And I can understand that it would be nice to throw out these shady politicians. But has anyone thought about the fact that in order to overthrow them, one is forced to replace them with another majority which will adhere to the same electoral principles?

The UDR, the reformers, and the Communist Party–Socialist Party are in competition. These parties stand on a common ground which consists of indirect representation (their hierarchic power, and the powerlessness of the citizens, in other words, the "bourgeois system"). Yet it should give us pause that the Communist Party, which claims to be revolutionary, has, since the beginning of peaceful coexistence, been reduced to seeking power in the bourgeois manner by accepting the institution of bourgeois suffrage. It is a matter of who can put it over on the citizens best. The UDR talks about order and social peace, and the Communist Party tries to make people forget its revolutionary image. At present the communists are succeeding so well in this, with the eager help of the socialists, that if they were to take power because of our votes, they would postpone the revolution indefinitely and would become the most stable of the electoral parties. Is there so much advantage in changing? In any case, the revolution will be drowned in the ballot boxes—which is not surprising, since they were made for that purpose.

Yet some people try to be Machiavellian, in other words, try to use their votes to obtain a result that is not serial. They aim to send a Communist Party–Socialist Party majority to the assembly in hopes of forcing Pompidou[6] to end the pretense—that is, to dissolve the chamber, force us into active battle, class against class or rather group against group, perhaps into civil war. What a strange idea—to serialize us, in keeping with the enemy's wishes, so that he will react with violence and force us to group together. And it is a mistaken idea. In order to be a Machiavelli, one must deal with certainties whose effect is predictable. Such is not the case here: one cannot predict with certainty the consequences of serialized suffrage. What can be foreseen is that the UDR will lose seats and the Communist Party–Socialist Party and the reformers will gain seats. Nothing else is likely enough for us to base a strategy on it. There is only one sign: a survey made by the IFOP [Institut français d'opinion publique] and published in *France-Soir* on December 4, 1972, showed 45 percent for the Communist Party–Socialist Party, 40 percent for the UDR, and 15 percent for the reformers. It also revealed a curious fact: there are many more votes for the Communist Party–Socialist Party than there are people convinced that this coalition will win. Therefore—and always allowing for the fallibility of surveys—many people seem to favor voting for the left, yet apparently feel certain that it will not receive the majority of the votes. And there are even more people for whom the elimination of the UDR is the most important thing but who are not particularly eager to replace it by the left.

So as I write these comments on January 5, 1973, I consider a UDR-reformer majority likely. If this is the case, Pompidou will not dissolve the assembly; he will prefer to make do with the reformers. The majority party will become somewhat supple, there will be fewer scandals—that is, the government will arrange it so that they are harder to discover—and Jean-Jacques Servan-Schreiber and Lecannet[7] will enter the government. That is all. Machiavellianism will therefore turn against the small Machiavellis.

If they want to return to direct democracy, the democracy of people fighting against the system, of individual men fighting against the seriality which transforms them into things, why not start here? To vote or not to vote is all the same. To abstain is in effect to confirm the new majority, whatever it may be. Whatever we may do about it, we will have done nothing if we do not fight at the same time—and that means starting today—against the system of indirect democracy which deliberately reduces us to powerlessness. We must try, each according to his own resources, to organize the vast anti-hierarchic movement which fights institutions everywhere.

From

"SELF-PORTRAIT AT SEVENTY"

FOR the past year there has been much concern over the rumors that have been circulating about the state of your health. You will be seventy years old this month. Tell us, Sartre, how are you feeling?

It is difficult to say that I am feeling well, but I can't say that I'm feeling bad either. During the last two years, I've had several mishaps. My legs begin to hurt, as soon as I walk more than one kilometer, so I don't usually walk any farther than that. I've also had considerable problems with my blood pressure, but recently, and quite suddenly, these problems have disappeared. I had rather serious high blood pressure, but now, after a course of treatments with medicine, the pressure is almost too low.

Worst of all, I had hemorrhages behind my left eye—the only eye that I can see out of, since I lost almost all vision in my right eye when I was three years old. Now I can still see forms vaguely, I can see light and colors, but I do not see objects or faces distinctly, and as a consequence, I can neither read nor write. More exactly, I can write—that is to say, form the words with my hands—more or less comfortably, but I cannot see what I am writing. And reading is absolutely out of the question. I can see the lines and the spaces between the words, but I can no longer distinguish the words themselves. Without the ability to read or write, I no longer have even the slightest possibility of being actively engaged as a writer: my occupation as a writer is completely destroyed.

However, I can still speak. That is why, if television manages to find the money, my next work will be a series of broadcasts in which I will try to talk about the seventy-five years of this century. I am working on this with Simone de Beauvoir, Pierre Victor [Benny Lévy], and Philippe Gavi, who have their own ideas and who will do the editing, which I am incapable of handling myself. I might speak to them while they take notes, for example, or we might have a discussion, after which they will put the project together. Sometimes I write, too: I make notes for speeches on subjects that should be included in these broadcasts. But only my associates can read the speeches and deliver them for me.

This is my situation at the moment. Apart from that, I am in fine shape. I sleep extremely well. This work with my comrades is going well and I am participating fully. My mind is probably just as sharp as it was ten years ago—no more, but no less—and my sensibility has remained the same. Most of the time my memory is good, except for names, which I recall only with great effort and which sometimes escape me. I can use objects when I know where they are in advance. In the street, I can get along by myself without too much difficulty.

Even so, not being able to write any more must be a considerable blow. You speak about it with serenity…

In a sense, it robs me of all reason for existing: I was, and I am no longer, you might say. I should feel very defeated, but for some unknown reason I feel quite good. I am never sad, nor do I have any moments of melancholy in thinking of what I have lost.

No feelings of rebellion?

Who, or what, should I be rebelling against? Don't take this for stoicism—although, as you know, I have always had sympathy for the Stoics. No, it's just that things are the way they are and there's nothing I can do about it, so there's no reason for me to be upset. I've had some trying times, because things were more serious two years ago. I would have attacks of mild delirium. I remember walking around in Avignon, where I had gone with Simone de Beauvoir, and looking for a girl who had made an appointment to meet me somewhere on a bench. Naturally there was no appointment...

Now, all I can do is make the best of what I am, become accustomed to it, evaluate the possibilities, and take advantage of them as best I can. It is the loss of vision, of course, which is most annoying, and the doctors I've consulted say it is irremediable. This is bothersome, because I feel moved by enough things to want to write—not all the time, but now and then.

You feel at loose ends?

Yes. I walk a little, the newspapers are read to me, I listen to the radio, sometimes I catch a glimpse of what is happening on television, and in fact these are the things you do when you are at loose ends. The only point to my life was writing. I would write out what I had been thinking about beforehand, but the essential moment was that of the writing itself. I still think, but because writing has become impossible for me, the real activity of thought has in some way been suppressed.

What will no longer be accessible to me is something that many young people today are scornful of: style, let us say the literary manner of presenting an idea or a reality. This necessarily calls for revisions— sometimes as many as five or six. I can no longer correct my work even once, because I cannot read what I have written. Thus what I write or what I say necessarily remains in the first version. Someone can read back to me what I have written or said, and if worst comes to worst I can change a few details, but that has nothing to do with the kind of rewriting I would do myself.

Couldn't you use a tape recorder, dictate, listen to yourself, and listen to your revisions?

I think there is an enormous difference between speaking and writing. One rereads what one writes. But one might read it slowly or quickly; in other words, you do not know how long you will have to spend deliberating over a sentence. It is possible that what is not right in the sentence will not be clear to you at the first reading: perhaps there is something inherently wrong with it, perhaps there is a poor connection between it and the preceding sentence, or the following sentence, or the paragraph as a whole, or the chapter.

All this assumes that you approach your text somewhat as if it were a magical puzzle, that you change words here and there one by one, and go back over these changes and replace, one change by another, and then modify something farther along, and so on and so forth. But if I listen to a tape recorder, the listening time is determined by the speed at which the tape turns and not by my own needs. Therefore I will always be either lagging behind or running ahead of the machine.

Have you tried it?

I will try it, I will give it an honest try, but I am certain that it will not satisfy me. Everything in my past, in my training, everything that has been most essential in my activity up to now has made me above all a man who writes, and it is too late for that to change. If I had lost my sight at the age of forty, perhaps it would have been different. Perhaps I would have learned to use other methods of expressing myself, such as a tape recorder. I know some authors do. But I do not see how it could give me the same freedom that writing gave me.

Within my own mind, my intellectual activity remains what it was, that is to say, a controlled form of reflection. On the reflexive level, therefore, I can revise what I am thinking, but this remains strictly subjective. Here again, stylistic work as I understand it necessarily assumes the act of writing.

Many young people today do not concern themselves with style. They think that what one says should be said simply and that is all. For me, style—which does not exclude simplicity, quite the opposite—is above all a way of saying three or four things in one. There is the simple sentence, with its immediate meaning, and then at the same time, below this immediate meaning, other meanings are organized. If one is not capable of giving language this plurality of meaning, then it is not worth the trouble to write.

What distinguishes literature from scientific communication, for example, is that literature is ambiguous. The artist of language arranges words in such a way that, depending on how he emphasizes them or gives weight to them, they will have one meaning, and another, and yet another, each time at different levels.

Your philosophical manuscripts are written in longhand, with almost no crossing-out or erasures, while your literary manuscripts are very much worked over, perfected. Why is there this difference?

The objectives are different. In philosophy, every sentence should have only one meaning. The work I did on *The Words*, for example, where I attempted to give multiple and superimposed meanings to each sentence, would be bad work in philosophy. If I have to explain the concepts of "for-itself" and "in-itself," that can be difficult. I can use different comparisons, different demonstrations, to make it clear, but I must deal with ideas that are self-contained. It is not on this level that the complete meaning is found, because the complete meaning can and must be multiple as far as the complete work is concerned. I do not actually mean to say that philosophy, like scientific communication, is unambiguous.

In literature, which in some way always has to do with *lived experience [le vécu]*, nothing that I say is totally expressed by what I say. The same reality can be expressed in a practically infinite number of ways. And it is the entire book that indicates the type of reading each sentence requires, and even the tone of voice this reading requires, no matter whether one is reading aloud or not.

The kind of sentence that is purely objective, like those found frequently in Stendhal, necessarily leaves out many things. Yet this sentence contains within itself all the others, and thus holds a totality of meanings that the author must have constantly in mind for them all to emerge. As a consequence, stylistic work does not consist of sculpting a sentence but of permanently keeping in mind the totality of the scene, the chapter, and beyond that the entire book. If this totality is present, you will write a good sentence. If it is not present, the sentence will jar and seem gratuitous.

For some authors stylistic work takes longer and is more laborious than for others. But generally speaking it is always more difficult to write, say, four sentences in one, as in literature, than one in one, as in philosophy. A sentence like "I think, therefore I am," can have infinite repercussions in all directions, but as a sentence it possesses the meaning that Descartes gave it. While when Stendhal writes, "As long as he could see the clock tower of Verrieres, Julien kept turning around,"[1] the sentence, by simply saying what the character does, also tells us what Julien feels, what Mme. de Renal feels, and so on.

Obviously it is much more difficult to invent a sentence that counts for several sentences than to invent a sentence like "I think, therefore I am." I suppose Descartes hit upon that sentence all at once, at the moment he thought it.

And you have even reproached yourself for including in Being and Nothingness *phrases that were too literary, such as "Man is a useless passion,"[2] which is excessively dramatic.*

Yes, I made the mistake—and most other philosophers have made it too—of using literary phrases in a text whose language should have been strictly technical. That is, the meaning of the words should have been unequivocal. In the phrase you quote, the ambiguity of the words "passion" and "useless" have obviously falsified the meaning and caused misunderstanding. Philosophy has a technical language that one must use—changing it whenever necessary, if one is forging new ideas. It is this accumulation of technical phrases which creates the total meaning, a meaning which has more than one level. Whereas in a novel, what produces the larger meaning is the superimposing of meanings within a single phrase—from the clearest, most immediate meaning to the most profound, the most complex meaning. This work which achieves meaning through style is exactly the kind of work I can no longer do, since I cannot revise what I have written.

Is it a burdensome handicap for you that you are no longer able to read?

For the moment, I would say no. I can no longer find out on my own about recent books that might interest me. But people talk to me about them or read them to me, and I pretty much keep abreast of what is coming out. Simone de Beauvoir has read many books to me all the way through—books of every sort.

I used to be in the habit of going through the books and reviews I received, and it is a loss that I can no longer do so. It does not matter, however, in my current work on the historical broadcasts. If I have to learn about a book on sociology or history, for example, it makes no difference whether I hear it read to me by Simone de Beauvoir or read it with my own eyes. On the other hand, simply hearing a book read is not adequate if I must do more than assimilate information—if I have to criticize it, examine it to hear whether or not it is coherent, decide whether or not it is consistent with its own principles, and the like. For those purposes I would have to ask Simone de Beauvoir to read it to me several times and to stop, if not after every sentence, at least after every paragraph.

Simone de Beauvoir reads and speaks extremely fast. I let her go at her usual speed and try to adapt myself to the rhythm of her reading. Naturally it requires a certain effort. And then we exchange ideas at the end of the chapter. The problem is that the element of reflective criticism, which is constantly present when one reads a book with one's own eyes, is never clear when something is read out loud. What dominates is the simple effort to understand. The critical element remains in the background, and it is only at the moment that Simone de Beauvoir and I begin discussing our opinions that I feel myself draw out of my mind what had been hidden by the reading.

Isn't it painful for you to be dependent upon others?

Yes—although "painful" would be too strong a word, since as I said before, nothing is painful to me now. In spite of everything, this dependence is hardly unpleasant. I was in the habit of writing alone and reading alone, and I still think that real intellectual work demands solitude. I am not saying that some intellectual work—even writing books—cannot be undertaken by several people. But I do not see how two or three people can perform real intellectual work of the kind that leads both to a written work and to philosophical reflections. At the present time, with our current methods of thought, the unveiling of a thought before an object implies solitude ...

... In general, your political statements are optimistic, even though in private you are very pessimistic.

Yes, I am. And my statements are never very optimistic, because in each social event that is important to us, that touches us, I see the contradictions—either manifest or hardly noticeable yet. I see the mistakes, the risks, everything that can prevent a situation from going in the direction of freedom. And there I am pessimistic because each time, the risks are in fact enormous. Look at Portugal, where the kind of socialism we want has a small chance now which it didn't have at all before April 25, and yet runs the greatest risk of being postponed again for a very long time.[3] Looking at everything generally, I say to myself: Either man is finished (and in that case not only is he finished but he has never existed—he will have been no more than a species, like the ant) or else he will adapt by bringing about some form of libertarian socialism. When I think about individual social acts, I tend to think man is finished. But if I consider all the conditions necessary for man to exist at all, I tell myself that the only thing to do is to point out, emphasize, and support with all one's strength whatever aspects of a particular political and social situation can produce a society of free men. If one does not do that, one is in effect agreeing that man is a piece of shit.

That is what Gramsci said: "We must fight with pessimism of the mind and optimism of the will."

That is not exactly how I would formulate it. It's true that we have to fight. But it has nothing to do with voluntarism. If I were convinced that any fight for freedom was necessarily doomed to failure, there would be no sense in fighting. No, if I am not completely pessimistic it is primarily because I sense in myself certain needs which are not only mine but the needs of every man. To express it another way, it is the experienced certainty of my own freedom, to the extent that it is everyone's freedom, which gives me at the same time the need for a free life and the certainty that this need is felt in a more or less clear, more or less conscious way by everyone.

The coming revolution will be very different from the previous ones. It will last much longer and will be much harsher, much more profound. I am not thinking only of France; today I identify myself with the revolutionary battles being fought throughout the world. That is why the situation in France, all choked up as it is now, does not drive me to greater pessimism. I can only say that at least fifty years of struggle will be necessary for the partial victory of the people's power over bourgeois power. There will be advances and retreats, limited successes and reversible defeats, in order finally to bring into existence a new society in which all the powers have been done away with because each individual has full possession of himself. Revolution is not a single moment in which one power overthrows another; it is a long movement in which power is dismantled. Nothing can guarantee success for us, nor can anything rationally convince us that failure is inevitable. But the alternatives really are socialism or barbarism.

In the end, like Pascal, you are making a wager.

Yes, with the difference that I am wagering on man, not on God.[4] But it is true that either man crumbles—and then all one could say is that during the twenty thousand years in which there have been men, a few of them tried to create man and failed—or else this revolution succeeds and creates man by bringing about freedom. Nothing is less sure. In the same way, socialism is not a certainty, it is a value: it is freedom choosing itself as the goal.

Which therefore presupposes a faith?

Yes, to the extent that it is impossible to find a rational basis for revolutionary optimism, since what *is* is the present reality. And how can we lay the foundations for the future reality? Nothing allows me to do it. I am sure of one thing—that we must engage in a radical politics.

But I am not sure that it will succeed, and there faith enters in. I can understand my refusals, I can demonstrate the reasons for refusing this society, I can show that it is immoral—that it is made not for people but for profit and that therefore it must be radically changed. All this is possible and does not imply faith, but action. All I can do as an intellectual is try to win over as many people as I can—that is, the masses—to radical action for changing society. That is what I have tried to do, and I cannot say either that I have succeeded or that I have failed, since the future is undecided.

You have lived through seventy years of this century's history, you have gone through two world wars, you have witnessed enormous social changes, you have seen hopes dashed and other hopes that were not foreseeable come to life. Would you say that we have better prospects than at the beginning of the century, or that we are in a situation where the risk of a definitive failure of the human adventure is as great as before?

I would say that we are more advanced, as we begin to move toward the decisive moment of history—that is, toward revolution—but also that the risks are the same. In other words, I don't see any reason to be more optimistic than we were fifty or sixty years ago. But on the other hand, I think that many dangers were avoided, and that there has been some progress, even so. If you had known the period 1914 to 1918, when I began to live, you would be able to take stock of the differences and see that they are encouraging.

In spite of the millions of deaths in the last world war, in spite of Hitler's camps, in spite of the atomic bomb, in spite of the Gulag?

Of course, yes. Don't think that the pharaohs wouldn't have wanted to kill fifty million of their enemies! They didn't do it because they couldn't. The fact that it is possible today should almost contribute to our optimism: it is an indication of progress on a certain level.

Which doesn't change the fact that the victims were individuals whose loss is irreparable...

Of course; I agree. From the point of view of the individuals, the harm done to them will never have any justification. I am only saying that the enormous number of victims in this century is also a function of the growth in world population, and that there is no reason to despair because of it.

Have you always been sincere in politics?

Insofar as possible. There were situations in which, politics being what it is, I undoubtedly supported ideas I was not very sure of. But I don't think I ever deliberately affirmed the opposite of what I believed.

Even where the USSR was concerned?

Oh, yes, I did actually lie about that after my first visit to the USSR in 1954. Well, "lie" is a strong word: I wrote an article—which Cau finished, as a matter of fact, because I was ill, I had just been in the hospital in Moscow—saying nice things about the USSR which I did not believe. I did that partly because I think that when you have just been invited somewhere by people, you can't dump on them as soon as you get home, and partly because I wasn't very sure where I stood in relation to the USSR and my own ideas.

But when you first went to the USSR, did you know of the existence of the camps?

Yes, I knew about them; I had denounced them four years earlier, along with Merleau-Ponty.[5] Actually it was a joke among the writers who received me—they would say, "Be sure not to go see the camps without us!" But I didn't know they still existed after the death of Stalin, and certainly not that the Gulag was involved! No one in the West knew it for certain at that time . . .

So aren't you afraid of learning some day that there is a Gulag in China?

But we are already somewhat aware of it; you read Jean Pasqualini's book on the Chinese prison camps![6] When I was in China in 1955, I was shown prisons, but they had nothing to do with what Pasqualini describes, which I have no doubt is true. But I think there are many fewer camps in China than in the USSR, even if they are undoubtedly terrible...

And don't you think we might be in for some nasty surprises?

Oh, yes, I think so. That's why we shouldn't put our faith in the Chinese revolution, any more than in any revolution today. But once again, that does not stop me from being optimistic.

One of the only political problems about which you have gone against the whole world in impenetrable intransigence is the Arab–Israeli conflict. And because you have done so, you have isolated yourself to a certain extent from your comrades in the struggle. Yet I think there are many people who are grateful to you for that independence.

I don't believe anyone is grateful to me. I think it is more the reverse: each of the two sides would like me to disassociate myself from the other. But I have friends on both sides and I recognize the rights of each. I know my position is purely a moral one, but this is precisely one of those cases which prove that one must reject political realism because it leads to war. I would say the Arab–Israeli conflict, with the emotional implications it had for me, played a part in making me abandon the political realism I went along with to a certain extent before 1968. And here, in fact, I did not agree with the Maoists.

Speaking of the influence of your ideas, the other day I had a strange experience. I was at the top of the Montparnasse tower watching a demonstration of lycée students go by. A woman of about thirty-five, an employee in the tower, happened to be next to me. We started talking about the demonstration. She was against it, because she disapproved of all revolts. And she disapproved of all revolts, she said, because she believed she herself was totally responsible for her fate. She didn't particularly like her life, but she believed that at each stage on the way to where she was today, she had always had a choice. For instance, she freely chose to marry at the age of seventeen instead of continuing her studies. "And everyone is as free as I am," she said, "and therefore responsible for his situation." What struck me is that she was using almost word for word a number of the best-known of your formulations. What would you have said to this woman, who had perhaps read you in school and who perhaps owed to you the ideas that justified her resignation?

Well, I would have talked to her about alienation. I would have told her that we are free, but that we have to free ourselves, and so freedom must revolt against forms of alienation. Isn't that what you would have said?

Yes, of course, that is roughly what I said to her. But she stuck to her opinion.

Well, as far as that goes, it is her business. And how did it end?

The way conversations like that always end; we went our separate ways. You know very well that in order to change someone, you have to love them very much. But I wanted to ask you one thing: Haven't you sometimes had the feeling that the most widely known part of your thinking—the notions of freedom and individual responsibility—is precisely the part that is most likely to become an obstacle to true political awareness?

Possibly. But I think this kind of misunderstanding always happens when someone's work becomes public. The most vivid and profound part of a thought can bring the most good and also, if it is understood in the wrong way, the most harm. I think that a theory of freedom which does not explain what the forms of alienation are—to what extent freedom can be manipulated, distorted, turned against itself—can cruelly deceive someone who does not understand all it implies and who thinks that freedom is everywhere. But I don't think a person who reads what I have written carefully can make a mistake like that.

In my broadcasts I will explain what I mean about this on a political level; it will be one of the larger themes of the three concluding talks. But I will explain it on the basis of precise, concrete cases. It will not be philosophy, or at least it will not be expressed philosophically.

And do you think you will convince people?

I have no idea. I will try.

In his last article in Les Temps modernes, *François Georges writes more or less the following: "If my ideas have failed to convince everyone, it is no doubt because they weren't completely true." Would you say something like that?*

It's well put, and it is what everyone thinks at some point. This does not prove that it's true; there are some ideas that take longer to convince people. Everyone has discouraging moments. At times I think I could actually have said something like that. But to do so is both to honor "everyone" too much—since it is the truth of the ideas that is in question and not everyone—and to assert that true ideas triumph right away, which is equally false. What if Socrates had said something like that as he died? It would have been laughable! His thought affected the whole world, but long afterward.

And how about you? Do you have the feeling that your thought has had an effect?

I hope it will. I think one has very little evidence about the importance of one's ideas during one's own lifetime, and it's good that way.

Letters from readers, for example, don't tell you anything?

Each is a letter from *one* reader: What does he represent? Besides, people write me less often now. At a certain time I did receive a lot of letters, but now hardly any come. And the letters I receive interest me less: people saying they like me very much does not have a great effect on me, it doesn't mean much. I have had correspondences with people I didn't know, who would write to me and whom I would answer. And one day the correspondence would end suddenly, either because they were dissatisfied with one of my answers or because they suddenly had other things to do. All that gave me fewer illusions about the letters I receive which seem sincere. And then I receive quite a few from crazy people. I don't know if Gide's correspondence, for example, had as large a proportion of crackpots. In any case, since I started publishing I have always had several of them trailing after me. I don't know if it's because of what I write or if all writers excite the demands or confidences of cranks. After *Nausea*, many people said that I was crazy and that I was telling the story of a crazy person: this could have induced psychotics to get in touch with me. After *Saint Genet*, I received many letters from homosexuals, simply because I had talked about a homosexual and they felt isolated. But as I say, the letters I still receive now and then hardly interest me anymore.

And do you have the feeling that this is what old age is—indifference?

I did not say I was indifferent!

What still has real interest for you?

Music, as I told you. Philosophy and politics.

But do they excite you?

No, there is not much that excites me anymore. I put myself a little above . . .

Is there anything you would like to add?

In one sense, everything, I suppose; and in another sense, nothing. Everything, because in connection with what we have said, there is everything else, and it should all be explored with care. But this cannot be done in an interview. That is what I feel every time I give an interview.

In a way they are frustrating, because there are so many things to say. The interview brings them to life, along with their opposites, at the very moment that one answers. But having said this, I think that our conversation has given a portrait of what I am at the age of seventy.

You will not conclude, as Simone de Beauvoir did, that you have been "gypped" by life ?

Oh no, I wouldn't say that. Besides, she herself, you know, says rightly that she did not mean that she had been gypped by life, but that she felt cheated in the circumstances in which she wrote that book,[7] since it came after the Algerian war, and so on. But I wouldn't say that; I have not been had by anything, I have not been disappointed by anything. I have known people, good and bad—moreover, the bad are never bad except in relation to certain goals. I have written, I have lived, I have nothing to regret.

In short, so far life has been good to you?

On the whole, yes. I don't see what I could reproach it with. It has given me what I wanted and at the same time it has shown that this wasn't much. But what can you do? [The interview ends in wild laughter brought on by the last statement.] The laughter must be kept. You should put: "Accompanied by laughter."

NOTES

Notes by original translator indicated as [Trans.]; by editors of this volume as [RA] or [AvdH].

A FUNDAMENTAL IDEA OF HUSSERL'S PHENOMENOLOGY: INTENTIONALITY

Written in 1933–34 and first published as "Une Idée fondamentale de la phénoménologie de Husserl: l'intentionnalité," *La Nouvelle Revue Française* (January 1939); reprinted in *Situations I* (Paris: Éditions Gallimard, 1947). This translation by Chris Turner was originally published in *Critical Essays* (Oxford: Seagull Books, 2010) and is used by permission of Seagull Books; copyright © 2010 by Chris Turner.

1. Léon Brunschvicg (1869–1944), André Lalande (1867–1963), and Émile Meyerson (1859–1933): prominent academic philosophers whose work had largely passed out of vogue by Sartre's day. [Trans.]

2. Henri-Frédéric Amiel (1821–81): Swiss philosopher and diarist. [Trans.]

ON JOHN DOS PASSOS AND *1919*

First published as "A propos de John Dos Passos et de *1919*," *La Nouvelle Revue Française* (August 1938); reprinted in *Situations I* (Paris: Éditions Gallimard, 1947). This translation by Chris Turner was originally published in *Critical Essays* (Oxford: Seagull Books, 2010) and is used by permission of Seagull Books; copyright © 2010 by Chris Turner.

1. The preterit, or the past historic (*passé simple*), is used in French literary texts such as novels and short stories with the notable exception of Albert Camus's *L'Étranger* (*The Stranger*). See Sartre's detailed comments on the use of the *passé composé* in "*The Stranger* Explained." [AvdH]

2. The reference is to Ramon Fernandez's *Messages I* (Paris: Éditions Gallimard, 1926), 59–77. Sartre makes extensive use in his literary criticism of Fernandez's distinction between the *récit*, which "has inner coherence and explains," and the novel, which allows the action to develop in time and creates characters who are free to evolve in time. See also Sartre's disparaging comments about Fernandez and the collaborationist press during World War II in "Drieu La Rochelle, or Self-Hatred," note 2. [AvdH]

3. John Dos Passos, "1919," in *U.S.A.* (Library of America, 1978), 421, 451, 470.

4. Ibid., 497.

5. Ibid., 607. Other editions of this work show that the hyphen in "*La Madel-lon*" is intended by Dos Passos. [Trans.]

6. Fabrice del Dongo is the central character of Stendhal's *La Chartreuse de Parme* (1839). He famously describes the battle of Waterloo solely from his own restricted point of view as a chaotic affair in which soldiers gallop one way, then another, while bullets plow the fields around them. This description inspired Tolstoy in his account of the battle of Borodino in *War and Peace*. [Trans. and AvdH]

7. See André Malraux, *L'Espoir* (Paris: Éditions Gallimard, 1979), 294. In fact, it is not Malraux who says this but the republican Hernandez just before he is to be executed. The novel was translated into English as *Man's Hope*. [AvdH]

8. Sartre mentions Fillette ("Daughter") but she does not appear as a character in Dos Passos's *1919*. [AvdH]

9. Dos Passos, *U.S.A.*, 509.

10. Ibid., 401.

11. Ibid., 420.

12. Ibid., 659.

13. Sartre is referring to the branches that the miners at Hallein near Salzburg throw down into the abandoned depths of the salt mine in winter. These are recovered two or three months later covered in sparkling crystals. [Trans.]

14. Dos Passos, *U.S.A.*, 238.

ON *THE SOUND AND THE FURY*:
TEMPORALITY IN FAULKNER

First published as "A propos de *Le Bruit et la Fureur*, La Temporalité chez Faulkner," *La Nouvelle Revue Française* (June–July 1939); reprinted in *Situations I* (Paris: Éditions Gallimard, 1947). This translation by Chris Turner was originally published in *Critical Essays* (Oxford: Seagull Books, 2010) and is used by permission of Seagull Books; copyright © 2010 by Chris Turner.

1. William Faulkner, *The Sound and the Fury*, Norton Critical Edition, 2nd ed. (New York: W. W. Norton & Company, 1994), 66.

2. Ibid., 49.

3. Ibid., 54.

4. Ibid., 51.

5. Ibid., 56.

6. Ibid., 110.

7. In fact both *Sartoris* and *The Sound and the Fury* were published in 1929, and in the concluding interview published in *Faulkner in the University: Class Conferences at the University of Virginia 1957–1958* [Frederick L. Gwynn and Joseph L. Blotner, eds. (New York: Knopf, 1959), 285], Faulkner commented that "[you should p]robably begin with... *Sartoris* ... I'd say that's a good one to begin with." [AvdH]

8. Faulkner, *The Sound and the Fury*, 100–4. See 102.

9. Ibid., 54.

10. Ibid., 48.

11. Ibid., 51.

12. Ibid.

13. Ibid., 112–13.

14. Ibid., 112.

15. Armand Salacrou (1899–1989): a French playwright, who is remembered particularly for *L'Inconnue d'Arras* of 1935. [Trans.]

16. Faulkner, *The Sound and The Fury*, 49.

17. William Shakespeare, *Macbeth*, Act V, Scene 5.

18. The reference is presumably to Heidegger's use of the term (*sich*) *zeiti-gen*. [Trans.]

19. "*Die stille Kraft des Möglichen.*" [Trans.]

20. Martin Heidegger, *Being and Time*, trans. John Macquarrie and Edward Robinson (Oxford: Basil Blackwell, 1978), 279. Translation modified to reflect Sartre's rendering of Dasein as "*la réalité humaine.*" [Trans.]

THE STRANGER EXPLAINED

First published as "Explication de *L'Étranger*," *Cahiers du Sud* (February 1943); reprinted in *Situations I* (Paris: Éditions Gallimard, 1947). This translation by Chris Turner was originally published in *Critical Essays* (Oxford: Seagull Books, 2010) and is used by permission of Seagull Books; copyright © 2010 by Chris Turner.

1. The armistice was signed on June 22, 1940, between the Third Reich and the Vichy government led by Maréchal Pétain. It divided France into the Occupied and the Free Zone. *The Stranger* is set in Algeria across the Mediterranean; at the time it was a French colony. [AvdH]

2. Albert Camus, *The Stranger*, trans. Matthew Ward (New York: Knopf, 1993), 90, 98, 117.

3. Henri Poincaré (1854–1912) and Pierre Duhem (1861–1916): prominent French mathematicians and philosophers of science; Émile Meyerson (1859–1933): a Polish-born, German-educated, French chemist and philosopher of science. [Trans.]

4. Albert Camus, *The Myth of Sisyphus*, trans. Justin O'Brien (New York: Vintage, 1991), 20.

5. Maurice Merleau-Ponty, *La Structure du Comportement* (Paris: La Renaissance du Livre, 1942), 1.

6. Camus, *The Myth of Sisyphus*, 4.

7. Charles Maurras (1868–1952): essayist and leader of the extreme right Action Française movement. [Trans.]

8. Camus, *The Myth of Sisyphus*, 12–13.

9. Ibid., 6.

10. Ibid., 51.

11. George Gissing (1857–1903): a prolific Yorkshire-born novelist, his *Born in Exile* (1892) was translated into French by Marie Canavaggia and published in 1932. [Trans.]

12. Camus, *The Myth of Sisyphus*, 14 (translation modified). [Trans.]

13. Ibid., 15.

14. Ibid., 63–64.

15. William Somerset Maugham (1874–1965): one of the most popular English novelists of his day. Sartre is probably thinking of novels such as *The Moon and Sixpence*, based on the life of Paul Gauguin among the "primitives" of Tahiti. [Trans.]

16. The central character of Dostoevsky's novel *The Idiot*. [Trans.]

17. Camus, *The Stranger*, 23.

18. Camus, *The Myth of Sisyphus*, 101.

19. Camus, *The Stranger*, 88.

20. Camus, *The Myth of Sisyphus*, 73.

21. Camus, *The Stranger*, 34, 92, 5.

22. Camus, *The Myth of Sisyphus*, 73 (translation modified). [Trans.]

23. Ibid., 59.

24. Camus, *The Stranger*, 109.

25. Camus, *The Myth of Sisyphus*, 10 (translation modified). [Trans.]

26. Ibid., 28.

27. Camus, *The Stranger*, 91.

28. The reference is to Joë Bousquet, *Traduit du Silence* (Paris: Éditions Gallimard, 1941). [Trans.]

29. Jean Paulhan (1884–1968): a French writer, literary critic, and publisher, and the director of the literary magazine *Nouvelle Revue Française*. [Trans.]

30. Camus, *The Myth of Sisyphus*, 25. Compare also Brice Parain's theory of language and his conception of silence. [Trans.]

31. Ibid., 51.

32. Camus, *The Stranger*, 116.

33. Ibid., 93.

34. Camus, *The Myth of Sisyphus*, 14–15.

35. Ibid., 15.

36. Camus, *The Stranger*, 13.

37. Ibid., 76–77.

38. The use of the present perfect in French is quite different from its use in English. In particular, it is used for completed actions in the past, whereas the English present perfect requires almost always either that an action is continuing into—or is of some continuing relevance to—the present. The *passé composé* is typical of spoken French; normally the *passé simple* is used in literary works such as novels and short stories, but *L'Étranger* is an exception to the rule. [Trans. and AvdH]

39. Camus, *The Stranger*, 34.

40. Ibid., 19.

41. Georges Courteline (1858–1929): one of the leading French dramatists in the early decades of the twentieth century. [Trans.]

42. For the distinction between the "*roman*" (the novel) and the "*récit*," see comments in "On John Dos Passos and *1919*," note 2, on the use Sartre makes of Fernandez's work *Messages I*: the story explains and coordinates as it reproduces events. [AvdH]

DRIEU LA ROCHELLE,
OR SELF-HATRED

First published as "Drieu La Rochelle ou la haine de soi" in an underground issue of *Les Lettres françaises* 6 (April 1943); reprinted in *Les Écrits de Sartre: Chronologie, Bibliographie commentée*, eds. Michel Contat and Michel Rybalka (Paris: Éditions Gallimard, 1970). This translation by Richard C. McCleary was first published in *The Writings of Jean-Paul Sartre, Volume 2: Selected Prose*, eds. Michel Contat and Michel Rybalka (Evanston, IL: Northwestern University Press, 1974) and is used by permission of Northwestern University Press; copyright © 1974 by Northwestern University Press.

1. Chateaubriant was the editor of *La Gerbe*, an anticommunist, anti-Semitic, fascistic, and pro-Nazi journal (1940–44). [AvdH]

2. Ramon Fernandez was a highly regarded literary figure whose critical writings Sartre knew well. He quotes his definition of the "*récit*" approvingly in "On John Dos Passos and *1919*," note 2. Fernandez became a fascist after 1937 and wrote for *La Gerbe*. He died of a heart attack in 1944. [AvdH]

3. André Fraigneau (1901–91) was a novelist, essayist, and editor and the author of more than a dozen works. He was indeed a homosexual; after the war he was denounced as a collaborator. [AvdH]

4. *La Nouvelle Revue Française* was a highly respected literary journal, which was started in 1908 and taken over by Gallimard in 1911. In 1940 Drieu La Rochelle became the editor, and Jewish and communist writers were prohibited from publishing in it. In 1943 its publication was halted because of its collaborationist editorial policies. [AvdH]

5. Gilles is the eponymous hero of Drieu's best-known novel. It was first published in 1939 by Éditions Gallimard. [AvdH]

6. *Esprit* was founded by Edouard Mounier in 1932 as a vehicle for his "personalist" philosophy. After 1940 it became more and more critical of Vichy, was suppressed in 1941, and then was published again after the war. [AvdH]

7. *La Nouvelle Revue boche* ("The New 'Kraut' Review"). [AvdH]

A NEW MYSTIC:
ON BATAILLE'S *INNER EXPERIENCE*
First published as "Un Nouveau Mystique," *Cahiers du Sud* (November 1943); reprinted in *Situations I* (Paris: Éditions Gallimard, 1947). This translation by Chris Turner was originally published in *Critical Essays* (Oxford: Seagull Books, 2010) and is used by permission of Seagull Books; copyright © 2010 by Chris Turner.

1. Jacques Delille (1738–1813): a poet renowned for his elaborate circumlocution. In his *Epistles* things are not called by their name but are hinted at by elaborate paraphrases, for example, "sugar" becomes "American honey." [Trans. and AvdH]

2. Alain was the pen name of the influential French philosopher Émile-Auguste Chartier (1868–1951). As a teacher at the Lycée Henri IV, Alain counted Simone Weil, Georges Canguilhem, and Raymond Aron among his pupils. [Trans.]

3. See "*The Stranger* Explained," note 29. [Trans.]

4. Sartre is making reference here to such polished and clever writers as Voltaire and Beaumarchais. [AvdH]

5. Georges Bataille, *Inner Experience*, trans. Leslie Anne Boldt (Albany: State University of New York Press, 1988), 102.

6. Pascal died in 1662. The manuscript entitled *Pensées* consists of jottings and ideas, not all of them complete. It was not published until 1669 and not in the order that Pascal had planned. [AvdH]

7. Michel Leiris, *Manhood* (London: Jonathan Cape, 1968).

8. Bataille, *Inner Experience*, xxxiii.

9. Ibid., 18.

10. Ibid., 55. It even seems at times that Bataille amuses himself by pastiching Pascal's style: "Should one look at last at the history of men, man by man," etc. (38). [Trans.]

11. Ibid., 135–36 (translation modified). [Trans.]

12. Ibid., 6.

13. Ibid., 28–29.

14. Ibid., 16.

15. "Invitation au Voyage" is the title of a famous and much translated poem in Baudelaire's *Les Fleurs du Mal*. In this poem the narrator invites his loved one to accompany him to an imaginary and exotic realm where "All is order and beauty, luxury, peace, and voluptuousness." In 1953, Sartre, in his adaptation of Dumas's *Kean*, has Anna use part of the refrain to entice Kean into marrying her; see Jean-Paul Sartre, *Théâtre complet* (Paris: Éditions Gallimard, 2005), 604–5. [Trans. and AvdH]

16. Alain wrote a series of "Propos," including *Propos sur le bonheur* (Paris: Éditions Gallimard, 1925), *Propos de politique* (Paris: Éditions Rieder, 1934), and *Propos de littérature* (Paris: Paul Hartmann, 1934); his *Histoire de mes pensées* was published by Éditions Gallimard in 1936. [Trans.]

17. This journal maintains the purported narrator's running commentary within the novel on André Gide's *Les Faux-Monnayeurs* (1925). [Trans.]

18. The latter journal, published separately in 1927, was (or at least claims to be) Gide's journal at the time of writing *Les Faux-Monnayeurs*. [Trans.]

19. Bataille, *Inner Experience*, 92.

20. Nathanaël is the disciple to whom André Gide's *Les nourritures terrestres* (1928) is addressed. [Trans.]

21. Bataille, *Inner Experience*, 92. The original French is: "*Même à prêcher des convaincus, il est dans la prédication un élément de détresse.*" It seems odd to read "*prédication*" here in the grammatical sense of "predication," rather than to take it to refer to its everyday meaning of "preaching." [Trans.]

22. Ibid., 66.

23. Ibid., 34 (translation modified). [Trans.]

24. This is an oblique reference to Gérard de Nerval's famous mid-nineteenth-century poem "El Desdichado": "I am the Dark One, the Widower, the Unconsoled, the Prince of Aquitaine whose Tower was abolished..." [AvdH]

25. Bataille, *Inner Experience*, 135.

26. Ibid., 69.

27. Ibid.

28. Ibid., 70.

29. Ibid., 69.

30. Ibid.: "Linked to the birth then to the union of a man and a woman, and even, at the moment of their union..."

31. Sartre refers to Henry Corbin's 1937 translation of Heidegger's *Qu'est-ce que la métaphysique?* (*Was ist der Metaphysik?*) for the first time in his *Les Carnets de la drôle de guerre: Septembre 1939–Mars 1940* (Paris: Éditions Gallimard, 1995), 406–7. [AvdH]

32. Bataille, *Inner Experience*, 78 (translation modified). [Trans.]

33. Ibid., 71.

34. Ibid., 72.

35. Ibid., 85, 74 (translations modified). [Trans.]

36. Ibid., 94 (translation modified). [Trans.]

37. Ibid., 74 (translation modified). [Trans.]

38. Ibid., 84.

39. Ibid., 85.

40. Sartre also refers to Meyerson's insights in *Notebooks for an Ethics*, trans. David Pellauer (University of Chicago Press, 1992), 35. [AvdH]

41. Jules Romains (1885–1972): a French novelist and the founder of the Unanimist literary movement. [Trans.]

42. Émile Durkheim (1858–1917): one of the founding fathers of modern sociology; Lucien Lévy-Bruhl (1857–1939): a sociologist and ethnologist with a strong interest in what was known in his day as "the primitive mind"; Célestin Bouglé (1870–1940): a philosopher who turned to the social sciences and became, alongside Durkheim, one of the first editors of *L'Année sociologique*. [Trans.]

43. Bataille, *Inner Experience*, 66.

44. Ibid., 85 (translation modified). [Trans.]

45. Ibid., 87–88.

46. Ibid., 87.

47. Ibid., 89.

48. Ibid., 91.

49. Ibid., 46.

50. Ibid., 48.

51. Ibid., 46 (translation amended). [Trans.]

52. Ibid., 49.

53. This a reference to the Pascal's *Pensées* section dealing with "*divertisse-ment*" (distraction or diversion), in which he explains that man is incapable of sitting still in a room because he is always agitated and in constant need of distraction. See Donna C. Stanton's detailed discussion in *The Aristocrat as Art* (New York: Columbia University Press, 1980), 100–2. [AvdH]

54. Bataille, *Inner Experience*, xxxi.

55. Friedrich Nietzsche, *Ecce homo: How One Becomes What One Is*, trans. R. J. Hollingdale (London: Penguin, 1979), 98.

56. Bataille, *Inner Experience*, xxxiii.

57. Ibid., 66.

58. Ibid., 89 (translation modified). [Trans.]

59. Ibid., 90 (translation modified). [Trans.]

60. Ibid., 66.

61. Ibid., 88 (translation modified). [Trans.]

62. Ibid., 47 (translation modified). [Trans.]

63. Ibid., 22.

64. Ibid., 23 (translation modified). [Trans.]

65. Ibid., 4 (translation modified). [Trans.]

66. Ibid., 9.

67. Ibid., 95 (translation modified). [Trans.]

68. Ibid., 55 (translation modified). [Trans.]

69. Ibid., x.

70. Ibid., 91.

71. Ibid., 80 (translation modified). [Trans.]

72. Ibid., 27.

73. Ibid., 130.

74. Ibid., 79.

75. See Friedrich Nietzsche, *Thus Spoke Zarathustra*, trans. R. J. Hollingdale (London: Penguin, 1961), 58.

76. Sartre refers to "what Nietzsche called 'the illusion of worlds-behind-the-scene'" in *Being and Nothingness*, trans. Hazel E. Barnes (New York: Philosophical Library, 1956), xlvi. [AvdH]

77. Karl Jaspers, *Philosophy* (University of Chicago Press, 1969–71).

78. Bataille, *Inner Experience*, 37, 36, 35.

79. Ibid., 4 (translation modified). [Trans.]

80. Ibid., 33, 36.

81. Ibid., Part Four, 99–157. [Trans.]

82. Ibid., 102–3 (translation modified). [Trans.]

83. Ibid., 34 (translation modified). [Trans.]

84. Ibid., 35.

85. Ibid., 55 (translation modified). [Trans.]

86. Ibid., 52.

87. Ibid.

88. From Blanchot, *Thomas the Obscure*, cited in Bataille, *Inner Experience*, 101 (translation modified; Sartre's italics). [Trans.]

89. Ibid. (translation extensively modified). [Trans.]

90. Ibid., 53.

91. See Hegel's *Phenomenology of Spirit*, trans. A. V. Miller (Oxford University Press, 1977), 9. Sartre uses the expression "At night all the cows are gray" in *Truth and Existence*, ed. Ronald Aronson, trans. Adrian van den Hoven (University of Chicago Press, 1992), 2. [AvdH]

92. Pierre Loti (1850–1923): a naval officer from Rochefort (Charente-Maritime) who became one of France's leading novelists. He first published *L'Inde (sans les Anglais)* in 1903. In 2008 it was republished by Phébus of Paris in the Libretto Collection. Since at the time that Loti wrote the book India was still a British colony and hence could not be imagined without the British, Sartre wished to stress the "absurdity" of such a work. [Trans. and AvdH]

THE REPUBLIC OF SILENCE

First published as "La République du silence," *Les Lettres françaises* (September 1944); reprinted in *Situations III* (Paris: Éditions Gallimard, 1949). This translation by Chris Turner was originally published in *The Aftermath of War* (Oxford: Seagull Books, 2008) and is used by permission of Seagull Books; copyright © 2008 by Chris Turner.

1. Sartre's sentiments echo those of Arthur Koestler after his liberation from jail and death row during the Spanish Civil War. See *Dialogue*

with Death (New York: Macmillan, 1966), p.195–96 (initially published in 1937 under the title *The Spanish Testament*): "Often when I wake at night I am homesick for my cell in the death-house in Seville and, strangely enough, I feel that I have never been so free as I was then.... Most of us were not afraid of death, only of the act of dying; and there were times when we overcame even this fear. At such moments we were free—men without shadows, dismissed from the ranks of the mortal; it was the most complete experience of freedom that can be granted a man." Sartre read *Un Testament espagnol* during the Phony War in November 1939. *Les Mots et autres écrits autobiographiques* (Paris: Gallimard, 2010), 331. NB: Sartre and Camus met Koestler in Paris after the Liberation. [AvdH]

EXISTENTIALISM: A CLARIFICATION

First published as "A propos de l'existentialisme: Mise au point," *Action* (December 29, 1944); reprinted in *Les Écrits de Sartre: Chronologie, Bibliographie commentée*, eds. Michel Contat and Michel Rybalka (Paris: Éditions Gallimard, 1970). This translation by Richard McCleary was first published as "A More Precise Characterization of Existentialism," in *The Writings of Jean-Paul Sartre, Volume 2: Selected Prose*, eds. Michel Contat and Michel Rybalka (Evanston, IL: Northwestern University Press, 1974) and is used by permission of Northwestern University Press; copyright © 1974 by Northwestern University Press.

1. *Action* was a communist weekly. Francis Ponge, the poet, was its cultural editor. After the Liberation it attacked Sartre and existentialism but allowed Sartre to reply. [AvdH]

2. René Marill-Albérès is the author of a study of Sartre entitled *Jean-Paul Sartre: Philosopher Without Faith* (New York: Philosophical Library, 1961). [AvdH]

3. In 1942 Albert Camus published *The Myth of Sisyphus*, which clearly spelled out his position regarding the absurdity of existence. [AvdH]

4. On the night of August 4, 1789, the Constituent Assembly put an end to the feudal system and all privileges. [AvdH]

5. Alain Laubreaux was one of the editors of *Je suis partout* (1930–44), which had become a racist and then a collaborationist weekly during the 1930s and World War II. [AvdH]

6. Association de la jeunesse internationale; Jeunesse ouvrière chrétienne. [AvdH]

ON THE AMERICAN WORKING CLASS

Sartre wrote thirty-two articles about his 1945 trip to the United States; the story of his trip is told in Annie Cohen-Solal, *Sartre: A Life* (New York: Pantheon, 1985); for a detailed discussion see Michael Scriven, *Sartre and the Media* (London: Macmillan, 1993). Twenty of the articles were published in *Combat* (February 2 to June 30, 1945) and a dozen in *Le Figaro* (January 24 to July 30, 1946). Seven of the articles from Le Figaro (gathered as "Individualism and Conformism in the United States" and "American Cities") were reprinted in *Situations III* (Paris: Éditions Gallimard, 1949) and later published in *Literary and Philosophical Essays*, trans. Annette Michelson (New York: Collier, 1955). The *Combat* articles gathered here, which were first translated by Adrian van den Hoven and published in *Sartre Studies International* and *Dissent* in 2000–2001, are the only ones to be reprinted in any language; translation copyright © 2000–2001 by Adrian van den Hoven.

1. Taken from André Siegfried, *America Comes of Age: A French Analysis*, trans. H. H. and Doris Hemming (New York: Harcourt Brace, 1927). [AvdH and RA]

2. On February 26, 1946, *Combat* published a front-page article entitled "With His Salary an American Can Buy Five Times More Manufactured Products Than a French Salaried Worker and Two to Five Times More Foodstuffs." [AvdH and RA]

3. Hendrik de Man (1885–1953) wrote studies of the Dutch and Belgian working classes as well as *Au-delà du Marxisme* (1929) and *The Psychology of Socialism* (1927). [AvdH and RA]

THE LIBERATION OF PARIS:
AN APOCALYPTIC WEEK

First published as "La Libération de Paris: Une Semaine d'apocalypse," *Clarté* (August 24, 1945); reprinted in *Les Écrits de Sartre: Chronologie, Bibliographie commentée*, eds. Michel Contat and Michel Rybalka (Paris: Éditions Gallimard, 1970). This translation by Richard McCleary was originally published in *The Writings of Jean-Paul Sartre, Volume 2: Selected Prose*, eds. Michel Contat and Michel Rybalka (Evanston, IL: Northwestern University

Press, 1974) and is used by permission of Northwestern University Press; copyright © 1974 by Northwestern University Press.

1. Les Forces Françaises de l'Intérieur (FFI) were the combined underground paramilitary forces of the French Resistance. [RA]

2. General der Infanterie Dietrich von Choltitz was the military governor of Paris at the time. He claimed to have disobeyed Hitler's order to destroy Paris during this stage of the war, but this is disputed. [RA]

3. Charles Maurras (1868–1952) became the editor of *L'Action Française*, a nationalist and counterrevolutionary journal. He supported Vichy and was sentenced to life imprisonment after the war. [RA]

NEW YORK, COLONIAL CITY
First published as "Manhattan: The Great American Desert," *Town and Country* (May 1946); retranslated into French as "Ville coloniale," *Spectateur* (July 2, 1946); published as "New York, ville coloniale," in *Situations III* (Paris: Éditions Gallimard, 1949). This translation by Chris Turner was first published in *The Aftermath of War* (Oxford: Seagull Books, 2008) and is used by permission of Seagull Books; copyright © 2008 by Chris Turner.

NICK'S BAR, NEW YORK CITY
First published in *Jazz 47*, a special issue of *America* (June 25, 1947); reprinted in *Les Écrits de Sartre: Chronologie, Bibliographie commentée*, eds. Michel Contat and Michel Rybalka (Paris: Éditions Gallimard, 1970). This translation by Richard McCleary was originally published in *The Writings of Jean-Paul Sartre, Volume 2: Selected Prose*, eds. Michel Contat and Michel Rybalka (Evanston, IL: Northwestern University Press, 1974) and is used by permission of Northwestern University Press; copyright © 1974 by Northwestern University Press.

INTRODUCING *LES TEMPS MODERNES*
First published in the premier issue of *Les Temps modernes* (October 1945); reprinted in *Situations II* (Paris: Éditions Gallimard, 1948). This translation by Jeffrey Mehlman was originally published in *"What Is Literature?" and Other Essays* (Cambridge, MA: Harvard University Press, 1988), 247–68, and

is reprinted by permission of Harvard University Press; copyright © 1988 by the President and Fellows of Harvard University Press.

1. Les Forces Françaises de l'Intérieur (FFI) were the combined underground paramilitary forces of the French Resistance. [AvdH]

2. Alain published *Le Citoyen contre les pouvoirs* in 1925. [AvdH]

3. *Ten Days That Shook the World*, by John Reed, was published in 1919; *Spanish Testament*, by Arthur Koestler, was published in 1937. [AvdH]

CALDER'S MOBILES

First published in the catalogue for a Calder exhibition (October–November 1946); reprinted in *Situations III* (Paris: Éditions Gallimard, 1949). This translation by Chris Turner was originally published in *The Aftermath of War* (Oxford: Seagull Books, 2008) and is used by permission of Seagull books; copyright © 2008 by Chris Turner.

1. *Corps glorieux*. The reference is to Philippians 3:21. [Trans.]

2. Jacques de Vaucanson (1709–82) was a French inventor who was responsible for the creation of automata, the most famous of which was *The Digesting Duck*. He also created the first automated loom for which he proposed using punch cards. Perfected, it became known as the Jacquard loom. [AvdH]

BLACK ORPHEUS

First published as the introduction to Léopold Sédar Senghor, *Anthologie de la nouvelle poésie nègre et malgache* (Paris: Presses Universitaires de France, 1948); reprinted in part in *Les Temps modernes* (October 1948); reprinted in full in *Situations III* (Paris: Éditions Gallimard, 1949). This translation by Chris Turner was first published in *The Aftermath of War* (Oxford: Seagull Books, 2008) and is used by permission of Seagull Books; copyright © 2008 by Chris Turner.

NB: Where the poems cited are from Senghor's anthology, the translator gives the references as: A, page number.

1. Senghor, "Femme noire," *Chants d'ombre* (A, 151).

2. Guy Tirolien, "Prière d'un petit enfant nègre" (A, 87).

3. Léon-G. Damas, "Un clochard m'a demandé dix sous," *Pigments* (A, 14).

4. Aimé Césaire, "Et les chiens se taisaient," *Les armes miraculeuses.*

5. Senghor, "A l'appel de la race de Saba" (A, 152).

6. Jaques Rabémananjara, "Lyre à sept cordes (Cantate)" (A, 201).

7. Césaire, "Cahier d'un retour au pays natal" (A, 59).

8. In fact Sartre uses the term "*le grand soir*" ("the great evening"). This notion defines a revolutionary break where everything becomes possible. This notion was shared by Marxists and anarchists of the nineteenth century and refers to the complete destruction of the old regime and the creation of a totally new society. [AvdH]

9. Damas, "Limbe," *Pigments* (A, 9).

10. Even though Gaelic is indeed Ireland's official language, it is English that is the mother tongue of the vast majority of the Irish people. [AvdH]

11. Léon Laleau, "Trahison" (A, 108).

12. See "A New Mystic," 50. [AvdH]

13. Stephen Mallarmé, "Magie," in *Oeuvres complètes* (Paris: Éditions Gallimard, 1945), 400.

14. Césaire, "Tam-tam II," *Les armes miraculeuses*, 156.

15. Tirolien, "L'âme du noir pays" (A, 87).

16. Césaire, "L'irrémédiable," *Les armes miraculeuses.*

17. Césaire, "Barbare," *Soleil cou coupé* (A, 56).

18. The hainteny is the traditional source of Malagasy oral literature and poetry, involving heavy use of metaphor. [AvdH]

19. Césaire, "Le cristal automatique," *Les armes miraculeuses.*

20. Césaire, "L'irrémédiable," *Les armes miraculeuses.*

21. Lero, "Châtaignes aux cils" (A, 53).

22. Césaire, "Barbare," *Soleil cou coupé* (A, 56).

23. Césaire, "Soleil serpent," *Les armes miraculeuses* (A, 63).

24. Césaire, "Cahier d'un retour au pays natal" (A, 58–9). This translation by Clayton Eshleman and Annette Smith, from Aimé Césaire, *The Collected Poetry* (Berkeley: University of California Press, 1983), 67–69. [Trans.]

25. Ibid., 67.

26. Ibid., 69.

27. Senghor, "Congo," *Éthiopiques* (A, 168).

28. Senghor, *Chant du printemps* (A, 166).

29. Rabéarivelo, "Cactus," *Presque–Songes* (A, 189).

30. Laleau, "Sacrifice" (A, 108).

31. Rabéarivelo uses the following French neologism: "*lactogène*." [AvdH]

32. Rabéarivelo, "10," *Traduit de la nuit* (A, 182).

33. Césaire, *Les armes miraculeuses* (A, 73).

34. "Cahier d'un retour au pays natal" (A, 57–58). The second of these lines precedes the first in the published poem.

35. Paul Niger, "Lune" (A, 104).

36. See also "Nick's Bar, New York City." [AvdH]

37. Niger, "Je n'aime pas l'Afrique" (A, 100).

38. Damas, "La complainte du nègre," *Pigments* (A, 10–11).

39. J.-F. Brière, "Me revoici, Harlem" (A, 122).

40. For Sartre it is "the project that the For-itself makes of itself in History: by deciding to undertake the coup d'état of the 18th Brumaire, Bonaparte historializes himself" [*Truth and Existence*, ed. Ronald Aronson, trans. Adrian van den Hoven (University of Chicago Press, 1992), 79]. Sartre borrows this notion from Henry Corbin, who used it in *Qu'est-ce que la métaphysique?*, his 1937 translation of Heidegger's *Was ist der Metaphysik?* [AvdH]

41. Jacques Roumain, "Bois-d'Ebène" (A, 114).

42. In English in the text. An obvious reference to Richard Wright's eponymous novel. [AvdH]

43. Brière, "Black Soul" (A, 128).

44. Roumain, "Bois-d'Ebène" (A, 114).

45. This is a reference to Descartes's opening statement in *Meditations*, namely that common sense is the human characteristic that is most commonly shared. [AvdH]

46. Roumain, "Bois-d'Ebène" (A, 116).

47. Oddly, there is no question mark in the original text. [AvdH]

48. There appears to be a mistake in the version Sartre quotes: *"Je périrai. Mais un. Intact."*: "I will perish. But *one*. Intact." [emphasis is mine—AvdH]

49. Césaire, "Et le chiens se taisaient," *Les armes miraculeuses.*

50. *"Qui perd gagne"* ("the loser wins all") is one of Sartre's favorite statements, so much so that Philippe Knee used it as the title of his study of Sartre's philosophy (Quebec: Presses de l'Université Laval, 1993). [AvdH]

51. See "A New Mystic," 47. [AvdH]

52. Césaire, *Les armes miraculeuses*, 156.

THE QUEST FOR THE ABSOLUTE: ON GIACOMETTI'S SCULPTURE

First published in the exhibition catalogue for a Giacometti show in New York in January 1948; published in *Les Temps modernes* (January 1948); reprinted in *Situations III* (Paris: Éditions Gallimard, 1949). This translation by Chris Turner was first published in *The Aftermath of War* (Oxford: Seagull Books, 2008) and is used by permission of Seagull Books; copyright © 2008 by Chris Turner.

1. This passage bears a striking resemblance to the description Sartre's protagonist, Roquentin, provides in *La Nausée* (1938) when he draws his face close to the mirror. See *Nausea*, trans. Lloyd Alexander (New Directions, 1964), 17. Orography is the branch of physical geography which pertains to mountains and to features directly connected to mountains. [AvdH]

PORTRAIT OF THE ADVENTURER

First published as the preface to Roger Stéphane, *Portrait de l'aventurier* (Paris: Editions du Sagittaire, 1950); reprinted in *Situations VI* (Paris: Éditions Gallimard, 1964). This translation by Adrian van den Hoven; copyright © 2013 by Adrian van den Hoven.

1. See Georges Politzer, *Critique of the Foundations of Psychology*, trans. Maurice Apprey (Pittsburgh: Duquesne University Press, 1994). [AvdH]

2. Elizabeth Roudinesco disputes Sartre's interpretation in *Jacques Lacan & Co: A History of Psychoanalysis, 1925–1985*, trans. Jeffrey Mehlman (University of Chicago Press, 1990), 7–66, especially 62. [AvdH]

3. Sartre is quoting from Franz Kafka, *Journal intime: Suivi de Esquisse d'une autobiographie, Considérations sur le péché, Méditations*, trans. Pierre Kossowski (Lausanne: La Guilde du Livre, 1945; Editions Grasset, 1945). The original text can be found in Franz Kafka, *Nachgelassene Schriften und Fragmente*, ed. Jost Schillemeit (Frankfurt am Main: Fischer, 1992), 234–35. According to Ritchie Robertson, Oxford Kafka Center, no English translation exists. [AvdH]

4. Jean Genet, *Funeral Rites*, trans. Bernard Frechtman (New York: Grove Press, 1969), 119. [AvdH]

5. Stéphane borrows this expression from the character Annie in Sartre's *Nausea*. [AvdH]

6. As Paul Nizan describes communists in *Aden, Arabie* (Paris: François Maspero, 1960). [AvdH]

7. In André Malraux's *La Condition humaine* (*Man's Fate*), Tchen is a terrorist. He attempts to assassinate Chiang Kai-shek but fails and dies. [AvdH]

8. Sartre is referring to Mallarmé's poem "Un Coup de dés" ("A Throw of the Dice"). [AvdH]

9. In *Saint Genet* Sartre makes the following comment about Jaspers: "At least [Genet] seeks a way out. I cannot say as much for Jaspers, whose intolerable chatter about failure is an act of studied humbug. Genet is a victim, Jaspers a charlatan" [trans. Bernard Frechtman (New York: New American Library, 1964), 214]. [AvdH]

10. See Jean-Paul Sartre, *Critique of Dialectical Reason, Volume I: Theory of Practical Ensembles*, trans. Alan Sheridan-Smith (London: Verso, 1976), chapter 1, "The Dogmatic Dialectic and the Critical Dialectic." [AvdH]

REPLY TO ALBERT CAMUS

Written in response to Albert Camus, "Lettre au directeur des *Temps modernes*," *Les Temps modernes* (August 1952) and published as "Réponse à Albert Camus" in the same issue; reprinted in *Situations IV* (Paris: Éditions Gallimard, 1964). This translation by Chris Turner was originally published in *Portraits* (London: Seagull Books, 2009) and is used by permission of Seagull Books; copyright © 2009 by Chris Turner.

1. Characters from Molière's play *Les femmes savantes* (*The Learned Ladies*, 1672). Trissotin is described as a wit, Vadius as a classical scholar; they quarrel over the quality of Trissotin's poetry. Sartre's "Who would have said, who would have believed" here is also a clear reference to the well-known exchange between Rodrigue and Chimène in Act III, Scene 4 of Corneille's *Le Cid*. [Trans.]

2. Sartre is referring to the 1632 painting by Rembrandt entitled *The Anatomy Lesson of Dr. Nicolaes Tulp*. It portrays the public dissection of an executed criminal. Obviously, Dr. Tulp is not pointing out "wounds" but rather the musculature of the left forearm. [AvdH]

3. Literally, "passage of evil." The great Catholic writer's third play—published by La Table ronde (Paris, 1948) and staged the same year—was a resounding critical failure. [Trans.]

4. Madame Boucicault was the widow of French philanthropist Aristide Boucicault (1810–77). He created the Bon Marché in Paris. She continued her husband's philanthropic works. [AvdH].

5. Jeanson enlisted in the French army in Algeria in 1943 under General Girard. [AvdH]

6. *The Rebel: An Essay on Man in Revolt*, trans. Anthony Bower (London: Hamish Hamilton, 1953) [*L'Homme révolté* (Paris: Éditions Gallimard, 1951)]. [Trans.]

7. *Accusateur public*: the Prosecutor of the French Revolutionary Tribunal. [Trans.]

8. Pierre Hervé wrote a highly critical review of *The Rebel* in April 1952 for *La Nouvelle critique*, the monthly magazine of the PCF. [AvdH]

9. Henry de Montherlant (1896–1972): a novelist, playwright, and essayist. [Trans.]

10. The police headquarters. [AvdH]

11. David Rousset, a survivor of Buchenwald, was the first person to bring the Gulag system to light within the French left. He was denounced by

Les Lettres françaises in 1949 as a "falsifying Trotskyite," but went on to fight a successful libel action against this charge. [Trans.]

12. Sartre is referring to Senator Joseph McCarthy's anticommunist campaign of the 1950s. [Trans.]

13. Sartre's comments here are somewhat perplexing because Camus does not use in his article—nor in *The Rebel*, for that matter—the expression "*liberté sans frein*"; however, he does speak of Sartre's "terrible and incessant freedom." [AvdH]

14. This is a reference to Roger Troisfontaines, *Le Choix de Jean-Paul Sartre. Exposé et critique de "L'Etre et le Néant"* (Paris: Montaigne, 1945). [Trans.]

15. Jean-Paul Sartre, *Being and Nothingness: An Essay on Phenomenological Ontology*, trans. Hazel E. Barnes (New York: Methuen and Co., 1957) [*L'Être et le néant: Essai d'ontologie phénoménologique* (Paris: Éditions Gallimard, 1943)]. [Trans.]

16. Albert Camus, *L'Étranger* (Paris: Éditions Gallimard, 1942) [*The Stranger*, trans. Stuart Gilbert (New York: A. A. Knopf, 1946)]. [Trans.]

17. Georges Bataille, "Torture," in *The Inner Experience*, Leslie Anne Boldt (Albany: State University of New York Press, 1988). [Trans.]

18. My translation of part of an enigmatic fragment from Stéphane Mallarmé, "Igitur," in *Œuvres complètes*, eds. Henri Mondor and G. Jean-Aubry (Paris: Éditions Gallimard, 1945), 428. [Trans.]

19. Ménalque, like the Nathanaël mentioned below, is a character in André Gide's *Les Nourritures terrestres* (1897) [*The Fruits of the Earth*, trans. Dorothy Bussy (New York: Alfred A. Knopf, 1949)], who reappears in *L'Immoraliste* (1902) [*The Immoralist*, trans. Dorothy Bussy (New York: Alfred A. Knopf, 1930)]. It has sometimes been suggested that Ménalque was based on Oscar Wilde, but André Maurois says Gide personally rejected this suggestion. [Trans.]

20. Albert Camus, "Nuptials at Tipasa," in *Selected Essays and Notebooks*, ed. and trans. Philip Thody (Penguin, 1967), 71–72 (translation modified). [Trans.]

21. See note 19. [Trans.]

22. The epistolary novel *Obermann* was written by Étienne Pivet de Sénancour in 1804. [Trans.]

23. "Lettres à un ami allemand." Published in French in 1945; published for the first time in English as "Letters to a German Friend," in *Resistance, Rebellion, and Death*, trans. Justin O'Brien (New York: Random House, 1961). [Trans.]

24. Ibid.

25. Albert Camus, *La Peste* (Paris: Gallimard, 1947) [*The Plague*, trans. Stuart Gilbert (New York: A. A. Knopf, 1948)]. [Trans.]

26. Passy is a leafy suburb in the fashionable 16th arrondissement of Paris. Boulogne-Billancourt is a working-class area in that city's western suburbs. [Trans.]

27. These three quotations are from Camus, "Nuptials," in *Selected Essays and Notebooks*, 90, 97, 98 (the translation of the passage cited on 97 has been modified). [Trans.]

FROM *THE GHOST OF STALIN*

First published as "La Révolte de la Hongrie," the 121-page introduction to the triple issue of *Les Temps modernes* (January 1957), which had been in preparation before the revolution; reprinted in *Situations VII* (Paris: Éditions Gallimard, 1967). This translation by Martha Fletcher was first published in *The Ghost of Stalin* (New York: George Braziller, 1968), 61–81 and is used by permission of George Braziller, Inc.

1. *Borba* was the official newspaper of the League of Communists of Yugoslavia. [RA]

2. Karl Marx, introduction to "Contribution to the Critique of Hegel's Philosophy of Right," in *The Marx-Engels Reader*, ed. Robert Tucker (New York: Norton, 1978), 64. [RA]

3. Claude Bourdet, leftist journalist and founder of *L'Observateur*, forerunner of *Le Nouvel Observateur*. [RA]

A VICTORY

First published as a review of Henri Alleg's book *Une Question*, in *L'Express* 350, March 6, 1958. Because of Sartre's denunciation of torture in Algeria in the review, that issue of the newspaper was confiscated by the authorities. During the next several weeks the review was published as a pamphlet, confiscated again, then appeared as a scroll that could only be read with a magnifying glass, and finally was published in Switzerland as a preface to a reprinted version of Alleg's text. It was reprinted in *Situations V* (Paris: Éditions Gallimard, 1964); an English translation by John Calder is in *The Question* (Lincoln, NE: Bison, 2006). This translation by Azzedine Haddour et al. was first published in *Sartre: Colonialism and Neocolonialism* (New York: Routledge, 2001) and is used by permission of Taylor & Francis.

1. It was on this street in Paris that French people were tortured during World War II. [AvdH]

2. Lacoste was the governor-general of Algeria. [AvdH]

3. Oradour is infamous in French history. On June 10, 1944, the Second Panzer Division destroyed Oradour-sur-Glane and killed 642 of its inhabitants. Women and children were herded into the church and burned to death. The town has never been rebuilt and its ruins remain standing as a national monument. [AvdH]

4. El Biar is a suburb of Algiers. [AvdH]

5. The Marchioness de Brinvilliers (1630–76) was accused of poisoning poor people. She was tortured with the "water cure" and beheaded. [AvdH]

6. General Jacques Massu seized power in the Algiers crisis of 1958 and insisted that de Gaulle be put in charge of the republic. De Gaulle accepted on the condition that a new constitution be voted on, thus the Fifth Republic was born. General Massu was relieved of his duties on January 14, 1960, after threatening that the army would seize power in Algeria. [AvdH]

7. Ben Saddok was tried for the assassination of All Chekkal, the onetime vice president of the Algerian National Assembly and a strong supporter of France. Sartre appeared as a defense witness. Ben Saddok was sentenced to life in prison. [AvdH]

8. On June 17, 1957, Alleg was arrested at the home of Professor Maurice Audin, whom he was visiting. The latter died later in prison under suspicious circumstances. [AvdH]

9. Abdelkader Guerroudj, who was the leader of the "*groupe d'action*" of the Algerian Communist Party, and his wife, Jacqueline, were condemned to death in December 1957. Neither was executed. [AvdH]

10.   The ALN was the military arm of the Front de Libération Nationale (FLN). [AvdH]

11.   Albert Memmi published *Portrait du colonisé, précédé par Portrait du colonisateur (The Colonizer and the Colonized)* in 1957, for which Sartre wrote the preface. [AvdH]

PAUL NIZAN

First published as the foreword to Paul Nizan, *Aden, Arabie* (Paris: François Maspero, 1960); reprinted in *Situations IV* (Paris: Éditions Gallimard, 1964). This translation by Chris Turner was first published in *Portraits* (London: Seagull Books, 2009) and is used by permission of Seagull Books; copyright © 2009 by Chris Turner.

1.   Paul Nizan, *Aden, Arabie*, trans. Joan Pinkham (New York: Monthly Review Press, 1960) [*Aden, Arabie* (Paris: François Maspero, 1960)]. Paul Nizan, *Antoine Bloyé*, trans. Edmund Stevens (Moscow: Co-operative Publishing Society of Foreign Workers in the USSR, 1935) [*Antoine Bloyé* (Paris: Grasset: 1933)]. [Trans.]

2.   "*Tu causes, tu causes, c'est tout ce que tu sais faire!*" This is the refrain of the parrot in Raymond Queneau, *Zazie dans le métro* (Paris: Éditions Gallimard, 1959). [Trans.]

3.   "Le Lac," a poem by Alphonse de Lamartine (1790–1869), is one of the classics of French poetry routinely learned by French schoolchildren in this period. Similarly, the sermons of Jaques-Bénigne Bossuet (1627–1704) were taught as models of French prose style. [Trans.]

4.   Antoine Pinay (1891–1994): a French conservative politician who served as the prime minister of France in 1952. [Trans.]

5.   SFIO: Section Française de l'Internationale Ouvrière—the French Section of the Workers' International—was founded in 1905. A French socialist political party, it was designed as the local section of the Second International. After the 1917 October Revolution, it split (during the 1920 Tours Congress) into two groups, the majority creating the Section Française de l'Internationale Communiste (SFIC), which became the French Communist Party (PCF). [Trans.]

6.   Georges-Augustin Bidault (1899–1983): a Christian Democratic French politician, active in the French Resistance during World War II. After

the war, he served as the foreign minister and prime minister on several occasions between 1945 and 1953. [Trans.]

7.   In English in the text. [AvdH]

8.   Jean-Paul Sartre, *Nausea*, trans. Lloyd Alexander (New York: New Directions, 1959) [*La Nausée* (Paris: Éditions Gallimard, 1938)]. [Trans.]

9.   On September 26, 1958, there was a 79.2 percent referendum vote in favor of the Constitution of the new Fifth Republic with de Gaulle as president. [Trans.]

10. Léon Brunschvicg (1869–1944): a French idealist philosopher who taught at the Sorbonne. Sartre and Nizan were both students of his and he supervised Simone de Beauvoir's thesis on Leibniz. [Trans.]

11. It was Paul Nizan who wrote *Les Chiens de garde* (Paris: Rieder, 1932) [*Watchdogs: Philosophers and the Established Order*, trans. Paul Fittingoff (New York: Monthly Review Press, 1972)]. [Trans.]

12. Paul Nizan, *The Conspiracy*, trans. Quintin Hoare (London: Verso, 1989) [*La Conspiration* (Paris: Éditions Gallimard, 1973)]. [Trans.]

13. Nizan, *Antoine Bloyé*, 299. All translations from this work are by me. [Trans.]

14. The first-year class of the two-year preparatory course for the arts section of the École normale supérieure. [Trans.]

15. Georges Valois (1878–1945): a once prominent member of the monarchist Action Française and the leader of France's first substantial fascist movement, Le Faisceau. [Trans.]

16. Nizan, *Aden, Arabie*, 61 (translation modified). [Trans.]

17. See Paul Valéry, *Monsieur Teste*, trans. Jackson Matthews (New York: Alfred A. Knopf, 1947); also available in Jackson Matthews, ed., *Collected Works of Paul Valéry, Volume 6: Monsieur Teste* (Princeton University Press, 1989). [Trans.]

18. Nizan, *Antoine Bloyé*, 310. It would seem that Sartre misquotes Nizan here, who does not write, as Sartre suggests, of the "*visage uniforme de sa vie*" but of the "*visage informe de toute sa vie*"—the *formless* countenance of his whole life. [Trans.]

19. Nizan, *Aden, Arabie*, 65.

20. Nizan, *Antoine Bloyé*, 260–61.

21. Nizan, *Aden, Arabie*, 65.

22. Nizan, *Antoine Bloyé*, 273.

23. Nizan, *Aden, Arabie*, 102–3.

24. Nizan, *Antoine Bloyé*, 140–41.

25. Ibid., 281–84.

26. The French expression here is *hurlait à la mort*, which reflects a folk belief that dogs have an intuitive sense of death. A particularly lugubrious style of barking is thought to derive from the dog's perception that someone in the surrounding area is dead or dying. [Trans.]

27. Nizan, *Antoine Bloyé*, 271.

28. Ibid., 276.

29. Nizan, *Aden, Arabie*, 83.

30. Nizan, *Antoine Bloyé*, 137.

31. See Paul Nizan, *Les matérialistes de l'antiquité. Démocrite, Épicure, Lucrèce* (Paris: François Maspero, 1965 [1938]). [Trans.]

32. Nizan, *Aden, Arabie*, 85 (translation modified). [Trans.]

33. Ibid., 159 (translation modified). [Trans.]

34. The quotation is from Stéphane Mallarmé, "Plusieurs sonnets, IV," in *Œuvres complètes*, eds. Henri Mondor and G. Jean-Aubry (Paris: Éditions Gallimard, 1945), 68. [Trans.]

35. Nizan, *Antoine Bloyé*, 135–36.

36. Ibid., 207.

37. Ibid., 285.

38. Sartre was at Brumath, Alsace, in November 1939 when he began writing the second of his surviving wartime notebooks, which were published as *Les carnets de la drôle de guerre: Septembre 1939–Mars 1940* (Paris: Éditions Gallimard, 1995, second edition) [*War Diaries: Notebooks from a Phony War 1939–40*, trans. Quintin Hoare (London: Verso, 1984)]. [Trans.]

39.   Nizan, *Antoine Bloyé*, 307–8.

40.   Ibid., 310.

MERLEAU-PONTY

A eulogy, first published as "Merleau-Ponty vivant," *Les Temps modernes* (October 1961); reprinted in *Situations IV* (Paris: Éditions Gallimard, 1964). This translation by Chris Turner was originally published in *Portraits* (London: Seagull Books, 2009) and is used by permission of Seagull Books; copyright © 2009 by Chris Turner.

1.   Joseph Rouletabille was a fictional detective created by Gaston Leroux, now perhaps better known as the author of *The Phantom of the Opera*. [Trans.]

2.   See Maurice Merleau-Ponty, *Signs*, trans. Richard McCleary (Evanston, IL: Northwestern University Press, 1964), 39 [*Signes* (Paris: Éditions Gallimard, 1960)]. Sartre is paraphrasing slightly. [Trans.]

3.   Maurice Merleau-Ponty, *Phenomenology of Perception*, trans. Colin Smith (London: Routledge and Kegan Paul Ltd, 1962) [*Phénoménologie de la Perception* (Paris: Éditions Gallimard, 1945)]. [Trans.]

4.   Maurice Merleau-Ponty, *Humanism and Terror: An Essay on the Communist Problem*, trans. John O'Neill (Boston: Beacon Press, 1969) [*Humanisme et terreur, essai sur le problème communiste* (Paris: Éditions Gallimard, 1947)]. [Trans.]

5.   Maurice Merleau-Ponty, "La guerre a eu lieu," *Les Temps modernes* 1 (October 1945). [Trans.]

6.   Ibid.

7.   Pierre Courtade (1915–63), Pierre Hervé (1913–93), and Jean-Toussaint Desanti (1914–2002). [Trans.]

8.   Sartre provides no references for this quotation and the following one, but this first passage can be found in Maurice Merleau-Ponty, *Sens et non-sens* (Paris: Éditions Gallimard, 1996), 201–2. [Trans.]

9.   Ibid., 205.

10.   Sartre writes "*nous-même*" here, singular, not "*nous-mêmes*," which suggests an authorial "we" that refers to himself alone: the context seems to

suggest, however, that he is thinking of those who remained at *Les Temps modernes* beyond its first beginnings, i.e., chiefly Merleau and himself. [Trans.]

Raymond Aron (1905–83) and Sartre went to the École normale supérieure together. He introduced Sartre to Husserl's phenomenology and was instrumental in Sartre obtaining a scholarship to study in Berlin in 1933. They were still friends when Sartre started *Les Temps modernes* but soon their political opinions began to diverge significantly. Jean Paulhan (1884–1968) was a prolific author and he recommended Sartre's *Nausea* to Gallimard. He was an active member of the Resistance and was arrested by the Gestapo. Recently, Anne Desclos revealed that she had written *The Story of O* as a series of love letters to Paulhan. Albert Ollivier (1915–64) was Gaston Gallimard's secretary and was also a member of the Resistance. Later on he became a Gaullist and director of the Office de la Radio Télévision Française. [AR and AvdH]

11. Literally, "cellar rats"—those who frequented the jazz-saturated cellar nightclubs of the immediate postwar years. [Trans.]

12. Sartre is referring to the article "The USSR and the Camps," reprinted in *Signs*, 263–73. It was published originally in January 1950. [Trans.]

13. Père Joseph—Father Joseph—was the éminence grise of Cardinal de Richelieu. [Trans.]

14. Maurice Merleau-Ponty, *La guerre a eu lieu* (Paris: Éditions Champ Social, 2007), 55. This work, originally published in *Les Temps modernes* 1 (October 1945): 48–66, is also reprinted in *Sens et non-sens*. [Trans.]

15. RDR: Le Rassemblement Démocratique Révolutionnaire. [Trans.]

16. PCF: Parti Communiste Français—the French Communist Party. [Trans.]

17. Yves Farge (1899–1953): one of the founders in February 1948 of Les Combattants de la liberté, the forerunner of the French Mouvement de la Paix, of which he was the president until his death in a car accident near Tbilisi (Georgia, USSR). [Trans.]

18. Merleau-Ponty, *Signs*, 265.

19. Ibid., 266.

20. Ibid., 267–68.

21. Ibid., 268–69 (translation modified). [Trans.]

22. Ibid., 268.

23. Ibid., 265.

24. Ibid., 269 (translation modified). [Trans.]

25. Ibid., 32–33.

26. Paul Rivet (1876–1958): one of the founders of the prewar Comité de vigilance des intellectuels antifascistes, which was one of the organizations that contributed to the emergence of the French Popular Front. [Trans.]

27. Henri Martin: a French sailor who was arrested for sabotage in March 1950 in French Indochina. Though cleared of that charge, he was sentenced to five years' imprisonment for distributing antiwar propaganda. He was freed in August 1953 after a national campaign to liberate him, in which Sartre played a prominent role. The book to which Sartre refers here, and which contained contributions from Michel Leiris, Vercors, Francis Jeanson, Jacques Prévert, and Hervé Bazin among others, is *L'Affaire Henri Martin* (Paris: Éditions Gallimard, 1953). [Trans.]

28. The Communist leader Jacques Duclos had been arrested after a demonstration. Two dead pigeons in his car were alleged to have been "carrier pigeons" for communicating with Moscow. [Trans.]

29. Jean-Paul Sartre, "Les Communistes et la paix," Part 1, *Les Temps modernes* 81 (July 1952); Part 2, *Les Temps modernes* 84–85 (October–November 1952); Part 3, *Les Temps modernes* (April 1954). Reproduced in Jean-Paul Sartre, *Situations VI* (Paris: Éditions Gallimard, 1964), 80–384 [*The Communists and Peace: With a Reply to Claude Lefort*, trans. Martha H. Fletcher and Philip R. Berk (New York: George Braziller, 1968)]. [Trans.]

30. Lucien Rebatet (1903–72): a fascist, anti-Semitic writer who had been a prominent journalist on the magazine *Je suis partout* before and during the Nazi occupation. [Trans.]

31. Jean-Bertrand Pontalis, better known today as a Lacanian psychoanalyst and man of letters. [Trans.]

32. The pseudonym of François Emmanuel (1914–99), the Romanian-born journalist, critic, and publisher. [Trans.]

33. The prolific writer Jean Cau (1925–93) was Sartre's secretary at this time. He was to win the Prix Goncourt in 1961 for his novel *La pitié de Dieu*. In later years, he switched political camps dramatically and became involved with GRECE and the so-called New Right. [Trans.]

34. Merleau-Ponty, "From Mauss to Claude Lévi-Strauss," in *Signs*, 123.

35. Merleau-Ponty, "Man and Adversity," in *Signs*, 229.

36. Maurice Merleau-Ponty, "Eye and Mind," in *The Primacy of Perception*, ed. James Edie, trans. Carleton Dallery (Evanston, IL: Northwestern University Press, 1964) [*L'Œil et l'esprit* (Paris: Éditions Gallimard, 1961)]. [Trans.]

37. Merleau-Ponty speaks of the eyes as *computeurs du monde*, "computers of the world." See "Eye and Mind," in *The Primacy of Perception*, 165. [Trans.]

38. *La Vie de Marianne*, begun in 1727, is an unfinished novel by Pierre de Marivaux. The novel was written in sections, eleven of which appeared between 1731 and 1745. [Trans.]

39. "Being" or "the Being." [Trans.]

40. Merleau-Ponty, "Man and Adversity," in *Signs*, 240.

41. Merleau-Ponty, "Reading Montaigne," in *Signs*, 202.

42. Maurice Merleau-Ponty, *Les aventures de la dialectique* (Paris: Éditions Gallimard, 1955) [*Adventures of the Dialectic*, trans. Joseph Bien (Evanston, IL: Northwestern University Press, 1973). [Trans.]

43. This is presumably a reference to *Le visible et l'invisible, suivi de notes de travail*, published posthumously, along with Merleau's notes for its continuation, by his friend Claude Lefort (Paris: Éditions Gallimard, 1964). See Maurice Merleau-Ponty, *The Visible and the Invisible, Followed by Working Notes*, trans. Alphonso Lingis (Evanston, IL: Northwestern University Press, 1968). [Trans.]

44. See Merleau-Ponty, "Eye and Mind," in *The Primacy of Perception*, 161. [Trans.]

45. Ibid., 190 (translation modified). [Trans.]

THE WRETCHED OF THE EARTH
First published as the preface to Frantz Fanon, *Les damnés de la terre* (Paris:

François Maspero, 1961); reprinted in *Situations V* (Paris: Éditions Gallimard, 1964). This translation by Azzedine Haddour et al. was first published
in *Sartre: Colonialism and Neocolonialism* (New York: Routledge, 2001) and
is used by permission of Taylor & Francis.

1.   On May 15, 1945, the nationalists organized a demonstration in Sétif,
      Algeria; it was violently suppressed. Historians estimated the number
      of deaths at between 8,000 and 15,000. The Indochina war started with
      the French naval shelling of Hanoi in December 1946, in which 6,000
      Vietnamese were killed. An insurrection broke out in Madagascar in
      1947–48; it too was suppressed, with between 11,000 and 19,000 deaths.
      [AvdH]

2.   In July 1960, Katanga, under Moise Tshombe, broke away from the
      newly independent Democratic Republic of the Congo that was led by
      Patrice Lumumba. This move was widely understood to have been en-
      couraged by foreign mining interests. [AvdH]

3.   Georges Sorel (1847–1922) is considered a precursor of fascism. His "an-
      timaterialist" revisions of Marxism are considered a basic element of the
      fascist synthesis. [AvdH]

4.   This a reference to Albert Camus's work of the same title. [AvdH]

5.   Marshal Bugeaud was responsible for the violent "pacification" of the
      Algerian countryside in the 1830s and 1840s. [AvdH]

6.   The port of Bizerte was the site of a military conflict between France
      and Tunisia in 1961, which resulted ultimately in the withdrawal of
      French troops and the independence of Tunisia toward the end of 1963.
      During a protest march in Paris on October 17, 1961, it is claimed that
      three hundred Algerians were killed and 2,300 wounded. However,
      there is no evidence of a lynching during the Algerian War. [AvdH]

KIERKEGAARD: THE SINGULAR UNIVERSAL

This was a lecture delivered to a UNESCO colloquium entitled "The Living
Kierkegaard," in April 1964; first published as "L'Universel singulier," in
Kierkegaard vivant (Paris: Éditions Gallimard, 1966) and reprinted in *Situa-
tions IX* (Paris: Éditions Gallimard, 1972). This translation by John Matthews
was originally published in *Between Existentialism and Marxism* (London:
Verso, 1974) and is used by permission of Verso.

1. Giuseppe Arcimboldo (1530–93) was a painter of fantastic faces and figures. [Trans.]

2. Epigraph to Søren Kierkegaard, *Philosophical Fragments*, trans. David Swenson (Princeton University Press, 1962). [Trans.]

3. Sartre uses "think" transitively. [Trans.]

4. Kierkegaard, *Philosophical Fragments*, 17. [Trans.]

5. Referred to by Kierkegaard in *Papirer, Edifying Discourses*, and *Concluding Unscientific Postscript*. [Trans.]

6. Emmanuel de Grouchy was a general under Napoleon at Waterloo. [Trans.]

7. Quoted from a letter concerning Kierkegaard from Pastor A. F. Schioedte to H. P. Barford, dated September 12, 1869. [Trans.]

8. Franz Kafka, "An Imperial Message." [Trans.]

9. Søren Kierkegaard, *Papirer*, VII A 181. [Trans.]

10. Paul-Henri Tisseau was one of Kierkegaard's French translators. [Trans.]

RUSSELL VIETNAM WAR CRIMES TRIBUNAL
INAUGURAL STATEMENT

This was the opening speech at the tribunal's first meeting on May 2, 1967, in Stockholm; first published in *Tribunal Russell: Le Jugement de Stockholm* (Paris: Éditions Gallimard, 1967). This translation is from *Prevent the Crime of Silence: Reports from the Sessions of the International War Crimes Tribunal founded by Bertrand Russell* (London: Allen Lane, 1971).

1. "In the language of the Nuremberg prosecutors, aggressive leaders who launch unjust wars commit 'crimes against peace.' What constitutes a just or unjust resort to armed force is disclosed to us by the rules of *jus ad bellum*." Entry entitled "War," in *Stanford Encyclopedia of Philosophy*, available at http://plato.stanford.edu/entries/war/#2.1. [Trans.]

2. "Law on the prevention of war." [Trans.]

3. Sartre is referring to Hegel. [Trans.]

ISRAEL AND THE ARAB WORLD

Interview by Claudine Chonez, *Le Fait public 3* (February 1969); reprinted in *Situations VIII* (Paris: Éditions Gallimard, 1972). This translation is by Adrian van den Hoven; copyright © 2013 by Adrian van den Hoven.

1.   Just before the beginning of the Six-Day War between Israel and the Arab countries, in June 1967, President Charles de Gaulle imposed an arms embargo, ending twenty years of strong military cooperation between France and Israel. That November in a news conference he created a scandal when he described the Jewish people as "this elite people, sure of themselves and domineering." [AvdH]

2.   Mapam was a leftist Zionist party that eventually became one of the constituents of the current Meretz. [AvdH]

THE SOCIALISM THAT CAME IN FROM THE COLD

First published as "Le Socialisme qui venait du froid," the preface to Antonín J. Liehm, *Trois Générations* (Paris: Éditions Gallimard, 1970), the French translation of the Czech work *Generace*; reprinted in *Situations IX* (Paris: Éditions Gallimard, 1972); first English translation as "The Socialism That Came in from the Cold," *Evergreen Review* 84 (November 1971). This translation by Helen R. Lane was first published as the introduction to Antonín J. Liehm, *The Politics of Culture*, trans. Peter Kussi (New York: Grove Press, Inc., 1968) and is used by permission of Grove/Atlantic; copyright © 1970 by Grove Press.

1.   In 1968 the Czech and Slovak republics were still one country called Czechoslovakia. This is the year of the Prague Spring, and "Socialism with a Human Face" was suppressed by the invading Soviet bloc countries. The Munich Agreement of 1938 allowed Hitler to annex the German-speaking parts of the country and soon led to the total occupation of the country by the Nazi regime. [AvdH]

2.   The Prague trials began on November 20, 1952. Rudolf Slánský and thirteen members of the Communist Party were accused of participating in a Trotskyite-Titoite-Zionist conspiracy. Slánský and ten others were executed and three others were sentenced to life imprisonment. [AvdH]

3.   In 1935 Edvard Beneš succeeded Masaryk as president. He opposed the Nazis' claim to the German-speaking Sudetenland. After the Munich Agreement he was forced to resign on October 5, 1938. [AvdH]

4. Sartre discusses Hegel's conception of truth in *Vérité et existence* (Paris: Éditions Gallimard, 1989), 27; see *Truth and Existence*, ed. Ronald Aronson, trans. Adrian van den Hoven (University of Chicago Press, 1992), 9. [AvdH]

5. Sartre discusses the USSR and "Socialism in One Country" in great detail in *Critique de la raison dialectique,* vol. II (Paris: Éditions Galliard, 1985); see *Critique of Dialectical Reason*, vol. II (London: Verso, 2006). [AvdH]

6. Rosa Luxemburg, "Democracy and Dictatorship," *The Russian Revolution,* available at http://www.marxists.org/archive/luxemburg/1918/russian-revolution/ch08.htm. [AvdH]

7. Vítězslav Nezval's novel *The Joke* dates from 1935. [AvdH]

8. The phrase is derived from Gorky's play *The Lower Depths* (1901), and was spoken by Sahtin, a thief and derelict, in an almost two-minute extemporization on the value of human dignity. [AvdH]

THE THIRD WORLD BEGINS IN THE SUBURBS

Presented as part of the discussion entitled "Le tiers-monde commence en banlieue," which was organized by the General Union of Senegalese Immigrants on the occasion of the publication of *Le Livre des travailleurs africains en France* (Paris: François Maspero, 1970); published under the title "Les pays capitalistes et leurs colonies intérieures," *Tricontinental* (Paris, 1970); reprinted as "Le tiers-monde commence en banlieue," in *Situations VIII* (Paris: Éditions Gallimard, 1972). This translation is by Adrian van den Hoven; copyright © 2013 by Adrian van den Hoven.

ELECTIONS: A TRAP FOR FOOLS

First published in *Les Temps modernes* 318 (January 1973); reprinted in *Situations X* (Paris: Éditions Gallimard, 1976). This translation by Paul Auster and Lydia Davis was first published in *Life/Situations: Essays Written and Spoken* (New York: Pantheon Books, 1977) and is used by permission of Pantheon Books, a division of Random House, Inc; copyright © 1977 by Random House, Inc.

1. The Le Chapelier law of June 1781 forbade workers, tradespeople, and peasants from organizing. [Trans.]

2. Marc Kravetz was a journalist at *Libération*. [Trans.]

3. Union pour la défense de la République (the Gaullist party). [Trans.]

4. Georges Séguy was the secretary-general of the Confédération générale du travail (CGT), a trade union with links to the French Communist Party. [Trans.]

5. Guy Mollet was a socialist politician. He formed the Republican Front in 1956 and promised to reestablish peace in Algeria. Instead he poured troops into the country, which resulted in the Battle of Algiers (June–October 1957). His government collapsed in June 1957 on the issue of taxation to pay for the Algerian War. [Trans.]

6. Georges Pompidou was elected president of the republic in 1969. He unexpectedly died in office on April 2, 1974. [Trans.]

7. Jean-Jacques Servan-Schreiber was the minister of government reform from May 27 until June 9, 1974. Jean Lecanuet was the minister of justice from 1974 to 1976. [Trans.]

FROM "SELF-PORTRAIT AT SEVENTY"

The full text of this interview with Michel Contat appeared in *Le Nouvel Observateur* (June 23, 30, and July 7, 1975); reprinted in *Situations X* (Paris: Éditions Gallimard, 1976). This translation by Paul Auster and Lydia Davis was first published in *Life/Situations: Essays Written and Spoken* (New York: Pantheon Books, 1977) and is used by permission of Pantheon Books, a division of Random House, Inc; copyright © 1977 by Random House, Inc.

1. This sentence is from Stendhal's novel *Le Rouge et le noir* (*The Red and the Black*). [Trans.]

2. See Jean-Paul Sartre, *Being and Nothingness: An Essay on Phenomenological Ontology*, trans. Hazel Barnes (New York: Philosophical Library, 1956), 615. [Trans.]

3. Portugal's Carnation Revolution started on April 25, 1974. The first free election was held on April 25, 1975. In 1976, after another election, the moderate socialist Mario Suares assumed office as prime minister. [Trans.]

4. In his *Pensées* (1670), Blaise Pascal formulates the wager as follows: "Let us weigh the gain and the loss by selecting 'heads' that God exists. Con-

sider then these two cases: if you win, you will have won everything; if you lose, you have lost nothing. Therefore wager that he exists without hesitating." [Trans.]

5. In January 1950 Sartre and Merleau-Ponty denounced the existence of the camps in an unsigned editorial in *Les Temps modernes*. [Trans.]

6. Jean Pasqualini, *Prisoner of Mao* (Harmondsworth, UK: Penguin, 1976). [Trans.]

7. Simone de Beauvoir, *Force of Circumstance* (Harmondsworth, UK: Penguin, 1964), 674. [Trans.]

TITLES IN SERIES

For a complete list of titles, visit www.nyrb.com or write to:
Catalog Requests, NYRB, 435 Hudson Street, New York, NY 10014

* *Also available as an electronic book.*

PAUL GOODMAN Growing Up Absurd: Problems of Youth in the Organized Society*
EDWARD GOREY (EDITOR) The Haunted Looking Glass
A.C. GRAHAM Poems of the Late T'ang
WILLIAM LINDSAY GRESHAM Nightmare Alley*
EMMETT GROGAN Ringolevio: A Life Played for Keeps
VASILY GROSSMAN An Armenian Sketchbook*
VASILY GROSSMAN Everything Flows*
VASILY GROSSMAN Life and Fate*
VASILY GROSSMAN The Road*
OAKLEY HALL Warlock
PATRICK HAMILTON The Slaves of Solitude
PATRICK HAMILTON Twenty Thousand Streets Under the Sky
PETER HANDKE Short Letter, Long Farewell
PETER HANDKE Slow Homecoming
ELIZABETH HARDWICK The New York Stories of Elizabeth Hardwick*
ELIZABETH HARDWICK Seduction and Betrayal*
ELIZABETH HARDWICK Sleepless Nights*
L.P. HARTLEY Eustace and Hilda: A Trilogy*
L.P. HARTLEY The Go-Between*
NATHANIEL HAWTHORNE Twenty Days with Julian & Little Bunny by Papa
PAUL HAZARD The Crisis of the European Mind: 1680–1715*
GILBERT HIGHET Poets in a Landscape
JANET HOBHOUSE The Furies
HUGO VON HOFMANNSTHAL The Lord Chandos Letter*
JAMES HOGG The Private Memoirs and Confessions of a Justified Sinner
RICHARD HOLMES Shelley: The Pursuit*
ALISTAIR HORNE A Savage War of Peace: Algeria 1954–1962*
GEOFFREY HOUSEHOLD Rogue Male*
WILLIAM DEAN HOWELLS Indian Summer
BOHUMIL HRABAL Dancing Lessons for the Advanced in Age*
DOROTHY B. HUGHES The Expendable Man*
RICHARD HUGHES A High Wind in Jamaica*
RICHARD HUGHES In Hazard*
RICHARD HUGHES The Fox in the Attic (The Human Predicament, Vol. 1)*
RICHARD HUGHES The Wooden Shepherdess (The Human Predicament, Vol. 2)*
INTIZAR HUSAIN Basti*
MAUDE HUTCHINS Victorine
YASUSHI INOUE Tun-huang*
HENRY JAMES The Ivory Tower
HENRY JAMES The New York Stories of Henry James*
HENRY JAMES The Other House
HENRY JAMES The Outcry
TOVE JANSSON Fair Play *
TOVE JANSSON The Summer Book*
TOVE JANSSON The True Deceiver*
RANDALL JARRELL (EDITOR) Randall Jarrell's Book of Stories
DAVID JONES In Parenthesis
KABIR Songs of Kabir; translated by Arvind Krishna Mehrotra*
FRIGYES KARINTHY A Journey Round My Skull
ERICH KÄSTNER Going to the Dogs: The Story of a Moralist*
HELEN KELLER The World I Live In
YASHAR KEMAL Memed, My Hawk
YASHAR KEMAL They Burn the Thistles